Environmental and Natural Resource Economics

Additional resources for students are available at
www.mesharpe-student.com.

Resources for instructors who adopt the book are available at
www.mesharpe-instructor.com.

Environmental and Natural Resource Economics

A Contemporary Approach

Third Edition

Jonathan M. Harris and **Brian Roach**

M.E.Sharpe
Armonk, New York
London, England

Library of Congress Cataloging-in-Publication Data

Harris, Jonathan M.
  Environmental and natural resource economics : a contemporary approach /
by Jonathan Harris & Brian Roach.—3rd ed.
  p. cm.
  Includes bibliographical references and index.
  ISBN 978–0–7656–3792–5 (hardcover : alk. paper) 1. Environmental economics. 2. Natural
resources. 3. Environmental policy. I. Title.

HC79.E5H356 2013
333.7—dc22   2012045232

Printed in the United States of America

The paper used in this publication meets the minimum requirements of
American National Standard for Information Sciences
Permanence of Paper for Printed Library Materials,
ANSI Z 39.48-1984.

∞

IBT (c)   10   9   8   7   6   5   4   3   2   1

Contents

Note to the Reader

Key Terms are bolded in the text, with a sidebar definition.

All Key Terms in a chapter are listed at the end of the chapter, and the definitions
are collected in the Glossary, noting the chapters in which they appear.

Preface to the Third Edition

The third edition of *Environmental and Natural Resource Economics: A Contemporary Approach* maintains its essential focus on making environmental issues accessible to a broad range of students. The text is a product of twenty years of teaching environmental and natural resource economics at the undergraduate and graduate levels. It reflects the conviction that environmental issues are of fundamental importance and that a broad approach to understanding the relationship of the human economy and the natural world is essential.

Typically, students come to an environmental economics course with an awareness that environmental problems are serious and that local, national, and global policy solutions are needed. Some students may be interested in careers in environmental policy; others in gaining an understanding of issues that are likely to be relevant in their careers, personal lives, and communities. In either case, the current importance of the topics gives the course a special spark of enthusiasm that is a heaven-sent boon to any instructor trying to breathe life into marginal cost and benefit curves.

There is a distinct danger, however, that this initial enthusiasm can be dampened rather quickly by the use of a strictly conventional approach to environmental economics. One major limitation of this approach is its almost exclusive use of neoclassical microeconomic techniques. The standard microeconomic perspective strongly implies that anything of importance can be expressed in terms of price—even though many important environmental functions cannot be fully captured in dollar terms. Also, this perspective makes it difficult to focus on the inherently "macro" environmental issues such as global climate change, ocean pollution, ozone depletion, population growth, and global carbon, nitrogen, and water cycles.

For these reasons, the authors have developed an alternative approach that draws on the broader perspective that has come to be known as ecological economics, in addition to presenting standard economic theory. In our view, these two approaches are complementary rather than in conflict. Many elements of standard microeconomic analysis are essential for analyzing resource and environmental issues. At the same time, it is important to recognize the limitations of a strictly cost-benefit approach and to introduce ecological and biophysical perspectives on the interactions of human and natural systems.

NEW TO THE THIRD EDITION

The third edition of *Environmental and Natural Resource Economics: A Contemporary Approach* has been updated in response both to developments in the world of environmental policy and to comments and suggestions based on classroom use. New material in the third edition includes:

- a new chapter on water economics, including analysis of water demand management, water pricing, and water privatization
- a new chapter on the relationship between environmental protection and the economy, including analysis of decoupling output from resource and energy inputs and policies to promote a green economy
- new scientific evidence on climate change and a new chapter on global climate change policy, including technological potential, abatement costs, and proposals for an Earth Atmospheric Trust and Greenhouse Development Rights
- more on the application of economic valuation techniques, including evaluating new mercury regulations, valuing life, and estimating the impacts of the Gulf oil spill
- new material on "green" national income accounting, including adjusted net savings, the Genuine Progress Indicator, the Better Life Index, and environmental asset accounts
- new sections on recent population developments, including changing fertility rates, projections for 2050 to 2100, and the human ecological footprint
- changing projections for food supply and the impact of the "food crisis," rising meat consumption, and biofuels
- new data on rising prices for minerals and new projections for fossil-fuel supply limits, discussion of fossil-fuel subsidies, and the potential for a transition to renewable energy

All data series have been updated to reflect recent trends. New appendices have been added to chapters dealing with formal analysis, providing greater depth in analytical techniques.

ORGANIZATION OF THE TEXT

The text is structured so as to be appropriate for a variety of courses. It assumes a background in basic microeconomics and can be used in an upper-level undergraduate course or a policy-oriented master's-level course. Part I provides a broad overview of different approaches to economic analysis of resources and environment and of the fundamental issues of economy/environment interactions. Part II covers the basics of standard environmental and resource economics, including the theory of externalities, resource allocation over time, common property resources, public goods, and valuation. Part III offers an introduction to the ecological economics approach, including "greening" national accounts and economic/ecological modeling.

Parts IV and V apply these analytical approaches to fundamental environmental and resource issues. Part IV focuses on population, agriculture, and the environment, reviewing different theories of population, giving an overview of the environmental impacts of world agricultural systems and discussing policy responses to population and food supply issues. Part V deals with the economics of renewable and nonrenewable resources at both the microeconomic and macroeconomic levels.

Part VI provides a standard analysis of the economics of pollution control, a new chapter on the relationship between environmental protection and the economy, and two chapters that address global climate change. Part VII brings together some of the themes from the specific topics of the earlier parts in a consideration of trade and development issues.

PEDAGOGICAL AIDS FOR STUDENTS AND INSTRUCTORS

Each chapter has discussion questions, and the more quantitative chapters have numerical problem sets. Key terms in each chapter are compiled in an extensive glossary. Useful Web sites are also listed. Instructors and students are urged to make full use of the text's supporting Web sites at http://www.gdae.org/environ-econ.

The instructor Web site includes teaching tips and objectives, answers to text problems, and test questions. The student site includes chapter review questions and Web-based exercises and will be updated periodically with bulletins on topical environmental issues.

ACKNOWLEDGMENTS

The preparation of a text covering such an extensive area, in addition to the supporting materials, is a vast enterprise, and our indebtedness to all those who have contributed to the effort is accordingly great. Colleagues at the Global Development and Environment Institute have supplied essential help and inspiration. Research associate Anne-Marie Codur cowrote the original version of Chapter 18 on global climate change and contributed material to the chapters on population and sustainable development. Especially significant has been the unwavering support of the Institute's codirector, Neva Goodwin, who has long championed the importance of educational materials that bring broader perspectives to the teaching of economics.

Our colleagues Timothy Wise, Frank Ackerman, Kevin Gallagher, Julie Nelson, Liz Stanton, and Elise Garvey provided insights on specific issues. Essential research assistance was given by Josh Uchitelle-Pierce, Adrian Williamson, Baoguang Zhai, Maliheh Birjandi Feriz, Lauren Jayson, Reid Spagna, and Mitchell Stallman, in addition to work by Dina Dubson and Alicia Harvey for the previous edition. Lauren Denizard and Erin Coutts offered administrative support.

The book has greatly benefited from the comments of reviewers including Kris Feder, Richard Horan, Gary Lynne, Helen Mercer, Gerda Kits, Gina Shamshak, Jinhua Zhao, John Sorrentino, Richard England, Maximilian Auffhammer, and Guillermo Donoso and reflects much that we have learned from the work of colleagues at Tufts University and elsewhere, especially William Moomaw, William Wade, Sheldon Krimsky, Molly Anderson, Ann Helwege, Kent Portney, Kelly Gallagher, Paul Kirshen, and Richard Wetzler. Others whose work has provided special inspiration for this text include Herman Daly, Richard Norgaard, Richard Howarth, Robert Costanza, Faye Duchin, Glenn-Marie Lange, John Proops, and many other members of the International Society for Ecological Economics. Fred Curtis, Rafael Reuveny, Ernest Diedrich, Lisi Krall, Richard Culas, and many other faculty members at colleges in the United States and worldwide have provided valuable feedback from class use. Our editor at M.E. Sharpe, George Lobell, provided support and advice throughout, and Stacey Victor guided us through the production process. Finally we thank the many students we have had the privilege to teach over the years—you continually inspire us and provide hope for a better future.

Jonathan M. Harris and *Brian Roach*
Global Development and Environment Institute
Tufts University
Jonathan.Harris@Tufts.edu
Brian.Roach@Tufts.edu

Environmental and Natural Resource Economics

PART ONE

INTRODUCTION

THE ECONOMY AND THE ENVIRONMENT

CHAPTER 1

Changing Perspectives on the Environment

1.1 ECONOMICS AND THE ENVIRONMENT

Over the past four decades, we have become increasingly aware of environmental problems facing communities, countries, and the world. During this period, natural resource and environmental issues have grown in scope and urgency. In 1970, the Environmental Protection Agency was created in the United States to respond to what was at that time a relatively new public concern with air and water pollution. In 1972, the first international conference on the environment, the United Nations Conference on the Human Environment, met in Stockholm. Since then, growing worldwide attention has been devoted to environmental issues.

In 1992 the United Nations Conference on Environment and Development (UNCED) met in Rio de Janeiro, Brazil, to focus on major global issues, including depletion of the earth's protective ozone layer, destruction of tropical and old-growth forests and wetlands, species extinction, and the steady buildup of carbon dioxide and other "greenhouse" gases causing global warming and climate change. Twenty years later, at the United Nations Rio + 20 Conference on Sustainable Development, countries of the world "reaffirmed commitments" to integrating environment and development but acknowledged limited progress toward these goals.[1] In 2012, the United Nations Environmental Programme (UNEP) report *Global Environmental Outlook 5* found that "burgeoning populations and growing economies are pushing ecosystems to destabilizing limits." According to the report:

> The twentieth century was characterized by exceptional growth both in the human population and in the size of the global economy, with the population quadrupling to 7 billion [in 2011] and global economic output increasing more than 20-fold. This expansion has

been accompanied by fundamental changes in the scale, intensity, and character of society's relationship with the natural world. Drivers of environmental change are growing, evolving, and combining at such an accelerating pace, at such a large scale and with such widespread reach that they are exerting unprecedented pressure on the environment.[2]

With the exception of ozone depletion, an area in which major reductions in emissions have been achieved by international agreement, the UNEP report offers evidence that the global environmental problems identified at UNCED in 1992 in the areas of atmosphere, land, water, biodiversity, chemicals, and wastes have continued or worsened. UNEP Global Environmental Outlook reports have identified nitrogen pollution in freshwater and oceans, exposure to toxic chemicals and hazardous wastes, forest and freshwater ecosystem damage, water contamination and declining groundwater supplies, urban air pollution and wastes, and overexploitation of major ocean fisheries as major global issues. Underlying all these problems is global population growth, which adds more than 70 million people a year. World population, which exceeded 7 billion in 2011, is expected to grow to around 9 billion by 2050.

Scientists, policy makers, and the general public have begun to grapple with questions such as: What will the future look like? Can we respond to these multiple threats adequately and in time to prevent irreversible damage to the planetary systems that support life? One of the most important components of the problem, which rarely receives sufficient attention, is an economic analysis of environmental issues.

Some may argue that environmental issues transcend economics and should be judged in different terms from the money values used in economic analysis. Indeed, this assertion holds some truth. We find, however, that environmental protection policies are often measured—and sometimes rejected—in terms of their economic costs. For example, it is extremely difficult to preserve open land that has high commercial development value. Either large sums must be raised to purchase the land, or strong political opposition to "locking up" land must be overcome. Environmental protection organizations face a continuing battle with ever-increasing economic development pressures.

Often public policy issues are framed in terms of a conflict between development and the environment. An example is the recent debate over "fracking," or hydraulic fracturing to obtain natural gas. Producing natural gas can be profitable and increase the nation's energy supplies, but there are social and environmental costs to communities. Similarly, opponents of international agreements to reduce carbon dioxide emissions argue that the economic costs of such measures are too high. Supporters of increased oil production clash with advocates of protecting the Arctic National Wildlife Refuge. In developing countries, the tension between the urgency of human needs and environmental protection can be even greater.

Does economic development necessarily have a high environmental price? Although all economic development must affect the environment to some degree, is "environment-friendly" development possible? If we must make a tradeoff between development and environment, how should the proper balance be reached? Questions such as these highlight the importance of environmental economics.

Two Approaches

In this book we explore two approaches to addressing natural resource and environmental economics. The first, or traditional, approach uses a set of models and

ecological economics
an economic perspective that views the economic system as a subset of the broader ecosystem and subject to biophysical laws.

nonrenewable resources
resources that are available in a fixed supply, such as metal ores and oil.

renewable resources
a resource that is supplied on a continuing basis by ecosystems; renewable resources such as forests and fisheries can be depleted through exploitation.

common property resources
a resource that is not subject to private ownership and is available to all, such as the oceans or atmosphere.

public goods
goods that are available to all (nonexclusive) and whose use by one person does not reduce their availability to others (nonrival).

externalities
an effect of a market transaction that changes the utility, positively or negatively, of those outside the transaction.

third-party effects
effects of market transactions that affect people other than those involved in the transaction, such as industrial pollution that affects a local community.

solar energy
the energy supplied continually by the sun, including direct solar energy as well as indirect forms such as wind energy and flowing water.

techniques rooted in the standard neoclassical mainstream of economic thought to apply economic concepts to the environment.[a] The second approach, known as **ecological economics**, takes a different perspective.[3] Rather than applying economic concepts *to* the environment, ecological economics seeks to place economic activity *in the context of* the biological and physical systems that support life, including all human activities.

The Traditional Economic Perspective

Several models in economic theory specifically address environmental issues. One important application of neoclassical economic theory deals with the allocation of **nonrenewable resources** over time. This analysis is important in understanding such issues as the depletion of oil and mineral resources and also has applications to **renewable resources** such as agricultural soils. Other economic analyses deal with **common property resources** such as the atmosphere and oceans and **public goods** such as national parks and wildlife preserves. Because these resources are not privately owned, the economic principles governing their use are different from those affecting goods traded in the market.

Another central concept in neoclassical economic analysis of the environment is that of **externalities**, or **external costs and benefits**. The theory of externalities provides an economic framework for analyzing the costs of environmental damage caused by economic activities or the social benefits created by economic activity that improves the environment. Externalities are also sometimes referred to as **third-party effects**, because a market transaction that involves two parties—for example, someone buying gasoline from a filling station—also affects other people, such as those exposed to pollution from producing and burning the gasoline.

Modern environmental economic theory, built on this foundation, addresses many issues, ranging from overfishing to fossil-fuel depletion to parkland conservation.[4] In this text, we investigate how these economic concepts can help frame environmental questions and provide guidance for environmental policy making.

The Ecological Economics Perspective

Ecological economics takes a broader perspective in framing environmental questions by incorporating laws derived from the natural sciences. For example, to understand the collapse of many important ocean fisheries, ecological economics refers to population biology and ecology as well as to the economic view of fish as a resource for production.

Ecological economics theorists emphasize the importance of energy resources, especially fossil fuels, in current economic systems. All ecological systems depend on energy inputs, but natural systems rely almost entirely on **solar energy**. The rapid growth of economic production during the twentieth century required enormous energy inputs, and global economic systems are making even greater energy demands in the twenty-first century. The availability and environmental implications of energy use are central issues for ecological economics.

---

[a] Neoclassical price theory, based on the concepts of marginal utility and marginal productivity, emphasizes the essential function of market price in achieving equilibrium between supply and demand.

A fundamental principle of ecological economics is that human economic activity must be limited by the environment's **carrying capacity**. Carrying capacity is defined as the population level and consumption activities that the available natural resource base can sustain without depletion. For example, when a herd of grazing animals exceeds a certain size, rangeland overgrazing will diminish the potential food supply, leading inevitably to a population decline.

For the human population, the issue is more complex. The issue of food supplies is certainly relevant as the world population, which surpassed 7 billion in 2012, grows to a projected 9 billion in 2050. But ecological economists also point to energy supplies, scarce natural resources, and cumulative environmental damage as constraints to economic growth. They argue that the standard theory gives these factors insufficient weight and that major structural changes in the nature of economic activity are required to adapt to environmental limits.

In this text, we consider insights from both the standard and the ecological versions of environmental economics.[5] Sometimes the theories show significant agreement or overlap, and sometimes there are widely differing implications. The best way to judge which approaches are most fruitful is to apply them to specific environmental issues, as we do throughout this book. First, however, we must understand the relationship between the economic system, natural resources, and the environment.

1.2 A Framework for Environmental Analysis

How can we best conceptualize the relationship between economic activities and the environment? One way is to start with the traditional **circular flow** diagram used in most economics courses to depict the economic process.

The Circular Flow Model

Figure 1.1 shows a simplified model of relationships between households and business firms in two markets: the market for goods and services and the market for factors of production. Factors of production are generally defined as land, labor, and capital. The services that these factors provide are "inputs" to the production of goods and services, which in turn provide the basis for households' consumption needs. Goods, services, and factors flow clockwise; their economic values are reflected in the flows of money used to pay for them, moving counterclockwise. In both markets, the interaction of supply and demand determines a market-clearing price and establishes an equilibrium level of output.

Where do natural resources and the environment fit in this diagram? **Natural resources**, including minerals, water, fossil fuels, forests, fisheries, and farmland, generally fall under the inclusive category of "land." The two other major factors of production, labor and capital, continually regenerate through the economic circular flow process, but by what processes do natural resources regenerate for future economic use? To answer this question, we need to consider a larger "circular flow" that takes into account ecosystem processes as well as economic activity (Figure 1.2).

Taking this broader view, we notice that the standard circular flow diagram also omits the effects of wastes and pollution generated in the production process. These wastes from both firms and households must flow back into the ecosystem somewhere, either through land disposal or as air and water pollution.

Figure 1.1   **The Standard Circular Flow Model**

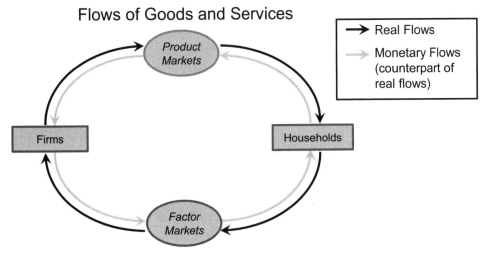

In addition to the simple processes of extracting resources from the ecosystem and returning wastes to it, economic activities also affect broader natural systems in subtler and more pervasive ways. For example, modern intensive agriculture changes the composition and ecology of soil and water systems, as well as affecting nitrogen and carbon cycles in the environment.

Figure 1.2, although still quite simple, provides a broader framework for placing the economic system in its ecological context. As you can see, the ecological system has its own circular flow, determined by physical and biological rather than economic laws. This broader flow has only one net "input"—solar energy—and only one net "output"—waste heat. Everything else must somehow be recycled or contained within the planetary ecosystem.

Points of Contact Between Economic and Ecological Flows

Understanding the relationships between economic systems, natural resources, and the environment begins with defining the different functions that natural systems serve.

source function
the ability of the environment to make services and raw materials available for human use.

resource depletion
a decline in the stock of a renewable resource due to human exploitation.

pollution
contamination of soil, water or atmosphere by discharge of harmful substances.

sink function
the ability of natural environments to absorb wastes and pollution.

- The environment's **source function** is its ability to make services and raw materials available for human use. Degradation of the source function can occur for two reasons: (1) **Resource depletion**: the resource declines in quantity because humans have drawn on it more rapidly than it could be regenerated; and (2) **Pollution**: contamination of the resource reduces its quality and usefulness.
- The environment's **sink function** is its ability to absorb and render harmless the waste by-products of human activity. The sink function is overtaxed when waste volume is too great within a given time period or when wastes are too toxic. When that happens, aspects of the environment on which we depend (most often soil, water, and atmosphere) become damaged, polluted, or poisoned.

Figure 1.2 **A Broader Circular Flow Model**

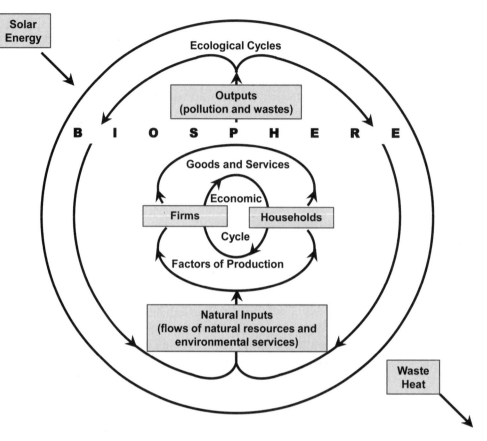

These relationships between human activity and the environment define the points of contact between the inner circle of economic flows and the outer circle of ecological flows. Natural resource and environmental economics analyzes the relationships between the two circular flows: the economic system and the ecosystem.

The Economic Valuation Approach

economic valuation
the valuation of a resource in monetary terms.

The traditional economic approach to analysis of natural resource and waste flows uses the same kind of **economic valuation** applied to factors of production, goods, and services. This analysis seeks to put a price on each natural resource and environmental input to the economy, including estimating a price for inputs not usually included in market transactions, such as clean air and water. Economic techniques can be used to assess the money value of damages caused by pollution and waste disposal.

By placing a money value on natural resources and environmental functions, we can include them in the inner, or economic, circular flow. This is the goal of much standard resource and environmental analysis. As we will see, a variety of methods can serve this end, including redefining or reassigning property rights, creating new institutions such as markets for pollution permits, or implicit valuation through surveys and other techniques. If we can be satisfied that these pricing mechanisms accurately reflect the "true value" of resources and of environmental damages, we can include these factors in a market-oriented economic analysis relatively easily.

The Ecological Systems Approach

The ecological economics approach views the economic system as a subset of the broader ecosystem. In this perspective, an economic valuation expressed in prices can only imperfectly capture the complexity of ecological processes and will sometimes result in serious conflict with ecosystem requirements.

Ecological economists have often argued that standard economic pricing and valuation techniques must either be altered to reflect ecosystem realities or be supplemented by other forms of analysis focusing on energy flows, the carrying capacity of the environment, and the requirements of ecological balance. As we will see in our discussion of analytical techniques and of specific issues in population, energy, resources, and pollution, the standard and ecological economics perspectives have similar practical implications in some cases, but in other cases the two approaches can lead to significantly different conclusions about appropriate resource and environmental policies.

For example, in dealing with the problem of global climate change (discussed at length in Chapter 18), a standard economic approach involves balancing the costs and benefits of avoiding future climate change. Damages caused by rising sea levels or stronger heat waves are estimated in economic terms and then compared to the costs involved in lessening climate change through reducing fossil-fuel use and other measures. Policy recommendations are then formulated to maximize net economic benefits. An ecological economics approach, by contrast, looks first at the physical requirements for a stable climate, in particular the limitation of carbon dioxide and other heat-trapping gases in the atmosphere. After the physical requirements for a stable climate are determined, the economic measures necessary to achieve this are analyzed.

Application of a standard economic approach to the problem of global climate change often results in a recommendation for more limited policy action, to avoid excessive economic costs. The ecological approach usually suggests more drastic action to preserve atmospheric balance. Cost minimization is also a concern for ecological economists, but only after the basic biophysical requirements for ecosystem stability have been met.

1.3 Environmental Microeconomics and Macroeconomics

environmental macroeconomics
an analysis approach that places the human economic system within an ecological context to balance the scale of the economic system within ecological constraints.

Another way of viewing the difference between standard and ecological approaches is in terms of a tension between microeconomic and macroeconomic perspectives on the environment. Standard environmental economic analysis relies largely on microeconomic theory, which focuses on individual resource and environmental issues. **Environmental macroeconomics**, however, can help place the economic system in its broader ecological context. The macroeconomic view gives insight into the interrelationship of economic growth and ecosystems.

Microeconomic and Valuation Techniques

To the extent that we can succeed in putting a price on natural resources and the environment, extensions of standard microeconomic theory can help explain the process

environmental services
ecosystem services such as nutrient cycling, water purification, and soil stabilization; these services benefit humans and support economic production.

environmental microeconomics
the use of microeconomic techniques such as economic valuation, property rights rules, and discounting to determine an efficient allocation of natural resources and environmental services.

internalizing external costs/externalities
using approaches such as taxation to incorporate external costs into market decisions.

assets
something with market value, including financial assets, physical assets, and natural assets.

intertemporal resource allocation
the way resource use is distributed over time.

discount rate
the annual rate at which future benefits or costs are discounted relative to current benefits or costs.

property rights
the set of rights that belong to the owner of a resource, such as the right of a landowner to prohibit trespassing.

cost-benefit analysis (CBA)
a tool for policy analysis that attempts to monetize all the costs and benefits of a proposed action to determine the net benefit.

of achieving equilibrium in markets for natural resources and for **environmental services**—the capacity of the environment to absorb wastes and pollutants, capture solar energy, and in other ways provide the basis for economic activity. Analytical techniques that play an important role in **environmental microeconomics** include:

- *Measuring external costs and benefits.* This means, for example, estimating a money value for damage caused by acid rain pollution. This value can then be compared to the costs of correcting the problem through pollution control technology or reduced output of polluting activities. We can **internalize externalities**, for example, by levying a tax on the polluting activity.
- *Valuing resources and the environment as* **assets**, *whether ownership is private or public.* This involves the consideration of **intertemporal resource allocation**, the choice between using a resource now and conserving it for future use. The standard economic technique to balance present and future benefits and costs is to use a **discount rate**. In this technique, a present benefit or cost is assigned a somewhat higher value than a future benefit or cost—how much higher depends on the discount rate employed and on how far into the future the comparison extends.
- *Devising appropriate* **property rights** *rules for environmental resources, and establishing rules for use of common property resources and for provision of public goods.*[b] For example, ownership of a fishery can be private or public, in which case access may be limited by government sale of fishing licenses. Similarly, a wildlife preserve can be privately owned and managed or maintained as a public park.
- *Balancing economic costs and benefits through some form of* **cost-benefit analysis**. This often involves a combination of values observable in the market, such as values of land or goods, and estimates of nonmarket values, such as natural beauty and maintenance of species diversity. For example, deciding whether to permit construction of a ski resort on a previously undeveloped hillside requires an estimate of the recreational value of skiing, the value of alternative uses of the land, and valuation of less easily quantifiable concerns such as impact on water supplies, wildlife, and the rural character of the area.

In the context of the double circular flow shown in Figure 1.2, the above analytical techniques are derived from the smaller "economic" circle: In effect, they apply pricing concepts drawn from the economic system to the intermediate flows of natural resources and wastes that connect the two circles. These approaches seem most appropriate when we focus on a specific, quantifiable problem, such as calculating the appropriate fee to charge for a license to cut timber on government land or the appropriate form of limits on emissions of air pollutants from factories.

Environmental Macroeconomics

Valuation techniques are less effective in handling important unquantifiable values such as aesthetics, ethical issues, and **biodiversity** (the maintenance of many different interrelated species in an ecological community). They may also fail to capture

---

[b]These are resources and goods that are available to the public without restriction. For a more precise definition, see Chapter 4.

the scope of the **global environmental problems** that have become increasingly important in recent years. Issues such as global climate change, ozone depletion, loss of species, widespread degradation of agricultural lands, water shortages, forest and ocean ecosystem damage, and other large-scale environmental issues require a broader perspective. For this reason, ecological economist Herman Daly has called for development of an environmental macroeconomics, which requires a different approach from the standard economic techniques discussed earlier.[6]

Developing such a macroeconomic perspective on environmental issues requires placing the economic system in its broader ecological context. As Figure 1.2 shows, the economic circular flow is really part of a larger ecological circular flow. This ecological flow is actually made up of many cycles. **Ecological cycles** include:

- the *carbon cycle,* in which green plants break down atmospheric carbon dioxide (CO_2) into carbon and oxygen. The carbon is stored in the plants, some of which are eaten by animals. Carbon is recombined with oxygen by animal respiration, and by decay or burning of organic matter, and is thus returned to the atmosphere.
- the *nitrogen cycle,* in which soil bacteria "fix," or chemically combine, nitrogen from the atmosphere with oxygen and make this essential nutrient available for plant growth.
- the *water cycle,* including precipitation, runoff, and evaporation, which continually make freshwater available for plant and animal life.
- other *organic cycles* of growth, death, decay, and new growth, in which essential nutrients are recycled through the soils to provide a continuing basis for plant and animal life.

All these cycles are driven by solar energy and operate in a complex balance that has evolved over millennia.

Seen in this context, economic activity is a process of speeding up the **throughput** of materials from the ecological cycles. The term "throughput" denotes the total use of energy and materials as both inputs and outputs of a process.

Modern agriculture, for example, applies vast quantities of artificially derived nitrogen fertilizer to obtain higher crop yields. Runoff of excess nitrogen creates environmental problems and water contamination. Both agriculture and industry make heavy demands on water supplies. Together with household use, this demand can exceed the capacity of the natural water cycle, depleting reservoirs and underground aquifers.

The most important way of speeding up resource throughput is using more energy to drive the economic system. More than 80 percent of the energy used in the global economic system is derived from fossil fuels. The carbon emissions from burning these fuels unbalances the global carbon cycle. Excessive amounts of CO_2 accumulate in the atmosphere, altering the processes that determine the planet's climate and thereby affect many global ecosystems.

As economic growth proceeds, the demands of the economic system on the ecological cycles grow larger. Energy use, resource and water use, and waste generation increase. Thus the environmental macroeconomic issue is how to balance the size of the economic system, or **macroeconomic scale**, with the supporting ecosystem. Viewing the problem in this way represents a significant paradigm shift for economic analysis, which has not usually considered overall ecosystem limitations.

Implications of Ecologically Oriented Economics

An ecologically oriented macroeconomics involves new concepts of national income measurement that explicitly take into account environmental pollution and natural resource depletion when calculating national income. In addition, ecological economists have introduced new forms of analysis at both microeconomic and macroeconomic levels. These new analytical techniques are based on the physical laws that govern energy and materials flows in ecosystems. Applying these laws to the economic process offers a contrasting perspective to the standard microeconomic analysis of environmental issues.

Seeking a balance between economic growth and ecosystem health has given rise to the concept of **sustainable development** (discussed in detail in Chapters 2 and 21). Forms of economic development that preserve rather than degrade the environment include renewable energy use, organic and low-input agriculture, and resource-conserving technologies. On a global scale, the promotion of sustainable development responds to the many resource and environmental issues outlined at the beginning of this chapter, viewing these issues in terms of ecosystem impacts rather than as individual problems.[7]

sustainable development
development that meets the needs of the present without compromising the ability of future generations to meet their own needs.

1.4 A Look Ahead

How can we best use these two approaches to economic analysis of environmental issues? In the following chapters, we apply the tools and methods of each to specific issues. In preparation, Chapter 2 provides an overview of the relationship between economic development and the environment. The microeconomic elements of resource and environmental economics are explored in detail in Chapters 3–6. Chapters 7 and 8 cover the concepts of ecological economics, environmental accounting, and ecosystem modeling.

In Chapters 9–19, we apply techniques of standard economic analysis and of ecological analysis to the major issues of population, food supply, energy use, natural resource management, pollution control, and climate change. Chapters 20 and 21 bring together many of these topics to focus on questions of trade, economic growth, and development as they relate to the environment.

Summary

National and global environmental issues are major challenges in the twenty-first century. Responding to these challenges requires understanding the economics of the environment. Policies aimed at environmental protection have economic costs and benefits, and this economic dimension is often crucial in determining which policies we adopt. Some cases may require tradeoffs between economic and environmental goals; in other cases these goals may prove compatible and mutually reinforcing.

Two different approaches address economic analysis of environmental issues. The standard approach applies economic theory to the environment using the concepts of money valuation and economic equilibrium. This approach aims to achieve efficient management of natural resources and the proper valuation of waste and pollution. The ecological economic approach views the economic system as a whole as a subset of a broader biophysical system. This approach emphasizes the need for economic activity that conforms to physical and biological limits.

Much of the analysis drawn from the standard approach is microeconomic, based on the workings of markets. Variations of standard market analysis can be applied to cases in which economic activity has damaging environmental effects or uses up scarce resources. Other economic analyses provide insight into the use of common property resources and public goods.

Environmental macroeconomics, a relatively new field, emphasizes the relationship between economic production and the major natural cycles of the planet. In many cases, significant conflicts arise between the operations of the economic system and these natural systems, creating regional and global problems such as global climate change from excess carbon dioxide accumulation. This broader approach requires new ways to measure economic activity, as well as analysis of how the scale of economic activity affects environmental systems.

This text outlines both analytical perspectives and draws on both to help clarify the major issues of population, food supply, energy use, natural resource management, and pollution. The combination of these analyses can help to formulate policies that can address specific environmental problems as well as promote a broader vision of environmentally sustainable development.

KEY TERMS AND CONCEPTS

assets
biodiversity
carrying capacity
circular flow
common property resources
cost-benefit analysis
discount rate
ecological cycles
ecological economics
economic valuation
environmental microeconomics
environmental macroeconomics
environmental services
external costs and benefits
externalities
global environmental problems

internalizing externalities
intertemporal resource allocation
macroeconomic scale
natural resources
nonrenewable resources
pollution
property rights
public goods
renewable resources
resource depletion
solar energy
source and sink functions
sustainable development
third-party effects
throughput

DISCUSSION QUESTIONS

1. Do economic growth and sound environmental policy necessarily conflict? Identify some areas where a choice must be made between economic growth and environmental preservation and others where the two are compatible.

2. Is it possible to put a money price on environmental resources? How? Are there cases in which this impossible? Identify specific instances of valuing the environment with which you are familiar or that you have read about.

3. In what ways do the principles of ecological circular flow resemble those of the economic circular flow? How do they differ? Give some specific examples in the areas of agriculture, water, and energy systems.

NOTES

1. See www.uncsd2012.org/rio20/index.html.
2. UNEP, 2012; figures on global economic output from Maddison, 2009; for background on human/environment interactions, see McNeill, 2000; Steffen et al., 2007.
3. For an overview of many issues in ecological economics, see Common and Stagl, 2005; Costanza, 1991; Krishnan et al., 1995; Martinez-Alier and Røpke, 2008.
4. For collections of articles on environmental economics, see Grafton et al., 2001; Hoel, 2004; Mäler and Vincent, 2003; Markandya, 2001; Stavins, 2012; van den Bergh, 1999.
5. For an approach specifically focused on ecological economics, see Daly and Farley, 2011.
6. See Daly, 1996, chap. 2.
7. For an overview of the relationship between environmental/ecological economics and sustainable development, see Daly, 2007; Harris et al., 2001; and López and Toman, 2006. For a discussion of global ecosystem impacts of human activity, see World Resources Institute et al., 2011.

REFERENCES

Common, Michael S., and Sigrid Stagl. 2005. *Ecological Economics: An Introduction.* Cambridge: Cambridge University Press.
Costanza, Robert, ed. 1991. *Ecological Economics: The Science and Management of Sustainability.* New York: Columbia University Press.
Daly, Herman E. 1996. *Beyond Growth: The Economics of Sustainable Development.* Boston: Beacon Press.
———. 2007. *Ecological Economics and Sustainable Development.* Northampton, MA: Edward Elgar.
Daly, Herman E., and Joshua Farley. 2011. *Ecological Economics: Principles and Applications,* 2d ed. Washington, DC: Island Press.
Grafton, R. Quentin, Linwood H. Pendleton, and Harry W. Nelson. 2001. *A Dictionary of Environmental Economics, Science, and Policy.* Cheltenham, UK: Edward Elgar.
Harris, Jonathan M., Timothy A. Wise, Kevin P. Gallagher, and Neva R. Goodwin, eds. 2001. *A Survey of Sustainable Development: Social and Economic Dimensions.* Washington, DC: Island Press.
Hoel, Michael. 2004. *Recent Developments in Environmental Economics.* Northampton, MA: Edward Elgar.
Krishnan, Rajaram, Jonathan M. Harris, and Neva R. Goodwin, eds. 1995. *A Survey of Ecological Economics.* Washington, DC: Island Press.
López, Ramón, and Michael A. Toman. 2006. *Economic Development and Environmental Sustainability: New Policy Options.* Oxford: Oxford University Press.
Maddison, Angus. 2009. *Historical Statistics for the World Economy: 1–2001 A.D.* www.ggdc.net/maddison/.
Mäler, Karl-Göran, and Jeffrey R. Vincent, eds. 2003. *Handbook of Environmental Economics.* Amsterdam: North-Holland/Elsevier.
Markandya, Anil. 2001. *Dictionary of Environmental Economics.* London: Earthscan.
Martinez-Alier, Joan, and Inge Røpke. 2008. *Recent Developments in Ecological Economics.* Northampton, MA: Edward Elgar.
McNeill, John R. 2000. *Something New Under the Sun: An Environmental History of the Twentieth Century.* New York: Norton.
Stavins, Robert N., ed., 2012. *Economics of the Environment: Selected Readings,* 6th ed. New York: Norton.
Steffen, W., P.J. Crutzen, and J.R. McNeill. 2007. "The Anthopocene: Are Humans Now Overwhelming the Great Forces of Nature?" *Ambio* 36(8): 614–621.

United Nations Environment Programme (UNEP). 2012. *Global Environmental Outlook 5: Environment for the Future We Want*. Malta: Progress Press. www.unep.org/geo/geo5.asp.

Van den Bergh, Jeroen C.J.M. 1999. *Handbook of Environmental and Resource Economics*. Northampton, MA: Edward Elgar.

World Resources Institute, United Nations Development Programme, United Nations Environment Programme, and World Bank. 2011. *World Resources 2010–2011: Decision Making in a Changing Climate*. Washington, DC: World Resources Institute.

WEB SITES

1. **www.worldwatch.org.** The homepage for the Worldwatch Institute, an organization that conducts a broad range of research on environmental issues. The Worldwatch annual "State of the World" report presents detailed analyses of current environmental issues.
2. **www.ncseonline.org.** Web site for the National Council for Science and the Environment, with links to various sites with state, national, and international data on environmental quality.
3. **www.unep.org/geo/.** Web site for the Global Environment Outlook, a United Nations publication. The report is an extensive analysis of the global environmental situation.

CHAPTER 2

Resources, Environment, and Economic Development

2.1 A BRIEF HISTORY OF ECONOMIC GROWTH AND THE ENVIRONMENT

Human population and economic activity remained fairly stable during much of recorded history. Before the Industrial Revolution in the eighteenth and nineteenth centuries, Europe's population grew slowly and standards of living changed little. The advent of the market economy and rapid technological progress altered this pattern dramatically. Population in Europe entered a period of rapid growth that led the British classical economist Thomas Malthus to theorize that populations would outgrow food supplies, keeping the mass of people perpetually at a subsistence standard of living.

Malthus's *Essay on the Principle of Population as It Affects the Future Improvement of Society*, published in 1798, initiated a long and continuing debate on the impact of population growth and the availability of natural resources. History has proved the simple **Malthusian hypothesis** wrong: Both population and living standards in Europe rose rapidly in the two centuries after publication of Malthus's *Essay*. But if we consider a more sophisticated argument, that a growing human population and economic system will eventually outrun their biophysical support systems, the debate turns out to have strong current relevance.

Malthusian hypothesis
the theory proposed by Thomas Malthus in 1798 that population would eventually outgrow available food supplies.

The controversy over population growth is intimately intertwined with resource and environmental issues. In the twenty-first century, these issues, rather than the simple race between population and food supply, will strongly affect the course of economic development. It is unlikely that we will see major shortfalls in food supply on a global scale, although local and regional food crises resulting from rising prices have already become significant. But it is

gross domestic product (GDP)
the total market value of all final goods and services produced within a national border in a year.

GDP growth rate
the annual change in GDP, expressed as a percentage.

population growth rate
the annual change in the population of a given area, expressed as a percentage.

per capita GDP growth rate
the annual change in per capita GDP, expressed as a percentage.

real GDP
gross domestic product corrected for inflation using a price index.

nominal GDP
gross domestic product measured using current dollars.

capital stock
the existing quantity of capital in a given region, including manufactured, human, and natural capital.

technological progress
increases in knowledge used to develop new products or improve existing products.

highly likely that the environmental stresses associated with a growing population and rising resource demands will require major changes in the nature of economic systems.

Measuring Growth Rates

In approaching complex growth issues, we can start with a simple economic analysis of the relationship between population and economic activity. Measuring economic output in conventional terms as **gross domestic product (GDP)**, we have the simple identity[a]

$$GDP = (Population) \times (per\ capita\ GDP)$$

which can then be expressed in terms of rates of growth as a relationship among **GDP growth rate, population growth rate,** and **per capita GDP growth rate:**[b]

$$GDP\ growth\ rate = (population\ growth\ rate) + (per\ capita\ GDP\ growth\ rate)$$

To correct for the effects of inflation, we should use **real GDP** rather than **nominal GDP** in this equation.[c] Real per capita GDP will rise steadily, as long as real GDP growth remains consistently higher than population growth. For this to occur, productivity must also rise steadily. This increasing productivity is, of course, the key to escaping the Malthusian trap.

Increased agricultural productivity means that the portion of the population working in farming can decrease, freeing labor for industrial development. Increased industrial productivity brings higher living standards. Broadly speaking, economic development has unfolded along these lines in Europe, the United States, and other industrialized countries.

Factors Essential to Economic Growth

What determinants of increased productivity make this steady growth possible? Standard economic theory identifies two sources of increasing productivity. First is accumulation of capital. Investment makes possible the growth of **capital stock** over time: As capital stock per worker increases, the productivity of each worker increases. Second, **technological progress** raises the productivity of both capital and labor. Standard economic growth models place no limits on this process. Provided that investment continues at adequate rates, productivity and per capita consumption can continue rising far into the future.

---

[a]GDP is defined as the total flow of goods and services produced within a country's borders over a specified time period, usually a year.

[b]This relationship is derived from the mathematical rule of natural logarithms stating that if $A = BC$, then $\ln (A) = \ln(B) + \ln (C)$. The rates of growth of B and C can be expressed in terms of natural logarithms, and when added together, they give the rate of growth of A.

[c]Nominal GDP is measured using current prices. Real GDP corrects for inflation by using a price index to calculate the constant dollar value of production.

The ecological economics perspective focuses on three other factors as essential to economic growth. The first is energy supply. Europe's economic growth in the eighteenth and nineteenth centuries depended heavily on coal as an energy source, and some writers at the time expressed concern that coal supplies might run out. In the twentieth century, oil displaced coal as the prime energy source for industry.

Currently oil, natural gas, and coal provide over 80 percent of energy supplies for the United States, Europe, Japan, and other industrial economies and about the same proportion of industrial energy for the world as a whole.[1] To a great extent, economic growth in both agriculture and industry has been a process of substituting fossil-fuel energy for human labor. This substitution has important resource and environmental implications, which in turn affect projections of future growth.

The second fundamental factor is supplies of land and natural resources, sometimes referred to as **natural capital**. Almost all economic activities require some land use. As these activities grow, pressures increase to convert land from a natural state to agricultural, industrial, and residential uses. Some uses conflict: Housing may compete with farming for rural land, and industry or road-building may make land less suitable for either residential or agricultural use.

natural capital
the available endowment of land and resources including air, water, soil, forests, fisheries, minerals, and ecological life-support systems.

Land, of course, is fixed in supply. Except in very limited areas such as the diked areas of the Netherlands, human technology cannot create more land. Natural resources vary in abundance, but mineral resources and the regenerative capacity of forests and other living resources have physical limits.

The third important factor is the **absorptive capacity of the environment** for the waste products of industrial development. This issue is not so critical when the scale of economic activity is small relative to the environment. But as national and global economic activity accelerates, the flow of waste products increases and may threaten to overwhelm environmental systems. Flows of solid wastes, sewage and liquid wastes, toxic and radioactive wastes, and atmospheric emissions all pose specific environmental problems that require local, regional, and global solutions.

absorptive capacity of the environment
the ability of the environment to absorb and render harmless waste products.

Growth Optimists and Pessimists

Debate is ongoing concerning the resource and environmental factors that contribute to, and could eventually limit, economic growth. In 1972 a Massachusetts Institute of Technology research team published a study titled *The Limits to Growth,* which used computer modeling to project severe future resource and environmental problems as a result of continued economic growth (Box 2.1).[2] This report touched off a vigorous debate between growth "optimists" and "pessimists."

For the most part, the optimists placed faith in future technological progress to tap new sources of energy, overcome any resource limitations, and control pollution problems. The pessimists pointed to the rapid growth of population and GDP, together with the already formidable array of existing environmental problems, to warn that humanity was in danger of "overshooting" the earth's capacity to sustain economic activity. In effect, the question was whether the successful experience of economic growth over the previous two centuries could be sustained in the future.

BOX 2.1 THE LIMITS TO GROWTH MODEL

The Limits to Growth model, presented by a research team from the Massachusetts Institute of Technology (MIT) in 1972, addressed the issue of physical limits to economic growth. The study employed a model called World 3, which attempted to capture interrelationships between population, agricultural output, economic growth, resource use, and pollution. At the time, public attention was just beginning to focus on environmental issues, and the message of the MIT study had a powerful impact. The team conclusion was that we would reach the environmental limits to global growth within a century and that without drastic changes there was a strong likelihood of an "overshoot/collapse" outcome: "a sudden and uncontrollable decline in both population and industrial capacity."[1]

The model relied heavily on exponential growth patterns and feedback effects. Exponential growth occurs when population, economic production, resource use, or pollution increases by a certain percentage each year. Feedback effects occur when two variables interact, for example, when capital accumulation increases economic output, which in turn leads to a more rapid accumulation of capital. Positive feedback effects strengthen growth trends, whereas negative feedback effects moderate them. Negative feedback effects, however, may be undesirable, for example when limits on food supply cause population decline through malnutrition and disease.

Figure 2.1 shows a portion of the complex pattern of feedback effects in the World 3 model. The results of the model's "standard run" are shown in Figure 2.2. Exponential growth in population, industrial output, and food demand generate declines in resources and increasing pollution, which force a catastrophic reversal of growth by the mid-twenty-first century.

The report also emphasized that aggressive policies to moderate population growth, resource consumption, and pollution could avoid this disastrous result, leading instead to a smooth transition to global economic and ecological stability. This conclusion received far less attention than the catastrophic predictions. The report was widely criticized for failing to recognize the flexibility and adaptability of the economic system and for overstating the danger of resource exhaustion.

In 1992, the authors of the 1972 report published another book reasserting their conclusions but with more emphasis on environmental problems such as ozone layer destruction and global climate change. Once again they stated that catastrophe was not inevitable, but warned of an even more urgent need for major policy changes to achieve sustainability, with some ecological systems already being forced beyond their limits.[2] With such policy changes, the results look significantly different. In a model run showing a "transition to sustainability," policies are implemented to stabilize population, limit growth of industrial output, conserve resources and agricultural land, and control pollution. This leads to a stable, wealthier world population by 2050, with declining pollution levels (Figure 2.3).

NOTES

1. Meadows et al., 1972.
2. Meadows et al., 1992.

In the 30-year update to *Limits to Growth*, published in 2002, the authors argued that "overshoot" had already occurred in major planetary systems.[3] In a fortieth anniversary report in 2012, one of the authors, Jorgen Randers, suggested that the most likely outcome would be a stabilization of population and GDP around 2050, but with significant damage to climate systems, coral reefs, oceans, forests, and other ecosystems.[4] Note that even if something like a "sustainable world" model (see Figure 2.3) were achieved, this would represent a radical change from the current model of exponential economic growth.

Figure 2.1 **Feedback Loops of Population, Capital, Resources, Agriculture, and Pollution**

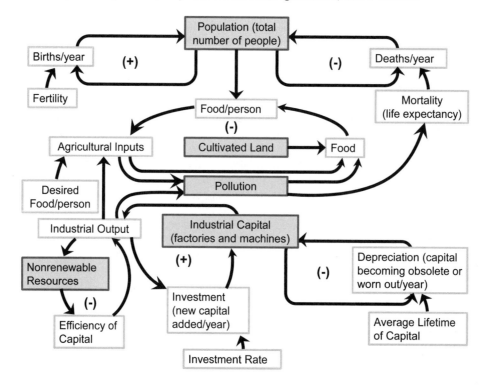

Source: Meadows et al., 1992.

Figure 2.2 **The Basic Limits to Growth Model**

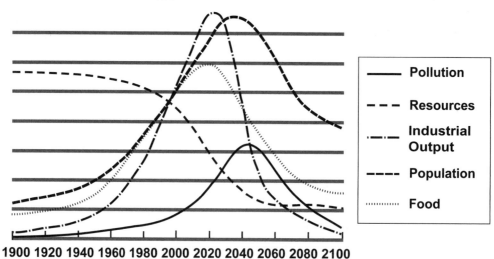

Source: Meadows et al., 1992.

Figure 2.3 **A Sustainable World Model**

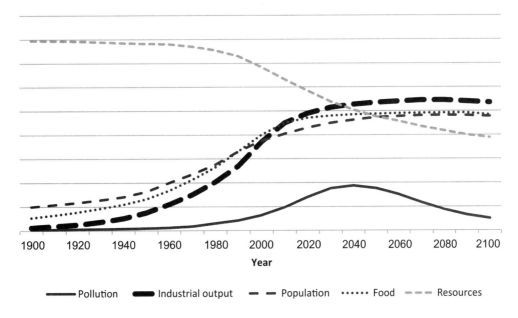

Year

———— Pollution   ━ ━ ━ Industrial output   — — Population   •••••• Food   — — — Resources

Source: Meadows et al., 1992.

We can explore some of the specifics of the limits to growth debate by reviewing the history of economic growth and looking at some of the specific possibilities for the future in terms of population, food supply, resources, energy, and pollution.

2.2 A SUMMARY OF RECENT GROWTH

It is worth noting that the economic growth since the conclusion of World War II has been extraordinary in its scope and character. In historical terms, world population and economic growth between 1800 and 1950 represented a significant increase over previous slow growth rates. But the rates since 1950 have been truly remarkable in historical context.

Between 1950 and 2010, world population more than doubled, world agricultural production more than tripled, and real world GDP and energy use more than quadrupled (Figure 2.4 shows trends since 1961). This, of course, has raised demands on resources and the environment to unprecedented levels. The growth process, however, is far from completed. Global population, which surpassed 7 billion in 2011, continues to increase by 1.2 percent per year, a net addition of more than 70 million people (more than the entire population of France) every year.

Together with population growth, the demand for improved living standards continues to drive overall production steadily upward. GDP growth faltered in the aftermath of the global economic crisis of 2008, but otherwise has averaged between 2 and 3 percent per year, adjusted for inflation, in both developing and developed countries, with much higher rates in many developing countries such as China. At this rate, by 2030 world GDP will be more than double the 2000 GDP level.

Figure 2.4 **Growth in Population, Agricultural Production, and Energy Use, 1961–2010**

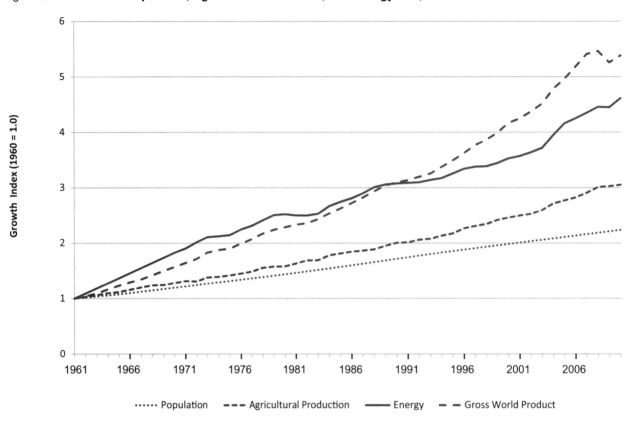

Sources: Population and agriculture: FAO, 2012; GWP: IMF, www.imf.org; energy data: US EIA, www.eia.gov.

As population and per capita GDP grow, increased demands for food, living space, and consumption goods put increased pressure on land, water, resources, and the atmosphere. Many of the stresses are already evident, with problems such as land degradation, depletion of water supplies, forest loss, ecosystem decline, and climate change affecting the functioning of basic life support systems.

Will we have enough energy, resources, and environmental capacity to sustain a much greater level of output? We examine many specific aspects of this question in succeeding chapters. As an introduction, we review the main dimensions of the problem and suggest some approaches to analyze them.

2.3 THE FUTURE OF ECONOMIC GROWTH AND THE ENVIRONMENT

In the economic history of the twentieth century, environmental issues gradually became more prominent. During the Great Depression of the 1930s, soil erosion drew attention, and in the 1950s and 1960s, concerns about pesticide use and air and water pollution emerged. Only in the last decades of the twentieth century, however, did environmental degradation gain recognition as a fundamental challenge to the whole economic growth process. In the global economy of the twenty-first century, by contrast, environmental considerations are becoming a determining factor in shaping economic development.

Population Growth

population momentum
the tendency for a population to continue to grow, even if the fertility rate falls to the replacement level, as long as a high proportion of the population is in young age cohorts.

The first essential fact of this new global economy is our dramatically increased population. The phenomenon of **population momentum**, discussed in Chapter 9, guarantees growing populations in most countries over the next forty years. Unlike many predictions that may be quickly disproved by events, this one is virtually certain; the largest generation of children in global history has already been born. We know that these children will grow to be adults and have children of their own. Even if they have small families (and large families are now the norm in much of the world), their children will significantly outnumber the present older generations that they will replace. Although some countries, such as Japan and some countries in Europe, are facing declining populations (see Chapter 9), most of the world is still experiencing growing population.

Thus only a huge increase in the death rate could alter the prediction of significantly higher population. Even the global AIDS crisis, despite its global spread, is unlikely to affect population projections except in a few regions. The lowest projections for 2050 show a population of 8 billion; median and higher-range projections show a global population of 9 billion or 10 billion. More than 95 percent of this increase will occur in currently developing countries.

Although global population growth rates have been falling since the 1970s, a decline projected to continue, the addition to world population (a smaller percentage of a larger total) will remain over 50 million per year over the next several decades.[5]

Such population growth raises the question of whether we can feed everyone in the world. Will agricultural capacity be sufficient to supply the needs of an extra 1 to 3 billion people? We can examine this problem in several ways. The simplest question is whether it is physically possible to produce sufficient grain and other foodstuffs to provide adequate nutrition for 8 billion to 10 billion people, given the limited global land area suitable for agriculture. The more difficult problem is whether it is possible to satisfy ever-growing per capita demand, including demand for "luxury" foods and meat-centered diets.

Global inequality means that widespread hunger and malnutrition persist even when the *average* food production on a national or global basis is adequate. Economic growth may improve the standard of living of the poorest (though this is not always true by any means), but it also encourages increased per capita consumption by the relatively affluent. Taking this into account, food consumption is likely to grow significantly more rapidly than population.

intensification of production
increasing production rates with a limited supply of resources, such as increasing agricultural yield per acre.

Increasing global food production will require **intensification of production**. This means that each acre of land must produce significantly higher food output. The stresses on land and water supplies, the increased fertilizer requirements, and the problems of erosion, chemical runoff, and pesticide pollution represent the real limits to agricultural expansion. In addition, a growing demand for biofuels also creates demand for agricultural land that is already competing with food production.

In Chapter 10 we examine in more detail this interplay between population, social inequality, food consumption, food production, and environmental impacts. Certainly a focus on productive capacity alone is insufficient. Resource and environmental factors, as well as issues of equity, are central in responding to the challenge of feeding much larger populations with limited resources.

In addition to agricultural land requirements, expanding populations require more space for urban, residential, and industrial development. These needs tend to encroach on farmland, forests, and natural ecosystems. This population pressure on land is acute in countries such as India (383 people per square kilometer), or Bangladesh (1,062 people per square kilometer). In less densely populated countries such as the United States (33 people per square kilometer),[6] land use is still a central environmental issue, with ever-increasing pressure from suburban developments on farmland and natural areas and continual conflict between large-scale agriculture or forestry and wilderness preservation.

Rising Resource Demand

Resource use issues also surround the question of future population and economic growth. The original argument of the 1972 *Limits to Growth* report stressed limited supplies of key **nonrenewable resources** such as metal ores and other minerals. Since then, the focus of the debate has shifted. Critics of the pessimistic position on growth limits have pointed out that new resource discoveries, new technologies for extraction, and the development of substitute resources as well as expanded recycling all extend the horizon of resource use. As with food supply, the real issue may not be absolute limits on availability but, rather, the environmental impacts of increased **resource recovery** (mining or extraction of resources for economic use).

Mining operations, for example, are notoriously damaging to the environment. If the "average" global consumer demand for iron, copper, zinc, and other metals rises toward the current U.S. consumption level at the same time as world population rises, requirements for extraction of mineral ores will rise drastically. Plenty of mineral ores remain to be extracted from the earth's crust—but at what environmental cost?

Common sense and economic theory both tell us that the highest-quality ores will be exploited first.[d] As we move toward the use of lower-quality ores, the energy requirements to obtain processed metal, as well as the volume of related industrial waste, rise steadily. Our present mining operations have left a legacy of scarred earth and polluted water—how will we deal with future higher-impact requirements including new demands for precious metals and rare earths essential for cell phones and other electronics?

Increasing Energy Use

Expansion of resource use, like expansion of agricultural output, depends on energy supply. Energy is fundamental to economic activity and to life itself, making possible the use of all other resources. Energy resource issues are therefore of special importance. Nineteenth-century economic development relied largely on coal, and twentieth century development on oil. Our current heavy dependence on fossil fuel resources poses major problems for the twenty-first century economy.

These issues arise in part from limited supplies of fossil fuels. Currently known reserves of oil and gas will be largely depleted within fifty years. Coal reserves will last much longer—but coal is the "dirtiest" of all fossil fuels. The burning of coal, oil, and gas all contribute to ground-level air pollution as well as to global carbon emissions, an important cause of **global climate change**.

nonrenewable resources
resources that are available in a fixed supply, such as metal ores and oil.

resource recovery
mining or extraction of resources for economic use.

global climate change
the changes in global climate, including temperature, precipitation, and storm frequency and intensity, that result with changes in the concentrations of greenhouse gases in the atmosphere.

---

[d]The economic theory of nonrenewable resources is explained in detail in Chapters 5 and 11.

Increased population and rising living standards are projected to require significantly increased energy use over the next forty years. As we have noted, world energy use has quadrupled since the end of World War II. A 2 percent annual rate of growth in energy use, barely sufficient to keep ahead of growing population, would cause it to double again in 35 years. It is more likely that energy use, especially in developing countries, will increase at a faster rate to fuel industrial growth. New less-polluting sources of energy, as well as reduction in present per capita energy use in developed countries, appear essential. The economics of this transition to alternative energy sources is discussed in Chapters 12 and 17.

Dwindling Resources

renewable resources
a resource that is supplied on a continuing basis by ecosystems; renewable resources such as forests and fisheries can be depleted through exploitation.

overharvesting of renewable resources
rates of harvest that decrease the stock or population of a resource over time.

Worldwide pressure on **renewable resources** such as forests and fisheries has become increasingly evident. **Overharvesting of renewable resources** has caused serious environmental losses. World forest cover has declined, with rapid loss of tropical forest during the past several decades, although temperate forest cover has remained steady or increased slightly.[7] After increasing steadily between 1950 and the mid-1980s, global fish catch appears to have reached a maximum, with some major fisheries now in decline.

Exploitation of natural resources is also causing an increasing rate of species loss, posing unknown ecological hazards and diminishing the natural "inheritance" of future generations. Clearly, these pressures will only increase with rising demands for food, fuel, wood products, and fiber.

Economic theory offers an explanation for the overharvesting phenomenon, as we will see in Chapters 4 and 13. Prescribing solutions is more difficult. Such prescriptions will certainly require a conceptual shift from regarding forests and fisheries as unrestricted **open-access resources** to perceiving them as part of a **global commons**.[e] Future economic development cannot simply take advantage of the "free" resources such as undeveloped land and open oceans but must be adjusted to ecological limits. In some cases, private property rights can create incentives for individual owners to conserve resources. Other situations require the development of effective regional or global common-property management policies.

open-access resource(s)
a resource that offers unrestricted access such as an ocean fishery or the atmosphere.

global commons
global common property resources such as the atmosphere and the oceans.

Pollution

cumulative pollutants
pollutants that do not dissipate or degrade significantly over time.

Economic growth also brings the problem of growing volumes of **cumulative pollutants** (pollutants that do not dissipate or degrade significantly over time) and of toxic and nuclear wastes. Controls on emissions, the traditional focus of pollution policy, are of limited use in dealing with these more insidious problems. When we deal with cumulative pollutants such as chlorofluorocarbons (CFCs), organochlorides such as DDT, or radioactive wastes, we must grapple with the legacy of all previous pollution and waste production as well as consider how our present activities will affect the future environment. This greatly complicates any economic evaluation of costs and benefits.

Air and water pollutants that are not cumulative can be controlled through specific regulatory policies. But economic growth often leads to an increased volume of such pollutants. In the area of emissions control, improved technology continually races

---

[e] "Commons" is a term used to refer to resources that are not privately owned but must be managed for the social good.

against increased consumption (automobile use is a prime example). Some major pollutants have declined in industrialized countries due to environmental regulation. But some others have increased, and developing countries like China are just beginning to grapple with their severe industrial pollution problems. The economic analysis of pollution control offers policy solutions for specific emissions problems, whereas the newer theory of **industrial ecology**, explored in Chapter 17, offers an overview of the relationship of pollution-generating activities to the natural environment.

industrial ecology
the application of ecological principles to the management of industrial activity.

An Ecological Approach to Economic Growth and the Environment

In reviewing these major environmental and resource challenges of the twenty-first century, we should not necessarily lean toward either an "optimistic" or "pessimistic" perspective. Much depends on policy responses. While analysts differ greatly regarding appropriate responses, few dispute the importance of global environment and resource issues. As we will see, both the market-oriented approach stressing economic system adaptability and the ecological assessment of biophysical problems have important roles to play in devising policy responses.

Chapters 9–19 give these issues more detailed attention. Although in each case specific policies may address individual problems, the issues together suggest a common need for a different kind of economic analysis, one that addresses a global economy in which resource and environmental considerations are much more prominent than in the past.

Rather than approaching environmental questions as a secondary issue after we have dealt with the basic economic issues of production, employment, and output growth, our concept of economics must consider the environment as fundamental to the production process. Of course, economic production has always depended on the environment, but the scale of economic activity makes a difference. Now that economic production produces such widespread environmental effects, it is essential to integrate our views of economics and environment.

environmental sustainability
the continued existence of an ecosystem in a healthy state; ecosystems may change over time but do not significantly degrade.

If we adopt a broader perspective, we must adapt the goals of economic activity to ecological realities. Traditionally, the main goals of economic activity have been to increase welfare though increased industrial production and rising per capita consumption. For all the reasons presented above, these goals may pose a threat to the **environmental sustainability** of our economic system. Either the goals or the methods we choose to achieve them must be modified as population and environmental pressures increase.

sustainable development
development that meets the needs of the present without compromising the ability of future generations to meet their own needs.

The effort to balance economic and environmental goals is addressed in the theory of **sustainable development**—economic development that provides for human needs without undermining global ecosystems and depleting essential resources. Some have complained that "sustainable development" is just a buzzword devoid of specific content. Others have quickly moved to appropriate the term "sustainable" to characterize only slightly modified forms of traditional economic growth. Nevertheless, the outlines of a new concept that redefines economic goals have begun to emerge.[8]

2.4 SUSTAINABLE DEVELOPMENT

Recall that the standard view of economic growth is defined in terms of per capita GDP, meaning that total GDP must grow faster than population. Sustainable development requires different measures. Increased output of goods and services can certainly be part of the desired outcome, but equally important is the maintenance of the ecological base of the economy—fertile soils, natural ecosystems, forests, fisheries, and water systems.

As we will see in Chapter 8, techniques for modifying the measurement of national income can take such factors into account. Even so, sustainable development means more than simply using a different yardstick. It also implies a different analysis of the process of production and consumption.

Sustainable Development Versus Standard Views of Economic Growth

On the production side, it is important to differentiate between renewable and nonrenewable resources. Every economy must use some nonrenewable resources, but sustainable development implies conservation or recycling of these resources and greater reliance on renewables. On the consumption side, an important distinction is drawn between wants and needs. In contrast to the standard economic paradigm, in which "dollar votes" command the marketplace and determine which goods are to be produced, sustainable development implies putting a priority on supplying basic needs before luxury goods.[9]

Also in contrast to standard economic growth theory, sustainability implies some limits to the **macroeconomic scale**. Rather than projecting rates of growth indefinitely into the future, a maximum level can be postulated based on the **carrying capacity** of the area (and ultimately of the planet). This in turn implies a maximum level of population above which carrying capacity—the level of population and consumption that can be sustained by the available natural resource base—will be exceeded and living standards must fall.[10]

Population and Sustainable Development

This introduction of population as a key variable in determining the limits to economic growth has implications for both developing and currently industrialized countries. For developing countries with rapid population growth rates, it means that limiting population growth is a critical element in successful development.

For industrialized countries, the role of population is different. In much of Europe and in Japan, population has stabilized, and for some countries concern has shifted to an emerging pattern of population decline (see Chapter 9). In the United States, however, population increase continues to put pressure both on national and on global ecosystems. Although the U.S. population growth rate is less dramatic than that in many developing countries (0.5 percent per annum as opposed to 2–3 percent in much of Latin America, Africa, and Asia), the much larger level of U.S. per capita consumption means that each additional U.S. resident creates a much greater additional resource demand than, for example, an additional resident of Nigeria or Bangladesh.

This means that population policy must be an essential element of sustainable development. Population policy must include elements of education, social policy, economic policy, and health care, including availability of contraception, and often runs into conflict with established religious and social mores. Still, this difficult area, generally little considered in standard economic development models, is crucial for sustainability.

macroeconomic scale
the total scale of an economy; ecological economics suggests that the ecosystem imposes scale limits on the macroeconomy.

carrying capacity
the level of population and consumption that can be sustained by the available natural resource base.

Agriculture and Sustainable Development

When we consider agriculture production systems, the general principle of relying as much as possible on renewable resources runs counter to much of standard agricultural "modernization." Modern food production is based on **input-intensive agriculture**, meaning that it depends heavily on additional fertilizer, pesticides, water for irrigation, and mechanization. All of these in turn depend on fossil-fuel energy. Traditional agriculture, based on solar energy, animal power, and human labor, has generally produced lower yields than modern agriculture.

The concept of **sustainable agriculture** combines elements of traditional and modern techniques. It emphasizes maximum use of renewable resources such as crop waste and animal manure, as well as crop rotation, intercropping of different plant types, agroforestry, efficient irrigation, minimum-till techniques, and integrated pest management (discussed in Chapter 10). It is still an open question whether this form of agriculture can achieve the yields achieved with input-intensive techniques, but its environmental impacts are less damaging or even beneficial to the environment.

Energy and Sustainable Development

A similar issue arises as to whether **renewable energy sources** (including **solar energy**) have the capacity to supplant dependence on fossil fuel. The challenge is a daunting one, because renewables now supply less than 10 percent of energy in industrialized countries. The picture is different in developing countries, where a large portion of current energy supply comes from **biomass** (wood, plant, and animal waste). Efficient use of biomass and maintenance of forest resources can thus play an important role in energy policy. Technological advances in solar, wind, and biomass energy systems have brought the prices of these renewable sources down, and their potential for future expansion is significant in both developed and developing countries.

Huge, often unrecognized, potential lies in conservation and improved efficiency—by some estimates the developed world could reduce its energy use by at least 30 percent through these techniques with little or no effect on living standards.[11] The traditional emphasis on **energy supply augmentation** (such as building new power plants) could thus give way to a focus on **demand-side management** (increasing efficiency and reducing energy consumption).

Because industrialized countries now account for three-quarters of global energy use (though only one-quarter of global population), increased energy consumption in developing countries could be offset by reductions in developed country energy use. Such reductions could come from increased efficiency rather than requiring reduced living standards. Negotiations over global climate policy (discussed in Chapter 19) suggest that such a tradeoff may be essential to reduce overall human impacts on world climate.

Sustainable Management for Natural Resources

Sustainable natural resource management implies a combination of economic and ecological perspectives. The economic theory of natural resource management, set forth in Chapters 13–15, shows how many management systems for resources such as forests

---

input-intensive agriculture
agricultural production that relies heavily on machinery, artificial fertilizers, pesticides, and irrigation.

sustainable agriculture
systems of agricultural production that do not deplete the productivity of the land or environmental quality, including such techniques as integrated pest management, organic techniques, and multiple cropping.

renewable energy sources
energy sources that are supplied on a continual basis such as wind, water, biomass, and direct solar energy.

solar energy
the energy supplied continually by the sun, including direct solar energy as well as indirect forms such as wind energy and flowing water.

biomass
an energy supply from wood, plant, and animal waste.

energy supply augmentation
an approach to energy management emphasizing increase in energy supplies, such as building more power plants or increasing oil drilling.

demand-side management
an approach to energy management that stresses increasing energy efficiency and reducing energy consumption.

and fisheries can lead to depletion or even extinction of the resource. Proper incentives and institutions can promote sustainable management. Current management systems for many of the world's fisheries and forests, however, are far from sustainable.

In the area of industrial pollution management, the standard economic approach is to analyze the costs and benefits of various forms of pollution control to determine an economically optimal policy. This approach has its merits, fully considered in Chapter 16, but it is insufficient for sustainability. The best pollution control policy can be overwhelmed by growth in pollution-generating activities, especially those that produce cumulative pollutants.

Attention has therefore begun to focus on the new concept of industrial ecology as a more comprehensive approach to pollution control. Using the analogy of a natural ecosystem's capacity to recycle its own wastes, this approach attempts to analyze industrial systems as a whole to identify ways in which to minimize or avoid the generation of pollutants and maximizing the recycling of resources. The application of industrial ecology techniques, discussed in Chapter 17, has potential both for restructuring existing industrial systems and for economic development in Latin America, Asia, and Africa.

In all these areas, sustainable development offers a new **theoretical paradigm,** which differs from the standard economic approach. Considering a new paradigm of thought is justified because the global reality has changed radically from an earlier period when economic policy could be formulated without much regard to environmental impacts.

Following this logic, we might distinguish roughly three periods of economic history. In the pre-industrial period, human population and economic activity remained at fairly stable levels, placing only limited demands on the planetary ecosystem. During the past two hundred years of rapid industrial and population growth, economic growth has had increasingly heavy environmental impacts. The process has not been uniform; in some cases, improved technology or changing industrial patterns have lessened pollution and resource demand. Nevertheless, the increasing pressures already discussed suggest that we are entering a third period during which population growth and economic activity must align with ecological carrying capacity.

The tools of economic analysis, which we study in Part II, are drawn from standard economic theory, while the perspectives presented in Part III respond to the issues of ecological limits on economic growth. The two in combination provide a powerful toolbox of analytical techniques with which to address the multifaceted questions of the interrelationship between environment and economy.

SUMMARY

Economic growth over time reflects both population and per capita GDP growth. This growth depends on increases in capital stock and technological progress, as well as increased supplies of energy, natural resources, and the capacity of the environment to absorb waste.

A simple model of the relationship between population, industrial output, resources, and pollution indicates that unlimited economic growth will lead to exhaustion of resources, rising pollution, and eventual collapse of economic systems and ecosystems. However, such a model depends on assumptions about technological progress and feedback patterns among the variables in the model. A more optimistic view considers increased efficiency, pollution control, and a transition to alternative, more sustainable technologies.

Between 1950 and 2010, unprecedented rates of growth more than doubled population, more than tripled world agricultural production, and more than quadrupled world GDP and energy use. Continuing population and economic growth will exert even greater demands on resources and the environment during the first half of the twenty-first century. Food production, nonrenewable resource recovery, energy supply, atmospheric pollution, toxic wastes, and renewable resource management are all major issues requiring detailed analysis and policy solutions. In addition, the nature of economic growth must adapt to environmental and resource constraints.

The concept of sustainable development attempts to combine economic and environmental goals. Sustainable techniques for agricultural production, energy use, natural resource management, and industrial production have significant potential but have yet to be widely adopted. A sustainable global economy also implies limits on population and material consumption. The question of the sustainability of economic activity has already become a major issue and will be even more important in coming decades.

KEY TERMS AND CONCEPTS

absorptive capacity of the environment	nominal GDP
biomass	nonrenewable resources
capital stock	open-access resources
carrying capacity	overharvesting of renewable resources
cumulative pollutants	per capita GDP growth rate
demand-side management	population growth rate
energy supply augmentation	population momentum
environmental sustainability	productivity per capita
GDP growth rate	real GDP
global climate change	renewable energy sources
global commons	renewable resources
gross domestic product (GDP)	resource recovery
industrial ecology	solar energy
input-intensive agriculture	sustainable agriculture
intensification of production	sustainable development
macroeconomic scale	sustainable natural resource management
Malthusian hypothesis	technological progress
natural capital	theoretical paradigm

DISCUSSION QUESTIONS

1. Can we safely say that history has refuted the Malthusian hypothesis? What main factors have worked against Malthus's perspective? How might that perspective still be relevant today?
2. Over the past several decades, people have worried about the world running out of oil or natural resources. Sufficient oil remains for current needs, however, and no important

resources have run short. Have these fears been exaggerated? How would you evaluate them, considering both past experience and future prospects?

3. Does an improved standard of living necessarily mean more consumption? Is it possible to envision a future in which consumption of many goods and natural resources would decline? If this happened, would it mean an end to economic growth? How might perception of these questions differ, for example, for a citizen of the United States and a citizen of India?

NOTES

1. U.S. Department of Energy, 2012.
2. Meadows et al., 1972.
3. Meadows et al., 2002, chap. 2.
4. Randers, 2012.
5. Population Reference Bureau, 2012; United Nations, 2010.
6. Population Reference Bureau, 2012.
7. Food and Agriculture Organization, 2011.
8. For a review of theory and practice in the area of sustainable development, see Harris et al., 2001; López and Toman, 2006.
9. The "basic needs" approach to development, first set forth by Streeten et al., 1981; it has been further developed in Stewart, 1985; Sen, 2000; and UNDP, 1990–2011.
10. See Daly, 1996, on limits to macroeconomic scale.
11. See, for example, Intergovernmental Panel on Climate Change (IPCC), 2007, and the American Council for an Energy-Efficient Economy, www.aceee.org.

REFERENCES

Daly, Herman E. 1996. *Beyond Growth: The Economics of Sustainable Development*. Boston: Beacon Press.

Food and Agruculture Organization, 2011. *State of the World's Forests 2011*. Rome.

Harris, Jonathan M., Timothy A. Wise, Kevin Gallagher, and Neva R. Goodwin, eds. 2001. *A Survey of Sustainable Development*. Washington, DC: Island Press.

Intergovernmental Panel on Climate Change (IPCC). 2007. *Climate Change 2007: Mitigation of Climate Change*. Cambridge: Cambridge University Press.

López, Ramón, and Michael A. Toman. 2006. *Economic Development and Environmental Sustainability: New Policy Options*. Oxford: Oxford University Press.

Malthus, Thomas Robert. 1993. *Essay on the Principle of Population as It Affects the Future Improvement of Society*. New York: Oxford University Press. (Original publication 1798.)

Meadows, Donnella H., et al. 1972. *The Limits to Growth*. New York: Universe Books.

———. 1992. *Beyond the Limits: Confronting Global Collapse, Envisioning a Sustainable Future*. White River Junction, VT: Chelsea Green.

———. 2002. *Limits to Growth: The 30-Year Update*. White River Junction, VT: Chelsea Green.

Population Reference Bureau. 2012. *2011 World Population Data Sheet*. Washington, DC.

Randers, Jorgen. 2012. *2052: A Global Forecast for the Next Forty Years*. White River Junction, VT: Chelsea Green.

Sen, Amartya. 2000. *Development as Freedom*. New York: Knopf.

Stewart, Frances. 1985. *Basic Needs in Developing Countries*. Baltimore: Johns Hopkins University Press.

Streeten, Paul, et al. 1981. *First Things First: Meeting Basic Needs in Developing Countries*. New York: Oxford University Press.

United Nations. Department of Economic and Social Affairs, Population Division. 2010. *World Population Prospects: The 2010 Revision*. http://esa.un.org/unpd/wpp/index.htm.

United Nations Development Programme (UNDP). 1990–2011. *Human Development Report*. New York: Oxford University Press.

U.S. Department of Energy. 2012. *International Energy Outlook*. Washington, DC: Energy Information Administration.

World Resources Institute, United Nations Development Programme, United Nations Environment Programme, and World Bank. 2011. *World Resources 2010–2011: Decision Making in a Changing Climate*. Washington DC: World Resources Institute.

WEB SITES

1. **www.iisd.org.** The homepage for the International Institute for Sustainable Development, an organization that conducts policy research toward the goal of integrating environmental stewardship and economic development.
2. **www.epa.gov/economics/.** The Web site for the National Center for Environmental Economics, a division of the U.S. Environmental Protection Agency that conducts and supervises research on environmental economics. Its Web site includes links to many research reports.
3. **http://ase.tufts.edu/gdae/.** The homepage for the Global Development and Environment Institute at Tufts University, "dedicated to promoting a new understanding of how societies can pursue their economic goals in an environmentally and socially sustainable manner." The site includes links to many research publications.
4. **www.wri.org.** The World Resources Institute Web site offers the biennial publication *World Resources* as well as extensive reports and data on global resource and environmental issues.

PART TWO

ECONOMIC ANALYSIS OF ENVIRONMENTAL ISSUES

The Theory of Environmental Externalities

CHAPTER 3 FOCUS QUESTIONS

- How can pollution and environmental damage be represented in economics?
- What economic policies can be instituted to respond to environmental problems?
- How and when can property rights be relied upon to solve environmental problems?

3.1 THE THEORY OF EXTERNALITIES

externalities
an effect of a market transaction that changes the utility, positively or negatively, of those outside the transaction.

third-party effects
effects of market transactions that affect people other than those involved in the transaction, such as industrial pollution that affects a local community.

negative externality/externalities
negative impacts of a market transaction affecting those not involved in the transaction.

positive externalities
the positive impacts of a market transaction that affect those not involved in the transaction.

marginal costs
the cost of producing or consuming one more unit of a good or service.

marginal benefit
the benefit of producing or consuming one more unit of a good or service.

How do environmental issues affect the economic analysis of markets? Markets reflect the benefits and costs of economic activities to those who participate in buying and selling goods and services. But how can we account for environmental impacts? Economists refer to the effects of a market transaction that affect someone other than those involved in it as **externalities**. Externalities are often called **third-party effects**, because they affect individuals or groups other than the market participants.

Externalities can be either positive or negative. The most common example of a **negative externality** is pollution. Without any regulation, the production decisions of companies will not account for the social and ecological damages of pollution. Consumers also typically will not limit their purchases because of pollution caused by the goods and services that they purchase. But when we analyze the overall social welfare of a market, we need to account for the damages from pollution.

In some cases, a market transaction can generate **positive externalities** if it benefits those external to the market. An example of a positive externality is a landowner who buys and plants trees. The trees provide benefits to those who appreciate the scenery and to society as a whole because they absorb carbon dioxide and provide habitat for wildlife.

In a basic economic analysis of markets, demand and supply curves represent the costs and benefits of a transaction. A supply curve tells us the **marginal costs** of production—in other words, the costs of producing one more unit of a good or service. Meanwhile, a demand curve can also be considered a **marginal benefit** curve because it tells us the perceived benefits consumers obtain from consuming one additional unit. The intersection of demand and supply curves gives the

Figure 3.1 **The Market for Automobiles**

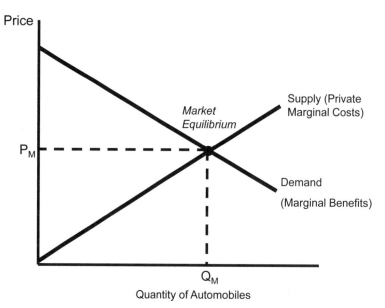

Note: Private marginal costs are the costs of production to private producers.

equilibrium price

the market price where the quantity supplied equals the quantity demanded.

economic efficiency

an allocation of resources that maximizes net social benefits; perfectly competitive markets in the absence of externalities are efficient.

internalizing external costs/externalities

using approaches such as taxation to incorporate external costs into market decisions.

external cost(s)

a cost, not necessarily monetary, that is not reflected in a market transaction.

equilibrium price at which supply and demand balance, as shown in Figure 3.1 for a hypothetical market for automobiles. This equilibrium represents a situation of **economic efficiency** because it maximizes benefits to buyers and sellers in the market—if there are no externalities.[a]

Accounting for Environmental Costs

But this market equilibrium does not tell the whole story. The production and use of automobiles create numerous negative externalities. Automobiles are a major contributor to air pollution, including both urban smog and regional problems such as acid rain. In addition, their emissions of carbon dioxide contribute to global warming. Automobile oil leaked from vehicles or disposed of improperly can pollute lakes, rivers, and groundwater. The production of automobiles involves toxic materials that can be released to the environment as toxic wastes. The road system required for automobiles paves over many acres of rural and open land, and salt runoff from roads damages watersheds.

Where do these various costs appear in Figure 3.1? The answer is that they do not appear at all. Thus the market overestimates the net social benefits of automobiles because the costs of the negative externalities are not considered. So we need to find ways of **internalizing externalities**—bringing the **external costs** into our market analysis.

The first problem in doing this is assigning a monetary value to environmental damages. How can we reduce the numerous environmental effects we have identified to a single monetary value? There is no clear-cut answer to this question. In some cases, economic damages are identifiable. For example, if road runoff pollutes a town's water supply, the cost of water treatment gives at least one estimate

---

[a]Benefits to buyers are known as consumer surplus, and benefits to sellers are called producer surplus. See Appendix 3.1 for an overview of benefits, costs, and efficiency in markets.

of environmental damages. However, this does not include less tangible factors such as damage to lake and river ecosystems.

If we can identify the health effects of air pollution, the resulting medical expenses will give us another monetary damage estimate, but this does not capture the aesthetic damage done by air pollution. Smoggy air limits visibility, which reduces people's welfare even it does not have a measurable effect on their health. Issues such as these are difficult to compress into a monetary indicator. Yet if we do not assign a monetary value to environmental damages, the market will automatically assign a value of zero, because none of these issues are directly reflected in consumer and producer decisions about automobiles.

Some economists have attempted to estimate the external costs of automobiles in monetary terms (see Box 3.1 and Table 3.1).[b] Assuming we have a reasonable estimate of these external costs, how can these be added to our supply and demand analysis?

Recall that the supply curve tells us the marginal costs of producing a good or service. But in addition to the normal private production costs, we now also need to consider the environmental costs—the costs of the negative externalities. So we can add the externality costs to the production costs to obtain the total social costs of automobiles. This results in a new cost curve, which we call a **social marginal cost curve**. This is shown in Figure 3.2.

The social marginal cost curve is above the original market supply curve because it now includes the externality costs. Note that the vertical distance between the two cost curves is our estimate of the externality costs of each automobile, measured in dollars. In this simple case, we have assumed that the external costs of automobiles are constant. Thus the two curves are parallel. This is probably not the

social marginal cost curve

the cost of providing one more unit of a good or service, considering both private production costs and externalities.

BOX 3.1   THE EXTERNAL COSTS OF MOTOR VEHICLE USE

What are the external, or social, costs of motor vehicle use in the United States? Annually in the United States, motor vehicles emit about 60 million tons of carbon monoxide, 10 million tons of nitrogen oxides, and other toxins, including formaldehyde and benzene. Annually, motor vehicle accidents in the United States kill more than 30,000 people and injure more than 3 million others. Additional external costs include the destruction of natural habitats from building roads and parking lots, the disposal of vehicles and parts, costs associated with national security in securing petroleum supplies, and noise pollution.

While some external costs are internalized through gasoline taxes, economic analyses find that these taxes are not sufficient to cover all external costs. Perhaps the most comprehensive attempt to monetize the external costs of motor vehicle use is a 20-volume study (Delucchi, 1997), which estimated the costs of such impacts as air pollution, crop losses, reduced visibility, national security, highway maintenance, and noise pollution.

Some of these costs are paid by the public sector while others are external social losses. Total annual externality costs were estimated at $167 billion under low-estimate assumptions and $1.483 trillion using high-estimate assumptions (in 2012 dollars). Annual public sector costs for motor vehicle infrastructure and services were estimated at $223 billion to $406 billion. Thus the total externality and public sector costs of automobile use range between 3 and 13 percent of the gross domestic product (GDP), depending on the underlying assumptions.

A 2007 article (Parry et al., 2007) summarized the existing literature on automobile externalities and presented a "best assessment" of automobile externalities in the United States, divided into several

---

[b]We discuss techniques of valuing environmental externalities in Chapter 6.

BOX 3.1 (*continued*)

categories as shown in Table 3.1. These estimates suggest that externalities from automobile use in the United States amount to about 3 percent of GDP. However, the Parry et al. study did not include public sector costs such as highway maintenance, which may be as much as the externality costs. Also, the Parry et al. estimate of climate change externalities, 6 cents per gallon, is based on social carbon damages of $20/ton. As we see in Chapter 18, other estimates of carbon damages are considerably higher.

As noted in both these studies, a range of policy approaches would be needed to fully internalize all the costs associated with motor vehicle use. For example, internalizing air pollution externalities should be based on a vehicle's emissions level rather than gasoline consumption. The externalities associated with congestion could be internalized through congestion tolls that charge drivers on busy roads depending on the time of the day, using electronic sensors.

Table 3.1

External Costs of Automobile Use in the United States

Cost Category	Dollars/gallon	Total ($billion/year)
Climate change	0.06	10
Oil dependency	0.12	20
Local pollution	0.42	71
Congestion	1.05	177
Accidents	0.63	106
Total externality costs	2.28	384

Sources: Delucchi, 1997; Parry et al., 2007.

Note: Total externality cost estimated by multiplying Parry et al.'s per-gallon damages by annual highway fuel consumption of 168 billion gallons, based on data from the 2012 *Statistical Abstract of the United States* (table 929).

Figure 3.2 **The Market for Automobiles with Negative Externalities**

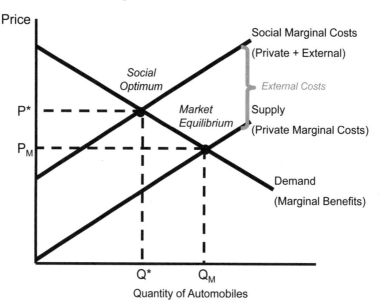

case in reality, as the external costs of automobiles can change depending on the number of automobiles produced. Specifically, the external costs of an additional automobile are likely to increase when more automobiles are produced as air pollution exceeds critical levels and congestion becomes more severe.

Considering Figure 3.2, is our market equilibrium still the economically efficient outcome? It is definitely not. To understand why, you can think of the social decision to produce each automobile to depend on comparing the marginal costs and marginal benefits. If the marginal benefit exceeds the marginal cost, considering all benefits and costs, then from the social perspective it makes sense to produce that automobile. But if the costs exceed the benefits, then it does not make sense to produce that automobile.

So in Figure 3.2 we see that it makes sense to produce the first automobile because the demand curve (reflecting the marginal benefits) is above the social marginal cost curve (reflecting the production and externality costs). Even though the first automobile creates some negative externalities, the high marginal benefits justify producing that automobile. We see that this is true for each automobile produced up to a quantity of Q^*. At this point, the marginal benefits equal the social marginal costs. But then notice that for each automobile produced beyond Q^*, the marginal social costs are actually above the marginal benefits. In other words, for each automobile produced above Q^*, society is becoming worse off!

So our unregulated market outcome, at Q_M, results in a level of automobile production that is too high. We should produce automobiles only as long as the marginal benefits are greater than the marginal social costs. Thus the optimal level of automobile production is Q^*, not the market outcome of Q_M. Rather than producing the maximum benefits for society, the equilibrium outcome is inefficient in the presence of a negative externality. We can also see in Figure 3.2 that from the perspective of society, the market price of automobiles is too low—that is, it fails to reflect the true costs including the environmental impacts of automobiles.[c] The **socially efficient** price for automobiles is P^*.

socially efficient
a market situation in which net social benefits are maximized.

Internalizing Environmental Costs

Pigovian (pollution) tax
a per-unit tax set equal to the external damage caused by an activity, such as a tax per ton of pollution emitted equal to the external damage of a ton of pollution.

polluter pays principle
the view that those responsible for pollution should pay for the associated external costs, such as health costs and damage to wildlife habitats.

What can we do to correct this inefficient market equilibrium? The solution to our problem lies in getting the price of automobiles "right." The market fails to send a signal to consumers or producers that further production past Q* is socially undesirable. While each automobile imposes a cost upon society, neither the consumers nor the producers pay this cost. So, we need to "internalize" the externality so that these costs now enter into the market decisions of consumers and producers.

The most common way to internalize a negative externality is to impose a tax. This approach is known as a **Pigovian tax**, after Arthur Pigou, a well-known British economist who published his *Economics of Welfare* in 1920. It is also known as the **polluter pays principle**, since those responsible for pollution pay for the damages they impose upon society.

For simplicity, assume that the tax is paid by automobile manufacturers.[d] For each automobile produced, they must pay a set tax to the government. But what is the proper tax amount?

---

[c]See Appendix 3.2 for a more formal analysis of the impact of a negative externality.
[d]If we imposed the tax on the consumer instead of the producer, we would reach the same result as we obtain here.

By forcing manufacturers to pay a tax for each automobile produced, we have essentially increased their marginal production costs. So you can think of a tax as shifting the private marginal cost curve upward. The higher the tax, the more we would be shifting the cost curve upward. So if we set the tax exactly equal to the externality damage associated with each automobile, then the marginal cost of production would equal the social marginal cost curve in Figure 3.2. This is the "correct" tax amount—the tax per unit should equal the externality damage per unit.[e] In other words, those responsible for pollution should pay for the full social costs of their actions.

In Figure 3.3, the new supply curve with the tax is the same curve as the social marginal cost curve from Figure 3.2. It is the operative supply curve when producers decide how many automobiles to supply, because they now have to pay the tax in addition to their manufacturing costs.

The new equilibrium results in a higher price of P^* and a lower quantity of Q^*. The tax has resulted in the optimal level of automobile production. In other words, automobiles are produced only to the point where the marginal benefits are equal to the social marginal costs. Also note that even though the tax was levied on producers, a portion of the tax is passed on to consumers in the form of a price increase for automobiles. This causes consumers to cut back their purchases from Q_M to Q^*. From the point of view of achieving the socially optimal equilibrium, this is a good result. Of course, neither producers nor consumers will like the tax, since consumers will pay a higher price and producers will have lower sales, but from a social point of view we can say that this new equilibrium is optimal because it accurately reflects the true costs of automobile use.

Our story tells a convincing argument in favor of government regulation in the presence of negative externalities. The tax is an effective policy tool for reaching a more efficient outcome for society. But should the government always impose a tax to counter a negative externality? The production of most good or services are associated with some pollution damage. So it may seem as if the government should tax all products on the basis of their environmental damage.

But two factors suggest we probably should not put a Pigovian tax on all products. First, recall that we need to estimate the tax amount in monetary terms, which requires economic research and analysis, perhaps along with toxicological and ecological studies. Some products cause relatively minimal environmental damages and the small amount of taxes collected may not be worth the costs of estimating the "right" tax. Second, we need to consider the administrative costs of imposing and collecting the tax. Again, if a product does not cause much environmental damage, then these costs might outweigh the revenues we would collect.

Determining the appropriate tax on every product that causes environmental damage would be a monumental task. For example, we might impose a tax on shirts because the production process could involve growing cotton, using petroleum-based synthetics, applying potentially toxic dyes, and so on. But we would ideally need to set a different tax on shirts made with organic cotton, or those using recycled plastics, or even shirts of different sizes!

Rather than looking at the final consumer product, economists generally recommend applying Pigovian taxes as far upstream in the production process as possible.

---

[e]Note that in our example, the externality damage is constant per automobile produced. If the externality damages were not constant, we would set the tax equal to the marginal externality damage at the optimal level of production.

Figure 3.3 Automobile Market with Pigovian Tax

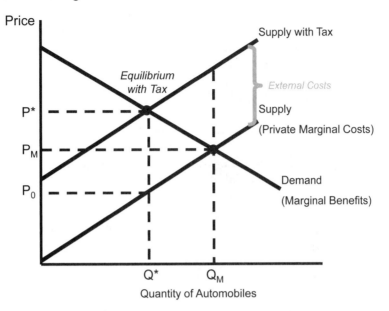

Quantity of Automobiles

upstream tax

a tax implemented as near as possible to the point of natural resource extraction.

An **upstream tax** is imposed at the level of the raw production inputs, such as the crude oil or cotton used to make a shirt. If we determine the appropriate Pigovian tax on cotton, then this cost will be reflected in the final selling price of the shirt. We could focus our taxation efforts on those raw materials that cause the most ecological damage. So we might tax fossil fuels, various mineral inputs, and toxic chemicals. This limits the administrative complexity of tax collection and avoids the need for estimating the appropriate tax for a multitude of products.

Another issue related to our externality analysis is to explore how the tax burden is distributed between producers and consumers. Many noneconomists claim that any taxes are simply passed on to consumers in terms of higher prices. While it is true that the automobile tax raised prices, was the full cost passed on to consumers? The answer is no. Note that the tax per unit was the difference between P_0 and P^* in Figure 3.3. But the price went up only by the difference between P_M and P^*. In this example, it seems that the tax burden was borne about equally by consumers and producers.

elasticity of demand

the sensitivity of quantity demanded to prices; an elastic demand means that a proportional increase in prices results in a larger proportional change in quantity demanded; an inelastic demand means that a proportional increase in prices results in a small change.

In some cases, the tax burden may fall more heavily on producers, while in other cases the burden may fall mostly on consumers. It depends on the **elasticities of supply and demand** with respect to price—how responsive supply and demand are to price changes. We discuss the topic of elasticities in more detail later in the text, including Appendix 3.1.

A final consideration is that a tax can fall disproportionately on certain income groups. One concern with most environmental taxes, such as taxes on fossil fuels, is that they hit low-income households the hardest. This is because the lower a household's income is, the more they tend to spend, as a share of their income, on fossil-fuel products, including gasoline and electricity. So we might wish to use some of the tax revenues to counteract the impact on low-income households, perhaps in the form of tax credits or rebates.

elasticity of supply

the sensitivity of quantity supplied to prices; an elastic supply means that a proportional increase in prices results in a larger proportional change in quantity supplied; an inelastic supply means that a proportional increase in prices results in a small change.

In practice, environmental policy often takes the form of other kinds of regulation besides taxes, such as, in the case of automobiles, fuel efficiency standards or mandated pollution control devices such as catalytic converters. These policies reduce fuel consumption and pollution without necessarily reducing the number of automobiles sold. They are also likely to drive up the purchase price of automobiles, so in this respect their effects are somewhat similar to a tax (although greater fuel efficiency reduces operating costs).

Positive Externalities

Just as it is in society's interest to internalize the social costs of pollution, it is also socially beneficial to internalize the social benefits of activities that generate positive externalities. As with a negative externality, the free market will also fail to maximize social welfare in the presence of a positive externality. Similarly, a policy intervention will be required to reach the efficient outcome.

A positive externality is an additional social benefit from a good or service beyond the private, or market, benefits. Because a demand curve tells us the private marginal benefits of a good or service, we can incorporate a positive externality into our analysis as an upward shift of the demand curve. This new curve represents the total social benefits of each unit.

Figure 3.4 shows the case of a good that generates a positive externality—solar panels. Each solar panel installed reduces emissions of carbon dioxide and thus benefits society as a whole. The vertical distance between the market demand curve and the social marginal benefits curve is the positive externality per solar panel, measured in dollars. In this example, the social benefits are constant per panel, so the two benefit curves are parallel.

The market equilibrium price is P_M, and quantity is Q_M. But notice in Figure 3.4 that between Q_M and Q^*, marginal social benefits exceed the marginal costs. Thus the optimal level of solar energy is Q^*, not Q_M. So we can increase net social benefits by increasing the production of solar energy.

Figure 3.4 **The Market for Solar Energy with Positive Externalities**

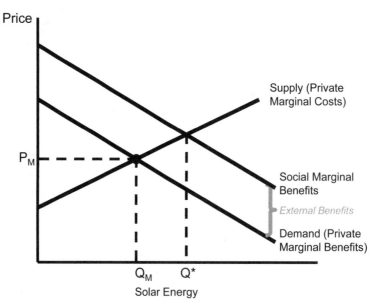

subsidy/subsidies

government assistance to an industry or economic activity; subsidies can be direct, through financial assistance, or indirect, through protective policies.

In the case of a positive externality, the most common policy to correct the market inefficiency is a subsidy. A **subsidy** is a payment to a producer to provide an incentive for it to produce more of a good or service. The way to illustrate a subsidy in our market analysis is to realize that a subsidy effectively lowers the cost of producing something. So a subsidy lowers the supply curve by the amount of the per-unit subsidy. In essence, a subsidy makes it cheaper to produce solar panels. The "correct" subsidy lowers the supply curve such that the new market equilibrium will be at Q^*, which is the socially efficient level of production. This is illustrated in Figure 3.5, with equilibrium at the point where the supply curve with the subsidy intersects the market demand curve.[f]

The principle parallels the use of a tax to discourage economic activities that create negative externalities—except that in this case we want to encourage activities that have socially beneficial side effects.

3.2 WELFARE ANALYSIS OF EXTERNALITIES

welfare analysis

an economic tool that analyzes the total costs and benefits of alternative policies to different groups, such as producers and consumers.

We can use a form of economic theory called **welfare analysis** to show why it is socially preferable to internalize externalities. The idea here is that *areas* on a supply and demand graph can be used to measure total benefits and costs. The area under the market demand curve shows the total benefit to consumers; the area under the market supply curve shows the total cost to producers. For each unit purchased, the demand curve shows the value of that unit to consumers.

This concept is illustrated in Figure 3.6, which presents a welfare analysis of the automobile market. Because the supply and demand curves, as noted above, show the *marginal* benefits and costs for each individual unit produced, the areas under these curves in effect sum up the *total* benefits and costs for all units produced. For consumers, the net benefit is called consumer surplus (area A)—representing the

Figure 3.5   **The Market for Solar Energy with a Subsidy**

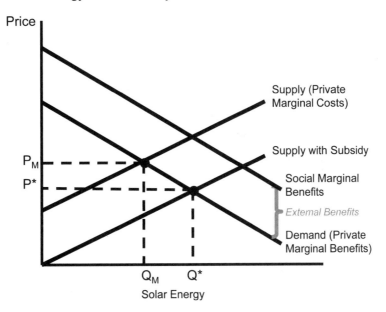

[f]See Appendix 3.2 for a detailed analysis of positive externalities.

difference between their benefits from the consumption of automobiles, as shown by the demand curve, and the price they pay, as shown by the horizontal line at P_M. Producers gain a net benefit defined as producer surplus (area B)—the difference between their production costs, shown by the supply curve, and the price P_M that they receive.[g]

In the absence of externalities, the market equilibrium is economically efficient because it maximizes the net social benefit (areas A + B). But if we introduce externalities, the market equilibrium is no longer economically efficient.

We can define the net social benefits of the automobile market as the sum of consumer and producer surplus minus the externality damage. Thus net benefits equal the market benefits (areas A and B in Figure 3.6) minus negative externality damages. This is shown in Figure 3.7. Here we superimpose externality damages, shown by the area between the private marginal cost curve and the social marginal cost curve, on Figure 3.6. (Figure 3.7 is equivalent to Figure 3.2, showing negative externalities in exactly the way we did earlier, but it also shows the total externality costs, equal to the dark area).

Note that the externality damages effectively offset parts of consumer and producer surplus. Net social welfare in the presence of the negative externality is (A′ + B′ − C), where C is just the triangular area to the right of Q^*. We have used the notation of A′ and B′ because these areas are smaller than areas A and B from Figure 3.6. A′ and B′ represent the areas of consumer and producer surplus that are not offset by subtracting the externality damage.[h] In addition to these smaller

Figure 3.6 **Welfare Analysis of the Automobile Market**

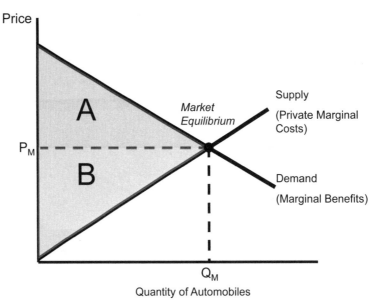

[g]Appendix 3.1 provides a background overview of market analysis, including a discussion of consumer and producer surplus.

[h]Note that consumer and producer surpluses are not lowered by the presence of the negative externality, which is external to the market benefits. Consumer surplus remains area A from Figure 3.6, and producer surplus remains area B. But parts of A and B are offset by the social loss from pollution, leaving a smaller net social gain. A more formal presentation of externality net benefits is presented in Appendix 3.2.

Figure 3.7 **Welfare Analysis of the Automobile Market with Externalities**

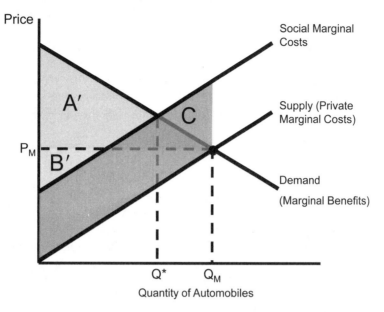

areas of net benefit, area C represents a net loss, because between Q^* and Q_M social marginal costs exceed marginal benefits, as shown by the demand curve.

Now consider the imposition of a Pigovian tax to internalize the externality. The tax will shift the equilibrium from Q_M to Q^*. We can prove that net social welfare has increased as a result of the tax by comparing the net welfare before the tax, area $(A' + B' - C)$ from Figure 3.7, to net welfare in Figure 3.8. With price at P^* and quantity at Q^*, our new consumer surplus is A'' and producer surplus is B''. Note that the sum of A'' and B'' is the same as the sum of A' and B' from Figure 3.7—as we will see shortly, this point is critical to our analysis.

Figure 3.8 **The Welfare-Improving Effect of a Pigovian Tax**

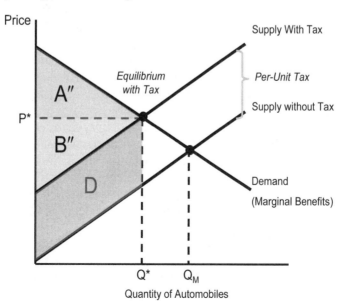

As we are only producing $Q*$ automobiles instead of Q_M, the externality damages are now area D, which is less than the externality damages from Figure 3.7. The per-unit tax is the vertical distance between the two supply curves. This tax is collected on a quantity of $Q*$ automobiles. Thus the total tax revenue is represented by area D. The tax revenue exactly equals the externality damages. In other words, the tax revenue is exactly sufficient to fully compensate society for the externality damages.

The net social welfare is the sum of consumer and producer surplus, minus the externality damages, plus the benefit of the tax revenue, or:

$$Net\ Social\ Welfare = A'' + B'' - D + D$$
$$= A'' + B''$$

As we mentioned above, area $(A'' + B'')$ equals area $(A' + B')$. Recall that net social welfare before the tax was $(A' + B' - C)$. Now net social welfare is effectively $(A' + B')$. Net social welfare has increased as a result of the Pigovian tax by area C. Society is better off with the tax than without it!

A similar welfare analysis of a positive externality and the impacts of a subsidy can be used to show that a subsidy in the presence of a positive externality increases net social welfare. The analysis is a bit more complex, and is presented in Appendix 3.2.

Optimal Pollution

optimal level of pollution
the pollution level that maximizes net social benefits.

Our analysis of negative externalities reveals an idea that may seem paradoxical—the concept of **optimal pollution**. Note that even after imposing an externality tax, society is still left with pollution damages of area D in Figure 3.8. According to our analysis, this is the "optimal" amount of pollution based on current production costs and technologies. But you might object, isn't the optimal level of pollution *zero*?

The economist's answer would be that the only way to achieve zero pollution is to have zero production. If we want to produce virtually any manufactured good, some pollution will result. We as a society must decide what level of pollution we are willing to accept. Of course, we can strive to reduce this level over time, especially through pollution-reducing technology, but as long as we have production we will have to determine an "optimal" pollution level.

Some people remain uneasy with the concept of optimal pollution. Note, for example, that if the demand for automobiles increases, the demand curve will shift to the right and the "optimal" pollution level will increase. This suggests that as global demand for automobiles rises steadily, ever-rising levels of pollution will, in some sense, be acceptable. We might choose instead to set a maximum level of acceptable pollution based on health and ecological considerations, rather than economic analysis. In fact, the main federal air pollution law in the United States, the Clean Air Act, sets pollution standards based on scientific data on health impacts, explicitly ruling out economic considerations in setting standards. We discuss pollution policies, and the concept of optimal pollution, in more detail in Chapter 16.

3.3 PROPERTY RIGHTS AND THE ENVIRONMENT

The idea of a Pigovian tax, which forces polluters to pay for the cost of their social and environmental damages, is intuitively appealing. Implicit in the imposition of a Pigovian tax is the idea that society has a legitimate right to be compensated for any pollution damages. Many people would contend that this is the appropriate allocation of rights. In other words, society has a right to clean air, but the polluters do not have a right to emit whatever they want into the atmosphere.

In other cases, the appropriate allocation of rights may be less clear cut. Suppose a farmer drains a wetland on his property to create a field suitable for growing crops. His downstream neighbor complains that without the wetland to absorb heavy rainfall, her land now floods, damaging her crops. Should the first farmer be obliged to pay the second the value of any crop damages? Or does he have the right to do what wants on his own land?

We can see that this is an issue not just of externalities but also of the nature of property rights. Does the ownership of land include a right to drain wetlands on that land? Or is this right separate, subject to control by the community or other property owners?

The property rights in this case could be allocated in one of two ways. Suppose we say that the first farmer (call him Albert) *does* have the right to drain the wetland on his land. Assume that the net value of crops grown on drained wetland is $5,000. Further, let's suppose that the second farmer (call her Betty) would suffer crop losses of $8,000 if the land were drained. Even though Albert has the right to drain the wetland, Betty could potentially pay Albert not to drain it. Specifically, she would be willing to pay Albert up to $8,000 to keep the wetland intact, because that is the value of the damage she would suffer if Albert exercises his right to drain it.[i] Meanwhile, Albert would be willing to accept any amount higher than $5,000, because that is what he stands to gain by draining the wetland.

Between $5,000 and $8,000 lies sufficient negotiation space for Albert and Betty to reach an agreement that satisfies both of them. Let's say that Albert accepts an offer of $6,000 from Betty to keep the wetland intact. He gains $1,000 relative to what he would have made by draining the wetland. Betty is not happy about paying $6,000, but she is better off than she would be if the wetland were drained and she lost $8,000. In effect, Betty purchases the right to say how the wetland will be used (without having to purchase the land).

We can also assign the relevant right to Betty, by passing a law stating that no one can drain a wetland without the agreement of any affected parties downstream. In that case, Albert would have to reach an agreement with Betty before he could drain the wetland. With the crop values that we have assumed, the same result will be reached—the wetland will not be drained, because the value of doing so to Albert ($5,000) is not enough to compensate Betty for her loss. Betty will demand at least $8,000 to grant her permission, and this price is too high for Albert. So regardless of who holds the property rights, the same outcome is achieved.

Now suppose that a new gourmet crop item becomes popular, a crop that grows well on former swampland and would bring Albert $12,000 in profit. A deal is now possible—Albert can pay Betty, say, $10,000 for the right to drain the swamp and earn $12,000 from the new crop, netting $2,000 profit for himself and leaving Betty $2,000 better off as well.[j]

---

[i] In this example we assume that Albert and Betty have accurate information regarding their costs or benefits.

[j] Note that Albert could offer Betty an amount lower than $10,000. In theory Betty would accept any payment greater than $8,000. But Albert would be willing to pay up to $12,000 for the right to drain the swamp. The actual price Albert would pay depends on the bargaining abilities of the two parties.

Coase theorem

the proposition that if property rights are well defined and there are no transactions costs, an efficient allocation of resources will result even if externalities exist.

transaction costs

costs associated with a market transaction or negotiation, such as legal and administrative costs to transfer property or to bring disputing parties together.

The principle at issue in this simple example has come to be known as the **Coase theorem**, after Ronald Coase, a Nobel prize–winning economist who discussed similar examples of property rights and externalities in his famous 1960 article "The Problem of Social Cost."[1] The Coase theorem states that if property rights are well defined, and there are no **transactions costs**, an efficient allocation of resources will result even if there are externalities. Transactions costs are costs involved in reaching and implementing an agreement, which can include costs of obtaining information (such as surveying the land), time and effort spent in negotiations, and costs of enforcing the agreement. In the case of Albert and Betty, these costs should be low, because they need only to reach an understanding about the amount of compensation, although legal costs may be involved in formalizing an agreement.

Through negotiations, the two parties will balance the external costs against the economic benefits of a given action (in this case, draining the wetland). In the example above, the external costs were $8,000. It is not worth incurring these costs for an economic benefit of $5,000, but an economic benefit of $12,000 makes it worthwhile. Regardless of which farmer is assigned the property right, the "efficient" result will occur through negotiation.

An Illustration of the Coase Theorem

We can illustrate the Coase theorem graphically, by showing the marginal benefits and marginal costs of an economic activity that generates an externality. Suppose, for example, a factory emits effluent into a river, polluting the water supply of a downstream community. The factory is currently emitting 80 tons of effluent. If the factory were forced to reduce effluent to zero, it would have to abandon a valuable production line. Thus we can say that the factory realizes marginal benefits from emitting pollution, and the community pays marginal costs as a result of the damage to their water supply. We can arrive at a reasonable quantitative estimate of these external costs by estimating the costs of water treatment. Both marginal costs and marginal benefits are shown in Figure 3.9.

What is the optimal solution? The emission of 80 tons of pollution clearly imposes high marginal costs on the community, while bringing the company lower marginal benefits. This is "too much" pollution. But suppose that emissions were limited to 50 tons. Marginal benefits to the company would then be equal to marginal costs to the community. A further limitation to, say, 20 tons, would result in high additional losses to the company while bringing only low additional benefits to the community. The efficient or "optimal" solution, therefore, is at a level of pollution of 50 tons. At this level the extra benefit to the company from production just balances the extra cost imposed on the community through pollution.[k]

The Coase theorem states that this solution can be achieved by assigning the pollution rights *either* to the company *or* to the community. Suppose that the community has the right to say how much pollution can be emitted. You might initially think that it would not allow the company to emit any pollution. But notice in Figure 3.9 that the company would be willing to pay the community up to about $400 for the right to emit the first ton of pollution. Meanwhile, the damages to the

---

[k]Note that the marginal benefit equation for the company in this example is $MB = 400 - 5T$, where T is tons of pollution. The marginal cost (damage) function for the community is $MC = 3T$. Thus the point of intersection is found by setting the two equations equal, $400 - 5T = 3T$, or $T = 50$.

Figure 3.9 **Application of the Coase Theorem**

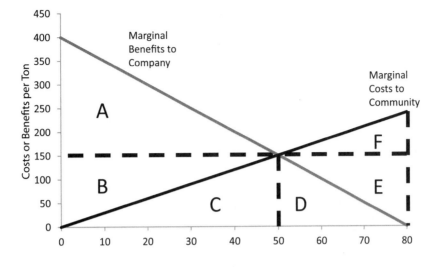

community from the first ton of pollution are quite small, only a few dollars. So there is a significant opportunity for a successful agreement in which the company would pay the community in order to be able to emit the first ton of pollution.

Note that this process of successful negotiation would continue as long as the marginal benefits to the company exceed the marginal damages to the community. However, the space for successful negotiation gradually declines as we move rightward in the graph. For example, after the company has already purchased the right to emit 40 tons of pollution, its marginal benefits of pollution have fallen to $200 per ton, while the marginal costs to the community have risen to $120/ton. Eventually, we reach a point, at 50 tons of pollution, where the company cannot offer the community enough to allow it to pollute any further. So after the marginal benefits to the company equal the marginal costs to the community, we reach the optimal level of pollution. If there is any further pollution, the marginal costs would exceed the marginal benefits.

At this level, the marginal benefits to the company and marginal costs to the community are both equal to $150. The company will not be willing to pay any higher price than $150 for the fiftieth unit of pollution, and the community will not be willing to accept any lower price.

We can analyze the effects of this outcome using welfare analysis (as explained above, and in more detail in Appendixes 3.1 and 3.2). For example, in Figure 3.9, area C represents the total costs of pollution damage at 50 tons of emissions. This area is $3,750 (using the formula for the area of a triangle, in this case 50 * 150 * ½).

If we assume that all rights to pollute sold for the same price of $150, then the community receives a total payment of $7,500 (area B + C). The total costs of pollution to the community are $3,750 (area C). So the community comes out ahead, with a net gain of $3,750.

What about the company? In purchasing the right to pollute 50 tons, it gains areas (A + B + C) in total benefits, or $13,750. But it has to pay the community $7,500 for the right to pollute 50 tons (area B + C). So the company comes out ahead by $6,250, compared with not polluting at all. Considering the gains to both the company and the community, the total welfare gain from the negotiation process is $10,000, as detailed in Table 3.2.

Table 3.2

Gains and Losses from Negotiation with Different Property Rights

	If community holds rights	If company holds rights
Net gain/loss to community	+ $7,500 payment − $3,750 environmental costs + $3,750	− $4,500 payment − $3,750 environmental costs − $8,250
Net gain/loss to company	+ $13,750 total benefits − $7,500 payment + $6,250	+ $13,750 total benefits + $4,500 payment + $18,250
Net social gain	+ $10,000	+ $10,000

What if we instead assume that the company has the right to pollute as much as it wants? In this case, we start off with the firm emitting 80 tons of pollutants—gaining the maximum possible amount of net benefits from polluting. Total benefits to the company would be areas (A + B + C + D), or $16,000. The total damage to the community would be areas (C + D + E + F), or $9,600. Thus net social benefits at 80 tons of pollution, prior to any negotiations, would be $6,400.

But notice that the company receives very small marginal benefits for the last ton emitted, just a few dollars. Meanwhile, the community suffered damages from the eightieth ton of $240. So the community could pay the company to reduce its pollution, as there is a significant negotiation space where both parties could benefit. Again, the final outcome would be 50 tons of pollution, with the community paying the company $150 per ton for pollution reduction.

In this case, the company receives the financial benefits from its remaining 50 tons of pollution, or areas (A + B + C), which equal $13,750 as shown in Table 3.2. Assuming that all rights are negotiated for a price of $150/ton, it also receives a payment of $4,500 from the community, for total benefits of $18,250. Note that this is higher than the $16,000 benefit it obtained from maximum pollution.

The community suffers remaining damages of area C, or $3,750. It also pays the company $4,500. So its total losses are now $8,250—not a great outcome for the community, but better than its initial losses of $9,600. Note that overall net social benefits are $10,000—the same exact outcome we obtained when the community held the property rights.

This more formal demonstration of the Coase theorem shows that the efficient solution is reached regardless of the assignment of the property right governing pollution. Provided that right is clearly defined, the party that values it most highly will acquire it, with the result that the external costs of pollution and the economic benefits of production are balanced through the marketplace.

Note, however, that the assignment of the right makes a big difference in distribution of gains and losses between the two parties (see Table 3.2). The net social benefit from production is the same in both cases, equal to area (A + B), or $10,000. But in one case this benefit is divided between the community and the company. In the other case, the community has a net loss while the company has a large net gain.

We can say that the value of the right to pollute, or to control pollution, is $12,000 in this case. By redistributing that right, we make one party $12,000 better off and the other $12,000 worse off. The different assignments of rights are equivalent in terms of efficiency, because the final result balances marginal benefits and marginal costs, but they clearly differ in terms of equity, or social justice.

A Practical Application

An example of environmental protection using Coase theorem principles is New York City's Watershed Land Acquisition Program. The city must provide clean water to its 8.2 million residents. This can be done through building filtration plants, but the cost of building these plants can be avoided through watershed protection. By preserving land around the main water supplies for the city, the quality of the water can be maintained at a level that does not require filtration. The watersheds are located upstate, on lands not currently owned by the city. According to the U.S. Environmental Protection Agency:

> The Watershed Land Acquisition Program is a key element in the City's long-term strategy to preserve environmentally sensitive lands in its upstate watersheds. Land acquisition is a critical element of the City's ability to obtain filtration avoidance. Through this program, New York City has committed to soliciting a minimum of 355,050 acres of land over a ten-year period. The goal of the Program is for the City to acquire, from willing sellers, fee title to or conservation easements on real property determined to be water quality sensitive, undeveloped land. The land will be bought at fair market value prices and property taxes will be paid by the City. No property will be acquired by eminent domain. (www.epa.gov/region02/water/nycshed/protprs.htm#land/)

As in our Coase theorem example, all the transactions here are voluntary, based on private property rights. The power of eminent domain, by which a government can compel a property owner to give up land in return for compensation (see Box 3.2), is not used. New York City has made the determination that it is less expensive to pay private property owners for conservation easements, which restrict the uses of the land, or to purchase the land outright, than to construct filtration plants. This market-based solution appears to be both environmentally effective and economically efficient.

BOX 3.2 PROPERTY RIGHTS AND ENVIRONMENTAL REGULATION

Under the principle of eminent domain, governments are permitted to appropriate private property for public purposes. However, the Fifth Amendment of the U.S. Constitution requires that the property owner be fairly compensated. Specifically, the Fifth Amendment concludes with the statement "nor shall private property be taken for public use, without just compensation."

An action by a government that deprives someone of his or her property rights is referred to as a "takings." In cases in which the property owner is deprived of all property rights, the Constitution clearly orders full compensation. For example, if a state government decides to build a highway through a parcel of private property, the landowner must be paid the fair market value of the property.

A more ambiguous situation arises when actions by a government limit the uses of property and, consequently, reduce the value of property. Instances of government regulations reducing the value of private property are often called "regulatory takings." For example, if a new law is created that regulates timber harvesting and reduces the value of private forests, are the landowners entitled to compensation under the Fifth Amendment?

The most notable case concerning a regulatory taking is *Lucas v. South Carolina Coastal Council*.

(continued)

BOX 3.2 (*continued*)

David Lucas, a real estate developer, purchased two oceanfront lots in 1986 and planned to construct vacation homes. However, in 1988 the South Carolina state legislature enacted the Beachfront Management Act, which prohibited Lucas from building any permanent structures on the property. Lucas filed suit claiming that the legislation had deprived him of all "economically viable use" of his property.

A trial court ruled in Lucas's favor, concluding that the legislation had rendered his property "valueless" and awarded him $1.2 million in damages. However, the South Carolina supreme court reversed this decision. It ruled that further construction in the area posed a significant threat to a public resource and in cases in which a regulation is intended to prevent "harmful or noxious uses" of property private, no compensation is required.

The case was appealed to the U.S. Supreme Court. Although the Supreme Court overturned the state court ruling, it delineated a distinction between total and partial takings. Compensation is necessary only in cases of total takings—when a regulation deprives a property owner of "all economically beneficial uses." If a regulation merely reduces a property's value, then compensation is not required.

In essence, this ruling represented a victory for environmentalists because cases of total takings are rare. Partial takings as a result of government regulations, however, are common. A requirement of compensation for partial takings would have created a legal and technical morass that would effectively render many environmental laws ineffective. Still, partial takings can result in significant costs to individuals, and the debate continues over equity when private costs are necessary to achieve the public good.

Sources: Ausness, 1995; Hollingsworth, 1994; Johnson, 1994.

Limitations of the Coase Theorem

According to the Coase Theorem, the clear assignment of property rights appears to promise efficient solutions to problems involving externalities. In theory, if we could clearly assign property rights to *all* environmental externalities, further government intervention would not be required. Individuals and business firms would negotiate all pollution control and other environmental issues among themselves after it was clear who had the "right to pollute" or the "right to be free from pollution." Through this process, fully efficient solutions to the problem of externalities would be achieved.

free market environmentalism
the view that a more complete system of property rights and expanded use of market mechanisms is the best approach to solving issues of resource use and pollution control.

This is the theoretical basis behind the idea of **free market environmentalism**. In effect, by setting up a system of property rights in the environment, this approach seeks to bring the environment into the marketplace, allowing the free market to handle issues of resource use and pollution regulation.

As we will see in dealing with specific examples in future chapters, this approach may have significant potential, especially in areas like water rights. But it also has crucial limitations. What are some of the problems in simply assigning property rights and letting unregulated markets address environmental and resource problems?

We mentioned above that the Coase theorem assumes there are no transaction costs preventing efficient negotiation. In the examples that we have used, there are only two parties negotiating. What happens if, for example, fifty downstream communities are affected by pollution from a factory's effluent? The process of negotiating effluent limits will be very cumbersome, perhaps impossible. This problem would be even worse if there were several factories instead of just one. Thus the efficient outcome may not be reachable because of significant transaction costs.

Free-Rider and Holdout Effects

Another problem may arise with a large number of affected communities. Suppose that we assign the factory the right to pollute. The communities can then offer compensation for reducing pollution. But which community will pay what share? Unless all fifty can agree, it might prove impossible to make a specific offer to the company. No single community, or group of communities, is likely to step forward to pay the whole bill. In fact, there is likely to be a tendency to hang back, waiting for other communities to "buy off" the factory—and thus gain pollution control benefits for free. This barrier to successful negotiations is known as the **free-rider effect**, in which there is a tendency not to pay one's share of the costs but still attempt to receive the benefits.

A similar problem arises if the communities are given the "right to be free from pollution" and the factory must compensate them for any pollution emitted. Who will determine which community gets how much compensation? Because all are situated on the same river, any single community can exercise a kind of veto power. Suppose that forty-nine communities have hammered out an agreement with the company on permissible pollution levels and compensation. The fiftieth community can demand a much higher rate of compensation, for if it withholds consent, the entire agreement will fail, and the company will be restricted to zero pollution (i.e., forced to shut down). This parallel to the free-rider effect is known as the **holdout effect**.

When large numbers of parties are affected, the Coase theorem generally cannot be applied. In this case, some form of government intervention is required, such as regulation or a Pigovian tax. The state or federal government could set a standard for a water-borne effluent or a tax per unit of effluent. This would not be a pure market solution (although a tax does have its impact through market processes) because government officials must decide on the strictness of regulation or the level of tax.

Issues of Equity and Distribution

Other lines of criticism of the Coase theorem concern its effects on equity. Suppose that in our original example the community suffering from pollution is a low-income community. Even if the water pollution is causing serious health impacts, which could be valued at many millions of dollars, the community may simply be unable to "buy off" the polluter. In this case, the market solution is clearly not independent of the assignment of property rights. Pollution levels will be significantly higher if the right to pollute is assigned to the company.

It is also possible that, even if the right is assigned to the community, poor communities will accept location of toxic waste dumps and other polluting facilities out of a desperate need for compensatory funds.[2] While this is apparently consistent with the Coase theorem (it is a voluntary transaction), many people believe that communities should not be forced to trade the health of their residents for needed funds. An important criticism of free market environmentalism is that under a pure market system, poorer communities and individuals will generally bear the heaviest burden of environmental costs.

A similar example relates to preservation of open space. Wealthy communities can afford to buy up open space for preservation, while poor communities cannot.

If communities are allowed to use zoning to preserve wetlands and natural areas, poor communities, too, will be able to protect their environment, because passing a zoning regulation has zero cost other than for enforcement.

Another point to note in considering the limitations of the Coase theorem principle is the issue of environmental impacts on nonhuman life forms and ecological systems. Our examples so far have assumed that environmental damage affects specific individuals or businesses. What about environmental damage that affects no individual directly, but that threatens plant or animal species with extinction? What if a certain pesticide is harmless to humans but lethal to birds? Who will step into the marketplace to defend the preservation of nonhuman species? No individual or business firm is likely to do so, except on a relatively small scale.

Consider, for example, the activities of a group like the Nature Conservancy, which buys up ecologically valuable tracts of land in order to preserve them. Here is an example of an organization that *is* prepared to pay to save the environment. But its purchases can reach only a tiny proportion of the natural areas threatened with destruction through development, intensive farming, and other economic activities. In the "dollar vote" marketplace, purely ecological interests will almost always lose out to economic interests.

We should also note that property rights are typically limited to the current generation. What about the rights of the next generation? Many environmental issues have long-term implications. Rights to non-renewable resources can be assigned today, but those resources will be used up at some time in the future. This important issue of resource allocation over time is the subject of Chapter 5. Long-term environmental impacts are also vital to the analysis of climate change, presented in Chapter 18.

In some cases, property rights are simply inappropriate tools for dealing with environmental problems. It may be impossible, for example, to establish property rights to the atmosphere or to the open ocean. When we confront problems such as global warming, ocean pollution, the decline of fish stocks, or endangered species, we find that the system of private property rights, which has evolved as a basis for economic systems, cannot be fully extended to ecosystems. It may be possible to use market transactions, such as tradable permits for air emissions or fishing rights, but these only apply to a limited subset of ecosystem functions. In many cases, some other techniques of economic analysis will be helpful in considering the interaction between human economic activity and aspects of the broader ecosystem. We consider some of these analyses in Chapter 4.

SUMMARY

Many economic activities have significant external effects—impacts on people who are not directly involved in the activity. Pollution from automobile use is an example. The costs of these external impacts are not reflected in the market price, leading to an excessive production of goods with negative externalities and an inefficient outcome.

One approach to pollution control is to internalize external costs using a tax or other instrument that requires producers and consumers of the polluting good to take these costs into account. In general, the use of such a tax will raise the price and reduce the quantity produced of the good, thereby also reducing pollution. In so doing, it shifts the market equilibrium to a socially more desirable result. In theory, a tax that exactly reflects external costs could achieve a social optimum, but it is often difficult to establish a proper valuation for negative externalities.

Not all externalities are negative. Positive externalities result when economic activities bring benefits to others not directly involved in the transaction. Preservation of open land benefits those who live nearby directly, often raising their property values. The use of solar energy benefits society as it reduces pollution levels. When a positive externality exists, there is an economic case for a subsidy to increase the market provision of the good.

An alternative to the use of a tax is the assignment of property rights to externalities. If there is a clear legal right either to emit a certain amount of pollution or to prevent others from emitting pollution, a market in "rights to pollute" can develop according to the Coase theorem. However, this solution depends on the ability of firms and individuals to trade these pollution rights with relatively low transactions costs. Where large numbers of people are affected, or where the environmental damages are not easy to define in monetary terms, this approach is not effective. It also raises significant questions of equity, because under a market system the poor generally bear a heavier burden of pollution.

KEY TERMS AND CONCEPTS

Coase theorem
consumer surplus
economic efficiency
elasticities of supply and demand
equilibrium price
external costs
externalities
free market environmentalism
free-rider effect
holdout effect
internalizing externalities
marginal benefit
marginal costs

negative externality
optimal pollution
Pigovian tax
polluter pays principle
positive externalities
producer surplus
social marginal cost curve
socially efficient
subsidy
third-party effects
transaction costs
upstream tax
welfare analysis

DISCUSSION QUESTIONS

1. "Solving the problems of environmental economics is simple. It is just a matter of internalizing the externalities." What is your reaction to this statement? Does the theory of externalities apply to most or all environmental issues? What are some of the practical problems involved in internalizing externalities? Can you think of some examples in which the principle works well and others in which it is more problematic?

2. A pollution tax is one policy instrument for internalizing externalities. Discuss the economic policy implications of a tax on automobiles, on gasoline, or on tailpipe emission levels as measured at an auto inspection. Which would be the most cost-efficient? Which do you think would be most effective in reducing pollution levels?

EXERCISES

1. Consider the following supply and demand schedule for steel:

Price per ton ($)	20	40	60	80	100	120	140	160	180
Q_D (million tons)	200	180	160	140	120	100	80	60	40
Q_S (million tons)	20	60	100	140	180	220	260	300	340

Pollution from steel production is estimated to create an external cost of $60 per ton. Show the external cost, market equilibrium, and social optimum in a graph.

What kinds of policies might help to achieve the social optimum? What would be the effects of these policies on the behavior of consumers and producers? What would be the effect on market equilibrium price and quantity?

2. A chemical factory is located next to a farm. Airborne emissions from the chemical factory damage crops on the farm. The marginal benefits of emissions to the factory and the marginal costs of damage to the farmer are as follows:

Quantity of emissions	100	200	300	400	500	600	700	800	900
Marginal benefit to factory ($000)	320	280	240	200	160	120	80	40	0
Marginal cost to farmer ($000)	110	130	150	170	190	210	230	250	270

From an economic point of view, what is the best solution to this environmental conflict of interest? How might this solution be achieved? How should considerations of efficiency and equity be balanced in this case?

NOTES

1. Coase, 1960.
2. See Bullard, 1994, and Massey, 2004.

REFERENCES

Ausness, Richard C. 1995. "Regulatory Takings and Wetland Protection in the Post-Lucas Era." *Land and Water Law Review*, 30(2): 349–414.

Bullard, Robert D. 1994. *Dumping in Dixie: Race, Class, and Environmental Quality.* Boulder: Westview Press.

Coase, Ronald. 1960. "The Problem of Social Cost." *Journal of Law and Economics* 3: 1–44.

Delucchi, Mark A. 1997. *The Annualized Social Cost of Motor Vehicle Use in the U.S., 1990–1991: Summary of Theory, Data, Methods, and Results.* Report # UCD-ITS-RR-96–3(1), Institute of Transportation Studies, University of California, Davis.

Hollingsworth, Lorraine. 1994. "Lucas v. South Carolina Coastal Commission: A New Approach to the Takings Issue." *Natural Resources Journal* 34(2): 479–495.

Johnson, Stephen M. 1994. "Defining the Property Interest: A Vital Issue in Wetlands Takings Analysis After Lucas." *Journal of Energy, Natural Resources & Environmental Law* 14(1): 41–82.

Massey, Rachel, 2004. *Environmental Justice: Income, Race, and Health.* Tufts University Global Development and Environment Institute, http://www.ase.tufts.edu/gdae/education_materials/modules.html#ej.

Parry, Ian W.H., Margaret Walls, and Winston Harrington. 2007. "Automobile Externalities and Policies." *Journal of Economic Literature* 45: 373–399.

WEB SITES

1. **www.journals.elsevier.com/journal-of-environmental-economics-and-management/.** Web site for the *Journal of Environmental Economics and Management,* with articles on environmental economic theory and practice.
2. **http://reep.oxfordjournals.org.** Web site for the *Review of Environmental Economics and Policy,* with articles on the application of environmental economic concepts to practical cases of environmental policy; the journal "aims to fill the gap between traditional academic journals and the general interest press by providing a widely accessible yet scholarly source for the latest thinking on environmental economics and related policy."
3. **www.iisd.org/susprod/browse.aspx and www.iisd.org/publications/.** A compendium of case studies and articles by the International Institute for Sustainable Development on economic instruments for promoting environmentally sound economic development.
4. **http://chicagopolicyreview.org/2012/02/15/when-costs-outweigh-benefits-accounting-for-environmental-externalities/.** A paper estimating the cost of environmental externalities in major industries to the U.S. economy, indicating that "the cost of environmental externalities in several industries exceeds the value they add to the economy."

APPENDIX 3.1: SUPPLY, DEMAND, AND WELFARE ANALYSIS

This text presupposes that you have had an introductory economics course. But if you have not, or if your basic economic theory is a little rusty, then this appendix provides you with the background economic knowledge you will need for this book.

Economists use models to help them explain complex phenomena. A model is a scientific tool that helps us understand something by focusing on certain aspects of reality yet ignoring others. No model can consider every possible factor that might be relevant, so scientists make simplifying assumptions. A scientific model can take the form of a simplified story, a graph, a figure, or a set of equations. One of the most powerful and widely used models in economics concerns the interaction of supply and demand. Based on several simplifying assumptions, this model provides us with insights about the changes we can expect when certain things happen as well as what types of economic policies are the most appropriate in different circumstances.

The Theory of Demand

The theory of demand considers how consumer demand for goods and services changes as a result of changes in prices and other relevant variables. In this appendix, we use the market for gasoline as an example. Obviously, many factors affect consumer demand for gasoline so we start by making a simplifying assumption. For now, let us consider only how consumer demand for gas changes when the price of gas changes—all other relevant factors are assumed to be held constant. Economists use the Latin term *ceteris paribus*, meaning "all other things equal" or "all else being equal," to isolate the influence of only one or a few variables.

law of demand
the economic theory that the quantity of a good or service demanded will decrease as the price increases.

How will the quantity of gas demanded by consumers change as the price of gas changes? The **law of demand** states that as the price of a good or service increases, consumers will demand less of it, ceteris paribus. We could conversely state the law of demand thus: Consumers demand more of a good or service when the price of it falls. This inverse relationship between the price of something and the quantity demanded can be expressed a couple of ways. One is a demand schedule—a table showing the quantity of a specific good or service demanded at different prices. The other way is to use a graph to illustrate a demand curve—just the graphical representation of a demand schedule. The convention among economists is to put the quantity demanded on the horizontal axis (the *x*-axis) and price on the vertical axis (the *y*-axis).

Suppose that we have collected some data about how much gasoline consumers in a particular metropolitan area demand at different prices. This hypothetical demand schedule is presented in Table A3.1. We can see that as the price of gas rises, people demand less of it. The data in Table A3.1 are expressed graphically, as a demand curve, in Figure A3.1. Notice that the demand curve slopes down as we move to the right, as we would expect according to the law of demand.

Table A3.1

Demand Schedule for Gasoline

Price ($/gal.)	$2.80	$3.00	$3.20	$3.40	$3.60	$3.80	$4.00	$4.20	$4.40	$4.60
Quantity demanded (thousand gal./week)	80	78	76	74	72	70	68	66	64	62

Figure A3.1 **Demand Curve for Gasoline**

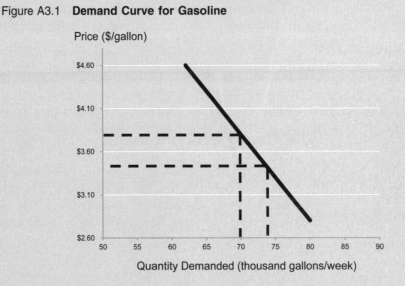

We can see in Figure A3.1 that at a price of $3.40 per gallon, consumers in the area will purchase 74,000 gallons of gas per week. Suppose that the price rises to $3.80 per gallon. At the higher price, we see that consumers decide to purchase less gas, 70,000 gallons per week. We call this movement along a demand curve at different prices a *change in the quantity demanded*. This is different from what economists call a *change in demand*. A change in demand occurs when the entire demand curve shifts.

What would cause the entire demand curve to shift? First, we need to realize that a change in the price of gasoline will *not* cause the demand curve to shift, it will only cause consumers to move along the demand curve in Figure A3.1 (i.e., a change in the quantity demanded). Our demand curve in Figure A3.1 is stable as long as we assume that no other relevant factors are changing—the ceteris paribus assumption. To expand our model, let us consider several factors that would cause the entire demand curve to shift. One factor is income. If the consumers' incomes were to rise, many would decide to purchase more gas at the same price. Higher incomes would result in a change in demand. This is shown in Figure A3.2 where the entire demand curve shifts to the right.[1]

Figure A3.2   **A Change in Demand**

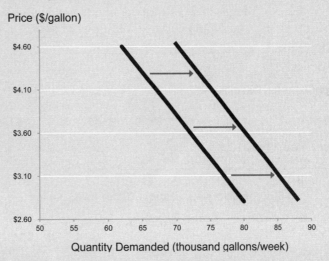

Another factor that would cause a change in demand is a change in the price of related goods. In our example of the demand for gas, suppose that the price of public transportation increases significantly. This would cause the demand for gas to increase (shift to the right) as some people decide to drive their own vehicles because public transportation is now too expensive for them. A change in consumer preferences could also cause the demand curve for gas to shift. For example, American consumer preferences toward smaller, fuel-efficient vehicles in recent years has caused a decrease in the demand for gas. A significant change in the number of people driving would also cause a change in the demand for gas. In what direction do you think the demand curve for gas would shift if the population of our metropolitan area were to decrease by 20 percent? Can you think of any other factors that would also cause a demand curve to shift?

---

[1]Economists generally describe demand curves as shifting to "the right" or "the left," not up or down. This is because it makes more intuitive sense to say that at a given price consumers will demand more or less than to say that consumers will purchase a given quantity at a higher or lower price.

The Theory of Supply

law of supply
the economic theory that the quantity of a good or service supplied will increase as the price increases.

The next step in our analysis is to consider the other side of the market. The theory of supply considers how suppliers respond to changes in the price of a good or service they offer or other relevant factors. While low prices appeal to consumers looking for a bargain, high prices appeal to suppliers looking to make profits. As you might expect, the **law of supply** is the opposite of the law of demand. The law of supply states that as the price of a good or service increases, suppliers will choose to offer more of it, ceteris paribus. According to the law of supply, price and the quantity supplied change in the same direction.

Once again, we can express the relationship between price and the quantity supplied using both tables and graphs. Table A3.2 illustrates a supply schedule for gas, with the quantity supplied increasing as the price of gas increases. Figure A3.3 simply converts the data in Table A3.2 into a graph. Notice that the supply curve slopes upward as we move to the right.

Table A3.2

Supply Schedule for Gasoline

Price ($/gal.)	$2.80	$3.00	$3.20	$3.40	$3.60	$3.80	$4.00	$4.20	$4.40	$4.60
Quantity demanded (thousand gal./week)	52	57	62	67	72	77	82	87	92	97

Figure A3.3 **Supply Curve for Gasoline**

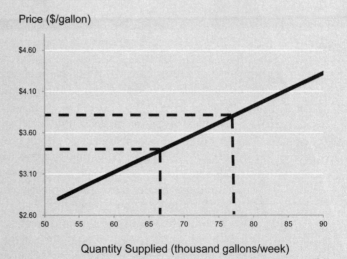

There is also a distinction between a *change in the quantity supplied* and a *change in supply*. A change in the quantity supplied occurs when we move along a supply curve as the price of the good or service changes. This is shown in Figure A3.3. We see that at a price of $3.40, suppliers are willing to supply 67,000 gallons of gas. But if the price were to increase to $3.80 the quantity supplied would increase to 77,000 gallons per week.

A change in supply occurs when the entire supply curve shifts. Again, several different factors might cause a supply curve to shift. One is a change in the price of input goods and services. For example, an increase in the wages paid to gasoline company employees would cause suppliers to raise the price that they charge for gas, meaning a shift in the supply curve to the left, as illustrated in FigureA3.4. Another factor that would cause a change in supply is a change in production technology. Suppose that an innovation reduces the costs of gasoline refining. In which direction would the supply curve shift in this case? Which other factors would cause a change in supply?

Figure A3.4 **A Change in Supply**

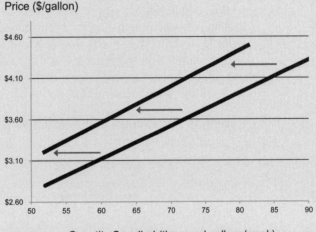

Price ($/gallon)

Quantity Supplied (thousand gallons/week)

Market Analysis

We can now bring together both sides of the gasoline market. The price of gasoline is determined by the interaction of consumers and suppliers. We can illustrate this interaction by putting our demand and supply curves on the same graph, as shown in Figure A3.5. We can use this figure to determine what the price of gas will be and how much will be sold. First, suppose the price of gas was initially $3.80 per gallon. We see in Figure A3.5 that at this price the quantity supplied exceeds the quantity demanded. We call this situation a **surplus** because suppliers have more gas than consumers are willing to buy. Rather than dumping the excess gas, suppliers will lower their price in order to attract more customers. So, in the case of a surplus, we expect a downward pressure on prices.

surplus
a market situation in which the quantity supplied exceeds the quantity demanded.

shortage

a market situation in which
the quantity demanded
exceeds the quantity
supplied.

market equilibrium

the market outcome where
the quantity demanded
equals the quantity
supplied.

What if the initial price were instead $3.20/gallon? We see in Figure A3.5 that at this price the quantity demanded exceeds the quantity suppliers are willing to supply. Suppliers will notice this excess demand and realize they can raise their prices. So, in the case of a **shortage**, there will be upward pressure on prices.

When a surplus or shortage exists, the market will adjust, attempting to eliminate the excess supply or excess demand. This adjustment will continue until we reach a price where the quantity demanded equals the quantity supplied. Only at this price is there no pressure for further market adjustment, ceteris paribus. We see in Figure A3.5 that this occurs at a price of $3.60/gallon.[m] At this price, both the quantity demand and the quantity supplied are 72,000 gallons per week. Economists use the term **market equilibrium** to describe a market that has reached this stable situation.

A market in equilibrium is stable as long as all other relevant factors stay the same, such as consumer incomes, the prices of related goods, and production technology. Changes in these variables will cause one (or both) curve(s) to shift and result in a new equilibrium, as illustrated in Figure A3.6. Assume that an increase in consumer income causes the demand curve for gas to shift from D_0 to D_1. This results in a new market equilibrium with a higher price and an increase in the quantity of gas sold. You can test yourself by figuring out what happens to the equilibrium price and quantity when the demand curve shifts in the opposite direction and when the supply curve shifts.

Figure A3.5 **Equilibrium in the Market for Gasoline**

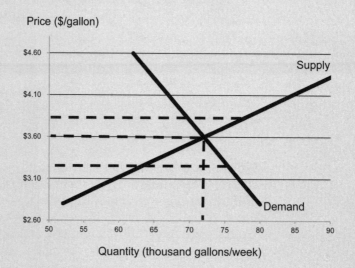

---

[m]This was the approximate market price of gasoline at the time this text was written. Of course, by the time you read this, the price of gas may be higher or lower. If so, after reading this appendix, you might try to explain why the price of gas has changed.

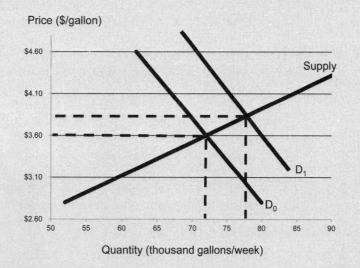

Figure A3.6 **A New Equilibrium with a Change in Demand for Gasoline**

Elasticity of Demand and Supply

price elasticity of demand

the responsiveness of the quantity demanded to price, equal to the percentage change in quantity demanded divided by the percentage change in price.

Demand and supply curves indicate consumers' and suppliers' responsiveness to changes in price. While we expect all demand curves to slope downward and all supply curves to slope upward, responses to changes in price can be large or small. Consider again how consumers would respond to an increase in the price of gasoline. Consumers would buy less gas but, at least in the short term, probably not that much less because they generally have fixed commutes to work, cannot buy a new vehicle, and so on. The degree of consumer responsiveness to a change in the price of a good or service is determined by the **price elasticity of demand**.

The demand for a good is relatively *price inelastic* if the quantity demanded changes little as the price changes. This can be illustrated graphically by a relatively steep demand curve. The formal expression of demand elasticity in mathematical terms is:

$$Elasticity\ of\ demand = \frac{Percent\ change\ in\ quantity\ demanded}{Percent\ change\ in\ price}$$

Because the quantity demanded moves in the opposite direction of the price, demand elasticity is a negative number. Gasoline is an example of a good with a demand that is price inelastic. But the demand for a good is relatively *price elastic* if the quantity demanded changes a great deal as the price changes (the demand curve would be relatively flat). Which goods have relatively elastic demand curves?

We can also talk about the **price elasticity of supply**. The supply of a good is considered price inelastic if the quantity supplied changes little as the price changes. A price-elastic supply curve would indicate a relatively large change in the quantity supplied with a change in the price. The mathematical expression for elasticity of supply is the same as for elasticity of demand, but because quantity and price move in the same direction, supply elasticity is positive.

Notice that the price elasticity of demand and supply can change as we consider a longer period. In the short term, the demand and supply curves for gasoline are relatively inelastic. But when we consider a longer time frame, consumers can respond to an increase in gas prices by moving closer to work or buying a more fuel-efficient vehicle, and suppliers can build new refineries or drill more oil wells. So the price elasticity of demand and supply for gasoline will be more elastic over a longer period.

Welfare Analysis

The final topic we consider in this appendix is welfare analysis. Welfare analysis looks at the benefits that consumers and suppliers obtain from economic transactions. Using welfare analysis, our supply and demand model becomes a powerful tool for policy analysis. Our understanding of welfare analysis begins with a more detailed look at demand and supply curves.

Why do people buy things? Economists assume that people will not purchase a good or service unless the benefits that they obtain from the purchase exceed what they have to pay for it. While the cost of something is expressed in dollars, quantifying benefits in dollar terms is not obvious. Economists define the net benefits a consumer obtains from a purchase as their maximum **willingness to pay** less the price they actually have to pay. For example, if someone is willing to spend a maximum of $30 for a particular shirt yet the actual price is $24, then he or she obtains a net benefit of $6 by buying it. This net benefit is called **consumer surplus**.

Note that if the price of the shirt were instead $32, the consumer would not purchase it because the costs are greater than their benefits. When we observe people purchasing goods or services, we conclude that they are doing so because the benefits that they obtain exceed their costs. If the price of a particular item rises, some people will decide not to purchase it—buying other things instead or saving their money. If the price rises further, more people will drop out of the market because the cost exceeds their maximum willingness to pay. In other words, a demand curve can also be viewed as a maximum willingness-to-pay curve.

We can now look at Figure A3.7, which shows the demand and supply curve for gasoline. The equilibrium values are the same as before ($3.60/gal. and 72,000 gallons sold), but the demand and supply curves have been extended to the y-axis. Given that the demand curve is a maximum willingness-to-pay curve, the vertical difference between the demand curve and the equilibrium price is consumer surplus. Total consumer surplus in the gasoline market is indicated by the triangle in Figure A3.7.

Figure A3.7 **Consumer and Producer Surplus**

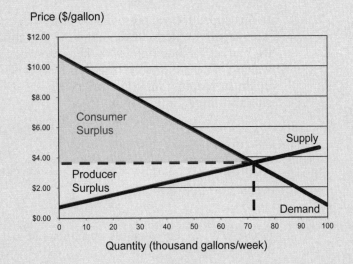

economies of scale
an expanded level of output increases returns per unit of input.

marginal cost
the cost of providing one more unit of a good or service, considering both private production costs and externalities.

producer surplus
the net benefits of a market transaction to producers, equal to the selling price minus production costs (i.e., profits).

We can also look at the supply curve in more detail. Economists assume that suppliers will supply an item only if the price exceeds their costs of production—in other words, if they can obtain a profit. The supply curve shows how much is needed to cover production costs. This explains the upward slope; as production increases, costs tend to rise. (At low levels of production, costs might fall as production increases, a phenomenon known as **economies of scale**. But eventually costs are likely to rise as raw materials run short, workers are paid overtime, and so forth.) In effect, the supply curve tells us how much it costs to supply each additional unit of an item. The cost to supply *one more* unit of a good is called the marginal cost. In other words, a supply curve is a **marginal cost** curve.

Economists define the benefits that producers obtain from selling an item as **producer surplus**. Producer surplus is calculated as the selling price minus the cost of production. Once again, we can look at our supply and demand graph to visualize producer surplus. We see in Figure A3.7 that producer surplus is the lower triangle between the supply curve and the equilibrium price. The total net benefits from a market are simply the sum of consumer and producer surplus.

We can use welfare analysis to determine the impacts of various government policies, such as taxes and price controls. While welfare analysis can indicate whether a policy increases or decreases net benefits, it normally does not tell us about the distribution of costs and benefits or the broader social and ecological impacts. Clearly, other impacts must be considered if we want to conduct a complete policy analysis.

APPENDIX 3.2: EXTERNALITY ANALYSIS: ADVANCED MATERIAL

Formal Presentation of Externality Analysis

In this appendix, we present a more formal analysis of externalities, starting with negative externalities. Figure A3.8 is similar to Figure 3.7, which shows the market for automobiles in the presence of a negative externality. The net welfare of the automobile market is market benefits (the sum of consumer and producer surplus) minus externality costs. Consumer surplus at the market equilibrium Q_M in Figure A3.8 is:

$$CS = A + B + C + D.$$

The producer surplus at the market equilibrium Q_M is:

$$PS = E + F + G + H.$$

Figure A3.8 **Welfare Analysis of Automobile Market with Externalities**

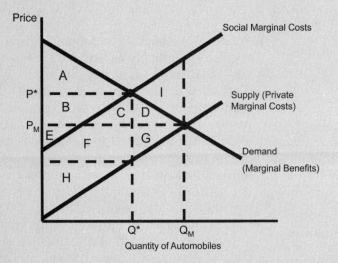

The vertical distance between the social marginal costs and the private marginal costs is the externality damage per automobile. These externality damages accrue for every automobile sold, up to the market equilibrium of Q_M. Thus the total externality damage is the parallelogram between the two cost curves up to Q_M, or:

$$Externality = C + D + F + G + H + I.$$

Since the externality represents a cost, to determine the net social welfare we need to subtract these costs from the market benefits. Thus the net social welfare of the unregulated automobile market is:

$$Net\ Benefits = (A + B + C + D) +$$
$$(E + F + G + H) - (C + D + F + G + H + I).$$

Canceling out the positive and negative terms, we are left with:

$$Net\ Benefits = A + B + E - I.$$

Next, we determine net social welfare with a Pigovian tax that fully internalizes the externality, shown in Figure A3.9.

Figure A3.9 **Welfare Analysis of Automobile Market with Pigovian Tax**

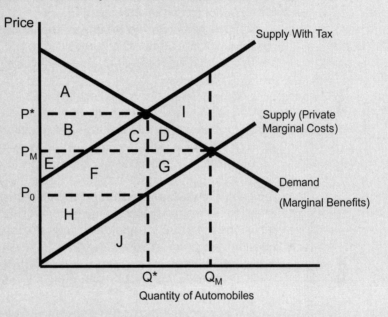

With a new price of P^*, the new consumer surplus is simply area A. Note that this is less than the original consumer surplus of $(A + B + C + D)$. So the tax has raised prices and clearly reduced the welfare of automobile consumers, which makes sense given that consumers generally do not like taxes, ceteris paribus.

The effect on producer surplus is a little more difficult to determine. We know that total revenue to producers is simply price times quantity, or (P^*Q^*). In Figure A3.9 this is the rectangle that includes the following areas:

$$Total\ Revenues = B + C + E + F + H + J.$$

Producer surplus, or profits, is total revenue minus all costs. In this case, producers have two costs. One is their production costs. This is the area under their original private marginal cost curve, or area J. Their other cost is the tax. The tax per automobile is equal to the difference between P^* and P_0 in Figure

A3.9. This tax must be paid for every automobile sold, which is Q^*. Thus the total tax paid is the rectangle including the following areas:

$$Tax = B + C + E + F.$$

When we subtract these two costs from total revenues, we obtain producer surplus as:

$$PS = (B + C + F + E + H + J) - J - (B + C + E + F) = H.$$

Note that producer surplus has also decreased. It used to be area $(E + F + G + H)$, but now it is only area H.[n]

If both consumer and producer surplus have decreased, how can the tax increase social welfare? First, we need to account for the reduced pollution. With quantity reduced to Q^*, the total externality damage is now:

$$Externality = C + F + H.$$

So the externality damage associated with production between Q^* and Q_M, or area $(D + G + I)$, has been avoided.

But there is another benefit to imposing the tax. The government has now collected area $(B + C + E + F)$ in taxes. It can use this money for any socially beneficial purpose. Thus the tax revenues represent a benefit to society as a whole.

So to determine the net social benefits with the tax, we need to add the tax revenues to consumer and producer surplus. We can now calculate the net social benefits as:

$$Net\ Benefits = (A) + (H) + (B + C + E + F) - (C + F + H).$$

If we cancel out the positive and negative terms, we get:

$$Net\ Benefits = A + B + E.$$

How does this compare to net benefits before the tax? Recall that benefits were $(A + B + E - I)$. So benefits have increased by area I as a result of tax. Another way of looking at this is that we have avoided the negative impacts of "too much" automobile production, represented by area I, which shows the excess of marginal costs (including external costs) over marginal benefits.

Negative Externalities—A Mathematical Approach

We can further demonstrate the welfare analysis of a negative externality by looking at a numerical example. Suppose that the demand schedule for new automobiles in the United States is given by:

---

[n]Note that producer surplus can also be measured as the difference between price and the supply curve with the tax. This would be area $(B + E)$. Since the two supply curves are parallel, this is the same as area H.

$$P_d = 100 - 0.09\,Q$$

where P_d is the price of new vehicles in thousands of dollars and Q is the quantity demanded per month in hundreds of thousands.

Assume the supply schedule for automobiles is:

$$P_s = 4 + 0.03\,Q$$

where again P_s is the price in thousands of dollars and Q is the quantity sold per month in hundreds of thousands.

We know that at equilibrium P_d must be equal to P_s. So we can set the two equations equal to each other to solve for the equilibrium quantity:

$$100 - 0.09\,Q = 4 + 0.03\,Q$$
$$96 = 0.12\,Q$$
$$Q = 800$$

We can insert this quantity into either the demand or supply equation to solve for the equilibrium price. Note that we should get the same price from both equations.

$$P_d = 100 - 0.09\,(800)$$
$$P_d = 100 - 72$$
$$P_d = 28$$

or

$$P_s = 4 + 0.03\,(800)$$
$$P_s = 4 + 24$$
$$P_s = 28$$

So, the equilibrium price of new automobiles is $28,000, and the quantity sold is 800,000 per month.[o]

We can next determine consumer and producer surplus in the automobile market. To do this, it is helpful to draw a graph of the market, as shown in Figure A3.10. Since our supply and demand curves are linear equations, both consumer and producer surplus will be the area of a triangle. For consumer surplus, we know the base of the triangle is the equilibrium quantity, or 800,000 automobiles. The height of the triangle is the difference between the equilibrium price and the intersection of the demand curve with the y-axis, as shown in Figure A3.10. To determine the point of intersection, we simply insert a quantity of zero in the demand curve and solve for price.

$$P_d = 100 - 0.09\,(0)$$
$$P_d = 100$$

---

[o] These values are relatively close to actual new monthly automobile sales in the United States and the average price of a new vehicle.

So the height of the consumer surplus triangle is (100 – 28), or $72,000. Thus total consumer surplus is:

$$CS = (\$72,000) * (800,000) * 0.5$$
$$CS = \$28.8 \text{ billion.}$$

(Note that we need to be careful with our units in this example to make sure we obtain the correct answer).

Figure A3.10 **Automobile Market Example**

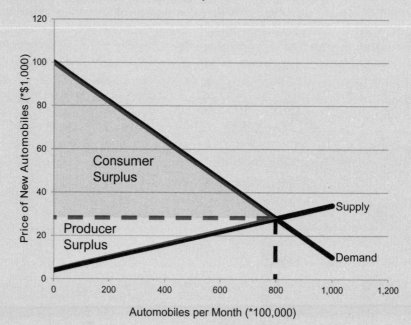

For producer surplus, the base of the triangle is again the equilibrium quantity of 800,000. To determine the height, we need to calculate the price where the supply curve intersects the y-axis. To do this, we insert a quantity of zero in the supply equation.

$$P_s = 4 + 0.03 (0)$$
$$P_s = 4$$

So the height of the producer surplus triangle is (28 – 4), or $24,000. Producer surplus is then:

$$P_S = (\$24,000) * (800,000) * 0.5$$
$$P_S = \$9.6 \text{ billion.}$$

Total market benefits are the sum of consumer and producer surplus, or $38.4 billion. But we also need to consider the negative externality costs. Suppose that the negative externality cost of each automobile is $6,000. We can calculate the total externality costs by simply multiplying this amount by the number of automobiles sold:

$$Externality = \$6,000 * 800,000$$
$$Externality = \$4.8\ billion.$$

So the net social welfare of the automobile market would $38.4 billion minus $4.8 billion, or $33.6 billion.

Next we consider the net social benefits if we were to institute a tax on automobiles that fully internalizes the externality. Thus we would impose a tax of $6,000 per automobile on vehicle manufacturers. As this reflects an additional cost, the new market supply curve would shift upward by $6,000, as shown in Figure A3.11. In other words, the intercept for the supply curve with the tax would increase by 6, to:

$$P_s = (4 + 6) + 0.03\ Q$$
$$P_s = 10 + 0.03\ Q.$$

As before, we can solve for the equilibrium quantity first by setting the supply curve with the tax equal to the demand curve:

$$100 - 0.09\ Q = 10 + 0.03\ Q$$
$$90 = 0.12\ Q$$
$$Q = 750.$$

Substituting this quantity into the demand curve (we could use the new supply curve as well), we solve for the equilibrium price as:

$$P_d = 100 - 0.09\ (750)$$
$$P_d = 32.5.$$

So with the externality tax in place, the price of new vehicles increases to $32,500 and the quantity sold per month falls to 750,000.

We can calculate the new consumer surplus CS* as a triangle with a base of 750,000 and a height equal to the difference between 100 (the intercept) and the new price of 32.5, or 68.5:

$$CS* = (\$68,500) * (750,000) * 0.5$$
$$CS* = \$25.6875\ billion.$$

So we can see that the tax has reduced consumer surplus by more than $3 billion.

Note that in Figure A3.11 producer surplus is the triangle above the market supply curve and below price, but we also need to deduct the tax revenue. Since the tax is $6,000, we know that the height of the producer surplus triangle is the difference between the intercept on the market supply curve ($4,000), and the new equilibrium price minus $6,000, or ($32,500 – $6,000) = $26,500. Thus the height is ($26,500 – $4,000), or $22,500. The new producer surplus is:

$$PS^* = (\$22,500) * (750,000) * 0.5$$
$$PS^* = \$8.4375 \text{ billion.}$$

Producer surplus has also decreased as a result of the tax, by more than $1 billion. So the market benefits have clearly declined as a result of the tax.

Since fewer automobiles are sold, the externality damage will decrease. The damage per automobile is still $6,000, so the externality costs are:

$$Externality = \$6,000 * 750,000$$
$$Externality = \$4.5 \text{ billion.}$$

Figure A3.11 **Automobile Market Example with Externality Tax**

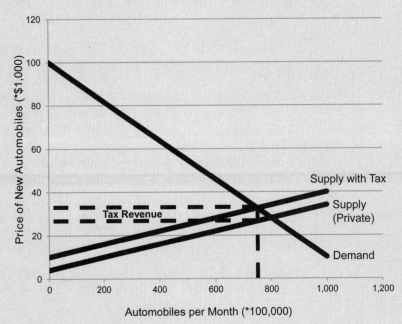

So externality costs have decreased by $300 million. Finally, we need to consider the tax revenue. The tax revenue is the $6,000 tax multiplied by the number of vehicles sold:

$$Tax\ Revenue = \$6,000 * 750,000$$
$$Tax\ Revenue = \$4.5 \text{ billion.}$$

We see that the tax revenue is exactly equal to the remaining externality damage. In other words, the market participants are fully compensating society for the external costs of their actions. Net social welfare with the tax is:

$$Net\ Benefits = CS + PS - externality\ costs + tax\ revenues$$
$$Net\ Benefits = \$25.6875 + \$8.4375 - \$4.5 + 4.5$$
$$Net\ Benefits = \$34.125\ billion.$$

Compared to our original net welfare of $33.6 billion, we see that net benefits have increased by $525 million. So society is actually better off with the tax than without it.

Welfare Analysis of Positive Externalities

We now present a formal analysis of a market in the presence of positive externalities, as shown in Figure A3.12, which again shows the market for solar energy. Market benefits are the usual areas of consumer and producer surplus. So consumer surplus is

$$CS = B + C$$

and producer surplus is

$$PS = D + E$$

The area of positive externalities is the parallelogram between the two benefit curves, up to Q_M:

$$Externality = A + F$$

Figure A3.12 **Welfare Analysis of a Positive Externality**

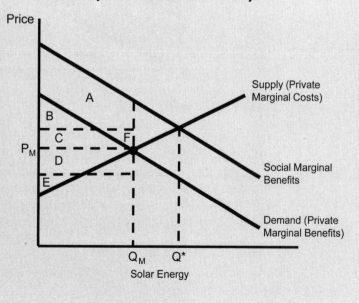

So total social benefits are simply the sum of the market and external benefits:

$$Net\ Benefits = A + B + C + D + E + F.$$

But notice in Figure A3.12 that between Q_M and Q^*, marginal social benefits exceed the marginal costs. Thus the optimal level of solar energy is Q^*, not Q_M. So we can increase net social benefits by increasing the production of solar energy. We can do this through the use of a subsidy on the production or installation of solar systems, illustrated in Figure A3.13.

With the subsidy in place, the new equilibrium price will fall to P_0, and the quantity will increase to Q^*. Consumer surplus will be the triangle above P_0 and below the market demand curve:

$$CS = B + C + D + G + L.$$

Figure A3.13   **The Market for Solar Energy with a Subsidy**

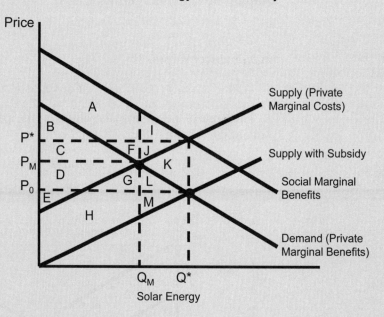

Determining the producer surplus is a little tricky. Let's start by not considering the subsidy payment, so the cost of producing Q^* is the area under the private marginal cost curve. Note that for the first few solar panels, price is above the marginal cost curve, yielding positive producer surplus of area E. But beyond this point, price is below the marginal cost curve, and solar energy producers are actually losing money. Thus losses accrue equal to the area (G + K + L). The producer surplus without the subsidy is:

$$PS = E - G - K - L.$$

So if the subsidy is not considered, producers appear to be losing money. But, of course, they also receive the subsidy payment. The per-panel subsidy is the vertical distance between P^* and P_0. Thus the total subsidy for producing Q^* is:

$$Subsidy = C + D + F + G + J + K + L.$$

Net producer surplus with the subsidy is:

$$Net\ PS = (E - G - K - L) + (C + D + F + G + J + K + L)$$
$$Net\ PS = E + C + D + F + J.$$

The area that represents the positive externality is the area between the two marginal benefit curves up to Q^*, or:

$$Externality = A + F + I + J + K.$$

Finally, we have to realize that society needs to pay for the subsidy, such as through higher taxes. So the subsidy payment must be considered a cost from the perspective of society. The subsidy area defined above must be deducted in order to determine net social welfare. Thus net benefits are:

$$Net\ Benefits = (B + C + D + G + L) + (E + C + D + F + J) +$$
$$(A + F + I + J + K) - (C + D + F + G + J + K + L).$$

If we cancel out the positive and negative terms, we are left with:

$$Net\ Benefits = A + B + C + D + E + F + I + J.$$

Comparing this to the estimate of net benefits without a subsidy, we can see that the net gain in social welfare as a result of the subsidy is $(I + J)$. Once again, society is better off with market intervention than without it. The subsidy moves us to the efficient outcome.

KEY TERMS AND CONCEPTS FROM APPENDICES

consumer surplus

economies of scale

law of demand

law of supply

marginal costs

market equilibrium

price elasticity of demand

price elasticity of supply

producer surplus

shortage

surplus

willingness to pay

CHAPTER 4

Common Property Resources and Public Goods

4.1 COMMON PROPERTY, OPEN ACCESS, AND PROPERTY RIGHTS

As we saw in the Chapter 3, clearly defined property rights can be used for efficient resource allocation. In market economies, private property rights are central. This has not always been the case. In traditional or tribal societies, private property rights over resources are rare. Resources important to the life of the tribe are either held in common (like a common grazing ground) or are not owned at all (like animals that are hunted for food). Economically developed societies—we like to think of ourselves as "advanced" societies—have generally evolved elaborate systems of property rights covering most resources as well as most goods and services. But modern industrialized countries also have resources, goods, and services, which are difficult to categorize as property.

A free-flowing river is one example. If we think of the river simply as a quantity of water that flows past people's land, we can devise rules for "ownership" of the water, allowing a certain amount of water withdrawal per landowner. But what about the aquatic life of the river? What about the use of the river for recreation: canoeing, swimming, and fishing? What about the scenic beauty of the riverside?

Some of these aspects of the river might also become specific types of property. For example, in Scotland trout-fishing rights on certain rivers are jealously guarded property. But it is difficult to parcel up every function of the river and define it as someone's property. To some degree, the river is a **common property resource**—it is accessible to everyone and not subject to private ownership. Technically speaking, a common property resource is a **nonexclusive good** because people cannot easily be excluded from using it.

common property resources

a resource that is not subject to private ownership and is available to all, such as the oceans or atmosphere.

nonexclusive good

a good that is available to all users; one of the two characteristics of public goods.

How can a common property resource be managed to maximize social benefits? Is government regulation required, and, if so, how might an efficient outcome be achieved? We address these questions using the example of an ocean fishery.

The Economics of a Fishery

open-access resource(s)
a resource that offers unrestricted access such as an ocean fishery or the atmosphere.

A classic example of a common property resource is an ocean fishery. While inland and coastal fisheries are often governed by private, traditional, or government management systems, fisheries in the open ocean are typically **open-access resources**. (An open-access resource is a common property resource that lacks any system of rules governing its use.) Anyone who wants to can fish in nonterritorial waters, which means that no one owns the basic resource, the wild stock of fish. We use this example to apply some of the basic concepts of production theory to an open-access resource.

How can we apply economic theory to a fishery? Let's start with common sense. If only a few fishing boats start operations in a rich fishery, their catch will certainly be good. This is likely to attract other fishers, and as more boats join the fishing fleet the total catch will increase.

As the number of fishing boats becomes very large, it is clear that the capacity of the fishery will be strained, and the catch of individual boats will diminish. We know from experience that if this process is taken too far, the output of the whole fishery can be badly damaged. At what point does it become counterproductive to put in more effort, in terms of more boat trips? Which forces can drive us past that point? Economic theory can give us some insights into these critical questions of common property resource management.

total product
the total quantity of a good or service produced with a given quantity of inputs.

We can envision the fishery's **total product** as shown in Figure 4.1. The horizontal axis shows fishing effort, measured in numbers of boat trips. The vertical axis shows the total catch of all the boats. As the number of boat trips increases, the total product curve shown in Figure 4.1 goes through three distinct phases.

constant returns to scale
a proportional increase (or decrease) in one or more inputs results in the same proportional increase (or decrease) in output.

The first is a period of **constant returns to scale** (here shown from 0 to 400 boats). In this range, each extra boat finds an ample supply of fish and is able to return to port with a catch of 10 tons.[a]

diminishing returns
a proportional increase (or decrease) in one or more inputs results in a smaller proportional increase (or decrease) in output.

The second is a period of **diminishing returns** to effort, shown from 400 to 850 boats. It is now becoming more difficult to catch a limited number of fish. When an extra boat puts out to sea, it increases the total catch of the fishery, but it also reduces by a small amount the catch of all the other boats. The natural resource is no longer ample for all; now there is intense competition for fish stocks, which makes the job tougher for all fishers.

absolutely diminishing returns
an increase in one or more inputs results in a decrease in output.

Finally, there is a period of **absolutely diminishing returns**, above 850 boats, a situation in which having more boats actually *decreases* the total catch. Here it is evident that **overfishing** is taking place. Stocks of fish are being depleted. The fish population's ability to replenish itself is damaged, and we have the makings of both an economic and an ecological collapse.[b]

overfishing
a level of fishing effort that depletes the stock of a fishery over time.

---

[a]For simplicity we assume that all boats are the same in this example. Thus each boat catches the same amount of fish.

[b]Note that in this example we use a long-term production function that represents the fishery product over time. Decline, or collapse, of fisheries, as shown in the absolutely diminishing returns section of the graph, would not take place in a single period but over several years.

Figure 4.1 **Total Product of the Fishery**

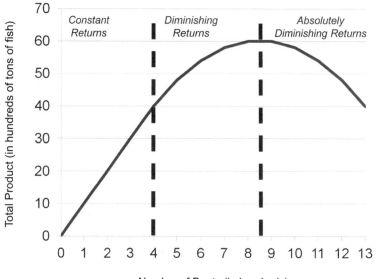

To understand the economic forces motivating the fishers, we must consider how different levels of total fishing effort affect their profits. We assume that fishers are interested only in making profits for themselves. The first step in determining profits is to convert the quantitative measure of tons of fish landed into a monetary figure showing total revenue earned. This can be done by simply multiplying the quantity of fish by the price per ton ($TR = P*Q$). We assume here that the price of fish is stable at $1,000/ton. We are implicitly assuming that this fishery is small enough relative to the total market that its output does not significantly affect the market price. If this fishery were the only source of fish for the market, we would have to consider price changes also.

We can now calculate the **total revenue** of the fishery, as shown in Table 4.1. Next, let's assume that cost of operating a fishing boat is constant at $4,000 per boat. Thus the **marginal cost** of a boat (i.e., the cost of sending one more boat into the fishery) is $4,000.[c] Since the cost of operating a boat is constant, the **average cost** of operating a boat is also always $4,000. The **total cost** for all boats in the fishery is equal to $4,000 multiplied by the number of boats. By subtracting the total revenue in the fishery from the total cost (TC) of operating the boats, we can obtain the **profits** ($TR - TC$) of the fishery, shown in Table 4.1.

We can see from Table 4.1 that total profits in the fishery are $3 million at 600 and 700 boats.[d] Figure 4.2 charts the total revenue, total costs, and profits of the fishery at each effort level. We see that profits are actually maximized between 600 and 700 boats, or at 650 boats. If fishing effort is too high (more than 1,200 boats), total profits of the fishery actually become negative.

total revenue
the total revenue obtained by selling a particular quantity of a good or service; equal to price multiplied by quantity sold.

marginal costs
the cost of producing or consuming one more unit of a good or service.

average cost
the average cost of producing each unit of a good or service; equal to total cost divided by the quantity produced.

total cost
the total cost to a firm of producing its output.

profits
total revenue received minus total cost to producers.

[c] Again, all boats are the same in this example, so the cost of operating each boat is assumed to be the same.
[d] In this example, we limit our analysis to maximizing the profits of the fishery. Thus we do not consider the benefits that consumers obtain from buying fish or any externality damage.

Table 4.1

Total Fish Catch, Revenue, Costs, and Profit

Number of boats (in hundreds)	1	2	3	4	5	6	7	8	9	10	11	12	13
Total fish catch (hundred tons)	10	20	30	40	48	54	58	60	60	58	54	48	40
Total revenue (in million $)	1	2	3	4	4.8	5.4	5.8	6	6	5.8	5.4	4.8	4
Total costs (in million $)	0.4	0.8	1.2	1.6	2	2.4	2.8	3.2	3.6	4	4.4	4.8	5.2
Total profits (in million $)	0.6	1.2	1.8	2.4	2.8	3	3	2.8	2.4	1.8	1	0	−0.8

Figure 4.2 **Total Revenue, Total Costs, and Profits for the Entire Fishery**

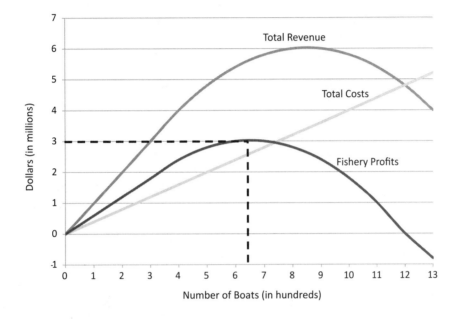

Incentives for Overfishing

We know that the profit-maximizing level of effort is 650 boats. But in the absence of any regulations governing how the fishery is managed, what level of fishing effort will occur? We assume that each fisher is only concerned with his or her profits. Thus individuals will not consider how their activities affect the fishery as whole, only whether fishing is profitable to them. So rather than looking at the values in Table 4.1 for the total fishery, we need to consider the perspective of the individual fisher.

We know that each boat costs $4,000 to operate. For each level of effort in Table 4.1, we can calculate the revenue for each fisher as the total revenue in the fishery divided by the number of boats. For example, with 800 boats operating total revenue is $6 million, and thus the revenue per boat is $7,500 ($6,000,000/800). This is the **average revenue** or revenue per boat, as shown in Table 4.2. In mathematical terms, $AR = TR/Q$. By subtracting the cost per boat of $4,000, we obtain the profit per boat, also shown in Table 4.2.

Suppose that 400 boats are operating. We see in Table 4.2 that each boat is bringing in revenues of $10,000, yielding an individual profit of $6,000. Other people will notice that fishing is rather profitable, and thus new fishers will be attracted

average revenue

the average price a firm receives for each unit of a good or service; equal to total revenue divided by the quantity produced.

Table 4.2

Revenue, Costs, and Profits for Individual Fishers

Number of boats (in hundreds)	1	2	3	4	5	6	7	8	9	10	11	12	13
Revenue per boat (in thousand $)	10	10	10	10	9.6	9	8.2	7.5	6.6	5.8	4.9	4	3.1
Cost per boat (in thousand $)	4	4	4	4	4	4	4	4	4	4	4	4	4
Profit per boat (in thousand $)	6	6	6	6	5.6	5	4.2	3.5	2.6	1.8	0.9	0	–0.9

open-access equilibrium
the level of use of an open-access resource that results from a market with free entry; this level of use may lead to depletion of the resource.

tragedy of the commons
the tendency for common property resources to be overexploited because no one has an incentive to conserve the resource while individual financial incentives promote expanded exploitation.

to enter the fishery. So long as fishers have free entry to the industry, the number of boats will continue to increase. Either existing fishers will acquire more boats, or new operators will enter the fishery.

Once we exceed 400 boats, in Table 4.2 profits per boat begin to decline as we enter the region of diminishing returns. But as long as operating each boat is profitable, there is an incentive for more boats to enter the industry—even into the region of absolutely diminishing returns. For example, when 1,000 boats are operating, the profits per boat are still $1,800. So even though additional boats actually reduce the total catch, and total revenue, of the fishery, there is still an economic incentive for individual fishers to send more boats into the fishery.

Only when we reach 1,200 boats do profits per boat finally fall to 0. If any more boats operate above 1,200, then profits per boat actually fall below 0 (i.e., every boat is losing money), and there would be an incentive for some fishers to leave the industry. Above 1,200 boats, the market is sending a "signal," through unprofitability, that the industry is overcrowded. Thus the **open-access equilibrium** is 1,200 boats, which is the point at which there is no further incentive for entry to or exit from the market.[e]

The open-access equilibrium is clearly not economically efficient. The market signal that the industry is overcrowded comes far too late—well above the efficient level of 650 boats. Looking at Table 4.1, we see that total profits in the industry at 1,200 boats are 0. Industry profits can actually be increased by *reducing* fishing effort.

In addition to being economically inefficient, the open-access equilibrium is also not ecologically sustainable. As the open-access equilibrium is in the region of absolutely diminishing returns, eventual collapse of the fishery is a likely outcome. The forces of free entry and profit maximization at the individual level, which usually work to promote economic efficiency, have exactly the opposite effect in the case of a common property resource. These forces encourage overfishing, which ultimately eliminates any profitability in the industry and destroys the natural resource. The economic explanation is that fishers have free access to a valuable resource—fish stocks. Economic logic tells us that an underpriced resource will be overused, and a resource priced at zero will be squandered.

This phenomenon is sometimes referred to as the **tragedy of the commons**.[1] Because common property resources belong to no one in particular, no one has an incentive to conserve them. On the contrary, the incentive is to use as much as

---

[e] You might wonder why more boats continue to operate even though the profit per boat, while still positive, becomes rather small. Our explanation assumes, for example, that even if the profit per boat is $50, more fishers will be attracted to enter the industry. We are assuming that the profits in this example represent *economic profits*, which are the profits measured relative to the fishers' next-best alternative. So as long as such profits are positive, fishing is more attractive than the next-best alternative, and there is further incentive to send more boats.

you can before someone else gets it. When resources are ample, as in precolonial America, when the stocks of fish were far beyond the needs or fishing abilities of the small population, there is no problem. When the population and demand are large enough, and fishing technologies more sophisticated, the economic logic that we have sketched out leads to a critical danger of overfishing and even complete collapse of the fishery.

Marginal Analysis of a Common Property Resource

marginal benefit
the benefit of producing or consuming one more unit of a good or service.

marginal revenue
the additional revenue obtained by selling one more unit of a good or service.

Economists seeking to determine efficient outcomes focus on comparing **marginal benefits** and marginal costs. This is really just common sense—if the benefits of doing something exceed the costs, then it normally makes sense to do it. So in our fishing example, as long as the benefits of one more boat exceed the costs of one more boat, then it makes sense for the industry as a whole to keep increasing the number of boats. In other words, if the **marginal revenue** of a boat exceeds the marginal cost, it is efficient to increase the number of boats. However, when the marginal costs equal or exceed the marginal revenue, we should stop adding boats. Thus the economically efficient outcome occurs where marginal revenue equals marginal cost.

We know the marginal cost per boat is constant at $4,000. To calculate the marginal revenue for each level of fishing effort, we calculate the additional revenue for each change in effort (effort being measured by the number of boats). We normally speak of the marginal change from one level of effort to another; thus we would calculate the marginal revenue between two levels of effort.

Let's consider the marginal revenue that results from increasing the number of boats from 400 to 500. Total revenue in the industry increases from $4 million to $4.8 million, an increase of $800,000. Since an additional 100 boats increases revenues by $800,000, the marginal revenue per boat when the number of boats increases from 400 to 500 is $800,000/100 = $8,000.[f] Expressed mathematically, $MR = \Delta TR/\Delta Q$.

It makes economic sense to increase from 400 to 500 boats because marginal cost is $4,000 per boat. In other words, marginal revenue exceeds marginal cost, so raising the number of boats from 400 to 500 increases economic efficiency in the fishery.

Table 4.3 calculates the marginal revenue per boat between each effort level, along with the marginal cost. Between 600 and 700 boats, the marginal revenue is exactly equal to the marginal cost of $4,000 per boat. So we can conclude that the efficient level of effort is between 600 and 700 boats, as illustrated in Figure 4.3.

The efficient outcome is where marginal revenue equals marginal cost, at 650 boats. But the open-access equilibrium occurs where average revenue equals the cost of a boat. In this example, due to our assumption of constant marginal costs, the marginal cost of $4,000 is also the average cost (i.e., the cost for each boat owner). Note that the difference between average revenue and average cost at 650 boats is about $4,500. This represents the profit that each boat makes at the efficient level of effort. We will see why this is important in the next section. If 650 boats

---

[f]Note that a true marginal analysis would require data on how total revenues change with each additional boat, rather than each additional 100 boats. Thus our analysis involves some approximation between the values given in the tables.

Table 4.3

Marginal Revenue and Cost Analysis of Fishery

Number of boats (in hundreds)	1	2	3	4	5	6	7	8	9	10	11	12	13
Total revenue (in $ million)	1	2	3	4	4.8	5.4	5.8	6	6	5.8	5.4	4.8	4
Marginal revenue (in $ 000)	10	10	10	8	6	4	2	0	−2	−4	−6	−8	
Marginal cost (in $ 000)	4	4	4	4	4	4	4	4	4	4	4	4	

Figure 4.3 **Economic Conditions in the Fishery**

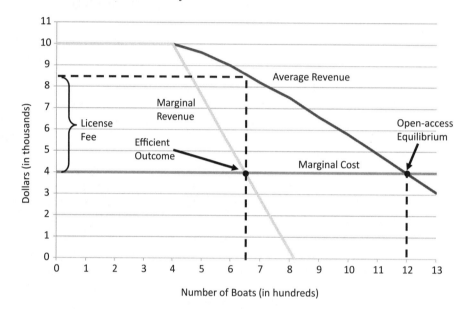

each obtain a profit of about $4,500, then total industry profits are maximized at $2.9 million. Obviously this represents a big improvement over total profits at the open-access equilibrium, which are zero at 12 boats.

The efficient outcome is also more likely to be ecologically sustainable. Referring back to Figure 4.1, we see that at 650 boats we are in the region of diminishing returns, rather than the area of absolutely diminishing returns. While fishing effort is high enough to cause some reduction in individual yields, it is unlikely to cause collapse of the fishery.

Policies for Fishery Management

What policies might be used to achieve the efficient outcome, as well as protecting the fishery by reducing effort? One option may be for all the fishers to voluntarily agree to limit fishing effort to 650 boats. But the problem is that each fisher will still have a strong economic incentive to send one more boat out, which may cause the agreement to break down. Plus, new fishers will be enticed to enter the fishery and would not be bound by the voluntary agreement.

As in the problem of externalities, achieving the efficient outcome requires regulation. One policy option is to use a **license fee** to discourage overfishing. The correct fee can be determined by referring to Figure 4.3. We want fishing to be profitable

license fee

the fee paid for access to a resource, such as a fishing license.

up to the efficient level of 650 boats, but we want to discourage fishing beyond this level. So the fee needs to be high enough to make the 651st boat unprofitable. At 650 boats, average revenue is $8,500 per boat, and profits are $4,500 per boat. The potential profit per boat at 651 boats would be slightly less than $4,500. So if we charge a license fee of $4,500, then the 651st boat would be unprofitable, and fishing effort would reach a new equilibrium at 650 boats. In other words, even with a license fee of $4,500 per boat, fishing remains profitable up to 650 boats, but then becomes unprofitable above 650 boats. Thus the "correct" license fee is the difference between average revenue and cost at the efficient level of effort. The license fee effectively moves us from the inefficient open-access equilibrium to the efficient outcome.

At 650 boats, each fisher will now be in the position of a perfect competitor, making minimal or "normal" profit.[g] But in this case the logic of competition now works to protect the ecosystem, not to destroy it. In effect, fishers will be charged a fee for the use of a previously free resource—access to fish stocks. This policy might be politically unpopular in fishing communities, but it will prevent the industry from destroying the means of its own livelihood.

Another advantage of charging a license fee is that the government receives a source of revenue. Charging $4,500 per boat, the government effectively collects the potential industry profits of $2.9 million. This revenue could be used for any purpose, such as to improve the habitat of the fishery, to compensate those who are forced out of the fishery when the fee is imposed, or to invest in technologies that reduce fishery damage.

Another policy to achieve the same goal would be the use of a **quota**, or catch limit. Government officials can determine a quota for the entire fishery, but determining who receives the rights to a limited fish catch can become controversial. If the right is allocated to current fishers, new entrants will be barred from the industry. Alternatively, fishers might receive **individual transferable quotas (ITQs)**, which could be sold to someone entering the business. In some cases, limited rights to hunt or fish certain species are allocated to indigenous peoples. Aleut people, for example, have the right to hunt a limited number of endangered bowhead whales. See Box 4.1 for another example of ITQs.

Yet another possibility is to sell fishing quotas at auction, which will lead to an economic result similar to that for the license fee. Suppose that the government correctly determines that 650 is the efficient levels of boats and makes this number of permits available in an auction. What would be the ultimate bidding price for these permits? If fishers can correctly estimate that potential economic profits at this effort level are $4,500 per boat (average revenue minus cost), then the permit price would get bid up to $4,500. In essence, the quota produces the same outcome as the license fee, both in terms of the number of boats and government revenue of $2.9 million. Whichever method is chosen, it requires a consciously planned government intervention. Although economists often argue that markets operate more efficiently without government intervention, here is a case in which government intervention is *required* to achieve an economically efficient (and ecologically sustainable) solution.

---

[g]A **normal profit** is the minimal profit a business needs to make to remain in the industry. It is equal to the profit that could be made in the next-best alternative.

BOX 4.1   COMMON-PROPERTY RESOURCE MANAGEMENT IN PRACTICE: INDIVIDUAL TRANSFERABLE QUOTAS

One real-world example of regulating a fishery through individual transferable quotas is the Long Island clam fishery. This example shows that the details of the quota system can significantly influence the efficiency of the industry.

The New York Department of Environmental Conservation allocates only 22 permits, which limit the total annual harvest to 300,000 bushels (about 13,600 bushels per permit). Based on 2011 clam prices, the gross revenue potential of each permit was about $135,000.

However, clam fishers claimed that after deducting operating costs, a single permit was insufficient to make a living. The permits are transferrable, meaning a single fisher could purchase multiple permits. But the permit system initially required each permit to be associated with one boat. If you purchased a second permit then you would have to also operate a second boat, effectively doubling your operating costs. This requirement meant that efficiency gains from applying multiple permits to the same boat could not be realized.

In 2011 the state changed the law to allow "cooperative harvesting"—meaning a fisher could buy additional permits without having to operate more boats. Given that the total quota allocation remained at 300,000 bushels the law change shouldn't affect the health of the fishery, but it offers the potential to increase the economic efficiency of the industry.

Source: Newsday (New York), July 6, 2012, p. A28.

We have not considered externalities yet in our analysis. It may be that high levels of fishing effort cause negative externalities, such as water pollution or reduced recreational opportunities. If this were the case, then the socially efficient outcome might be less than 650 boats, and we would also need to take these externalities into account when setting the license fee or the quota. If we could monetize the externality damage, we would add this amount to the fee to further reduce effort.

The need for social regulation to manage common-property resources has been well recognized throughout history. Many traditional societies have maintained flourishing fisheries through the implementation of socially accepted rules governing fishing activity. This approach reflects a longstanding principle of limited catch and conservation of resources.

Population growth, high demand, and advanced technology have complicated the implementation of such sound principles. As demand for fish increases globally, and more areas become overfished, the price of fish will tend to rise. A higher price will make the problems of open access worse, since it increases the profitability of fishing and encourages more entry. Improved technology also worsens the problem—usually increased productivity is good for society, but in the case of an open access resource, it hastens the pressure on the resource and makes ecosystem collapse more likely. For example, sonar systems that enable tracking of fish make it easier for large fishing boats to increase their catch—but also accelerate the depletion of fish stocks.

Both economic theory and ecological principles tell us that we must find ways to manage common property resources or risk having them destroyed through overuse.[2] As we will see in future chapters, the principles of common property resource management illustrated in this fishery example apply to many other resources, such as forests, open land, and even the atmosphere.

4.2 THE ENVIRONMENT AS A PUBLIC GOOD

public goods
goods that are available to all (nonexclusive) and whose use by one person does not reduce their availability to others (nonrival).

nonrival good
a good whose use by one person does not limit its use by others; one of the two characteristics of public goods.

Economists have long recognized the concept of **public goods**. Ordinary goods, such as automobiles, are generally purchased by one person, and their benefits are enjoyed only by the purchaser. Public goods, in contrast, benefit a large number of people, often the whole society. Like common property resources, public goods are defined as goods that are nonexclusive but are also said to be **nonrival**. If a good is nonrival, its use by one person does not reduce its availability or quality to others.[h]

One example is the National Park system of the United States. National Parks are open to all, and (except where overcrowding becomes a significant problem) their use by some people does not reduce others' ability to enjoy them. Public goods are not necessarily environmental in character: The highway system and the national defense are often cited as examples of public goods. Another nonenvironmental example is public radio, because anyone with a radio can listen to it and additional people listening to public radio does not reduce its availability to others. Many aspects of environmental preservation, however, do fall into the public goods category, since virtually everyone has an interest in a sound and healthy environment.[i]

Can we rely upon private markets to provide us with the appropriate level of public goods? The answer is clearly no. In many cases, private markets will not provide public goods at all. With market goods, the ability to charge a price, along with recognition of property rights, acts as a means to exclude nonbuyers from the benefits that buyers enjoy. Because of the nonexclusive and nonrival characteristics of public goods, no individual consumer has an incentive to pay for something that everyone else can freely enjoy.

A second possibility is to rely on donations to supply public goods. This is done with some public goods, such as public radio and television. Also, some environmental groups conserve habitats that, while privately owned, can be considered public goods (see Box 4.2). Donations, however, generally are not sufficient for an efficient provision of public goods. Since public goods are nonexclusive, each person can receive the benefits of public goods regardless of whether they pay. So while some people may be willing to donate money to public radio, many others simply listen to it without paying anything. Those who do not pay choose to be **free riders**. It is obvious that a voluntary donation system would not work for, say, the provision of national defense.

free riders
an individual or group that obtains a benefit from a public good without having to pay for it.

Although we cannot rely upon private markets or voluntary donations to supply public goods, their adequate supply is of crucial interest to the whole society. Once again, the solution to the dilemma requires some degree of government involvement. Decisions regarding the provision of public goods are commonly decided

[h]The formal definition of a public good is a commodity or service that, if supplied to one person, can be made available to others at no extra cost (Pearce, 1992). A "pure" public good is one for which the producer is unable to exclude anyone from consuming it. Thus a pure public good demonstrates both nonrival consumption and nonexcludability.

[i]Technically, National Parks are not a "pure" public good since it is possible to charge an entry fee, thereby excluding those who do not pay the fee. But the National Parks remain a public good so long as it is national policy to allow free or low-fee entry.

BOX 4.2   THE NATURE CONSERVANCY

While voluntary donations cannot be relied on to provide an efficient level of public goods, voluntary efforts can effectively supplement government efforts. A successful example is The Nature Conservancy, an environmental group founded in 1951. Rather than focusing on political lobbying or advertising, The Nature Conservancy directs most its efforts toward purchasing land with the donations that it receives. This approach essentially creates a voluntary market in which people can express their preference for habitat conservation.

The organization started in the United States and now operates in more than thirty countries. The Nature Conservancy has protected over 119 million acres globally—an area equal in size to the U.S. state of New Mexico. Most of its protected areas are open for recreation, although it also allows logging, hunting, and other extractive uses on some properties.

In addition to directly purchasing and managing land, The Nature Conservancy also works with landowners to establish *conservation easements.* In a conservation easement agreement a landowner sells the rights to develop his or her land in certain ways (e.g., creating a housing subdivision), while still retaining ownership and continuing with traditional uses such as ranching and timber harvesting. Other efforts include their "Plant a Billion Trees" campaign to plant trees in the tropical rainforest of Brazil. Each $1 donated is used to plant one tree.

The Nature Conservancy's nonconfrontational, pragmatic approach is widely respected and generally considered effective. It is normally ranked as one of the most trusted nonprofit organizations and is praised for its efficient use of donations. While some environmentalists are critical of some of its policies, for example, selling parcels of donated land for a profit rather than conserving them, its efforts provide a means for individuals to use the market to promote habitat conservation.

Source: Nature Conservancy, www.nature.org.

in the political arena. This is generally true of, for example, national defense. A political decision must be made, taking into account that some citizens may favor more defense spending, others less. But a decision must be made, and after the decision is made, we all pay a share of the cost through taxes.

Similarly, decisions on the provision of environmental public goods have to be made through the political system. Congress, for example, must decide on funding for the National Park system.[j] Will more land be acquired for parks? Might some existing park areas be sold or leased for development? In making decisions like this, we need some indication of the level of public demand for environmental amenities. Can economic theory be of any help here?

Economics of Public Goods

The problem of public good provision cannot be solved through the ordinary market process of supply and demand. In the fishery example discussed above, the problem lay on the production side—the ordinary market logic led to overexpansion of production and excessive pressure on resources. In the case of public goods, the problem is on the demand side. Recall that in Chapter 3 we referred to a demand curve as both a marginal benefit curve and a willingness-to-pay curve. A consumer

---

[j]The National Park system does receive some funding from voluntary donations to the National Park Foundation, a nonprofit organization set up by Congress to support the National Parks.

is willing to pay, say, up to $30 for a shirt because that is his or her perceived benefits from owning the shirt. But in the case of a public good, the marginal benefits that someone obtains from a public good are not the same as their willingness to pay for it. In particular, their willingness to pay is likely to be significantly lower than their marginal benefits.

A simple example illustrates this point. Consider a society with just two individuals: Doug and Sasha. Both individuals value forest preservation—a public good. Figure 4.4 shows the marginal benefits each person receives from the preservation of forest land. As with a regular demand curve, the marginal benefits of each acre preserved decline with more preservation. We see that Doug receives greater marginal benefits than Sasha does. This may be because Doug obtains more recreational use of forests, or it may simply reflect different preferences.

vertical addition

adding the price of more than one demand curve at the same quantity demanded.

The social marginal benefits from preserved forest land are obtained by the **vertical addition** of the two marginal benefit curves. In the top graph in Figure 4.4, we see that Doug receives a marginal benefit of $5 for an additional acre of forest preservation if 10 acres are already preserved. Sasha receives a marginal benefit of only $2. So the social, or aggregate, benefits of an additional acre of preserved forest are $7, as shown in the bottom graph. Note that the aggregate curve is kinked because to the right of the kink the curve only reflects Doug's marginal benefits, since Sasha's marginal benefits are zero in this range.

social benefits

the market and nonmarket benefits associated with a good or service.

Suppose for simplicity that forest preservation costs society a constant $7/acre, in terms of administrative and management costs. This is shown in the bottom graph in Figure 4.4. In this example, the optimal level of forest preservation is 10 acres—the point where the marginal **social benefits** just equal the marginal costs. But we have not addressed the question of how much Doug and Sasha are willing to pay for forest preservation. In the case of a public good, one's marginal benefit curve is not the same as his or her willingness-to-pay curve. For example, while Doug receives a marginal benefit of $5 for an acre of forest preservation, he has an incentive to be a free rider and he may be willing to pay only $3 or nothing at all.

The problem is that we do not have a market in which people accurately indicate their preferences for public goods. Perhaps we could use a survey to collect information on how much people value certain public goods (we discuss economic surveys in Chapter 6), but even then people might not provide accurate responses. Ultimately, decisions regarding public goods require some kind of social deliberation. One possibility is to rely on elected officials to make public goods decisions for their constituents. Another is to rely on a democratic process such as direct voting or local town meetings.

Even if we reach the "correct" level of provision from a social perspective, another problem arises due to differences across individuals. Suppose that we correctly determine that the appropriate level of forest preservation in Figure 4.4 is 10 acres. At a marginal cost of $7/acre, we need to raise $70 in revenues to pay for preservation. We might tax Doug and Sasha $35 each to cover these costs. Doug receives at least $5 in benefits for every acre preserved, or a total of at least $50 in benefits, so he probably would not object to the $35 tax. However, Sasha receives significantly lower benefits, and she may view the tax as excessive.

Suppose that we extend our two-person example to the entire population of the United States—about 114 million households. If preferences in the general population are similar to Doug and Sasha's, we will need to raise about 114 million × $35

Figure 4.4 **The Economics of Forest Preservation**

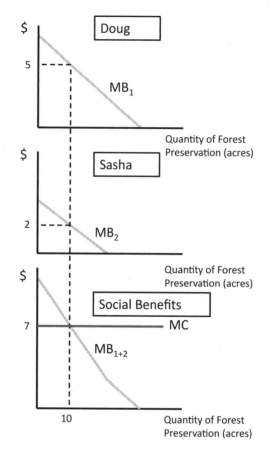

or about $4 billion for forest preservation in order to reflect its true social benefits. This could be done with a tax of $35 per household. But, of course, marginal benefits vary across households. It is clearly impractical to assess the actual marginal benefit of each household. A society-wide decision must be made. Some people might think that they have to pay too much; others that the allocation of money for forest preservation is inadequate. But assessing a tax on everyone is essential to achieve the goal. Debates regarding efficiency and fairness in the case of public goods are thus inevitably both political and economic in nature.

4.3 THE GLOBAL COMMONS

In examining these examples of common property resources and public goods, we have extended the scope of our resource and environmental analysis. A little thought should make it clear that these cases are closely related to the theory of externalities discussed in Chapter 3. In a sense, we are dealing here with special cases of externalities. The fisher who adds an extra boat to the fishing grounds imposes an external cost on all the other fishers by slightly lowering the average catch. An environmental organization that purchases and conserves important habitats confers an external benefit on all the rest of us, who may not have contributed to the effort but who gain a slightly improved environment.

The extension of the analysis to these examples, however, seems to raise another question. Can we really continue to define all these environmental issues as "externalities"? The use of the term seems to imply a secondary role in economic theory—external costs are added to economic analysis after the rest of the theory is essentially complete. But are these numerous externalities really symptoms of something more fundamental?

As we consider the multitude of environmental problems that have gained increased attention in recent years, we see the rising importance of cases involving common property resources and public goods. Global warming, ozone layer depletion, ocean pollution, freshwater pollution, groundwater overdraft, and species loss all have clear similarities to the cases discussed in this chapter. The increasing prevalence of such examples has led to a new focus on the concept of the **global commons**. If so many of the earth's resources and environmental systems show the characteristics of common property resource or public goods, perhaps we need to revise our way of thinking about the global economy.[3]

global commons
global common property resources such as the atmosphere and the oceans.

Rather than focusing on the goals of economic growth and dealing with the externalities as an afterthought, we need to recognize that the global economic system is highly dependent on the health of global ecosystems. Evaluation of the state of these systems and an assessment of how economic development can best be adapted to planetary limits is essential. This implies the need for new approaches to economic policy and new or reformed institutions at the national and international level. Clearly, this raises issues that go beyond the management of individual fisheries or national parks.

Proper management of the global commons poses special challenges because of the need to secure agreement among many different governments. Despite the many possibilities for conflicting views and free-rider temptations, several important international agreements, such as the Montreal Protocol on depletion of the ozone layer, have been put into place to deal with threats to the global atmosphere, oceans, and ecosystems. In other cases, such as the Kyoto Protocol on global climate change, effective agreement on implementation has been harder to achieve, as many countries wait for others to act or disagree about who should bear the costs.

We examine some of the implications of this broader perspective on common property issues in Chapter 7 and consider some issues of managing the global commons in later chapters, in particular in relation to the issue of global climate change in Chapters 18 and 19.

SUMMARY

Common property resources are those that are owned by a community, without specific assignment of private property rights to individuals or firms. Various systems are possible for managing such resources, including traditional use customs and government management. When no rules limit use, the resource is open access, meaning that anyone can use it without restriction. This situation leads to overuse of the resource and sometimes to the collapse of its ecological functions.

A classic case of the tragedy of the commons is overfishing of the oceans. Since there are no restrictions on access to fisheries in the open ocean, economic incentives lead to an excessive number of boats in operation. Depletion of the fish stocks results, with declining revenues for all fishers. But until economic profits (revenue minus costs) reach zero, there will continue to be an incentive for new participants to enter the fishery. This open-access equilibrium is both economically inefficient and ecologically damaging.

Possible policies to respond to overuse of the open-access resource include the use of licenses or quotas. Quotas can be assigned to individual fishing boats and can be made transferable (saleable). In smaller traditional societies, social principles of resource management are often followed. But in large industrialized societies, with advanced technology for fishing and other resource extraction, government management of open-access resources is essential.

Similarly, active government policy is needed in the area of public goods provision. Public goods, once provided, benefit the general public rather than selected individuals. They include goods and services such as parks, highways, public health facilities, and national defense. No individual or group of individuals is likely to have sufficient incentive or funds to provide public goods, yet their benefits are great and often essential to social well-being. Many environmental public goods, such as forest and wetlands preservation, cannot be adequately supplied through the market. Government intervention and public funds are needed to achieve the social benefits that flow from providing these public goods.

The global scope of many common property resources and public goods, including the atmosphere and oceans, raises many issues regarding proper management of the global commons. New and reformed institutions are needed to manage common property resources at the global level. The difficulty often lies in establishing effective international authority to regulate activities that threaten global ecosystems.

KEY TERMS AND CONCEPTS

absolutely diminishing returns	nonrival
average cost	normal profit
average revenue	open-access equilibrium
common property resource	open-access resources
constant returns to scale	overfishing
diminishing returns	profits
economic profit	public goods
free riders	quota
global commons	social benefits
individual transferable quotas	total cost
license fee	total product
marginal benefit	total revenue
marginal costs	tragedy of the commons
marginal revenue	vertical addition
nonexclusive good	

DISCUSSION QUESTIONS

1. Would a good policy for fishery management aim to obtain the maximum sustainable yield? Why or why not? When we speak of an optimal equilibrium from an economic

point of view, will this equilibrium also be generally ecologically sound? What might cause economic and ecological principles to conflict with fisheries management?

2. Suppose that the fishery example discussed in the chapter was *not* a common property resource but a fishery in a lake owned by an individual or a single firm. The owner could choose to allow fishing and charge a fee for access to the lake. How would the economic logic differ from the common property resource case? Would there be a greater net social benefit? Who would receive this net social benefit?

3. Discuss the effects of technological improvement in an industry that uses a common-property resource. For example, consider a technological improvement in fishing equipment that makes it possible to cut the costs of a fishing boat trip in half. Technological progress usually increases net social benefit. Does it do so in this case? How would your answer be affected by government policies relating to this industry?

4. Do you think it is possible to draw a clear distinction between private and public goods? Which of the following might be considered public goods: farmland, forest land, beachfront property, highways, a city park, a parking lot, a sports arena? What rules of the market or of public policy should apply to the provision of these goods?

EXERCISES

1. Farmers in an arid region of Mexico draw their irrigation water from an underground aquifer. The aquifer has a natural maximum recharge rate of 340,000 gallons per day (i.e., 340,000 gal./day filter into the underground reservoir from natural sources). The total product schedule for well operations looks like this:

Wells Operating	10	20	30	40	50	60	70	80	90
Total Water Output (Thousand Gal./Day)	100	200	280	340	380	400	400	380	340

The cost of operating a well is 600 pesos per day; the value of water to the farmer is 0.1 peso per gallon. Calculate Total Revenue ($TR = PQ$) for each level of output.

If each well is privately owned by a different farmer, how many wells will operate? (To calculate this you will need to calculate Average Revenue, which is TR/Q. Note that the quantity of wells is given in units of 10.) Analyze this result in terms of economic efficiency and long-term sustainability.

What would be the economically efficient number of wells? (To calculate this, you will need Marginal Revenue, which is $MR = TR/Q$, best shown *between* two levels of output). Show that net social benefit is maximized at this level of output.

How could the socially efficient equilibrium be achieved? In this case, is the socially efficient equilibrium also ecologically sustainable?

How would the answers change if the cost of well operation was 400 pesos per day?

2. Four towns share a common water source. By buying open land along the watershed (area from which the water flows) they can preserve its purity from sewage, road runoff, etc.

The land demand schedule for each town based on water treatment costs saved can be expressed as:

$$P = \$34{,}000 - 10Q_d$$

where Q_d is acres purchased, and P is the price the town would be willing to pay.

If the cost of land is $30,000 per acre, how much land will be purchased if each town operates independently? How much if they form a joint commission for land purchases? Show the situation graphically. (If the economic theory is not clear, imagine representatives of the four towns sitting around a table, discussing the costs and benefits of purchasing different amounts of land.)

Which is the socially efficient solution and why? How would the answers change if the price of land were $36,000 per acre?

Discuss this in terms of the demand for clean water. Is clean water a public good in this case? Can water generally be considered to be a public good?

NOTES

1. This concept was first introduced in Hardin, 1968. A more recent assessment of the issue is given in Feeny et al., 1999.

2. For an extensive treatment of the economic analysis of fisheries and other natural resources, see Clark, 1990.

3. See Heal, 1999, and Johnson and Duchin, 2000, on the concept of the global commons.

REFERENCES

Clark, Colin W. 1990. *Mathematical Bioeconomics: The Optimal Management of Renewable Resources.* New York: Wiley.

Feeny, David, Fikret Berkes, Bonnie J. McCay, and James M. Acheson. 1999. "The Tragedy of the Commons: Twenty-Two Years Later." In *Environmental Economics and Development*, ed. J.B. (Hans) Opschoor, Kenneth Button, and Peter Nijkamp, 99–117. Cheltenham, UK: Edward Elgar.

Hardin, Garrett. 1968. "The Tragedy of the Commons." *Science* 162: 1243–1248.

Heal, Geoffrey. 1999. "New Strategies for the Provision of Public Goods: Learning for International Environmental Challenges," in *Global Public Goods: International Cooperation in the 21st Century*, ed. Inge Kaul et al. New York: Oxford University Press.

Johnson, Baylor, and Faye Duchin. 2000. "The Case for the Global Commons," in *Rethinking Sustainability*, ed. Jonathan M. Harris. Ann Arbor: University of Michigan Press.

Pearce, David W., ed. 1992. *The MIT Dictionary of Modern Economics*, 4th ed. Cambridge, MA: MIT Press.

WEB SITES

1. **www.iasc-commons.org.** Links to articles related to management of common pool resources. The site is managed by the International Association for the Study of Common Property, "a nonprofit Association devoted to understanding and improving institutions for the management of environmental resources that are (or could be) held or used collectively by communities in developing or developed countries."

2. **www.sciencemag.org/site/feature/misc/webfeat/sotp/commons.xhtml.** A special issue of *Science* magazine focusing on the tragedy of the commons, including the original article on the subject by Garrett Hardin and more recent commentary.

CHAPTER 5

Resource Allocation Over Time

- How should we decide whether to use or conserve nonrenewable resources?
- How can we value resource consumption that will take place in the future?
- What will happen to prices and consumption if resources start to run out?

5.1 ALLOCATION OF NONRENEWABLE RESOURCES

renewable resources
a resource that is supplied on a continuing basis by ecosystems; renewable resources such as forests and fisheries can be depleted through exploitation.

nonrenewable resources
resources that are available in a fixed supply, such as metal ores and oil.

Resources can be **renewable** or **nonrenewable**. Renewable resources, if properly managed, can last indefinitely. Think of a well-managed farm, forest, or fishery—we expect that such resources can continue to be productive for centuries. Nonrenewable resources, by contrast, cannot last forever. Some may be in relatively short supply. Examples include high-grade deposits of copper ore or crude oil supplies. This raises the issue of how much of these nonrenewable resources we use today and how much we save for future generations.

A common concern is that we are using up Earth's resources too rapidly. Another point of view is that technological progress and adaptation will avoid resource shortages. What does economic theory have to say about this issue?

A simple version of nonrenewable resource analysis begins by assuming that we have a known, limited quantity of a resource that we can use during two different periods. The supply of high-grade copper, for example, is relatively fixed in amount. How should we allocate this limited resource between current and future periods?

A simple initial model of nonrenewable resource allocation deals only with two time periods. (If we consider all possible future periods, the problem becomes more complex, though not theoretically insoluble, as we will see). Our economic analysis weighs the economic value of copper in the present as compared with the value of copper in the future. Owners of copper deposits will decide whether to exploit them immediately or to hold them for a future period based on an estimate of probable future prices. We can formulate the problem as a simple extension of standard supply and demand theory.[a]

[a]This analysis assumes that there is no recycling of copper; the economics of recycling is considered in Chapters 11 and 17.

Equilibrium in the Current Period

marginal net benefit

the net benefit of the consumption or production of an additional unit of a resource; equal to marginal benefit minus marginal cost.

First, let us consider only the present period. Figure 5.1a shows a hypothetical supply and demand for copper. From this, we can derive the **marginal net benefit** curve for copper, which shows the difference between the value to the consumer and the cost of supply for each unit of copper. (For example, if we can extract a unit of copper for $50 and its value to the purchaser is $150, its marginal net benefit is $100).

Figure 5.1a **Supply, Demand, and Marginal Net Benefit for Copper**

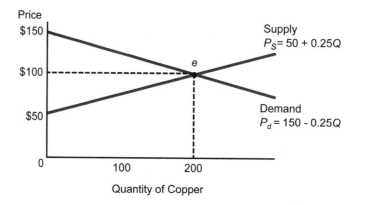

Graphically, marginal net benefit is the vertical difference between price on the supply curve and price on the demand curve. Marginal net benefits are generally largest for the first units extracted, then decline to zero at equilibrium (where the supply and demand curves meet). If we were to produce more than the equilibrium quantity, marginal net benefits would become negative as supply costs rise above the value to the purchaser (i.e., maximum willingness to pay).

The marginal net benefit concept is a handy way of compressing into one curve information about both supply and demand in one period. The marginal net benefit of copper in the present period is shown by curve MNB in Figure 5.1b.

Figure 5.1b **Marginal Net Benefit for Copper**

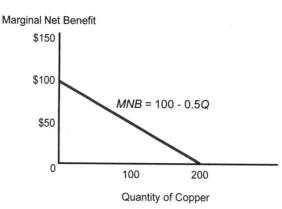

Algebraically, if the demand and supply schedules are given by

$$P_d = 150 - 0.25Q$$

and

$$P_s = 50 + 0.25Q$$

then marginal net benefit is given by

$$MNB = P_d - P_s = [(150 - 0.25Q) - (50 + 0.25Q)] = 100 - 0.5Q_1$$

total net benefit

total benefit minus total cost.

At the supply and demand equilibrium of $Q = 200$, marginal net benefit is 0, indicating that producing and consuming more than 200 units of copper will provide no additional net benefit. The area under the marginal net benefit curve shows **total net benefit** (just as the area under a demand curve shows total benefit and the area under a supply curve shows total cost).

static equilibrium

a market equilibrium that results when only present costs and benefits are considered.

When marginal net benefits are just equal to zero, total net benefits are maximized (as shown by the area under the marginal net benefit curve in Figure 5.1b). This corresponds to the ordinary supply and demand equilibrium for the first period, at a quantity of 200 and a price of 100. We will call this the **static equilibrium**—the market equilibrium that will prevail if only present costs and benefits are considered.[b]

Now let's consider the marginal net benefit of copper in the second period. We cannot know this value for sure, of course, because no one can foretell the future, but we *do* know that a fixed quantity of copper must be divided between the two periods. Let's make a simplifying assumption that the marginal net benefits of the copper market in Period 2 will be *exactly the same* as in Period 1. In other words, the supply and demand curves will be unchanged in the second time period. (This assumption is not necessary for the analysis, but it will make our first example simpler.)

A graphical trick allows us to compare the two periods. We use the horizontal axis to measure the total available quantity of copper—say, 250 units—and put the marginal net benefit curve for the first period, MNB_1, on this graph in the usual way. Then we put the marginal net benefit curve for the second period, MNB_2, on the graph in mirror-image fashion, going from right to left. Thus we have two horizontal scales, with the quantity used in Period 1 (Q_1) shown left-to-right, and the quantity used in Period 2 (Q_2) shown right-to-left (Figure 5.2). At any point on the horizontal axis, the total quantity used in the two time periods adds up to 250 units, the total available.

present value

the current value of a stream of future costs or benefits; a discount rate is used to convert future costs or benefits to present values.

discount rate

the annual rate at which future benefits or costs are discounted relative to current benefits or costs.

One more step will complete our analysis. Because we want to compare two time periods, we must translate future values into their equivalent in present values. The economic concept of **present value** relies on the use of a **discount rate** to convert future to present monetary values. Suppose, for example, I promise to give you $1,000—ten years from now. What is the value of this promise today?

---

[b]In this chapter we assume that copper production has no associated externalities. The impact of externalities on nonrenewable resource extraction is discussed in Chapter 11.

Figure 5.2 Allocation of Copper over Two Time Periods

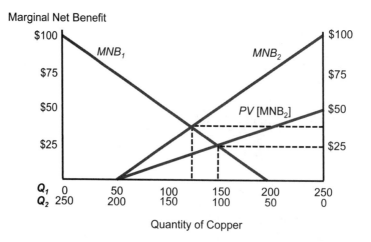

Assuming I am trustworthy, and you will definitely receive the money, the answer depends on the discount rate, reflected in financial terms as a rate of interest on deposits. Suppose there is a 7.25 percent interest rate.[c] Five hundred dollars put in the bank today at compound interest would be worth almost exactly $1,000 in ten years. We can say that the present value of the $1,000 to be received ten years from now is equal to $500 in cash today. In other words, you would be equally well off with $500 today or $1,000 ten years from now.[d]

Applying this principle to our copper example, let's assume that the two periods in our copper extraction example are ten years apart. (This assumption of only two extraction periods separated by ten years is, of course, unrealistic—but the principle that emerges from this mathematically simple example can be generalized to an n-period model.) Using the present value method, we can convert the marginal net benefits of copper in Period 2 into equivalent Period 1 values. We do this using the formula

$$PV[MNB_2] = MNB_2 / (1+r)^n,$$

where r is the annual discount rate and n is the number of years between periods.

If $r = 0.0725$ or 7.25 percent, and $n = 10$, then we can closely approximate $PV[MNB_2]$ as

$$PV[MNB_2] = MNB_2 / (1.0725)^{10} = MNB_2 / 2.$$

This present value of marginal net benefit schedule for Period 2 is shown in Figure 5.2 as a line exactly half the height of the undiscounted MNB_2.

---

[c]We assume here this is a real interest rate, corrected for expected inflation.

[d]You might object that you would prefer to have an actual $500 to spend today. But if this is your choice you can do it by borrowing $500 at 7.25 percent interest. When the loan comes due in ten years, amounting to $1,000 with interest, you can pay it off with my $1,000 gift.

Dynamic Equilibrium for Two Periods

The reason for the special graphical format now becomes apparent. Consider the point where the two curves *MNB1* and *PV[MNB2]* cross. At this point the present value of the marginal net benefit of 1 unit of copper is *the same* in both time periods. This is the optimal economic allocation between periods, since at this point no additional net benefit can be obtained by shifting consumption from one period to another. As you can see from the graph, this optimal allocation is 150 units in Period 1 and 100 units in Period 2. Algebraically this solution is obtained by solving a system of two equations:

$$MNB_1 = PV[MNB_2]$$

and

$$Q_1 + Q_2 = 250.$$

The second equation is the **supply constraint**, which tells us that the quantities used in the two periods must sum to exactly 250, the total quantity available.

We can solve the system of equations by first setting the two marginal net benefit curves equal to each other:

$$MNB_1 = 100 - 0.5Q_1 = PV[MNB_2] = (100 - 0.5Q_2) / 2$$
$$100 - 0.5Q_1 = 50 - 0.25Q_2$$

Because $Q_1 + Q_2 = 250$, $Q_2 = 250 - Q_1$. Substituting this in, we have:

$$100 - 0.5Q_1 = 50 - 0.25(250 - Q_1)$$
$$0.75\ Q_1 = 112.5$$

$Q_1 = 150$, and because $Q_1 + Q_2$ must equal 250:
$$Q_2 = 100.$$

We can check the assertion that this solution is economically optimal by using the same kind of welfare analysis introduced earlier (see Figure 5.3). By choosing the equilibrium point where $Q_1 = 150$ and $Q_2 = 100$, we have achieved maximum total net benefit, shown by the shaded area A + B in Figure 5.3a. (Area A is the net benefit in the first period, area B the net benefit in the second period.)

Compare this result with the welfare effects of any other allocation, for example the allocation $Q_1 = 200$, $Q_2 = 50$. As shown in Figure 5.3b, total welfare for the two periods is less with this new allocation (by the area B_2). By shifting 50 units from Period 2 use to Period 1 use, we have gained a Period 1 benefit equal to A_2, but lost a Period 2 benefit equal to $A_2 + B_2$, for a net loss of B_2. Total welfare is now $A_1 + A_2 + B_1$, less than the area A + B in Figure 5.3a. Similarly, any other allocation we can try will prove inferior to the optimal solution of $Q_1 = 150$, $Q_2 = 100$. (Try, for example, $Q_1 = 100$, $Q_2 = 150$. Show the effect of this allocation on total net benefits.)

Figure 5.3a **Optimal Intertemporal Resource Allocation**

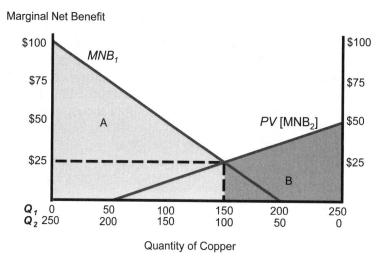

Figure 5.3b **Suboptimal Intertemporal Resource Allocation**

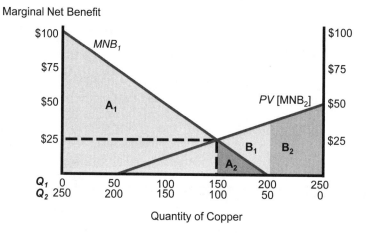

User Costs and Resource Depletion

Let's translate what we have learned from this algebraic and graphical analysis into more commonsense terms. We know that we can increase our benefit today by using more copper (in this example up to 200 units, which is the most we would use today if we took no account of future needs). If we chose to use only 50 units today, 200 would be left for the next period—enough to fulfill the maximum demand in that period. But at any use level greater than 50 units, we start to cut into the amount of copper available for future use.

Another way of putting this is to say that we start *imposing costs on future consumers of copper* by using up copper today. On our graph, those **user costs** show up as the steadily rising curve *PV[MNB₂]*. The more we use today, the higher these costs become. User costs are really just a different kind of third-party cost or externality—an **externality in time**.

user costs

opportunity costs associated with the loss of future potential uses of a resource, resulting from consumption of the resource in the present.

externality in time

an externality that affects future periods or generations.

We can justify using up copper today so long as the benefits from doing so outweigh the user costs imposed on future citizens. But when the user costs become higher than the marginal benefits from consumption today—in our example, at any level of present consumption above 150 units—we are reducing total economic welfare (i.e., the sum of welfare in both time periods) by our excessive present consumption.

Going back to our algebraic and graphical analysis, we define an exact value for the user cost at the Period 1 consumption level that we have defined is optimal. The vertical distance to the intersection point of MNB_1 and $PV[MNB_2]$ shows the user cost at equilibrium. We can calculate this easily by evaluating either MNB_1 or $PV[MNB_2]$ at the intersection point where $Q_1 = 150$ and $Q_2 = 100$:

$$User\ Cost = MNB_1 = 100 - 0.5(150) = 25$$

or:

$$= PV[MNB_2] = 50 - 0.25(100) = 25.$$

The user cost at equilibrium is thus $25.

What does this mean? Suppose we go back to the original supply and demand schedules for Period 1 (redrawn in Figure 5.4a). If we do not consider Period 2 at all, the market equilibrium in Period 1 will be 200 units of copper at a price of $100. Now suppose we add to the ordinary supply costs the user cost derived from Figure 5.2—just as we added an environmental external cost to the ordinary supply costs in the previous section. The result is shown in Figure 5.4a as the **social cost** schedule S'.

A new equilibrium appears at 150 units of copper consumption, with a price of $112.50. The user cost at this new equilibrium is $25—the vertical distance between the old supply curve S and the new social cost curve S'.

social cost

the market and nonmarket costs associated with a good or service.

Figure 5.4a **Market for Copper with User Costs** (first period)

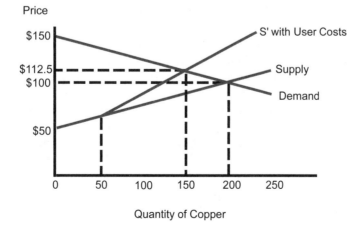

We can calculate the new first and second period prices using the original equations for the supply and demand schedules, with $25 added to the first period supply schedule to reflect the user cost.[e] For the first period this gives us:

$$P_d = 150 - 0.25Q_1 \text{ and } P_s = 75 + 0.25Q_1.$$

Setting these equal and solving we get the first period equilibrium:

$$Q_1 = 150, P_1 = 112.5.$$

With a first-period consumption of 150 units, 100 units will remain for consumption in the second period, at a second-period price of $125 (assuming demand conditions are unchanged). This is shown in Figure 5.4b. Using the demand curve equation, the equilibrium price can be calculated mathematically as:

$$P_2 = 150 - 0.25(100) = 150 - 25 = 125.$$

Figure 5.4b **Market for Copper** (second period)

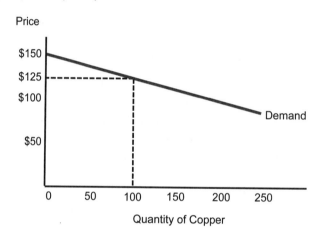

If user costs are internalized in this fashion, the new market equilibrium, known as a **dynamic equilibrium**, reflects *both* the needs of the present and of the future. The higher price will send a signal to producers and consumers of the resource to produce and use less today, thereby conserving more for the future. But how will user costs be reflected in the market?

dynamic equilibrium
a market equilibrium that results when present and future costs and benefits are considered.

One possibility is a **resource depletion tax** imposed on copper ore production and sale. Like a pollution tax, this tax will raise the effective supply schedule to the real social cost S'. Other policy mechanisms could include direct government control of resource exploitation, setting aside resource deposits or maintaining stockpiles.

resource depletion tax
a tax imposed on the extraction or sale of a natural resource.

In certain cases, however, the market may not need government intervention to internalize user costs. This would be true especially if the period until expected resource exhaustion is relatively short. In this case, private owners of the resource will anticipate the second-period situation and act accordingly.

If resource shortages are foreseen, profit-seeking resource owners will hold some copper stocks off the market or leave copper ores in the ground and wait for the

---

[e]This equation does not quite represent the supply curve accurately (to do that we would need a more complex equation reflecting the change in slope at 50 units) but it will give a correct result for the equilibrium price and quantity, since at that level we know the user cost is $25.

higher prices likely to prevail in a period of shortage. This supply limitation will have exactly the same effect (a leftward and upward shift of the supply curve to S′) as the imposition of a resource depletion tax. So in this case the imposition of a tax is not necessary—the market process will automatically adjust for anticipated future limits on copper resources.

5.2 HOTELLING'S RULE AND TIME DISCOUNTING

What if we want to consider the real world, which presents not two periods but an infinite number of future periods? How much copper should we be prepared to set aside for fifty years from now? One hundred years? Extending our two-period analysis to a more general theory offers perspective on these issues. Such questions test the limits of our economic model and also address the interrelationship between social values and the more specific market values that we deal with in economic theory.

Our simple two-period example makes clear that the discount rate is a critical variable. At different discount rates, the optimal allocation of copper between the two periods will vary significantly. Let's start at one extreme—a discount rate of zero. In our example, the equilibrium allocation of copper would be 125 units consumed in each period. At a discount rate of zero, future net benefits are given *exactly the same value* as if they were current net benefits. The available copper is therefore divided evenly between the periods.

At any discount rate above zero, we favor present consumption over future consumption to some degree. At a very high discount rate—say 50 percent per year—the first period allocation of copper is 198 units, close to the 200 units consumed in the static equilibrium case, and user costs fall nearly to zero. At high discount rates has the effect of weighing present benefits much more heavily than future benefits (see Figure 5.5 and Table 5.1).

Figure 5.5 **Intertemporal Resource Allocation with Different Discount Rates**

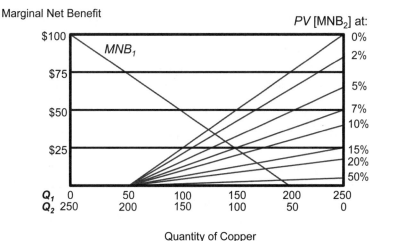

Quantity of Copper

Hotelling's rule
a theory stating that in equilibrium the net price (price minus production costs) of a resource must rise at a rate equal to the rate of interest.

We can extend this logic from one period to many periods, and even to an infinite future. The principle involved is known as **Hotelling's rule**. This rule states that

Table 5.1

Intertemporal Resource Allocation with Different Discount Rates

Discount Rate (%)	(1 + r)10	Q1	Q2
0	1	125	125
2	1.2	132	118
5	1.6	143	107
7.5	2	150	100
10	2.6	158	92
15	4	170	80
20	6.2	179	71
50	57.7	198	52

in equilibrium the resource net price (defined as the price minus extraction costs) must rise at a rate equal to the rate of interest.[f]

Consider an example from the perspective of a copper ore deposit owner. The owner's profit per unit extracted is equal to the net price. In deciding whether to produce and sell the copper, the owner will weigh the net price available today against a possible higher future net price. If the present net price, plus interest, exceeds the probable future net price, the owner will profit more by extracting the resource today and invest the proceeds, rather than waiting. If the expected future net price is higher than the net price today plus interest, it will be more profitable to wait and sell at the future date.

If all resource owners follow this logic, the quantity of copper supplied today will increase until today's copper price falls low enough to encourage resource owners to conserve, hoping for a better future price. At this point, Hotelling's rule will hold: The expectations of future price increases will exactly follow an exponential curve $P_1(1+r)^n$, where P_1 is today's price, r is the discount rate, and n is the number of years from the present (see Figure 5.6).

If this sounds confusing, consider this simpler, common sense formulation: High discount rates create an incentive to use resources quickly (since their present value is greater relative to their future value); low discount rates create greater incentive to conserve. More generally, we can say that economic theory implies the existence of an **optimal depletion rate**. Under market conditions, a nonrenewable resource will be used up at a certain "optimal" rate, and this rate will be faster at higher discount rates.[g]

Interestingly, according to this theory it is optimal to deplete certain resources to complete exhaustion over time—the higher the discount rate, the shorter the time. Like the theory of optimal pollution, this sounds wrong to many people. What about the ethical imperative to leave something for future generations?

One way of answering this question is to say that we do not have an ethical imperative to leave untouched resources to future generations. Rather, we can leave them an economic system including an accumulation of capital that has been developed using these resources. If we use the resources today and squander the proceeds on frivolous consumption, that would indeed be unfair to future generations. But if we invest the proceeds wisely, resource use today will benefit both us and our descendants. This principle, expressed in economic terms, is known as the **Hartwick rule**

optimal depletion rate
the depletion rate for a natural resource that maximizes the net present value of the resource.

Hartwick rule
a principle of resource use stating that resource rents—the proceeds of resource sale, net of extraction costs—should be invested rather than consumed.

[f]The rule is named for Harold Hotelling, who originated the modern theory of nonrenewable resources in the 1930s (see Hotelling, 1931). There is a debate about how well Hotelling's rule works to describe the prices of real-world resources; we discuss this further in Chapter 11.

[g]We examine the relationship of resource prices and resource extraction patterns in more detail in Chapter 11.

Figure 5.6 **Hotelling's Rule on Equilibrium Resource Price**

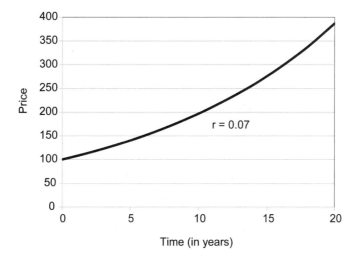

(not to be confused with the similarly named and closely related Hotelling's rule). The Hartwick rule states that we should invest **resource rents**—the proceeds of resource sale, net of extraction costs—rather than consuming them. Thus we replace diminished natural resources with an equal value of produced capital.[1]

resource rents
income derived from the ownership of a scarce resource.

A broader critique of discounting focuses on the fact that a discount rate based on standard commercial rates of interest will give a low weight to the well-being of future generations. This leads some people to question whether we can justifiably apply present-value analysis, based on a discount rate, over long periods. This issue will be important in our discussion of valuation and cost/benefit analysis in Chapter 6 and of long-term sustainability in Chapter 7.

Another issue that affects the theory of exhaustible resources concerns the presence of environmental externalities in resource extraction. In this chapter we simply assume no externalities in the production of copper, so the supply and demand cures for copper accurately reflect its social costs and benefits. In the real world, copper mining is likely to have significant environmental impacts. As higher-quality copper ores are used up, the environmental costs of recovering copper from lower-grade ores will probably rise. Internalizing these costs would affect the market price and intertemporal allocation of copper. In addition, a market for recycled copper is likely to develop, providing a new source of market supply not considered in our basic analysis. Issues such as these are dealt with more fully in Chapter 11.

SUMMARY

Nonrenewable resources can be used in the present or conserved for future use. Economic theory offers some guidance concerning the principles of nonrenewable resource allocation over time. In essence, the net value gained from using a resource today must be balanced against the net value of its potential future use. To compare values across time periods, we use a discount rate to measure the present value of future consumption.

The concept of user costs captures the idea that by using resources today, we impose some cost on future potential consumers. User cost is a kind of externality in time and, like other externalities, should be reflected in market price to internalize all social costs. Including user costs in market price will reduce consumption today, leaving more for future use.

If resource owners foresee future resource shortages, current prices will reflect user costs. The expectation that prices will rise creates an incentive to hold resources off the market today, in order to sell them at a higher price in the future. According to Hotelling's rule, in equilibrium the net price of a resource (market price minus extraction costs) must rise at a rate equal to the rate of interest. The higher the interest rate, the more likely the owner is to profit from extracting and selling a nonrenewable resource today rather than waiting for higher prices in the future.

Especially when figuring for long periods, discounting reduces the significance of user costs almost to zero and creates little market incentive for conserving nonrenewable resources. If governments wish to ensure a long-term supply of certain resources, they can internalize user costs through a resource depletion tax—much as a pollution tax can be used to internalize current externalities.

The alternative may be to exploit nonrenewable resources to exhaustion, leaving no reserves for future use. A major question is whether it is appropriate to use current discount rates to determine the allocation of resources over the long term or whether there is a social obligation to conserve resources for future generations.

KEY TERMS AND CONCEPTS

discount rate
dynamic equilibrium
externality in time
Hartwick rule
Hotelling's rule
marginal net benefit
net price
nonrenewable resources
optimal depletion rate

present value
renewable resources
resource depletion tax
social cost
static equilibrium
supply constraint
total net benefit
user costs

DISCUSSION QUESTIONS

1. It has been argued that any government policy aimed at nonrenewable resource conservation is an unwarranted interference with the free market. According to this point of view, if a resource is likely to become scarce, the people most likely to realize this are the private investors and traders who deal in the resource. If they anticipate scarcity, they will hold stocks of the resource for future profit, driving up its price and leading to conservation. Any action by government bureaucrats is likely to be less well informed than those of profit-motivated private firms. Evaluate this argument. Do you think that there are cases in which government should step in to conserve specific resources? If so, which policy tools should they use?

2. How could the principle of allocation of resource over time be applied to environmental resources such as the atmosphere and the oceans? Would the same kind of conclusions about optimal depletion apply or not?

EXERCISES

We can modify the interperiod allocation model to deal with the issue of intergenerational allocation of resources. Suppose a generation is thirty-five years, and we are concerned with only two generations. Demand and supply functions for oil in the present generation are given by:

$$Demand: Q_d = 200 - 5P \text{ or } P = 40 - 0.2Q_d$$
$$Supply: Q_s = 5P \text{ or } \qquad P = 0.2Q_s$$

(a) Draw a demand and supply graph showing the equilibrium price and quantity consumed in this generation in the absence of any consideration of the future. Now draw a graph showing the marginal net benefits from consumption in this period at all levels of consumption up to the equilibrium level. Express the net benefit (benefit minus cost) algebraically.

(b) Suppose that the net benefit function is expected to be the same for the next generation. But there is a discount rate (interest rate) of 4 percent per annum, which for thirty-five years works out to $(1.04)^{35}$, which is approximately equal to 4. Total oil supply for both generations is limited to 100 units. Calculate the efficient allocation of resources between the two generations and show this graphically. (Set marginal benefits equal for the two periods, remembering to include the discount rate.)

(c) What is marginal user cost for this efficient allocation? If you include this user cost in your original supply and demand graph, what is the new equilibrium? What is the scarcity rent? If the demand curve is the same in the second generation, what will the price and quantity consumed in that period be?

(d) How would the answers differ if we used a zero discount rate? What can you conclude from this example about the general problem of allocation of resources over long periods?

NOTES

1. See Hartwick, 1977; Solow, 1986.
2. See, for example, Howarth and Norgaard, 1995.

REFERENCES

Hartwick, J.M. 1977. "Intergenerational Equity and the Investing of Rents from Exhaustible Resources." *American Economic Review,* 66(1977): 972–974.

Hotelling, Harold. 1931. "The Economics of Exhaustible Resources." *Journal of Political Economy*, 39(2): 137–75.

Howarth, Richard B., and Richard B. Norgaard. 1995. "Intergenerational Choices under Global Environmental Change." In *Handbook of Environmental Economics*, ed. Daniel W. Bromley. Cambridge, MA; Oxford: Basil Blackwell.

Solow, R.M. 1986. "On the Intertemporal Allocation of Natural Resources." *Scandinavian Journal of Economics*, 88(1986): 141–149.

WEB SITES

1. **http://ideas.repec.org/a/aen/journl/1998v19–04-a06.html#abstract/.** A paper that examines the application of Hotelling's rule to exhaustible resource pricing and depletion.
2. **https://www.nber.org/jel/Q3.html.** National Bureau of Economic Research working papers that deal with nonrenewable resources and conservation.
3. **http://dieoff.org/page87.htm.** Robert Costanza, "Three General Policies to Achieve Sustainability," including discussion of a resource depletion tax.

CHAPTER 6

Valuing the Environment

6.1 TOTAL ECONOMIC VALUE

Almost everyone would agree that the environment has tremendous value to humanity, from the natural resources that provide the basic material inputs for our economy to the ecological services that provide us with clean air and water, arable soil, flood protection, and aesthetic enjoyment. Some of these values are expressed through market transactions. Using market data, economists can estimate the benefits consumers and producers obtain from marketed goods and services.

But many of the benefits we obtain from nature are not necessarily derived from market transactions. Coastal wetlands provide protection from storm surges during extreme weather events. Hikers obtain enjoyment and a sense of renewal from visiting a National Park. Others simply receive satisfaction from knowing that efforts are made to protect endangered species or conserve wilderness. Despite common perceptions, economists do recognize these values when analyzing various policy options. It is incorrect to assume that an economist will necessarily recommend, say, cutting down trees to obtain financial benefits over keeping the forest intact for the purposes of wildlife habitat and recreation.

The economist's notion of "value," however, is generally not based on broad ethical or philosophical grounds. In standard economic theory, nature has value *only* because humans ascribe some value to it. Thus according to this viewpoint, species do not have an inherent right to exist. Instead, their "worth" derives from any values placed on their existence by humans. Similarly, no one has an inherent right to clean air. Instead, the benefits of clean air should be weighed against the value of the market goods that can be produced along with the pollution.

Some theorists—primarily noneconomists—have challenged this view, suggesting instead a "rights-based" notion of value.[1] The idea that nonhuman species may have rights goes beyond the human-centered or **anthropocentric viewpoint** usually adopted by economists. A **biocentric viewpoint**, by contrast, suggests that the most fundamental source of value derives from ecosystem functioning and should not be limited by the human perceptions of value that form the basis for economic analysis. It may be impossible to reconcile theories of inherent rights and biocentric perspectives with monetary valuation, but it is certainly possible to go beyond market value to take into account environmental and social factors, and economists have devoted considerable effort to doing so.

How can we analyze tradeoffs between the market benefits of goods and services and the **nonmarket benefits** of ecological services and environmental amenities? Many economists believe that in order to make a valid comparison we need to first quantify all these benefits using a common metric. As you might guess, the standard metric normally used by economists is some monetary unit, such as dollars. Thus the central challenge for nonmarket valuation becomes expressing various benefits and costs in dollar terms.

First, let's consider the benefits that we receive from natural resources and the environment. Recall from Chapter 3 that marketed goods and services provide benefits to consumers as defined by the difference between their maximum willingness to pay and price, that is, consumer surplus. The same notion can be applied to nonmarket goods and services. The economic value that people obtain from a specific resource is defined as their maximum **willingness to pay (WTP)** for it. For many nonmarket goods there is not a direct "price" that must be paid to receive benefits. Clean air, for example, is something for which most people would be willing to pay. While they cannot necessarily express a valuation of clean air in markets, they can express their support in other ways, such as by voting or donations.

What if a specific policy would damage or destroy a certain environmental resource or decrease environmental quality? We can also ask how much people would be willing to accept in compensation for these changes. This is the **willingness to accept (WTA)** approach to environmental valuation. Both WTP and WTA are theoretically correct measures of economic value. They can be applied to any potential policy situation. We will consider various economic techniques used to estimate WTP or WTA shortly, but first we turn to the different types of economic value.

Economists have developed a classification scheme to describe the various types of values that we place on the environment. These values are classified as either **use values** or **nonuse values**.[a] Use values are tangible benefits that can be physically observed. They are further classified into direct use value and indirect use value. **Direct-use value** is obtained when we make a deliberate decision to use a natural resource. These values may derive from the financial benefits that we could obtain by extracting or harvesting a resource, such as the profits from drilling for oil. They may also derive from the well-being that we obtain by interacting with a natural environment, such as fishing or going for a hike or fishing.

Indirect-use values are tangible benefits obtained from nature without any effort on our part. Also referred to as **ecosystem services**, they include flood prevention, the mitigation of soil erosion, pollution assimilation, and pollination by bees. While

---

[a]Nonuse values are also called passive-use values.

these benefits may not be as apparent as direct use benefits, they are still real economic benefits and should be included in an economic analysis.

Nonuse values are derived from the intangible well-being benefits that we obtain from the environment. While these benefits are psychological in nature, they are nonetheless "economic" as long as people are willing to pay for them. Economists have defined three types of nonuse values. First, there is **option value**, or the amount that people are willing to pay to preserve a resource because they wish to use it in the future. One example is someone's willingness to pay to ensure the protection of the Arctic National Wildlife Refuge because he or she might visit it in the future. Another expression of option value would be the value placed on preservation of the Amazon rainforest because the cure for a disease might someday be dicovered using one of the species found there.

The second type of nonuse value is **bequest value**, or the value that one places on a resource because he or she wishes it to be available for future generations. For example, one might wish to have the Arctic National Wildlife Refuge preserved so that his or her children will be able to visit it. Thus while option value is derived from the benefits individuals may obtain in the future, bequest values are based upon one's concern for future generations.

Finally there is **existence value**, the benefit that an individual obtains from knowing that a natural resource exists, assuming that he or she will never physically use or visit the resource, separate from any bequest value. Again, as long as someone is willing to pay for the existence of a resource, it is a valid economic benefit. For example, consider the decrease in welfare that many people experience as a result of knowing that a pristine coastal environment has been damaged by an oil spill. From an economic perspective, these losses are just as valid as, and may even be larger than, the spill's impact on commercial fishing—even if the individuals involved never personally visit the affected area.

Figure 6.1 summarizes the different types of economic values, using a forest as an example. Note that direct use values can include extractive uses, such as harvesting timber and nontimber products, as well as nonextractive uses such as hiking or bird watching. Indirect use values for a forest include the protection trees provide through soil erosion and flood control and their ability to store carbon to limit climate change. Option values can include future recreation benefits as well as the possibility that forest products may provide a source for drugs to treat diseases.

It is important to note that the various types of economic values we have discussed are additive. Thus the **total economic value** of a resource is simply the sum of the different use and nonuse values. Some types of values may not be relevant for a particular resource. For example, a small local park may not have any measurable existence value. But the total economic value of a major National Park is likely to include every type of value presented in Figure 6.1.

We have already seen one example in which information regarding total economic value is needed—the internalization of externalities from Chapter 3. In order to set the "correct" price of a resource that generates externalities, we need to estimate these externalities in monetary terms. The valuation of externalities applies to a situation in which a particular good or service has market value to begin with, and we need to add or subtract the value of external costs or benefits. Externalities may involve changes to both use and nonuse values. For example, the negative externalities of oil drilling include the lost ecological services from habitat degradation as well as potential loss of existence values.

option value
the value that people place on the maintenance of future options for resource use.

bequest value
the value that people place on the knowledge that a resource will be available for future generations.

existence value
the value people place on a resource that they do not intend to ever use, such as the benefit that one obtains from knowing an area of rain forest is preserved even though he or she will never visit it.

total economic value
the value of a resource considering both use and nonuse values.

Figure 6.1 **Components of Total Economic Value**

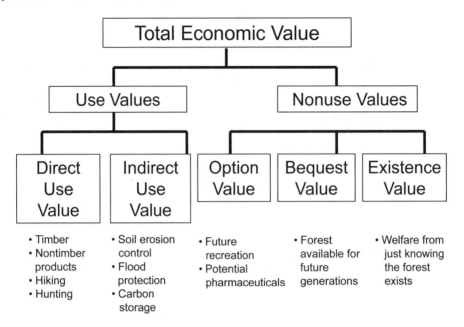

Another application of environmental valuation is the analysis of existing or proposed policies, which often involve assessing nonmarket values. Examples would include a proposal to establish a new National Park or a regulation that restricts use of a particular chemical. In such cases, we can use valuation techniques to develop a **cost-benefit analysis (CBA)** of the proposed policy. Before looking at methods for cost-benefit analysis in greater detail, we need to look more specifically at the techniques that economists use to measure economic values.

cost-benefit analysis (CBA)

a tool for policy analysis that attempts to monetize all the costs and benefits of a proposed action to determine the net benefit.

6.2 OVERVIEW OF VALUATION TECHNIQUES

We can classify environmental valuation techniques into five basic categories:[2][b]

1. Market Valuation
2. Cost of Illness Method
3. Replacement Cost Methods
4. Revealed Preference Methods
5. Stated Preference Methods

We have already discussed how markets can be used to determine economic values directly in Chapter 3. Many environmental goods, such as forests, fish stocks, minerals, and groundwater, can be sold in existing markets. By estimating consumer and producer surplus, economists can calculate the social benefits of these resources as market commodities—a type of direct use value. In the case of

---

[b]These valuation techniques are classified differently by some environmental economists. In particular, Market Valuation may be classified together with Revealed Preference Methods and in some cases with Replacement Cost Methods as well. We keep the categories disaggregated to emphasize the differences among the techniques.

cost of illness method
an approach for valuing the negative impacts of pollution by estimating the cost of treating illnesses caused by the pollutant.

human capital
the knowledge, skills, and abilities of the labor force, reflecting investments in education and training.

replacement cost methods
an approach to measuring environmental damages that estimates the costs necessary to restore or replace the resource, such as applying fertilizer to restore soil fertility.

habitat equivalency analysis (HEA)
a method used to compensate for the damages from a natural resource injury with an equivalent amount of habitat restoration.

revealed preference methods
methods of economic valuation based on market behaviors, including travel cost models, hedonic pricing, and the defensive expenditures approach.

producer surplus, the benefits are direct financial gains to the producers. In the case of consumer surplus, the benefits represent increases in welfare.

Environment impacts often include damages to human health. The **cost of illness method** monetizes the direct and indirect costs associated with illnesses attributed to environmental factors. The direct costs include medical costs, such as office visits and medication, paid by individuals and insurers, and lost wages due to illness. Indirect costs can include decreases in **human capital** (such as when a child misses a significant number of school days due to illness), welfare losses from pain and suffering, and decreases in economic productivity due to work absences.

If society is paying these costs as a result of an environmentally attributed illness, then it follows that the cost of illness method provides us with a lower-bound estimate of the willingness to pay to avoid these illnesses. The true WTP could be greater, since the market-based costs may not capture the full losses to individuals from illness, but even the lower-bound estimate could provide policy guidance. For example, the cost of asthma in the United States in 2007 was estimated at $56 billion, based on direct medical costs and productivity losses from missed days of school and work.[3] The cost for a typical worker amounted to about $3,500. These estimates provide a starting point for determining whether efforts to reduce asthma cases are economically efficient.

Replacement cost methods can be used to estimate the indirect use value of ecosystem services. These approaches consider the costs of actions that provide human-made substitutes for lost ecosystem services. For example, a community could construct a water treatment plant to make up for the lost water purification benefits from a forest habitat. The natural pollination of plants by bees could, to some extent, be done by hand or machine. If we can estimate the costs of these substitute actions, in terms of construction and labor costs, these can be considered an approximation of society's WTP for these ecosystem services.

One important point, however, is that potential replacement costs are not measures of WTA or WTP. Suppose that a community could construct a water treatment plant for $50 million to offset a hypothetical loss of forest land. This estimate does not tell us whether the community would actually be willing to pay the $50 million should the forest loss occur. Actual WTP could be greater or less than $50 million and is fundamentally unrelated to the cost of the water purification plant. So in this sense, replacement costs should be used with caution. However, if we know that the community would be willing to pay the $50 million cost for the plant, then we could conclude that $50 million represents a lower bound of the value of the water purification benefits of the forest.

One replacement cost method that has been used often in recent years is **habitat equivalency analysis (HEA)**. HEA is commonly applied to estimate the economic damages of accidental releases of hazardous chemicals, such as oil spills.[4] An oil spill reduces the ecological functioning of natural habitats until they eventually recover to baseline conditions. Under existing U.S. legislation, the responsible parties must provide compensation in terms of funding for ecological restoration. Thus the objective of HEA is to determine the appropriate amount of ecological restoration to offset the ecological losses from the spill. (See Box 6.1 on the *Deepwater Horizon* oil spill of 2010).

The two remaining valuation methods—revealed preference and stated preference—are the most studied techniques regarding environmental valuation. **Revealed preference methods** indirectly infer the values that people place on environmental goods or services based on market decisions. For example, as we see in more detail

BOX 6.1 ESTIMATING ECOLOGICAL DAMAGES FROM THE 2010 GULF OIL SPILL

The explosion of BP's *Deepwater Horizon* oil rig in the Gulf of Mexico in April 2010 produced the largest marine oil spill in history, with an estimated release of 4.9 million barrels. For comparison, the *Exxon Valdez* spill in Alaska in 1989 was between 0.3 million and 0.8 million barrels. The spill despoiled about 600 miles of coastline and killed at least 7,000 animals, mostly seabirds.

The *Deepwater Horizon* spill caused financial losses to the commercial fishing and tourism industries, and cost BP more than $14 billion in cleanup and containment costs and $8 billion in payments to individuals and businesses who suffered losses as a result of the spill. In addition, a preliminary settlement of a further $7.8 billion for individuals and businesses was announced (*New York Times,* April 18, 2012), and in January 2013 BP agreed to plead guilty to manslaughter and other charges and pay a record $4 billion in criminal penalties (*Associated Press,* January 29, 2013). But what of the ecological damage caused by the spill?

Under the Oil Pollution Act of 1990, those determined to be responsible for oil spills must compensate society for ecological damage by providing an equivalent amount of ecological restoration. In particular, the compensation must equal the lost ecological services that accrue during the period between the spill and recovery to baseline conditions. The normal unit of measurement is "acre-years" of habitat loss. So, for example, the loss of 10 acres of wetland habitat for 5 years would be 50 lost acre-years of wetland ecological services. Through the technique of habitat equivalency analysis, this damage could be offset, in principle, by providing 50 acre-years of wetland restoration.

The restoration should ideally take place in a habitat similar to the one affected by the spill and relatively close to the affected site. Various factors to consider in habitat equivalency analyses include the productivity of restored ecosystems relative to natural habitats, the possibility that restoration projects will fail, and the lifespan of restored habitats. Making adjustments for these factors, the affected states and the federal government choose one or more ecological restoration projects that provide the appropriate compensation for the ecological losses from a spill. The responsible parties are then required to fund these projects.

A preliminary analysis of the damage from the *Deepwater Horizon* spill suggests that lost ecological services, including coastal habitat degradation and wildlife deaths, may comprise 58–70 percent of the damages from the spill. Commercial fishing losses were estimated at 5–22 percent of the damage. Fines for ecological damage under the Clean Water Act could range from $5.4 billion to $21 billion, but estimates for loss of ecosystem function could run even higher (Roach et al., 2010). BP has set aside $37.2 billion for spill costs, but this may not be sufficient to cover the full ecological damage.

Sources: J. Schwartz, "Papers Detail BP Settlement in Gulf Oil Spill," *New York Times,* April 18 2012; M. Kunzelman, "Judge OKs $4B BP oil spill criminal settlement," *Associated Press,* January 29, 2013; Roach et al., 2010.

below, the value that people place on clean drinking water can be inferred from the amount that they spend on bottled water.

stated preference methods

economic valuation methods based on survey responses to hypothetical scenarios, including contingent valuation and contingent ranking.

With **stated preference methods** we use surveys to ask people their preferences for hypothetical scenarios regarding environmental quality or natural resource levels. The main advantage of stated preference methods is that we can survey people about any type of value shown in Figure 6.1. Thus an estimate of total economic value can theoretically be obtained. With revealed preference methods, we typically can only estimate one particular type of value. The main disadvantage of stated preference methods is that there are concerns about the validity of the estimates. We consider these issues below, but first we summarize the different types of revealed preference approaches.

6.3 REVEALED PREFERENCE METHODS

Market decisions are based on many considerations, including environmental quality. Thus even if an environmental good or service is not directly traded in a market, it may be a relevant factor for decisions made in related markets. Economists have come up with various techniques to extract meaningful valuation information from existing markets. We now take a look at the three most common revealed preference methods.

Travel Cost Method

travel cost method (TCM)
the use of statistical analysis to determine people's willingness to pay to visit a natural resource such as a national park or river; a demand curve for the resource is obtained by analyzing the relationship between visitation choices and travel costs.

The **travel cost method (TCM)** can be used to estimate the use value of natural recreation sites, such as National Parks, beaches, and wilderness areas. Visitors to recreation sites typically must pay various trip costs such as gas and other vehicle costs (if they drive), other transportation costs such as air fares and public transportation, entrance fees, lodging, food, and so on. Assuming that visitors are behaving rationally, we can conclude that their actual visitation expenditures represent a lower bound to their maximum willingness to pay to visit the site. For example, if an individual spends $300 for a week-long camping visit to a National Park, then her maximum willingness to pay must be at least $300.

While potentially useful, data on actual expenditures do not capture consumer surplus—the true measure of net economic benefits. In order to estimate consumer surplus, we need an estimate of how the quantity demanded varies with price. Note that the cost to travel to a park varies for different visitors primarily based on their distance from it. Those who live nearby face relatively low travel costs, while those who travel from far away must pay higher travel costs to visit the site. This effectively provides us with variation in the "price" that different visitors must pay in order to visit a particular site. We can use this variation to estimate a full demand curve and thus obtain an estimate of consumer surplus (for more on techniques used to estimate TCMs, see Appendix 6.1).

Numerous TCMs have estimated the recreational benefits of natural sites. For example, a study of recreational visitors to the Murray River in Australia found that the average visitor received a consumer surplus of US$155 per day.[5] Another study found that the annual aggregate consumer surplus for a recreation beach on Galveston Island, Texas, was about $128,000.[6] TCMs have been used to explore how changes in the fish catch rate affect the consumer surplus of anglers visiting sites in Wisconsin[7] and how a drought affects the benefits of visitors to reservoirs in California.[8]

Given that TCMs are based on actual market decisions about recreation choices, the estimates are considered relatively valid. Perhaps the main limitation of TCMs is that they can only estimate recreational use values. A TCM cannot provide the total economic value for a natural area because it cannot estimate indirect use or nonuse benefits.

meta-analysis
an analysis method based on a quantitative review of existing research to identify explanatory variables for differences in results.

Also, like any statistical model, the results of a TCM can vary considerably based on the model's structure and assumptions. For example, how a researcher values travel time can influence the resulting consumer surplus estimates. In a **meta-analysis** of twenty-five different TCMs that estimated forest recreation benefits in Europe, consumer surplus ranged from less than $1 to over $100 per trip.[9][c] This

---

[c] A meta-analysis analyzes the results from numerous existing studies of a particular topic to determine common patterns. For example, a meta-analysis of travel cost models includes the consumer surplus estimates from numerous studies as the dependent variable. Potential independent variables may include characteristics of the recreation sites, how travel time was valued, and the modeling techniques employed by the researchers.

demonstrates that the results from one study are rarely directly transferable to a different situation—an issue we discuss further later in the chapter.

Hedonic Pricing

The second revealed preference method is based on the idea that environmental quality can affect the market prices of certain goods and services. **Hedonic pricing** attempts to relate the price of a marketed good to its underlying characteristics. The most common environmental application of hedonic pricing is to residential housing prices.

The price of a house is determined by characteristics of the property and community, such as the number of bedrooms, square footage, quality of the school system, and proximity to public transportation. Housing prices may also be affected by environmental quality or natural resource variables, including air quality, visibility, noise pollution, and proximity to a natural area. Using statistical methods, a researcher can attempt to isolate the relationship between housing prices and these environmental variables. The results indicate how much buyers are willing to pay for improved environmental quality.

A hedonic pricing model is typically based on analysis of a large number of home sales. Public data are available on sale prices and some property characteristics. The researcher supplements this with information on the environmental variable(s) of interest. The statistical model then determines whether there is a significant relationship between the environmental quality variable and the selling price.

The results from hedonic models have been mixed.[10] In some hedonic models studying the effects of local air quality on real estate prices, no statistically significant relationship was found. But other studies conclude that real estate prices are positively correlated with better air quality. A study based on data from 242 metropolitan areas in the United States found that the marginal willingness to pay for a 1 $\mu g/m^3$ reduction in particulate matter concentration was \$148–\$185.[11]

Other research has found that homes located near hazardous waste sites or sources of noise such as airports and highways are associated with lower prices, ceteris paribus. A 2010 meta-analysis found that high-volume landfills (500 tons per day or more) decrease property values by an average of 14 percent while low-volume landfills decrease property values by only 3 percent.[12]

The Defensive Expenditures Approach

In some cases, individuals may be able to reduce or eliminate their exposure to environmental harms by buying certain consumer goods or taking other actions. For example, households with concerns about their drinking water quality may purchase bottled water, install a home water purification system, or obtain their drinking water from another source. Exposure to air pollutants can be reduced by purchasing home air purifiers. If we observe individuals spending money or time for environmental quality improvements, then we can use this information to infer the WTP for quality changes.

The **defensive expenditures approach** collects data on actual expenditures to obtain a lower-bound WTP for environmental quality changes.[d] The most common

---

[d]The defensive expenditures approach is also called the averting expenditures or averting behavior approach.

application of the defensive expenditures approach is to drinking water quality. The premise is that if a household is observed paying, say, $20 per month for bottled water in response to concerns about the quality of their tap water, then their WTP for an improvement in drinking water quality is at least $20 per month.

For example, one study surveyed households in Pennsylvania to identify the actions that they were taking in response to a municipal water contamination incident.[13] Defensive expenditures in the community during the incident ranged from about $60,000 to $130,000, depending on how time was valued. As a lower-bound estimate of the WTP to avoid similar contamination incidents, the results can indicate whether investments to safeguard municipal water supplies are economically efficient.

An analysis in Brazil found that households were paying US$16–$19 per month on defensive expenditures to improve drinking water quality.[14] In this study, 79 percent of households were taking some measures to improve the quality of the water that they drink. Given concerns about drinking water quality in developing countries, the defensive expenditures approach provides a means for estimating the benefits of better access to safe drinking water.

One limitation of the defensive expenditures approach is that it only provides a lower-bound estimate to WTP. A household may be willing to spend much more than it actually is to improve the quality of its drinking water, but this approach does not allow us to estimate its maximum WTP. Another potential problem with the defensive expenditures approach is that individuals who take actions to reduce their exposure to environmental harms may also be taking such actions for other reasons.[e] For example, someone who buys bottled water for a perceived improvement in water quality may also be motivated by its convenience or taste. In this case, only a portion of one's defensive expenditures should be attributed to a desire for better water quality, meaning that defensive expenditures could overestimate the true WTP for better water quality. To reduce this problem, a researcher would need to identify expenditures made solely to reduce environmental exposure.

6.4 STATED PREFERENCE METHODS

While revealed preference methods have the advantage of being based on actual market decisions, these methods are applicable only in certain situations (e.g., hedonic models mainly estimate environmental benefits that affect housing prices) and only to obtain use benefits. Revealed preference methods cannot be used to obtain estimates of nonuse benefits, so they normally do not reveal the total economic value of a natural resource. Stated preference methods, in contrast, can be applied to any situation to determine the WTA or WTP for a hypothetical scenario. Using a survey, we can ask respondents about the total economic value that they place on a resource, including use and nonuse benefits.

contingent valuation (CV)
an economic tool that uses surveys to question people regarding their willingness to pay for a good or , such as the preservation of hiking opportunities or air quality.

The most common stated preference method is **contingent valuation (CV)**.[15] The name indicates that a respondent's valuation is contingent on that person's reaction to a hypothetical scenario presented in a survey format. CV questions can be phrased in terms of either WTA, for a scenario that decreases utility, or WTP, for a scenario that increases utility. So a researcher could ask respondents what minimum

---

[e]This issue is called the "jointness in production" problem.

amount they would accept as compensation for a 10 percent decrease in air quality or what maximum amount they would pay for a 10 percent increase in air quality. In theory, for a marginal (i.e., small) change in environmental quality WTA and WTP should be rather similar. However, in practice WTA tends to be much larger than WTP—by an average of seven times according to one meta-analysis.[16]

You can imagine that a WTA question asking people how much money they would need for compensation creates an incentive for them to overstate that value. This divergence is one reason that some critics question the validity of contingent valuation estimates. However, the divergence may illustrate the **endowment effect**, in which people evaluate gains and losses differently. After someone already possesses something, such as a physical good or a certain level of air quality, their utility, or level of satisfaction decreases significantly if it is taken away from them, because the person believes that s/he has established a right to it. Thus a loss from a baseline situation is viewed in a fundamentally different light than a gain from baseline.

In addition to deciding whether a CV question will be phrased in terms of WTP or WTA, other considerations in designing a CV survey include different ways of asking CV questions and whether the survey should be conducted by mail, over the phone or Internet, or in person. More details on CV survey design are discussed in Appendix 6.1. Hundreds of contingent valuation studies have been conducted over the past several decades.[f] Table 6.1 provides a sampling of some of the results of CV analyses. We can see that CV has been applied to various environmental issues all over the world. See Box 6.2 for a discussion of one of these studies.

Despite such voluminous research, fundamental concerns about the validity of CV questions remain. A classic article whose title begins with "Ask a Silly Question . . ." concludes that "CV measurements of nonuse values are so speculative that the costs of using CV to assess damages to natural resources almost always outweigh the benefits."[17] Other researchers "conclude that many of the alleged problems with CV can be resolved by careful study design and implementation."[18] While the debate about CV's validity was initially limited to academic discussion, the 1989 *Exxon Valdez* oil spill in Alaska brought the CV debate under wider scrutiny.[19]

While some of the damages from the *Exxon Valdez* oil spill were lost use values, such as lost commercial fishing profits and recreation benefits, the federal government and the state of Alaska argued that Exxon should also compensate the public for lost nonuse values. Thus a large-scale CV survey was funded to determine the nonuse damages of the spill to the country.[20] The results estimated the total lost nonuse values at around $3 billion, significantly more than the claimed lost use value. Thus the validity of CV results suddenly became central to the damage claim being made by the government against Exxon.

To explore the validity of CV questions, the National Oceanic and Atmospheric Administration (NOAA) assembled a panel of prestigious economists, including two Nobel Prize winners, to report on the validity of the technique. After reviewing the CV literature and hearing testimony from many economists, the NOAA panel concluded that:

endowment effect

the concept that people tend to place high value on something after they already possess it, relative to its value before they possess it.

---

[f]A search for the term "contingent valuation" in the title of journal articles in scholarly journals results in nearly 700 matches, using the search engine EconLit.

Table 6.1

Sample of Recent Environmental Contingent Valuation Results

Good or Service Valued	WTP Estimate(s), U.S. Dollars
Reduced highway noise and air pollution in Spain[1]	$22/year
Increased biodiversity in Hungary[2]	$23–$69/year
Increased supplies of renewable energy in the United States[3]	$10–$27/month
Urban greening in China[4]	$20–$29/year
Increased forest reserves in Norway[5]	$261–$303 (one-time payment)
Clean drinking water supplies in Pakistan[6]	$7–$9/month
Grassland conservation in Italy[7]	$11–$19/year
Marine biodiversity in the Azores islands[8]	$121–$837 (one-time payment)
River recreation in Australia[9]	$113/day

Sources:
  1. Lera-Lopez et al., 2012; 2. Szabó, 2011; 3. Mozumder et al., 2011; 4. Chen and Jim, 2011; 5. Lindhjem and Navrud, 2011; 6. Akram and Olmstead, 2011; 7. Marzetti et al., 2011; 8. Ressurreicao et al., 2011; 9. Rolfe and Dyack, 2010.
  Note: WTP = willingness to pay.

BOX 6.2   WILLINGNESS TO PAY FOR RENEWABLE ENERGY

At least sixty-six countries and twenty-nine U.S. states have set targets for the percentage of energy that they obtain from renewable sources. For example, Germany has set an ambitious goal of obtaining 100 percent of its electricity from renewable sources by 2050. To determine the effects of such targets on social welfare, it is necessary to identify how electricity consumers value renewable energy.

A 2011 paper used contingent valuation to determine New Mexico residents' willingness to pay for an increasing share of renewable energy in their electricity supplies. An Internet-based survey was conducted, and 367 responses were obtained (a response rate of 27 percent). Respondents were first asked an open-ended question about their willingness to pay to have 10 percent of New Mexico's energy generated from renewable sources, as an additional charge above their current electricity bill. A subsequent question asked them their additional willingness to pay for a 20 percent share from renewable sources.

The results of the survey showed that the average household was willing to pay about $10 more per month to have 10 percent of the state's energy generated from renewable sources, which represented a 14 percent increase in the typical monthly bill. The average willingness to pay for a 20 percent share was about $26/month—a 36 percent increase in their bill.

While the results of the survey indicate a significant willingness to pay for renewable energy, the results are not necessarily representative of New Mexico residents, particularly since the survey was conducted over the Internet. The average respondent was only twenty-five years old and, with fifteen years of schooling, was more educated than normal. So clearly, extrapolation of the results to the entire state may not be a valid use of the results. Still, the authors "hope that results from this study will offer useful insights to energy regulators, utility companies and other related agencies that can design effective mechanisms and charge appropriate premiums to support a larger share of renewable energy in the energy" (p. 1125).

Source: Mozumder et al., 2011.

CV studies can produce estimates reliable enough to be the starting point of a judicial process of damage assessment, including lost passive-use values. To be acceptable for this purpose, such studies should follow the guidelines described in [the NOAA panel report]. The phrase "be the starting point" is meant to emphasize that the Panel does not suggest that CV estimates can be taken as automatically defining the range of compensable damages within narrow limits. [CV studies contain] information that judges and juries will wish to use, in combination with other evidence, including the testimony of expert witnesses.[21]

While the NOAA panel concluded that CV studies may produce valid estimates of nonuse values, it also provided a long list of recommendations in order for a CV survey to be considered acceptable, including:

- In-person surveys are preferred because they best maintain a respondent's concentration and allow for the use of graphics.
- WTP questions are preferred over WTA questions.
- The WTP question should be phrased using a "Yes/No" format with a specific price. For example, a question might ask whether the respondent is willing to pay $20 per year to preserve endangered species. The Yes/No format with a single price aligns with actual consumer decisions about whether to buy something. Rarely must consumers actually think about their maximum WTP.
- The sensitivity of WTP to the scope of the damage should be explored. One CV study used separate survey versions to elicit respondent's WTP to protect 2,000, 20,000, or 200,000 migratory birds from oil spills.[22] The WTP amounts were insensitive to the number of birds protected, leading the authors to conclude that CV results are not valid.
- Follow-up questions should be included to determine whether respondents understood the hypothetical scenario and why they answered the valuation question as they did.
- The respondents should be reminded of their income constraints and that funds used for the scenario under study cannot be used for other purposes.

The NOAA panel recognized the "likely tendency to exaggerate willingness to pay" in CV surveys and thus its recommendations tend to produce conservative WTP estimates "as a partial or totally offset" to this bias. In practice, very few CV surveys follow all the recommendations of the NOAA panel. Even if all the recommendations are followed, the survey's validity checks may lead the researchers to conclude that the results are not valid.

Ultimately, the debate over whether CV can provide valid estimates of nonuse values may never be settled because no real-world markets exist to test its validity explicitly. But as one article phrased it, isn't some number better than no number?[23] Nonuse values are part of total economic value and theoretically should be included in any economic analysis. And in the case of the *Exxon Valdez* oil spill, these nonuse values may exceed values that are more observable.

While estimating lost nonuse values may be necessary in legal cases, some economists believe that CV should not be used to guide environmental policies because of the methodological concerns stated above or for ethical reasons. One ethical issue is that a person's WTP in a CV survey may be a function of his ability to pay. Thus CV results, like markets in general, tend to be more responsive to the preferences of wealthier participants. Instead of "one person, one vote" CV results embody a "one dollar, one vote" principle.

Another ethical critique states that putting a price on the environment fails to address issues of rights and responsibilities.

> In essence, the economists' position is that everything has a price and that the price can be discovered by careful questioning. But for most people, some matters of rights and principles are beyond economic calculation. Setting the boundaries of the market helps to define who we are, how we want to live, and what we believe in.[24]

contingent ranking (CR)
a survey method in which respondents are asked to rank a list of alternatives.

Some of the problems with contingent valuation can be avoided by using the technique of **contingent ranking (CR)** instead. CR is also a stated preference method, but the respondents are not asked directly about their WTP. Instead, they are presented with various scenarios and asked to rank them according to their preferences.[g]

For example, in a UK study, respondents were asked to rank four scenarios regarding the water quality of an urban river: the current water quality, a small improvement, a medium improvement, and a large improvement.[25] Maintaining the current water quality necessitated no tax increase, but each improvement in water quality required progressively higher tax increases. Through statistical analysis, the researchers were able to estimate the average WTP for each of the three improved water quality scenarios.

protest bids
responses to contingent valuation questions based on the respondent's opposition to the question or the payment vehicle, rather than the underlying valuation of the resource.

strategic bias/strategic behavior
the tendency for people to state their preferences or values inaccurately in order to influence policy decisions.

Respondents may be more comfortable with the CR format since they do not have to value a scenario explicitly. Another advantage of CR over CV is that biases such as **protest bids** and **strategic behavior,** which occur when people exaggerate their responses to promote their point of view, may be reduced (see Appendix 6.1 for a discussion of these potential problems with CV). However, CR questions can become quite difficult when each scenario consists of several different attributes or when the number of scenarios becomes large. As with CV, the validity of CR estimates for nonuse values is difficult to establish. While economists continue to conduct research on stated preference methods, making improvements in survey design and statistical analysis, it remains unclear whether a consensus will ever be reached regarding the validity of these techniques.

6.5 Cost-Benefit Analysis

One common definition of economics is that it is about the allocation of scarce resources. Like individuals and businesses, governments often have to make decisions about the allocation of limited resources. Budgetary constraints prevent us from pursuing all proposed public projects. How should governments decide which projects should be undertaken and which ones should be passed over? For example, should public funds be allocated to build more roads, provide health care, or improve environmental quality? Further, how should governments decide which policy proposals to enact?

The valuation techniques discussed above allow for a decision-making framework in which all impacts can theoretically be assessed and compared using a common metric—a monetary measure, such as dollars. Cost-benefit analysis (CBA) seeks to measure all the costs and all the benefits of a proposed project or policy in monetary units.[h] In principle, using a common metric makes it easier to assess tradeoffs objectively.

---

[g]A similar methodology is contingent choice, in which respondents are asked to pick one scenario from a list as their preferred option.

[h]The term "benefit-cost analysis" (BCA) is also used. The two are synonymous.

For example, consider a federal government decision about the appropriate level of mercury emissions from power plants. Suppose that, compared to baseline conditions, a stricter standard would cost the country an additional $10 billion per year but prevent an estimated 10,000 premature deaths. Is the cost of the stricter standard worth it? In other words, is the benefit of 10,000 avoided deaths worth the cost of $10 billion per year? (See Box 6.3. for an answer to this real-world question.) CBA provides one tool for helping us make such decisions. In fact, under existing U.S. law, federal agencies, including the Environmental Protection Agency, are required to conduct CBA for major policy proposals.

The basic steps of a CBA are rather straightforward:

1. List all the costs and benefits one can think of in relation to a proposed action.
2. For costs and benefits ordinarily measured in monetary units, obtain reliable estimates.
3. For costs and benefits not ordinarily measured in monetary units, such as human health or ecosystem impacts, use nonmarket valuation techniques to obtain estimates.
4. If actual nonmarket values cannot be estimated due to budgetary or other constraints, consider transferred values or expert opinions.
5. Add up all the costs and all the benefits, preferably under a range of plausible assumptions or scenarios.
6. Compare total costs to total benefits to obtain a recommendation.

CBAs normally consider various alternatives, including a baseline or "no action" option. For example, the current mercury air pollution standard might be compared to several stricter standards.

Of course, in practice CBA can be a technically difficult undertaking. In particular, estimating all nonmarket impacts in monetary units may not be feasible or even desirable. Thus most CBAs are incomplete to some extent. This does not necessarily mean that it is not possible to obtain definite policy recommendations, as we will see below.

Suppose for now that we are able to estimate all the costs and benefits of a policy proposal in monetary units. Let's say that the benefits of the mercury standard mentioned above are $12 billion per year and the costs are $10 billion per year. The bottom-line result of a CBA can be presented in two main ways:

1. Net benefits: This is total benefits minus total costs. In this example, net benefits are $12 billion minus $10 billion or $2 billion. Note that if costs were greater than benefits, net benefits would be negative.
2. Benefit/cost ratio: This is total benefits divided by total costs. In this case, the benefit/cost ratio would be $12 billion divided by $10 billion, or 1.2. A ratio of less than 1 indicates costs greater than benefits.

If a proposal yields positive net benefits (or a benefit/cost ratio greater than 1), does this mean we should proceed with it? Not necessarily. Recall that economics is about trying to maximize net benefits. So while the mercury standard yields positive net benefits, there may well be an alternative proposal that could generate more than $12 billion in annual benefits for the same cost. We should make sure that we have considered a range of options before proceeding with a particular recommendation.

It is also important to note that a bottom-line estimate of net benefits does not tell us anything about the distribution of costs and benefits across society. Suppose that the benefits of a proposal accrue primarily to wealthy households while the costs fall on poorer households. Even though such a proposal might yield positive net benefits, we could reject it on equity grounds. Thus one should be careful about relying solely on CBA to make policy decisions, as we discuss further at the end of the chapter. But first let's consider several important topics in conducting a CBA.

Balancing Present and Future: The Discount Rate

real or **inflation-adjusted dollars**
monetary estimates that account for changes in price levels (i.e., inflation) over time.

In most CBAs, some of the costs and benefits occur in the future. We know that a cost of $100 now is not equivalent to a cost of $100 in ten or twenty years due to inflation. We can control for inflation by presenting all result in **real**, or **inflation-adjusted, dollars**.[i]

Even if all costs and benefits are expressed in real terms, we may still prefer a benefit now rather than later. Money available now can usually be invested to get a positive real (inflation-adjusted) return. That means that $100 today will grow into, say, $200 ten years from now. In this sense, $100 today is equivalent to $200 ten years from now. Another reason for preferring money now may be uncertainty about the future—if we get the benefit now we don't have to worry about whether we will actually get it in the future. Then there is simple impatience—the natural human tendency to focus on the present more than the future.[j] So beyond adjust-

---

[i]Dollar values are adjusted for inflation by the use of a price index that represents the general price level compared to a base year (a well-known example is the Consumer Price Index [CPI]). For example, if the price index is 120, compared to 100 in the baseline year, a current dollar value of $240 would be equivalent to an inflation-adjusted value of $240/(120/100) = $200.

[j]Numerous examples of this tendency exist, such as people running up large credit card bills or failing to save adequately for retirement.

discounting

the concept that costs and benefits that occur in the future should be assigned less weight (discounted) relative to current costs and benefits.

discount rate

the annual rate at which future benefits or costs are discounted relative to current benefits or costs.

present value

the current value of a steam of future costs or benefits; a discount rate is used to convert future costs or benefits to present values.

ing for inflation, most economists believe that a further adjustment is necessary to compare present and future impacts. This adjustment is known as **discounting**.

Discounting essentially "devalues" any impacts that occur in the future as less relevant than a similar impact that occurs now. Thus a $100 benefit in 10 years is not as valuable as a $100 benefit now, even if both are expressed in real terms. In other words, the $100 benefit in 10 years would be worth less than $100 now. We would use the following formula to calculate the present, or discounted, value of a future benefit or cost:

$$PV(X_n) = X_n / (1 + r)^n$$

where n is the number of years in the future the benefit or cost occurs and r represents the **discount rate**—the annual rate by which future values are reduced, expressed as a proportion (i.e., $r = 0.03$ for a 3 percent discount rate). Using this formula, at a 3 percent discount rate, a benefit (or cost) of $100 in 10 years is equivalent to getting a $74.41 benefit now. At a higher discount rate of 7 percent, a benefit (or cost) of $100 in ten years is worth only $50.83 today.

As you can see by the formula, the **present value** is lower the further out in time we go (since a higher exponent makes the denominator larger) or the higher the discount rate (which also makes the denominator larger). Table 6.2 and Figure 6.2 illustrate how the present value of $100 varies depending on the discount rate and the time period. The range of discount rates shown, from 1 percent to 10 percent, is typical of the ones used in economic analyses.

Note that the higher discount rates dramatically reduce the relevance of impacts that occur just a few decades in the future. For example, a $100 cost that occurs fifty years in the future has a present value of only $3.39 at a 7 percent discount rate and just $0.85 at a 10 percent rate. Also, small changes in the discount rate can have a dramatic effect over longer horizons. While the difference between a 1 percent and 3 percent discount rate is not that large 10 years into the future, after a hundred years the present value is about seven times greater with the 1 percent discount rate.

We see in Table 6.2 that even moderate discount rates essentially render irrelevant any impacts that occur several decades or more in the future. For example, with a 5 percent discount rate it would not be worth spending even $1 now to avoid a damage of $100 that occurs a hundred years in the future.

Clearly, the choice of a discount rate is an important decision in any CBA. A high discount rate will highly favor the present over the future, while a low discount rate will give more weight to future costs or benefits. In many environmental applications, the benefits occur in the future while the costs are paid in the short term. Climate change is perhaps the best example of this. The costs of mitigating climate change would occur in the near term while the benefits (i.e., reduced damages) would occur decades and even centuries in the future (as discussed in detail in Chapter 18). Thus a low discount rate will generally support a higher degree of environmental protection.

So what is the "correct" discount rate? There is no clear consensus in the economics profession that one discount rate should be used in all circumstances. One approach to determining the discount rate is to set it equal to the rate of return on low-risk investments such as government bonds. The rationale behind this is that funds used for a beneficial public project could otherwise be invested to provide

Table 6.2

Present Value of a $100 Impact, by Discount Rate

Years	Discount Rate				
	1%	3%	5%	7%	10%
0	$100.00	$100.00	$100.00	$100.00	$100.00
10	$90.53	$74.41	$61.39	$50.83	$38.55
20	$81.95	$55.37	$37.69	$25.84	$14.86
30	$74.19	$41.20	$23.14	$13.14	$5.73
50	$60.80	$22.81	$8.72	$3.39	$0.85
100	$36.97	$5.20	$0.76	$0.12	$0.01

Figure 6.2 **Present Value of a $100 Impact, by Discount Rate**

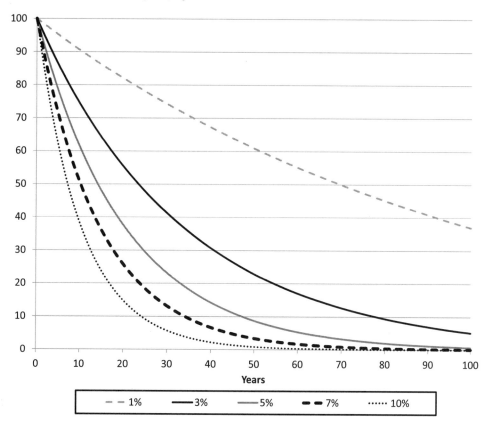

society with greater resources in the future. In other words, the market rate of return represents the opportunity cost of spending it now.

By using investment rates as the discount rate in a CBA, we are evaluating the proposal relative to the opportunity cost of other investments that could be made instead. In 2012 the rates of return on medium- to long-term government bonds were 1.6–3.8 percent in nominal terms and 0.0–2.0 percent in real terms.[26]

Of course, the rates of return on government bonds vary over time. Returns were unusually low in 2012, but in the early 1980s these rates reached 13 percent in nominal terms. This leads some economists to wonder whether we should base the valuation of long-term effects upon an interest rate that is subject to the whims of financial market conditions.

A different approach to determining the discount rate reasons that there are two justifications for discounting:

pure rate of time preference

the rate of preference for obtaining benefits now as opposed to the future, independent of income level changes.

1. The natural human tendency to prefer the present over the future. This is known as the **pure rate of time preference**.
2. Assuming that real economic growth continues, people in the future will be richer than people now. So $100 in damages (in real terms) to them is "less damaging" than a $100 damage now because it will represent a smaller share of their wealth and thus have a smaller effect on their welfare. Similarly, $100 in benefits will be less valuable to people in the future than $100 to people today, just as $100 is less important to a rich person than to a poor person. In more technical terms, utility is assumed to be a diminishing marginal function of consumption.

social discount rate/ social rate of time preference (SRTP)

a discount rate that attempts to reflect the appropriate social valuation of the future; the SRTP tends to be less than market or individual discount rates.

These two factors can be combined to estimate the **social discount rate**, or **social rate of time preference (SRTP)**, as:

$$SRTP = \rho + (\varepsilon * c)$$

where ρ is the pure rate of time preference, c is the growth rate of consumption, and ε is the elasticity of the marginal utility of consumption. Multiplying the growth rate of consumption by the rate at which the extra satisfaction from increased consumption declines as consumption increases (in economic terms, the elasticity of the marginal utility of consumption) tells us how much better off a society is as it gets richer.

Estimates of the historical growth rate of consumption can be obtained from government data sources. In projecting real consumption growth rates into the future, the Stern Review (a famous cost-benefit analysis of global climate change that we discuss in Chapter 18) uses a value of $c = 1.3$ percent.[27] Estimates of the value of ε are about 1.0–2.0, with one recent analysis finding a value of 1.4.[28]

A vigorous debate among economists has focused on the value of ρ. The Stern Review used a value of $\rho = 0.1$. The justification for setting the pure rate of time preference to near zero is that one generation's welfare is not inherently more important than another generation's welfare.

Thus with the Stern Review using $c = 1.3$ percent, $\varepsilon = 1.0$, and $\rho = 0.1$, a final discount rate of 1.4 percent is obtained. In another commonly referenced analysis of climate change, the value of ρ was set higher at 1.5.[29] Many economic analyses use higher discount rates based on higher values for ρ and ε. The justification for these higher values of ρ and ε is that these values more closely align with the time preference implied by financial market decisions. For example, using the same value of $c = 1.3$ percent, setting $\rho = 1.5$ and $\varepsilon = 1.4$ yields a final discount rate of 3.4 percent. Compared with a 1.4 percent discount rate, using a rate of 3.4 percent will yield a present value for an impact a hundred years in the future only one-seventh as large.

What do economists think the discount rate should be? In 2001 over 2,000 economists were surveyed for their opinion on "the appropriate real discount rate to be used for evaluating environmental projects over a long time horizon."[30] The average response was 4.0 percent, with a median value of 3.0 percent.

One might question whether the opinions of economists should be the ultimate factor in determining the discount rate for environmental analyses. In particular, if economists devote so much effort to asking people their preferences for environmental values using contingent valuation questions, why not also ask people their opinions regarding time preferences? In an innovative 2003 paper, Colorado residents were asked to reveal their willingness to pay to prevent future forest loss as a result of climate change. From their responses the researchers were able to imply the time preferences of respondents:

> Our estimates conclude that the public's discount rate is somewhat less than 1 percent. Interestingly, and probably not surprisingly to non-economists, the public's estimated discount rate is lower than that suggested by economists. [31]

Risk and Uncertainty

In many CBAs, the future outcome of a specific project or proposal is not known with certainty. For example, the operation of a nuclear power plant involves some risk of a serious accident and major release of radiation. Any CBA of a nuclear power plant would have to take this issue into account. How can we incorporate this possibility into a CBA framework?

First, we must realize that risk and uncertainty mean different things to economists.[32] In terms of CBA, **risk** is defined as variability or randomness that can be quantified. For example, statistical studies can define the risks associated with smoking. While no one can tell whether a particular smoker will suffer an early onset of a serious disease or live to a ripe old age, it is clear that smoking increases the chances of early disease and death, and for a large population these risks can be calculated fairly precisely. In situations of risk, the full range of possible outcomes can be listed in a CBA, and likely probabilities can be attached to each outcome. Of course, we do not know which particular outcome will occur, but we believe that we know the probabilities with a reasonable degree of confidence.

For example, in the case of a CBA of a nuclear power plant proposal, we may estimate that the risk of a catastrophic accident is, say, one in 1,000 over the lifespan of the plant.[k] Or in a proposal to develop an offshore oil well, we might estimate the risk of a major oil spill as one in 5,000.[l]

Uncertainty, in contrast, is defined as variability or randomness that cannot be accurately quantified. The issue of global climate change, discussed in depth in Chapter 18, demonstrates this. The full effects of global climate change resulting from emissions of greenhouse gases are not accurately predictable. While scientists have generally agreed on a range of possible temperature increases from 1 to 6 degrees Centigrade (about 2 to 10 degrees Fahrenheit) likely to result over the next century, the global weather system is so complex that dramatic and unpredictable events are possible.

risk
term used to describe a situation in which all potential outcomes and their probabilities are known.

uncertainty
term used to describe a situation in which some of the outcomes of an action are unknown or cannot be assigned probabilities.

---

[k]About 400 nuclear plants have operated worldwide in the past four decades, with two catastrophic accidents, in Chernobyl, Ukraine, and Fukushima, Japan. This implies an accident likelihood of one in several hundred, so 1 in 1,000 would be a conservative estimate.

[l]This rough estimate might be based on the actual experience of one major oil spill in the Gulf of Mexico, out of several thousand wells drilled.

For example, it is possible that positive feedback effects such as the release of CO_2 from melting of the Arctic tundra could add huge additional volumes of greenhouse gases to the atmosphere, greatly accelerating warming. Climate change could also lead to changes in ocean currents such as the Gulf Stream, changing the climate of Northern Europe to something like that of Alaska. Despite recent advances in climate change modeling, no one can accurately determine the likelihood of these events.

Risk can be quantitatively incorporated into a CBA, while uncertainty cannot. For a single possible outcome x_i, the **expected value** of that outcome is equal to its probability $P(x_i)$ multiplied by its net benefit (or cost). Thus:

expected value
the weighted average of potential values.

$$EV(x_i) = P(x_i) * NB(x_i)$$

In a situation of risk, we would list all possible outcomes, their probabilities, and their associated net benefits. The expected value of these various possible outcomes is then calculated as:

$$EV(X) = \Sigma_i [P(x_i) * NB(x_i)]$$

where $P(x_i)$ is the probability that outcome i will occur, and $NB(x_i)$ is the net benefit of outcome i.

Let's consider an example of a proposal to build a dam for flood control for a cost of $7 million. The expected benefits of the dam will depend on the future risks of a flood, which is a function of precipitation. Suppose that four precipitation scenarios are defined: low, average, high, and extremely high precipitation. In all precipitation scenarios except the extremely high scenario, the dam prevents flooding and thus provides society with benefits. With extremely high precipitation, the dam bursts and society actually ends up suffering significant damages.

Table 6.3 illustrates these hypothetical outcomes, along with the probability and net benefits of each outcome. The benefits of flood control increase with greater precipitation. The likelihood of a dam failure is only 1 percent, but the damages are very high. When we calculate the expected value across all four scenarios, we obtain a value of $9.85 million. Assuming that the net benefit estimates reflect all costs and benefits, we would recommend building the dam based on this analysis, assuming no other proposed dam project yields greater net benefits.

risk aversion
the tendency to prefer certainty instead of risky outcomes, particularly in cases when significant negative consequences may result from an action.

The formula for expected value does not take into account **risk aversion**—the common tendency to avoid risky situations, particularly those that involve losses. For example, suppose that you were offered the chance to receive $100 with certainty versus a 50/50 chance of either winning $300 or losing $100. The expected value (EV) of the latter scenario is:

$$EV = [(+\$300 * 0.5) + (-\$100 * 0.5)]$$
$$= [+\$150 - \$50]$$
$$= \$100.$$

So in expected value terms, the two scenarios are equal. But many people would prefer to take the $100 with certainty because of risk aversion.

Going back to our dam example above, we see that the possibility of a dam failure does not have a significant impact on the expected net benefits of the dam.

Table 6.3

Hypothetical Example of Risk Analysis

Scenario	Net Benefit	Probability	Expected Value
Low precipitation	+ $5 million	0.27	+ 1,350,000
Average precipitation	+ $10 million	0.49	+ 4,900,000
High precipitation	+ $20 million	0.23	+ 4,600,000
Extremely high precipitation	– $100 million	0.01	– 1,000,000
Total expected value			+ 9,850,000

precautionary principle
the view that policies should account for uncertainty by taking steps to avoid low-probability but catastrophic events.

safe minimum standard
the principle that environmental policies on issues involving uncertainty should be set to avoid possible catastrophic consequences.

Even though the damages from a dam failure are very high, the low probability of this scenario means that it does not sway the final result very much. If we are risk averse, we may wish to give greater consideration to the possibility of a dam failure. In a quantitative analysis, we could give added weight to any significant negative outcomes. Or we may apply the **precautionary principle**. People living below the dam may not be willing to take the chance, even if remote, of such a huge catastrophe. A similar logic applies to the unpredictable possibilities of extreme global warming effects. We cannot tell whether they will occur, but the unknown risk of such major planetary disruptions makes us properly nervous and lends urgency to efforts to reduce greenhouse gas emissions.

The precautionary principle is especially appropriate when impacts are irreversible. Some types of pollution and environmental damage can be remedied by reducing emissions or allowing time for natural systems to regenerate. Others, like species loss, are irreversible. In cases in which we can adjust for mistakes or change our policies to adapt to new circumstances, an economic balancing of costs and benefits may be appropriate. But when essential natural systems could suffer irreversible damage, it is better to apply a **safe minimum standard** of environmental protection. Damage to the atmospheric ozone layer, for example, could threaten all life on earth by removing an essential barrier to destructive radiation. As a result, international treaties have sought to impose a complete ban on many ozone-depleting substances, regardless of any economic benefits that they might offer.

In dealing with issues involving risk and uncertainty, good judgment is required regarding which risks can reasonably be estimated and given an expected monetary value. Just because outcomes are not known with certainty does not mean that economic analysis of environmental impacts is inappropriate. But caution is needed to recognize cases in which economic valuation of possible outcomes fails to capture the full impact on human health or ecosystems.[33]

Benefit Transfer

benefit transfer
assigning or estimating the value of a resource based on prior analysis of one or more similar resources.

Conducting a CBA can be time consuming and expensive. Often federal and state agencies require quantification of environmental costs and benefits but lack the resources to fund original analyses. In such cases, the agency may locate similar studies and rely upon them to obtain estimates. The practice of using existing studies to obtain an estimate for a new situation is known as **benefit transfer**.

Consider an example of benefit transfer. In 2001 the U.S. EPA was conducting a CBA of different standards for arsenic in drinking water. One of the human health impacts of arsenic consumption is bladder cancer, which does not tend to be fatal. Rather than conduct an original study of the willingness to pay to avoid a case of nonfatal bladder cancer, the EPA applied benefit transfer. However, no studies were available on the valuation of damages from bladder cancer or any other nonfatal cancer. According to the EPA study, the most-similar estimate was a study that used contingent valuation to estimate people's willingness to pay to avoid a case of chronic bronchitis.[34] Obviously, bladder cancer and chronic bronchitis are two rather different diseases. Thus one may question the validity of such a transfer.

Other applications of benefit transfer appear more reasonable. For example, in 1996 an oil spill off the coast of Rhode Island caused a reduction in recreational marine fishing. As part of the claim for legal damages, the government agencies involved in the case needed an estimate of the consumer surplus of a day of marine fishing in the area of the spill. Again, an original analysis was not conducted, and the agencies sought to transfer a benefit estimate. After reviewing more than a hundred studies, the agencies ended up transferring an estimate based on a travel cost study of marine recreational fishing off the coast of New York.[35]

Several studies have tested the validity of benefit transfer. By comparing the results from original analyses to the results of transferred values, a researcher can test the accuracy of the transferred values. The results suggest that significant errors are common if one relies upon transferred values, ranging from about 30 percent to over 7,000 percent![36] In one study of recreation benefits, errors averaged 80–88 percent with a range of 12–411 percent.[37]

Benefit transfer is rather common in practice, but should economists use this practice so often if the validity is questionable? Of course, primary studies are preferable to benefit transfer if the resources are available. But benefit transfer does provide an estimate when information would not be available otherwise. Benefit transfer may be more suitable for some situations, such as preliminary screening of policy options, and less suitable for other applications, such as determining damages in a legal case. Ultimately,

> decision makers will have to use their own judgment to make a tradeoff between us-
> ing benefit transfer values and conducting a primary study to generate original WTP
> estimates. [I]n principle, an analyst might be able to correct for some of the errors
> in the [transferred] values to be used in real world benefit transfer. It is important to
> acknowledge, however, that benefit transfer is not a panacea . . . but an approach to
> effectively utilize existing information and resources to provide a rough estimate when
> a "first best" valuation study is not affordable.[38]

Valuing Life

Perhaps the most controversial topic in CBA is the valuing of human lives. Many environmental policies, such as those setting standards for air pollution or contaminants in drinking water, affect mortality rates. Toxicological studies can provide estimates of the number of deaths that can be prevented by specific policies. Say, for example, that a policy to improve air quality would cost $500 million in terms of pollution control equipment and administrative costs but reduce the number of deaths associated with air pollution by fifty per year. Is such a policy "worth it" to society?

In one sense, we must at least implicitly value human lives when determining environmental policies. Even if it were technically feasible to eliminate all mortality associated with environmental pollution, surely the cost would be prohibitive. Thus society must make a tradeoff between expenditures to limit impacts and mortality rates. Of course, technological improvements can always be sought to reduce exposure to harmful contaminants, but for the foreseeable future policy makers will need to determine "acceptable" standards for such contaminants.

It is obviously unreasonable to ask someone how much she would be willing to pay to avoid dying from environmental pollution. Thus economists do not value any specific individual's life. Instead, economists seek to estimate how people value relatively minor changes in risk and use this information to infer the **value of a statistical life (VSL)**. A VSL estimate, in theory, indicates how much society is willing to pay to reduce the number of deaths from environmental pollution by one without any specific reference to whose death will be avoided.

An example best illustrates how a VSL can be estimated. Suppose that we conduct a contingent valuation survey to ask people how much they would be willing to pay for a policy that would improve air quality such that the number of people who die from air pollution would be reduced by fifty per year. If we assume that the respondents to the survey are representative of the broader population, then they have just as much chance of benefiting from the policy as anyone else, on average. Suppose that the survey results indicate that the average household is willing to pay $10 per year for such a policy. If society comprises 100 million households, then the total willingness to pay for the policy would be:

*100 million * $10 / year = $1 billion.*

Since this is the WTP to reduce annual deaths by fifty, the VSL would be:

$1 billion / 50 = $20 million.

Thus this society is implicitly willing to pay $20 million for each avoided death from air pollution.

While this example is based on a contingent valuation study, the most common approach for estimating a VSL is **wage-risk analysis**. In this approach, statistical analysis is used to determine the wage premium that needs to be paid to attract workers to particularly risky jobs, while controlling for other factors. Assuming that workers are aware of the risks and have a degree of freedom in choosing jobs, wage-risk analysis can determine the wage necessary to induce workers to undertake riskier jobs such as being loggers, airline pilots, and commercial fishermen.

According to a recent meta-analysis, the results of VSL studies have varied significantly, producing estimates from $0.5 to $50 million per avoided death.[39] Across the thirty-two studies included in this meta-analysis, the mean VSL was $8.4 million but the standard deviation was $7.9 million. Another meta-analysis recognizes the large variation in estimates, but notes that half the studies based on the U.S. labor market range between $5 million and $12 million.[40]

The VSLs used by government agencies in the United States have varied but generally increased over time, from around $2 million in the 1980s to nearly $10 million more recently. For more on the economic, and political, debate about the VSL in the United States, see Box 6.4.

Some economists (and many noneconomists) are critical of VSL estimates, based on methodological grounds or ethical objections. The two main methodologies used to derive VSL estimates—contingent valuation and wage-risk analysis—both raise

---

value of a statistical life (VSL)
the willingness to pay of society to avoid one death based on valuations of changes in the risk of death.

wage-risk analysis
a method used to estimate the value of a statistical life based on the required compensation needed to entice people to high-risk jobs.

validity concerns. We already discussed the potential problems with contingent valuation. Critics of wage-risk studies point out that those who undertake relatively risky jobs are not representative of the broader population. In particular, the wage premium that would be required to attract the average person to a risky job is likely to be higher than the observed wage premium. This could be because the people who undertake risky jobs likely are inherently more accepting of risks and may actually seek risky jobs. It could also be that people in risky jobs have fewer options and are not really undertaking the risk voluntarily in return for higher compensation.

Another methodological issue is that the majority of risky jobs are undertaken by men. About half the wage-risk studies include data only on male job choices. If men and women evaluate risks differently, then extrapolating results from male job choices to the broader population would not be valid.

In most policy applications, the same VSL estimate has been used by an agency regardless of the situation. But people may not evaluate, say, the risk of cancer from an environmental contaminant in the same way as the risk of a nuclear accident. As seen in Box 6.4, agencies have recently considered assigning different VSL estimates to different policy situations.

Other critics reject the entire premise that we should place a numerical value of human lives. They suggest that human life is inherently priceless, and therefore it makes no sense to value risks to human life.[41] Further, some consider the process of reducing human lives to economic analysis fundamentally objectionable on ethical grounds. They suggest that methods other than CBA should be used to make decisions about policies that affect human mortality levels.

Cost-Benefit Analysis Example

A relatively simple example of a CBA can illustrate some of the practical issues that often arise. Suppose that we are evaluating a proposal to build a dam. We start by listing some of the costs and benefits associated with the dam, as summarized in Table 6.4.

Table 6.4

Potential Costs and Benefits Associated with Dam Construction Proposal

Potential Costs	Potential Benefits
1. Construction costs	1. Flood control
2. Operations and maintenance costs	2. Recreation
3. Environmental damages	3. Hydropower supply
4. Risk of dam failure	

The list is not meant to be comprehensive—these are only the impacts we consider in this example. You may well think of other costs and benefits that should be included.

Let's assume that the construction costs of the dam are $150 million, to be paid $50 million per year over a three-year construction period. Normally, construction costs would be paid over a longer time period, funded by a loan, but in this case we assume three annual payments. During the construction period, the dam generates no benefits. The discount rate is set at 5 percent. Thus the costs, in present value, over the three-year construction period would be (all impacts will be expressed in millions of dollars):

$$PV = 50 + (50/1.05) + (50/1.05^2)$$
$$= 50 + 47.62 + 45.35$$
$$= 142.97.$$

Note that this calculation assumes that we do not discount in the first (current) year. Suppose that we collect information on the other categories of costs and benefits as:

- Annual operations and maintenance costs are $8 million.
- Annual recreation benefits are $15 million. Note that the reservoir obviously is not available for study until after the dam is constructed. Thus we need to rely on some kind of benefit transfer in order to provide an estimate of the recreation benefits before the site is built.
- Annual hydropower benefits are $5 million. This estimate would be based on the consumer surplus of those using the electricity and the producer surplus (profits) of the electricity provider.
- Environmental damages from the dam are $10 million annually. These damages likely include lost habitats and reduced fish population, as dams can prevent the spawning of certain species.
- Annual flood control benefits depend upon the distribution of expected precipitation patterns. In normal years, assume that there is no risk of flooding and thus no benefits. Assume that normal years occur 70 percent of the time (probability of 0.7). In a wet year, assume that the damage prevented by the dam is $20 million in crop damage, property damage, and other impacts. Suppose that wet years occur every five years (a probability of 0.2). Further, assume that a very wet year occurs every 10 years, and in these years the damage prevented is $50 million.

We thus have a situation of risk in which we know the probability of all possible outcomes and their economic impacts. The expected value of annual benefits using the formula from earlier in the chapter is:

$$EV = (0.7 * 0) + (0.2 * 20) + (0.1 * 50)$$
$$= 0 + 4 + 5$$
$$= 9.$$

- Finally, let's assume that the dam is in an area prone to earthquakes, and there is a chance that a major earthquake will cause the dam to fail and produce catastrophic damages. Let's suppose that an engineering estimate indicates that the risk of dam failure from an earthquake is only 0.01 percent per year or a probability of 0.0001. However, if the dam does fail, damages would $5 billion in terms of material damage and human lives lost. A VSL would be needed to value the predicted human deaths. The annual expected damage from a dam failure would be:

$$EV = \$5,000 * 0.0001$$
$$= 0.5.$$

This annual value is much lower than any of the other impacts. Thus it will not have a significant impact on our final results. However, we may want to adjust this calculation if we are risk averse.

The other piece of information that we need is the expected lifespan of the dam. We assume that the dam will last for fifty years, after which no costs and benefits will occur. Again, this is perhaps unrealistic and we do not consider any permanent ecological damage, but we keep the example relatively basic.

We are now able to bring all our impacts together to produce a net benefit estimate. For the purposes of discounting, realize that in the first year of the dam's operation the value of n in our discounting formula will be 3. A spreadsheet can be used to calculate the present value of each category of impacts for each year. (For instructions on how to use Microsoft Excel to calculate present values, see Appendix 6.2.)

Table 6.5 presents the detailed calculations for the first few and last few years of the analysis (the results for Years 6–48 have been omitted), as well as the total present value for each impact.

Consider the environmental costs, which start to occur in Year 3. The environmental costs in Year 3 are $10 million, which convert to a present value of:

$$PV = \$10 \text{ million} / (1.05)^3$$
$$= \$8.64 \text{ million}.$$

By the time we get to the end of the dam's lifetime, the effect of discounting becomes much more significant. Impacts are reduced by more than a factor of 10 in the last few years.

Over the dam's lifetime, the present value of all costs is:

$$PV_{costs} = 142.97 + 132.47 + 165.59 + 8.28$$
$$= 449.31.$$

Table 6.5

Annual Present Value of Costs and Benefits of Dam Construction Proposal (in Millions), Selected Years

Year	Costs Construction	Operations	Environmental	Dam Failure	Benefits Recreation	Hydropower	Flood Control
0	50.00	0.00	0.00	0.00	0.00	0.00	0.00
1	47.62	0.00	0.00	0.00	0.00	0.00	0.00
2	45.35	0.00	0.00	0.00	0.00	0.00	0.00
3	0.00	6.91	8.64	0.43	12.96	4.32	7.77
4	0.00	6.58	8.23	0.41	12.34	4.11	7.40
5	0.00	6.27	7.84	0.39	11.75	3.92	7.05
...	...	...	...	...	...	...	...
49	0.00	0.73	0.92	0.05	1.37	0.46	0.82
50	0.00	0.70	0.87	0.04	1.31	0.44	0.78
51	0.00	0.66	0.83	0.04	1.25	0.42	0.75
52	0.00	0.63	0.79	0.04	1.19	0.40	0.71
Total Present Value	142.97	132.47	165.59	8.28	248.38	82.79	149.03

The present value of all benefits is:

$$PV_{benefits} = 248.38 + 82.79 + 149.03$$
$$= 480.20.$$

So should we build the dam based on this example? Benefits exceed costs by about $30 million, so that would suggest building the dam. But as mentioned earlier, we do not know whether building the dam will necessarily produce the most social benefits for a given cost. Perhaps investing the $150 million construction cost in building schools or reducing air pollution would yield greater net benefits. We should also consider whether the scale of the dam project is optimal. Perhaps a smaller, or larger, dam would produce greater net benefits.

A good CBA should include **sensitivity analysis**. This considers whether the recommendation changes when we change some of the assumptions of the analysis. Perhaps the most common type of sensitivity analysis is to change the discount rate. In our example, the construction costs are paid first, whereas net benefits occur in the future (i.e., for each year starting in Year 3 in Table 6.5, the benefits exceed the costs). So increasing the discount rate tends to reduce net benefits and make the project seem less appealing. In fact, if we change the discount rate to 8 percent instead of 5 percent, the proposal has a net present value cost of about $30 million, and we would not recommend building the dam.

Another type of sensitivity analysis might consider the effect of risk aversion to the possibility of a dam failure. Even with a 5 percent discount rate, an adjustment for risk aversion (such as increasing the present value of this impact by a factor of five) could result in net costs, and a recommendation not to build the dam.

Sensitivity analysis is important because it tells us whether our results are robust to changes in the underlying assumptions. If the recommendation does not change after our sensitivity analysis, we can feel relatively confident in proceeding with that recommendation. However, if our recommendation differs with reasonable changes in the assumptions, we may be unable to make a firm recommendation. Finally, we also need to determine whether we have excluded any costs and ben-

sensitivity analysis
an analytical tool that studies how the outputs of a model change as the assumptions of the model change.

efits or left some impacts unquantified. This may be another reason why a CBA could be inconclusive.

6.6 CONCLUSION: THE ROLE OF COST-BENEFIT ANALYSIS IN POLICY DECISIONS

Valuing the environment is necessarily a troublesome endeavor. Some argue that what nature gives us is priceless and that we should not even think about reducing these "services" to mere monetary values; others maintain that putting a value on ecological functions is essential, since the primary alternative is to allow the economic system to value them at zero. According to one famous analysis, the value that humans obtain from nature's services may exceed the value of global economic production (see Box 6.5).

BOX 6.5   VALUING THE GLOBAL ECOSYSTEM

Economists have devised various techniques to estimate nonmarket values for ecological services. These values allow us to incorporate ecosystem services in cost-benefit analyses. Most nonmarket applications estimate the value of a particular ecosystem or service, such as the value of a wetland or the value of clean air. A much more ambitious approach is to consider the value of the entire global ecosystem.

Although many would argue that the value of the global ecosystem is priceless, large-scale application of nonmarket techniques is feasible. In fact, in a 1997 article in the journal *Nature*, a group of researchers estimated the global value of ecosystem services (Costanza et al., 1997). The researchers considered the value of seventeen ecosystem services, including climate regulation, erosion control, waste treatment, food production, and recreation. They extensively reviewed nonmarket valuation studies to obtain estimates for the value of these seventeen ecosystem services for each of sixteen ecological areas, or biomes (see Table 6.6).

The total annual value of the global ecosystem was estimated at $33 trillion, with a range of $16 trillion to $54 trillion (for comparison, global gross national product is currently around $30 trillion). Slightly more than half the total is for nutrient cycling services. The biomes with the highest total values are open oceans, continental shelves, and estuaries. The highest per-hectare ecosystem values are for estuaries, swamps/floodplains, and seagrass/algae beds.

The paper has been criticized for its attempt to use fairly simple economic methods to reduce all ecological functions to money values (El Serafy, 1998; Turner et al., 1998). But even the critics acknowledge "the article's potential to influence environmental discourse" and generate "rich methodological discussions" (Norgaard et al., 1998). Although any specific dollar value estimate is necessarily controversial, attempts to value the global ecosystem certainly demonstrate the significant value of ecological services and their importance in policy decisions.

Critics of CBA point to the many difficulties involved in obtaining reliable estimates and the fact that some things, like spiritual values or the value of community, are essentially impossible to estimate in dollar terms. Economists generally maintain that CBA is a useful tool, provided that it is used with the proper caution. It would be unreasonable to assume that we can place a precise dollar value on everything—but in many cases economic valuations can assist decision makers by providing specific estimates of policy impacts.

Table 6.6

The Global Value of Ecosystem Services

Biome (ecosystem)	Area (millions of hectares)	Annual value (1994 $ millions)
Open ocean	33,220	8,381
Estuaries	180	4,110
Seagrass/algae beds	200	3,801
Coral reefs	62	375
Shelf	2,660	4,283
Tropical forest	1,900	3,813
Temperate/boreal forest	2,955	894
Grass/rangelands	3,898	906
Tidal marsh/mangroves	165	1,648
Swamps/floodplains	165	3,231
Lakes/rivers	200	1,700
Desert	1,925	NA[1]
Tundra	743	NA[1]
Ice/rock	1,640	NA[1]
Cropland	1,400	128
Urban	332	NA[1]
Total	51,645	33,268

[1]No estimate was provided.

CBAs of environmental policies are particularly difficult and controversial because several of the most important benefits of environmental improvements are difficult to quantify. First, nonuse values can only be estimated using contingent valuation. We have seen that the validity of this method is a subject of debate among economists. Second, the benefits of reduced mortality rates are estimated using the VSL methodology—another controversial valuation approach. Third, environmental policies often involve up-front costs and longer-term benefits. This makes the choice of a discount rate critically important. A lower discount rate tends to support greater environmental protection.

While CBA can provide definite policy recommendations in some instances, commonly the results will produce ambiguous results because of excluded factors or sensitivity analysis. Thus some economists believe that CBA cannot and should not be used to provide specific policy recommendations. One alternative is to rely on a different process for setting policy objectives and having economics play a more limited role. With **cost-effectiveness analysis**, economic analysis merely determines the least-cost way of achieving a policy goal.

Suppose, for example, that we have established a goal of cutting sulfur dioxide pollution, a major cause of acid rain, by 50 percent.[m] This might be done by requiring highly polluting plants to install scrubbers; by imposing taxes or fines based on emission levels; or by issuing tradable permits for certain levels of emissions, with the total number of permits not exceeding 50 percent of current levels. Assuming economic analysis can provide reliable estimates of the costs arising from each of these policies, cost-effectiveness analysis can tell us which option is the most economically efficient way to achieve our policy goal.

Clearly it makes sense to adopt the least-cost method of reaching a given goal. In this approach, we do not rely on economic analysis to tell us *how much* we

cost-effectiveness analysis

a policy tool that determines the least-cost approach for achieving a given goal.

---

[m]This was, in fact, the goal set by the U.S. Environmental Protection Agency under the Clean Air Act Amendments of 1990.

ought to reduce pollution—that decision is made based on other factors including scientific evidence, political discussion, and ordinary common sense. But economic analysis is used to tell us how to choose the most efficient policies to achieve a desired result.

Another alternative to CBA, involving consideration of broader social and political factors, has been called **positional analysis**. In this, estimates of the economic costs of a particular policy are combined with an evaluation of the effects on different groups of people, possible alternative policies, social priorities, individual rights, and goals and objectives other than economic gain. There is no single "bottom line," and it is recognized that particular outcomes may favor some groups over others.[42]

For example, the construction of a major dam may require relocation of large numbers of people. Even if the dam's economics appear favorable, these people's right to remain in their homes may be given a greater social priority. Such judgments cannot be made on a purely economic basis. However, some of the valuation techniques we have discussed may be useful in defining economic aspects of what must ultimately be a social and political decision.[43]

Up to this point, we have seen that traditional environmental economics has several core theories and methods that can provide environmental policy guidance. The theories discussed in Chapters 3–5 generally point out how policy interventions can produce more economically efficient, and environmentally beneficial, outcomes. To use economic analysis to provide specific policy recommendations, we must rely upon the valuation approaches discussed in this chapter. We have seen that this is a challenging task, raising numerous issues of validity, assumptions, and ethics.

In the next few chapters, we turn to some of the issues that define the core of what is known as ecological economics. Ecological economics does not necessarily dismiss the theories and methods presented in Chapters 3–6. But ecological economics does place greater emphasis on the limitations of economic valuation of the environment. It also asks some broader questions that have not been fully addressed by more traditional environmental economics.

positional analysis
a policy analysis tool that combines economic valuation with other considerations such as equity, individual rights, and social priorities; it does not aim to reduce all impacts to monetary terms.

SUMMARY

Economists have devised various techniques to estimate the total economic value of environmental resources. Some values can be inferred from markets, either directly or indirectly. Revealed preference methods can be used to estimate the benefits of outdoor recreation, drinking water quality, air quality, and a few other environmental services. Nonuse values, often an important component of the value of natural resources, can only be measured using stated preference methods such as contingent valuation. CV uses surveys to ask respondents about their willingness to pay for environmental improvements. Contingent valuation is controversial because of potential biases that cast doubt on the validity of the method.

Cost-benefit analysis can be used to evaluate proposed projects and government actions. Environmental factors are often involved in cost-benefit analysis and can be some of the most controversial to value. One important issue is the valuation of future costs and benefits. Economists use the technique of discounting to balance the needs of the present and future. Selection of an appropriate discount rate is important and can significantly affect the results of cost-benefit studies. The socially appropriate discount rate may be different from the commercial discount rate used to evaluate financial investment returns.

Another important, and controversial issue is the valuation of human lives. While we must somehow evaluate tradeoffs between environmental protection expenditures and mortality risks, the VSL methodology seeks to estimate society's willingness to pay to avoid a death due to environmental contaminants in terms of economic value.

Some have argued that pricing the environment is inherently wrong, since dollar values are an inadequate metric for the benefits of ecological systems. Others maintain that some valuation is essential for comparing policy options and if done with caution will not misrepresent environmental values.

KEY TERMS AND CONCEPTS

anthropocentric viewpoint
benefit transfer
bequest value
biocentric viewpoint
contingent ranking (CR)
contingent valuation (CV)
cost of illness method
cost-benefit analysis
cost-effectiveness analysis
defensive expenditures approach
direct-use value
discount rate
discounting
ecosystem services
endowment effect
existence value
expected value
habitat equivalency analysis (HEA)
hedonic pricing
human capital
indirect-use values
meta-analysis
nonmarket benefits
nonuse values
option value

positional analysis
precautionary principle
present value
protest bids
pure rate of time preference
real or inflation-adjusted dollars
replacement cost methods
revealed preference methods
risk
risk aversion
safe minimum standard
sensitivity analysis
social discount rate/social rate of time preference
 (SRTP)
stated preference methods
strategic behavior
total economic value
travel cost method (TCM)
uncertainty
use values
value of a statistical life (VSL)
wage-risk analysis
willingness to accept (WTA)
willingness to pay (WTP)

DISCUSSION QUESTIONS

1. Suppose that you are asked to conduct a cost-benefit study of a proposed coal-fired power plant. The plant will be built on the outskirts of a residential area and will emit a certain volume of pollutants. It will require a substantial amount of water for its cooling system. Industries in the region argue that the additional power is urgently needed, but local residents oppose construction. How would you evaluate social and environmental costs and weigh them against economic benefits?

2. As mentioned in the text, under U.S. law federal agencies must use cost-benefit analysis to evaluate major policy proposals. Do you agree with this requirement, in particular for environmental policies? How much weight do you believe should be given to the results of cost-benefit analyses when making policy decisions? Discuss how economic, health, and environmental criteria should be balanced in formulating regulations.

3. Suppose that the government of a developing country is considering the establishment of a national park in a scenic forested area. Local opposition arises from those who wish to use the forest land for timbering and agriculture. But the national park would draw both local and foreign visitors as tourists. Could cost-benefit analysis aid the decision on whether to establish the park? What factors would you consider, and how would you measure their economic value?

EXERCISE

1. The World Bank is considering an application from the country of Equatoria for a large dam project. Some costs and benefits of the project (dollar values) are as follows:

   Construction costs: $500 million/year for three years
   Operating costs: $50 million/year
   Hydropower to be generated: 3 billion Kilowatt hours/year
   Price of electricity: $0.05/Kilowatt hour
   Irrigation water available from dam: 5 billion gallons/year
   Price of water: $0.02/gallon
   Agricultural product lost from flooded lands: $45 million/year
   Forest products lost from flooded lands: $20 million/year

   There are also additional, less easily quantifiable, losses: human costs to villagers who will be forced to move, watershed damage, and ecological costs of habitat destruction. It is also possible that the new lake area may contribute to the spread of water-borne diseases.

   a. Do a formal cost-benefit analysis using the quantifiable factors previously listed. Assume that the lifespan of the dam is 30 years. As in the example in Table 6.5, assume that construction begins now (in Year 0). All other impacts start once the dam is completed (in Year 3) and continue for 30 years (until Year 32). Refer to Appendix 6.2 to make the necessary calculations using Excel.

For costs C_i or benefits B_i that extend into the indefinite future, use the formulae $PV[C] = C_i/r$ or $PV[B] = B_i/r$ to obtain the value of the (infinite) stream of benefits. You may assume that the dam will operate for the foreseeable future.

Do a complete cost/benefit analysis for *two* possible interest rates: 10 percent and 5 percent. Do your figures indicate a definite "yes," definite "no," or uncertain result in each case?

b. Now consider an alternative project: a number of smaller dams constructed so as not to flood significant agricultural or forest lands. For this project, total construction costs are exactly half the costs of the big dam project, and power/irrigation benefits are also half as much. But there is no damage to farmland or forest, and there are no ecological or resettlement costs. Evaluate this project, and compare it to the larger project at the two interest rates.

NOTES

1. See, for example, Sagoff, 2004.
2. For a more in-depth overview of environmental valuation techniques, see Ulibarri and Wellman, 1997.
3. Barnett and Nurmagambetov, 2011.
4. Roach and Wade, 2006.
5. Rolfe and Dyack, 2010.
6. Marvasti, 2010.
7. Murdock, 2006.
8. Ward et al., 1996.
9. Zanderson and Tol, 2009.
10. For a summary of hedonic pricing model results, see Boyle and Kiel, 2001; Palmquist and Smith, 2002.
11. Bayer et al., 2009. 1 µg/m3 is one milligram per cubic meter, a measure of pollutant levels in air.
12. Ready, 2010.
13. Abdalla et al., 1992.
14. Rosado et al., 2006.
15. For an overview of contingent valuation, see Breedlove, 1999; Whitehead, 2006.
16. Horowitz and McConnell, 2002.
17. Anonymous, 1992.
18. Carson et al., 2001.
19. See Portney, 1994.
20. Carson et al., 2003.
21. Arrow et al., 1993.
22. Desvouges et al., 1993.
23. Diamond and Hausman, 1994.
24. Ackerman and Heinzerling, 2004, p. 164.
25. Bateman et al., 2006.
26. The rate varies depending upon the length to maturity (3 to 30 years). See U.S. OMB, 2012.
27. Stern, 2007.
28. Evans, 2005.
29. Nordhaus, 2007.
30. Weitzman, 2001.
31. Layton and Levine, 2003, p. 543.

32. For a discussion of the difference, see Staehr, 2006.

33. For discussion of the limitations of economic valuation, see, for example, O'Brien, 2000; Toman, 1994.

34. U.S. EPA, 2001.

35. NOAA et al., 1999.

36. Spash and Vatn, 2006.

37. Shrestha and Loomis, 2003.

38. Ibid., p. 95.

39. Bellavance et al., 2009.

40. Viscusi and Aldy, 2003.

41. See Ackerman and Heinzerling, 2004.

42. For an exposition of the basis of positional analysis, see Söderbaum, 1999.

43. For a discussion of the interaction between estimation techniques and underlying values, see Gouldner and Kennedy, 1997.

REFERENCES

Abdalla, Charles W., Brian Roach, and Donald J. Epp. 1992. "Valuing Environmental Quality Changes Using Averting Expenditures: An Application to Groundwater Contamination." *Land Economics* 68(2): 163–169.

Ackerman, Frank, and Lisa Heinzerling. 2004. *Priceless: On Knowing the Price of Everything and the Value of Nothing.* New York, London: New Press.

Akram, Agha Ali, and Sheila M. Olmstead. 2011. "The Value of Household Water Service Quality in Lahore, Pakistan," *Environmental and Resource Economics* 49(2): 173–198.

Anonymous. 1992. "'Ask a Silly Question' . . . Contingent Valuation of Natural Resource Damages." *Harvard Law Review* 105(8): 1981–2000.

Arrow, Kenneth, Robert Solow, Paul R. Portney, Edward E. Leamer, Roy Radner, and Howard Schuman. 1993. "Report of the NOAA Panel on Contingent Valuation." *Federal Register,* 58(10): 4601–4614.

Barnett, Sarah Beth L., and Tursynbek A. Nurmagambetov. 2011. "Costs of Asthma in the United States, 2002–2007." *Journal of Allergy and Clinical Immunology* 127(1): 142–152.

Bateman, I.J., M.A. Cole, S. Georgiou, and D.J. Hadley. 2006. "Comparing Contingent Valuation and Contingent Ranking: A Case Study Considering the Benefits of Urban River Water Quality Improvements." *Journal of Environmental Management* 79: 221–231.

Bayer, Patrick, Nathaniel Keohane, and Christopher Timmins. 2009. "Migration and Hedonic Valuation: The Case of Air Quality." *Journal of Environmental Economics and Management* 58(1): 1–14.

Bellavance, François, Georges Dionne, and Martin Lebeau. 2009. "The Value of a Statistical Life: A Meta-analysis with a Mixed Effects Regression Model." *Journal of Health Economics* 28: 444–464.

Boyle, Melissa A., and Katherine A. Kiel. 2001. "A Survey of House Price Hedonic Studies of the Impact of Environmental Externalities." *Journal of Real Estate Literature* 9(2): 117–144.

Breedlove, Joseph. 1999. "Natural Resources: Assessing Nonmarket Values through Contingent Valuation." CRS Report for Congress, RL30242, June 21, 1999.

Carson, Richard T., Nicholas E. Flores, and Norman F. Meade. 2001. "Contingent Valuation: Controversies and Evidence." *Environmental and Resource Economics,* 19: 173–210.

Carson, Richard T., Robert C. Mitchell, Michael Hanemann, Raymond J. Kopp, Stanley Presser, and Paula A. Ruud. 2003. "Contingent Valuation and Lost Passive Use: Damages from the *Exxon Valdez* Oil Spill." *Environmental and Resource Economics* 25: 257–286.

Chen, Wendy Y., and C. Y. Jim. 2011. "Resident Valuation and Expectation of the Urban Greening Project in Zhuhai, China," *Journal of Environmental Planning and Management* 54(7): 851–869.

Costanza, Robert, Ralph d'Arge, Rudolf de Groot, Stephen Farber, Monica Grasso, Bruce Hannon, Karin Limburg, Shahid Naeem, Robert V. O'Neill, Jose Paruelo, Robert G. Raskin, Paul Sutton, and Marjan van den Belt. 1997. "The Value of the World's Ecosystem Services and Natural Capital." *Nature* 387: 253–260.

Desvousges, William H., F. Reed Johnson, Richard W. Dunford, Sara P. Hudson, and K. Nicole Wilson. 1993. "Measuring Natural Resource Damages with Contingent Valuation: Tests of Validity and Reliability." In *Contingent Valuation: A Critical Assessment,* ed. J.A. Hausman, 91–114. Amsterdam: North-Holland.

Diamond, Peter A., and Jerry A. Hausman. 1994. "Contingent Valuation: Is Some Number Better Than No Number?" *Journal of Economic Perspectives* 8(Fall): 45–64.

Eilperin, Juliet. 2011. "Environmental Protection Agency Issues New Regulation on Mercury." *Washington Post*, December 11.

El Serafy, Salah. 1998. "Pricing the Invaluable: The Value of the World's Ecosystem Services and Natural Capital." *Ecological Economics* 25(1): 25–27.

Evans, David J. 2005. "The Elasticity of Marginal Utility of Consumption: Estimates for 20 OECD Countries." *Fiscal Studies* 26(2): 197–224.

Gouldner, Lawrence H., and Donald Kennedy. 1997. "Valuing Ecosystem Services: Philosophical Bases and Empirical Methods." In *Nature's Services: Societal Dependence on Natural Ecosystems.* Washington, DC: Island Press.

Horowitz, John K., and Kenneth E. McConnell. 2002. "A Review of WTA/WTP Studies." *Journal of Environmental Economics and Management* 44: 426–447.

Layton, David F., and Richard A. Levine. 2003. "How Much Does the Future Matter? A Hierarchical Bayesian Analysis of the Public's Willingness to Mitigate Ecological Impacts of Climate Change." *Journal of the American Statistical Association* 98(463): 533–544.

Lera-Lopez, Fernando, Javier Faulin, and Mercedes Sanchez. 2012. "Determinants of the Willingness-to-Pay for Reducing the Environmental Impacts of Road Transportation," *Transportation Research: Part D: Transport and Environment* 17(3): 215–220.

Lindhjem, Henrik, and Stale Navrud. 2011. "Are Internet Surveys an Alternative to Face-to-Face Interviews in Contingent Valuation?" *Ecological Economics* 70(9): 1628–1637.

Marta-Pedroso, Cristina, Helena Freitas, and Tiago Domingos. 2007. "Testing for the Survey Mode Effect on Contingent Valuation Data Quality: A Case Study of Web Based versus In-person Interviews." *Ecological Economics* 62: 388–398.

Marvasti, Akbar. 2010. "A Welfare Estimation of Beach Recreation with Aggregate Data." *Applied Economics* 42: 291–296.

Marzetti, Silva, Marta Disegna, Giulia Villani, and Maria Speranza. 2011. "Conservation and Recreational Values from Semi-Natural Grasslands for Visitors to Two Italian Parks." *Journal of Environmental Planning and Management* 54(2): 169–191.

Mozumder, Pallab, William F. Vásquez, and Achla Marathe. 2011. "Consumers' Preference for Renewable Energy in the Southwest USA." *Energy Economics* 33(6): 1119–1126.

Murdock, Jennifer. 2006. "Handling Unobserved Site Characteristics in Random Utility Models of Recreation Demand." *Journal of Environmental Economics and Management* 51(1): 1–25.

National Oceanic and Atmospheric Administration (NOAA), Rhode Island Department of Environmental Management, U.S. Department of the Interior, and U.S. Fish and Wildlife Service. 1999. "Restoration Plan and Environmental Assessment for the January 19, 1996, *North Cape* Oil Spill."

Nordhaus, William D. 2007. "A Review of the Stern Review on the Economics of Climate Change." *Journal of Economic Literature* 45: 686–702.

Norgaard, Richard B., Collin Bode, and Values Reading Group. 1998. "Next, the Value of God, and Other Reactions." *Ecological Economics* 25(1): 37–39.

O'Brien, Mary. 2000. *Making Better Environmental Decisions: An Alternative to Risk Assessment.* Cambridge, MA: MIT Press.

Palmquist, Raymond B., and V. Kerry Smith. 2002. "The Use of Hedonic Property Value Techniques for Policy and Litigation." In *The International Yearbook of Environmental and Resource Economics 2002/2003: A Survey of Current Issues*, ed. Tom Tietenberg and Henk Folmer, 115–164. Cheltenham, UK; Northampton, MA: Edward Elgar.

Portney, Paul. 1994. "The Contingent Valuation Debate: Why Economists Should Care." *Journal of Economic Perspectives* 8(Fall): 3–17.

Ready, Richard C. 2010. "Do Landfills Always Depress Nearby Property Values?" *Journal of Real Estate Research* 32(3): 321–339.

Ressurreição, Adriana, James Gibbons, Tomaz Ponce Dentinho, Michel Kaiser, Ricardo S. Santos, and Gareth Edwards-Jones. 2011. "Economic Valuation of Species Loss in the Open Sea." *Ecological Economics* 70(4): 729–739.

Roach, Brian, and William W. Wade. 2006. "Policy Evaluation of Natural Resource Injuries using Habitat Equivalency Analysis." *Ecological Economics* 58: 421–433.

Roach, Brian, Kevin J. Boyle, and Michael Welsh. 2002. "Testing Bid Design Effects in Multiple-Bounded Contingent-Valuation Questions." *Land Economics* 78(1): 121–131.

Roach, Brian, Jonathan M. Harris, and Adrian Williamson. 2010. *The Gulf Oil Spill: Economics and Policy Issues.* Tufts University Global Development And Environment Institute educational module, available at www.ase.tufts.edu/gdae/education_materials/modules/Gulf_Oil_Spill.pdf.

Rolfe, John, and Brenda Dyack. 2010. "Testing for Convergent Validity Between Travel Cost and Contingent Valuation Estimates of Recreation Values in the Coorong, Australia." *Australian Journal of Agricultural and Resource Economics* 54: 583–599.

Rosado, Marcia A., Maria A. Cunha-e-Sa, Maria M. Dulca-Soares, and Luis C. Nunes. 2006. "Combining Averting Behavior and Contingent Valuation Data: An Application to Drinking Water Treatment in Brazil." *Environment and Development Economics* 11(6): 729–746.

Sagoff, Mark. 2004. *Price, Principle, and the Environment.* Cambridge: Cambridge University Press.

Söderbaum, Peter. 1999. "Valuation as Part of a Microeconomics for Ecological Sustainability." In *Valuation and the Environment: Theory, Method, and Practice*, ed. Martin O'Conner and Clive Spash. Cheltenham, UK: Edward Elgar.

Shrestha, Ram K., and John B. Loomis. 2003. "Meta-Analytic Benefit Transfer of Outdoor Recreation Economic Values: Testing Out-of-Sample Convergent Validity." *Environmental and Resource Economics* 25(1): 79–100.

Spash, Clive L., and Arlid Vatn. 2006. "Transferring Environmental Value Estimates: Issues and Alternatives." *Ecological Economics* 60(2): 379–388.

Staehr, Karsten. 2006. "Risk and Uncertainty in Cost Benefit Analysis." Environmental Assessment Institute Toolbox Paper.

Stern, Nicholas. 2007. *The Economics of Climate Change: The Stern Review.* Cambridge: Cambridge University Press.

Szabó, Zoltan. 2011. "Reducing Protest Responses by Deliberative Monetary Valuation: Improving the Validity of Biodiversity Valuation." *Ecological Economics* 72(1): 37–44.

Toman, Michael A. 1994. "Economics and 'Sustainability': Balancing Trade-offs and Imperatives." *Land Economics* 70: 399–413.

Turner, R.K., W.N. Adger, and R. Brouwer. 1998. "Ecosystem Services Value, Research Needs, and Policy Relevance: A Commentary." *Ecological Economics* 25(1): 61–65.

Ulibarri, C.A., and K.F. Wellman. 1997. "Natural Resource Valuation: A Primer on Concepts and Techniques." Report prepared for the U.S. Department of Energy under Contract DE-AC06–76RLO 1830.

U.S. Environmental Protection Agency (U.S. EPA). 2001. *National Primary Drinking Water Regulations; Arsenic and Clarifications to Compliance and New Source Contaminants Monitoring; Final Rule.* Federal Register 40 CFR Parts 9, 141, and 142, vol. 66(14): 6975-7066, January 22.

U.S. Office of Management and Budget (U.S. OMB). 2012. "Memorandum for the Heads of Departments and Agencies." January 3, 2012, www.whitehouse.gov/sites/default/files/omb/memoranda/2012/m-12–06.pdf.

Viscusi, Kip W., and Joseph E. Aldy. 2003. "The Value of a Statistical Like: A Critical Review of Market Estimates Throughout the World." *Journal of Risk and Uncertainty* 27(1): 5–76.

Ward, Frank, Brian Roach, and Jim Henderson. 1996. "The Economic Value of Water in Recreation: Evidence from the California Drought." *Water Resources Research* 32(4): 1075–1081.

Weitzman, Martin L. 2001. "Gamma Discounting." *American Economic Review* 91(1): 260–271.

Whitehead, John C. 2006. "A Practitioner's Primer on the Contingent Valuation Method." In *Handbook on Contingent Valuation,* ed. Anna Alberini and James R. Kahn. Cheltenham, UK; Northampton, MA: Edward Elgar.

Zanderson, Marianne, and Richard S.J. Tol. 2009. "A Meta-analysis of Forest Recreation Values in Europe." *Journal of Forest Economics* 15(1–2): 109–130.

Web Sites

1. **www.rff.org.** Home page for Resources for the Future, a nonprofit organization that conducts policy and economic research on natural resource issues. Many RFF publications available on their Web site use nonmarket techniques to value environmental services.
2. **https://www.evri.ca/Global/HomeAnonymous.aspx.** Web site for the Environmental Valuation Reference Inventory (EVRI), developed by the government of Canada. The EVRI is a "searchable storehouse of empirical studies on the economic value of environmental benefits and human health effects. It has been developed as a tool to help policy analysts use the benefits transfer approach. Using the EVRI to do a benefits transfer is an alternative to doing new valuation research."

Appendix 6.1: Advanced Material on Valuation Methods

Zonal Travel Cost Models

One type of travel cost model is called a zonal model.[n] With a zonal TCM, we first divide up the area around one or more recreation sites into different zones. These zones are normally defined based on typical geographic divisions, such as counties, zip codes, or townships. Then we need information on visitation rates to the recreation sites from the various zones. We can collect this information either by surveying visitors on-site and asking them their origin or by conducting a general population survey. In a general population survey people are contacted randomly, normally by phone or mail, and asked to report on their visitation patterns to one or more recreation sites over a period, such as the past year. In either an on-site or general population survey, we ask various other questions such as party size, expenditure information, length of stay, the activities undertaken during the visit, and demographic data such as age and income level.

The survey data are aggregated and extrapolated to estimate how many people visit the site, or several sites in the case of a multisite model, from each origin zone. Dividing the estimate of total visits by the zonal population produces visitation per capita, which controls for differences in population across zones. This variable is used as the dependent variable in a statistical model. The primary independent, or explanatory, variable is the travel cost from each origin zone to each destination site. Travel costs can be measured using software that estimate driving distances and costs. Normally, the cost of travel time is also included, assuming that travel time is another "cost" that must be paid in order to visit a site. The cost of travel time is normally estimated as a function of the wage rate of visitors. This may be based on survey data on income or the average wage rate for a zone.

In order to estimate a robust statistical model, TCMs include other independent variables besides travel cost. These include:

- Zone demographics such as age levels, family size, and income levels
- Site characteristics (for a multisite model) such as facility levels and the presence of different amenities

---

[n]Another common type of travel cost model is called a random utility model. Since zonal models are simpler, we limit our discussion here to them.

- Quantity and quality of substitute sites—a zone with nearby, high-quality substitutes would be expected to have lower visitation rates to a site, ceteris paribus
- Other pertinent variables, such as weather conditions and the timing of weekends and holidays

The model is estimated statistically, with a negative coefficient on the travel cost variable indicating that visitation rates go down as the travel costs increase—essentially a standard downward-sloping demand curve. Using the estimated model, one can then plot the demand curve by calculating expected visitation rates at different travel costs. Figure A6.1 illustrates an example showing the demand curve for a visitation site.[o] Suppose that for a particular zone, the average cost to visit the site is $30. Inserting a cost of $30 into the estimated model results in an estimated visitation rate of 5 annual visits per capita, as shown in Figure A6.1. We can then estimate consumer surplus as the area below the demand curve and above the cost of a visit—the shaded area in the figure. In this case, consumer surplus is a triangle with a base of 5 visits and a height of $50 (the difference between the y-axis intercept of $80 and the cost of $30/visit). So consumer surplus (CS) is:

$$CS = \tfrac{1}{2} * 5 * 50 = \$125.$$

Figure A6.1 **Travel Cost Demand Curve Example**

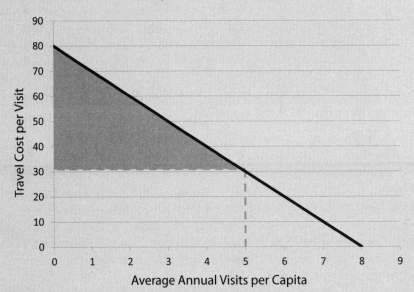

Note that this is the consumer surplus for 5 trips. The consumer surplus for an individual trip would be $25 ($125 divided by 5). If we had an estimate of the total number of trips from this zone, we could then estimate the total consumer surplus. The benefits to other zones could be obtained using the same approach, and then these benefits could be aggregated to obtain the total consumer surplus for the site, or the average consumer surplus per visitor.

_____

[o]The figure shows a linear demand curve for simplicity. Normally, a travel cost demand model is estimated as a nonlinear demand curve.

Contingent Valuation Survey Design

An important issue in assessing the validity of contingent valuation (CV) is how the valuation question is asked. There are several basic ways to ask contingent valuation questions, as illustrated in Figure A6.2 using an example of wetlands preservation:

Figure A6.2 **Contingent Valuation Question Formats**

Open-Ended Format:
What is the maximum amount you would be willing to pay annually, as a tax surcharge, to fund a wetlands protection program?

Payment Card Format:
Which of the amounts below most closely indicates your maximum willingness to pay annually, as a tax surcharge, for a wetlands protection program? Please circle your answer.

$5	$40	$80	$200	$750
$10	$50	$100	$300	$1000
$20	$60	$125	$400	$1500
$30	$75	$150	$500	$2000

Single-Bounded Format:
Would you be willing to pay $75 annually, as a tax surcharge, to fund a wetlands protection program?
Yes
No
Unsure

Double-Bounded Format:
Would you be willing to pay $75 annually, as a tax surcharge, to fund a wetlands protection program?
- If respondent answers "Yes," then ask: "Would you be willing to pay $150?"
- If respondent answers "No," then ask: "Would you be willing to pay $40?"

Multiple-Bounded Format:
For each dollar amount below, indicate whether you would be willing to pay that amount annually, as a tax surcharge, to fund a wetlands protection program?

$5	Yes	No	Unsure
$10	Yes	No	Unsure
$25	Yes	No	Unsure
$50	Yes	No	Unsure
$75	Yes	No	Unsure
$100	Yes	No	Unsure
$200	Yes	No	Unsure
$300	Yes	No	Unsure
$500	Yes	No	Unsure
$1000	Yes	No	Unsure

- *Open-ended:* Perhaps the simplest form of CV question is the open-ended format, in which a respondent is directly asked to state a maximum WTP for a desirable scenario. Thus the respondent can offer any monetary value.
- *Payment card*: The respondent is presented with numerous potential WTP amounts and picks the one that most closely represents her maximum WTP.
- *Single-bounded:* The respondent is given a single WTP amount and asked whether he would be willing to pay this amount for the scenario being studied. The WTP amount is not the same for all respondents—a range is used to provide variation and more precisely estimate average WTP. An "unsure" option may be given to allow for uncertainty. If the question is phrased as a vote on a hypothetical ballot issue, it is called a **referendum format**.
- *Double-bounded:* A limitation of the single-bounded format is that we only know whether a respondent's WTP is above or below a certain amount. In a double-bounded question, the initial WTP is followed by a second ques-

referendum format
a contingent valuation question format where the valuation question is presented as a vote on a hypothetical referendum.

tion with a different WTP amount, as shown in Figure A6.2. This format provides more precise information about someone's WTP.

- *Multiple-bounded*: Even more precise information can be obtained using the multiple-bounded format, which asks respondents to indicate whether they would be willing to pay several different amounts.

So which question format is preferred? CV questions have several potential sources of bias, so we can consider how each format reduces or exacerbates biases. One bias common in CV questions is strategic bias—when a respondent intentionally provides an incorrect WTP amount in order to advance a particular policy outcome. For example, a single-bounded question might ask a respondent whether she is willing to pay $100 per year to support protection of endangered species. While she actually would not pay this amount, she might answer "yes" because she basically supports protection of endangered species. Another bias is **yea-saying**—when a respondent agrees to pay the indicated amount because he perceives it as a "correct" answer or the answer that the researcher wants to hear. Thus yea-saying will result in an upward bias to WTP amounts. **Range bias** can be a problem with the payment card and multiple-bounded formats. This is when the respondent's answers are influenced by the range of values presented. In particular, respondents may be biased to give a WTP amount in the middle of the range.[1] While most biases lead to overestimates of WTP, protest bids occur when someone states that he is not willing to pay for something because he thinks that he already pays enough in taxes or objects to the question for another reason. Another potential bias that is an issue in any survey is **non-response bias**—when those who respond to a survey are not representative of the population under study. In such cases, the survey results cannot be extrapolated to the entire population.

Another issue in designing a CV survey is how it is administered to respondents. CV surveys can be administered by mail, phone, in person, or over the Internet. Regardless of the method used, researchers wish to obtain a high response rate, which reduces the chance of non-response bias. Response rates can be increased through follow-up contacts, such as continuing to call someone who does not answer with a phone survey or multiple mailings with a mail survey. While Internet surveys are the cheapest to administer, they also suffer from low response rates.[2] In-person surveys allow researchers to present detailed valuation scenarios and generally encourage more focus on the survey questions but are normally the most expensive to administer. As discussed in the chapter, the NOAA panel recommended in-person surveys because they allow the CV scenario to be presented in the greatest detail.

yea-saying
responding "yes" to a contingent valuation WTP question even though one's true valuation of the scenario is less, for reasons such as perceiving "yes" to be a correct answer.

range bias
a potential bias with payment card or multiple-bounded contingent valuation questions whereby the responses are influenced by the range of values presented to the respondent.

non-response bias
bias as a result of survey respondents not being representative of survey non-respondents.

APPENDIX 6.2: USING EXCEL TO PERFORM PRESENT VALUE CALCULATIONS

Present value calculations for analyses that cover many years can be performed easily using Microsoft Excel. Let's assume that we want to calculate the present value of a $20,000 annual benefit that occurs over a twenty-year period starting in Year 3 (relative to now, which is Year 0). The discount rate is 3 percent.

We would first set up a column in our spreadsheet for the years, shown as Column A in Table A6.1. The benefit will occur for twenty years starting in Year 3, so the numbers go up to 22. Note that the benefits for Years 0–2 are zero. We entered the annual benefit of $20,000 in Cell E2 and the discount rate in Cell E5. Entering these on the side will allow us to change these values easily if we want to consider a different scenario, such as a different discount rate.

Table A6.1

Using Excel to Perform Present Value Calculations

	A	B	C	D	E
1	Year	Benefit			
2	0	0		Benefit =	20,000
3	1	0			
4	2	0		Discount	
5	3	18,303		Rate =	0.03
6	4	17,770			
7	5	17,252			
8	6	16,750			
9	7	16,262			
10	8	15,788			
11	9	15,328			
12	10	14,882			
13	11	14,448			
14	12	14,028			
15	13	13,619			
16	14	13,222			
17	15	12,837			
18	16	12,463			
19	17	12,100			
20	18	11,748			
21	19	11,406			
22	20	11,074			
23	21	10,751			
24	22	10,438			
26					
27		280,469	TOTAL PV		

For Year 3 the present value of the benefit is:

$$PV = \$20,000 / (1 + 0.03)^3$$
$$= \$18,303.$$

To perform this calculation in Excel, we would enter the following exactly into Cell B5:

$$=E2 / ((1+E5)^{\wedge}A5).$$

The = is necessary to indicate you are entering a formula. Entering E2 tells Excel to use the value in Cell E2 (20,000) as the numerator of the equation. The denominator refers to the cells with the discount rate and the year. When you enter this formula, you should get a value of 18,303.

Next, copy the formula from Cell B5 to Cell B6, to obtain the present value for Year 4. You should get a value of 0—obviously not correct. If you look at the copied formula (click on Cell B6), you will see that every cell reference has been shifted down by one line. The copied formula should read:

$$=E3 / ((1+E6)^\wedge A6)$$

while we wanted to refer to Cell A6 instead of Cell A5 (Year 4 instead of Year 3), we wanted to maintain the references to Cells E2 and E5. To do this in Excel, when we enter a formula we place "$" before the column and the row to fix a reference to a specific cell. Then whenever the formula is copied, the reference won't change.

Go back to the formula in Cell B5 and revise it as follows:

$$=\$E\$2 / ((1+\$E\$5)^\wedge A5).$$

Now the references to Cells E2 and E5 are fixed, and only the reference to Cell A5 will adjust when the formula is copied. The value in Cell B5 should still be 18,303. If we copy this revised formula to Cell B6, the new value should be 17,770. The formula is Cell B6 should be:

$$=\$E\$2 / ((1+\$E\$5)^\wedge A6).$$

So we are now discounting by four years instead of three. We can then copy this formula down to all the remaining years. With each additional line down, we are discounting by an additional year. The value for the last year should be 10,438. Summing over all the years (Excel has a simple summation command), we get a total present value of $280,469, as shown in Cell B27.

With the input variables on the side, we can easily revise our analysis. Suppose that we want to redo our calculations with a 5 percent discount rate. All we would need to do is change the value in Cell E5 from 0.03 to 0.05. All calculations will automatically update. The new total present value should be $226,072 instead of $280,469.

KEY TERMS AND CONCEPTS FOR APPENDIX 6.1 AND APPENDIX 6.2

non-response bias
protest bids
range bias

referendum format
strategic bias
yea-saying

NOTES FOR APPENDIX 6.2

1. See Roach et al., 2002, for a study that found range bias with the multiple-bounded format.

2. See, for example, Marta-Pedroso et al., 2007. They conducted a CV survey using both in-person and Internet formats. While they obtained a response rate of 84 percent for in-person contacts, the response rate for the Internet survey was only 5 percent. Mail and phone survey response rates can typically exceed 50 percent when follow-up contacts are employed.

PART THREE

ECOLOGICAL ECONOMICS AND ENVIRONMENTAL ACCOUNTING

Ecological Economics: Basic Concepts

CHAPTER 7 FOCUS QUESTIONS

- Are natural resources a form of capital?
- How can we account for and conserve resources and environmental systems?
- What limits the scale of economic systems?
- How can we sustain economic well-being and ecosystem health in the long term?

7.1 AN ECOLOGICAL PERSPECTIVE

The relationships between economic and environmental issues can be viewed from a variety of perspectives. In Chapters 3–6 we applied concepts derived from standard economic analysis to environmental issues. The school of thought known as **ecological economics**, however, takes a different approach. Ecological economics attempts to redefine basic economic concepts to make them more applicable to environmental problems. As noted in Chapter 1, this often means viewing problems from a macro rather than a micro perspective, focusing on major ecological cycles and applying the logic of physical and biological systems to the human economy, rather than viewing ecosystems through a lens of economic analysis.

methodological pluralism

the view that a more comprehensive understanding of problems can be obtained using a combination of perspectives.

Unlike standard economic analysis, ecological analysis does not have a single methodological framework based on markets.[a] The ecological economist Richard Norgaard has identified this approach as **methodological pluralism**, maintaining that "multiple insights guard against mistaken action based on one perspective."[1] Through a combination of analyses and techniques, we can achieve a more comprehensive picture of the problems that we study.

This pluralist approach means that ecological economics is not necessarily incompatible with market analysis. The analyses reviewed in Chapters 3–6 offer many insights that are complementary to a broader ecological perspective. But some of the assumptions and concepts used in market analysis may need to be modified or replaced in order to gain an understanding of the interaction between the economic system and ecological systems.[2]

---

[a] "Methodology" means the set of techniques and approaches used to analyze a problem.

7.2 Natural Capital

natural capital

the available endowment of land and resources including air, water, soil, forests, fisheries, minerals, and ecological life-support systems.

One fundamental concept emphasized by ecological economists is **natural capital**. Most economic models of the production process focus on two factors of production: capital and labor. A third factor, usually referred to as "land," is acknowledged but usually has no prominent function in economic models. Classical economists of the nineteenth century, especially David Ricardo, author of *The Principles of Political Economy and Taxation*, were concerned with land and its productivity as a fundamental determinant of economic production.[3] Modern economics, however, generally assumes that technological progress will overcome any limits on the productive capacity of land.

Ecological economists have reintroduced and broadened the classical concept of "land," renaming it natural capital. Natural capital is defined as the entire endowment of land and resources available to us, including air, water, fertile soil, forests, fisheries, mineral resources, and the ecological life-support systems without which economic activity, and indeed life itself, would not be possible.

In an ecological economics perspective, natural capital should be considered at least as important as human-made capital as a basis for production. Further, a careful accounting should be made of the state of natural capital and of its improvement or deterioration, and this should be reflected in national income accounting.

Accounting for Changes in Natural Capital

net investment and disinvestment

the process of adding to, or subtracting from, productive capital over time, calculated by subtracting depreciation from gross, or total, investment.

Defining natural resources as capital raises an important economic implication. A central principle of prudent economic management is preservation of the value of capital. It is generally desirable to add to productive capital over time, a process that economists call **net investment**. A country whose productive capital decreases overtime (**net disinvestment**) is a country in economic decline.

Sir John Hicks, Nobel laureate in economics and author of *Value and Capital* (1939), defined income as the amount of goods and services that an individual or country can consume over a period while remaining at least as well off at the end of the period as at the beginning. In other words, you cannot increase your income by reducing your capital.

To see what this means in practice, imagine that you receive an inheritance of $1 million (few of us will ever be so lucky, but we can dream). Suppose that the $1 million is invested in bonds that yield a real return of 5 percent.[b] This will give an annual income of $50,000. However, if you decide to spend $100,000 per year from the inheritance, you will be spending $50,000 of capital in addition to the $50,000 income. This means that in future years, the income will be reduced, and eventually the capital will be entirely depleted. Clearly, this is different from a prudent policy of living only on income, which would allow you (and your heirs) to receive $50,000 per year indefinitely.

capital depreciation

a deduction in national income accounting for the wearing-out of capital over time.

This principle is generally accepted insofar as human-made capital is concerned. National income accounting includes a calculation of the depletion of human-made capital over time. This **capital depreciation** is estimated annually and subtracted from gross national product to obtain net national product. To maintain national wealth requires at least enough investment to replace the capital that is depleted

---

[b]Real return is return in excess of inflation.

each year. We recognize this also by distinguishing between gross and net investment. Net investment is gross investment minus depreciation and can be zero or below zero if insufficient replacement investment occurs. A negative net investment implies a decline in national wealth.

But no similar provision is made for **natural capital depreciation**. If a country cuts down its forests and converts them to timber for domestic consumption or export, this enters the national income accounts only as a positive contribution to income, equal to the value of the timber. No accounting is made of the loss of standing forest, either as an economic resource or in terms of its ecological value. From the standpoint of ecological economics, this is a serious omission that must be corrected. Ecological economists have proposed revisions to national income accounting systems so as to include natural capital depreciation (we consider these proposals in detail in Chapter 8).

The Dynamics of Natural Capital

The natural capital concept further implies that a purely economic analysis cannot fully capture the stock and flow dynamics of natural resources. As we saw in Chapter 6, economists have many techniques for expressing natural resource and environmental factors in money terms suitable for standard economic analysis. But this captures only one dimension of natural capital.

The basic laws governing behavior of natural capital elements such as energy resources, water, chemical elements, and life forms are physical laws described in the sciences of chemistry, physics, biology, and ecology. Without specific consideration of these laws, we cannot gain a full understanding of natural capital.

For example, in agricultural systems, soil fertility is determined by complex interactions among chemical nutrients, micro-organisms, water flows, and plant and animal waste recycling. Measuring soil fertility in terms of, say, grain output, will be valid for short-term economic calculations, but may be misleading over the long term as subtler ecological processes come into play. A purely economic analysis could result in insufficient attention to long-term maintenance of soil fertility.

Thus it is necessary to combine insights from economic analysis with ecological principles when dealing with issues of the maintenance of natural capital. This does not render the economic techniques of Chapters 3–6 irrelevant; rather, they must be complemented by ecological perspectives on natural systems to avoid misleading results. Techniques advocated by ecological economists for natural capital accounting and conservation include the following:

- **Physical accounting** for natural capital. In addition to the familiar national income accounts, **satellite accounts** can be constructed to show the abundance or scarcity of natural resources and to estimate their variations from year to year. These accounts can also show pollutant build-up, water quality, soil fertility variations, and other important physical indicators of environmental conditions. Accounts that indicate significant **resource depletion** or **environmental degradation** call for measures to conserve or restore natural capital.
- Determination of **sustainable yield** levels. As we saw in Chapter 4, economic exploitation of natural resources often exceeds ecologically sustainable levels. An ecological analysis of a natural system harvested for human use

---

natural capital depreciation

a deduction in national accounting for loss of natural capital, such as a reduction in the supply of timber, wildlife habitat, or mineral resources.

physical accounting

a supplement to national income accounting that estimates the stock or services of natural resources in physical, rather than economic, terms.

satellite accounts

accounts that estimate the supply of natural capital in physical, rather than monetary, terms; used to supplement traditional national income accounting.

resource depletion

a decline in the stock of a renewable resource due to human exploitation.

environmental degradation

loss of environmental resources, functions, or quality, often as a result of human economic activity.

sustainable yield

a yield or harvest level that can be maintained without diminishing the stock or population of the resource.

can help to determine the sustainable yield level at which the system can continue to operate indefinitely. If the economic equilibrium yield exceeds the sustainable yield, the resource is threatened, and specific protective policies are necessary. This has happened with many fisheries and forests, a topic dealt with in Chapters 13 and 14.

absorptive capacity of the environment

the ability of the environment to absorb and render harmless waste products.

- Determination of the **absorptive capacity of the environment** for human-generated wastes, including household, agricultural, and industrial wastes. Natural processes can break down many waste products over time and reabsorb them into the environment without damage. Other waste and pollutants, such as chlorinated pesticides, chlorofluorocarbons (CFCs), and radioactive waste are difficult or impossible for the environment to absorb. Scientific analysis can offer a baseline estimate of acceptable levels of waste emissions. This will not necessarily coincide with the economic concept of "optimal pollution levels" introduced in Chapter 3.

natural capital sustainability

conserving natural capital by limiting depletion rates and investing in resource renewal.

All these measures point toward a general principle of **natural capital sustainability**. According to this principle, countries should aim to conserve their natural capital by limiting its depletion or degradation and investing in its renewal (e.g., through soil conservation or reforestation programs). The difficult and controversial process of translating this general principle into specific policy rules brings into focus the differences between economic and ecological analyses. We deal with some of these questions in more detail in future chapters.

7.3 ISSUES OF MACROECONOMIC SCALE

Standard macroeconomic theory recognizes no limitation on an economy's scale. Keynesian, classical, and other economic theories deal with the conditions for equilibrium among the macroeconomic aggregates of consumption, savings, investment, government spending, taxes, and money supply. But with economic growth, the equilibrium level can rise indefinitely, so that a country's gross domestic product (GDP) can multiply tenfold or a hundredfold over time.

With a 5 percent growth rate, for example, GDP would double every fourteen years, becoming more than a hundred times as large within a century. Even at a 2 percent growth rate, GDP doubles in thirty-five years, growing sevenfold in a century. From the point of view of mathematical computation of economic equilibrium, such growth poses no problem. But ecological economists, in particular Robert Goodland and Herman Daly, have argued that resource and environmental factors impose practical limits on feasible levels of economic activity and that economic theory must include a concept of **optimal macroeconomic scale**.[4]

optimal macroeconomic scale

the concept that economic systems have an optimal scale level beyond which further growth leads to lower well-being or resource degradation.

This concept is relevant both for individual economies dependent on limited resource bases and for the global economy. Its implications for the global economy are especially important, because national economies can overcome resource limitations through international trade. The situation is illustrated in Figure 7.1. Although reminiscent of our original schematic showing the relationship between economic and ecological systems (see Figure 1.2 in Chapter 1), Figure 7.1 also shows the economy growing within the supporting ecosystem to the point where it applies significant physical and life-cycle stress.

In Figure 7.1, we see that the economic system (shown as a rectangle) uses both energy and resources as inputs and releases waste energy and other wastes into the

Figure 7.1a **The Economic Subsystem Relative to the Global Ecosystem (Small Scale)**

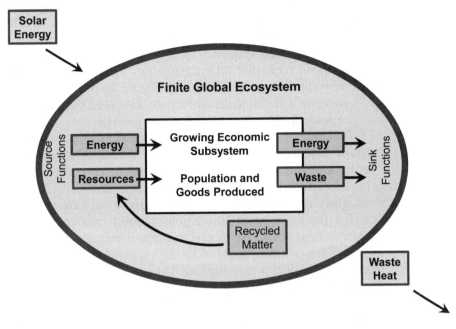

Source: Goodland, Daly, and El Serafy, 1992, p. 5.

Figure 7.1b **The Economic Subsystem Relative to the Global Ecosystem (Large Scale)**

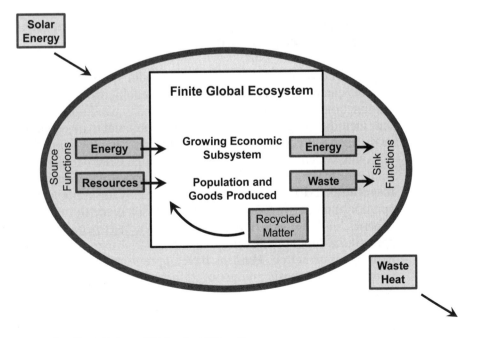

Source: Goodland, Daly, and El Serafy, 1992, p. 5.

throughput

the total use of energy and materials as both inputs and outputs of a process.

open system

a system that exchanges energy or natural resources with another system; the economic system is considered an open system because it receives energy and natural resources from the ecosystem and deposits wastes into the ecosystem.

closed system

a system that does not exchange energy or resources with another system; except for solar energy and waste heat, the global ecosystem is a closed system.

scale limit

a limit to the size of a system, including an economic system.

dematerialization

the process of achieving an economic goal through a decrease in the use of physical materials, such as making aluminum cans with less metal.

decoupling

breaking the correlation between increased economic activity and similar increases in envrionmental impacts.

net primary product of photosynthesis (NPP)

the biomass energy directly produced by photosynthesis.

ecosystem (shown as a circle). The combined input and waste flows can be called **throughput**.[5] The economic system as shown here is an **open system**, exchanging energy and resources with the global ecosystem within which it is located. The global ecosystem has an inflow of solar energy and an outflow of waste heat, but is otherwise a **closed system**.

As the open economic subsystem grows within the closed planetary ecosystem (shown by the enlarged rectangle in Figure 7.1b), its resource needs and waste flows are more difficult to accommodate. The fixed size of the planetary ecosystem places a **scale limit** on economic system growth.

This diagram refers to the *physical* growth of the economic system, measured in terms of its resource and energy demands and waste flows. It is possible for GDP to grow without higher resource requirements, especially if growth is concentrated in the service sector. Expanded automobile production, for example, requires more steel, glass, rubber, and other material inputs, as well as gasoline to operate the vehicles. But more opera productions or child-care services require few physical resources. Energy and physical resource use may also become more efficient, thus requiring fewer throughputs of resources per unit of output, a process known as **dematerialization** or **decoupling**, discussed in greater detail in Chapter 17. In general, though, growing GDP is associated with higher throughput of energy and resources.

Economic activity undoubtedly faces some scale limits. How can we determine whether the economic subsystem is straining the limits of the ecosystem? One way is simply by noting the increased prevalence of large-scale or global environmental problems, such as global climate change, ozone layer destruction, ocean pollution, soil degradation, and species loss.[6] In commonsense terms as well as in ecological analysis, these pervasive problems suggest that important environmental thresholds had been reached by the late twentieth century.[7]

Measuring the Relationship Between Economic and Ecological Systems

Ecological economists have also suggested a specific measure by which the two systems can be linked theoretically. Both ecological and economic systems have the function of using energy to support and expand the functions of life. We can thus identify energy as in some sense fundamental to all economic activity: human labor, capital investment, and natural resource exploitation all require energy.

Living systems obtain solar energy through plant photosynthesis. As the human economic system grows, a larger proportion of this **net primary product of photosynthesis (NPP)** is used directly or indirectly to support economic activity. This appropriation of photosynthetic energy takes place through agriculture, forestry, fisheries, and fuel use. In addition, human activities convert land from natural or agricultural functions for urban and industrial uses, transportation systems, and housing construction. Humans have appropriated about 40 percent of terrestrial (land) photosynthesis and about 25 percent of the global total, including ocean ecosystems.[8]

This NPP figure implies that a doubling of economic activity will bring us close to absolute limits. As we saw in Chapter 2, such a doubling is virtually certain unless population growth or economic growth rates change dramatically. We must, therefore, take the question of scale limits seriously. We look at specific implications of this issue for agriculture, energy use, and other resources in Chapters 10–19, but general implications for economic theory also emerge.

Herman Daly has argued that rapid economic growth brought us from **empty-world economics** to **full-world economics**. In the "empty world" phase, when the economic system is small relative to the ecosystem, resource and environmental limits are unimportant, and the main economic activity is the exploitation of natural resources to build up human-made capital stocks and to expand consumption. At this stage, economic activity is constrained mainly by limited quantities of human-made capital.

In the "full-world" phase, however, when the dramatically expanded human economic system presses against ecosystem limits, the conservation of natural capital becomes far more important. If we do not implement adequate measures to conserve resources and protect the "full-world" environment, environmental degradation will undermine economic activity regardless of how large stocks of human-made capital become.[9]

This perspective differs in significant respects from standard economic theory, which generally assumes **substitutability** between resources. For example, industrially produced fertilizer might compensate for loss of fertile soil. The ecological perspective tells us that substitution is not so easy—the natural resource base for economic activity is in a sense irreplaceable, unlike human-made factories or machinery. In the case of fertilizer, heavy applications of fertilizer can deplete other nutrients in the soil as well as polluting waterways with fertilizer runoff.

In many cases, natural capital displays **complementarity** rather than substitutability with manufactured capital—meaning that both are needed for effective production. For example, increasing the stock of fishing boats will be of no use if stocks of fish are depleted (as discussed in Chapters 4 and 13). The essential function of natural capital means that we need to modify standard theories of economic growth to take into account issues of ecological limits and long-term sustainability.[10]

7.4 LONG-TERM SUSTAINABILITY

We have already mentioned sustainability in terms of natural capital. But how can this term be defined more precisely? We want to limit the loss or degradation of natural capital and to invest in its conservation and renewal. Taken in its strictest sense, this would mean that we could never use any depletable resource or conduct any economic activity that would substantially alter natural systems. In a world of more than 7 billion people, largely either industrialized or rapidly industrializing, this is clearly impossible. But unrestrained resource use and ever-increasing waste generation is also unacceptable. How can we strike the balance?

We have already examined elements of the standard economic answer to this question. The theories of external economies, resource allocation over time, and common-property and public goods management, which we outlined in Chapters 3–5, offer economic principles on when to use and when to conserve resources and on "optimal" pollution levels. In the long-term global context, however, these theories may be insufficient. Oriented toward individual markets, they may fail to guarantee environmental sustainability at the macroeconomic level. We need guidelines for overall conservation of the national and global resource bases. Within these guidelines, market solutions to specific resource and environmental management problems will become relevant.

empty-world and full-world economics

the view that economic approaches to environmental issues should differ depending on whether the scale of the economy relative to the ecosystem is small (an empty world) or large (a full world).

substitutability (of human-made and natural capital)

the ability of one resource or input to substitute for another; in particular, the ability of human-made capital to compensate for the depletion of some types of natural capital.

complementarity

the property of being used together in production or consumption, for example, the use of gasoline and automobiles.

We can distinguish between the concepts of **strong sustainability** and **weak sustainability**. (The use of the terms "strong" and "weak" in this context refers to how demanding our assumptions are and does not imply that one is necessarily better or worse than the other.) Strong sustainability is based on an assumption of very limited substitutability between natural and human-made capital. Weak sustainability assumes that natural and human-made capital are generally substitutable.[11]

Taking the strong sustainability approach, we would keep separate accounts for human-made and natural capital and ensure that overall natural capital stocks were not depleted. It would be acceptable, for example, to cut down forests in one area only if similar forests were being expanded elsewhere so that the overall forest stock remained constant. Petroleum stocks could be depleted only if alternative energy sources of equal capacity were simultaneously developed. The implementation of strong sustainability would require extensive government intervention in markets and a radical change in the nature of economic activity.

Weak sustainability is easier to achieve. This principle allows for substitutability between natural and human-made capital, provided that the total value of capital is maintained. This may allow us, for example, to cut down forests in order to expand agriculture or industry. It does require, however, that there be an adequate accounting for the *value* of the cleared forest. The forest-clearing activity would not be acceptable unless the value generated in new human-made capital was greater than the value lost.

This principle is closer to standard economic theory. A private owner presumably would make such a calculation and would not willingly exchange a higher-valued resource for a lower-valued one. Government intervention would, however, be required to maintain even weak sustainability when:

- Private owners fail to consider the full ecological value of natural capital (say, a forest products company that considers timber values but is indifferent to endangered species).
- Property rights in natural resources are poorly defined, as is often true in developing countries. This can lead to the rapid plundering of a natural resource base by holders of short-term concessions or illegal users.
- Private property owners have short-term perspectives and fail to consider long-term effects such as cumulative soil erosion.
- Common property resources or public goods are involved.
- Truly irreplaceable resources are at issue, as in the case of species extinction or limited water supplies in arid areas.

Policy Choices and Discounting the Future

The choice between strong and weak sustainability may be difficult. In managing forest resources, for example, strong sustainability may be too restrictive, requiring a country to maintain the same area of forest cover under all circumstances. Weak sustainability, however, places no inherent limits on the amount of forest that can be cut, requiring only a sound economic accounting of its value. Although a middle ground must be defined, this cannot happen simply through the market process. It must be a conscious social choice.

One crucial factor in defining this middle ground is the issue of *discounting the future*. Our discussions of resource allocation over time (Chapter 5) and of cost-benefit analysis (Chapter 6) have highlighted the importance of the discount rate in market choices regarding resource use. In general, the higher the discount rate, the greater the incentive to exploit resources in the present. According to Hotelling's rule, private owners must expect a resource's net price to rise at a rate at least equal to the interest rate before they will conserve that resource for the future. This rarely occurs for most depletable natural resources.

Consider that at a 5 percent discount rate, net resource prices would be expected to double every fourteen years to induce conservation. Otherwise it is more profitable for the owner to extract the resource immediately and invest the proceeds at 5 percent. For renewable resources such as forests, the annual yield must be at least equal to the market rate of interest for private owners to practice sustainable management (see Chapter 14 for a full treatment of this issue). At lower yields, economic incentives favor clear-cutting the forest for immediate monetary gains. In effect, this means treating the renewable resource as a depletable resource and "mining" it out as fast as possible.

The logic of discounting imposes a stiff test on natural resource systems. Unless they can meet a certain yield level, immediate exploitation will take precedence over sustainable management. If major ecological systems and important natural resources fail this test, the resulting rush to exploit resources as fast as possible will make little provision for the future.

Here the strong sustainability principle becomes relevant: Can we trust that a world with much more human-made capital but a severely depleted resource base will meet the needs of the future? Or should we impose a stronger principle of resource conservation to guard our own and future generations' interests?

This is not a philosophical debate about the long-term future. Many high-quality mineral resources could be largely used up within thirty to forty years; tropical forests could be virtually eliminated in the same period; ocean and atmospheric systems could be severely degraded; soil erosion could destroy the fertility of hundreds of millions of acres of cropland within a generation. Applying a strict commercial discounting principle, all this destruction could be seen as quite "rational" and even "optimal."

Norgaard and Howarth have argued against using market-based discount rates to guide decisions on long-term resource use. They recommend using a sustainability criterion to promote **intergenerational equity**.[12] In this view, it is wrong to decide issues of long-term investment and conservation in the present simply by applying profit-maximizing criteria. This calls for social judgment on conservation of resources for the future.

Complexity, Irreversibility, and the Precautionary Principle

Another major justification for a sustainability criterion relates to **ecological complexity** and **irreversibility**. Current ecological systems have evolved over many centuries to achieve a balance involving interactions among thousands of species of plants and animals (the total number of species is unknown but is in the millions), as well as delicately balanced physical and chemical relationships in the atmosphere, oceans, and in freshwater and terrestrial ecosystems.

Extensive exploitation of natural resources permanently alters these ecological balances, with effects that are not fully predictable. In some cases, upsetting

intergenerational equity
the distribution of resources, including human-made and natural capital, across human generations.

ecological complexity
the presence of many different living and nonliving elements in an ecosystem, interacting in complex patterns; ecosystem complexity implies that the impacts of human actions on ecosystems may be unpredictable.

irreversibility
the concept that some human impacts on the environment may cause damage that cannot be reversed, such as the extinction of species.

the ecological balance can lead to disaster—desertification, collapse of ocean food systems, destruction of the ozone layer, pollution of aquifers, outbreaks of superpests resistant to insecticides, and the like. Species extinction is a clear example of irreversible damage, imposing unknown economic and ecological costs in the future.

Ecological economists therefore argue for a **precautionary principle**—we should strive for minimum interference with the operation of natural systems, especially where we cannot predict long-term effects. This principle obviously defies easy definition in economic calculations of resource value and use. Such calculations, therefore, are of value only if we can place them in the broader ecological context, whose priorities must sometimes override market equilibrium logic.

7.5 ENERGY AND ENTROPY

As noted above, ecological economics places a special focus on energy. This implies looking to the laws of physics to understand fundamental drivers and limitations on ecosystems and economies. The **first law of thermodynamics** states that matter and energy can be neither created nor destroyed (although matter can be transmuted into energy through nuclear processes). This means that any physical process, including all economic processes, can be seen as a transformation of matter and energy from one form to another. The **second law of thermodynamics** tells us something more about the nature of this transformation. It states that in all physical processes energy is degraded from an *available* to an *unavailable* state.

The formal measure of this process is called **entropy**. Entropy is a measure of the *unavailable* energy in a system, so according to the second law entropy increases as natural processes proceed. The concept of entropy can also be applied to resources other than energy. An easily usable resource, for example a high-grade metal ore, has low entropy. A poorer grade of ore has higher entropy; it can also be used, but only through the application of energy from some other source to refine it.

The best way to understand this rather slippery entropy concept is to think in terms of a specific example, such as burning a lump of coal. In its original state, coal has low entropy—that is, it contains available energy. This energy can be obtained by burning the coal. Once burned, the coal is transformed into ashes and waste heat. The energy can now no longer be used, and the system has moved to a high entropy state.

Nicholas Georgescu-Roegen, a pioneer of ecological economic thought, argued that this law of entropy should be seen as the fundamental governing principle of economics.[14] All economic processes require energy, and transform energy from a usable to an unusable form. The physical outputs of any economic process thus can be said to contain **embodied energy**.

For example, an automobile embodies energy used to produce steel and to shape the steel into auto parts, as well as the energy used by workers to assemble it (or the energy used to run assembly-line robots). It also, of course, will require additional fuel energy to run. But eventually all this energy ends up in an unusable form. The fuel energy is dissipated in waste heat and pollution. The car is eventually scrapped and itself becomes waste. In the process, it has provided transportation services to its users, but the net result is the degradation of usable energy and resources into an unusable form.

precautionary principle
the view that policies should account for uncertainty by taking steps to avoid low-probability but catastrophic events.

first and second laws of thermodynamics
physical laws stating that matter and energy cannot be destroyed, only transformed, and that all physical processes lead to a decrease in available energy (an increase in entropy).

entropy
a measure of the unavailable energy in a system; according to the second law of thermodynamics entropy increases in all physical processes.

embodied energy
the total energy required to produce a good or service, including both direct and indirect uses of energy.

If we think about the economic process from this perspective, two points become clear. One is that the economic process requires a continual stream of usable energy and resources (low entropy). The other is that it produces a continual stream of waste energy and other waste products (high entropy). Thus the input and output flows of resources and energy to and from the economic system become the fundamental governing mechanisms of production.

This perspective differs dramatically from standard economic theory, in which labor and capital inputs usually rank as the fundamental productive factors. Energy and resource inputs are often not specifically considered and sometimes omitted altogether. Energy and resource prices have no special significance over other input prices, and waste-flow effects, as we have seen, are generally defined as externalities rather than as a central reality of production.

The standard approach works well enough when energy and resources are abundant and cheap and when the environment easily absorbs waste and pollution damage. But as energy and resource demands grow, along with waste and pollution, the entropy perspective emerges as an important factor in understanding the relationship between the economic and ecological systems.

Energy Flows and the Economic Production System

solar flux
the continual flow of solar energy to the earth.

Existing ecological systems are precisely organized for the efficient capture of energy. Millennia of evolution have developed complex and interdependent life systems that draw energy from the environment, using the **solar flux** (flow of sunlight). The fundamental process in all ecosystems is photosynthesis, by which green plants use the sun's energy to produce the organic compounds necessary for life. All animal life is completely dependent on plant photosynthesis, since animals lack the ability to utilize the solar flux directly.

Viewed from the perspective of the entropy law, the economic process is essentially an extension of the biological process of using low entropy to support life activity and, at the same time, increasing overall entropy. Industrial systems greatly increase the use rate of entropy. Low-entropy mineral deposits and stored low-entropy in the form of fossil fuels are mined to support the industrial process. Intensive agriculture also "mines" the stored resources of the soil. At the same time, the industrial system greatly increases the emission of high-entropy waste products into the environment.

In standard economic theory, there are no inherent limits to growth. But the entropy theory implies that there are limits; economic systems must operate subject to the constraints of:

- Limited stocks of low-entropy resources, in particular high-grade ores and easily available fossil fuels;
- Limited capacity of soils and biological systems to capture solar energy to produce food and other biological resources;
- Limited capacity of the ecosystem to absorb high-entropy waste products.

In some cases, it may be possible to evade specific constraints. For example, we can increase the productivity of soils through adding artificial fertilizers. We cannot evade the entropy law, however, since fertilizer production itself requires energy. In effect, we can expand the limits of the agricultural system by "borrowing" low entropy from somewhere, but only with more rapid use of energy resources (and faster generation of waste and pollution). The one truly "free" source of low entropy is solar energy. Even in the case of solar energy, there are usually material and labor costs involved in capturing and using the available energy.

We can apply the entropy perspective to many different sectors of production: the energy sector itself, agriculture, mining, forestry, fishing, and other industrial sectors. This often gives a different picture of how these economic activities operate. A mining industry, for example, may show increasing productivity over time, measured in standard terms of output relative to labor or capital inputs. But if we concentrate on output per unit of energy inputs, we could well see declining productivity. In other words, we need increasing amounts of energy to achieve the same output as the quality of the mined ore declines.

In this case, we are substituting energy for labor and capital, an economically advantageous choice so long as energy is cheap. However, it means that our economic system becomes more dependent on fossil fuels, which as we will see in Chapter 13, provide over 80 percent of our industrial energy. Pollution problems associated with fossil fuels also increase.

Ecological economic analysis thus emphasizes the physical basis of production, as opposed to the economic costs of production. This provides a direct link to the physical realities of planetary ecosystems. If we focus only on economic costs, even though we attempt to internalize resource depletion and environmental costs, we may miss the full scope of resource and environmental impacts of economic activity.

Modeling Economic and Ecological Systems

Ecological economics has also sought different techniques of modeling economic and ecological systems. It may be possible to integrate the analysis of different processes to give a comprehensive picture of economic and ecological activity. Such an integrated analysis is depicted in Figure 7.2. This example shows a schematic of economic and ecological flows in the city of Brabant, the Netherlands.

Local natural resource systems provide inputs to the farms and industries of Brabant. Other inputs, including fossil fuels, are imported, and the products of industry are exported. Agricultural production in Brabant provides products both for local consumption and for export. Industry, agriculture, and households all draw on local water systems, which suffer some pollution from nitrate and pesticides runoff. Forests provide outdoor recreation as well as inputs for wood-processing industries. Agricultural runoff also affects forests as well as heathlands (upland moors).

A model of this kind can be used to gain insight into patterns of economic production, land use, and environmental change. While some of the flows in the system are governed by economic rules, others are biophysical in nature. The model attempts to capture the interactions between the two systems as well as their changes over time.

As we explore resource and environment topic areas in Chapters 9–19, we bear in mind the tension between the standard economic techniques outlined in Chapters

Figure 7.2 **Ecological-Economic Model of Brabant, the Netherlands**

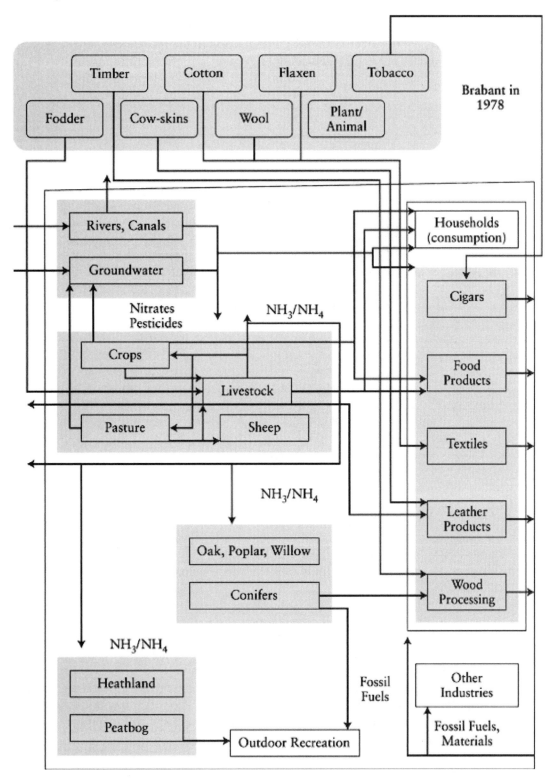

Source: Adapted from Braat and Steetskamp, 1991, p. 283.

3–6 and the general principles of ecological economics set forth in this chapter. In addition, before moving to consideration of specific topic areas, we examine some new analytical techniques developed by ecological economists. One important issue is adding an environmental dimension to the measurement of economic output or GDP, or perhaps replacing GDP with a more inclusive measure of human well-being and ecosystem health. We deal with this topic in Chapter 8.

SUMMARY

Ecological economics takes a different approach from standard environmental economic analysis based on markets. It emphasizes the dependence of the human economy on natural ecosystems and gives special emphasis to the concept of natural capital. While much of standard economics is concerned with the accumulation and productivity of human-made capital, ecological economics focuses on the maintenance of the natural capital systems that support life and economic activity. Natural capital includes all the natural resources, oceans, atmosphere, and ecosystems of the planet. These must be accounted for and should be managed according to sustainable principles, so that their functions are not degraded over time.

In this perspective, economic systems cannot grow without limit but must achieve a sustainable scale for economic activity at which the planet's ecosystems are not subjected to undue stress. Significant evidence indicates that current economic activity exceeds these limits or badly strains them. One measure of this is the proportion of photosynthetic energy appropriated for human use, now about 40 percent of terrestrial photosynthesis. Significant further growth in human demand would thus leave little room for other living systems of the earth.

The concept of sustainability, although important to managing natural capital, is difficult to define. A "weak" definition relies on the possibility of replacing natural ecosystem functions with human-made substitutes. A "strong" definition assumes that humans have limited ability to replace natural system functions and that a sustainable society must therefore maintain most of its natural systems without significant depletion or degradation.

Long-term sustainability involves issues of discounting the future and the question of our responsibility to provide for future generations. Economic incentives and property rights systems affect decisions regarding resource use, as does public policy on resource management. A precautionary principle is appropriate in cases in which irreversible effects may result from damage to complex ecosystems. Resource conservation for future generations requires social judgment in addition to economic calculation.

A special focus on energy in the economic system emphasizes the principle of entropy: Available energy is limited, and its use governs all physical processes, including ecological and economic systems. This places a special importance on the use of solar energy and the limits of fossil-fuel energy. In general, an entropy analysis shows the limits of economic activity and the ecological price to be paid for exceeding these limits.

The principles of ecological and of standard economics are both relevant to resource management issues. Sometimes the principles will conflict, but it is important to consider how best to apply both to specific resource and environmental issues as well as to the measurement of economic output, human well-being, and ecosystem health.

KEY TERMS AND CONCEPTS

absorptive capacity of the environment
capital depreciation
closed system
complementarity
decoupling
dematerialization
discounting the future
ecological complexity
ecological economics
embodied energy
empty-world economics
entropy
environmental degradation
first and second laws of thermodynamics
full-world economics
intergenerational equity
irreversibility
methodological pluralism

natural capital
natural capital depreciation
natural capital sustainability
net investment and disinvestment
net primary product of photosynthesis (NPP)
open system
optimal macroeconomic scale
physical accounting
precautionary principle
resource depletion
satellite accounts
scale limit
solar flux
strong and weak sustainability
substitutability
sustainable yield
throughput

DISCUSSION QUESTIONS

1. In what respects is "natural capital" similar to human-made capital, and in what respects does it differ? We often speak of a "return to capital," meaning the stream of income generated by a capital investment. Can we speak of a return to natural capital? What are examples of investment in natural capital? Who is motivated to make such investments? Who would suffer if such investments were not made, or if "disinvestment" occurs due to resource depletion or environmental degradation?

2. Is the concept of optimal scale for an economy useful? If so, how would you go about determining it? Do you think that economies such as those in the United States, Europe, and Japan have reached optimal scale? Exceeded it? How about the economies of Latin America? of Asia? of Africa? How would you relate the concept of optimal scale in the global economy to economic growth in national economies at different levels of development?

3. Distinguish the concepts of strong and weak sustainability, and give some practical examples, other than those cited in the text, for their application. Where is each concept most appropriate? Which economic policy measures are relevant to achieving sustainability?

NOTES

1. Norgaard, 1989.
2. For a more detailed account of the development of ecological economics and its relation to economic theory, see Costanza et al., 2012; Krishnan et al., 1995; Martinez-Alier and Røpke, 2008.

3. See Ricardo, 1951 (original publication 1817).
4. See Daly, 1996; Goodland et al., 1992.
5. See Daly, 2007.
6. See, for example, Goodland et al., 1992, chaps. 1 and 2; Meadows et al., 2002; Randers, 2012.
7. For a detailed assessment of environmental limits, see Millennium Ecosystem Assessment, 2005.
8. Vitousek et al., 1986.
9. See Daly and Farley, 2011, chap. 7.
10. For discussion of the implications of an ecological economics perspective for growth theory, see Daly, 1996; Harris and Goodwin, 2003.
11. A discussion of the principles of strong and weak sustainability is in Daly, 2007; Martinez-Alier and Røpke, 2008, part VI A; Neumayer, 2003.
12. Norgaard and Howarth, 1991; see also Padilla, 2002; Page, 1997.
13. Application of the precautionary principle is discussed in Tickner and Geiser, 2004.
14. Georgescu-Roegen, 1993.

REFERENCES

Braat, Leon C., and Ineke Steetskamp. 1991. "Ecological Economic Analysis for Regional Sustainable Development." In *Ecological Economics,* ed. Robert Costanza. New York: Columbia University Press.

Costanza, Robert, John Cumberland, Herman Daly, Robert Goodland, and Richard Norgaard, eds. 2012. *An Introduction to Ecological Economics,* 2d ed. Boca Raton, FL: CRC Press.

Daly, Herman E., 1996. *Beyond Growth: The Economics of Sustainable Development.* Cheltenham, UK; Northampton, MA: Edward Elgar.

———. 2007. *Ecological Economics and Sustainable Development: Selected Essays of Herman Daly.* Cheltenham, UK; Northampton, MA: Edward Elgar.

Daly, Herman E., and Joshua Farley. 2011. *Ecological Economics: Principles and Applications.* Washington, DC: Island Press.

Georgescu-Roegen, Nicholas. 1993. "The Entropy Law and the Economic Problem." In *Valuing the Earth: Economics, Ecology, Ethics,* ed. Herman E. Daly. Cambridge, MA: MIT Press.

Goodland, Robert, Herman Daly, and Salah El-Serafy, eds. 1992. *Population, Technology, and Lifestyle: The Transition to Sustainability.* Paris, France: United Nations Educational, Scientific and Cultural Organization (UNESCO).

Harris, Jonathan M., and Neva R. Goodwin. 2003. "Reconciling Growth and Environment." In *New Thinking in Macroeconomics,* ed. Jonathan M. Harris and Neva R. Goodwin. Cheltenham, UK: Edward Elgar.

Harris, Jonathan M., Timothy A. Wise, Kevin P. Gallagher, and Neva R. Goodwin, eds. 2001. *A Survey of Sustainable Development: Social and Economic Dimensions.* Washington, DC: Island Press.

Hicks, Sir John R. 1939. *Value and Capital.* Oxford: Oxford University Press.

Krishnan, Rajaram, Jonathan M. Harris, and Neva R. Goodwin, eds. 1995. *A Survey of Ecological Economics.* Washington, DC: Island Press.

Martinez-Alier, Joan, and Inge Røpke. 2008. *Recent Developments in Ecological Economics.* Cheltenham, UK; Northampton, MA: Edward Elgar.

Meadows, Donnella, et al. 2002. *Limits to Growth: The Thirty Year Update.* White River Junction, VT: Chelsea Green.

Millennium Ecosystem Assessment. 2005. *Ecosystems and Human Well-Being: Synthesis* and *Volume 1: Current State and Trends.* Washington, DC: Island Press.

Neumayer, Eric. 2003. *Weak Versus Strong Sustainability: Exploring the Limits of Two Opposing Paradigms.* Cheltenham, UK: Edward Elgar.

Norgaard, Richard B. 1989. "The Case for Methodological Pluralism." *Ecological Economics* 1 (February): 37–57.

Norgaard, Richard B., and Richard B. Howarth. 1991. "Sustainability and Discounting the Future." In *Ecological Economics,* ed. Robert Costanza. New York: Columbia University Press.

Padilla, Emilio. 2002. "Intergenerational Equity and Sustainability." *Ecological Economics* 41 (April): 69–83.

Page, Talbot. 1997. "On the Problem of Achieving Efficiency and Equity, Intergenerationally." *Land Economics* 73 (November): 580–596.

Randers, Jorgen. 2012. *2052: A Global Forecast for the Next Forty Years.* White River Junction, VT: Chelsea Green.

Ricardo, David. 1951. "On the Principles of Political Economy and Taxation." In *The Works and Correspondence of David Ricardo*, ed. Piero Sraffa. Cambridge: Cambridge University Press. Original publication 1817.

Tickner, Joel A., and Ken Geiser. 2004. "The Precautionary Principle Stimulus for Solutions- and Alternatives-based Environmental Policy." *Environmental Impact Assessment Review* 24: 801–824.

Vitousek, P.M., P.R. Ehrlich, A.H. Ehrlich, and P.A. Matson. 1986. "Human Appropriation of the Products of Photosynthesis." *BioScience* 36 (6): 368–73.

WEB SITES

1. **www.ecoeco.org.** Web site for the International Society for Ecological Economics, "dedicated to advancing understanding of the relationships among ecological, social, and economic systems for the mutual well-being of nature and people." Their site includes links to research and educational opportunities in ecological economics.

2. **www.uvm.edu/giee/.** Web site for the Gund Institute for Ecological Economics at the University of Vermont, which "transcends traditional disciplinary boundaries in order to address the complex interrelationships between ecological and economic systems in a broad and comprehensive way." The Gund Institute sponsors the EcoValue project, which "provides an interactive decision support system for assessing and reporting the economic value of ecosystem goods and services in geographic context."

3. **www.biotech-info.net/precautionary.html.** Information provided by the Science and Environmental Health Network (SEHN), which promotes the precautionary principle as it relates to biotechnology and food engineering. Includes articles on definitions and applications of the precautionary principle.

National Income and Environmental Accounting

CHAPTER 8 FOCUS QUESTIONS

- Do traditional national income accounting measures fail to account for the environment?
- How can traditional measures be adjusted to better reflect the importance of natural capital and environmental quality?
- What is the potential for alternative "green" measures of national welfare?

8.1 GREENING THE NATIONAL INCOME ACCOUNTS

natural capital
the available endowment of land and resources including air, water, soil, forests, fisheries, minerals, and ecological life-support systems.

gross national product (GNP)
the total market value of all final goods and services produced by citizens of a particular country in a year, regardless of where such production takes place.

gross domestic product (GDP)
the total market value of all final goods and services produced within a national border in a year.

Taking **natural capital** and environmental quality seriously affects the way that we evaluate measures of national income and well-being. Can we say that a country with a higher per capita income is necessarily better off than a similar country with a lower per capita national income? The overall well-being of a country is dependent on many factors other than income levels, including health, education levels, social cohesion, and political participation. But most important from the point of view of environmental analysis, a country's well-being is also a function of natural capital levels and environmental quality.

Standard measures of **gross national product (GNP)** or **gross domestic product (GDP)** are commonly used to measure a country's level of economic activity and progress in development, with GDP being the most frequently used measure.[a] (See Appendix 8.1 for an introduction to national income accounting.) Macroeconomic analyses and international comparisons are based on these measures, and they are widely recognized as important standards of economic progress.

Many analysts have pointed out that these measures can give a highly misleading impression of economic and human development. To be fair, GDP was never intended to be an accurate measure of a country's well-being. But politicians and economists often place disproportionate importance on GDP and act as if maximiz-

---

[a] The difference between GNP and GDP concerns whether foreign earnings are included. GNP includes the earnings of a country's citizens and corporations regardless of where they are located in the world. GDP includes all earnings within a country's borders, even the earnings of foreign citizens and corporations. GDP is the measure more commonly used when comparing international statistics.

ing it is the primary objective of public policy. But maximizing GDP can conflict with other goals such as promoting social equity or protecting the environment.

While GDP accurately reflects the production of marketed goods and services, it fails to provide a broader measure of social welfare. Some of the common critiques of standard accounting measures such as GDP include:

- *Volunteer work is not accounted for.* Standard measures do not count the benefits of volunteer work, even though such work can contribute to social well-being as much as paid work.
- *Household production is not included.* While standard accounting measures include the paid labor from such market household activities as housekeeping and gardening, these services are not counted when they are unpaid.
- *No consideration is made for changes in leisure time.* A country's GDP rises if, ceteris paribus, total work hours increase.[b] However, no accounting is made for the loss of leisure time.
- **Defensive expenditures** *are included.* One example is expenditures on police protection. If police expenditures are increased to counter a rise in crime levels, the increased spending raises GDP, but no consideration is made for the negative impacts of higher crime rates.
- *The distribution of income is not considered.* Two countries with the same GDP per capita may have significantly different income distributions and, consequently, different levels of overall well-being.
- *Non-economic contributors to well-being are excluded.* GDP does not consider the health of a country's citizens, education levels, political participation, or other social and political factors that may significantly affect well-being levels.

In our study of environmental issues, we must add another major criticism of standard accounting measures—they fail to account for environmental degradation and resource depletion. This issue can be important especially in developing countries, which depend heavily on natural resources. If a country cuts down its forests, depletes its soil fertility, and pollutes its water supplies, this surely makes the country poorer in some very real sense. But national income accounts merely record the market value of the timber, agricultural produce, and industrial output as positive contributions to GDP. This may lead policy makers to view the country's development in an unrealistically rosy light—at least until the effects of the environmental damage become apparent, which in some cases may be decades.

If we are measuring social welfare with, so to speak, the wrong ruler, we may obtain policy prescriptions that could actually make a country worse off, rather than better off. Economic growth alone does not necessarily represent true economic development and may even lower human well-being if it is accompanied by growing inequity and environmental degradation. The attempt to define better measures of development has led to new proposals to adjust or replace traditional accounting measures in order to take into account resource and environmental factors. In this chapter, we discuss the estimation and application of several of these alternatives.

defensive expenditures (approach)

a pollution valuation methodology based on the expenditures households take to avoid or mitigate their exposure to a pollutant.

---

[b]*Ceteris paribus*, a Latin phrase that means "other things equal," is used by economists to make clear what assumptions are used as the basis of an analysis.

System of Environmental and Economic Accounts (SEEA)

a guidebook developed by the United Nations to provide standards for incorporating natural capital and environmental quality into national accounting systems.

Efforts to develop "greener" accounting measures are relatively new. Interest in inclusion of the environment in national accounting began in the 1970s and 1980s, when several European countries began to estimate physical accounts for natural resources such as forests, water, and land resources.[1] In 1993 the United Nations published a comprehensive handbook on environmental accounting, which was revised in 2003 and further systematized in 2012.[2] The 2003 **System of Environmental and Economic Accounts** (commonly referred to as SEEA-2003) describes four basic approaches to environmental accounting:[3]

1. *Measuring the relationships between the environment and the economy in both directions.*[c] This approach seeks to quantify the ways various economic sectors are dependent upon natural resources as well as the way the environment is affected by different economic activities. For example, one might seek to estimate how much air pollution results when different industrial sectors increase their production levels. These accounts combine monetary data with information on the flow of materials, pollution, and energy in an economy. A key motivation for this approach is to determine how closely economic activity is linked to material inputs and pollution outputs.

2. *Measuring environmental economic activities.* This approach measures expenditures on environmental protection and the impact of economic policies, such as taxes and subsidies, to reduce environmental damages.

3. *Environmental asset accounts.* This approach collects data on the levels of various types of natural capital, such as forests, minerals, and groundwater. As we discuss later in this chapter, these accounts (also called natural resource or **satellite accounts**) can be kept in either physical units or monetary terms.

4. *Adjusting existing accounting measures to account for natural capital degradation.* This approach seeks to monetize the damages associated with the depletion of natural resources and environmental quality degradation, as well as identify defensive expenditures made in response to, or in order to avoid, environmental damages. This approach essentially takes existing national accounting measures and makes a monetary deduction to represent environmental damages.

satellite accounts

accounts that estimate the supply of natural capital in physical, rather than monetary, terms; used to supplement traditional national income accounting.

Note that these approaches are not necessarily mutually exclusive—we could theoretically implement all of them simultaneously. While many countries have adopted one or more of these accounts to some extent, no country has fully implemented the SEEA-2003 provisions. In this chapter, we focus mainly on the last two of these approaches. In addition, we consider proposals for entirely new national welfare measures that seek to provide a fundamentally different perspective on measuring national welfare.

Before we delve into specific measures, it is important to note that there is no universally accepted approach to environmental accounting. While various measures have been developed and implemented, there is no uniform standard for alternative national accounting. We consider the future of environmental accounting at the end of the chapter.

---

[c]This approach is referred to as "physical flow accounts" or "hybrid accounts."

8.2 Environmentally Adjusted Net Domestic Product

green accounting
general term applied to efforts to incorporate natural resources and environmental quality into national accounting techniques.

net domestic product (NDP)
gross domestic product minus the value of depreciation of produced, or human-made, capital.

Perhaps the most basic approach to **green accounting** is to start with traditional measures and make adjustments that reflect environmental concerns (the fourth approach previously described in the SEEA-2003). In current national income accounting, it is commonly recognized that some of each year's economic production is offset by the depreciation of manufactured, or fixed, capital, such as buildings and machinery.[d] In other words, while economic activity provides society with the benefits of new goods and services, each year the value of previously produced assets declines, and this loss of benefits should be accounted for. Thus standard national accounting methods produce estimates of **net domestic product** (NDP), which starts with GDP and then deducts the annual depreciation value of existing fixed capital:

$$NDP = GDP - D_m$$

where D_m is the depreciation of fixed capital. In 2011 the GDP of the United States was $15.1 trillion. But the depreciation of fixed capital that year totaled $1.9 trillion.[e] Thus the NDP of the United States in 2011 was about $13.2 trillion.

environmentally adjusted net domestic product (EDP)
a national accounting measure that deducts a monetary value from net domestic product to account for natural capital depreciation.

Taking this logic a step further, we realize that each year the value of natural capital may also depreciate as a result of resource extraction or environmental degradation. In some cases, the value of natural capital could increase as well if environmental quality improves. The net annual change in the value of natural capital in a country can simply be added or subtracted from NDP to obtain what has been called **environmentally adjusted NDP** (EDP). So we would obtain EDP as:

$$EDP = GDP - D_m - D_n$$

natural capital depreciation
a deduction in national accounting for loss of natural capital, such as a reduction in the supply of timber, wildlife habitat, or mineral resources.

where D_n is the depreciation of natural capital. This measure requires estimating **natural capital depreciation** in monetary terms, rather than physical units such as biomass volume or habitat area. The methods discussed in Chapter 6 can theoretically be used to estimate such values, but obviously estimating all types of natural capital depreciation in monetary terms is a daunting task that would require many assumptions. Thus the estimates of EDP that have been produced focus on only a few categories of natural capital depreciation.

One of the earliest attempts at green accounting estimated EDP for Indonesia over a fourteen-year period, 1971–1984.[4] This pioneering analysis deducted the value of depreciation for three categories of natural capital: oil, forests, and soil. The values of GDP and EDP over this time period are displayed in Figure 8.1.[f]

While the data in Figure 8.1 are somewhat older, the results present several important points that will continue to be relevant as we proceed through this chapter:

[d]Depreciation is simply a measure of the loss of capital value through wear and tear. For accounting purposes, it can be calculated using a "straight-line" formula according to which, for example, a new machine is estimated to lose 10 percent of its original value each year over a ten-year period, or using more complex valuation methods.

[e]Estimates of fixed capital depreciation are obtained from tax records. Businesses are not taxed on the value of their fixed capital depreciation—thus they have a strong incentive to claim this deduction.

[f]The analysis actually refers to EDP as NDP, which they called "adjusted net domestic product." But to avoid confusion with the more common usage of the term "net domestic product"—only deducting for fixed capital depreciation—we call their environmentally adjusted values EDP.

Figure 8.1 **Indonesian GDP Adjusted for Resource Depreciation, 1971–1984**

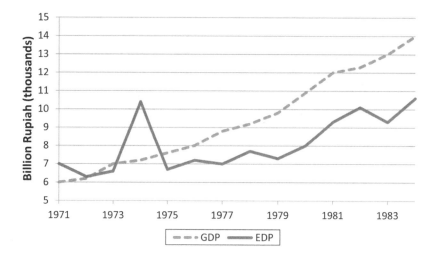

Source: Repetto et al., 1989.

1. *Natural capital depreciation can amount to a significant portion of GDP.* According to this analysis, EDP is normally about 20 percent lower than GDP. In other words, natural capital depreciation offsets about 20 percent of total economic production. Thus GDP presents an overly positive assessment of social welfare and can be a misleading guide for national policy (see Box 8.1).

2. *Measuring the growth of GDP to illustrate changes in social welfare may not produce accurate results.* Over the period covered in Figure 8.1, GDP grew at an annual rate of 7.1 percent. However, EDP only grew at an annual rate of 4.0 percent. So this case demonstrates that only looking at GDP to determine the trend in national welfare may lead policy makers to conclude that growth is robust. But accounting for environmental degradation shows that much of the apparent growth was at the expense of the environment.

3. *Monetization of natural capital needs to be approached carefully.* In Figure 8.1 there is a noticeable spike in EDP in 1974. Does this indicate an appreciation of natural capital and an environmental improvement? Not necessarily—this spike is mainly a result of a dramatic increase in world oil prices because of the 1973–1974 Arab oil embargo, rather than a change in the actual oil reserves in Indonesia. Similarly, in some years the total volume of timber decreased, but since the market price went up, the overall value of timber resources increased. However, this masks the physical degradation of timber resources. So if we measure the value of natural capital at market prices, we can lose important information regarding the actual physical stock of those resources.

A more recent attempt to measure EDP in Sweden looked at a broader set of natural resource categories, including soil erosion, recreation values, metal ores, and water quality.[5] The results found that EDP in Sweden was about 1–2 percent lower than NDP for 1993 and 1997. The author notes that while the overall adjustment may seem relatively minor, the analysis did not consider all potential environmental damages, such as climate change and loss of biodiversity. Also, looking at the effects of environmental degradation on the overall economy fails to recognize that some sectors are particularly affected, such as agriculture, forestry, and fisheries.

Another study estimated the value of changes in forest resources in India in 2003.[6] Based on timber and firewood market prices, the results indicated that while the overall stock of timber decreased, EDP was actually slightly higher than NDP. Again, this illustrates the potential distortionary effect of looking only at adjustments in monetary terms without looking in more detail at the actual physical environment.

8.3 ADJUSTED NET SAVING

net domestic savings (NDS)
a national accounting measure equal to gross domestic savings less manufactured capital depreciation.

In addition to GDP, traditional national accounting methods also estimate saving and investment rates. These accounts provide some insight into how much a country is saving for its future. Starting with gross savings, including savings by governments, businesses, and individuals, **net domestic saving** is obtained after adjustments for borrowing and fixed capital depreciation. Thus net domestic saving can be positive or negative. For example, in 2010 the United States had a net domestic saving rate that was negative: –1.1 percent of national income.

adjusted net saving (ANS)

a national accounting measure developed by the World Bank which aims to measure how much a country is actually saving for it future.

We can propose that how a country manages its natural resources and environmental quality also provides information about whether it is saving for the future or causing depletion that may make future generations worse off. As in the calculation of EDP, we can adjust net domestic saving to incorporate a country's management of its natural resources. The World Bank has developed such a measure, called **adjusted net saving (ANS)**.[g] Unlike standard measures of national saving, ANS

> takes the broader view that natural and human capital are assets upon which the productivity and therefore the well-being of a nation rest. Since depletion of a non-renewable resource (or over-exploitation of a renewable one) decreases the value of that resource stock as an asset, such activity represents a *dis*investment in future productivity and well-being.[7]

An ANS analysis, particularly appropriate for developing countries, may show that what appears to be a development "success story" can conceal serious natural capital depletion and in some cases even a negative adjusted net saving rate.

ANS is normally calculated as a percentage of national income, although it could also be expressed in monetary units. The calculation of ANS is summarized in Figure 8.2. ANS is obtained using the following steps:[h]

- Start with gross national saving.
- Make a deduction to account for the depreciation of fixed capital to obtain net national saving.
- *Adjust for education expenditures.* Unlike standard measures, ANS considers expenditures on education to be investments in the future of a society.[i] So expenditures on education are added to net national saving to reflect investment in human capital.
- *Adjust for energy resource depletion.* A deduction is made for the depletion of nonrenewable fossil fuels—oil, coal, and natural gas. The deduction is calculated as the total market value of the resource minus its extraction cost.
- *Adjust for metal and mineral depletion.* A deduction is made for the extraction of nonrenewable mineral resources, including copper, gold, lead, nickel, phosphate, and several other resources. The deduction is again calculated as the total market value of each mineral minus its extraction cost.
- *Adjust for net forest depletion.* Unsustainable depletion of a country's forest resources is considered a disinvestment in the future. As forests are renewable resources, it is possible that a country could actually increase its forest resources. Thus net forest depletion is calculated as the annual value of extraction for commercial uses such as timber and fuelwood, combined with an estimate of the net change in forest area.
- *Adjust for carbon dioxide damages.* Carbon dioxide emissions represent a disinvestment in a country's future as they contribute to damage from climate change. A country's annual emissions are multiplied by an assumed damage of $20 per ton of carbon.[j]

---

[g]Adjusted net savings is also called genuine savings.

[h]In addition to the steps presented in the text, some calculations of ANS also include a deduction for particulate matter emissions.

[i]Gross saving already includes fixed capital education expenditures, such as spending on buildings and buses. However, teacher salaries are not included nor is spending on books and other educational supplies. ANS adds in these nonfixed capital expenditures.

Figure 8.2 **Calculation of Adjusted Net Saving**

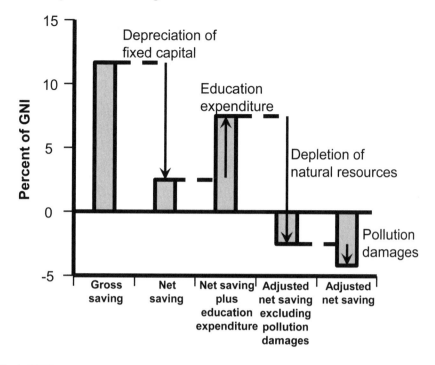

Source: World Bank, 2012.
Note: GNI = gross national income.

The World Bank has calculated ANS rates for most countries of the world, as seen in Table 8.1. For most countries, the environmental adjustments are relatively minor. For example, the ANS rates of France and the United States are primarily a result of their respective net national saving rates and education expenditures. But the environmental adjustments can be quite significant in some countries.

The Republic of Congo, Saudi Arabia, Indonesia, and Russia offset relatively robust net national saving by depleting their energy resources. So based on traditional saving measures, these countries may appear to be investing heavily in their future, but after we account for their extraction of nonrenewable fossil fuels, the ANS measure suggests that they are actually disinvesting in their future. Chile is an example of a country that may be overly dependent on nonrenewable minerals for its wealth. Uganda has a significant deduction for forest depletion—about 5 percent of national income.

The World Bank has also tracked ANS rates over time. Figures 8.3a and b present the results for several country aggregates. Figure 8.3a shows that ANS in high-income countries has generally been decreasing over the past couple of decades. Meanwhile, ANS in South Asia (which includes India, Bangladesh, and Pakistan) has shown a clear upward trend in the past decade. This reflects high levels of investment in these countries but does not indicate that environmental depletion

---

[j]Some analysts consider this a low value for carbon damages (see e.g., Ackerman and Stanton, 2011). We consider this issue in Chapter 18.

Table 8.1

Adjusted Net Saving (ANS) Rates, Selected Countries in Percent of Gross Domestic Product, 2008

Country	Gross national saving	Fixed capital depreciation	Education expenditure	Energy depletion	Mineral depletion	Net forest depletion	Carbon damage	ANS
Chile	24.23	−12.86	3.60	0.26	−14.32	0.00	0.31	0.08
China	53.89	−10.08	1.80	−6.74	−1.70	0.00	−1.26	35.92
Congo, Rep.	26.68	−14.08	2.25	−71.19	0.00	0.00	−0.16	−56.50
France	18.74	−13.86	5.05	−0.03	0.00	0.00	−0.10	9.80
India	38.17	−8.49	3.17	−4.86	−1.42	−0.78	−1.16	24.64
Indonesia	22.25	−10.66	1.15	−12.60	−1.38	0.00	−0.61	−1.85
Russia	32.78	−12.39	3.54	−20.47	−1.00	0.00	−0.85	1.62
Saudi Arabia	48.33	−12.46	7.19	−43.51	0.00	0.00	−0.62	−1.06
Uganda	12.63	−7.42	3.27	0.00	0.00	−5.06	−0.15	3.27
United States	12.60	−13.96	4.79	−1.93	−0.11	0.00	−0.31	1.07

Source: World Bank, 2012.

Figure 8.3a **Adjusted Net Saving, 1982–2008, World Bank Country Aggregates: High Income Countries, South Asia, Middle East and North Africa**

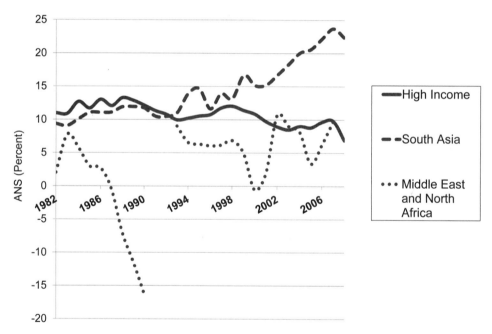

has declined. ANS rates in the Middle East and North Africa have fluctuated considerably, depending on oil extraction relative to domestic investment.

Figure 8.3b shows similar variation among other country groups. ANS rates are particularly high in East Asia (which includes China, Thailand, Indonesia, and Vietnam). This is because of very high savings and investment rates, but in many of these countries resource and environmental depreciation is also high (see Box 8.2). ANS rates in Latin America have been moderate—between 5 percent and 10 percent—over the past couple of decades. Finally, ANS rates in sub-Saharan Africa have declined in recent years and have actually turned negative, with significant resource depletion in many of these countries.

Figure 8.3b **Adjusted Net Saving, 1982–2008, World Bank Country Aggregates: East Asia and Pacific, Latin America and Caribbean, Sub-Saharan Africa**

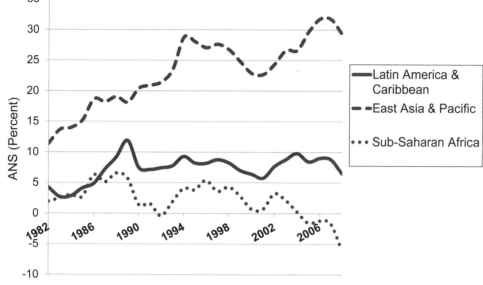

Source: World Bank, 2012.
Note: ANS = adjusted net saving.

BOX 8.2   ENVIRONMENTAL ACCOUNTING IN CHINA

In 2004 China's State Environmental Protection Agency (SEPA) announced that it would undertake a study to estimate the cost of various types of environmental damage. The initial findings released in 2006 indicated that environmental costs equaled about 3 percent of China's gross domestic product (GDP). The report was widely criticized because it failed to include numerous categories of environmental damage, such as groundwater contamination. Shortly afterward, Zhu Guangyao, the deputy chief of SEPA, released a separate report that concluded that environmental damage was closer to 10 percent of China's GDP—a value similar to what many observers were expecting.

In a 2007 report jointly produced by the World Bank and SEPA, the health and nonhealth costs of air and water pollution alone were estimated at 5.8 percent of China's GDP (World Bank and SEPA, 2007).

The results indicate that much of China's recent economic growth has been partially offset by increased resource depletion and pollution. Recognizing the costs of environmental damage, the Chinese government set targets in 2006 for such variables as energy consumption per unit of GDP, releases of major air pollutants, and total forest cover. China's investment in pollution control and renewable energy is growing rapidly. However, the Chinese government's efforts to develop green GDP measures have abated somewhat in recent years, and some of the targets set in 2006 were not met.

In early 2013, pollution levels in Beijing reached record heights: " . . . popular anger over air quality had reached a level where Communist Party propaganda officials felt that they had to allow the officially sanctioned press to address the growing concerns of ordinary citizens. [At] the 18th Party Congress, a meeting of party elites held in Beijing last November, Hu Jintao, the president and departing party chief, said China must address environmental problems worsened by rapid development. The inclusion of sections in the report on the need for "ecological progress" could be opening the door for greater dialogue

(continued)

on such issues under the watch of Xi Jinping, the new party chief, and his colleagues on the Politburo Standing Committee" ("China Lets Media Report on Air Pollution Crisis," *New York Times*, January 14, 2013).

> Past policies and decisions have been made in the absence of concrete knowledge of the environmental impacts and costs. [New], quantitative information based on Chinese research under Chinese conditions [can] reduce this information gap. At the same time . . . substantially more information is needed in order to understand the health and non-health consequences of pollution, particularly in the water sector. (World Bank and SEPA, 2007, p. xix)

8.4 THE GENUINE PROGRESS INDICATOR

genuine progress indicator (GPI)

a national accounting measure that includes the monetary value of goods and services that contribute to well-being, such as volunteer work and higher education, and deducts impacts that detract from well-being, such as the loss of leisure time, pollution, and commuting.

EDP and ANS adjust traditional national accounting measures to account for natural capital depreciation and environmental damage. But as with GDP, neither of these alternatives purport to measure social welfare. So another approach to greening the national accounts is to think about how to create a measure of social welfare if one were starting from scratch. Perhaps the most ambitious attempt to date to design a replacement to GDP is the **genuine progress indicator (GPI)**.[k]

One critique of GDP is that it includes all economic activity as a positive contribution to welfare. For example, all expenditures by the U.S. government Superfund for cleaning up toxic waste sites are contributions to GDP. The medical costs of treating diseases caused by air or water pollution are similarly added to GDP. If coastal homeowners or businesses whose property is damaged by an oil spill sue for damages, the legal expenditures involved as well as the cleanup costs also contribute to GDP. By this logic, the more pollution damage and resulting cleanup expense a country makes, the better off it is. Clearly this is irrational. Thus the GPI differentiates

> between economic activity that diminishes both natural and social capital and activity that enhances such capital. [The GPI is] designed to measure sustainable economic welfare rather than economic activity alone. In particular, if GPI is stable or increasing in a given year the implication is that stocks of natural and social capital on which all goods and services flows depend will be at least as great for the next generation while if GPI is falling it implies that the economic system is eroding those stocks and limiting the next generation's prospects.[8]

Like the previous measures discussed in this chapter, the GPI is measured in monetary units. The starting point of the GPI is personal consumption, based on the rationale that it is consumption that directly contributes to current welfare.

In the United States, about 70 percent of GDP consists of personal consumption (the remainder is government consumption, investment, and net exports). The GPI then adds to personal consumption several goods and services that are considered to increase social welfare, some of which are not counted in GDP. The next step in

---

[k]An earlier version of the GPI was called the Index of Sustainable Economic Welfare (ISEW).

calculating GPI is to deduct factors that are considered to decrease social welfare. Some of these deductions account for defensive expenditures—these are expenses associated with cleaning up pollution or attempting to repair or compensate for other environmental or social damage. In standard accounting, all such expenditures simply add to GDP.

The various steps in calculating the GPI are:[1]

- *Weighing consumption by income inequality.* Personal consumption is adjusted to reflect the degree of income inequality in a society.
- *Add in the value of household labor and parenting.* GDP includes only paid household and parenting work, such as house-cleaning and day-care services. The GPI estimates the market value of unpaid household labor and parenting.
- *Add in the value of higher education.* This component of the GPI reflects the external benefit society receives from well-educated citizens—a positive externality estimated at $16,000 annually for each educated individual.
- *Add in the value of volunteer work.* GDP excludes the value of volunteer work, even though society clearly derives benefits from these services. The value of volunteer work hours is estimated using a market wage rate.
- *Add in the service value of consumer durables.* This category is meant to capture the annual benefits consumers obtain from long-lasting goods such as motor vehicles, appliances, and furniture.
- *Add in the service value from highways and streets.* The GPI excludes most government spending, such as military expenditures, because it considers them responses to various threats to living standards rather than enhancements to consumer welfare. However, the ability to use public highways and streets is assumed to provide consumers with direct benefits.
- *Subtract the cost of crime.* As crime detracts from social welfare, the GPI counts costs associated with crime as a deduction—unlike GDP, which would count these costs as positive additions. The cost of crime includes the costs of prisons and defensive expenditures such as buying locks and alarms.
- *Subtract the loss of leisure time.* GDP may increase simply because people work longer hours. However, the associated loss of leisure time is not considered in GDP. Based on estimates of total working hours, the GPI calculates the reduction of leisure time since 1969.
- *Subtract the cost of underemployment.* Underemployed people includes those who have become discouraged and given up looking for a job, people working part-time who would prefer a full-time job, and people who are willing but unable to work because of circumstances such as an inability to afford child care.
- *Subtract the cost of consumer durables.* As discussed above, the GPI counts the annual service value of consumer durables. To avoid double counting, the annual expenditures on durable goods are subtracted.
- *Subtract the cost of commuting and auto accidents.* While GDP counts the costs of commuting as positive contributions, the GPI considers commuting

[1]These steps describe the calculation of the GPI for the United States. The GPI has been estimated for other countries, and for some U.S. states, using similar methods and data.

costs and lost time as deductions, as well as deaths and injuries from auto accidents.

- *Subtract the cost of household environmental defensive expenditures.* The cost of such products as air filters and water purifications systems do not increase welfare but simply serve to compensate for existing pollution.
- *Subtract the costs of pollution (air, water, and noise).* Relying on studies using the valuation methodologies discussed in Chapter 6, the GPI estimates the economic damage from each type of pollution.
- *Subtract the value of lost wetlands, farmlands, and forests.* The GPI subtracts for losses of natural capital including reductions in ecosystem services, lost recreation opportunities, and declining nonuse values.
- *Subtract the costs of depleting nonrenewable energy sources.* While GDP counts the market value of extracted nonrenewable energy sources as positive contributions, it fails to consider that a diminishing stock of resources imposes a cost on future generations. The GPI attempts to estimate this implied cost.
- *Subtract the damages from carbon dioxide emissions and ozone depletion.* As we discuss in Chapter 18, numerous economists have attempted to estimate the damage associated with carbon emissions. The GPI multiples an estimate of the marginal damage from a ton of CO_2 by the cumulative tons emitted. Even though production of CFCs in the United States has been virtually phased out as a result of the 1987 Montreal Protocol (see Chapter 16), ozone damage continues as a result of past emissions.
- *Adjust for net capital investment and foreign borrowing.* **Net investment** (gross investment minus depreciation) is assumed to increase social welfare, while net depreciation or foreign borrowing is assumed to decrease social welfare.

net investment and disinvestment

the process of adding to, or subtracting from, productive capital over time, calculated by subtracting depreciation from gross, or total, investment.

As we might expect with all these adjustments, the GPI differs significantly from GDP in magnitude and trends. The detailed results for U.S. GPI in 2004 are listed in Table 8.2. The largest positive adjustments to inequality-adjusted personal consumption are the value of household work and parenting and the benefits of higher education. But the additions are more than offset by the various deductions, most important are the deductions for nonrenewable energy depletion and carbon emissions. Thus the GPI is significantly less than personal consumption, with the implication that the various adjustments result in an overall reduction in social welfare.

Comparing the relative trends in GDP and the GPI, we see in Figure 8.4 that GDP per capita steadily increase from 1950 to 2004. While the GPI grew along with GDP until about the mid-1970s, since that time the GPI has remained relatively constant. This implies that the gains in economic production have been approximately offset by negative factors such as the loss of leisure time, pollution, and the depletion of natural capital. Relying on the GPI, instead of GDP, would obviously present significantly different policy recommendations, focusing more on reducing environmental damages, preserving natural capital, and developing renewable energy resources.

GPI estimates have been developed for countries other than the United States, including Germany, Australia, China, and India. The GPI has also been applied at the subnational level. For example, a 2009 analysis of the Auckland region in

Table 8.2

Genuine Progress Indicator (GPI), United States, 2004

Component of GPI	Value (billions of dollars)
Personal consumption	7,589
Personal consumption after inequality adjustment	6,318
Value of household work and parenting	+2,542
Value of higher education	+828
Value of volunteer work	+131
Service value of consumer durables	+744
Service value of highways and streets	+112
Costs of crime	−34
Loss of leisure time	−402
Costs of underemployment	−177
Cost of consumer durables	−1,090
Costs of commuting and auto accidents	−698
Costs of environmental defensive expenditures	−21
Costs of pollution	−178
Value of lost wetlands, farmland, and forests	−368
Costs of nonrenewable energy depletion	−1,761
Damages from carbon emissions and ozone depletion	−1,662
Adjustment for capital investment and foreign borrowing	+135
Total	4,419

Source: Talberth et al., 2007.

Figure 8.4 **Comparison of GDP and GPI per Capita, United States, 1970–2004**

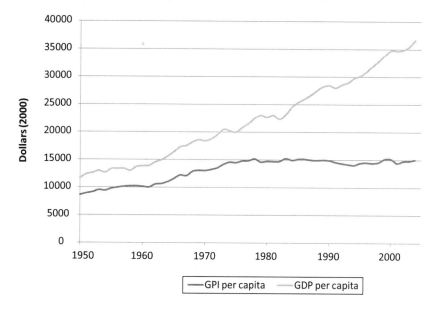

Source: Talberth et al., 2007.
Note: GPI = genuine progress indicator, GDP = gross domestic product.

New Zealand showed that, unlike in the United States, the GPI grew at nearly the same rate as the region's GDP during 1990–2006 (Figure 8.5).[9] However, even in this case environmental losses grew at a faster rate than the GPI—rising 27 percent during this period while the GPI rose 18 percent. But the positive contributions to the GPI, in particular the growth of personal consumption, were enough to more

Figure 8.5 **New Zealand's Auckland Regional GPI vs. GDP, 1990–2006**

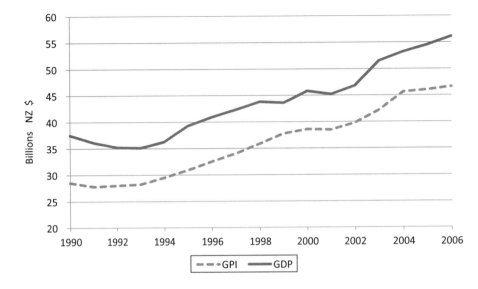

Source: McDonald et al., 2009.
Note: GPI = genuine progress indicator, GDP = gross domestic product.

than offset the environmental losses. So we need to recognize that a growing GPI can still occur despite increasing environmental damages.

This finding is further illustrated in Figure 8.6, which shows the economic, social, and environmental components of the GPI for Maryland from 1960–2010.[10] We see that while the economic contributions to the GPI rose steadily, the net social contributions increased only slightly and the environmental costs more than doubled.

This demonstrates a potential problem with any index that reduces all economic, social, and environmental factors into a single value. The overall index may fail to reflect important positive and negative trends that offset each other. Thus we should always refer to disaggregated results, such as the data in Figure 8.6, to achieve a more complete understanding of the changes occurring in a society and the potential policies that may be necessary to increase social welfare.

Like EDP and ANS, the GPI requires converting various environmental factors into a single metric—dollars. While this raises numerous methodological issues, as discussed in Chapter 6, we may also question whether disparate environmental resources and natural capital can be directly compared. Other approaches to measuring national well-being have been developed that avoid the use of a monetary metric but consider different aspects of the quality of life rather than using a dollar value. One recent approach, the Happy Planet Index, incorporates data on life expectancy, ecological impacts, and self-reported happiness (for more on the Happy Planet Index, see Box 8.3). We look at another recent index in the following section.

8.5 THE BETTER LIFE INDEX

While indices such as the GPI provide useful information and have been used by some policy makers, it currently seems unlikely that their adoption will become

Figure 8.6 **Components of the GPI for Maryland, 1960–2010**

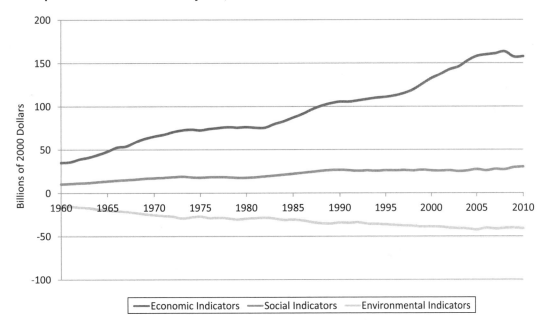

Source: www.green.maryland.gov/mdgpi/mdgpioverview.asp.

BOX 8.3   THE HAPPY PLANET INDEX

The Happy Planet Index (HPI) is perhaps the most novel attempt to devise an entirely new approach to measuring national welfare in the context of environmental sustainability. The HPI, created by the British New Economics Foundation (NEF), asserts that the goal of society is to create long and happy lives for its members. To do this, natural resources must be used and wastes generated. The HPI consists of three variables to reflect these concepts:

1. *Average life expectancy:* This measures whether a society's members lead long lives.
2. *Average subjective well-being:* This measures whether a society's members lead happy lives. The data are obtained from surveys that ask people how satisfied they are with their lives. Despite the simplicity of the approach, years of research have demonstrated that the results provide reasonably accurate estimates of an individual's welfare.
3. *Ecological footprint:* This measures a society's overall ecological impact. It is defined as the amount of land required to provide a society with the resources that it consumes and assimilate the waste that it generates. While it has been subject to methodological critiques, by converting all ecological impacts into a single value it provides an overall assessment of sustainability.

Average subjective well-being, measured on a scale between 0 and 1, is multiplied by life expectancy to obtain the "happy life years" of a society. Then the HPI is calculated as:

HPI = Happy Life Years/Ecological Footprint

(continued)

The HPI has been calculated for 143 countries. The countries with the highest HPI scores are those whose citizens tend to be rather happy and long-lived but have a relatively modest ecological footprint, including Costa Rica, the Dominican Republic, Jamaica, Guatemala, and Vietnam. One interesting aspect of the HPI is that a country's HPI ranking tends to be unrelated to its gross domestic product (GDP). The United States ranks 114th, just above Nigeria.

The interpretation and policy implications of the HPI are unclear. For example, India and Haiti have a higher HPI score than Germany or France. Does this imply that India and Haiti are more desirable to live in, or more ecologically sustainable, than Germany or France? Probably not. Another issue is whether a country's policies can affect happiness levels, which may be more a construction of inherent social and cultural factors rather than policy choices.

But despite its limitations, the HPI has received attention as an alternative or supplement to GDP, especially in Europe. A 2007 report to the European Parliament cites several strengths of the HPI, including:
- It considers the ends of economic activity, namely, happiness and life expectancy
- The innovative way that it combines well-being and environmental factors
- Its calculations are easy to understand
- Data can be easily compared across countries

So while the HPI is unlikely to become a widespread alternative to GDP, it does provide information that is not currently captured in any other national accounting metric.

Sources: Goossens, 2007; New Economics Foundation, 2009.

Human Development Index (HDI)

a national accounting measure developed by the United Nations, based on three factors GDP levels, education, and life expectancy.

widespread around the world. More attention is paid to indices and measures published by international organizations such as the World Bank and United Nations. The most referenced quality-of-life index is probably the United Nations' **Human Development Index (HDI)**.

The HDI is calculated based on three components of well-being: life expectancy, education, and income. A report on the HDI is produced every year, with rankings and policy recommendations. In 2011 the countries with the highest HDI scores were, in order: Norway, Australia, the Netherlands, the United States, and New Zealand.[11] The HDI is highly, although not perfectly, correlated with GDP. For example, of the thirty countries with the highest HDI scores in 2011, all but one was also ranked in the top 40 by national income per capita. But there are some significant differences. For example, Panama has about the same GDP per capita as Namibia, and Vietnam has about the same GDP per capita as Angola. But Panama has a much higher HDI score than Namibia, and Vietnam has a much higher HDI score than Angola. This is because both life expectancy and literacy measures in Panama and Vietnam are higher than in Namibia and Angola. So in some cases the HDI provides significantly more information than income alone.

A much more comprehensive attempt to assemble data on well-being in different nations is the Better Life Initiative launched by the Organization for Economic Cooperation and Development (OECD).[m] Its 2011 report "How's

---

[m]The OECD is a group of the world's advanced industrial countries, now including some developing countries such as Mexico.

Life?" describes the construction of the **Better Life Index (BLI)**.[12] The report recognizes that well-being is a complex function of numerous variables. While material living conditions are important for well-being, so are quality of life and environmental sustainability. Further, the distribution of well-being across a society is important. The report argues that we need "better policies for better lives":

> Better policies need to be based on sound evidence and a broad focus: Not only on people's income and financial conditions, but also on their health, their competencies, on the quality of the environment, where they live and work, their overall life satisfaction. Not only on the total amount of the goods and services, but also on equality and the conditions of those at the bottom of the ladder. Not only on the conditions "here and now" but also those in other parts of the world and those that are likely to prevail in the future. In summary, we need to focus on well-being and progress.[13]

The BLI considers well-being a function of eleven dimensions:

1. *Income, Wealth, and Inequality:* The two main variables used for this dimension are disposable household income and net financial wealth.[n] The BLI also considers the degree of inequality in income and wealth.
2. *Jobs and Earnings:* The three main variables comprising this dimension are the unemployment rate, the long-term unemployment rate, and average earnings per employee.
3. *Housing Conditions:* Sufficient housing is important to provide security, privacy, and stability.
4. *Health Status:* The BLI includes life expectancy and a subjective evaluation of one's overall health status.
5. *Work and Life Balance:* The BLI measures the proportion of employees working long (fifty or more) hours per week, the time available for leisure and personal care, and the employment rate for women with school-age children.
6. *Education and Skills:* This is measured as the percentage of the adult (25–64 years old) population that has a secondary (i.e., high school) degree and students' cognitive skills based on standardized tests.
7. *Social Connections:* This dimension is measured by people's responses to a standardized question asking whether they have friends or relatives that they can count on in times of need.
8. *Civic Engagement and Governance:* This dimension is based on data on voter turnout and a composite index that measures citizen input in policy making.
9. *Environmental Quality:* The main variable used to measure environmental quality is air pollution levels, specifically particulate matter. Secondary environmental variables include an estimate of the degree to which diseases are caused by environmental factors, people's subjective satisfaction with their local environment, and access to green space.
10. *Personal Security:* This dimension focuses on threats to one's safety. It is measured using homicide and assault rates.

---

[n] In addition to the main variables discussed here, most of the dimensions also consider secondary variables. For example, the dimension of income and wealth also includes data on household consumption and subjective evaluation of material well-being.

11. **Subjective Well-Being:** This dimension measures people's overall satisfaction with their lives as well as reported negative feelings.

The results for each dimension are standardized across countries, resulting in a score from 0 to 10. While the BLI includes many components, it is designed to produce an overall well-being index. But how do we assign weight to the various components? One basic approach is to simply weigh each of the eleven dimensions equally. But it seems likely that some dimensions contribute to well-being more than others. The BLI report makes no specific recommendations on weighing the different dimensions. An interesting feature of the BLI is that a Web site allows users to select their own weights for each of the dimensions. The OECD is collecting users' input and will use this information to gain a better understanding of the factors that are most important for measuring well-being.

The BLI has been measured for the thirty-four OECD member countries, as well as Brazil and Russia, with plans to expand it to China, India, Indonesia, and South Africa. Even for the OECD members, some results have to be estimated because of a lack of consistent data. Improving the standardization of data collection and reporting is one of the objectives of the Better Life Initiative.

Based on equal weighing of each dimension, Figure 8.7 shows how selected countries rank. We see that Australia, Canada, and Sweden are the top three countries. The United States ranks seventh among OECD nations, performing well in terms of housing and income but ranking lower in terms of work-life balance and

Figure 8.7 **Better Life Index Values for Selected Countries**

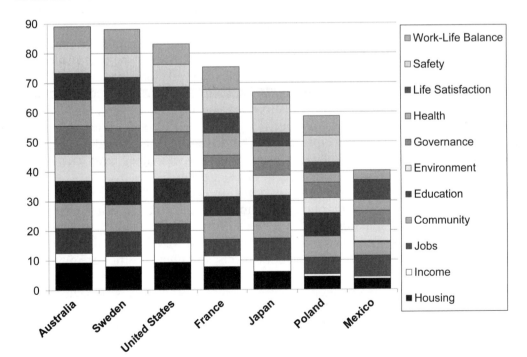

Source: OECD, 2011.

health. Realize that the equal weighing of each dimension reduces the importance of income levels relative to most other national accounting approaches, such as the GPI and EDP. As far as environmental rankings, the lowest pollution is found in Sweden and the United Kingdom, and the highest pollution, among the countries evaluated, in Chile, Turkey, and Greece.

The BLI thus provides a comprehensive view of the many factors that influence well-being. Income is not presented as the starting point but as one component of many. BLI indicators can be used to design policies that improve well-being. One of the criteria used to choose the BLI variables is policy relevance. Several of the dimensions, such as education, housing, and environmental quality, can be directly improved with effective policies, although the linkage between other dimensions (such as subjective well-being) and policies needs further study. While the main focus of BLI is not on environmental and natural resource issues, its measures of environmental quality could be expanded or given greater weight in future.

BLI calculations also indicate data collection needs in various countries. The development of a consistent statistical agenda would improve the validity of the results across OECD countries and provide a basis for extending the results to other countries. At least one country, Bhutan, has created its own measure, **gross national happiness (GNH),** which measures some of the same dimensions as BLI (see Box 8.4).

gross national happiness (GNH)

the concept, originating in Bhutan, where a society and its policies should seek to improve the welfare of its citizens, as opposed to maximizing GDP.

BOX 8.4   BHUTAN'S GROSS NATIONAL HAPPINESS

Perhaps no country has advocated the need to devise alternatives to the gross national product (GNP) as much as the small Himalayan country of Bhutan. In 1972, King H.M. Jigme Singye Wangchuck introduced the concept of **gross national happiness (GNH)** to provide an alternative development philosophy to simply maximizing economic growth. He sought to achieve progress toward GNH by focusing on four policy objectives: equitable economic development, environmental preservation, cultural resilience, and good governance (Braun, 2009).

While initially it was just a guiding concept, in recent years the Centre for Bhutan Studies (CBS) has sought to operationalize GNH (CBS, 2011). The Centre has defined GNH as encompassing nine domains:

- Psychological well-being
- Standard of living
- Good governance
- Health
- Education
- Community vitality
- Cultural diversity and resilience
- Time use
- Ecological diversity and resilience

In 2010 the Centre conducted an extensive survey of over 7,000 Bhutanese households to assess the country's GNH. Each domain was addressed by asking several questions. For example, for the ecological

(continued)

domain respondents were asked questions such as how concerned they were about air pollution, water pollution, waste disposal, flooding, and soil erosion. Based on "sufficiency" thresholds set by the CBS, the responses determine whether each household is sufficient in each of the nine domains. The results indicate that 41 percent of Bhutanese households have sufficiency in at least six domains and are thus considered happy. Bhutanese have the most sufficiency in health and then in ecology and psychological well-being. Sufficiency is greater in urban areas, among the young, and among those with a formal education.

Bhutan, unlike most other countries, appears to not only be implementing an alternative to GDP but also using these results to guide future policies in a democratic manner.

> Gross National Happiness seems to promote democracy in that it facilitates the process of citizens voicing their opinions on various dimensions of their lives to the Bhutanese government. The GNH survey and the index that the CBS constructs from it open a channel of communication between the government and society at large. People's voices on an array of domains reflected in the GNH index are the practical guiding forces for policy making in Bhutan.

Source: Braun, 2009, p. 35.

8.6 ENVIRONMENTAL ASSET ACCOUNTS

An important issue to consider when evaluating any "green" national accounting approach is how its results can be used to assess the environmental sustainability of a society. As discussed in Chapter 7, we can define different levels of sustainability, which we identified as "weak" and "strong" sustainability. (Recall that these terms refer to different definitions, and do not imply that one is preferable to the other.) How well do the indicators introduced so far in this chapter reflect sustainability?

Any index that monetizes various environmental factors and combines the results with traditional monetary aggregates, such as GDP, implicitly assumes a degree of substitutability among natural capital and economic production. For example, the GPI could remain constant if an increase in pollution damage is offset by an increase in personal consumption. Thus the GPI, along with other aggregate indices like EDP and ANS, can be considered appropriate metrics to address **weak sustainability** but not stronger forms of sustainability.[14]

weak sustainability
the view that natural capital depletion is justified as long as it is compensated for with increases in human-made capital; assumes that human-made capital can substitute for most types of natural capital.

strong sustainability
the view that natural and human-made capital are generally not substitutable and, therefore, natural capital levels should be maintained.

If we are interested instead in achieving **strong sustainability**, we need to concern ourselves with the preservation of natural capital. A further distinction emphasized by some analysts is between "strong sustainability" and "very strong sustainability." Strong sustainability seeks to maintain the overall level of natural capital but allows the substitutability of different types of natural capital, at least for noncritical resources. Very strong sustainability seeks to maintain the levels of various types of natural capital, allowing for substitutability only within each category of natural capital.

The indicators discussed so far in this chapter are not necessarily designed to provide information on stronger forms of sustainability. Still, a few of them do provide some insight into strong sustainability objectives. The environmental components of the GPI, for instance, provide information on natural capital depletion, although not the overall level of natural capital.

An alternative approach is to maintain national accounts that track the levels of different types of natural capital. The SEEA-2003 provides guidance on the maintenance of **environmental asset accounts** or (**natural resource accounts**), in both physical and monetary terms. These accounts are based on defining various natural capital categories, such as timber resources, mineral resources, agricultural land, and groundwater. The accounts may have different degrees of **aggregation**. For example, the account for mineral resources might include a separate account for each mineral or be disaggregated even further based on mineral quality, degree of accessibility, or location. The units would vary for different accounts based on the resource in question. So mineral accounts might be measured in tons, forest accounts in hectares of forest cover or board-feet of timber, groundwater accounts in acre-feet of water, and so on.

The two main strengths of environmental asset accounts in physical units are:

1. They provide a detailed picture of a country's natural capital levels and trends over time. A particular focus can be on ensuring that levels of **critical natural capital** are maintained.
2. They provide a means for assessing very strong sustainability. Since each category of natural capital is quantified in a separate account, policy makers can determine whether the levels of each are being maintained.

Environmental asset accounts can also be expressed in monetary units. In most cases, this simply involves multiplying a physical unit estimate by the market price per unit. For example, if a society has a standing timber stock of 500,000 board-feet of lumber and the market price is $5.00 per board-foot, then the asset value of their timber is $2.5 million. Environmental asset accounts in monetary terms offer the benefit of comparability, both among different types of natural capital and to traditional economic aggregates such as GDP. Unlike accounts in physical units, environmental asset accounts in monetary units can be used to give an overall measure of sustainability because gains and losses in different categories can be compared.

This is illustrated in Figure 8.8. For simplicity, assume there are only two natural resource assets in a society: timber and agricultural land. In Year 1 the society has a stock of 500,000 board-feet of timber and 6,000 hectares of agricultural land. At the market prices indicated in Figure 8.8, the total value of the environmental assets in the society is $8.5 million in Year 1. In the next year, the society harvests some of its timber stock but brings some additional land into agricultural production, as shown in the figure. If we kept asset accounts only in physical units (i.e., in this example, board-feet of timber and hectares of land), we would not be able to assess whether this society has maintained its overall level of natural capital. But Figure 8.8 indicates that the value of its natural assets has actually increased by $500,000, indicating that the overall value of natural capital is being sustained.

Comparing different assets in monetary units has both advantages and disadvantages. Suppose that the price of timber increased in Year 2 to $7.00 per board-foot. Even though the stock of timber was reduced by 100,000 board-feet, the value of

---

environmental asset accounts or (**natural resource accounts**)
national accounts that track the level of natural resources and environmental impacts in specific categories, maintained in either physical or monetary units.

aggregation
in reference to environmental asset accounts, the degree to which different types of natural capital are combined.

critical natural capital
elements of natural capital for which there are no good human-made substitutes, such as basic water supplies and breathable air.

Figure 8.8 **Example of Natural Resource Accounts**

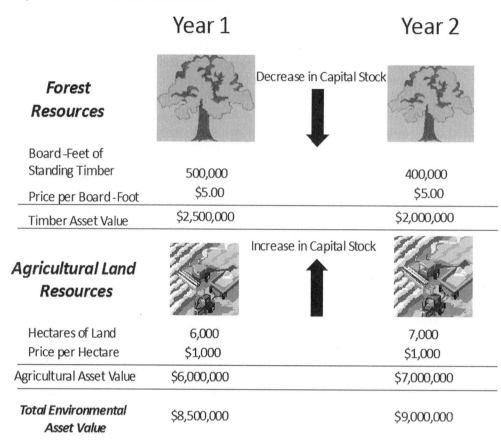

	Year 1	Year 2
Forest Resources		
Board-Feet of Standing Timber	500,000	400,000
Price per Board-Foot	$5.00	$5.00
Timber Asset Value	$2,500,000	$2,000,000
Agricultural Land Resources		
Hectares of Land	6,000	7,000
Price per Hectare	$1,000	$1,000
Agricultural Asset Value	$6,000,000	$7,000,000
Total Environmental Asset Value	$8,500,000	$9,000,000

the stock in Year 2 would be $2.8 million (= 400,000 board feet × $7.00). Even though the physical stock of timber was reduced, its market value increased relative to Year 1. So if we looked only at the monetary units, we could wrongly conclude that the society's stock of timber had increased due to factors such as increased planting or conservation. This demonstrates that we need to be wary of the effect of changing prices on the value of a society's natural assets. This is particularly problematic for mineral and oil assets because the price of these commodities can fluctuate considerably.

Another problem with the monetary value approach is that the estimates in Figure 8.8 do not consider the loss of ecosystem services from harvesting timber. In addition to the loss of timber, there may have been a loss of wildlife habitat, erosion control, carbon storage, and other services. Ideally, assessing strong sustainability by aggregating various asset accounts should consider nonmarket benefits as well as market values. But estimating nonmarket values, such as ecosystem services and nonuse values, can be problematic, as discussed in Chapter 6. Thus any attempt to assess strong sustainability based on monetary values is likely to be incomplete or dependent on numerous controversial assumptions.

Several countries have started to maintain environmental asset accounts. The United Kingdom's Office for National Statistics provides estimates for the following three categories of natural resources:[15]

- Oil and gas reserves—these accounts are maintained in both physical and monetary units.
- Forest account—this account includes the total area under forest cover, as well as an estimate of the market value of standing timber. The report mentions other benefits of forests, including recreation and wildlife habitat, but it makes no attempt to quantify these benefits.
- Land account—this account maintains the total area of nineteen categories of habitat including woodlands, grasslands, marsh, open water, and built-up areas. Data over time track changes, with some habitats increasing over time and others decreasing.

Other countries that have prepared environmental asset accounts include Australia, Canada, Denmark, and Norway. Perhaps the most extensive system of environmental accounts, measured in physical units, are maintained by Sweden (see Box 8.5).

Compared to the other indicators discussed in this chapter, environmental asset accounts provide a means for assessing "strong" and "very strong" sustainability.

BOX 8.5   ENVIRONMENTAL ACCOUNTS IN SWEDEN

In 2003 the Swedish government adopted sustainable development as an overall objective of government policy. In order to monitor progress toward sustainability objectives, an extensive database of environmental indicators is published on the Internet by Statistics Sweden (see "Web Links" at the end of the chapter). The government recognizes that:

no generally accepted set of indicators for sustainable development has been worked up yet. . . . [But] Sweden is engaged in an ongoing effort to improve its environmental accounting, monitoring of environmental objectives, public health, green key ratios and index for development in the segregated districts of its metropolitan areas. (Ministry of Sustainable Development, 2006, p. 69)

Currently, categories of environmental indicators include:

- Material flow statistics
- Chemical indicators
- Water accounts
- Waste
- Environmentally related subsidies
- Emissions to air

Tracking trends over time have revealed some positive outcomes, along with the need for improvement in other areas. Analysis of these trends indicates where policies could be most effective in reducing environmental impacts.

The indicators show that although the state of several issues appears good in an international perspective, there are trends that run counter to [sustainable development] goals. These [include], for example, the climate change issue, where the decrease of emissions needed for the year 2050 is not evident. More energy efficiency and more non-fossil fuels are likely to be needed to bring about [further progress]. It is noted that for some of the areas where emission trends are most conspicuous, namely shipping, air traffic and goods transports, there are economic instruments lacking. (Statistics Sweden, 2007, p. 4)

environmental services

ecosystem services such as nutrient cycling, water purification, and soil stabilization; these services benefit humans and support economic production.

If we maintain these accounts solely in physical units, we can assess very strong sustainability. If we convert physical units to monetary values, we can assess strong sustainability, but only to the extent that we can accurately value different types of natural resources and **environmental services** in monetary terms.

8.7 THE FUTURE OF ALTERNATIVE INDICATORS

As we have seen in this chapter, numerous proposals have been made to address the deficiencies of traditional national accounting approaches in order to account for the environment or to better reflect social welfare, the ultimate goal of economic analysis. Most of these indicators provide some guidance on sustainability objectives as well. However, their implementation has been limited.

> The current state of environmental information around the world is, by most accounts, unacceptable. Environmental statistics are scattered among too many organizations. They are not coherent with one another, let alone with other types of statistics. They are incomplete and not consistent over time. This situation greatly restricts national and international capacity to develop and monitor progress toward environmental policy goals.[16]

While the SEEA-2003 provides guidance on various ways to approach environmental accounting, it indicates no particular preference for one approach over another. Instead it provides a menu of options from which a given country can choose to implement some but not others. We remain a long way away from a universally accepted approach to environmental accounting that is adopted by the majority of countries.

Recognizing the limitations of GDP and the need to develop indicators that incorporate social and environmental factors, in 2008 French president Nicolas Sarkozy created the Commission on the Measurement of Economic Performance and Social Progress. The commission was chaired by Nobel Prize–winning economist Joseph Stiglitz and the chair adviser was another Nobel laureate economist, Amartya Sen. Other members of the commission included numerous prominent economists. The goals of the commission were:

> to identify the limits of GDP as an indicator of economic performance and social progress, to consider additional information required for the production of a more relevant picture, to discuss how to present this information in the most appropriate way, and to check the feasibility of measurement tools proposed by the Commission.[17]

In September 2009 the commission produced a nearly 300-page report. The commission noted that policies promoting economic growth, as measured by GDP, may be unsuccessful in increasing well-being because they fail to account for other factors, such as environmental degradation:

> traffic jams may increase GDP as a result of the increased use of gasoline, but obviously not the quality of life. Moreover, if citizens are concerned about the quality of air, and air pollution is increasing, then statistical measures which ignore air pollution will provide an inaccurate estimate of what is happening to citizens' well-being. Or a tendency to measure gradual change may be inadequate to capture risks of abrupt alterations in the environment such as climate change.[18]

The commission concluded that it is necessary to shift from an emphasis on measuring economic production to measuring well-being. It also distinguished between current well-being and sustainability. Whether current well-being can be sustained depends on the levels of capital (natural, physical, human, and social) passed on to future generations.

The commission hoped that its report would spur additional research on the topic of alternative indicators and encourage countries to investigate which indicators could provide the best information for measuring well-being and sustainability. Several countries have already taken action.[19] In the UK, the Office of National Statistics was directed to conduct a survey asking people which indicators they thought should be used to measure well-being. In Germany a commission on "Growth, Prosperity, and Quality of Life" was established. Other countries attempting to reform national accounting include Canada, South Korea, Italy, and Australia. In the United States, the "State of the USA Project" has been funded by the National Academy of Sciences to develop a Key National Indicator System that:

> will assemble the highest quality quantitative measures and related data, and will be presented on the Web in a simple and straightforward way so that interested people can assess whether progress is being made, where it is being made, by whom and compared to what.[20]

Perhaps the most comprehensive attempt to date to respond to the commission's recommendations has been the Better Life Index discussed above. The OECD report on the Better Life Index notes that

> The work of the Commission has been critical in giving impetus to our path-finding work on measuring progress and to a range of initiatives around the world aimed at developing better indicators of peoples' lives.[21]

The research agenda now appears focused on developing a range of indicators that are most relevant to measuring well-being and sustainability. Some environmental variables are rather obvious, such as measuring air pollution levels and carbon emissions. But the measurement of a broader range of environmental impacts, such as biodiversity and ecosystem services, requires further research. It also remains to be seen whether each country will rely on its own chosen set of indicators or whether a particular menu of indicators will become universally accepted. Another important objective is to develop consistent methods for measuring different variables, such as measuring carbon emissions and administering surveys to collect subjective data.

Improvement of data collection and international agreement on relevant indices may lead to better measures of "green" national income accounts and better ways to measure progress in terms of well-being and sustainability rather than simply marketed economic production. But measuring well-being and sustainability is only a first step toward determining and implementing polices to promote social and environmental progress. The chapters that follow examine the implications of environmental analysis and policy for a range of different areas, including population, agriculture, renewable and nonrenewable resources, pollution control, and climate change, concluding by returning to the overall issue of sustainable development.

Summary

Standard measures of national income such as gross domestic product (GDP) fail to capture important environmental and social factors. This can result in misleading measurements of national well-being, potentially ignoring important environmental problems. A variety of methods can be used to correct GDP measures or to provide alternatives.

Estimates of natural capital depreciation measure the depletion of natural resources such as oil, timber, minerals, and agricultural soils, in monetary units. Figures for these losses are subtracted from the standard measures of national income and investment. The results for many developing countries indicate a substantial impact of natural resource depletion and environmental degradation.

For developed countries, expenditures on pollution control and cleanup, as well as the cumulative impacts of long-lived pollutants, are significant factors. It is also possible to estimate the value of environmental services such as water purification, nutrient recycling, flood control, and provision of wildlife habitat. Systematic calculation of such factors can give a measure of social progress that often differs significantly from GDP.

The application of modified national income accounting has wide-ranging policy implications. Countries for which a large proportion of export earnings come from resource exports may be overestimating their economic progress. Natural resources may be sold below their true costs, leading to a net loss for the country despite an apparent trade surplus.

Social as well as environmental conditions affect calculations of national income. Questions of human development, including educational expenditures and measures of equity, are often interrelated with issues of environmental degradation. Despite the evident importance of these factors, there is no consensus on how to include them in national accounts. An alternative approach is to maintain natural resource accounts, measuring social and environmental indicators separately from GDP. International institutions have moved toward more extensive reporting of such data, creating a basis for more accurate assessments of true national well-being.

Key Terms and Concepts

adjusted net saving (ANS)
aggregation
Better Life Index (BLI)
critical natural capital
defensive expenditures
environmental asset accounts
environmental services
environmentally adjusted net domestic
    product (EDP)
genuine progress indicator (GPI)
green accounting
gross domestic product (GDP)
Gross National Happiness (GNH)

gross national product (GNP)
Human Development Index (HDI)
natural capital
natural capital depreciation
natural resource accounts
net domestic product (NDP)
net domestic savings (NDS)
net investment and disinvestment
satellite accounts
strong sustainability
System of Environmental and Economic
    Accounts (SEEA)
weak sustainability

Discussion Questions

1. What kinds of problems arise from the focus on standard GDP measures in discussing economic policy? How do these problems differ for highly industrialized countries like the United States and developing countries like Indonesia?
2. What are the main approaches that can be used to correct GDP for natural resource depletion and environmental damage? What difficulties and controversies arise in calculating these adjustments to GDP?
3. Do you think that a revised national income measure would be an improvement over current GDP concepts, or would it be better to keep GDP and resource/environmental considerations separate by using natural resource accounts?
4. What are some of the policy implications of using a revised measure that takes into account environmental and resource depreciation? How might the use of revised measures affect such policy areas as macroeconomic policy, trade policy, and resource pricing policy?

Exercises

1. Suppose you have been hired by the developing country of Equatoria to calculate its environmentally adjusted net domestic product (EDP). Assume for simplicity that only three adjustments need to be made to account for natural capital depreciation and pollution damages: timber capital, oil capital, and carbon dioxide damages. You have been given the following data:

Economic Data

Gross domestic product:	$40 billion
Depreciation of manufactured capital:	$6 billion

Timber Data

End-of-year timber stocks (board-feet):	2.0 billion
Start-of-year timber stocks (board-feet):	2.4 billion
End-of-year timber price ($/board-foot):	$6
Start-of-year timber price ($/board-foot):	$4

Oil Data

End-of-year oil stocks (barrels):	500 million
Start-of-year oil stocks (barrels):	550 million
End-of-year oil price ($/barrel):	$60
Start-of-year oil price ($/barrel):	$50

Carbon Data

CO_2 emissions (tons):	75 million
Damage per ton of CO_2 emissions:	$20

For timber and oil, you will need to calculate the value of depreciation, or appreciation, as the change in the total market value of the resource during the year, where total market value is the physical quantity times the resource price. What is the EDP for Equatoria? Would you recommend that Equatoria use EDP to measure its progress toward sustainability objectives? Why or why not? Would you make any other recommendations to policy makers in Equatoria?

NOTES

1. For a history of environmental accounting, see Hecht, 2007.
2. European Commission et al., 2012; United Nations et al., 2003.
3. Smith, 2007.
4. Repetto et al., 1989.
5. Skånberg, 2001.
6. Gundimeda et al., 2007.
7. Bolt et al., 2002, p. 4.
8. Talberth et al., 2007, pp. 1–2.
9. McDonald et al., 2009.
10. Posner and Costanza, 2011.
11. United Nations, 2011.
12. OECD, 2011.
13. Ibid., p. 3.
14. Dietz and Neumayer, 2006.
15. Office for National Statistics, 2011.
16. Smith, 2007, p. 598.
17. Stiglitz et al., 2009.
18. Ibid., p. 8.
19. Press, 2011.
20. www.stateoftheusa.org/about/mission/.
21. OECD, 2011, p. 3.

REFERENCES

Ackerman, Frank, and Elizabeth Stanton. 2011. "The Social Cost of Carbon." *Environmental Forum* 28(6) (November/December): 38–41.

Bolt, Katharine, Mampite Matete, and Michael Clemens. 2002. Manual for Calculating Adjusted Net Savings, Environment Department, World Bank.

Braun, Alejandro Adler. 2009. "Gross National Happiness in Bhutan: A Living Example of an Alternative Approach to Progress." Wharton International Research Experience, September 24.

Centre for Bhutan Studies (CBS). 2011. www.grossnationalhappiness.com.

Dietz, Simon, and Eric Neumayer. 2006. "Weak and Strong Sustainability in the SEEA: Concepts and Measurement." *Ecological Economics* 61(4): 617–626.

El Serafy, Salah.1997. "Green Accounting and Economic Policy," *Ecological Economics* 21(3): 217–229.

El Serafy, Salah. 2013. *Macroeconomics and the Environment: Essays on Green Accounting.* Cheltenham, UK: Edward Elgar.

European Commission, Food and Agriculture Organization, International Monetary Fund, Organization for Economic Cooperation and Development, United Nations, and World Bank. 2012. *System of Environmental-Economic Accounting: Central Framework.*

Goossens, Yanne. 2007. "Alternative Progress Indicators to Gross Domestic Product (GDP) as a Means Towards Sustainable Development." Policy Department, Economic and Scientific Policy, European Parliament, Report IP/A/ENVI/ST/2007–10.

Gundimeda, Haripriya, Pavan Sukhdev, Rajiv K. Sinha, and Sanjeev Sanyal. 2007. "Natural Resource Accounting for Indian States—Illustrating the Case of Forest Resources." *Ecological Economics* 61(4): 635–649.

Harris, Jonathan M., Timothy A. Wise, Kevin P. Gallagher, and Neva R. Goodwin, eds. 2001. *A Survey of Sustainable Development: Social and Economic Dimensions*. Washington, DC: Island Press.

Hecht, Joy E. 2007. "National Environmental Accounting: A Practical Introduction." *International Review of Environmental and Resource Economics* 1(1): 3–66.

McDonald, Garry, Vicky Forgie, Yanjiao Zhang, Robbie Andrew, and Nicola Smith. 2009. *A Genuine Progress Indicator for the Auckland Region*. Auckland Regional Council and New Zealand Centre for Ecological Economics.

Ministry of Sustainable Development (Sweden). 2006. "Strategic Challenges: A Further Elaboration of the Swedish Strategy for Sustainable Development." Government Communication 2005/06:126.

New Economics Foundation. 2009. "The (Un)Happy Planet Index 2.0." www.neweconomics.org.

Office for National Statistics. 2011. *UK Environmental Accounts 2011*. Statistical Bulletin, June 29.

Organization for Economic Cooperation and Development (OECD). 2011. "How's Life? Measuring Well-Being." Paris.

Posner, Stephen M., and Robert Costanza. 2011. "A Summary of ISEW and GPI Studies at Multiple Scales and New Estimates for Baltimore City, County, and the State of Maryland." *Ecological Economics* 70:1972–1980. www.green.maryland.gov/mdgpi/mdgpioverview.asp.

Press, Eyal. 2011. "The Sarkozy-Stiglitz Commission's Quest to Get Beyond GDP." *The Nation*, May 2.

Repetto, Robert, et al. 1989. *Accounts Overdue: Natural Resource Depreciation in Costa Rica*. Washington, DC: World Resources Institute.

Skånberg, Kristian. 2001. "Constructing a Partially Environmentally Adjusted Net Domestic Product for Sweden 1993 and 1997." National Institute of Economic Research, Stockholm, Sweden.

Smith, Robert. 2007. "Development of the SEEA 2003 and Its Implementation." *Ecological Economics* 61(4): 592–599.

Statistics Sweden. 2007. "Sustainable Development Indicators Based on Environmental Accounts."

Stiglitz, Joseph E., Amartya Sen, and Jean-Paul Fitoussi. 2009. *Report by the Commission on the Measurement of Economic Performance and Social Progress*. www.stiglitz-sen-fitoussi.fr/en/index.htm.

Talberth, John, Clifford Cobb, and Noah Slattery. 2007. *The Genuine Progress Indicator 2006: A Tool for Sustainable Development*. Redefining Progress.

United Nations. 2011. *Human Development Report 2011*. Sustainability and Equity: A Better Future for All, United Nations Development Programme, New York.

United Nations, European Commission, International Monetary Fund, OECD, and World Bank. 2003. *Integrated Environmental and Economic Accounting 2003*.

World Bank. 2012. Adjusted Net Saving website, http://go.worldbank.org/3AWKN2ZOY0.

World Bank and State Environmental Protection Agency (World Bank and SEPA), People's Republic of China. 2007. "Cost of Pollution in China," Rural Development, Natural Resources and Environment Management Unit, East Asia and Pacific Region, World Bank, Washington, DC.

WEB SITES

1. **www.beyond-gdp.eu/index.html.** The Web site for "Beyond GDP," an initiative to develop national indicators that incorporate environmental and social concerns. The project is sponsored by the European Union, the Club of Rome, the WWF, and the OECD.
2. **http://go.worldbank.org/3AWKN2ZOY0/.** The World Bank's Adjusted Net Saving Web site, which includes detailed data at the country level.
3. **www.green.maryland.gov/mdgpi/index.asp.** The Web site for the state of Maryland's calculation of its Genuine Progress Indicator.
4. **www.oecdbetterlifeindex.org.** The Web site for the OECD's Better Life Index. Note that you can adjust the weights applied to each dimension to create your own version of the BLI.
5. **www.mir.scb.se/Eng_Default.htm.** The Web site for environmental accounts in Sweden.

APPENDIX 8.1: BASIC NATIONAL INCOME ACCOUNTING

gross national product (GNP)
the total market value of all final goods and services produced by citizens of a particular country in a year, regardless of where such production takes place.

gross domestic product (GDP)
the total market value of all final goods and services produced within a national border in a year.

In this chapter we have discussed several modifications and alternatives to traditional national income accounting. Standard accounting measures, such as **gross national product (GNP)** and **gross domestic product (GDP)**, are widely accepted estimates of the health of a national economy. However, these measures have numerous technical and conceptual limitations. Some background knowledge of how they are calculated and interpreted is useful for understanding the arguments for adjusting or replacing these measures. If you have not taken an introductory macroeconomics course or need to refresh your knowledge, this appendix will help you work through the concepts presented in the chapter.

National income accounting was first developed in the United States in the 1930s to provide policy makers with information on the overall level of economic activity in the country. National income accounting was not designed to estimate the welfare of society—only the aggregate level of economic production. Also, at the time the accounts were being designed, environmental degradation was not an important issue.

For many years, the official measure of national economic activity in the United States was the gross national product, defined as the final market value of all new goods and services produced by the citizens of the country over a period of time (typically one year). GNP includes goods and services produced by U.S. citizens and corporations in foreign countries but not goods and services produced within U.S. borders by foreign citizens and corporations.

In the early 1990s the United States switched to gross domestic product as its official measure to conform with international standards developed by the United Nations. GDP measures the value of goods and services produced within the national boundaries of a country regardless of the producer's nationality. Thus GDP excludes production by U.S. citizens and corporations in foreign countries. In practice, there is normally little quantitative difference between GNP and GDP. In 2011 the values differed only by about 1 percent in the United States.

It is important to note that GNP and GDP measure only the final value of goods and services. Intermediate values are excluded to avoid double counting. For example, consider some of the steps involved in producing this textbook. First, a lumber company harvested wood and sold the wood to a paper mill. Then, the paper mill produced paper and sold it to a printing company. The printing company then printed the text under contract with the publisher. The publisher then sold the book to a retail store for final sale to you. If we add up the prices paid by the paper mill, printing company, publisher, retail store, and you, we end up with a value much higher than the price you paid for the book. The greater the number of intermediate production steps taken to produce an item, the higher the sum of all the prices paid. So all the intermediate steps are not counted, and only the final price you paid is included in GNP.

value-added method
the additional value of a good or service from each step in the production process.

Since it may be difficult in practice to distinguish intermediate from final goods, the accounting method generally used to compute GNP/GDP is the **value-added method**, in which the extra value added at each step of the production process is counted. In the textbook example, the value added for the paper mill is the value of its output minus the cost of inputs purchased from the lumber company. The sum of the values added at all stages of production is equal to the value of the final good.

GNP and GDP only count the production of new goods. If you purchased this book secondhand from a store or other student, then it would not be included in the national account. The sale of used products does not contribute to current economic production.

Calculating the Value of Gross Domestic Product

product, spending, and income approaches to calculating GDP
different approaches for calculating GDP; in theory each approach should produce the same value.

As you might imagine, calculating the total value of all goods and services produced in a national economy is not a simple task. Economists use a variety of data sources to estimate aggregate production including data from tax returns, surveys of businesses and households, and government records. An estimate of GDP can be obtained in three ways: the **product approach**, the **spending approach**, and the **income approach**. The product approach simply adds up the dollar value of all final goods and services produced in the economy. The spending approach adds up the expenditures of consumers, businesses, governments, and institutions for final goods and services. The income approach adds up the earnings of everyone in the economy, including wages, profits, investment income, and rental income.

In a simplified closed economy with no depreciation or inventories and where all business earnings are paid out as income, all three approaches should produce the same value.[o] In other words, if an economy produces $7 billion worth of goods and services we can conclude that $7 billion was spent to purchase these goods and services and $7 billion in income was earned to make these purchases. Of course, the real economy is more complex and the different approaches may produce different values. For example, not everything produced in a year may be sold during that year. Economists have devised adjustment methods, so the different approaches should produce the same values, but even so there remain statistical discrepancies arising from the complexity of the data or missing information.

The national accounts divide the economy into four sectors: businesses, households and institutions, governments, and the foreign sector. Using the product approach, we add up the final goods and services produced by all businesses, households and institutions, and governments. As you might guess, using the product approach we discover that the business sector produces most of the marketed final goods and service in the economy (75 percent in 2011 for the U.S. economy). Household production, as defined in the national accounts, includes rental values and paid work in households such as maid services, child care, and gardeners. However, similar household work that

---

[o]By a closed economy we mean one without any imports or exports.

is not marketed, such as people cooking their own meals or cleaning their own homes, is not included in GDP. This is one common criticism of GDP. For example, essentially the same service is produced whether members of a household clean their own home or hire someone to do it, but only in the latter case is the value of the service included in GDP.

Using the spending approach, we need to consider the foreign sector in calculating GDP. We add demands by foreigners for goods produced in the United States (exports) and subtract demand by U.S. residents and institutions for foreign goods (imports). Spending by businesses on machinery, buildings, and other goods is called **gross investment**. Governments also purchase goods and services and make investments. Using the spending approach, we find that households and institutions purchase most of the final goods and services produced in the economy (about 71 percent). The spending approach can be summarized by the equation:

$$Y = C + I + G + (X - M)$$

where Y represents GDP, C is consumer expenditures, I is business investment, G is government spending on goods and services, and $(X-M)$ is net exports (exports minus imports).

Calculating GDP using the income approach, we only include income received for production that occurs within the national boundaries. The income approach includes corporate profits and rental income as well as wages and salaries. Most of the U.S. national income, about 55 percent in 2011, is paid to workers as wages and salaries.

Adjusting for Depreciation, Population Growth, and Inflation

One reason GDP is not the best measure of national income is that a portion of investment in capital equipment, such as factories and machinery, simply replaces worn-out capital. Since capital that wears out or becomes obsolete decreases national wealth, the **depreciation** of this capital should be counted as a deduction from GDP. Gross investment minus depreciation is called **net investment**. If we deduct capital depreciation from GDP we get a measure called **net domestic product (NDP)**. The depreciation of fixed capital amounts to about 10–15 percent of GDP in the United States.

Of course, politicians and economists hope that the economy expands over time and GDP increases. But an increase in GDP does not necessarily indicate greater wealth for a country's citizens. GDP could increase simply because the country has a higher population. We can account for population growth (or decline) in national accounting by calculating **GDP per capita**, equal to GDP divided by population. Data on GDP per capita also allows us to compare economic production across different countries. For example, U.S. GDP is

gross investment
total investment in produced, or manufactured, capital.

depreciation
the reduction in value of a capital stock over time due to wearing out or exploitation.

net investment and disinvestment
the process of adding to, or subtracting from, productive capital over time, calculated by subtracting depreciation from gross, or total, investment.

net domestic product (NDP)
gross domestic product minus the value of depreciation of produced, or human-made, capital.

GDP per capita
GDP divided by population.

much greater than Swedish GDP, but when we adjust for population size we find that GDP per capita is higher in Sweden than in the United States.

The other factor we need to control for when comparing GDP values across time is inflation. Remember that GDP is based on market prices and it could grow simply because market prices have risen. So when comparing GDP data from different years, we need to use **constant dollars**. For example, suppose that the general level of prices in 2012 was twice as high as it was in 1990. So if we wanted to compare GDP for these two years, we could compare them using 2012 dollars by doubling the GDP from 1990. Or we could compare them using 1990 dollars by dividing the GDP for 2012 in half. The first method gives us **real GDP** in 2012 dollars, while the second gives us real GDP in 1990 dollars.

U.S. GDP has grown tremendously in recent decades. As seen in Table 8.A1, GDP increased by a factor of 51 between 1950 and 2011 if we do not consider any adjustments. Adjusting for population, we find that economic production per person has increased by about a factor of 25. But most of this increase is due to inflation. When we adjust for differences in price level by calculating real GDP per capita in 2011 dollars, we discover that economic production per person has actually increased by a factor of 3.2. This still suggests a large increase in the standard of living for the average American, but a much less significant increase than would be implied looking at the unadjusted aggregate GDP data.

Table 8.A1

Historical Gross Domestic Product (GDP) Data, United States

Year	Unadjusted U.S. GDP ($ billion)	Unadjusted GDP per capita (dollars)	GDP per capita in 2011 dollars
1950	294	1,929	14,920
1960	526	2,914	17,747
1970	1,038	5,064	23,586
1980	2,788	12,270	29,105
1990	5,801	23,252	36,476
2000	9,952	36,170	46,214
2011	15,094	48,409	48,409

Source: U.S. Bureau of Economic Analysis and U.S. Census Bureau Web sites.

Comparing GDP for Different Countries

A final adjustment that is made when comparing GDP data across countries is to adjust for **purchasing power parity (PPP)**. Even if we use currency exchange rates to put all countries' GDP per capita in U.S. dollars, we should still adjust for differences in what a dollar can purchase in different countries. For example, a U.S. dollar converted into Chinese currency will buy a lot more in China than it will in the United States. As mentioned above, Sweden has a higher GDP per capita than the United States, but when we adjust for PPP, GDP per capita is higher in the United States than in Sweden because of the relatively high prices in Sweden.

Of course, GDP per capita varies widely by country. In 2011 the World Bank classified 36 countries as "low income," with a per capita gross national income (GNI, a measure similar to GDP) of less than $1,025 annually. A total of about 800 million people in 2011 lived in countries classified as low income, mainly in Africa. There were 108 middle-income countries—those with a GNI per capita between $1,025 and $12,475. These countries include the majority of the world's population, about 5 billion people, in countries such as China, India, Brazil, Mexico, Russia, and Indonesia. Finally, there were 70 high-income countries with a per capita GNI above $12,475. These countries, including the United States, Japan, Australia, and those in Western Europe, had a total population of about a billion people in 2011.

National income accounting data illustrate the varying economic conditions of people in different countries. We can use the data to compare rates of economic development and to determine income inequality between countries. But we need to be careful about interpreting national accounting data. GDP measures only the aggregate level of economic production; it does not measure social welfare. If GDP per capita rises only because people are working longer hours, we cannot conclude that they are happier. Also, GDP per capita could increase only because the wealthy members of society are becoming wealthier. GDP data tell us nothing about the level of economic inequality in a country. This and other known problems with GDP make it important to be aware of its limits as a measure of well-being—even before we consider the environmental and resource issues discussed in this chapter.

KEY TERMS AND CONCEPTS FOR APPENDIX 8.1

constant dollars
depreciation
gross domestic product (GDP)
gross domestic product (GDP) per capita
gross investment
gross national product (GNP)

product, spending, and income approaches to calculating GDP
net investment
net domestic product (NDP)
purchasing power parity (PPP)
real GDP
value-added method

PART FOUR

POPULATION, AGRICULTURE, AND THE ENVIRONMENT

CHAPTER 9

Population and the Environment

9.1 THE DYNAMICS OF POPULATION GROWTH

Human population has grown slowly throughout most of our history. Only within the past two hundred years has rapid global population growth become a reality. Figure 9.1 shows the history of global population increase during the nineteenth and twentieth centuries, with a baseline projection for the twenty-first century. As the figure shows, in the past hundred years, population growth has accelerated at a pace unprecedented in global history.

In 1800, global population stood at about 1 billion after many centuries of slow growth. By 1950, the total had reached 2.5 billion. Rapid acceleration in growth rates after World War II doubled world population to 5 billion in less than forty years (by 1987). By 2000, world population had passed 6 billion, and by the end of 2011, it reached 7 billion. Current median projections show population eventually leveling off at around 10 billion by 2100.[1]

Extraordinarily rapid population growth—about 2 percent per year—occurred from 1960 to 1975. At first glance, 2 percent may not sound so remarkable, but at this rate of growth, population doubles in about thirty-five years. After 1975, the growth rate slowed, but the much larger size of total population meant that the absolute number of people added each year continued to increase until the first decade of the twenty-first century (Figure 9.2).

During this period of extremely rapid growth, various authors sounded the alarm regarding the dangers of **exponential growth**. A population of 5 billion that continued to grow at 2 percent per year, for example, would reach 20 billion in seventy years and 40 billion in a little over a century. Finding food, water, and

exponential growth
a value that increases by the same percentage in each time period, such as a population increasing by the same percentage every year.

Figure 9.1 **Global Population Growth and Projections, 1750–2100**

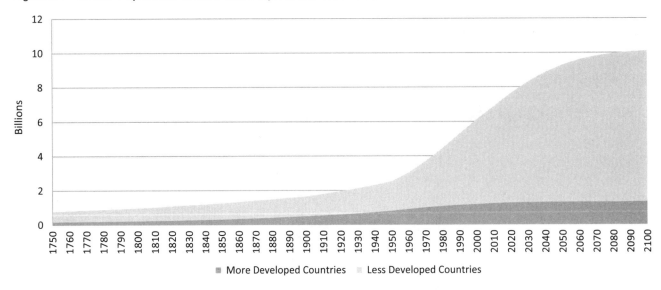

Sources: Caldwell and Schindlmayr, 2002; United Nations, 2010.

Figure 9.2 **Net Annual Increase in Population by Decade, 1750–2100**

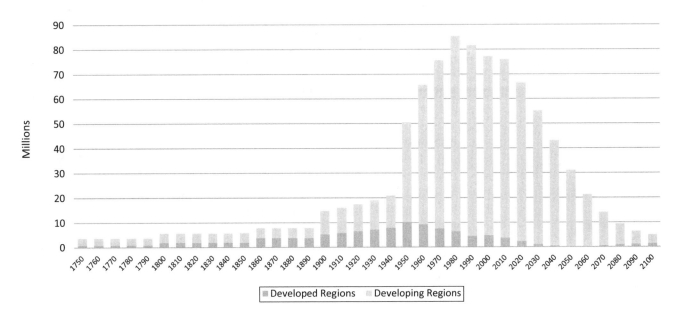

Sources: Repetto, 1991; United Nations, 2010.

living space for such a vastly increased population would be impossible; the grim Malthusian controls of famine and disease would take over.[a]

Authors such as Paul and Anne Ehrlich have repeatedly warned since the late 1960s that humanity was on a collision course with the natural world and that runaway population growth could overcome all the benefits of modern science and economic growth, leaving a devastated and miserable planet.[2] This **neo-Malthusian perspective** has gained much attention and provides the starting point for the modern debate on population growth.

Those who find the Ehrlichs' perspective overly negative often point out that **population growth rates** have been declining since the 1970s; as of 2011, the overall global rate had fallen to 1.1 percent and was continuing to fall. Does this mean that population will soon stabilize, and fears of rapid growth are mere alarmism? Unfortunately not.

First, the growth rate is declining at a time when total population is much higher than ever before. According to UN figures, the global **gross annual population increase** as of 2011 was 77 million.[b] This annual addition to the planet's human inhabitants is the equivalent of more than the entire population of Germany. Every year, the population increases by more people than during the 1960s, when the rate of growth (expressed in percentage terms) was highest (see Table 9.1 and Figures 9.2 and 9.3). The equivalent of a new New York City every five weeks, a new France every nine months, a new India in about fourteen years—this is hardly cause for complacency.

neo-Malthusian perspective

the modern version of Thomas Malthus's argument that human population growth can lead to catastrophic ecological consequences and an increase in the human death rate.

population growth rate

the annual change in the population of a given area, expressed as a percentage.

gross annual population increase

the total numerical increase in population for a given region over one year.

Table 9.1

Global Population Growth Rates and Average Gross Annual Increase

	1950s	1960s	1970s	1980s	1990s	2000s
Population growth rate (%)	1.80	2.00	1.90	1.80	1.40	1.20
Average annual increase (millions)	50.6	65.7	75.6	85.3	81.6	76.5

Source: United Nations, 2010.

Median projections by the United Nations indicate that population will reach 8 billion in 2025, 9 billion in 2043, and 10 billion in the last two decades of the twenty-first century.[3] The global demographic picture is far from stabilized, and this reality will continue to underlie environmental issues for many more decades.

The second reason for focusing on population has to do with its regional growth pattern. Population growth will be most rapid precisely in the poorest and most hard-pressed countries. More than 90 percent of the projected growth will come in currently developing countries in Asia, Africa, and Latin America (Table 9.2). Many of these countries, especially in Africa, have trouble providing adequate food supplies and basic goods to their present population.

---

[a]As noted in Chapter 2, Thomas Malthus predicted in the nineteenth century that population growth would outpace food supplies, leading to population control due to famine and disease.

[b]The Population Reference Bureau estimates the net annual addition to population in 2011 at a slightly higher level of 83 million (Population Reference Bureau, 2011).

Figure 9.3 **World Population Growth Rate, 1950-2010, with Projections to 2050**

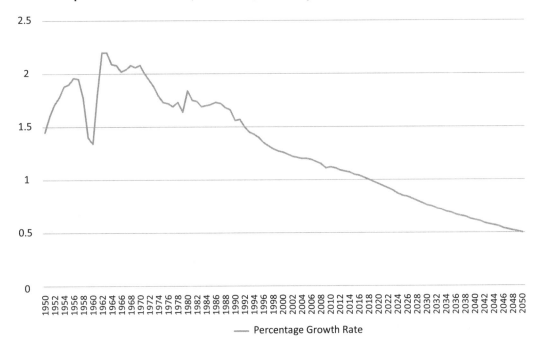

— Percentage Growth Rate

Source: United States International Census Bureau, www.census.gov/population/international/data/idb/informationGateway.php.
Note: The sharp temporary decline in the late 1950s was a result of famine in China.

Table 9.2

Population Projects for Three Fertility Scenarios

Regions	2010 Population (millions)	2050 population projections (millions)		
		Low fertility	Medium fertility	High fertility
Africa	1,022	1,932	2,192	2,470
Asia	4,164	4,458	5,142	5,898
Latin America and Caribbean	590	646	751	869
Europe	738	632	719	814
Northern America	345	396	447	501
Oceania	37	49	55	62
More developed regions	1,236	1,158	1,312	1,478
Less developed regions	5,660	6,955	7,994	9,136
World	6,896	8,112	9,306	10,614

Source: United Nations, 2010.

Developed countries currently create the greatest environmental impact through their high per capita demand on resources, as well as pollution generation. If the developing countries succeed in raising living standards for their expanding populations—as China and other East Asian countries have done—their per capita demands for food and resources, as well as their pollution generation, will also increase. The combined effects of population and economic growth will significantly increase environmental pressures.

9.2 PREDICTING FUTURE POPULATION GROWTH

How well can we predict future population growth? The projected population shown in Figure 9.1 is a baseline median prediction. Could the actual figures be much higher or much lower? As Table 9.2 and Figure 9.4 show, assumptions about changes in birth rates significantly influence projections. The three scenarios shown cover a range of possibilities for global population in 2050, from 8.1 to 10.6 billion people. Within this range, the major factor lending credibility to projections of continued population growth is the phenomenon of **population momentum**.

Figure 9.4   **Population Projections Through 2100, with Three Fertility Scenarios**

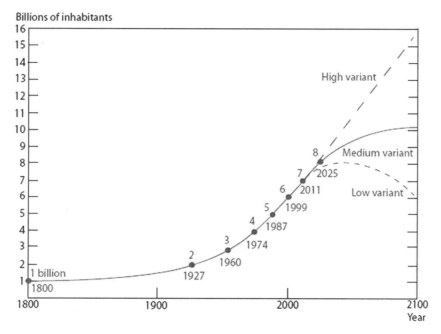

Sources: United Nations, 2010.
Notes: Future population growth is highly dependent on the path that future fertility takes.
The United Nations uses three scenarios or "variants" for the future evolution of fertility:

- Medium variant: assumes that world average fertility will decline from 2.52 children per woman in 2005–2010 to 2.17 children per woman in 2045–2050.
- High variant: assumes that fertility levels will remain about half a child above the levels projected in the medium variant, i.e., will reach 2.64 children per woman in 2045–2050. In this scenario, world population would reach 10.6 billion by 2050 and 15.8 billion by 2100.
- Low variant: assumes that world average fertility will drop to a level of about half a child below the medium variant, i.e., to 1.71 children per woman in 2045–2050. In this scenario, world population peaks at mid-century at about 8.1 billion, then decreases to 6.2 billion by the end of the century.

To understand population momentum, let's consider a hypothetical country, Equatoria, which has been experiencing rapid population growth for several generations. For the sake of simplicity, we define a generation as equal to twenty-five years and divide the population of Equatoria into three age categories: under 25, 25 to 50, and more than 50 years old. The population age structure in Equatoria depends on the birth rate in previous generations. Suppose that, up to the present, each generation has been roughly twice as large as the preceding generation. This will create a **population age profile** shaped like a pyramid (Figure 9.5). With this

Figure 9.5 **Projected Population Age Structure for "Equatoria"**

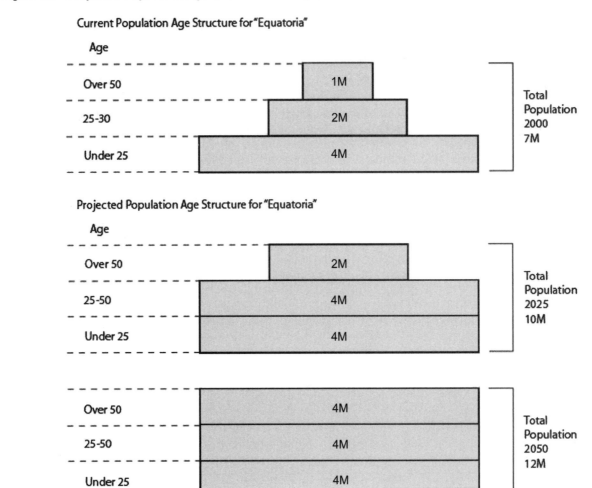

Current Population Age Structure for "Equatoria"

Age

Over 50	1M
25-30	2M
Under 25	4M

Total Population 2000 7M

Projected Population Age Structure for "Equatoria"

Age

Over 50	2M
25-50	4M
Under 25	4M

Total Population 2025 10M

Over 50	4M
25-50	4M
Under 25	4M

Total Population 2050 12M

age structure, the total population will double every twenty-five years, since each new generation is twice as large as its parents' generation. The overall population growth rate of the country will average about 3 percent per annum.[c]

This is a high but not unprecedented rate in developing countries—the current population growth rates in Liberia, Niger, Gambia, and Mali, for example, are close to 3 percent.

Now consider the future demographics of Equatoria. If this growth rate continues, with the population doubling every twenty-five years, there will be a situation of exponential growth. If the population was 7 million in 2000, as shown in our diagram, it will be 14 million by 2025, 28 million by 2050, and 56 million by 2075. No country can long withstand the environmental and social pressures of such growth. But, of course, the growth rate may decline.

[c]According to the "rule of 70," the doubling time for a population with growth rate x percent is approximately $70 / x$, so in this case $25 = 70 / x$ and $x = 70 / 25$ or about 3 percent.

fertility rate
the average number of live births per woman in a society.

For this to happen, the average **fertility rate** must fall. The fertility rate is defined as the number of children borne by the average woman during her lifetime. The fertility rate in Equatoria must be around 5 children per woman to account for such rapid rates of growth. Again, this is not unusual in developing countries. The average fertility rates in sub-Saharan Africa in 2011 were often higher than 5 children per woman: 5.7 in Nigeria, 6.4 in Mali, and 7.0 in Niger. In other parts of the world, high levels of fertility can be found in countries such as Guatemala (3.6 children per woman), Iraq (4.7), and Afghanistan (6.3).[4]

replacement fertility level
the fertility level that would result in a stable population.

Stabilizing population requires achieving a **replacement fertility level**, which is just over 2 children per woman (the precise number depends on the rate of infant and child mortality). At replacement fertility level, each new generation will be exactly the size of the preceding one. Lowering the fertility rate usually takes many years in a country such as Equatoria. Suppose that Equatoria reaches this goal. Does this mean that the population growth problem is over? Absolutely not!

Imagine a fantastically effective population policy that lowers fertility to replacement level *immediately*. Equatoria's demographic future would then be as shown in the second and third parts of Figure 9.5. Each new generation would be exactly the size of the last. The current generation of under-25s, however, is Equatoria's largest ever. Even at replacement-level fertility rates, the population will continue to grow for two more generations.

The next generation of children will be four times as large as the current over-50 generation, meaning that the birth rate will be several times as high as the death rate for another twenty-five years. For the twenty-five years after that, the birth rate will still be around double the death rate. The population growth rate, which is the difference between the birth and death rates, will continue to be positive. Only when people now aged 0–25 reach the end of their life span will *their* grandchildren no longer outnumber them. Thus Equatoria's population will continue to grow for fifty years before it stabilizes, reaching a total of 12 million, 71 percent higher than its current level, before it stabilizes.

This is the meaning of population momentum. When a country has a history of rapid population growth, continued growth for the next several generations is virtually guaranteed, short of some massive Malthusian catastrophe that dramatically raises death rates. A more realistic projection for Equatoria might be that fertility rates, rather than falling instantaneously as in our hypothetical case, would take about a generation to reach replacement level. In that case, population would continue to grow for seventy-five years, finally stabilizing at a level that would be more than double the 2000 level.

The case of Equatoria is not merely an abstract example (see Box 9.1). As Figure 9.6 shows, the simplified population pyramid described is very close to the reality for much of Africa. (Use Figure 9.5, frame 3, to visualize a future Africa in which all population age groups or **population cohorts** are at least as large as the present cohorts of young children.) Also recall that the medium projection for Africa in Table 9.2 indicated a doubling of population by 2050, consistent with our simplified example.

population cohort
the group of people born within a specific period in a country.

Population momentum is also considerable throughout Asia and Latin America. Projections of population growth for these regions are therefore well founded. The inexorable logic of population momentum guarantees growing human numbers well into the twenty-first century. The stable age structure of Western Europe shown

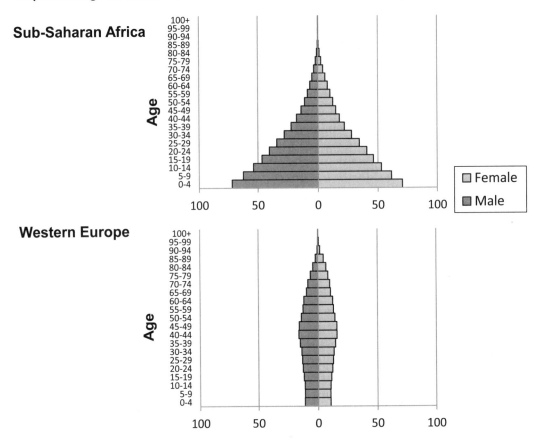

Source: U.S. Census Bureau, International Data Base, 2011, www.census.gov/population/international/data/idb/informationGateway.php.

BOX 9.1 RAPID POPULATION GROWTH STRESSES NIGERIA

Nigeria is the world's sixth most populous nation, with 167 million people. At the rate Nigeria is growing, in a quarter of a century, 300 million people—a number equal to the present-day United States—will live in a country roughly the combined size of Arizona, New Mexico, and Nevada. The population growth rate in Nigeria is similar to that of other sub-Saharan African countries, posing severe problems to governments as they struggle to keep up with resource and infrastructure demands. As a result, many governments have started to reverse pro-natalist policies that encouraged large families. In 2011, Nigeria made contraceptives free, and stated official promotion of the advantages of small families. "Population is key," said Peter Ogunjuyigbe, a demographer at Obafemi Awolowo University in the small central city of Ile-Ife. "If you don't take care of population, schools can't cope, hospitals can't cope, there's not enough housing—there's nothing you can do to have economic development."

Source: E. Rosenthal, "Nigeria Tested by Rapid Rise in Population," *New York Times*, April 14, 2012.

in the second frame of Figure 9.5 is the exception, not the rule. This is why even the lowest global population projections for 2050 are still about 8.1 billion (see Table 9.2).[5]

Population momentum makes substantial increase inevitable, but a huge difference remains between "low" and "high" forecasts for 2050 and beyond (see Table 9.2 and Figure 9.7). The critical variable in these differing projections is the rate of future fertility decline. If fertility falls rapidly throughout the developing world, the global population age pyramid could approach a more stable pattern within the next thirty-five years. (Compare the global low fertility scenario for 2030 in Figure 9.7 with the West European population age structure in Figure 9.6.) But a slow decline would leave the world with both a higher population and considerable remaining momentum in 2030 (see Figure 9.7).

Figure 9.7 **Alternative Futures for World Population**

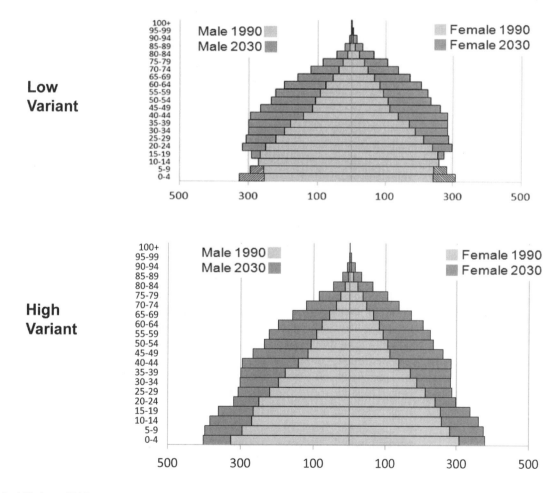

Source: United Nations, 2010.

Notes: Male population on left, female on right. In low variant, 2030 age groups 0–4 and 5–9 are smaller than comparable 1990 groups.

The Impact of AIDS

World population projections take into account the impact of diseases such as malaria, which kill millions annually. But the recent spread of HIV/AIDS has altered the picture of disease mortality. According to a 2010 UN report, more than 32 million people worldwide have died of HIV/AIDS in the past three decades. This huge number makes HIV/AIDS one of the deadliest epidemics of all times, comparable to the Black Death in fourteenth-century Europe, which killed more than 20 million people.

Fortunately, prevention policies and medical discoveries have made dramatic progress since the HIV/AIDS virus was first identified thirty years ago. In 2009, 33.3 million people were living with HIV/AIDS, including 2.5 million children under age fifteen. The number of people newly infected peaked in 1999 at 3.1 million per year, but as a result of better prevention, has been slowly decreasing since then, reaching 2.6 million in 2009. Efficient treatments were developed in the 1990s that slow the effects of AIDS in HIV-positive people and significantly improve their life expectancy. But these treatments were accessible to only 5 million of the 33 million people infected in 2009 because the needed medications are so costly that they are out of reach for many of the poor people infected in Africa. Of the 1.8 million people who died of AIDS in 2009, 72 percent (1.3 million) lived in sub-Saharan Africa.

International efforts by governments and private foundations have focused on making new medications more broadly available. The effects of antiretroviral therapy are especially evident in sub-Saharan Africa, where an estimated 320,000 (or 20 percent) fewer people died of AIDS-related causes in 2009 than in 2004, when antiretroviral therapy began to be dramatically expanded. In 2009 alone, 1.2 million people received HIV antiretroviral therapy for the first time—an increase in the number of people receiving treatment of 30 percent in a single year. In Asia, an estimated 4.9 million people were living with HIV in 2009, about the same as five years earlier. Most national HIV epidemics appear to have stabilized.[6]

What is the effect of AIDS on world population growth? The epidemic affects population growth directly in terms of increased mortality related to AIDS and indirectly through the reduction in the number of births caused by the sickness or premature death of potential parents. In projections made in 2007 by the United Nations for the sixty-two countries most significantly affected by the epidemic, the population projection for 2015 is 2 percent smaller if the impact of HIV/ AIDS is taken into account than it is in the absence of the disease. In southern Africa, the most affected region, the reduction in the population projection for 2015 is 14 percent.[7] But overall population in southern Africa is still growing, with a projected increase of 9 percent by 2025 and 17 percent by 2050.[8]

Thus AIDS, while creating a massive worldwide public threat and humanitarian disaster, will certainly not reverse population growth, not even in the hardest-hit countries in southern Africa, where the increased death rates due to AIDS are still lower than birthrates driven by some of the highest fertility rates in the world. The AIDS epidemics will, however, add enormously to the public health burden on countries already struggling with the needs of a large population of children. Many of these children are or will become orphans, creating enormous stress on family, social, and medical systems.[d]

---

[d]In 2009, more than 16.6 million orphans worldwide had lost their parents to AIDS, 14.8 million of whom lived in sub-Saharan Africa.

9.3 THE THEORY OF DEMOGRAPHIC TRANSITION

From the 1960s to the 1990s, the international community showed growing concern about rapid population growth, expressed at the third United Nations International Conference on Population and Development in Cairo in 1994. This conference adopted the ambitious goal of stabilizing world population at about 7.27 billion by 2015—an increase of roughly 30 percent over 1994 levels.

This objective obviously will not be reached since, as of late 2012, the population has already passed 7 billion, and will not stabilize any time soon. Current median projections by the United Nations indicate a world population of 8 billion by 2025, a net addition of 1 billion people over 2012 levels, with growth continuing after that to reach a possible 9 billion in 2045 and 10 billion by 2100. Certainly the task of supplying the needs of an extra 2 billion–3 billion people is a daunting one. The course of population growth and fertility levels over the next twenty years will profoundly affect all the issues of food production, resource use, and pollution generation, which we consider in upcoming chapters. What, then, can an environmental or ecological economics analysis tell us about population policy?

Much thinking about the relationship of population to economic growth rests on the experience of Western Europe. Western Europe's situation is considered the final stage of **demographic transition** from high to low birth and death rates. Figure 9.8 shows the pattern of this demographic transition.

demographic transition
the tendency for first death rates and then birth rates to fall as a society develops economically; population growth rates first increase and eventually decrease.

Figure 9.8 **The Demographic Transition**

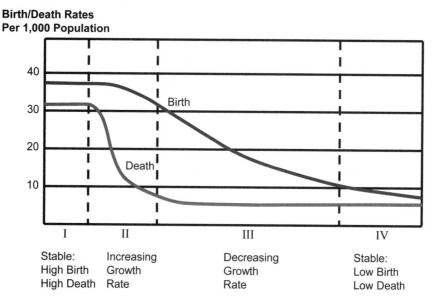

In the first stage, corresponding to preindustrial Europe, both birth and death rates are high. Large families are common, but medical care is poor, and many children die young. On average, a family produces only two surviving children. Thus the population remains stable from generation to generation. These social conditions resemble in many ways the state of nature, in which birds and animals typically produce numerous progeny to offset high rates of predation and disease. It is a harsh but ecologically stable regime.

In the second stage industrialization takes off, as in nineteenth-century Europe. Death rates fall rapidly as standards of living, public health, and medical care improve. Birthrates remain high, however, because families still view a large number of children as valuable, both to work on the farm or in the factory (child labor is still legal and common) and as a form of old-age insurance (no social security institutions exist). Since net population growth rate is equal to the birthrate minus the death rate (the distance between the two lines in Figure 9.8), the result is a rapidly growing population.

Population Growth Impact

Is growing population a good or bad thing for the country as a whole? If resources are abundant, the country's leaders may welcome it. A large labor force promotes rapid economic growth, making it possible to take advantage of unexploited resources and new technology. However, this period of rapid population and economic growth probably contains some self-limiting factors.

One such factor is the improvement in social conditions that is likely to accompany economic growth. This development, by no means automatic, often requires hard-fought battles for social and economic reform. Eventually, however, the country may achieve social changes characteristic of economically developed countries, including child labor laws, unemployment compensation, social security systems, private pension plans, and greater educational opportunity.

In this changed atmosphere, people's attitude toward family size changes. Smaller families are now seen as more desirable—a large family is an economic burden rather than a benefit, and greater opportunities arise, especially for women, as family size shrinks. Contraceptive methods become more available. For all these reasons, fertility rates fall—often quite rapidly. The country enters the third stage, of declining birthrates and declining net population growth rates.

Figure 9.8 shows only the *rate* of population growth (the difference between birth and death rates in Figure 9.8). The total population, of course, is considerably larger in the third stage, so a lower *rate* of growth may still mean a higher net addition to population (gross annual population increase) each year. Population, as we have seen, could double or triple during this period of declining birthrates. But if birthrates continue to decline, eventually the country will reach the fourth and final stage of stabilized population with low birthrates and low death rates.

As a retrospective view of European history, this process appears relatively benign. Despite the great hardships involved in the early stages, overall it appears that population growth, economic growth, and social progress went hand in hand and that population growth was eventually self-limiting. The Malthusian vision failed to be realized—on the contrary, larger populations typically led to better living conditions.

In both Europe and the United States, the third phase of the demographic transition, corresponding to the decrease of fertility rates (average number of children per women), was strongly correlated with an improvement in living conditions. Indeed, that strong relationship between better economic conditions and lower fertility is universally observed, both in long-term trends and in comparative perspectives. Figure 9.9 shows this pattern for all countries in the world, with fertility rate (y-axis) generally falling with increasing GDP per capita (x-axis).

Figure 9.9 **Total Fertility Rate vs. GDP per capita, 2009**

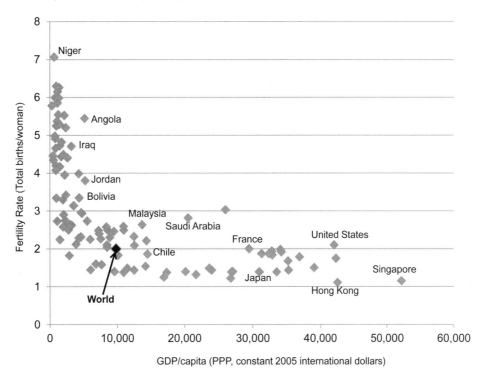

Source: World Bank, World Development Indicators, http://data.worldbank.org/data-catalog/world-development-indicators.
Notes: Countries with population over 5 million plotted. GDP = gross domestic product, PPP-purchasing power parity. PPP adjusts GDP to take account of price levels for domestically-consumed goods and services.

How well does the theory of demographic transition apply to present global population trends? Certainly the first two stages of the demographic transition theory apply well to the developing world's experience in the second half of the twentieth century. Death rates have fallen much faster than birthrates; fertility and population growth rates rose to historic highs between 1950 and 1975. Since then, strong evidence indicates that most countries have entered the third phase, with overall growth rates falling. In many respects, however, currently developing countries experiences differ significantly from Europe's:

- The total population numbers in developing countries are much larger, unprecedented in history. Every decade, the developing countries add population equal to the *entire* population of Europe, including Russia.
- In their expansion, Europe and the United States drew on the rest of the world for supplies of natural resources. The currently developed countries have disproportionately exploited the global environment's waste absorption capacities (contributing by far the highest proportion of greenhouse gas emissions, ozone-depleting chemicals, and other environmental pollutants). The developing world obviously will not have these options.
- There is significant uncertainty concerning the pace of fertility decline. Factors that contribute to fertility decline, such as education of females, access to health care, and access to contraception, may be present in some countries

but absent in others. Projections of population stabilization depend strongly on rapid fertility decline, which may or may not occur.

- The rapid economic growth that accompanied population growth in Europe has occurred in some developing countries but not in others. Those in Africa, in particular, have experienced high population growth together with stagnant or declining output and food production per capita. In places where economic growth has been strong, its benefits have not "filtered down" to the poor, resulting in increased inequality and a greater absolute number of people living in extreme poverty. In the "dual economies" of many countries in Latin America and South Asia, modern urban development coexists with extreme rural poverty and huge slums surrounding major cities. Many people have not yet achieved the improved living standards that contribute to fertility decline.

These arguments suggest that "looking back" to the history of population and economic growth offers insufficient insight into the population-related issues of the next forty or fifty years. Social, economic, and environmental factors intertwine with demographics. The impacts of population growth are not limited to developing countries; the United States faces significant continuing population growth based on a combination of natural increase and immigration (see Box 9.2). We cannot simply wait for the second, global process of demographic transition to play itself out. Rather, we must apply the best analysis and policy response possible to an issue of fundamental importance to the economic and environmental parameters of the twenty-first century.

BOX 9.2   U.S. POPULATION CONTINUES TO GROW

When we think of population problems, we tend to focus on rapid population growth rates in developing countries. But population is far from stable in the United States. Although Europe has completed the demographic transition to stable population levels, both natural increase and immigration keep the U.S. population growing. U.S. fertility rates are at replacement levels, but population growth since 1950 has generated large cohorts of people who are still in their reproductive years, creating significant continuing population momentum.

A larger increase in U.S. population occurred in the 1990s than in any other ten-year period in the country's history, surpassing even the baby boom decade of the 1950s. Population grew from 248.7 million to 281.4 million during the 1990s. In the decade between 2000 and 2010 the population grew another 30 million, and had reached 315 million by 2013.

U.S. population is projected to continue growing for at least the next three decades. According to the United Nations, projected U.S. population for 2025 is 350 million, an increase of 68 million, or 24 percent, over 2000 levels. Projected population for 2050 is over 400 million. While there is some uncertainty about the longer-term figures, these numbers indicate the continuing power of population momentum combined with immigration.

Since U.S. residents have the highest resource consumption and waste generation rates on the planet, the environmental impacts of consumption by these additional people will be much greater than that of a comparable number in a low-income country. Thus even though the projected U.S. population increase is only about 3 percent of likely global population growth, it has considerable significance for global environmental issues like greenhouse gas emissions.

(continued)

An increased U.S. population will also put growing pressure on domestic land and resources. Urban and suburban sprawl, overdraft of water supplies, and air and automobile traffic congestion will all become more difficult to manage. In considering these various environmental issues, we should not forget the underlying importance of population. Population policy is clearly as relevant for the United States as it is for developing countries.

Sources: E. Schmitt, "U.S. Population Has Biggest 10-Year Rise Ever," *New York Times*, April 3, 2001; Population Reference Bureau, *2012 World Population Data Sheet* (Washington, DC, 2011); U.S. Census Bureau, *Largest Census-to-Census Population Increase in U.S. History as Every State Gains*, www.census.gov/Press-Release/www/2001/cb01cn64.html.

9.4 POPULATION GROWTH AND ECONOMIC GROWTH

constant returns to scale
a proportional increase (or decrease) in one or more inputs results in the same proportional increase (or decrease) in output.

per capita output
the total product of a society divided by population.

law of diminishing returns
the principle that a continual increase in production inputs will eventually yield decreasing marginal output.

capital shallowing
a decrease in the availability of capital per worker, leading to reduced productivity per worker.

technological progress
increases in knowledge used to develop new products or improve existing products.

capital formation
addition of new capital to a country's capital stock.

What does economic theory say about population? A typical economic model, the Cobb-Douglas production function, shows economic output as a function of labor input, capital input, and technological parameters:

$$Q_t = A_t \, K^{\alpha}_t \, L^{\beta}_t$$

where Q is total output, K is the capital stock, L is the labor force, and α and β are parameters related to the productivity of capital and of labor respectively; A reflects a given state of technology, and t indicates a particular time period. The values of α and β are assumed to be fractions between 0 and 1; if $\alpha + \beta = 1$, the function shows **constant returns to scale**. This means that if labor and capital inputs were both doubled, output would also double.

Suppose that we increase only one factor, labor. Output will also increase, but by a smaller amount than labor input.[e] If labor is roughly proportional to total population, **per capita output** will decline. As more and more labor is added, the **law of diminishing returns** comes into play, giving smaller output boosts for each additional unit of labor input. Thus in a simple economic model, population increase alone would yield falling living standards. This is a result of **capital shallowing**, which means that each worker has less capital to work with and is thus less productive.

However, few economists would view this simple logic as an accurate representation of the effects of population growth. They would point to the capital stock variable K, noting that if K grows at a rate at least equal to that of L, output per capita will remain constant or rise. In addition, they would argue that we can safely bet that **technological progress** will increase the variable A over time, leading to greater output for each unit of labor or capital input. In this theoretical framework, provided that **capital formation** and technological progress are adequate, population and labor force growth can be accompanied by a rising standard of living.

---

[e]This is because the exponent α is less than 1. If, for example, $\alpha = \beta = 1/2$, then a doubling of labor alone would increase output by a factor of 1.414. A doubling of both labor and capital would increase output by a factor of 2.

What about the issue of **natural resource limitations**? We can modify the Cobb-Douglas production function to take account of **natural capital**—natural resources such as arable land and water for agricultural products, and minerals and fossil fuels as key inputs for all economic activities. If we denote natural capital by N and its productivity by the exponent γ, we get a revised equation:

$$Q_t = A_t \, K^{\alpha}_t \, L^{\beta}_t \, N^{\gamma}$$

In this formulation, limitations on natural capital could cause diminishing returns even if labor and capital both increase. For example, if $\alpha = \beta = \gamma = 1/3$, a doubling of labor and human-made capital while natural resources remain constant would increase output by a factor of 1.59, leading to a fall in per capita output. This decline could still be avoided by sufficiently rapid technological progress, but the natural resource limitation would be a steady drag on output expansion.

There is some evidence that population growth can actually spur technological progress in some cases. Ester Boserup has argued that increased population pressure forces the adoption of more efficient agricultural techniques.[9] At least in the early stages of development, **economies of scale** may prevail; increasing population density may make it possible to develop more productive, larger-scale industry.

From the point of view of economic theory, then, population growth is inherently neither good nor bad. Its effects depend on the context in which it occurs. If economic institutions are strong, markets work well, and environmental **externalities** are not great, then population growth can be accompanied by higher living standards.

Does Population Growth Promote or Retard Economic Development?

Some analysts present a positive view of population growth both as a proof of successful advance in human technological skill and as a spur to further progress. One of the strongest proponents of this point of view, Julian Simon, suggested that we should welcome further population growth because human ingenuity will always overcome resource limitations and environmental problems.[10] Most economists and ecologists, however, reject this unqualified optimism. While acknowledging the importance of technological progress, most analyses of the overall impact of population growth present the issue as significantly more complex.

Economic theory recognizes a number of ways in which population growth may negatively affect economic development, including:

- **Increased dependency ratios**. Comparing the total number of people who are not working (primarily children and elderly) to the total population gives the dependency ratio for a country. We have seen that a growing population typically includes a high proportion of children. Families must spend more on supporting dependent children and thus have less to save, lowering the national saving rate. Higher spending on health and education is required, reducing funds available for capital investment. These effects tend to slow capital accumulation and economic growth. As population eventually stabilizes, dependency ratios are raised by a high proportion of elderly people, creating a different set of economic problems (see Box 9.3 on p. 222).

- **Increased income inequality**. A rapidly growing population creates an excess supply of labor, which brings down wage rates. High rates of unemployment and underemployment are likely, and a large class of extremely poor people receives no benefit from economic growth. This situation prevails in many Latin American countries as well as in India, where unemployed rural laborers migrate to large cities in search of jobs, creating vast slums surrounding city centers.
- **Natural resource limitations**. As previously noted, the inclusion of **fixed factors**, such as a limited supply of land or nonrenewable natural resources, in the production function can lead to diminishing returns to labor and capital. In general, economists have tended to assume that technological progress can overcome these limitations,[11] but as resource and environmental problems become more pervasive and complex, this assumption may not hold.
- **Market failure**. As we saw in the case of the open-access fishery discussed in Chapter 4, increased population accelerates depletion of the resource. Where private or social property rights are poorly defined, as in the African Sahel or the Brazilian Amazon, population pressure contributes to rapid desertification and deforestation. Also, where externalities such as air and water pollution are uncontrolled, population growth will worsen existing pollution problems.

This more complex view of the relationship between population and economic development has been addressed by Nancy Birdsall, who has suggested that "the long debate over population growth and development is entering a new phase. The emphasis is now on the interaction of rapid population growth with market failures."[12] In a review of economic studies, she points out that policy also plays a crucial role:

> Countries with higher rates of population growth have tended to see less economic growth. An analysis of the role of demography in the "Asian economic miracle" strongly suggests that changes in age structures resulting from declining fertility create a one-time "demographic gift" or window of opportunity, when the working-age population has relatively few dependents, of either young or old age, to support. Countries which recognize and seize on this opportunity can, as the Asian tigers did, realize healthy bursts in economic output.
>
> But such results are by no means assured: only for countries with otherwise sound economic policies will the window of opportunity yield such dramatic results. Finally, several of the studies demonstrate the likelihood of a causal relationship between high fertility and poverty. While the direction of causality is not always clear and very likely is reciprocal (poverty contributes to high fertility and high fertility reinforces poverty), the studies support the view that lower fertility at the country level helps create a path out of poverty for many families.[13]

In view of these recent observations, the question arises: Were the "positive" effects of population growth mainly characteristic of an earlier period in world history—what Herman Daly has referred to as the "empty world" stage, in which resources and environmental absorptive capacities are abundant relative to the scale of the human economy?[14] As global population rises to 8 billion or more, will the negative impacts become dominant? Answering these questions requires a consideration of a broader, more ecologically oriented perspective on population growth.

BOX 9.3 FERTILITY DECLINE: IS THERE A BIRTH DEARTH?

Fertility, the most volatile variable in population projections, has declined worldwide, in many countries at a faster rate than expected. Does this mean that the "population problem" has gone into reverse? Some analysts think so. According to Phillip Longman, "Some people think overpopulation is one of the worst dangers facing the globe. In fact, the opposite is true. As countries get richer, their populations age and their birthrates plummet. And this is not just a problem of rich countries: the developing world is getting older fast. Falling birthrates might seem beneficial, but the economic and social price is too steep to pay" (Longman, 2004).

Longman is really referring to two issues. One is in areas like Europe and Japan, where fertility rates have largely fallen below replacement levels. These countries face the prospect of a high dependency ratio of elderly people, with a diminished workforce to support them. Another is in the developing world, where a small number of countries are now approaching, or have reached, replacement fertility levels. Slower population growth is likely to be beneficial in these developing countries, lowering the child dependency ratio, and providing a higher proportion of working-age people to contribute to national productivity.

Lower fertility in India, for example, has gone hand in hand with improvement of women's status and economic well-being (B. Crossette "Population Estimates Fall as Poor Women Assert Control," *New York Times*, March 10, 2002). Stabilizing populations also reduce pressure on scarce water supplies, arable land, and other resources. According to an expert panel on population issues, "fertility decline in high-fertility countries, by slowing population growth, makes many environmental problems easier to solve and development easier to achieve" (International Institute for Applied Systems Analysis, 2001).

A different story is unfolding in Japan, where the birthrate has been in sharp decline since the 1950s and reached an all-time low of 1.3 live births per woman in 2010. If these trends continue, the population of Japan is projected to fall from 128 million to 95 million by 2050 (Population Reference Bureau, 2011).

The elderly population has been growing steadily, so by 2040 more than a third of the population will be older than sixty-five, and "there will almost be one centenarian to welcome each Japanese newborn" (Eberstadt, 2012). The problems of supporting an increasing number of elderly with a shrinking workforce also affect Europe and within the next several decades will have a major impact in China and other developing countries.

The problems of population stabilization, however, will have to be faced to prevent global population from growing indefinitely. As we have seen, even the lowest global projections show population increasing by well over a billion by 2025, and areas that still have high fertility, such as Africa, are likely to experience a doubling of population before 2050. Rates of population growth are slower in Latin America and Asia, but increases of 150 million and 1 billion, respectively, are projected for these areas. Thus Longman's prescription of trying to deal with the situation by policies to promote fertility seems unwise for the developing world, even if it might be relevant for Europe or Japan, where fertility has fallen well below replacement levels.

9.5 ECOLOGICAL PERSPECTIVES ON POPULATION GROWTH

Whereas the standard economic perspective sees no inherent limitations on population or output growth, the ecological approach is based on the concept of **carrying capacity**, which implies some practical limits to the population that can occupy a certain region. This certainly applies to animal populations in nature.

If, for example, a herd of grazing animals exceeds the land's carrying capacity, food will run short, many individuals will starve, and the population will be reduced to more sustainable levels. Predator species are even more tightly constrained in numbers, based on the available prey populations. Since animals live by consum-

carrying capacity
the level of population and consumption that can be sustained by the available natural resource base.

solar flux
the continual flow of solar energy to
the earth.

ing either plants or other animals, all life on earth depends on the ability of green plants to capture solar energy. The available **solar flux**, or flow of sunlight to the earth's surface, is thus the ultimate determinant of carrying capacity.

Can human populations escape the logic of carrying capacity? Certainly we have been very successful at stretching its limits. The use of artificial fertilizers has greatly increased agricultural outputs. Fossil fuel and nuclear energy provide far more power for industrialization than any solar flux that we currently capture, either directly through solar energy systems or indirectly through hydroelectric and wind power. Through these means, 7 billion people can live on a planet that a century ago supported only 1.5 billion.

However, this expansion of carrying capacity has a significant ecological cost. The extraction of large quantities of fossil fuels and mineral stocks causes environmental degradation both in production and through the waste products generated. Some of the wastes and pollutants are cumulative—their negative environmental effects build up over time.

A prime example is global climate change caused by burning fossil fuels. Soil erosion, depletion of aquifers, and buildup of long-lived toxic and nuclear wastes are also cumulative processes. While increasing the earth's carrying capacity today, we build up problems for the future. Many of these issues already pose major problems—how much worse will they become if a significantly larger population is consuming at higher per capita levels than today? How can we accommodate an additional 2 billion or more people with their food demands, carbon emissions, and other ecological impacts?[15]

Ecologists have identified three major areas in which current economic activities are systematically undermining the planet's long-term carrying capacity. The first is erosion and degradation of topsoil; topsoil losses worldwide are currently estimated at 24 billion tons annually, with nearly 11 percent of the world's vegetated land suffering moderate to extreme degradation. The second is overuse and pollution of fresh water supplies—a problem in virtually every country but especially China, India, and parts of the former Soviet Union, where it has reached critical levels. The third, and perhaps most serious, is the loss of biodiversity, with more species driven to extinction every year than at any time in the preceding 65 million years.[16]

Reviewing evidence gathered by dozens of scientists, Paul and Anne Ehrlich conclude that "there is considerable evidence that the enormous expansion of the human enterprise has already caused *Homo sapiens* to overshoot the long-term carrying capacity of Earth—the number of people that could be sustained for many generations without reducing the resources necessary to similarly maintain an equal population size in the future."[17]

The Impacts of Population, Affluence, and Technology

We can conceptualize the interrelationship of population, economic growth, and environment in an equation linking all three, which has come to be known as IPAT. The equation states that:

$$I = P \times A \times T$$

where:

identity

a mathematical statement that is true by definition.

I = Ecological impact (e.g., pollution or natural resource depletion)
P = Population
A = Affluence measured as output/population
T = Technology variable measuring ecological impact per unit of output

This equation is an **identity**, a mathematical statement that is true by definition. The right-hand side of the equation can be mathematically stated as follows:

$$Population \times Output / Population \times Ecological\ Impact / Output$$

"Population" and "Output" cancel each other out since they occur in both the numerator and the denominator, leaving only ecological impact—which is the same as the left-hand variable. Thus we cannot argue with the equation itself. The only questions are what the levels of the variables will be, and what determines them. What do we know about these questions?

We have seen that global population (P) is projected to increase by 2 billion, or about 30 percent, over the next forty years, according to the UN medium-variant projection (see Table 9.2 and Figure 9.4). We also know that average per capita consumption (A), is steadily increasing throughout the world. If per capita consumption grows at 2 percent per year, which most development economists would view as a minimally satisfactory rate, it will increase by a factor of 2.7 in fifty years. The combined impacts of A and P will therefore multiply the right-hand side of the equation by a factor of 3.5.

What about T? Improved technology could lower the ecological impact per unit of GDP—let us say by a factor of 2. This would still leave us with a significantly increased level of overall environmental impact (in terms of pollution and pressure on natural resources, land, water, forests, biodiversity, etc.). Given the current level of concern about environmental problems, this seems unacceptable. In order to project a lower overall environmental impact, we will need technological improvements that would lower the environmental impact by a factor of 4 or more.

Of course, a mathematical abstraction such as IPAT gives little insight into the specifics behind these very broad concepts. IPAT has been criticized because it assumes that P, A, and T are independent of one another when in fact they are related—the true nature of that relationship being a subject of controversy, as we have seen earlier. In a review on the theoretical implications of the use of the IPAT equation, Marian Chertow stresses:

> The chicken-and-egg nature of this debate—whether population or technology is a bigger contributor to environmental damage—is revealing. Does an increased population call for improved technology or does improved technology increase carrying capacity? (Boserup 1981; Kates 1997). Cross-country comparisons show that different types of ecological impacts present very different types of relation with the level of affluence (factor A) or economic prosperity as measured by GDP per capita. For instance, many types of air pollutants typically decrease with the level of GDP per capita, whereas CO_2 emissions increase with the level of affluence (Shafik and Bandyopadhyay, 1992).[18]

While the IPAT formulation has been mostly used by scientists (biologists, ecologists, engineers, etc.), it has faced strong criticism from social scientists and economists on the grounds that it covers up some basic issues concerning causes of population growth, consumption distribution, and the working of markets. The field of industrial ecology (discussed in Chapter 17) has focused its attention mostly on T in the IPAT equation, emphasizing the need for a major technological leap forward that would reduce T by a factor of 4 or even 10.[19]

One obvious concern is highly unequal consumption per capita throughout the world. The one-quarter of the world's population living in developed countries accounts for roughly three-quarters of global consumption. Poverty, a lack of basic health services, and poor education in many developing countries contribute to high population growth rates. This suggests a crucial need to focus on issues of inequality rather than only on total population or economic output.

Perhaps the economic and ecological perspectives can converge. Even if we cannot identify a fixed carrying capacity for the planet, it is clear that population growth at the levels that we are now experiencing increases virtually all resource and environmental stresses (see Box 9.4). This means that it is vital to have progress on all fronts—reducing population growth, moderating the growth of consumption, improving social equity, and introducing environmentally friendly technologies.[20]

BOX 9.4   HUMANITY'S ECOLOGICAL FOOTPRINT

Substantial research has focused on measuring humanity's impact on the environment. Humans affect the environment in multidimensional ways, including disruption of natural cycles, depletion of the ozone layer, species extinction, and disposal of toxic pollutants. From a policy perspective, converting all these effects to a single index may have some advantages. Furthermore, this index should be measured in units that people can easily understand and interpret. Finally, the necessary data for the measurement of this index should be available at all scales, from an individual to a country, and in all societies and countries of the world, to allow for comparisons.

One such index calculates environmental impacts using "ecological footprints." Originally developed by Wackernagel and Rees (1996), the ecological footprint (EF) concept attempts to convert all human impacts into equivalent units of biologically productive land area. In other words, a person's ecological footprint is the amount of land required to support his or her lifestyle.

Some effects convert easily to land-area footprints. For example, demand for meat converts to pasture area needed to raise livestock. Other impacts are more difficult to translate into land-area equivalents. For instance, carbon dioxide emissions from burning fossil fuels are accounted for in the EF approach based on the area of vegetation that would be required to absorb the carbon emitted.

Calculation of a country's ecological footprint requires data on more than 100 factors, including demand for food products, timber, energy, industrial machinery, office supplies, and vehicles. A demonstration of the detailed calculations involved in obtaining a country's ecological footprint, using Italy as an example, is available at www.footprintnetwork.org. An individual ecological footprint calculation is at www.myfootprint.org.

Comparing a region's ecological footprint to its available land helps determine whether the region creates a sustainable environmental impact. Tables 9.3 and 9.4 present the per capita and total ecological footprints and available productive land for major regions and the world. The per capita ecological footprints are much higher in developed countries than in developing countries.

Most countries, developed or developing, are currently running an ecological deficit. The global per capita impact of 2.69 hectares per person exceeds the available biologically productive land on earth (2.0 ha/cap). Thus, the EF approach indicates that current global environmental impacts are not sustainable, implying a depletion of natural capital.

(continued)

BOX 9.4 *(continued)*

Table 9.3

Per-Person Ecological Footprint of Consumption, 2005

Country/Region	Population (millions)	Ecological footprint of consumption (gha* per person)	Biocapacity (gha per person)	Ecological deficit or reserve (gha per person)
World	6,476	2.69	2.06	−0.63
High income	972	6.40	3.67	−2.71
Middle income	3,098	2.19	2.16	−0.03
Low Income	2,371	1.00	0.88	−0.12

Source: Ecological Footprint Atlas 2008, Global Footprint Network, Research and Standards Department.
Note: gha = global hectare (a measure of area = 10,000 square meters or 2.47 acres). A global hectare represents one hectare of global average productivity.

Table 9.4

Total Ecological Footprint of Consumption, 2005

Country/Region	Population (millions)	Ecological footprint of consumption (gha*)	Biocapacity (gha)	Ecological deficit or reserve (gha)
World	6,476	17,444	13,361	−4,083
High income	972	6,196	3,562	−2,634
Middle income	3,098	6,787	6685	−102
Low income	2,371	2,377	2,090	−287

Source: Ecological Footprint Atlas 2008, Global Footprint Network, Research and Standards Department.
Note: gha = global hectare (a measure of area = 10,000 square meters or 2.47 acres). A global hectare represents one hectare of global average productivity.

The concept and methodology of ecological footprints remain controversial. The March 2000 volume of the journal *Ecological Economics* presented a forum of twelve articles related to the ecological footprint concept. Some of the articles were particularly critical of the approach. For example, Ayres (2000) claims that the EF concept "is too aggregated (and too limited in other respects) to be an adequate guide for policy purposes at the national level." Other researchers, while recognizing that the EF approach requires further refinement, believe it is a valuable analytical tool with policy relevance. Herendeen (2000) notes that the "EF, as modified and improved, is an excellent tool to illustrate the larger picture, and the details." At a minimum, the debate over the EF methodology has raised awareness of the need to go beyond the rhetoric of sustainability toward quantifiable results.

Sources: Ayres, 2000; Herendeen, 2000; Wackernagel and Rees, 1996.

9.6 POPULATION POLICIES FOR THE TWENTY-FIRST CENTURY

In recent years, the discussion of population policy has shifted. Past debate was dominated by the conflict between "optimists," who saw no problem in increasing population, and "pessimists," who predicted catastrophe. Now, elements of consensus are emerging. Most analysts accept that increasing population places extra stress on the environment and resources and agree that slower population growth in the future is essential. How can we accomplish this?

Countries have sometimes attempted to control population growth by government compulsion. The most prominent example of this is China's draconian "one-child family" policy. While effective in a strongly controlled economy and civil society such as China's, such policies have been discredited in most other countries both on human rights grounds and because they fail to alter basic incentives regarding fertility. Rather than changing people's desires to have children, they rely on penalties including forced abortions and sterilization of women.

Birthrates can fall rapidly, however, when people—especially women—reach higher levels of education and literacy and enjoy better employment opportunities and access to family planning. Significant voluntary reduction in the birthrate in many East Asian countries as well as in many parts of India has resulted from higher levels of basic education, health care, and job security.[21]

In analyzing which population policies are most effective, Nancy Birdsall focuses on the link between high fertility and poverty and the resulting vicious circle of negative social and environmental outcomes. She identifies a significant range of policies that can help both to slow population growth and to improve economic efficiency and output. Prominent among these are the promotion of education and other social programs, improvement in the status of women, and improved nutrition and health care, including the availability of contraception.[22]

All these policies tend to lower fertility rates and are identified by Birdsall as "win-win" policies—policies that benefit both the economy and the environment through voluntary moderation of population growth. Sound macroeconomic policies, improved credit markets, and improved conditions for agriculture are also important in promoting broad-based growth and poverty reduction, which in turn is critical for population/environment balance.

Such policies are essential for averting serious environmental and social breakdown in many developing countries. As people struggle to respond to higher demands on the land, slower population growth allows crucial breathing space—time to innovate and adapt. Higher population growth rates can push rural communities over the edge into neo-Malthusian collapse—not because of an absolute limit on carrying capacity but because the means and incentives to adopt new techniques were not forthcoming in time.

Urban areas, where population growth is most rapid due to a combination of natural increase and migration, often experience major social and infrastructure problems. Urban populations in Asia and Africa are projected to double over the next thirty years.[23] Inadequate housing and sanitation, congestion, air and water pollution, deforestation, solid waste problems, and soil contamination are typical of large cities in developing countries. Attempts to respond to massive social and environmental problems in cities are made more difficult by continuing rapid and unplanned growth. Moderation of overall population growth will have to be an essential component of efforts to achieve urban sustainability.[24]

Population growth was a major factor in shaping development patterns during the second half of the twentieth century and will continue to play a central role during the first half of the twenty-first. The differing perspectives of economists, ecologists, demographers, and other social theorists can all contribute to the development of effective policies aimed at population stabilization and an appropriate population/environment balance.

In later chapters, we use this overview of population as our basis for examining specific stresses associated with growing population and higher consumption levels—in agriculture, energy use, demands on natural resources, and pollution generation. In Chapter 21 we return to the issue of a sustainable global future for a growing human population.

SUMMARY

Global population grew very rapidly during the second half of the twentieth century. Although population growth rates are now slowing, total annual additions to global population are still at an all-time high, with a global population of 7 billion in 2011. Growth is projected to continue for at least the next four decades, reaching a level of 8 billion by 2025 and 9 billion by 2045. More than 90 percent of the projected growth will be in the developing countries of Asia, Africa, and Latin America.

Population projections offer no certainty about actual future numbers, but the population momentum phenomenon guarantees significant further growth. Currently, average fertility rates (number of children per woman) are still high throughout the developing world. Although fertility rates are generally falling, it will be decades before population stabilizes.

In Europe, the demographic transition from rapid population growth to relatively stable population has been achieved. In the United States, growth continues due to both population momentum and annual immigration. In the developing world, the demographic transition is far from finished, and significant uncertainty remains about future birthrates. Economic growth, social equity, access to contraception, and cultural factors all play a role.

The economic analysis of population growth emphasizes the potential of other factors, such as technological progress, to offset the effects of population growth. Under favorable conditions for economic and technological progress, population growth may be accompanied by rising living standards. However, rapid population growth accompanied by social inequity and significant environmental externalities may lead to a decline in living standards.

An ecological perspective recognizes more stringent limits to the population carrying capacity of regional and global ecosystems. Greater population increases the demand for materials, energy, and natural resources, which in turn increases pressures on the environment. Given the extent of existing environmental damage, especially where this damage is cumulative or irreversible, the challenge of providing for significantly larger populations poses severe challenges to the earth's ecosystems.

Compulsory population control policies generally fail to alter basic incentives regarding fertility. More effective population policy measures include improved nutrition and health care, greater social equity, women's education, and availability of contraception.

KEY TERMS AND CONCEPTS

capital formation
capital shallowing
carrying capacity
constant returns to scale
demographic transition
dependency ratios
economies of scale
exponential growth
externalities
fertility rate
fixed factors
gross annual population increase
growth rate
identity

income inequality
law of diminishing returns
market failure
natural capital
natural resource limitations
neo-Malthusian perspective
per capita output
population age profile
population cohorts
population growth rate
population momentum
replacement fertility level
solar flux
technological progress

DISCUSSION QUESTIONS

1. What criteria would you use to evaluate the argument between the neo-Malthusians, who see population growth as the major problem facing humanity, and those who argue that population growth is a neutral or even positive factor for economic development? How would you assess the relative urgency of population concerns in the United States (population growth rate 0.7 percent per annum), India (1.9 percent per annum), and Kenya (3.3 percent per annum)?

2. "Every extra mouth brings with it an extra pair of hands. Therefore we do not have to worry about growing population." Relate this statement to the more formal economic analysis of labor force and production. To what extent is the statement true? To what extent is it misleading?

3. The concept of carrying capacity is a useful one for the ecological analysis of animal and plant populations. Is it also useful for the analysis of human population growth? Why or why not?

NOTES

1. United Nations, 2010, Medium Variant.
2. Ehrlich, 1968; Ehrlich and Ehrlich, 1990, 2004.
3. United Nations, 2010.
4. Population Reference Bureau, 2011.
5. United Nations, 2010.
6. *UNAIDS Report on the Global Aids Epidemic, 2010,* www.unaids.org/globalreport/documents/20101123_GlobalReport_full_en.pdf.
7. United Nations, Department of Economic and Social Affairs, Population Division, *Population and HIV/AIDS 2007,* www.un.org/esa/population/publications/AIDS_Wallchart_web_2007/HIV_AIDSchart_2007.pdf. "Southern Africa" includes Botswana, Lesotho, Namibia, South Africa, and Swaziland.

8. Population Reference Bureau, 2011.
9. Boserup, 1981.
10. Simon, 1996.
11. See, for example, Solow, 1986.
12. Birdsall, 1989.
13. Birdsall, Kelley, and Sinding, 2001.
14. Daly, 1996, chap. 2.
15. On the relationship between population and other environmental issues, see, e.g., Ryerson, 2010.
16. Ehrlich, Ehrlich, and Daily, 2003; Postel, 2003.
17. Ehrlich and Ehrlich, 2004.
18. Chertow, 2000.
19. Weizsäcker, Lovins, and Lovins, 1997.
20. Cohen, 1995; Engelman, 2008; Harris et al., 2001, part IV; Halfon, 2007.
21. The cases of China and Kerala are reviewed in Sen, 2000, 219–224. On India, see also Pandya, 2008.
22. See Birdsall, Kelley, and Sinding, 2001; Engelman, 2008; Halfon, 2007; Singh, 2009.
23. United Nations, 2010.
24. See Harris et al., 2001, part IV.

REFERENCES

Ayres, Robert U., 2000. "Commentary on the Utility of the Ecological Footprint Concept," *Ecological Economics*, 32(3): 347–349.

Birdsall, Nancy. 1989. "Economic Analyses of Rapid Population Growth." *World Bank Research Observer* 4(1): 23–50.

Birdsall, Nancy, Allen Kelley, and Stephen Sinding. 2001. *Population Matters: Demographic Change, Economic Growth, and Poverty in the Developing World*. New York: Oxford University Press.

Boserup, Ester. 1981. *Population Growth and Technological Change: A Study of Long-Term Trends*. Chicago: University of Chicago Press.

Caldwell, John C., and Thomas Schindlmayr. 2002. "Historical Population Estimates: Unraveling the Consensus." *Population and Development Review* 28(2): 183–204.

Chertow, Marian R. 2000. "The IPAT Equation and Its Variants: Changing Views of Technology and Environmental Impact." *Journal of Industrial Ecology* 4(4): 13–29.

Cohen, Joel E. 1995. *How Many People Can the Earth Support?* New York: W.W. Norton.

Daly, Herman E. 1996. *Beyond Growth: The Economics of Sustainable Development*. Boston: Beacon Press.

Eberstadt, Nicholas. 2002. "The Future of AIDS." *Foreign Affairs* 81 (November/December). www.foreignaffairs.com/articles/58431/nicholas-eberstadt/the-future-of-aids.

———. 2012. "Japan Shrinks." *Wilson Quarterly* (Spring): 30–37.

Ehrlich, Paul R. 1968. *The Population Bomb*. New York: Ballantine Books.

Ehrlich, Paul R., and Anne H. Ehrlich. 1990. *The Population Explosion*. New York: Simon and Schuster.

———. 2004. *One with Nineveh: Politics, Consumption, and the Human Future*, Washington, DC: Island Press.

Ehrlich, Paul R., Anne H. Ehrlich, and Gretchen Daily. 2003. "Food Security, Population, and Environment." In *Global Environmental Challenges of the Twenty-first Century*, ed. David Lorey. Wilmington, DE: Scholarly Resources.

Engelman, Robert. 2008. *More: Population, Nature, and What Women Want*. Washington, DC: Island Press.

Ewing, Brad, et al., *Ecological Footprint Atlas 2008*. Oakland, California: Global Footprint Network.

Halfon, Saul. 2007. *The Cairo Consensus: Demographic Surveys, Women's Empowerment, and Regime Change in Population Policy*. Lanham, MD: Lexington Books.

Harris, Jonathan M., Timothy A. Wise, Kevin Gallagher, and Neva R. Goodwin, eds. 2001. *A Survey of Sustainable Development: Social and Economic Perspectives*. Washington, DC: Island Press.

Herendeen, Robert A., 2000. "Ecological Footprint Is a Vivid Indicator of Indirect Effects." *Ecological Economics*, 32(3): 357–358.

International Institute for Applied Systems Analysis. 2001. *Demographic Challenges for Sustainable Development: The Laxenburg Declaration on Population and Sustainable Development.* www.popconnect.org/Laxenburg/.

Kates, R. 1997. "Population, Technology, and the Human Environment: A Thread Through Time." In *Technological Trajectories and the Human Environment,* ed. J. Ausubel and H. Langford, 33–55. Washington, DC: National Academy Press.

Kelley, Allen C. 1988. "Economic Consequences of Population Change in the Third World." *Journal of Economic Literature* 26 (December): 1685–1728.

Longman, Phillip. 2004. "The Global Baby Bust." *Foreign Affairs* 83 (May/June). www.foreignaffairs.com/articles/59894/phillip-longman/the-global-baby-bust.

Lorey, David E., ed. 2003. *Global Environmental Challenges of the Twenty-first Century: Resources, Consumption, and Sustainable Solutions.* Wilmington, DE: Scholarly Resources.

Pandya, Rameshwari, ed. 2008. *Women, Welfare and Empowerment in India: A Vision for the 21st Century.* New Delhi: New Century Publications.

Population Reference Bureau. 2011. *2011 World Population Data Sheet.* Washington, DC.

Postel, Sandra. 2003. "Water for Food Production: Will There Be Enough in 2025?" In *Global Environmental Challenges of the Twenty-first Century,* ed. David Lorey. Wilmington, DE: Scholarly Resources.

Repetto, Robert. 1991. *Population, Resources, Environment: An Uncertain Future.* Washington, DC: Population Reference Bureau.

Ryerson, William N. 2010. "Population: The Multiplier of Everything Else." In *The Post-Carbon Reader: Managing the 21st Century's Sustainability Crisis* ed. Richard Heinberg and Daniel Lerch. Healdsburg, CA: Watershed Media.

Sen, Amartya. 2000. *Development as Freedom.* New York: Alfred A. Knopf.

Shafik, N., and S. Bandyopadhyay. 1992. *Economic Growth and Environmental Quality: Time Series and Cross-country Evidence.* World Bank, Policy Research Working Paper Series, no. 904. Washington, DC.

Simon, Julian L. 1996. *The Ultimate Resource 2.* Princeton: Princeton University Press.

Singh, Jyoti Shankar. 2009. *Creating a New Consensus on Population: the Politics of Reproductive Health, Reproductive Rights and Women's Empowerment.* London: Earthscan.

Solow, Robert. 1986. "On the Intertemporal Allocation of Natural Resources." *Scandinavian Journal of Economics* 88: 141–149.

United Nations. Department of Economic and Social Affairs, Population Division. 2010. *World Population Prospects: The 2010 Revision,* http://esa.un.org/unpd/wpp/index.htm.

Von Weizsäcker, Ernst, Amory B. Lovins, and Hunter Lovins. 1997. *Factor Four: Doubling Wealth, Halving Resource Use.* London: Earthscan.

Wackernagel, Mathis, and William Rees, 1996. *Our Ecological Footprint: Reducing Human Impact on Earth.* Stony Creek, CT: New Society.

WEB SITES

1. **www.prb.org.** Home page for the Population Reference Bureau, which provides data and policy analysis on U.S. and international population issues. Its World Data Sheet provides demographic data for every country in the world.
2. **www.un.org/esa/population/unpop.htm.** Web site for the United Nations Population Division, which provides international information on population issues including population projections.
3. **www.populationconnection.org.** Home page for Population Connection, a nonprofit organization that "advocates progressive action to stabilize world population at a level that can be sustained by Earth's resources."

Agriculture, Food, and Environment

CHAPTER 10 FOCUS QUESTIONS

- Can we produce enough food for growing a growing global population?
- Are agricultural production systems degrading the environment?
- What are the impacts of new agricultural technologies?
- How can we develop a sustainable agricultural system for the future?

10.1 FEEDING THE WORLD: POPULATION AND FOOD SUPPLY

Food supply constitutes a fundamental relationship between any human society and its environment. In the wild, animal populations wax and wane based largely on food availability. For many centuries, human numbers were also linked closely to food abundance or scarcity. In the past two centuries, increasingly productive agricultural technology has spurred a significant increase in human population.

Despite unprecedented population growth, average world per capita food production has risen steadily for the past six decades (Figure 10.1). Many economic theorists assert, based on this trend, that history has disproved the Malthusian argument that population would outrun food supply. Before we dismiss concerns over food limitations, however, we must consider several factors that cast a different light on the issues of population, agriculture, and the environment:

- *Land Use.* In the period following World War II, agricultural land use expanded considerably, but the expansion appeared to end around 1990 (see Figure 10.2a). The land most suitable for agriculture is already being farmed, and most remaining lands are marginal in quality. Also, urban and industrial encroachment are cutting into agricultural land and available farmland per person is steadily decreasing as population continues to grow (Figure 10.2b). To feed the world better, we must increase productivity on this shrinking per capita acreage.
- *Consumption Patterns.* Existing food supplies are distributed according to market demand, which strongly favors upper-income consumers. Per capita direct and indirect grain consumption in the United States, for example, is more than three times that in the developing world. This is not because U.S.

Figure 10.1   **World Food Production per Capita, 1961–2010**

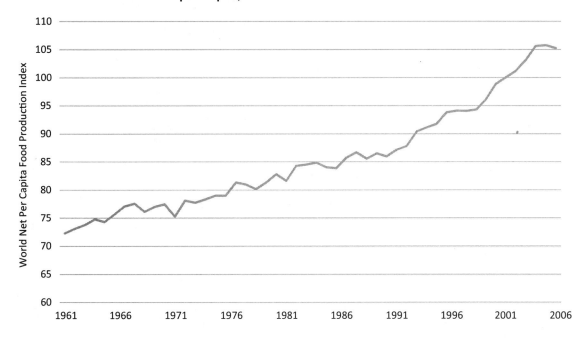

Source: FAO, 2012, Per Capita Production Index Number (2004–2006 = 100).
Note: Production quantities of each commodity are weighted by average international commodity prices and summed for each year.

Figure 10.2 (a)   **Total World Arable and Permanent Cropland, 1961–2009**

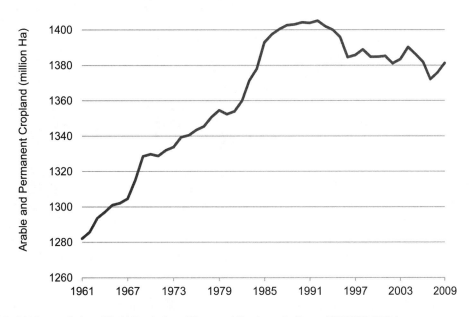

Sources: FAO, 2012; population: World Bank, http://data.worldbank.org/indicator/SP.POP.TOTL/.

Figure 10.2 (b) Arable and Permanent Cropland per Capita, 1961–2009

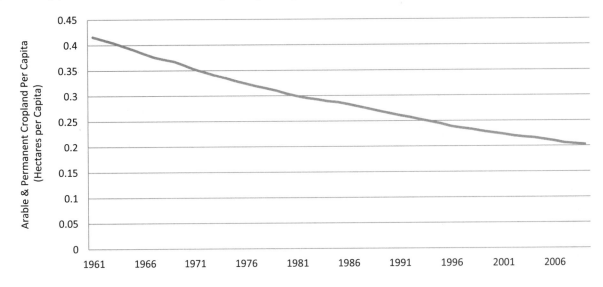

Sources: FAO, 2012; population: World Bank, http://data.worldbank.org/indicator/SP.POP.TOTL/.

nutritional deficit
the failure to meet human demands for basic levels of nutrition.

renewable resources
a resource that is supplied on a continuing basis by ecosystems; renewable resources such as forests and fisheries can be depleted through exploitation.

depletable resource
a renewable resource that can be exploited and depleted, such as soil or clean air.

biodiversity (biological diversity)
the maintenance of many different interrelated species in an ecological community.

citizens eat more grains, but because about three-quarters of U.S. domestic grain use goes to animal feed. The meat-centered U.S. diet thus requires about four times as much agricultural output per person as a typical diet for, say, a citizen of India.

- *Inequalities in Food Distribution.* On average, enough food is produced to provide an adequate diet for everyone on earth. In practice, however, many low-income areas suffer from a **nutritional deficit**, meaning that between 800 million and 1 billion people receive inadequate nutrition.[a]
- *Environmental Impacts of Agriculture.* As agricultural land use has expanded, more marginal and fragile lands have come into cultivation. The result is increased erosion, deforestation, and loss of wildlife habitat. Erosion and depletion of nutrients in the soil mean that a **renewable resource** is being turned into a **depletable resource**, and soil fertility is being "mined" over time. Increased irrigation, crucial to modern agriculture, also brings many environmental problems in its wake, including salinization, alkalinization, and waterlogging, as well as overdraft of ground water and pollution of surface water.

Runoff from chemical fertilizer and pesticide use pollutes land and water and contributes to atmospheric problems such as global warming and ozone depletion. Depletion of **biodiversity** and the creation of "superpests" resistant to pesticides are also results of intensive agriculture. At a minimum, the management of these problems is an important issue in the economics of agriculture. More broadly, these

---

[a]See FAO, 2011. An updated assessment of world hunger statistics, "World Hunger and Poverty Facts and Statistics" is available at http://www.worldhunger.org/.

environmental issues raise questions about the global agricultural system's capacity to sustain growing populations without unacceptable environmental damage.

These factors contribute to a more sophisticated perception of the problems involved in feeding an expanded world population. Rather than focusing on the simple dichotomy of population and food, we must examine interactions between population, per capita food consumption, and the environment.

10.2 TRENDS IN GLOBAL FOOD PRODUCTION

First, let us take a more careful look at the trends in global food production. Figure 10.3 shows trends for total and per capita production of grains. Grain, or cereal, output is easily measured and is significant because it provides the basis for the global diet, especially in poorer countries. Grain consumption is about 50 percent of food consumption worldwide and up to 70 percent in many developing countries.

Figure 10.3 **World Grain Production, Total and per Capita, 1961–2010**

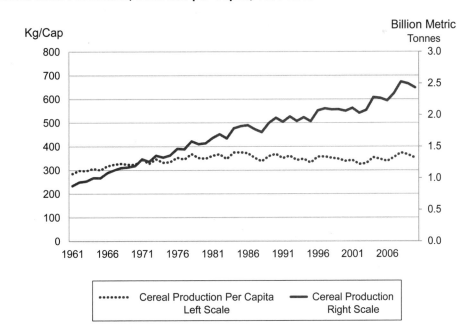

Sources: FAO, 2012; population: World Bank, http://data.worldbank.org.

The total output of grains rose from 1961 to 2010, but the per capita production figures tell a different story. From 1961 to 1985, output per capita increased slowly but steadily. This increase—about 0.5 percent per year—is of crucial importance. It means that people throughout the world experienced gradually improving average nutritional levels. Of course, as we have noted, not all benefited equally, but to some extent "a rising tide lifted all boats."

During the later years, however, we notice a change. Per capita output no longer increases and appears to decline slightly after 1985. Even though, as noted earlier, total food output per capita has continued to increase, grain output has a particular significance. The total food output index is weighted by price, so "luxury" foods will weigh more heavily in the index, while grains such as rice, wheat, and corn provide basic nutrition for most of the world's people.

Some analysts, such as Lester Brown of the Earth Policy Institute, have suggested that this represents a fundamental change in the dynamics of world agricultural production. Citing many of the environmental problems mentioned above, Brown argues that ecological limits already reached will prevent further rapid expansion in agricultural output.[1] Because of slowing growth in agricultural yields, growth in total grain production has no longer outpaced population growth. Growing demand, supply limits, and yield reduction due to extreme climate events mean that "the world may be much closer to an unmanageable food shortage than most people realize."[2] This, of course, would have enormous implications for economic development and for the nutritional status of the world's poorest people.

elasticity of supply
the sensitivity of quantity supplied to prices; an elastic supply means that a proportional increase in prices results in a larger proportional change in quantity supplied; an inelastic supply means that a proportional increase in prices results in a small change.

How can we evaluate Brown's hypothesis? From an economic perspective, the main question is one of price. If, indeed, agriculture experiences supply limitations, we would expect to see rising food prices as demand grows. The simple supply and demand analysis in Figure 10.4 shows this principle. Where **elasticity of supply** is high, as in the left half of the graph, demand increases from D_1 to D_2 with no significant upward pressure on price. With inelastic supply, in the right-hand portion of the graph, rising demand (D_2 to D_3) causes a sharp upward move in price.

Figure 10.4 **Elastic and Inelastic Food Supply**

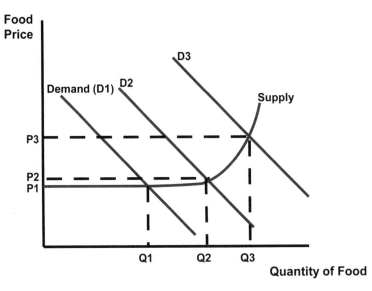

As shown in Figure 10.5, before 2006 there was no sustained increase in prices for cereal crops. Taking inflation into account, real food prices declined from the 1970s through the first decade of the twenty-first century. What, then, explains the change in per capita production trends after 1985? Economists such as Amartya Sen argue that it was primarily a demand-side rather than a supply-side phenomenon. In this view, a general slowdown in economic growth during the 1980s, a result of world recession and debt problems in many developing countries, lowered people's purchasing power for food as well as for other goods. Thus "food output [was] held back by a lack of effective demand in the marketplace" rather than by environmental constraints on production.[3]

Figure 10.5 **U.S. Producer Price Indices of Selected Cereal Crops, 1991–2009**

Figure 10.5 **U.S. Producer Price Indices of Selected Cereal Crops, 1991–2009**

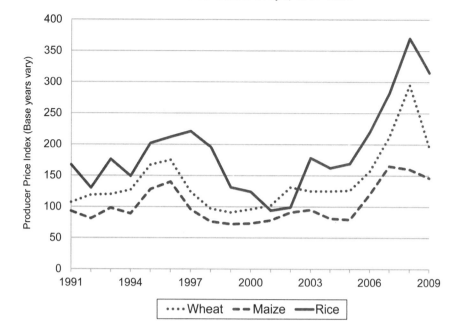

Source: FAO, 2012.

In addition, much of the global slowdown in cereal production during the 1990s can be attributed to lower farm subsidies in the United States and Europe, as well as the economic breakdown in the former Soviet Union.[4] Brown also acknowledges that part of the decline in per capita grain production is associated with an increase in the efficiency with which grain is converted into animal protein. To the extent that this is the case, lower per capita consumption of grain would not indicate any decrease in nutritional status.

Global trends changed, however, starting in 2006. Food prices started to rise, and with the onset of the "food crisis" in 2008, prices reached dramatically higher levels, which led to crises and food riots in many countries (Figure 10.5). After falling back somewhat in 2009 and 2010, food prices again reached all-time highs in 2011 and 2012.[5]

Increased food prices are attributable in part to a growing "global middle class" with higher demands for meat and other luxury food products and in part to demand for **biofuels**, which compete with food crops for limited arable land. Since the U.S. government mandated use of ethanol in fuel, corn ethanol as a share of U.S. corn production has risen from 5 percent in 2000 to 40 percent in 2012, significantly increasing the price of corn exports.[6]

At the same time, new land for agriculture has become scarce. The steady increase in land in cultivation from the 1950s to the 1980s, which helped to accommodate growing world food demand, appeared to reach its limits around 1990, and since then there has been a slight decline in world arable area (see Figure 10.2a). It appears that a higher price world food regime may well be a permanent change, not a temporary spike.

In many developing countries, the poor bear the greatest burden of economic recession, increasing the problem of inequality of distribution. At the same time,

biofuels

fuels derived from crops, crop wastes, animal wastes, or other biological sources.

Figure 10.6 **Per Capita Cereals Production in South America and Sub-Saharan Africa, 1961–2009 (kg/capita)**

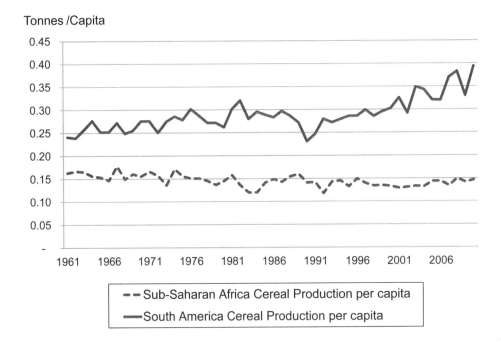

Source: FAO, 2012; U.S. Census, 2012, www.census.gov.

the marginal lands farmed by the poor suffer the greatest damage from erosion and other environmental problems. Loss of food-buying power for the poor, combined with a decline in the productive capacity of marginal farmlands, damages the nutritional status of the poor, even as overall world grain production increases. While per capita grain production has recently increased in South America, it has stagnated or declined in sub-Saharan Africa (see Figure 10.6) as a result of both population increase and weak yield growth.

Combined with rising food prices, these trends indicate continuing problems with food security in the developing world. According to the Food and Agriculture Organization of the United Nations (FAO), "[food] **price volatility** makes both smallholder farmers and poor consumers increasingly vulnerable to poverty." Globally, the number of people suffering from malnutrition has not declined, remaining steady at about 850 million.[7] There is a dramatic contrast between countries such as China, where per capita food production has risen steadily, and areas such as Africa, where it has barely increased since the 1960s (Figure 10.7).

price volatility
rapid and frequent changes in price, leading to market instability.

Land Use and Equity Issues

The issue of unequal distribution is linked to that of land use. We have already noted that most good agricultural land is currently in production. In a market economy, land will generally be used for the highest-valued crop, as shown in Figure 10.8.

Figure 10.7 **Per Capita Food Production Indices for China and Africa, 1961–2009**

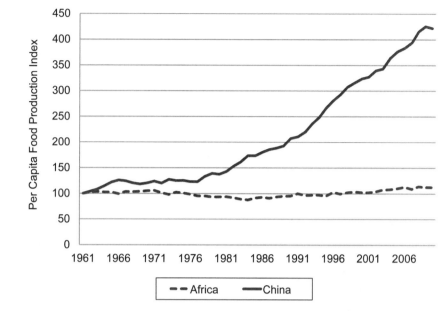

Source: FAO, 2012.

Figure 10.8 **Land Quality, Crop Value, and Land Use**

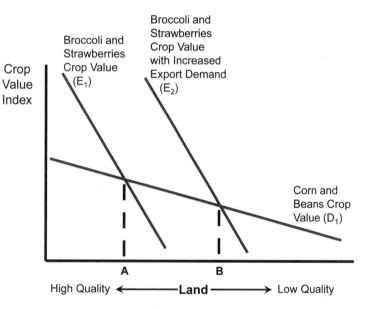

In the figure, land is rated by quality on the *x*-axis, with the highest quality land on the left side, and quality declining as we move rightward. The *y*-axis shows the value of crops grown on the land. This **crop value index** will differ depending on how the land is used. Some crops require higher-quality land and produce higher value per acre. Other crops grow on land of varying quality but produce less market value per acre. In economic terms, the crop value index represents the

crop value index

an index indicating the relative value of production of different crops on a given quantity of land.

marginal revenue product
the additional revenue obtained by increasing an input level by one unit; equal to marginal physical product multiplied by marginal revenue.

marginal physical product
the additional quantity of output produced by increasing an input level by one unit.

marginal revenue product of the land, which is the **marginal physical product** (additional quantity of a particular crop) times the price of the crop.

For example, in Mexico much land is devoted to growing corn and beans for local consumption. But growing broccoli and strawberries for export produces higher revenues. The intersection of the two crop value lines D_1 and E_1 shows how the land will be divided between production for export and production for domestic use. On the high quality land to the left of point A, the most valuable product is the export crop, for which the land will be used. Corn and beans will be grown on the lower-quality land to the right of point A.

Now suppose that the demand for export crops increases, as shown by crop value line E_2, while demand for domestic foods remains the same. The crop value line for exported products rises, reflecting higher prices for broccoli and strawberries. As a result, the land use pattern changes, with export production expanding up to point B and domestic production squeezed onto lower-quality land to the right of Point B. In Mexico, this land use trend has accelerated as a result of the North American Free Trade Agreement (NAFTA).[8]

What does this imply for the environment and for the nutritional status of the population? One likely result is that larger commercial farms will displace smaller farmers who lack good access to export markets. This will increase pressure on the marginal farmlands (to the right in the graph). Hill slopes, forest margins, and arid lands are all especially vulnerable to the kind of environmental degradation that results when displaced people move to whatever land is available. We see the effects of this throughout much of Africa, Latin America, and Asia.

If revenues from export crops are unequally distributed, poorer people's diets will worsen as less corn and beans are produced for domestic consumption. Small farmers who share in export revenues can buy imported foods with the proceeds from cash crops, but more frequently they will lose out to larger producers in export markets.

10.3 PROJECTIONS FOR THE FUTURE

Population projections for the first half of the twenty-first century, as discussed in Chapter 9, show total world population reaching a level of around 9 billion by 2050. What new stresses will the additional demand for food place on the environment? Will we exceed agricultural **carrying capacity**? Will we experience food shortages? The grain production figures shown in Table 10.1 (p. 242) illustrate some implications of projected increases in global population.

carrying capacity
the level of population and consumption that can be sustained by the available natural resource base.

As of 2007–9 the world produced about 2.5 billion metric tons of grain (column 2).[b] If evenly distributed, this would provide each person with about 350 kilograms (kg) of grain (cereals) per year—approximately 1 kg, or 2.2 pounds, per day (column 3). This grain crop requires about half the world's cropland. The other half is devoted to vegetables, fruits, oilseeds, root crops, and nonfood crops such as cotton.

This level of output, evenly distributed, would be adequate to provide each person with a mostly vegetarian diet, supplemented with a little meat, fish, or eggs—a diet characteristic of much of the developing world. The largely meat-centered diet characteristic of most of the developed world, however, requires much larger

---

[b]In analyzing agricultural production statistics, it is useful to calculate a three-year average in order to smooth out year-to-year variations in harvests.

Figure 10.9 **Global Meat Production Per Capita (kg/cap/year), 1961–2009**

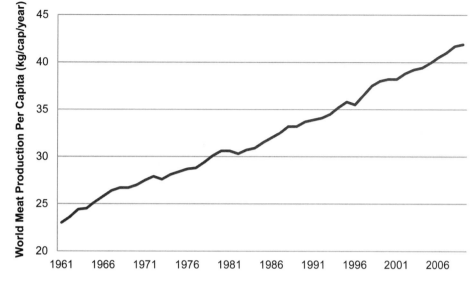

Source: FAO, 2012.

amounts of grain per person—not consumed directly, of course, but used for livestock feed. About three-quarters of the U.S. domestic consumption of cereal, for example, goes to feed cattle, pigs, and poultry.

Globally, therefore, distribution of the existing output is significantly unequal. Annual grain consumption in the United States is about 900 kg per capita, including direct consumption and feedgrains for livestock. In the developing world, it averages under 300 kg per capita. Consumption levels throughout much of the developing world are sufficient for an adequate non–meat-centered diet, but inequality of distribution within countries leaves many of the poorest with inadequate levels of food consumption.

As economic development proceeds, per capita demand for food rises. This is partly because poorer people can afford to buy more basic foods and partly because middle-class consumers shift to a meat-based diet (Figure 10.9). As we look ahead to the future, we must prepare to provide for both an increased total population, and a higher average consumption per person.

Future Production and Yield Requirements

The population projections in Table 10.1 for 2025 (column 4) are in the middle range of published estimates.[9] Note that over 95 percent of the population growth will take place in developing countries. When we combine this population growth with a modest projected increase in per capita consumption, it is clear that grain consumption will increase by about 50 percent in the developing world excluding China (column 5).[c] However, agricultural land area will increase little (as discussed earlier). Output per hectare of land in developing countries must rise by at least 35 percent (compare yield columns 3 and 6).[d]

---

[c]The rate of increase in per capita consumption assumed here is 0.5 percent per annum. Faster economic growth could increase this significantly if diets shift to meat products as incomes rise.

[d]1 hectare = 2.477 acres.

Table 10.1

Population and Cereal Consumption Projections for 2025

Region	1. Population in 2008 (millions)	2. Cereal production 2007-2009 average (mmt)	3. Cereal yields 2007-2009 average (kg/ha)	4. Projected population 2025	5. Projected cereal requirements in 2025 (mmt)	6. Projected yield requirements for self-sufficiency in 2025 (kg/ha)
World	6,715	2,457	3,500	7,989	2,931	3,967
Developed countries	1,225	963	4,358	1,272	783	3,421
Developing countries	5,489	1,506	3,119	6,717	2,149	4,214
Developing countries (excluding China)	4,172	1,033	2,608	5,323	1,570	3,703
Africa	980	149	1,446	1,431	315	2,942
Latin America and Caribbean	576	178	3,513	682	222	4,262
Asia	4,051	1,178	3,583	4,715	1,626	5,052
Asia (excluding China)	2,734	705	2,915	3,321	1,032	4,376
China	1,317	473	5,439	1,394	570	6,629
United States and Canada	337	464	6,089	388	374	4,407
Europe (excluding Russia)	595	360	4,490	601	328	4,002
Russia	140	94	2,220	128	57	1,157
Oceania	34	32	1,604	41	16	1,258

Sources: Population: www.census.gov/population/international/data/idb/informationGateway.php; production: http://faostat.fao.org. Projections assume an increase in 0.5% in per capita consumption in the developing world. Projections updated from Harris, 1996.

Notes: kg/ha = kilograms per hectare; mmt = million metric tons.

Column 6 in Table 10.1 shows the agricultural yields that will be required for self-sufficiency in grain production (supplying domestic demand without imports) in developed and developing countries. Average yields in the developing world must rise from the present 2.8 metric tons per hectare to more than 4 metric tons per hectare.[e] For the developing world, excluding China, yields must increase by 40 percent over present levels. Yields in Asia as a whole must rise from 3.5 metric tons per hectare to 5 metric tons per hectare. Yields in Africa would need to more than double for self-sufficiency in 2025.

Of course, not every region must achieve self-sufficiency; grains can be imported from countries with surplus capacity. The possibilities for meeting demand through increased trade, however, are limited. If we assume that most countries can achieve, but not exceed, yield levels similar to those now reached in developed countries, both Asia and Africa will significantly increase import demands.

According to recent studies, net cereal imports by developing countries will nearly double by 2020, from 104 million metric tons to 201 million metric tons and rise further to 265 million tons by 2030.[10] Where will this extra export production come from? Current world cereal exports are predominantly from North America and Europe. Both of these areas already have very high yields, suggesting that future yield increases in these areas may be difficult to achieve.[11] In addition, current Census Bureau projections show U.S. population rising from 314 million in 2012 to 351 million by 2025 and more than 420 million by 2050.[12] If this larger U.S. population consumes the same kind of meat-centered diet Americans now favor, there will be a significant added grain demand for

---

[e]1 metric ton = 1000 kilograms.

animal feed. These combined demand pressures, together with the demand for biofuels previously mentioned, could lead to rising grain prices, confronting the world's poorest countries with the problem of purchasing a larger volume of more expensive food imports.

Analysts who offer a more optimistic view of the future rely on two factors. The first is reduced population growth. As we have seen, population growth estimates show significant variation. If we accept the low-range projections, the pressures on the global agricultural system are significantly smaller.[13] The second factor is yield increases. Some regions have achieved grain yields of 6 to 9 metric tons per hectare (6,000 to 9,000 kg per hectare). If this success could be extended worldwide, grain production would be more than ample.[14]

However, these population and yield variables may move in the opposite direction. Population may rise higher than the level in medium projections. Environmental problems, including water shortages and global climate change, might endanger even present levels of yields in major regions. It seems prudent to prepare for unpleasant as well as pleasant surprises.[15] According to the FAO, "Achieving [an increase of 1 billion tons in global cereal output] should not be taken for granted, as land and water resources are now more stretched than in the past and the potential for continued growth of yield is more limited."[16]

If we take this approach, the critical question becomes the **environmental sustainability** of agricultural production. To assess the likelihood of an adequate solution to the food problem, we must consider in more detail the environmental stresses associated with pushing our agricultural systems to their limits.

10.4 AGRICULTURE'S IMPACT ON THE ENVIRONMENT

Soil Erosion and Degradation

With the exception of some hydroponics and aquaculture, almost all agriculture depends on soil. Soil, as we have noted, can be either a renewable or a depletable resource. Ideally, agricultural techniques should not degrade soils and should replenish soil productivity over time through **nutrient recycling** from crop residues. If this were the case, agricultural output would be truly sustainable and could continue at present levels indefinitely.

Unfortunately, the situation in almost all the world's major agricultural areas is quite different: Soil erosion and degradation is widespread. Between 30 and 50 percent of the earth's surface is affected by erosion and soil degradation. Erosion damages crop productivity by reducing the availability of water, nutrients, and organic matter. Water resources are also degraded by sediments and pollutants associated with erosion. Soil loss rates are typically highest in developing countries:

> Severe soil erosion is occurring in most of the world's agricultural regions, and the problem is growing as more marginal land is brought into production and less crop residues are returned to the soil. Soil loss rates in Europe range between 10 and 20 tons/hectare/year. In the United States, soil erosion on cropland averages 16 t/ha/yr. In Asia, Africa, and South America, soil erosion rates on cropland range between 20 and 40 t/ha/yr.[17]

The United Nations Environmental Programme's Global Assessment of Soil Degradation (GLASOD) estimates that erosion severely degrades an additional

---

environmental sustainability

the continued existence of an ecosystem in a healthy state; ecosystems may change over time but do not significantly degrade.

nutrient recycling

the ability of ecological systems to transform nutrients such as carbon, nitrogen, and phosphorus into different chemical forms.

5 million to 6 million hectares of land each year.[18] As well as soil loss from erosion, further soil degradation occurs from excessive irrigation, overgrazing, and destruction of trees and ground cover.

The Economics of Erosion and Erosion Control

crop rotation and fallowing
an agricultural system involving growing different crops on the same piece of land at different times and regularly taking part of the land out of production.

In many cases, farmers can greatly reduce erosion and soil degradation by **crop rotation and fallowing**—alternating grain and legume crops and taking the land out of production every few years. The farmer's costs include forgoing revenues in any year when the land is out of production and possibly settling for lower revenues in years when the land produces crops other than those with the highest value. Farmers must make an economic calculation as to whether the immediate costs of erosion control are worth the long-term benefits.

Consider a simple example. Suppose that a farmer can obtain $100,000 in annual revenues by continually growing the highest-value crops with no provision for rebuilding soils or erosion control. Under these conditions, erosion will cause an annual decline of about 1 percent in yield. An effective erosion control program will reduce revenues by $15,000 per year. Is the program worth it to the farmer?

discount rate
the annual rate at which future benefits or costs are discounted relative to current benefits or costs.

present value
the current value of a steam of future costs or benefits; a discount rate is used to convert future costs or benefits to present values.

The answer depends on the **discount rate** used to balance present versus future costs. One percent yield loss means a monetary loss of $1,000. But this is not just a one-time loss; it will continue into the future. How do we evaluate this stream of losses resulting from one year's erosion? In economic terms, we apply a discount rate as discussed in Chapters 5 and 6. Suppose that we select a 10 percent discount rate. The **present value** (PV) of the stream of losses extending indefinitely into the future is equal to:

$$PV = (-\$1,000)(1/0.10) = -\$10,000.$$

The benefits of erosion control are thus $10,000—not enough, in this example, to justify $15,000 in lost revenue. Under these conditions, it is economically optimal to continue the erosive practices—but it is certainly not ecologically sustainable. Following this economic logic, the farmer will leave severely degraded land for the next generation.

Unfortunately, many farmers are under exactly this kind of economic pressure to maximize short-term revenues. Note that if we used a lower interest rate—say 5 percent—the benefits of erosion control, calculated at $20,000, would exceed the costs and in theory make erosion control economically beneficial. Even so, the short-term losses might still be difficult to accept. An ecologically sound soil management policy is thus dependent on the farmer's foresight, relatively low interest rates, and the financial flexibility to invest in erosion control today for long-term benefits. Erosion control can be promoted by targeted government low-interest loan programs to support soil conservation measures.

externalities
an effect of a market transaction that changes the utility, positively or negatively, of those outside the transaction.

Off-farm effects of erosion are an additional problem. In many areas, major dams have silted up with eroded soil, ultimately destroying their potential for power generation and wasting billions in investment. Heavy siltation also causes extensive damage to river ecology. Because these costs are **externalities** from the farmer's point of view, a social decision is required to respond to this aspect of erosion impacts.

Environmental Effect of Fertilizer Use

The steady increase in average characteristic of modern agriculture depends strongly on increased fertilizer use. Figure 10.10 shows this pattern for major world regions over a forty-year period from 1960 to 2000. Increased fertilizer use is clearly associated with higher yields. The lines for each region, followed from lower left to upper right, indicate trends. Over time, countries tend to shift from traditional agriculture with low fertilizer input to modern agriculture's heavy fertilizer use and high yields. All major regions except Africa have followed this trend, resulting in food output generally outpacing population growth over the long term.[f]

Figure 10.10   **Yield/Fertilizer Relationship for Major Regions: Averaged Data for Periods 1961–1970, 1971–1980, 1981–1990, and 1991–2001**

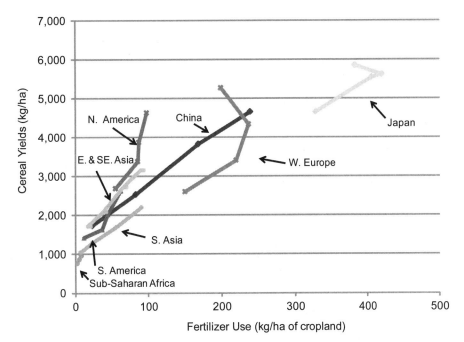

Source: FAO, 2012 (some fertilizer series have been discontinued).

What are the environmental implications of this "modernizing" process in agriculture? In general, modern agricultural techniques rely on a "package" of inputs including fertilizer, pesticides, irrigation, mechanization, and high-yielding crop varieties. In Figure 10.10, fertilizer per hectare serves as what economists call a **proxy variable** for this package. Higher use of fertilizer is so strongly associated with higher use of the other inputs that measuring fertilizer use alone gives us a good idea of the degree of agricultural modernization. Each of these inputs, however, relates to specific environmental problems, and as high-yield input use has increased, so has the seriousness of these environmental problems.

proxy variable
a variable that is meant to represent a broader concept, such as the use of fertilizer application rates to represent the input-intensity of agricultural production.

---

[f]Africa has seen little increase in use of fertilizer and other agricultural inputs and concomitantly little increase in yields over the forty-year period.

Fertilizer supplies nutrients to the soil and therefore to crops. Most fertilizers supply the three major nutrients of nitrate, phosphate, and potassium. But a significant portion of the nutrients applied do not reach the crops as intended. Instead, they leach into ground and surface water, where they become serious pollutants.

Excessive nitrate in water is damaging to human health. Nitrates and phosphates also promote unwanted algae growth that chokes out other life in rivers, lakes, and even oceans. Most agricultural areas in the U.S. Midwest and West suffer from these problems. In the Gulf of Mexico, a huge "dead zone" caused by agricultural runoff covers an area of 18,000 square kilometers and threatens commercial and recreational fisheries. In the Mediterranean, large portions of the sea have suffered severe ecological damage from agricultural runoff pollution, with giant mats of algae blanketing coastlines in the Aegean Sea and elsewhere. Inefficient and excessive fertilizer use has created especially severe agricultural problems in Russia and Eastern Europe. Inland seas such as the Black and Caspian Seas have experienced extinctions of numerous local species as a result.

Another damaging effect of excessive fertilizer use is more subtle. As large amounts of nitrate, phosphate, and potassium are added to the soil year after year, other nutrients present in smaller quantities—called **micronutrients**—become depleted.[g] This gradually reduces both yields and nutritional values of the crops. Like erosion, these are long-term effects, giving farmers little incentive to respond to them so long as current yields are high.

micronutrients

nutrients present in low concentrations in soil, required for plant growth or health.

Fertilizer production is energy intensive. In effect, modern agriculture replaces solar energy and human labor with energy extracted from fossil fuels.[19] Agricultural energy consumption thus contributes to all the environmental problems associated with fossil-fuel energy consumption discussed in Chapters 13, 18, and 19. Agriculture accounts for about 3–5 percent of total energy use. Although not the major component of energy-related issues, this percentage is not insignificant, particularly for developing countries with growing populations that must buy imported energy.[20] Rising oil prices have been one of the primary causes for the recent crisis of high food prices. Fertilizer use also contributes directly to various global atmospheric problems, including global warming and ozone depletion.

Some analysts find it significant that artificial nitrogen applied to crops now exceeds the amount supplied through natural nitrogen fixation by soil microorganisms. Such a large intervention in the earth's **nitrogen cycle** must clearly have ecological consequences. Furthermore, the use of fertilizer is projected to increase steadily to provide the yields needed for the twenty-first century. Perhaps the most encouraging trends in Figure 10.10 are the reductions in fertilizer use seen in recent years in Western Europe and Japan, implying more efficient use since at the same time yields have continued to increase. If this pattern could be duplicated more widely, agricultural productivity could increase at lower environmental cost—but given the overall pattern of rising fertilizer use seen in Figure 10.10—this experience seems to be unusual.

nitrogen cycle

the conversion of nitrogen into different forms in the ecosystem, including the fixation of nitrogen by symbiotic bacteria in certain plants such as legumes.

Pesticide Use

Like fertilizer use, pesticide use has risen rapidly with the spread of modern agriculture (see Figure 10.11). Pesticide use in the United States has leveled off after

---

[g]Micronutrients include boron, copper, cobalt, and molybdenum. While some of these substances can be damaging in large amounts, trace amounts are important for plant growth and human nutrition.

Figure 10.11 **U.S. Conventional Pesticide Usage, 1964–2001**

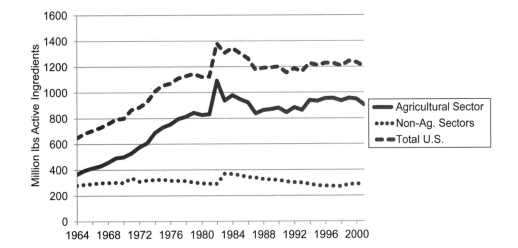

Source: U.S. EPA, 1995, 2001.

approximately doubling between the 1960s and 1980s, but worldwide pesticide use is still rising. Numerous health and environmental problems have accompanied this increase. Pesticides may affect agricultural workers directly—pesticide poisoning is a serious and widespread problem throughout much of the developing world.[21] Residues in food affect consumers: measurable levels of chlorinated pesticides can be found in breast milk, and the cumulative impact of many pesticides on the human body is a serious concern. The carcinogenic effects of many pesticides are well known, and a more recent focus of research has been effects on reproductive systems.

Pesticides also affect ecosystems in various ways. Groundwater pollution from pesticides is a common problem in agricultural areas (see Box 10.1). Unintended extermination of beneficial species can lead to pest outbreaks far worse than the original problem. Since World War II (when the chemistry for many pesticides emerged), rapidly expanding pesticide use has paralleled an equally rapid expansion in **resistant pest species** (Figure 10.12, p. 249). Similarly, excessive use of antibiotics in animal feed has encouraged the development of antibiotic-resistant microbes.

resistant pest species
pest species which evolve resistance to pesticides, requiring either higher pesticide application rates or new pesticides to control the species.

These developments are no surprise to ecologists, who understand the dangers of upsetting a natural species balance. However, such consequences are difficult to quantify in monetary terms or to introduce into farm-level decision making. In addition, vested interests—the manufacturers of agricultural chemicals—seek to promote the expanded use of pesticides.

information asymmetry
a situation in which different agents in a market have different knowledge or access to information.

Like other issues of technological impacts on the environment, **information asymmetry** is a problem.[h] Pesticide producers generally know the most about the chemical composition and potential effects of pesticides. Because thousands of different compounds are on the market, mastering this information—even if it is available—is practically impossible for pesticide consumers. Government regula-

---

[h]*Information asymmetry* is a term used by economists to denote a situation in which participants in a market economy have different levels of access to information. In the case of agricultural technologies, consumers of food products, and even government regulators, may be unaware of the nature and dangers of pesticide residues.

BOX 10.1 CONTROLLING AGRICULTURAL POLLUTION

Agricultural pollution from erosion, fertilizers, and pesticides is often a more difficult policy problem than pollution from well-defined industrial sources. Runoff from agriculture is called **nonpoint-source pollution**, meaning that it originates from a wide area, affecting water supplies and downstream communities. In addition, factory farms pose a huge problem of animal waste released into water supplies. According to the Environmental Protection Agency, hog, chicken, and cattle waste has polluted 35,000 miles of rivers in 22 states and contaminated groundwater in 17 states. Pollution from livestock is associated with many types of waterborne disease, as well as problems like bacterial outbreaks, which have plagued the Chesapeake Bay, red tides, algae blooms, and the dead zone in the Gulf of Mexico.

Reducing nonpoint source pollution requires altering production methods in agriculture. The use of fertilizers, pesticides, and intensive farming methods can bring benefits in terms of reduced prices to consumers. But while these benefits are automatically internalized into market mechanisms—farmers who can produce at lower cost will gain greater market share—external costs are not considered. Thus government policies must be oriented toward making sure that agricultural input and output prices reflect true social costs and benefits.

This implies reducing subsidies for agricultural inputs, as well as subsidies directed at increasing production. But support for research and promotion of alternative, lower-polluting techniques can be justified on the grounds of internalizing positive externalities. Strict regulation of factory farming and incentives for nonfactory livestock production may raise prices to consumers—but lower prices cannot be justified on economic grounds if they fail to reflect full social costs.

Particularly in the developing world, where the use of pesticides is steadily rising, information and support for production methods with lower pesticide use requires government commitment and investment. In the 1980s Indonesia invested as much as $1 million per year in research and training in ecologically oriented pest control, following a destructive infestation of the brown planthopper, which had spiraled out of control when excessive pesticide use eliminated its natural predators. The Indonesian program has been a success—crop yields increased by 12 percent with lower environmental impacts—but replication of such programs depends on initial investments, often hard to come by in developing nations.

Sources: Karlsson, 2004; U.S. Environmental Protection Agency, "Animal Feeding Operations," www.epa.gov/agriculture/anafoidx.html; Wilson and Tisdell, 2001.

---

nonpoint-source pollution
pollution that is difficult to identify as originating from a particular source, such as groundwater contamination from agricultural chemicals used over a wide area.

external cost(s)
a cost, not necessarily monetary, that is not reflected in a market transaction.

tors have trouble keeping up with the rapid rate of introduction of new compounds and usually must narrow their focus to, for example, carcinogenicity.

In such circumstances it is unlikely that the **external costs** of pesticide use will be fully understood and internalized. Regulatory issues have become even more complex with the introduction of genetically modified crops, often by the same chemical companies that are major producers of agricultural pesticides (see Box 10.2).

Irrigation and Water Resources

The spread of irrigation has been just as important as increased fertilizer use in expanding agricultural output. Irrigation greatly improves yields and often

Figure 10.12   **Increase in Pesticide-Resistant Species in the Twentieth Century**

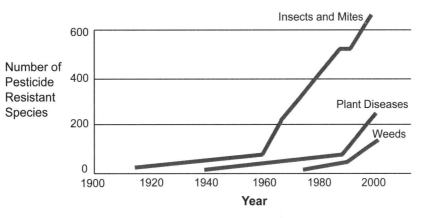

Source: Adapted from Gardner, 1996.

BOX 10.2 *(continued)*

ISSUES OF CORPORATE CONTROL

Formulating GM crops requires a large investment in research and development. To earn returns on their investment, companies must ensure that their products are being used only by those who pay for them. Traditionally farmers, especially in developing countries, buy the initial consignment of seeds and subsequently save a part of their crops as seeds for future cultivation. Biotechnology corporations can patent the products that they manufacture and ensure, through threat of legal action, that farmers buy a new consignment of seed for every season or pay royalties. Some companies have attempted to genetically modify seeds so that the subsequent crop seeds are sterile or create crops that can be used only with another product made by the same company. Critics claim that such developments can lead to a monopolistic situation in which a small number of companies have control over the supply of major crop seeds. Such a market would place small-scale farmers and developing countries at a strong disadvantage.

The staunch anti-GM foods stance taken by some countries is causing trade conflicts between GM food producers in the United States and importing countries. European governments, some Asian governments, and U.S. activists are calling for the labeling of foods that contain GM ingredients and the right to exclude GM products from their markets. Some farmers and industry lobbyists, mainly in the United States, contend that this will result in higher prices because GM and non-GM foods will have to be grown, transported, stored, and processed separately and that the labeling will stigmatize the products. Most countries have agreed that further research needs to be done on the safety of GM foods. In 2003, the U.S. Department of Agriculture announced stricter rules for crops that are genetically modified to produce pharmaceuticals or industrial chemicals.

The debate on GM foods includes powerful arguments on both sides, with implications for environmental sustainability, food security, international trade, and politics.

NOTES

1. U.S. Department of Agriculture (USDA) Economic Research Service, 2012, www.ers.usda.gov/data-products/adoption-of-genetically-engineered-crops-in-the-us.aspx.

2. "Genes from Engineered Grass Spread for Miles," *New York Times*, September 21, 2004; "Mexico Is Warned of Risk from Altered Corn," *New York Times*, March 13, 2004.

3. "U.S. Imposes Stricter Rules for Genetically Modified Crops," *New York Times*, March 7, 2003.

4. For more on both sides of this debate, see Paarlberg (2000); Rissler and Mellen (1996).

---

multiple cropping
an agricultural system involving growing more than one crop on a piece of land in the same year.

salinization and alkalinization of soils
the buildup of salt or alkali concentrations in soil from the evaporation of water depositing dissolved salts, with the effect of reducing the productivity of the soil.

permits **multiple cropping** in areas dependent on seasonal rains. The most optimistic projections of further yield increases in developing-country agriculture rely heavily on expanded irrigation. But, as with fertilizer and pesticides, the short-term benefits of irrigation are often linked to long-term environmental damage.

Poor drainage causes irrigation water to build up underground, eventually causing fields to be waterlogged. In tropical areas, water that reaches the surface evaporates rapidly, leaving behind a buildup of dissolved salts and leading to **salinization and alkalinization of soils**. In the Indian state of Punjab, for example, millions of hectares of land have been damaged by salinization. Irrigation also increases fertilizer and pesticide runoff, polluting local surface and groundwater.

common property resources

a resource that is not subject to private ownership and is available to all, such as the oceans or atmosphere.

The farmland most dependent on irrigation often lies in precisely those arid regions where water is in short supply. This leads to overdraft of groundwater—pumping out underground reservoirs faster than the natural water cycle can refill them—a classic example of the **common property resource** problem discussed in Chapter 4. No individual farmer has an incentive to limit water use. As a result, currently productive agricultural regions face a waterless future after the aquifers are exhausted. The Ogallala aquifer, which supports much of the irrigated agriculture of the western United States, is as much as 50 percent depleted in some areas, and its level continues to fall. Rapid declines in groundwater levels are also taking place in India, North China, and Central Asia (discussed further in Chapter 15).

Withdrawals from rivers in arid areas can be equally damaging. Agricultural water demand has led to serious salinization problems in the Colorado River in the western United States as well as an international dispute over the increased salinity of the river water crossing the border into Mexico. Perhaps the worst case of excessive irrigation demand is the Aral Sea in the former Soviet Union; this inland sea lost 88 percent of its surface area and 92 percent of its water volume between 1960 and 2009 as a result of water withdrawals (primarily for cotton production) from the rivers that feed it. (In recent years efforts by the World Bank and the government of Kazakhstan have led to a slow partial recovery, but large parts of the sea have been lost forever.) [22]

Limits on water supplies may be the most significant constraint on future agricultural expansion in large areas of the world. Irrigation accounts for 65 percent of total water withdrawal worldwide and more than 80 percent in developing countries.[23] Most of China and the Indian subcontinent are close to the limits of their available water supply, and urban/industrial water demand is rising steadily. Much of Africa is arid or semiarid, as are large areas in West and Central Asia and in the western United States. Despite clear economic incentives to expand irrigation, both the externality and the common property resource problems associated with irrigation mean that this expansion is likely to intensify resource and environmental problems.

10.5 SUSTAINABLE AGRICULTURE FOR THE FUTURE

user costs

opportunity costs associated with the loss of future potential uses of a resource, resulting from consumption of the resource in the present.

Many of the resource and environmental issues discussed in Chapters 3–5 are relevant to the analysis of agricultural production. Erosion and soil degradation, as we have noted, treat soil as a depletable resource, imposing **user costs** on future generations. Fertilizer runoff and pesticide pollution are classic examples of externalities. Excessive pumping of water from rivers and aquifers demonstrates the problem of overuse of common-property resources. Problems such as resistant pest species and loss of biodiversity impose ecological costs that may be difficult to evaluate in monetary terms, as we saw in Chapter 6.

Ecological analysis offers us a somewhat different understanding of the relationship between agriculture and the environment. Rather than seeing agricultural production as a process of combining inputs (including land, water, fertilizer, and pesticides) to maximize output, the ecological economist would argue that agriculture has to be understood as a process of intervention in the natural **biophysical cycles** responsible for plant growth. These include the carbon cycle, nitrogen cycle, water cycle, and similar cycles for other plant nutrients.

biophysical cycles

the circular flow of organic and inorganic materials in ecosystems.

sustainable agriculture

systems of agricultural production that do not deplete the productivity of the land or environmental quality, including such techniques as integrated pest management, organic techniques, and multiple cropping.

intercropping

an agricultural system involving growing two or more crops together on a piece of land at the same time.

agroforestry

growing both tree and food crops on the same piece of land.

integrated pest management (IPM)

the use of methods such as natural predators, crop rotations, and pest removal to reduce pesticide application rates.

species diversity or **biodiversity**

the maintenance of many different interrelated species in an ecological community.

monoculture

an agricultural system involving the growing of the same crop exclusively on a piece of land year after year.

labor-intensive techniques

production techniques that rely heavily on labor input.

information-intensive techniques

production techniques that require specialized knowledge; usually these techniques substitute knowledge for energy, produced capital, or material inputs, often reducing environmental impacts.

In a natural state, solar energy drives these cycles. Traditional agriculture departs little from these natural cycles. Modernized agriculture relies on extra inputs of energy, water, nitrogen, and synthetic chemicals. This gives higher yields, but creates imbalances in all the natural cyclical processes. From this perspective, soil degradation, fertilizer and pesticide pollution, and water over-draft are results of disrupting natural cycles. To use another ecological concept, modern agriculture expands carrying capacity but does so at the cost of increasing ecological stresses.

Both the economic and the ecological perspectives can influence our definition of **sustainable agriculture**. A sustainable agricultural system should produce a stable level of output without degrading the environmental systems that support it. In economic terms, this means no significant uninternalized externalities, user costs, or excessive use of common property resources. From an ecological point of view, a sustainable system minimizes disruption to natural cycles. This suggests some supply-side and demand-side techniques that may be appropriate for sustainable agriculture.

Production techniques such as organic fertilization by recycling of plant and animal waste, crop rotation, and **intercropping** of grains and legumes help to maintain the soil's nutrient balance and minimize the need for artificial fertilizer. The use of reduced tillage, terracing, fallowing, and **agroforestry** (planting trees in and around fields) all help to reduce erosion. **Integrated pest management (IPM)** uses natural pest controls such as predator species, crop rotation, and labor-intensive early pest removal to minimize the use of chemical pesticides.

Efficient irrigation techniques and the use of drought- and salt-tolerant crop varieties can reduce water use. **Species diversity** is promoted by multiple cropping (planting several different crops in the same field) rather than the **monoculture** (extensive planting of a single crop) pattern typical of modernized agriculture.

According to the National Research Council report *Alternative Agriculture*, farms that use organic techniques have been fairly successful in equaling the yields and economic record of neighboring farms using conventional inputs in Iowa, Pennsylvania, Ohio, Virginia, and California.[24] This is a positive indication that environmentally friendly techniques may be economically feasible on a larger scale in agriculture. However, the barriers to implementing this kind of farming in the United States and worldwide are considerable.

One major problem is access to information. Alternative techniques tend to be both **labor-intensive** and **information-intensive**. In developed countries, only a minority of farmers are sufficiently knowledgeable about the complex techniques of organic and low-input (minimum chemical use) agriculture to be able to make them pay. It is much easier to read the instructions on a bag of fertilizer or a canister of pesticide. In developing countries, traditional low-input farming systems have often been displaced by modernized "Green Revolution" techniques.

In recent years, organic agriculture has expanded rapidly, but it still represents a small portion of total agricultural production (see Box 10.3). Government policies, such as the establishment of organic standards and reform of agricultural subsidy policies, will have an important influence on the future of organic farming.

BOX 10.3 ORGANIC AGRICULTURE ON THE RISE

Organic production, which earned about $27 billion in the United States and $55 billion worldwide in 2010, is the most rapidly growing sector of agriculture. According to a report by the Organization for Economic Cooperation and Development (OECD), organic agriculture now constitutes only 2–3 percent of production within the OECD (essentially the world's higher-income countries), but is growing at a rate of 15–30 percent annually. The growth is in response to the demand of consumers in high-income countries who are prepared to pay a premium for foods grown without pesticides or genetic modification. The advantages of organic foods are perceived to include health and environmental benefits, improved food quality and taste, accessibility of fresh produce, and assistance to small-scale local producers.

While yields tend to be lower and labor costs higher on organic farms, profitability is also higher as a result of price premiums and, in some cases, government support payments. Market-based policy approaches to promote organic agriculture include certification and labeling schemes, now adopted by almost all OECD countries. The European Union has a single, "harmonized" standard for organic agriculture, and the United States has put federal organic standards in place. Compliance with these standards helps exporters to expand organic production, but the variety of different standards can sometimes be confusing.

Some European governments have undertaken promotional campaigns to encourage the consumption of organic products. A few countries require the purchase of organic food by public institutions such as schools and hospitals. Many governments provide direct financial support to organic farmers, justifying this subsidy as a return for providing external benefits of environmental protection—for example, reducing nitrate, phosphate, and pesticide flows into water supplies. A small percentage of public agricultural research is also devoted to organic systems.

The OECD report concludes that conventional agriculture still retains an advantage due to government production subsidies and failure to address the problems of negative externalities associated with conventional systems. "Such polices provide incentives to adopt farming practices that increase production rather than those, like organics, which stress quality. . . . Governments need to address the externalities in conventional agriculture to provide a better use of resources and a more level playing field for organic systems."

Source: Organization for Economic Cooperation and Development, *Organic Agriculture: Sustainability, Markets, and Policies* (Wallingford, UK: CABI, 2003); M. Saltmarsh, "Strong Sales of Organic Foods Attract Investors," *New York Times,* May 23, 2011.

Policies for Sustainable Agriculture

Without strong economic incentives to alter production methods, combined with widespread information and support for alternative techniques, most farmers will stay with established methods. A shift to alternative agriculture will require a combination of government policy and market incentives.

Important market incentives include the prices of fertilizer, pesticides, irrigation water, and energy. Many governments have policies that directly or indirectly subsidize these prices. According to a well-established principle of agricultural economics, price ratios for agricultural inputs determine the course of **induced innovation** in agriculture.[25] If fertilizer is cheap relative to land and labor, the farm sector will develop and implement fertilizer-intensive methods. By providing low-cost fertilizer, farm chemicals, and water for irrigation, governments promote agricultural productivity—but at environmental cost.

induced innovation
innovation in a particular industry resulting from changes in the relative prices of inputs.

Policies to subsidize energy development also promote the trend to more highly mechanized and input-dependent agriculture. Changing these policies would support the development of a more labor- and information-intensive agriculture with less environmental impact. In developing countries with large pools of unemployed and underemployed labor, promotion of labor-intensive agricultural development might have considerable employment as well as environmental benefits.[26]

Removing energy and input subsidies would send a price signal to farmers to use less input-intensive techniques. Before they can respond effectively to these price incentives, however, farmers need information on alternative techniques—otherwise higher input prices will simply make food more expensive. Developing countries can combine valuable knowledge of traditional agricultural techniques with modern innovations, provided that energy-intensive monoculture does not sweep away traditional knowledge.

Agricultural subsidies in developed countries have been estimated at $250–$300 billion.[27] Most of these subsidies are environmentally destructive, promoting increased input and energy use. While developed countries typically promote production, resulting in agricultural surpluses, developing countries often reduce incentives for agricultural production by policies that lower prices paid to farmers. The goal is to provide cheap food for consumers, but the effect is to discourage local production. Widespread use of these counterproductive economic policies in agriculture leaves much scope for policy reforms that could benefit both food supply and the environment. Damaging subsidies could be removed or shifted to favor environmentally sound techniques and agricultural research. Better prices and improved credit systems for farmers can encourage both increased production and investment in soil conservation.

An example of an environmentally positive agricultural subsidy is the U.S. Conservation Reserve Program. Started in 1985, this program now covers 30 million acres of former cropland. Farmers receive payments to remove environmentally sensitive land from production, reducing erosion, protecting wetlands and water supplies, and providing habitat for wildlife, including endangered species. This program internalizes positive externalities, helps to preserve family farms, and provides greater land-use options for the future.

On the demand side, it is clear that population size is a major determinant of food demand and indirectly of agricultural pressures on the environment. The ecological concept of carrying capacity implies a maximum population that the planet's resources can sustainably support. Our discussion of agricultural futures indicates that we are close to reaching that capacity and may have exceeded it if we consider long-term issues of soil erosion and water overdraft. Population policy is therefore a central element in limiting the impact of agricultural production on the environment.

The other major demand-side variable is diet. As we have seen, a meat-centered diet implies much higher land, water, and fertilizer requirements per capita than a mostly vegetarian diet. Using land resources to produce meat for export also increases environmental pressures in developing countries. Thus, reducing meat consumption in developed countries and slowing the trend toward meat-centered diets in newly industrializing countries are important components of long-term sustainability.

Abolishing input subsidies will increase the price of meat compared to more input-efficient foods, and health motivations may lead to reduced demand for meat in developed countries. To the extent that consumers shift their preferences toward more vegetables, including more organically grown produce, the incentives to producers to employ less environmentally damaging techniques will grow.

The environmental problems associated with agriculture are complex and cannot be solved by simple cost internalization policies—though these will help. It will take major changes in consumer behavior, production techniques, and government price and agricultural policies to move to a sustainable agricultural system. The urgency of these issues will grow as population increases and cumulative soil and water impacts increase. The high-input agriculture that has been so successful in increasing world output during recent decades will not meet the needs of the twenty-first century without significant changes to promote sustainability.

SUMMARY

Food production has outpaced population since 1950, allowing for slowly rising global per capita consumption. However, food distribution is significantly unequal, with around 850 million people receiving inadequate nutrition. Most suitable agricultural land is already being farmed, leaving relatively little room for further expansion. Yields have increased and continue to rise, but greater productivity has been accompanied by greater environmental impact, including erosion, soil degradation, and fertilizer and pesticide runoff.

Rates of growth in agricultural output have slowed, and in recent years prices of basic foods have risen significantly. In some developing countries, especially in Africa, per capita consumption has grown slowly, stagnated, or declined. Inequitable access to food means that basic food crops can be displaced by luxury or export food crops, increasing pressure on the poor and on environmentally vulnerable marginal lands.

Projections of future demand show a 50 percent increase in food demand in the developing world over the next several decades. Because little potential exists for land expansion, this demand will require dramatic increases in yields. The challenge is to achieve this in an environmentally sustainable manner. Existing environmental effects associated with agricultural production make this a formidable task.

Erosion causes declining soil fertility as well as significant off-farm damage. Farmers facing short-term financial pressures often find investment in long-term conservation difficult. Fertilizer use has led to extensive runoff pollution and excessive nitrate release, affecting both water supplies and the atmosphere. Pesticide application is associated with a steady increase in the number of resistant pest species as well as with other negative impacts on ecosystems. Poorly planned irrigation systems have led to water overdraft and pollution as well as soil damage.

Future policies must promote agricultural sustainability. Practices such as crop rotation, intercropping, agroforestry, and integrated pest management can reduce input requirements and environmental impacts while maintaining high yields. Efficient irrigation and land management techniques have great potential, but require appropriate economic incentives for farmers to adopt them. Removing energy and input subsidies and providing information on environmentally sound techniques must accompany more equitable and efficient distribution and consumption patterns.

KEY TERMS AND CONCEPTS

agroforestry
biodiversity
biofuels
biophysical cycles
carrying capacity
common property resources
crop rotation and fallowing
crop value index
depletable resource
discount rate
elasticity of supply
environmental sustainability
external costs
externalities
induced innovation
information asymmetry
information-intensive techniques
integrated pest management

intercropping
labor-intensive techniques
marginal physical product
marginal revenue product
micronutrients
monoculture
multiple cropping
nitrogen cycle
nutrient recycling
nutritional deficit
present value
proxy variable
renewable resources
resistant pest species
salinization and alkalinization of soils
species diversity
sustainable agriculture
user costs

DISCUSSION QUESTIONS

1. What evidence would you use to evaluate the proposition that the world is reaching the maximum carrying capacity in terms of food supply? Some analysts believe that the world's agricultural capacity is adequate for a population of 10 billion people. Are you comfortable with this assertion? Is it useful to attempt to evaluate maximum carrying capacity, or should we just wait and see how markets adjust to increased food demand?

2. Which environmental impacts of agriculture are most amenable to market solutions? Consider the on-farm and off-farm impacts of erosion, for example. What kinds of incentives are required to induce greater erosion control? How much can be done through private initiative and how much through government policy?

3. How can we define the concept of sustainable agriculture? Can high-input agriculture be sustainable? Is organic agriculture sustainable? In what respects is our current agricultural system *not* sustainable and what kinds of policies are appropriate to respond to problems of unsustainability? How would you evaluate the economic costs and benefits of such policies?

NOTES

1. See Brown, 2004, 2011.
2. Lester R. Brown, "The World Is Closer to a Food Crisis Than Most People Realize," *The Guardian,* July 24, 2012, www.guardian.co.uk/environment/2012/jul/24/world-food-crisis-closer/. See also Brown, 2004, 2011.

3. Sen, 2000.
4. Smil, 2000.
5. www.fao.org/worldfoodsituation/wfs-home/foodpricesindex/en/.
6. See, e.g., Wise, 2012.
7. FAO, 2011.
8. See Wise, 2011.
9. See, e.g., Conforti, 2011; FAO, 2003, 2006.
10. FAO, 2003; Pinstrup-Andersen and Pandya-Lorch, 2001.
11. See Brown, 2004, chap. 4.
12. U.S. Census, 2012, www.census.gov/population/international/data/idb/informationGateway.php.
13. See, e.g., Seckler, 1994.
14. A good example of optimism on yields is Waggoner, 1994.
15. For a more pessimistic view of world food supplies, see Brown, 2004, 2011.
16. FAO, 2006, 5.
17. Pimentel, 1993; Zuazo et al., 2009.
18. Oldeman et al., 1990. For detailed assessment of soil degradation, see www.isric.org.
19. See Cleveland, 1994; Martinez-Alier, 1993.
20. See, e.g., Hall, 1993.
21. Wesseling et al., 1997.
22. See http://news.nationalgeographic.com/news/2010/04/100402-aral-sea-story. For an extensive discussion of the problems of irrigated agriculture, see Postel, 1999.
23. Harris, 1990.
24. National Research Council, 1989.
25. Ruttan and Hayami, 1998.
26. See Cleveland, 1994.
27. Myers and Kent, 2001, chap 3; OECD, 2010.

REFERENCES

Brown, Lester R. 2004. *Outgrowing the Earth*. New York: W.W. Norton.
———. 2011. *World on the Edge: How to Prevent Environmental and Economic Collapse*. New York: W.W. Norton.
Cleveland, Cutler J. 1994. "Reallocating Work Between Human and Natural Capital and Agriculture: Examples from India and the United States." In *Investing in Natural Capital: The Ecological Approach to Sustainability*, ed. Jannson et al., Washington, DC: Island Press.
Conforti, Piero, ed. 2011. *Looking Ahead in Food and Agriculture: Perspectives to 2050*. Rome: United Nations Food and Agriculture Organization.
Food and Agriculture Organization (FAO). 2003. *World Agriculture: Towards 2015/2030*. Rome. www.fao.org/docrep/005/y4252e/y4252e00.htm.
———. 2006. *World Agriculture: Towards 2030/2050*. Rome.www.fao.org/docrep/009/a0607e/a0607e00.htm.
———. 2011. *The State of Food Insecurity in the World 2011*. Rome. www.fao.org/publications/sofi/en/.
———. 2012. FAOSTAT Agriculture Database.
Gardner, Gary. 1996. "Preserving Agricultural Resources." In *State of the World 1996*, ed. Brown et al., Washington, DC: Worldwatch Institute.
Hall, Charles A.S. 1993. "The Efficiency of Land and Energy Use in Tropical Economies and Agriculture." *Agriculture, Ecosystems and Environment* 46: 1–30.
Harris, Jonathan M. 1990. *World Agriculture and the Environment*. New York: Garland.
———. 1996. "World Agricultural Futures: Regional Sustainability and Ecological Limits." *Ecological Economics* 17 (May): 95–115.

Karlsson, Sylvia I., 2004. "Agricultural Pesticides in Developing Countries," *Environment* 46 (4): 22–42.

Martinez-Alier, Juan. 1993. "Modern Agriculture: A Source of Energy?" In *Ecological Economics: Energy, Environment, and Society*. London: Blackwell.

Myers, Norman, and Jennifer Kent. 2001. *Perverse Subsidies: How Tax Dollars Can Undercut the Environment and the Economy*. Washington, DC: Island Press.

National Research Council. 1989. *Alternative Agriculture*. Washington, DC: National Academy Press.

OECD, 2010. *Agricultural Policies in OECD Countries at a Glance 2010*. Paris: OECD. http://www.oecd.org/agriculture/agriculturalpoliciesandsupport/45539870.pdf.

Oldeman, L.R., R.T.A. Hakkeling, and W.G. Sombroek. 1990. *Global Assessment of Soil Degradation*. Wageningen, Netherlands: ISRIC/UNEP.

Paarlberg, Robert. 2000. "The Global Food Fight." *Foreign Affairs* 79 (3) (May/June): 24–38.

Pimentel, David, ed. 1993. *World Soil Erosion and Conservation*. Cambridge: Cambridge University Press.

Pinstrup-Andersen, Per, and Rajul Pandya-Lorch. 2001. *The Unfinished Agenda: Perspectives on Overcoming Hunger, Poverty, and Environmental Degradation*. Washington, DC: International Food Policy Research Institute.

Postel, Sandra. 1999. *Pillar of Sand: Can the Irrigation Miracle Last?* New York: W.W. Norton.

Rissler, Jane, and Margaret Mellen. 1996. *The Ecological Risks of Engineered Crops*. Cambridge, MA: MIT Press.

Ruttan, Vernon W., and Yujiro Hayami. 1998. "Induced Innovation Model of Agricultural Development." In *International Agricultural Development* (3d ed.), ed. Carl K. Eicher and John M. Staatz. Baltimore: Johns Hopkins University Press.

Seckler, David. 1994. "Trends in World Food Needs: Toward Zero Growth in the 21st Century." Arlington, Virginia: Winrock International Institute for Agricultural Development, Center for Economic Policy Studies Discussion Paper no. 18.

Sen, Amartya. 2000. "Population, Food and Freedom." In *Development as Freedom*. New York: Alfred A. Knopf.

Smil, Vaclav. 2000. *Feeding the World: A Challenge for the Twenty-First Century*. Cambridge, MA: MIT Press.

U.S. Environmental Protection Agency. 1995. *Pesticides Industry Sales and Usage Report, 1994/1995*. Washington, DC.

———. 2001. *Pesticide Market Estimates, 2000/2001*. Washington, DC.

Waggoner, Paul E. 1994. *How Much Land Can Ten Billion People Spare for Nature?* Ames, Iowa: Council for Agricultural Science and Technology, Task Force Report no. 121, February.

Wesseling, C., et al. 1997. "Agricultural Pesticide Use in Developing Countries: Health Effects and Research Needs." *International Journal of Health Services* 27(2): 273–308.

Wilson, Clevo, and Clem Tisdell, 2001. "Why Farmers Continue to Use Pesticides Despite Environmental, Health, and Sustainability Costs," *Ecological Economics* 39: 449–462.

Wise, Timothy A. 2011. *Mexico: The Cost of U.S. Dumping*. www.ase.tufts.edu/gdae/policy_research/MexicoUnderNafta.html.

———. 2012. "The Cost to Mexico of U.S. Corn Ethanol Expansion," Tufts University Global Development and Environment Institute Working paper 12–01. http://ase.tufts.edu/gdae/policy_research/EthanolCostMexico.html.

Zuazo, Victor H.D., and Carmen R.R. Pleguezuelo. 2009. "Soil Erosion and Runoff Prevention by Plant Covers: A Review." In *Sustainable Agriculture*, ed. Eric Lichtfouse, et al. Berlin and New York: Springer.

WEB SITES

1. **www.ers.usda.gov.** Web site for the Economic Research Service, a division of the U.S. Department of Agriculture with a mission to "inform and enhance public and private decision-making on economic and policy issues related to agriculture, food, natural resources, and rural development." Their Web site provides links to a broad range of data and analysis on United States agricultural issues.

2. **www.fao.org.** Web site for the Food and Agricultural Organization of the United Nations, an organization "with a mandate to raise levels of nutrition and standards of living, to improve agricultural productivity, and to better the condition of rural populations." Their Web site includes extensive data on agriculture and food issues around the world.

3. **www.ota.com.** Home page for the Organic Trade Association, "a membership-based business association representing the organic industry in Canada, the United States, and Mexico." Their Web site includes press releases and facts about the organic agriculture industry.

4. **http://nabc.cals.cornell.edu.** Home page for the National Agricultural Biotechnology Council, a nonprofit group with membership from more than 30 research and teaching institutions designed to provide a forum for the evaluation of agricultural biotechnology. Several reports are available on their Web site concerning the impacts of agricultural biotechnology.

5. **www.oecd.org/agr/.** Web site for the Food, Agriculture, and Fisheries division of the Organisation for Economic Co-operation and Development. The site includes data, trade information, and discussions of environmental issues. Note that the OECD also maintains a Web page on biotechnology.

6. **www.isric.org.** Web site for the International Soil Resource Information Center, providing information on global soil degradation and agricultural productivity loss, and on measures to conserve and reclaim soil productivity.

PART FIVE

ENERGY AND RESOURCES

CHAPTER 11

Nonrenewable Resources: Scarcity and Abundance

CHAPTER 11 FOCUS QUESTIONS

- Are we running out of nonrenewable resources?
- Will prices for metals, minerals, and other resources rise?
- What are the environmental costs of mining for mineral resources?
- How do economic incentives affect recycling of nonrenewable resources?

---

nonrenewable resources
resources that are available in a fixed supply, such as metal ores and oil.

user costs
opportunity costs associated with the loss of future potential uses of a resource, resulting from consumption of the resource in the present.

Hotelling's rule
a theory stating that in equilibrium the net price (price minus production costs) of a resource must rise at a rate equal to the rate of interest.

economic supply (of a resource)
the quantity of a resource that is available based on current prices and technology.

physical supply (of a resource)
the quantity of a resource that is available, without taking into account the economic feasibility of extraction.

11.1 THE SUPPLY OF NONRENEWABLE RESOURCES

The planet has a fixed quantity of **nonrenewable resources**, including metal and nonmetal minerals, coal, oil, and natural gas. We have extensive supplies of certain resources, such as iron; others, such as mercury or silver, are in relatively limited supply. The global economy is using up these resources—often at increasing rates. Is this cause for alarm?

Limited, nonrenewable resources cannot, of course, last forever, but issues regarding their use are complex, involving changes in resource supply and demand as well as the waste and pollution generated in their consumption. In this chapter we examine the dynamics of nonrenewable resource use, with a focus on minerals. Issues of nonrenewable energy resources, such as coal, oil, and natural gas, are addressed in Chapter 12.

Physical Supply and Economic Supply

In our initial analysis in Chapter 5, we considered the allocation of a mineral resource over two periods. We assumed that both the resource quantity and quality were fixed. The economic principles derived from this simple example, including the analysis of **user costs** and **Hotelling's rule** for resource pricing, are important, but a more sophisticated analysis must deal with real-world conditions. We usually see many different resource qualities (e.g., different grades of copper ore), and we rarely know with complete certainty the location and total quantity of resource deposits.

The **economic supply** of a nonrenewable resource differs from its **physical supply**. The physical supply (in the earth's crust) is finite but generally not pre-

economic reserves (economically recoverable reserves)
the quantity of a resource that is identified as economically feasible to extract given current prices and technology.

identified reserves
the quantity of a resource that has been identified; includes both economic and subeconomic reserves.

measured (reserves)
resources that have been identified and whose quantity is known with certainty.

indicated or inferred (reserves)
resources that have been identified but whose exact quantity is not known with certainty.

hypothetical (resources)
the quantity of a resource that is not identified with certainty but is hypothesized to exist.

economic reserves (economically recoverable reserves)
the quantity of a resource that is identified as economically feasible to extract given current prices and technology.

subeconomic resources
term used to describe mineral resources that cannot be profitably extracted with current technology and prices.

static reserve index
an index that divides the economic reserves of a resource by the current rate of use for the resource.

resource lifetime
the number of years the economic reserves of a resource are projected to last under expected consumption rates.

recycling
the process of using waste materials as inputs into a production process.

cisely known. The **economically recoverable reserves** provide the measure most commonly used in, for example, calculations of a resource's lifetime. However, this figure changes over time for three main reasons:

- The resource is extracted and used over time, diminishing reserves.
- New resource deposits are discovered over time, increasing reserves.
- Changing price and technological conditions can make more (or less) of the known reserves economically viable. These factors make predictions of resource lifetimes an inexact science.

A mineral resource such as copper is classified through a combination of geologic and economic measures (Figure 11.1).

In geological terms, resources are classified in terms of the available quantities, shown as the horizontal dimension in Figure 11.1. **Identified reserves** are those whose quantity and quality are already known. A portion of these identified reserves have been **measured** within a 20 percent margin of error; another portion is **indicated** or **inferred** based on geological principles. In addition, **hypothetical** amounts of the resource are yet undiscovered, but are likely to exist in certain geological situations.

Economic factors create another dimension to resource classification, shown vertically in Figure 11.1, with the most economically profitable resources at the top. Resources of high enough quality to be profitably extracted are identified as **economic reserves** (the shaded area in Figure 11.1). **Subeconomic resources** are those whose costs of extraction are too high to make production worthwhile. However, if prices rise or extraction technologies improve, it may become profitable to exploit these deposits. Note that undiscovered reserves are not counted toward economic reserves, as their quality is uncertain.

One measure of the availability of nonrenewable resources is a **static reserve index**. A static reserve index simply divides economic reserves by the current annual rate of use to get an estimate of **resource lifetime**:

$$\textit{Expected Resource Lifetime} \; = \; \frac{\textit{Economic Reserves}}{\textit{Annual Consumption}}$$

The fact that resource reserves can be expanded in both geological and economic dimensions renders projections using a static reserve index unreliable. Current consumption is not necessarily a good indication of future use. Because of growing population and economic output, we can expect nonrenewable resource use to grow—although substitution, changing consumption patterns, and **recycling** will affect rates of growth. An **exponential reserve index** assumes that consumption will grow exponentially over time, leading to more rapid resource exhaustion.

Calculations made in 1972 using both static and exponential reserve indices indicated that major mineral reserves would be exhausted within several decades—projections clearly not borne out.[1] Why not? Because reserves have grown with new discoveries and new extractive technologies. However, we cannot simply dismiss predictions of resource exhaustion. Even with reserve expansion, planetary resources are ultimately limited.

Figure 11.1   **Classification of Nonrenewable Resources**

	Identified			Undiscovered	
	Demonstrated		Inferred	Hypothetical (in known districts)	Hypothetical (in un-discovered districts)
	Measured	Indicated			
Economic	Reserves				
Subeconomic					

Increasing Economic Feasibility →

← *Increasing Geologic Assurance* ←

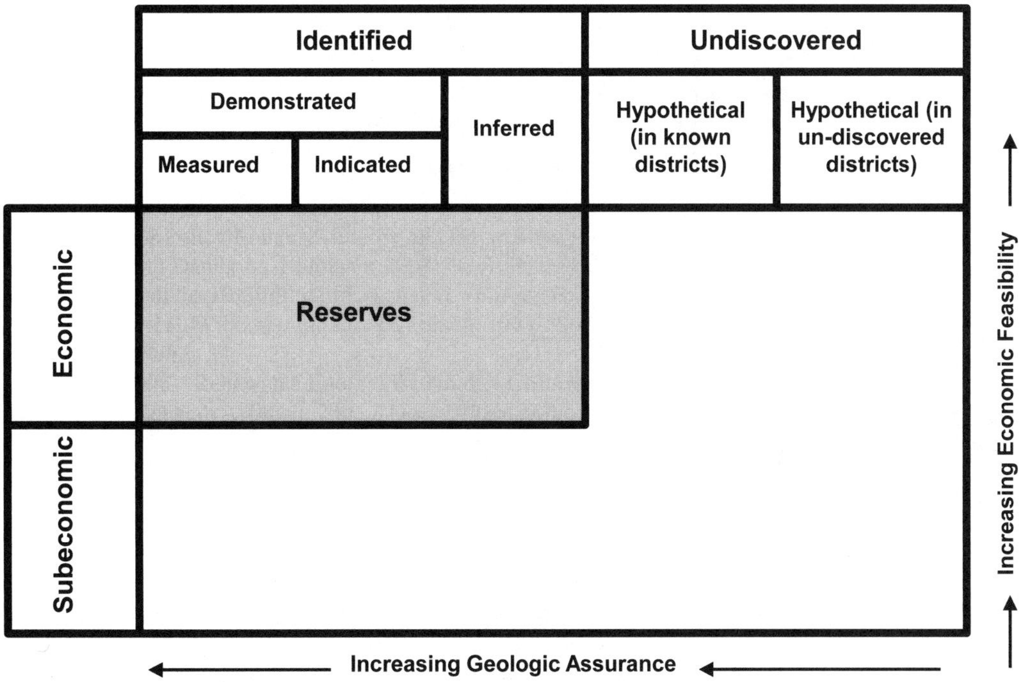

Source: Adapted from U.S. Bureau of Mines and U.S. Geological Survey, 1976.

exponential reserve index
an estimate of the availability of a mineral resource based on an assumption of exponentially increasing consumption.

The relevant question is how resource consumption, new technology, and discovery will interact to affect prices, which in turn will affect future patterns of resource demand and supply. To gain a better understanding of these factors, we need a more sophisticated economic theory of nonrenewable resource use.

11.2 ECONOMIC THEORY OF NONRENEWABLE RESOURCE USE

resource rents
income derived from the ownership of a scarce resource.

price taker
a seller in a competitive market who has no control over the price of the product.

marginal extraction cost
the cost of extracting an additional unit of a nonrenewable resource.

What determines the rate at which we extract and use nonrenewable resources? An individual firm operating a mine or other resource extraction operation is guided by the principle of maximization of **resource rents**.[a] Consider a firm that operates a bauxite mine (aluminum ore). If the firm is in a competitive industry, it is a **price taker**, selling its output at the market price, over which it has no control. It can, however, control the amount of the resource extracted during any period.

In general, as more of the resource is extracted, the marginal cost of extraction will rise. Obviously, if the **marginal extraction cost** rises above the market price, it will not be worthwhile to produce the bauxite. Price must at least equal marginal cost to make production worthwhile. Unlike other competitive industries where price equals marginal costs in equilibrium, resource-extracting firms typically operate at an output level at which price exceeds marginal cost (Figure 11.2). While firms could make small profits on the last few units produced, they have the option of

---

[a]**Economic rent** is the income derived from ownership of a scarce resource. In a resource-extracting industry, the usual principle of profit maximization thus becomes the maximization of resource rents.

Figure 11.2 **Nonrenewable Resource Production Decisions**

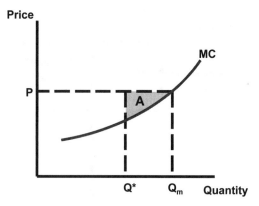

Source: Adapted from Hartwick and Olewiler, 1998, which provides a more advanced discussion of the economic theory of nonrenewable resource extraction.

postponing extraction until future periods when the profitability of those units may be higher. Thus rather than maximizing total current profits at Q_m, long-term profit maximization may imply production at Q^*. The forgone current profits (shaded area A) would be more than offset by higher profits in the future.

In addition to expectations about future prices and costs, prevailing interest rates will also influence firms' production decisions. Higher interest rates tend to encourage increased current production, as firms have a strong incentive to make immediate profits and invest them at the high rates. But increased production will drive down the current price of the resource, as well as reduce the available reserves and raise expected future prices. Both of these factors will shift production toward the future.

As we saw in Chapter 5, the expected outcome of this adjustment is that equilibrium is reached when firms' resource rents grow at the same rate as the interest rate—Hotelling's rule. Note that Hotelling's rule equates the rate of growth of **net price** (market price minus extraction cost), not of market price, to the interest rate. Thus information solely on resource market prices is not sufficient to test the validity of Hotelling's rule. Additional information is needed on extraction costs and external factors that may, at least temporarily, push resource rents away from the path implied by Hotelling's rule.

Economists have tested the accuracy of Hotelling's rule by studying trends in resource prices, extraction costs, and other variables. A 1998 paper summarized the empirical tests of Hotelling's rule and found that these analyses:

> have not completely reconciled the economic theory of nonrenewable resources with the observed data. . . . The variety of possible outcomes makes it difficult, if not impossible, to make any general predictions about the overall impact on price and extraction paths.[2]

The paper notes that the discovery of new deposits and technological progress has so far been sufficient to avoid increasing economic scarcity of nonrenewable resources. However, just because past advances have kept pace with increasing demands, there is no assurance that this will continue indefinitely. There is still a need for improved management of nonrenewable resources.

net price (of a resource)

the price of a resource minus production costs.

Given the open access and public good nature of these resources and services, market interventions are necessary to prevent inefficient use of these resources. Because of this, the attention focused on the environmental impacts of nonrenewable resource use will continue to increase with increased emphasis on the details of ecological interactions and the management of global public assets.[3]

physical reserves
the quantity of a resource that has been identified; includes both economic and subeconomic reserves.

resource use profile
the consumption rates for a resource over time, typically applied to nonrenewable resources.

price path
the price of a resource, typically a nonrenewable resource, over time.

extraction path
the extraction rate of a resource over time.

A less controversial theory of nonrenewable resource management is that higher-quality resources will be exploited first. Suppose, for example, that a firm owns two bauxite deposits, one high grade and one low grade. Marginal costs of production for the high-grade resource will be relatively low, so a high rent can be obtained by producing today. Costs of extracting the low-grade deposit are significantly higher. Even if extracting the low-grade deposit today would be marginally profitable, waiting until market prices rise or until better technology makes extraction less costly will often be a better strategy. This explains why resources that are subeconomic today (see Figure 11.1) can become economic in the future, possibly increasing the amount of economically recoverable reserves—at the same time that extraction has diminished the **physical reserves**.

During the early stages of nonrenewable resource extraction, high-quality supplies are likely to be abundant. As exploration expands and technology improves, initially we would expect prices to decline even as extraction rapidly increases. This is shown as Stage I in Figure 11.3, which presents a stylized long-term **resource use profile** for a nonrenewable resource. Figure 11.3 shows the **price path** and **extraction path** for a resource stock being exploited over time.

Figure 11.3 **Hypothetical Nonrenewable Resource Use Profile**

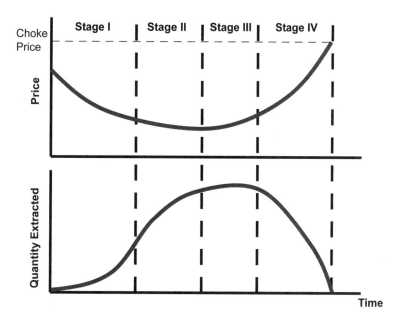

Source: Adapted from Hartwick and Olewiler, 1998,

During Stage II, prices are fairly stable as increasing demand (tending to pull prices up) balances further discovery and technological improvement (tending to pull prices down). During Stage III, demand starts to press against resource limitations, prices begin to rise, and reserves that were subeconomic in earlier years become economic. Technological progress is no longer sufficient to offset increasing resource scarcity.

choke price
the minimum price on a demand curve where the quantity demanded equals zero.

As reserves are depleted even further, we finally reach Stage IV, when rising prices begin to reduce demand. Ultimately, the price reaches the **choke price**, at which the quantity demanded falls to zero. By the time the choke price is reached, producers will have extracted and sold all economically viable reserves, although some physical subeconomic reserves will still be available. As a resource approaches its choke price, the motivation to find appropriate substitutes and raise recycling rates will increase.

Considerable controversy exists as to whether a resource profile similar to Figure 11.3 applies to most minerals. Where it does apply, an interesting question is whether we are currently in Stage I, II, III, or IV, and therefore whether we can expect falling, stable, or rising prices. We review this debate in the next section.

11.3 GLOBAL SCARCITY OR INCREASING ABUNDANCE?

resource substitution/ substitutability
the use of one resource in a production process as a substitute for another resource, such as the use of aluminum instead of copper in electrical wiring.

A classic study from the 1960s found that most mineral resource prices fell from the Industrial Revolution through the mid-twentieth century.[4] At the same time, global nonrenewable resource consumption steadily expanded. These findings are consistent with Stages I and II of Figure 11.3. Three major factors were responsible for these trends:

- Continual resource discovery
- Improved resource extraction technology
- **Resource substitution**, such as use of plastics in place of metals

Minerals prices continued to generally decline or remain steady during the second half of the twentieth century. However, starting around 2004 the price of many minerals increased rapidly as a result of surging global demand, as shown in Figure 11.4 for the common minerals copper, lead, and zinc. In the aftermath of the global financial crisis in 2008 and 2009, prices fell significantly but then began to rise again.

Based on the recent increase in prices, have we entered Stage III in the price path of most minerals, and can we expect prices to generally increase in the future? One indication is to look at data on mineral reserves. While global extraction of minerals has increased, reserves for many minerals are actually at record levels, as shown in Figure 11.5, again for copper, lead, and zinc.

Considering a broader range of minerals, Table 11.1 shows expected resource lifetimes based on current economic reserves. The static reserve indices indicate that supplies of some minerals are quite abundant, for example, lithium, aluminum, and copper. Meanwhile, reserves of lead, tin, and zinc are sufficient to meet only about twenty years of current demand. But, as mentioned earlier, the usefulness of a static reserve index is limited because it fails to account for new discoveries, changes in demand, and technological change. For example, while current reserves of lead are sufficient for only twenty years of global demand, Figure 11.5 shows that lead reserves have remained steady in recent years.

Figure 11.4 **Prices for Selected Minerals, 1996–2011**

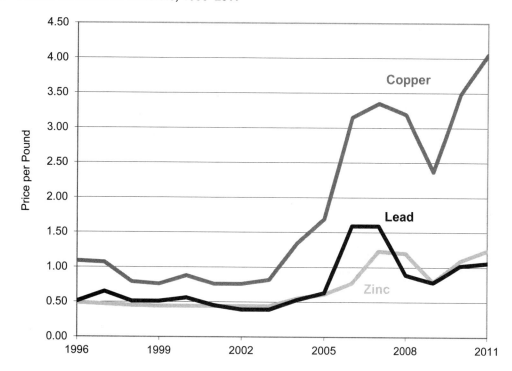

Source: U.S. Geological Survey, *Minerals Commodities Summaries*, various years.

Figure 11.5 **Global Economic Reserves for Selected Minerals, 1996–2012**

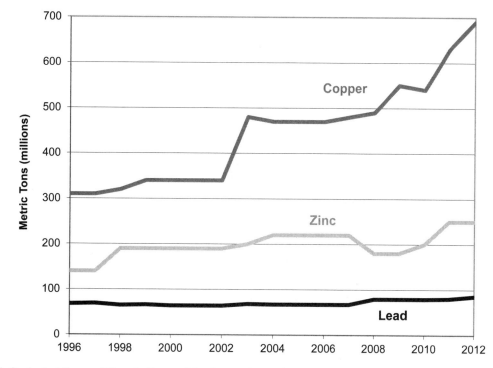

Source: U.S. Geological Survey, *Minerals Commodities Summaries*, various years.

Table 11.1

Expected Resource Lifetimes, Selected Minerals

Mineral	2011 global production (thousand metric tons)	Global reserves (thousand metric tons)	Expected resource lifetime, years (static reserve index)
Aluminum	220,000	29,000,000	132
Cadmium	22	640	29
Copper	16,100	690,000	43
Iron ore	2,800,000	80,000,000	29
Lead	4,500	85,000	19
Lithium	34	13,000	382
Mercury	2	93	47
Nickel	1,800	80,000	44
Tin	253	4,800	19
Tungsten	72	3,100	43
Zinc	12,400	250,000	20

Source: U.S. Geological Survey, *Minerals Commodities Summaries,* various years.
Note: Aluminum data for bauxite ore, the primary source of aluminum.

In general, global mineral supplies do not appear to be running low in the short term, although this does not imply that we should not worry about future supplies. According to a recent analysis:

> Global mineral reserves are adequate to supply world mineral demand for the next 50 years, at least in theory. Presently estimated global mineral reserves are 20 to almost 1,000 times larger than present annual production, depending on the commodity of interest. . . . Exactly when supply will become the dominant factor is difficult to predict and will undoubtedly vary from commodity to commodity and be heavily dependent on the form and cost of industrial energy. In fact, the failure of earlier predictions of mineral supply and demand relations, many of which foresaw mineral shortages by the year 2000, has led to a dangerous complacency about future world mineral supplies and might lead us to misinterpret these reassuring reserve figures.
>
> Although mineral reserves are large and seem adequate for the next 50 years or so when considered as a single global number, it is important to remember that these reserves are made up of many separate deposits, all of which have to be considered in the local context of which they are a part. Each of these deposits is subject to geologic, engineering, economic, environmental, and political constraints that undergo continuous change.[5]

A similar sentiment is expressed by the British Geological Survey, which also notes the potential problem of environmental impacts.

> As demand for metals and minerals increases, driven by relentless growth in the emerging economies in Asia and South America, competition for resources is growing. Human factors such as geopolitics, resource nationalism, along with events such as strikes and accidents are the most likely to disrupt supply. Policy-makers, industry and consumers should be concerned about supply risk and the need to diversify supply from Earth resources, [to] recycling more and doing more with less, and also about the environmental implications of burgeoning consumption.[6]

In addition to concerns about resource depletion, the environmental impacts of minerals mining can be significant. We now turn to the environmental impacts of mining in more detail.

11.4 ENVIRONMENTAL IMPACTS OF MINING

As discussed in Chapter 3, the price of a product should reflect both the private and social (or external) costs of production. While some regulations have been implemented to reduce the environmental impacts of mining,

> the full social and environmental costs of mining are not included in the price of mineral products and that more may yet need to be done to bring the private and social marginal costs of production more into line.[7]

tailings
the unwanted material from mining operations, often highly toxic.

smelting
the production of a metal from a metallic ore.

Table 11.2 presents some of the environmental impacts of minerals mining. When minerals ores are extracted from the earth, they must be processed in order to separate out the economically valuable material. The nonvaluable waste, known as **tailings**, can pollute the environment by contaminating rivers and lakes, leaching into groundwater, or being blown into the air. The refining of mineral ores, known as **smelting**, is also a potential source of environmental damage, including air and water pollution (see Box 11.1).

Table 11.2

Potential Environmental Impacts of Mining

Activity	Potential impacts
Excavation and ore removal	Destruction of plant and animal habitat, human settlements, and other features (surface mining) Land subsidence (underground mining) Increased erosion; silting of lakes and streams Waste generation Acid drainage and metal contamination of lakes, streams, and groundwater
Ore concentration	Waste generation (tailings) Organic chemical contamination Acid drainage and metal contamination
Smelting/refining	Air pollution (including sulfur dioxide, arsenic, lead, cadmium, and other toxics) Waste generation (slag) Impacts of producing energy (most energy used for mineral production goes into smelting and refining)

Source: Young, 1992.

Unfortunately, no economic analyses estimate the total externality costs of mining. Some recent examples of mining activities that have caused significant environmental impacts include:

- *Gold mining in the Peruvian Amazon*: Small-scale illegal gold mining relies on highly toxic mercury to extract gold from the rocks. In addition to the human health impacts, at least 2,000 square miles have been deforested as a result of mining.[8]

- *Phosphate mining in Nauru:* About 80 percent of the small island country has been strip mined. By 2000, the phosphate reserves were essentially depleted. Not only has the island become an environmental catastrophe, but the mining revenues were placed in a trust fund that was depleted due to poor investments and corruption.[9]
- *Copper mining disaster in the Philippines:* In 1996 a tailings dam from copper mining failed, releasing more than 1.6 million cubic meters of contaminated waste. The waste left the Boac River virtually dead, and the United Nations declared it a major environmental disaster.[10]

Another environmental problem is contamination from abandoned mines. For example, in the United States:

> one legacy of hardrock mining in the United States is the presence of many abandoned mines around the West. Some of these sites are causing severe environmental problems. The chief one is acid drainage, contaminated water that leaks from the mines into streams and rivers. Current government policies to cope with these abandoned mines are counterproductive. . . . Public reclamation of old sites does occur, but the available funds have many restrictions that keep them from being used efficiently. The total amount of money available from these sources is small compared to the apparent need.[11]

Reforming Mining Policies

General Mining Act of 1872
a U.S. federal law that regulates mining for economic minerals on federal lands.

The primary mining law in the United States is the **General Mining Act of 1872**. Little changed since the mid-nineteenth century, the Act allows the extraction of minerals from many public lands without royalty payments to the government. Mining rights are preserved as long as the claimant performs $100 of drilling or excavating in a year.[12] Some public lands can be purchased by individuals or corporations for a *maximum* of $5 per acre—prices that were set in 1872 and have never been adjusted. Since the Act was passed, more than 3 million acres of public lands have been purchased by mining interests, an area the size of Connecticut. The Act contains no provisions for environmental damage, although some regulations have been enacted since then. Numerous attempts to modernize the Act have failed (see Box 11.2).

One policy to address mining pollution is a Pigovian tax, as discussed in Chapter 3. However, a tax levied in proportion to mining pollution would be difficult to implement because of the problems involved in accurately measuring mining pollution. A tax could instead be levied on a mine's mineral output, rather than directly on pollution. But the problem with this proposal is that a firm would have no clear incentive to reduce its pollution for a given level of output, as it would be taxed the same amount.

Instead of a tax, requiring a mining company to post a bond before being allowed to mine would provide the public with compensation in case of environmental dam-

---

BOX 11.2   A MINING LAW WHOSE TIME HAS PASSED

The General Mining Act of 1872 was designed to spur development of the western United States by giving mining precedence over other uses of federal lands. Mining claims for copper, gold, uranium, and other minerals cover millions of acres, and the Act makes it extremely difficult to block mining regardless of the potential environmental impacts. Rising mineral prices in recent years have spurred an increase in mining claims under the Act.

Oregon's Chetco River is one example. The river's clear waters teem with wild trout and salmon. In 1998 Congress designated the Chetco a national wild and scenic river "to be protected for the benefit of present and future generations." But the river is now threatened by proposals to mine gold along almost half of its approximately 55-mile length. Suction dredges would vacuum up the river bottom searching for gold, muddying water and disrupting clean gravel that salmon need to spawn. Despite the Chetco's status as a wild and scenic river, the U.S. Forest Service is virtually powerless to stop the mining because of the 1872 law.

As Michael P. Dombeck, a former chief of the Forest Service, explained to a Senate committee in 2008, "It is nearly impossible to prohibit mining under the current framework of the 1872 mining law, no matter how serious the impacts might be."

According to the Environmental Protection Agency (EPA), streams in 40 percent of western watersheds are polluted by mining. A 2006 analysis of 25 western mines by the environmental group Earthworks concluded that more than three-fourths caused water contamination. Under the Mining Act, mine owners can abandon a mine without any responsibility for subsequent environmental damages. The EPA has estimated that it will cost $20 billion to $54 billion to clean up abandoned mine sites.

Potential reforms to the Act include giving the government the power to prevent mining based on a complete review of environmental impacts, clear environmental standards for operating mines, a fund for mine cleanup to be paid by mine operators, and charging royalty fees that reflect the market value of the minerals. So far, reform proposals have failed as a result of lobbying and opposition by legislators from mining states.

Source: Hughes and Woody, 2012.

age. The bond would need to be large enough to cover potential cleanup costs. For example, the state of Colorado required a $2.3 million cash bond from a company operating a gold mine, but when the company went bankrupt in 1992 the bond was insufficient to pay for cleanup costs of more than $150 million.[13]

Mining pollution is a problem that may be best addressed through effective standards and operational requirements. Nearby surface water and groundwater can be constantly monitored to identify contamination problems early. Stronger regulations can mandate certain practices for the management of tailings. In addition, mining activities can be limited by increasing the recycling of existing metal products. We consider the potential for recycling in the next section.

11.5. THE POTENTIAL FOR RECYCLING

virgin resource
a resource obtained from nature, as opposed to using recycled materials.

In Stages I and II of the resource use profile in Figure 11.3 there is little incentive for recycling as the price of the **virgin resource** is falling. But in Stage III, when prices begin to rise but demand remains high, recycling is likely to become more economically attractive. Over time, the proportion of total demand met from recycled material rather than virgin resources will rise as extraction costs rise in Stages III and IV. Even with decreasing extraction of the virgin resource in Stage IV, the total supply of a mineral need not fall, with efficient recycling.

This is illustrated in Figure 11.6. The dashed line shows a resource extraction path without recycling, similar to the one shown in Figure 11.3 but only for Stages III and IV. Now we consider the effect of recycling. At the start of Stage III, recycling is low, as virgin materials can still be obtained relatively cheaply. But as extraction costs of the virgin resource increase, and demand continues to rise, more of the total supply is met from recycled materials. Eventually, most of the total supply is met from recycled materials rather than the virgin resources. Note that recycling allows us to continue to use the virgin resource for a longer period, but at low rates. Recycling may provide a steadily increasing proportion of the resource supply. With technological improvements and high recycling rates, the choke price occurs later, if at all.

The shift toward recycled material would occur even earlier if prices reflected environmental externalities. In general, the environmental impacts are reduced by producing a product with recycled materials than virgin materials. For example, obtaining aluminum from recycled beverage cans requires 90–95 percent less energy than extracting virgin aluminum.[14] Thus a tax based on environmental externalities would increase the relative advantage of recycled materials over virgin resources.

backstop resource
a substitute resource that becomes a viable alternative after the price of the initial resource reaches a certain high price.

Another alternative to a virgin resource is a **backstop resource**, defined as a resource that can substitute for the original product but at a higher price. Thus we can view the choke price as the price at which it becomes cheaper to shift production to a backstop resource. With effective recycling, the shift to a backstop resource would be postponed or possibly eliminated.

Recycling resources today reduces both present and future costs from primary resource use. The recycling process also has its own costs, including capital costs of recycling facilities and labor, transportation, and energy costs. It makes sense, therefore, to examine the economics of recycling and its effects on resource use in more detail.

Figure 11.6 **Impact of Recycling on Virgin Resource Extraction Path**

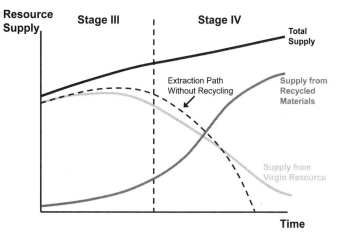

The Economics of Recycling

In theory, effective recycling could significantly extend the lifetime of many non-renewable resources. However, recycling has both economic and physical limits.

second law of thermodynamics

the physical law stating that all physical processes lead to a decrease in available energy, that is, an increase in entropy.

The **second law of thermodynamics** (the principle of increasing entropy, discussed in Chapter 7) implies that perfect recycling is impossible. Some loss or degradation of material will always occur during the process of fabrication, use, and recycling. In addition, recycling requires new inputs of energy. In economic terms, we must compare recycling costs to the costs of using virgin materials to determine when recycling will be both physically possible and economically advantageous.

Figure 11.7 shows the economics of recycling, considering the perspectives of an industry and of social welfare. The x-axis indicates the proportion of industrial demand for a resource met from recycled materials. Our analysis assumes that the marginal cost of recycled materials (MC_r) is initially low, but as we approach a theoretical 100 percent recycling, increasing the proportion of recycled materials becomes difficult and expensive. The marginal private cost of extracting a virgin resource (MPC_v) is also initially relatively low, as the cheapest reserves are extracted first. Reserves that are deeper underground or of lower quality become increasingly expensive to extract. (The MPC_v curve should be read from right to left, showing increasing use of virgin materials at lower levels of recycling supply.)

Reading from left to right, it makes sense for the industry to increase its reliance on recycled materials as long as the marginal costs are lower than the marginal costs of the virgin resource. In this simple example, the industry will minimize its production costs when it relies upon recycled materials for 40 percent of its supply.

From the social perspective, we need to also consider the environmental externalities. The MSC_v curve shows the marginal social cost of extracting the virgin resource, with the difference between MSC_v and MPC_v representing the additional environmental externalities associated with the extraction of the virgin resource. Thus the socially optimal level is to rely on recycled materials for 60 percent of the total supply. Internalization of environmental costs through a tax on virgin resource extraction could achieve this social optimum. As the marginal costs of

Figure 11.7 **Marginal Costs of Recycling**

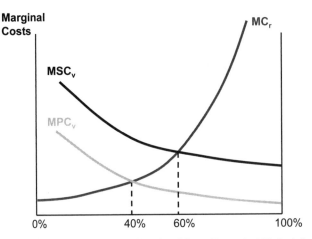

Proportion of Supply Obtained from Recycled Materials

recycled and virgin materials shift over time, even further reliance on recycling may be justified.

Policies to Promote Recycling

Even without significant policies to internalize environmental costs, metal recycling has generally expanded. In the United States, about 65 percent of total metal consumption came from recycled scrap in 2010. As shown in Figure 11.8, recycling rates are about 30 percent for zinc, copper, and tin, around 50 percent for nickel and aluminum, and close to 70 percent for iron and steel. Lead recycling, at about 80 percent, significantly reduces highly toxic lead residues in the environment.

These recycling rates are significant in terms of extending resource lifetimes as well as reducing economic and environmental costs. If global metal recycling rates could be boosted to over 50 percent, resource lifetimes would be more than double those based on using only virgin materials. In addition, pollution from metal mining and fabrication, as well as problems of waste disposal, would drop significantly.

What kinds of policies would best promote increased recycling of nonrenewable minerals? Policy options for increasing recycling include the following:

- *Altering public policies that encourage rapid resource extraction.* Governments often make mineral resources available for exploitation at extremely low cost. As mentioned above, the General Mining Act of 1872 clearly needs to be reformed. In addition to lost revenues, low prices for valuable resources promote resource overuse and excessive social costs.
- *Imposing taxes on the use of primary resources.* As Figure 11.7 shows, internalizing environmental costs through a tax promotes increased use of recycled materials. However, because the cost of virgin materials usually represents only a small portion of the final product cost, a tax alone may have little effect on consumption pattern.[15]

Figure 11.8 **Scrap Metal as a Percentage of Total U.S. Consumption, 2010**

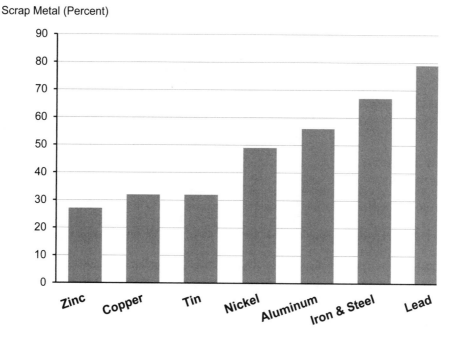

Scrap Metal (Percent)

Zinc | Copper | Tin | Nickel | Aluminum | Iron & Steel | Lead

Source: USGS, 2012.

technological (and social) lock-in

the tendency of an industry or society to continue to use a given technology despite the availability of more efficient or cheaper technologies.

government procurement

programs that guarantee a certain government demand for a good or service.

- *Combining market incentives for recycling with measures to promote the technology and infrastructure needed for recycling systems.* A phenomenon known as **technological lock-in** leads an industry that has once acquired a certain kind of plant and machinery—in this case production technology using nonrenewable resources—to continue investing in the same kind of plant. Changing over a whole industry from one production system to another involves heavy costs and requires a significant amount of initial capital. Tax incentives, support for research and development of recycling technologies, and **government procurement**—programs that guarantee a certain government demand for recycled materials—can help to jump-start this process.
- *Municipal programs and institutions to promote recycling.* Curbside recycling pickup makes recycling waste materials much easier for consumers and businesses. Communities can often recoup the costs of curbside recycling through sale of recyclable materials, as well as through reduced disposal costs. Even if these programs require a subsidy, they can often be justified on environmental grounds. Municipal recycling institutions create the basis for mining the waste stream—obtaining metals and other materials from waste rather than from mineral deposits or other virgin resources (more on this topic in Chapter 17). Increased supplies of recycled materials will lower their prices, making them more attractive to manufacturers as inputs.
- *Consumer incentives such as **deposit/return** systems or **pay-by-the-bag** rules for collecting nonrecyclable garbage.* These give consumers a financial incentive to recycle and impose a cost for failing to recycle. In general, these

consumer incentives prove much more effective if combined with other institutional mechanisms for recycling such as curbside pickup or rules requiring manufacturers to identify different kinds of material to facilitate recycling.

Promoting recycling can be environmentally beneficial both for nonrenewable and renewable resources. Metal recycling reduces the need for ore mining, plastics recycling reduces the demand for petroleum products, and paper recycling (as we discuss in Chapter 14) reduces demand pressures on forests.

Energy resources, however, cannot be recycled, and energy is required for both virgin resource extraction and recycling. According to the second law of thermodynamics, usable energy is inevitably degraded into waste heat after use.[b]

For this reason, energy deserves special attention in our analysis of resource use. In the following chapters, we consider the full cycle of resource use, including the pollution and waste generation from resource consumption. We focus our attention on energy resources in Chapter 12, consider the economics of renewable resources in Chapters 13–15, and analyze pollution control policies in Chapter 16.

SUMMARY

Nonrenewable resources are limited in supply, but available reserves can be expanded either by new discovery or technological improvements. Concerns over the exhaustion of major nonrenewable resources have so far not been borne out. Despite growing demand, new discoveries and improved technology have increased available reserves of key minerals.

While prices for most minerals generally declined or remained stable for most of the twentieth century, prices have increased in recent years. Whether this signals resource scarcity is difficult to determine, as many mineral reserves are at record levels. Even if reserves are adequate, improved management of mineral resources is needed to address environmental impacts. The mining process generates large quantities of toxic waste and has extensive negative environmental effects on land and water. Internalizing the full environmental cost of resource recovery would encourage a shift to renewable resource use or recycling, rather than increased consumption of virgin resources.

In the United States, about 65 percent of metal production currently uses recycled scrap. Although complete recycling is impossible, recycling rates for most major metals can increase considerably. In addition to extending nonrenewable resource lifetimes, recycling significantly reduces the environmental damage associated with the production of virgin materials.

Public policies to promote recycling include raising royalty payments for access to minerals on public lands, internalizing environmental costs through taxes on virgin resource use, developing technology and infrastructure, and government procurement of recycled products.

---

[b]It is possible to capture waste energy from industrial processes for heating buildings, a process called cogeneration, but after a single use this energy, too, will escape into the atmosphere as waste heat.

KEY TERMS AND CONCEPTS

backstop resource
choke price
cogeneration
deposit/return systems
economic rent
economic reserves (economically recoverable
  reserves)
economic supply (of a resource)
exponential reserve index
extraction path
General Mining Act of 1872
government procurement
Hotelling's rule
hypothetical (resources)
identified reserves
indicated or inferred (reserves)
marginal extraction cost
measured (reserves)
net price (of a resource)

nonrenewable resources
pay-by-the-bag rules
physical reserves
physical supply (of a resource)
price path
price taker
recycling
resource lifetime
resource rents
resource substitution
resource use profile
second law of thermodynamics
smelting
static reserve index
subeconomic resources
tailings
technological lock-in
user costs
virgin resource

DISCUSSION QUESTIONS

1. Is scarcity of nonrenewable resources a major problem? What kinds of physical and economic measures are relevant to understanding this issue, and in what ways can some of the measures be misleading? What do you think are the main issues relating to nonrenewable use?

2. Do you expect mineral prices to continue to increase, as shown in Figure 11.4? Which factors do you think will determine future mineral prices?

3. Some critics of municipal recycling programs have argued that they are uneconomic because they cost more than ordinary waste disposal. Which economic factors would you use to evaluate this argument? What relationship exists between recycling incentives for end-users and incentives for manufacturers to use recycled materials? How can environmental costs be internalized at various stages of the production cycle?

NOTES

1. Meadows et al., 1992.
2. Krautkraemer, 1998, p. 2102.
3. Ibid., p. 2103.
4. Barnett and Morse, 1963.
5. Kesler, 2007, p. 58.
6. British Geological Survey, Risk List 2012, www.bgs.ac.uk/mineralsuk/statistics/riskList.html.

7. Darmstadter, 2001, p. 11.
8. Ashe, 2012.
9. http://en.wikipedia.org/wiki/Phosphate_mining_in_Nauru/.
10. http://en.wikipedia.org/wiki/Marcopper_Mining_Disaster/.
11. Buck and Gerard, 2001, p. 19.
12. General Accounting Office, 1989.
13. Buck and Gerard, 2001.
14. New Jersey Department of Environmental Protection, www.state.nj.us/dep/dshw/recycling/env_benefits.htm.
15. See Ackerman, 1996, chap. 2.

REFERENCES

Ackerman, Frank. 1996. *Why We Recycle*. Washington, DC: Island Press.

Ashe, Katy. 2012. "Gold Mining in the Peruvian Amazon: A View from the Ground." Mongabay.com (March). http://news.mongabay.com/2012/0315-ashe_goldmining_peru.html.

Barnett, Harold J., and Chandler Morse. 1963. *Scarcity and Growth: The Economics of Natural Resource Availability*. Baltimore: Johns Hopkins University Press.

Berck, Peter, and Michael Roberts. 1996. "Natural Resource Prices: Will They Ever Turn Up?" *Journal of Environmental Economics and Management* 31: 65–78.

Buck, Stuart, and David Gerard. 2001. "Cleaning Up Mining Waste." *Political Economy Research Center*, Research Study 01–1 (November).

Canadian Press, 2012. "b.c. Mining Giant Admits Polluting U.S. Waters." CBC News, September 10.

Cleveland, Cutler J. 1991. "Natural Resource Scarcity and Economic Growth Revisited: Economic and Biophysical Perspectives." In Robert Costanza, ed., *Ecological Economics: The Science and Management of Sustainability*. New York: Columbia University Press.

Darmstadter, Joel. 2001. "The Long-Run Availability of Minerals: Geology, Environment, Economics." Summary of an Interdisciplinary Workshop, *Resources for the Future* (April).

General Accounting Office. 1989. "The Mining Law of 1872 Needs Revision." GAO/RCED-89–72 (March).

Goeller, H.E., and A. Zucker. 1984. "Infinite Resources: The Ultimate Strategy." *Science* 27: 456–462.

Hartwick, John M., and Nancy D. Olewiler. 1998. *The Economics of Natural Resource Use*, 2nd ed. Reading, MA: Addison Wesley Longman.

Hodges, Carol A. 1995. "Mineral Resources, Environmental Issues, and Land Use." *Science* 268 (June): 1305–1311.

Hughes, Robert M., and Carol Ann Woody. 2012. "A Mining Law Whose Time Has Passed." *New York Times*, January 11.

Kesler, Stephen E. 2007. "Mineral Supply and Demand into the 21st Century." Proceedings, Workshop on Deposit Modeling, Mineral Resource Assessment, and Sustainable Development.

Krautkraemer, Jeffrey A. 1998. "Nonrenewable Resource Scarcity." *Journal of Economic Literature*, 36 (4) (December): 2065–2107.

Meadows, Donella, et al. 1972. *The Limits to Growth*. New York: Universe Books.

———. 1992. *Beyond the Limits: Confronting Global Collapse, Envisioning a Sustainable Future*. Post Mills, VT: Chelsea Green.

Skinner, B.J. 1976. "A Second Iron Age Ahead?" *American Scientist* 64: 263.

Slade, Margaret E. 1982. "Trends in Natural Resource Commodity Prices: An Analysis of the Time Domain." *Journal of Environmental Economics and Management* 9 (June): 122–37.

Spofford, Walter O., Jr. 2012. "Solid Residual Management: Some Economic Considerations." *Natural Resources Journal* 11 (July): 561–89.

Tietenberg, Tom. 2000. *Environmental and Natural Resource Economics*, 5th ed. Reading, MA: Addison Wesley Longman.

United States Bureau of Mines and United States Geological Survey. 1976. *Geological Survey Bulletins* 1450-A and 1450-B.

United States Geological Survey (USGS). 2012. *2010 Minerals Yearbook*.

———. *Mineral Commodity Summaries*. Various years.

World Resources Institute. 1994. *World Resources 1994–95*. Oxford: Oxford University Press.

Young, John E. 1992. *Mining the Earth*. Worldwatch Paper 109. Washington, DC: Worldwatch Institute.

WEB SITES

1. **http://minerals.usgs.gov/minerals/.** The Web site for the Minerals Resource Program of the U.S. Geological Survey. The site includes links to extensive technical data as well as publications.
2. **www.epa.gov/waste/basic-solid.htm.** The EPA's Web site on nonhazardous waste management. It includes information about recycling, landfills, and the management of waste nationally and in each state.
3. **www.earthworksaction.org.** The Web site for Earthworks, a nonprofit environmental organization "dedicated to protecting communities and the environment from the impacts of irresponsible mineral and energy development while seeking sustainable solutions."

Energy: The Great Transition

CHAPTER 12 FOCUS QUESTIONS

- What is the special role of energy in economic systems?
- What are current and future demands for energy?
- Is there a danger of energy shortages?
- Can we shift from fossil fuel-based energy to renewable energy systems?

12.1 ENERGY AND ECONOMIC SYSTEMS

Energy is fundamental to economic systems and, indeed, to all life. On deep ocean floors, far below the reach of sunlight, giant tubeworms and other strange life forms cluster around heat vents. Energy from the earth's interior drives their metabolic processes. On the earth's surface and at shallower ocean levels, all plant life depends on sunlight, and all animal life is dependent directly or indirectly on plants.[a] Our own equally critical need for energy is partially camouflaged in a modern economy. Measured in terms of the gross domestic product (GDP), energy resources represent only about 5 percent of economic output, but the other 95 percent is absolutely dependent on energy inputs.

In less developed, agrarian economies, the dependence is more evident. People's basic need for food calories is, of course, a need for energy input. Traditional agriculture is essentially a method of capturing **solar energy** for human use. Solar energy stored in firewood meets other basic needs for home heating and cooking. As economies develop and become more complex, energy needs increase greatly. Historically, as supplies of firewood and other **biomass** proved insufficient to support growing economies, people turned to **hydropower** (also a form of stored solar energy), then to coal, and then to oil and natural gas as major energy sources. In the 1950s nuclear power was introduced into the energy mix.

Each stage of economic development has been accompanied by a characteristic **energy transition** from one major fuel source to another. Today, fossil fuels—coal,

solar energy
the energy supplied continually by the sun, including direct solar energy as well as indirect forms such as wind energy and flowing water.

biomass
an energy supply from wood, plant, and animal waste.

hydropower
the generation of electricity from the energy in flowing water.

energy transition
an overall shift of energy consumption away from fossil fuels toward renewable energy sources.

---

[a]The few plants that can live without direct sunlight make use of nutrients in the soil deposited by the decay of other plants.

oil, and natural gas—are by far the dominant energy source in industrial economies. In the twenty-first century, the next great transition in energy sources has started—from nonrenewable fossil fuels to renewable energy sources. This transition is being motivated by many factors, including concerns about environmental impacts (particularly climate change), limits on fossil fuel supplies, and prices.

Government policies will have significant influence on the nature and speed of this transition. Current energy markets bear little resemblance to the efficient unregulated markets described in Adam Smith's *Wealth of Nations*. Instead, energy markets are heavily subsidized and regulated. In particular, fossil-fuel subsidies by governments around the world total about $500 billion per year, dwarfing the subsidies for renewables.[1] (For more on energy subsidies, see Box 12.1.)

BOX 12.1 FOSSIL FUEL SUBSIDIES

According to analysis by Bloomberg New Energy Finance, global subsidies for fossil fuels are about twelve times higher than the subsidies allocated toward renewable energy. In 2009, global subsidies for renewable energy were $43 to $46 billion, mainly in the form of tax credits and feed-in tariffs. Meanwhile, the International Energy Agency estimated that governments spent about $550 billion to subsidize fossil fuels.

The G20 countries have agreed to phase out fossil subsidies over "the medium term" but progress has been slow and no specific target date has been set. Meanwhile, many countries are ramping up their commitment toward renewable energy. The most expensive renewable energy subsidy in 2009 was Germany's feed-in tariff, which cost nearly $10 billion. Other feed-in tariffs in Europe totaled another $10 billion.

The United States spent more than any other country toward renewable energy subsidies, around $18 billion. China provided about $2 billion, although this figure is likely too low as it does not include the value of low-interest loans offered for renewable energy projects by state-owned banks.

Source: Morales, 2010.

Energy prices also generally fail to reflect the costs of negative externalities. As we saw in Chapter 3, economic theory suggests that a commodity be taxed according to its externality damages. In the case of energy markets, externalities are rarely fully internalized. Removing distortionary subsidies and instituting appropriate externality taxes could significantly speed the transition from fossil fuels to renewable energy sources.

While getting the prices of different energy sources "right" is critically important, we should also note a different, more ecologically oriented, perspective on energy. Theorists of the ecological economics school see energy as fundamental to economic development and focus on a crucial distinction between the **nonrenewable stock** of fossil-fuel reserves and the **renewable flow** of solar energy.[2] In this perspective, the period of intensive fossil-fuel use that began with coal in the eighteenth century was a one-time, unrepeatable bonanza—the rapid exploitation of a limited stock of high-quality resources.[3]

The fossil-fuel age has obviously brought significant economic progress to much of the world, but this particular route to development cannot be followed universally. Even if sufficient supplies of fossil fuels were available, if everyone

nonrenewable stock
See "nonrenewable resources."

renewable flow
the continuous quantity of a renewable energy source supplied over time, such as the quantity of solar energy available each year.

consumed fossil fuels at the rate of the average American, global greenhouse gas emissions would increase by about a factor of four. Fortunately, the earth receives enough solar energy every hour to supply all human energy needs for an entire year.[4] This figure is theoretical—the capture and use of solar energy, either directly or indirectly through such sources as wind power or biomass, involves costs and limitations. Nonetheless, renewable energy potential is very great. Operating our economies on this renewable flow, as opposed to depletable stock resources, represents a key component of any conception of sustainable development.

Because so much of the **capital stock** and infrastructure of modern economic systems are based on fossil-fuel energy use, any transition from fossil fuel dependence will involve massive restructuring and new investment. While private markets will play a critical role in this process, major changes in government policies are necessary to foster the transition. The considerable economic implications of this justify a special focus on energy use as a central economic and environmental issue.

capital stock

the existing quantity of capital in a given region, including manufactured, human, and natural capital.

12.2 EVALUATION OF ENERGY SOURCES

We obtain energy from numerous sources for many different purposes. Figure 12.1a shows the main energy sources consumed globally. We see that about 81 percent of the world's energy comes from fossil fuels—oil, coal, and natural gas. Biomass provides over 10 percent of the world's energy, which developing countries rely upon for a disproportionate share of their energy. In most respects, the energy shares for the United States, shown in Figure 12.1b, are similar to the global proportions. The United States is slightly more reliant upon fossil fuels and nuclear energy, and less reliant upon biomass. Both the United States and the world receive about 2.5 percent of energy from hydropower and only about 1 percent from wind, solar, and geothermal energy.

Figure 12.1a **Global Energy Consumption 2010, by Source**

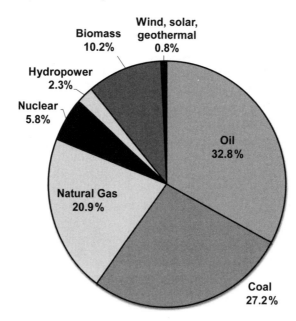

Source: International Energy Agency, 2011b.

Figure 12.1b   **United States Energy Consumption 2010, by Source**

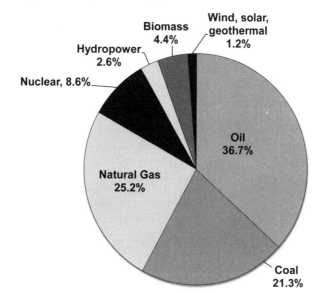

Source: U.S. Energy Information Administration, 2011a.

One objective of this chapter is to analyze whether our current energy supply mix is appropriate and how it may need to change in the future. But first we need to consider how we should evaluate various energy sources. This will help explain why our current energy mix is allocated as shown in Figure 12.1b. We consider five criteria to evaluate different energy sources:

Price: This is perhaps the most obvious factor to consider. We should consider both the average price of a particular energy source and also its variability over time. As you might expect, our heavy reliance on fossil fuels is driven largely by price considerations.

Availability: Fossil fuels are limited in supply. We consider later in the chapter whether we are in danger of running out of fossil fuels. Renewable energy sources such as wind and solar cannot be depleted but have variable geographic availability and may fluctuate daily and seasonally.

Environmental impacts: Analysis of the environmental impacts of different energy sources should consider the full life-cycle impacts. For example, for coal we should look at the impacts associated with mining coal, the air pollution generated from burning coal, the disposal of the waste from coal plants, and the eventual decommissioning of power plants.

Net energy: It takes energy to get energy. For example, the energy required to explore for, to extract, and to process crude oil should be deducted from the energy obtained to determine the net available energy. Net energy is normally expressed as a ratio of the energy available for final consumption divided by the energy required to produce it.[b]

Suitability: Different types of energy are more useful for certain applications. For example, oil is particularly suitable for powering motor vehicles, nuclear power is primarily used to generate electricity, and geothermal energy is well suited for heating buildings.

---

[b]Another term for "net energy" is "energy return on (energy) invested," or EROI. See Cleveland, 1991.

Net Energy and Suitability of Energy Sources

We discuss price, availability, and environmental impacts of energy in more detail later in this chapter. First, we discuss the other two factors: net energy and suitability of energy sources.

If net energy is expressed as a ratio, a higher value means that we can obtain a significant amount of available energy without using much energy to obtain it. Table 12.1 shows the net energy ratios for various energy sources, based on U.S. data. We see that net energy ratios for fossil fuels range from 5 for shale oil (oil extracted from hydrocarbon-rich rocks) to 80 for coal. The net energy ratio for hydropower is even greater—over 100. Nuclear power, wind energy, and photovoltaic cells have moderate net energy ratios.

Table 12.1

Net Energy Ratios for Various Energy Sources

Energy source	Net energy ratio
Oil (global)	35
Natural gas	10
Coal	80
Shale oil	5
Nuclear	5–15
Hydropower	>100
Wind	18
Photovoltaic cells	6.8
Ethanol (sugarcane)	0.8–10
Ethanol (corn-based)	0.8–1.6
Biodiesel	1.3

Source: Murphy and Hall, 2010.

The lowest net energy ratios are found for some biofuels. In fact, the energy needed to produce corn ethanol is about equal to the energy obtained. This implies that without significant technological improvements, corn ethanol is not a very attractive energy option based on the net energy criterion, although other biofuels might achieve higher net energy ratios.

Energy statistics normally divide energy use among four sectors in an economy: transportation, industrial, residential and commercial, and electricity.[c] Different energy sources are better suited for different sectors. Table 12.2 shows the three main energy sources used by each sector in the United States. Transportation is heavily dependent upon oil, which supplies 94 percent of U.S. transportation needs. Oil is well suited for transportation because it has a high energy density and is relatively easy to store. But oil is less prevalent in the other energy sectors. The industrial sector relies about equally on natural gas and oil. Natural gas demands are highest in such industries as chemicals manufacturing, agriculture, and metal manufacturing. The residential and commercial sector relies on natural gas for about three-quarters of its nonelectricity energy demands, mainly for heating.

---

[c]Note that the "industrial" and "residential and commercial" sectors exclude electricity use and transportation demands by these sectors.

Table 12.2

Energy Consumption by Sector in the United States, 2010

	Sector			
	Transportation	Industrial	Residential and commercial	Electricity
Percent of total U.S. energy consumption	28%	20%	11%	40%
Primary fuel source	Oil (94%)	Natural gas (41%)	Natural gas (76%)	Coal (48%)
Secondary fuel source	Biomass (4%)	Oil (40%)	Oil (18%)	Nuclear (21%)
Tertiary fuel source	Natural gas (2%)	Biomass (11%)	Biomass (5%)	Natural gas (19%)

Source: U.S. Energy Information Administration, 2011a.

In the electricity sector, the United States gets about half its electricity from coal, with about 20 percent each from nuclear power and natural gas. Renewable energy is most prevalent in electricity generation, with about 10 percent of U.S. electricity coming from renewable sources, mainly hydropower and wind. Biomass supplies 11 percent of industrial energy and 5 percent of residential and commercial energy.

12.3 ENERGY TRENDS AND PROJECTIONS

World energy demand has grown rapidly and is expected to continue to grow in the foreseeable future. As seen in Figure 12.2, world energy consumption increased by about a factor of three between 1965 and 2011. World population approximately doubled during this same period, so about half the growth in global energy demand can be attributed to a higher population and the other half can be attributed to greater demand per capita.

Figure 12.2 **World Energy Consumption, by Source, 1965–2011**

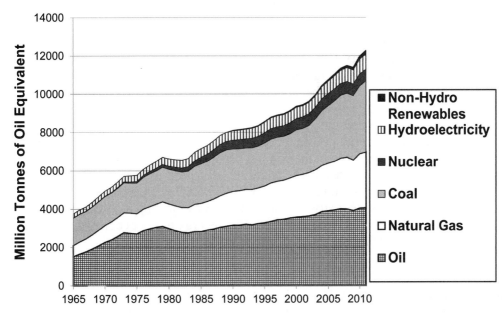

Source: British Petroleum, 2012.

Higher global demand has been met by expanding the use of all forms of energy. From 1965 to 2011, energy consumption from coal increased 161 percent, from oil 189 percent, from hydropower 278 percent, and from natural gas 395 percent. The most rapid growth in recent years has occurred for renewables. Since 1990, global consumption of wind energy has increased by about 12,000 percent and solar energy more than 14,000 percent! Despite such growth, solar and wind energy currently provide only a minuscule percentage of global energy supplies—less than 1 percent. Also, between 2000 and 2010 about half the increase in global energy demand was met by expanding coal use, mainly in new electricity plants in emerging countries such as China and India.[5]

Projections of future global energy demand depend on assumptions regarding prices, technology, and economic growth. Projections by the major energy agencies, including the U.S. Energy Information Administration and the International Energy Agency (IEA), typically include a baseline, or business-as-usual (BAU), scenario that assumes no significant policy changes and no dramatic shifts in prices and technology. Other scenarios consider what might be expected if, for example, oil prices are significantly higher in the future or if major policy changes are implemented.

Figure 12.3 presents one such comparison, produced by the IEA. In the BAU scenario, global energy consumption increases by about 50 percent from the current 12,000 million tonnes of oil equivalent (Mtoe) to over 18,000 Mtoe in 2035.[d] Compared to the energy mix shown in Figure 12.1, the percentage of global energy obtained from oil is expected to decline, while the share obtained from coal is expected to increase. Overall, the share of global energy obtained from fossil fuels stays about the same at 80 percent. Nuclear energy becomes a smaller share of energy supplies (going from 11 percent to 6 percent), while the share from renewable energy increases.[e]

Figure 12.3 also predicts the global energy mix under an aggressive policy scenario intended to keep global warming to no more than 2 degrees Celsius over preindustrial levels—the target agreed on during the 2009 international meeting on climate change in Copenhagen.[6] In this scenario, global energy demand grows by only about 25 percent. We also see significant differences in the global energy mix. Compared to the BAU scenario, coal use is dramatically lower, while renewable energy and nuclear power comprise much higher shares. In this case, the share of global energy obtained from fossil fuels falls from over 80 percent to about 62 percent.

These results demonstrate that our energy future is not predetermined, but that total energy consumption and the energy supply mix will depend on the policy choices made in the coming years. In fact, concerted policy efforts can make dramatic changes in a relatively short period of time (see Box 12.2).

In addition to looking at energy statistics based on different energy sources, it is also instructive to analyze energy consumption across different countries and regions. As we see in Table 12.3, energy use per capita varies tremendously across countries.

---

[d]A tonne is one metric ton, equal to 1,000 kilograms (kg) or 2,204.6 pounds.

[e]Note that the categories in Figure 12.3 are slightly different than those presented in Figure 12.1. In Figure 12.3 biomass energy is combined with wind, solar, and geothermal energy.

Figure 12.3 **Projected 2035 Global Energy Demand, by Source**

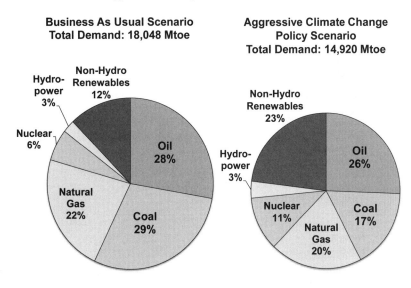

Source: International Energy Agency, 2011b.

BOX 12.2 PORTUGAL GIVES ITSELF A CLEAN-ENERGY MAKEOVER

Back in 2005 Portugal initiated an ambitious program to increase its reliance on renewable energy. The results have been impressive—the share of Portugal's electricity coming from renewable energy increased from 17 percent to about 45 percent from 2005 to 2010. Over that time period, the energy obtained from wind power increased by a factor of seven. Portugal is putting in place a national grid of charging stations for electric cars.

Portugal was able to expand its use of renewable energy rapidly because it had large supplies of untapped wind and hydroelectric power. As it previously relied heavily on costly imports of fossil fuels for its electricity, Portugal's shift toward renewable energy required no tax or debt increases. Portugal now plans to begin closing down some of its conventional power plants that are no longer needed.

"I've seen all the smiles—you know: It's a good dream. It can't compete. It's too expensive," said Prime Minister José Sócrates, recalling the way Silvio Berlusconi, the Italian prime minister, mockingly offered to build him an electric Ferrari. Mr. Sócrates added, "the experience of Portugal shows that it is possible to make these changes in a very short time. "

Source: Rosenthal, 2010.

Countries with the highest per capita energy use tend to be either countries with a cold climate, such as Canada and Iceland, or oil-producing countries such as the United Arab Emirates and Qatar. Per capita energy use in the United States is relatively high, especially when compared with European countries such as France and Italy. Per capita energy use in China has grown rapidly in recent years (increasing about 140 percent between 2000 and 2009), but it is still only about one-quarter of the typical energy use of an American. Energy use per person in India is only about one-sixteenth the U.S. level, and energy use in the poorest countries is less than 1 percent of the U.S. level.

Table 12.3

Energy Consumption per Capita, 2009, Selected Countries

Country	Million BTUs per person
United Arab Emirates	679
Canada	389
United States	308
Sweden	230
Russia	191
France	169
Germany	163
United Kingdom	143
Italy	126
China	68
Thailand	60
Brazil	52
India	19
Nigeria	5
Ethiopia	2

Source: U.S. Energy Information Administration, International Energy Statistics online database.
Note: BTU = British thermal unit.

Total global energy consumption is currently split about evenly between developed (OECD) and developing (non-OECD) countries, as shown in Figure 12.4. However, more than 80 percent of future growth in global energy demand is expected to occur in developing countries, under the BAU scenario shown in Figure 12.4. Even with such rapid growth in energy consumption in developing countries, energy use per capita will still be only about one-third of the levels in developed countries. In fact, if energy use per capita continued to grow at current rates in both developed and developing countries, it would be more than three hundred years before energy use per person became equal for developed and developing nations. Thus global inequality in energy access will continue for the foreseeable future.

Figure 12.4 **Past and Projected Energy Consumption, OECD vs. Non-OCED Nations**

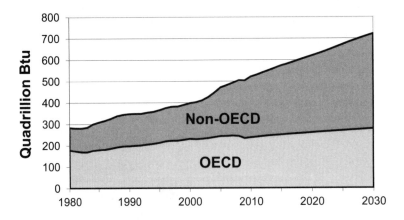

Source: U.S. Energy Information Administration, International Energy Statistics online database.
Note: OECD = Organization for Economic Cooperation and Development.

12.4 Energy Supplies: Fossil Fuels

Even with aggressive energy policies, global energy demand is projected to continue to increase in the coming decades, and we will continue to meet most of our energy needs with fossil fuels. But is the supply of fossil fuel sufficient to meet future demands?

Much of the discussion about energy supplies has focused on oil. The authors of this text can recall concerned discussions about limited supplies of oil during the energy crises of 1973 and 1979. But during the 1980s oil prices fell about 50 percent, and many people spoke of an oil glut. More recently, oil prices have moved back up, reaching a high of around $140/barrel in 2008 and hovering around $100/barrel during most of 2011 and 2012 (Figure 12.5). Some people have suggested that the era of cheap oil is over.

How can we evaluate projections of oil supply limits? According to a theory advanced by petroleum geologist M. King Hubbert in 1956, the typical pattern of oil production over time resembles a bell curve. In the early period of resource exploitation, discovery and production expand, leading to falling prices and exponentially rising consumption. Eventually production becomes more expensive as the most-accessible supplies are depleted. New discoveries decline, and production eventually peaks. Beyond the peak, production falls and, assuming constant or increasing demand, prices continue to increase.

Hubbert curve

a bell-shaped curve showing the production quantity of a nonrenewable energy resource over time.

As Figure 12.6 shows, the **Hubbert curve** projection for U.S. crude oil production matches up rather well to the actual data so far. Oil output in the United States peaked in the early 1970s and has generally declined since then. Figure 12.6 also shows U.S. oil consumption. While the United States was essentially oil

Figure 12.5 **Oil Prices in Constant Dollars, 1970-2012**

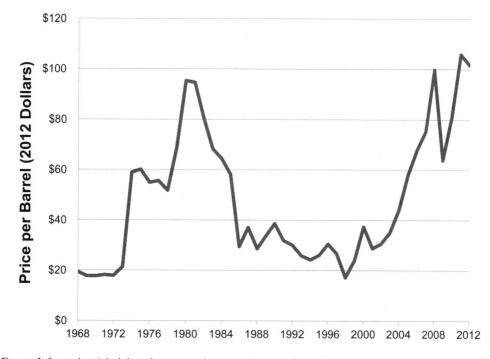

Sources: U.S. Energy Information Administration, www.eia.gov and http://inflationdata.com.

Figure 12.6 **United States Domestic Oil Production and Consumption**

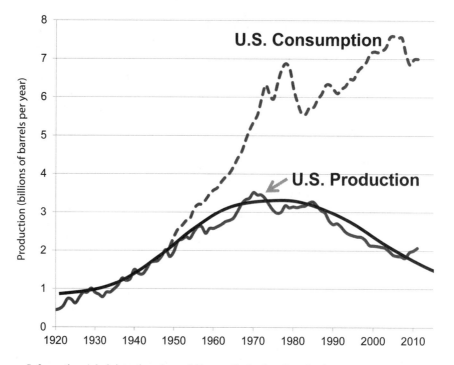

Source: U.S. Energy Information Administration, Annual Energy Outlook online database.

independent until the 1950s, the share of oil demand met from imports has generally increased since then. In the mid-2000s the United States obtained about 60 percent of its oil from imports. A common myth is that the United States obtains most of its imported oil from the Middle East. Actually, the top exporter of oil to the United States, with 28 percent of all U.S. imports, is Canada. Other top sources of U.S. oil imports are Saudi Arabia (15 percent), Mexico (9 percent), Venezuela (8 percent), Nigeria (5 percent), and Colombia (4 percent).

As recently as the mid-2000s, it was expected that the share of U.S. oil demand met from imports would continue to increase. However, in Figure 12.6 we see a recent increase in U.S. oil production. This is primarily a result of an increase in production of unconventional oil sources, mainly "tight oil"—oil from shale and other rock formations. Current projections by the U.S. Energy Information Administration estimate that U.S. domestic crude oil production will hold steady or slightly increase in the coming decades. So while the Hubbert Curve may continue to be representative of conventional U.S. crude oil production, the availability of unconventional oil sources may prevent further declines in U.S. total oil production.

Global Oil Supplies

More important is the availability of oil supplies at the global level. As discussed in Chapter 11, the reserves of a nonrenewable resource can fluctuate over time with changes in prices, technology, and new discoveries. Recall that the expected lifetime of a resource can be calculated as the economic reserves divided by annual consumption. Table 12.4 shows that in 1980 proven oil reserves would be sufficient to meet thirty-one years of demand if demand levels stayed constant. Rather than staying constant, global demand for oil continued to increase. But did the world run out of oil in 2011, or earlier? Of course not. We see in Table 12.4 that oil reserves are now 2.4 times higher than they were in 1980 as a result of new discoveries, technological improvements, and higher oil prices, which have made more oil deposits economically viable. Even with higher global demand in 2011 than in 1980, proven reserves can now meet global demands for a further fifty-one years.

However, the increase in oil reserves in recent years does not signal a return to lower oil prices. In fact, global production of oil from conventional sources may have already peaked. Figure 12.7 shows past and projected global oil production under a scenario that takes into account recent pledges by countries to reduce greenhouse gas emissions and phase out subsidies for fossil fuel. Even with new discoveries, conventional crude oil production stabilizes at around 70 million barrels per day. Global oil production is able to continue to increase only by reliance on unconventional oil sources and natural gas liquids.

Table 12.4

Global Oil Reserves, Consumption, and Resource Lifetime, 1980–2011

Year	Proven reserves (billion barrels)	Annual consumption (billion barrels)	Resource lifetime (years)
1980	683	22	31
1981	696	22	32
1982	726	21	34
1983	737	21	35
1984	774	21	36
1985	803	22	37
1986	908	22	41
1987	939	23	41
1988	1,027	23	44
1989	1,027	24	43
1990	1,028	24	42
1991	1,033	24	42
1992	1,039	25	42
1993	1,041	25	42
1994	1,056	25	42
1995	1,066	26	42
1996	1,089	26	42
1997	1,107	27	41
1998	1,093	27	40
1999	1,238	28	45
2000	1,258	28	45
2001	1,267	28	45
2002	1,322	29	46
2003	1,340	29	46
2004	1,346	30	45
2005	1,357	31	44
2006	1,365	31	44
2007	1,405	32	45
2008	1,475	31	47
2009	1,518	31	49
2010	1,622	32	51
2011	1,653	32	51

Source: British Petrolem, 2012

When global oil production peaks might depend as much upon policy as on resource availability. According to the IEA:

> Clearly, global oil production will peak one day, but that peak will be determined by factors affecting both demand and supply.... [I]f governments act more vigorously than currently planned to encourage more efficient use of oil and the development of alternatives, then demand for oil might begin to ease soon and, as a result, we might see a fairly early peak in oil production. That peak would not be caused by resource constraints. But if governments do nothing or little more than at present, then demand will continue to increase, supply costs will rise, the economic burden of oil use will grow, vulnerability to supply disruptions will increase and the global environment will suffer serious damage.
>
> Unconventional oil is set to play an increasingly important role in world oil supply through to 2035, regardless of what governments do to curb demand.... Unconventional oil resources are thought to be huge—several times larger than conventional oil resources. The rate at which they will be exploited will be determined by economic and environmental considerations, including the costs of mitigating their environmental impact. Unconventional sources of oil are among the more expensive available. Consequently, they play a key role in setting future oil prices.[7]

Figure 12.7 **Past and Projected Global Oil Production, 1990–2035**

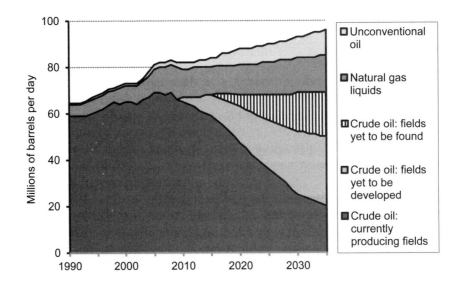

Source: International Energy Agency, 2010.

So in an absolute sense, we are unlikely to run out of oil anytime soon, especially when unconventional sources are taken into account. But the era of cheap oil may well be over as conventional production stops increasing and we rely upon more expensive unconventional oil to meet the increase in global demand.

Economics suggests that higher oil prices will lead to substitution of other fuels for oil. But there is a steady increase in demand for oil in developing countries:

> All of the net increase in oil demand comes from the transport sector in emerging economies, as economic growth pushes up demand for personal mobility and freight. Alternative vehicle technologies emerge that use oil much more efficiently or not at all, such as electric vehicles, but it takes time for them to become commercially viable and penetrate markets.[8]

Other Fossil Fuels: Natural Gas and Coal

The other fossil fuels, coal and natural gas, are alternatives to oil in the transportation sector. Natural gas can be used to fuel vehicles directly; there are an estimated 5 million natural gas vehicles worldwide.[9] Coal can be used to generate electricity to fuel electric vehicles. As we saw in Table 12.1, coal and natural gas play a relatively large role in the industrial, residential, commercial, and electricity sectors. Globally, coal and natural gas provide nearly 50 percent of energy supplies. What about the availability of these resources?

Both coal and natural gas are more abundant than oil in the United States and globally. While the United States has only 2 percent of global oil reserves, it has 4 percent of the world's natural gas reserves and 28 percent of coal reserves. In recent years, the United States has experienced a natural gas boom, with an increase in production of 27 percent between 2005 and 2011. According to the U.S. Energy Information Administration, U.S. production of natural gas is expected to grow by about 1 percent per year over the next couple of decades.

Natural gas is generally viewed as the cleanest fossil fuel, producing comparatively low amounts of air pollutants and greenhouse gases. Yet environmentalists have expressed concerns in recent years over the process of hydraulic fracturing, or "fracking," to obtain natural gas (see Box 12.3). Some analysts have suggested that leakages of methane, a powerful greenhouse gas, can make fracked natural gas as bad or worse than coal in terms of greenhouse gas emissions.[10] Globally, natural gas reserves are sufficient for more than sixty years of supply at current demand levels. Under a BAU scenario, global consumption of natural gas is expected to increase by about 23 percent between 2013 and 2035.[11]

BOX 12.3 E.P.A. LINKS TAINTED WATER IN WYOMING TO HYDRAULIC FRACTURING FOR NATURAL GAS

In 2011 a report published by the U.S. Environmental Protection Agency (EPA) found that the hydraulic fracturing of rocks in the process of drilling for natural gas, commonly known as fracking, is the likely cause of contaminated water supplies in Wyoming. The report raises questions about the environmental safety of fracking, which is being used to extract previously unrecoverable natural gas in dozens of places around the United States. However, the energy industry claims that water contamination from fracking has not been conclusively proven.

The report is based on a three-year study initiated when local residents complained about the smell and taste of their water. The study site, known as the Pavillion field, is a natural gas well that is unusually shallow. The shallow depth means that natural gas can seep upward into underground aquifers, contaminating water supplies.

"This investigation proves the importance of having a federal agency that can protect people and the environment," said John Fenton, the chairman of Pavillion Area Concerned Citizens. "Those of us who suffer the impacts from the unchecked development in our community are extremely happy the contamination source is being identified."

Another potential threat from fracking is the chemicals companies use to extract natural gas, which can also contaminate water supplies. While Wyoming now requires companies to disclose the ingredients in their fracking fluids, in other states disclosure is not required. The EPA has begun a national study of the effects of fracking on drinking water supplies.

Source: Johnson, 2011.

Coal is the most environmentally damaging fossil fuel. It is estimated that particulate-matter pollution from coal power plants leads to the deaths of more than 13,000 people in the United States every year.[12] Coal also emits more carbon dioxide, the primary greenhouse gas, per unit of energy. Coal is, however, the most abundant fossil fuel. The United States is the world leader in coal reserves—its reserves alone could satisfy current world demand for thirty-one years. Global reserves are sufficient for 111 years of world consumption at current demand levels. As with natural gas, under a BAU scenario, global coal demand is projected to increase by 23 percent between 2013 and 2035.

Renewable Energy Sources

In one sense, renewable energy is unlimited, as supplies are continually replenished through natural processes. As noted earlier, the daily supply of solar energy is theoretically sufficient to meet all human energy needs for an entire year. But solar energy and other renewable energy sources are limited in the sense that their availability varies geographically and across time. Some regions of the world are particularly well suited for wind or solar energy. For example, solar energy potential is highest in the southwestern United States, northern Africa, the Middle East, and parts of Australia and South America. Some of the best regions for wind energy include northern Europe, the southern tip of South America, and the Great Lakes region of the United States. Geothermal energy is abundant in countries such as Iceland and the Philippines.

One important question is whether renewable energy is available in sufficient quantities to replace our dependence on fossil fuels while also being comparably reliable and suitable for different purposes (we consider the issue of cost in the next section). A recent study concluded that renewable energy sources, based on wind, water, and sunlight (WWS), could provide all new energy globally by 2030 and replace all current nonrenewable energy sources by 2050.[13] Table 12.5 shows estimates of the potential energy from various renewable energy sources, converted into trillions of watts. Projected global energy demand in 2030 is 17 trillion watts. Thus we see in Table 12.5 that the availability of energy from wind and solar in likely developable locations is more than sufficient to meet all the world's energy needs. The report authors' analysis envisions:

Table 12.5

Availability of Global Renewable Energy

Energy source	Total global availability (trillion watts)	Availability in likely developable locations (trillion watts)
Wind	1700	40–85
Wave	> 2.7	0.5
Geothermal	45	0.07–0.14
Hydroelectric	1.9	1.6
Tidal	3.7	0.02
Solar photovoltaic	6500	340
Concentrated solar power	4600	240

Source: Jacobson and Delucchi, 2011a.

a world powered entirely by WWS, with zero fossil-fuel and biomass combustion. We have assumed that all end uses that feasibly can be electrified use WWS power directly, and that the remaining end uses use WWS power indirectly in the form of electrolytic hydrogen (hydrogen produced by splitting water with WWS power). The hydrogen would be produced using WWS power to split water; thus, directly or indirectly, WWS powers the world.

The authors then estimate the infrastructure that would be necessary to supply all energy worldwide from WWS in 2030. Table 12.6 presents their results, based on the assumption that 90 percent of global energy is supplied by wind and solar and 10 percent by other renewables. They also consider the land requirements for renewable **energy infrastructure**, including the land for appropriate spacing between wind turbines. Land requirements total about 2 percent of global land area, with most of this the space between wind turbines that could be used for agriculture, grazing land, or open space. Also, wind turbines could be located offshore to reduce the land requirements.

energy infrastructure
a system that supports the use of a particular energy source, such as the supply of gas stations and roads that support the use of automobiles.

Table 12.6

Infrastructure Requirements for Supplying All Global Energy in 2030 from Renewable Sources

Energy source	Percent of 2030 global power supply	Number of plants/devices needed worldwide
Wind turbines	50	3,800,000
Wave power plants	1	720,000
Geothermal plants	4	5,350
Hydroelectric plants	4	900
Tidal turbines	1	490,000
Rooftop solar photovoltaic systems	6	1.7 billion
Solar photovoltaic power plants	14	40,000
Concentrated solar power plants	20	49,000
Total	100	

Source: Jacobson and Delucchi, 2011a.

The technology already exists to implement these renewable energy sources. While construction of this renewable energy infrastructure would require significant investment, the authors conclude that the primary hurdles are not economic. "Barriers to the plan are primarily social and political, not technological or economic. The energy cost in a WWS world should be similar to that today."[14]

The issue of cost is central to the question of whether an energy transition will occur and, if so, how rapidly. The availability of energy supplies, whether fossil fuels or renewables, is not the determining factor. Rather, it is the relative costs, including the cost of energy infrastructure investment and the cost of day-to-day energy supply. In analyzing costs, we should consider both the market cost of supply and the environmental costs of various energy sources. It is to this analysis that we now turn.

12.5 THE ECONOMICS OF ALTERNATIVE ENERGY FUTURES

The world currently gets about 80 percent of its energy supplies from fossil fuels because these sources generally provide energy at the lowest cost. However, the cost advantage of fossil fuels over renewable energy sources has been decreasing in recent years, and certain renewables can already compete with fossil fuels on solely financial terms. The price of fossil fuels, especially for oil, in the future is difficult to predict, while the costs of renewable energy are expected to decline further. Thus even without policies to promote a transition toward renewables, economic factors are currently moving us in that direction.

Comparing the costs of different energy sources is not straightforward. Capital costs vary significantly—a new nuclear power plant can cost $10 billion to $20 billion. Some energy sources require continual fuel inputs, while other sources, such as wind and solar, only require occasional maintenance. We also need to account for the different lifespans of various equipment and plants.

Cost comparisons between different energy sources are made by calculating the **levelized cost** of obtaining energy. Levelized costs represent the **present value** of building and operating a plant over an assumed lifetime, expressed in real terms to remove the effect of inflation. For energy sources that require fuel, assumptions are made about future fuel costs. The levelized construction and operations costs are then divided by the total energy obtained to allow direct comparisons across different energy sources.

Different studies have produced different estimates of the costs of various energy sources. Some of these differences are attributed to cost variations in different regions of the world. Figure 12.8 provides a comparison of the projected levelized costs of generating electricity in the United States and Europe. Data for the United States provide cost estimates based on new electricity sources, equalized to 2016 to account for the time lag needed to bring certain new facilities, such as nuclear and coal plants, into production. The European data show a range of costs, projected for 2015.

levelized costs

the per-unit cost of energy production, accounting for all fixed and variable costs over a power source's lifetime.

present value

the current value of a steam of future costs or benefits; a discount rate is used to convert future costs or benefits to present values.

Figure 12.8 **Levelized Cost of Different Energy Sources, United States (2016) and Europe (2015)**

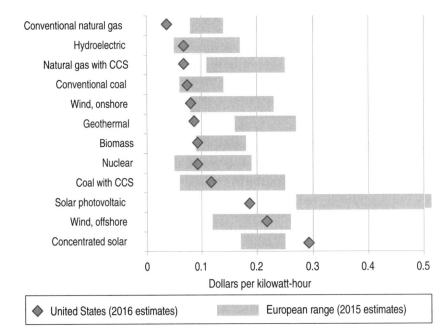

Sources: Department of Energy and Climate Change, 2011; International Energy Agency et al., 2010; Parsons Brinckerhoff, 2010; U.S. Energy Information Administration, 2011c.

Note: CCS = Carbon captured and storage.

In the United States, the cheapest energy sources are natural gas, hydroelectric power, and conventional coal. Natural gas prices in the United States fell from more than $10 per thousand cubic feet in 2008 to less than $2 in 2012, making natural gas cheaper than coal. The most expensive electricity sources in the United States are solar photovoltaic and offshore wind. However, the cost of onshore wind is comparable to conventional coal electricity, with biomass and geothermal also near the cost of coal.

In Europe, we see a wide range of price variability across countries and data sources. Conventional coal, nuclear, and hydropower tend to produce the lowest energy costs. However, onshore wind, natural gas, and biomass can also be cost competitive with these sources. As in the United States, solar and offshore wind tend to be the most expensive methods for generating electricity in Europe.

Figure 12.9 shows another way to compare the cost of renewables with traditional fossil-fuel costs. In order for renewables to be cost competitive with fossil fuels, their costs generally need to fall to the existing price of wholesale power. This has already occurred for some renewables, such as hydropower and biomass. Figure 12.9 indicates that wind and geothermal are nearly cost competitive with traditional power sources. Solar is more costly, but since solar photovoltaics (PV) can be installed by individual consumers the price of PV only needs to fall to the retail power price to be competitive.

Figure 12.9 **Cost Comparison of Renewable Energy Sources to Fossil Fuel Electricity Costs**

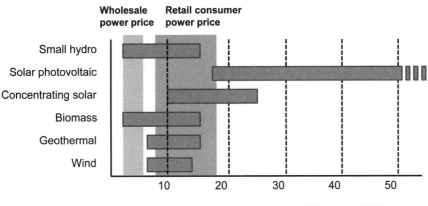

Power generation costs in USD cents/kWh

Source: International Energy Agency and Organization for Economic Cooperation and Development, 2007.

Oil does not appear in Figures 12.8 and 12.9 because it is rarely used to generate electricity. In the United States, only about 0.5 percent of electricity is generated using petroleum products. But as we saw in Table 12.2, oil dominates the transportation sector. Various alternative options are available for road vehicles, including fully-electric vehicles, hybrids which use fossil fuels only for long-distance trips (such as the Chevrolet Volt), and potentially hydrogen fuel cells. The electricity to charge vehicles or generate hydrogen could be generated by wind power, solar energy, geothermal power, or other renewable sources.

Cost comparisons between traditional internal combustion vehicles and renewable energy alternatives depend on such factors as the price of gasoline, the price of electricity, and the availability of tax credits or rebates for clean vehicles. A recent review of studies comparing the costs of different vehicle energy options finds that renewable alternatives, particularly using wind energy to power batteries of electric vehicles, may already be cost competitive with traditional vehicles, even in the United States, where gasoline is relatively cheap.[15]

Overall, fossil fuels generally currently have a cost advantage over renewable energy alternatives, although in some cases renewables such as onshore wind and geothermal energy can be competitive. But looking to the future, it is reasonable to expect that the cost of renewables will continue to decline, while the future price of fossil fuels is highly uncertain.

Consider the past and projected cost trends for wind and solar energy in Figures 12.10a and b. Particularly with solar PV, we can be confident that its cost will continue to decline. As technologies improve and prices decline, the utilization of these energy sources is increasing rapidly. As mentioned earlier, production of both wind and solar energy has increased dramatically in recent years.

Not only are the costs of renewable energy sources expected to decline in the future, but Figure 12.10 also projects that cost range will decrease for wind and solar energy. Thus the future prices for renewable energy are expected to be predictable within a relatively narrow band. This is not the case for fossil fuels, particularly oil.

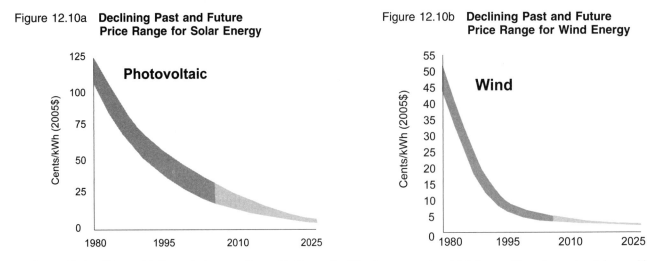

Figure 12.10a **Declining Past and Future Price Range for Solar Energy**

Figure 12.10b **Declining Past and Future Price Range for Wind Energy**

Source: National Renewable Energy Laboratory, Renewable Energy Cost Trends, www.geni.org/globalenergy/library/energytrends/renewable-energy-cost-trends/renewable-energy-cost_curves_2005.pdf.
Note: kWh = kilowatt hours.

Figure 12.11 shows the past and projected price of oil. The price of oil has varied considerably in the past, and there is great uncertainty about the future price of oil. Even just a few years into the future, the price of oil is projected to be between about $60 and $175 per barrel. Under the reference scenario, the price of oil increases about 50 percent in real terms by 2035, a sharp contrast to the projected declines in the costs of renewable energy sources. But perhaps the most relevant message from Figure 12.11 is that we really have no idea what the future price of oil will be—very different from the relative certainty about future renewable prices. Not only does the price of oil depend on technology and future discoveries, but it is highly dependent on political factors and other world events.

Figure 12.11 **Past and Projected Price of Oil**

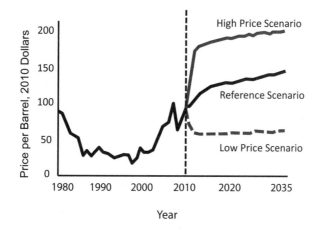

Source: U.S. Energy Information Administration, 2012.

The price of coal and natural gas normally does not vary as much as that of oil, but the future costs of these are also highly unpredictable. The reference projections for the price of coal and natural gas, like those for oil, indicate that prices will increase in the future. If these trends are borne out, the current price advantage of fossil fuels over renewables will decline and may cease to exist in the future.

So far we have been comparing the costs of different energy sources based on current market prices. But we need to consider two other factors that affect current and future energy prices: energy subsidies and environmental externalities.

Energy Subsidies

Energy subsidies can take various forms, including:

depletion allowances
a tax deduction for capital investments used to extract natural resources, typically oil and gas.

feed-in tariffs
a policy to provide renewable energy producers long-term contracts to purchase energy at a set price, normally based on the costs of production (but higher than the cost of production).

- *Direct payments or favorable loans*: A government can pay a company a per-unit subsidy for producing particular products or provide them with a loan at below-market interest rates.
- *Tax credits and deductions*: A government can allow individuals and businesses to claim tax credits for actions such as installing insulation or purchasing a fuel-efficient vehicle. **Depletion allowances** are a form of tax credit widely used for oil production.
- *Price supports*: For example, the price that producers of renewable energy receive may be guaranteed to be at or above a certain level. **Feed-in tariffs**, commonly used in Europe, guarantee producers of solar and wind power a certain rate for sales of power to the national grid.
- *Mandated purchase quotas*: These include laws requiring that gasoline contain a certain percentage of ethanol or that governments buy a certain percentage of their energy from renewable sources.

As we saw in Chapter 3, subsidies can be justified to the extent that they support goods and services that generate positive externalities. All energy sources currently receive a degree of subsidy support, but, as discussed in Box 12.1, subsidies heavily favor fossil fuels. Given that fossil-fuel use tends to generate negative, rather than positive, externalities, it is difficult to justify such subsidies on the basis of economic theory. Directing the bulk of energy subsidies to fossil fuels tilts the playing field in their favor relative to renewables.

In 2009, the members of the G20, a group of major economies including both developed and developing countries, agreed to "rationalize and phase out over the medium term inefficient fossil-fuel subsidies that encourage wasteful consumption" and "adopt policies that will phase out such subsidies worldwide."[16] The International Energy Agency notes:

> Energy subsidies—government measures that artificially lower the price of energy paid by consumers, raise the price received by producers or lower the cost of production—are large and pervasive. When they are well-designed, subsidies to renewables and low-carbon energy technologies can bring long-term economic and environmental benefits. However, when they are directed at fossil fuels, the costs generally outweigh the benefits. [Fossil-fuel subsidies] encourage wasteful consumption, exacerbate energy-price volatility by blurring market signals, incentivize fuel adulteration and smuggling, and undermine the competitiveness of renewables and other low-emission energy technologies.[17]

Global subsidies to fossil fuels in the electricity sector total about $100 billion annually.[18] Data on subsidies to nuclear power are difficult to obtain, but the limited information available suggests global nuclear subsidies of at least $10 billion.[f] Global subsidies to renewable forms of electricity total about $30 billion annually but are growing faster than other subsidies.

While the majority of electricity-sector subsidies go to fossil fuels, on a per-kilowatt-hour basis subsidies actually give renewables a price advantage. Subsidies effectively lower the price of electricity provided by fossil fuels by about one cent per kilowatt-hour. But according to one estimate, subsidies in 2007 lowered the per-kilowatt-hour price of wind energy by 7 cents, of concentrated solar energy by 29 cents, and of solar PV by 64 cents.[19] Thus electricity-sector subsidies are generally encouraging a shift to renewables.

In the transportation sector, global oil subsidies averaged about $200 billion annually in 2007–2009.[20] With annual global oil consumption around 1.3 trillion gallons, this amounts to a subsidy of about $0.15 per gallon. If we assume that this value is applicable for the United States, oil subsidies approximately cancel out the federal gasoline tax of 18 cents per gallon. The other major recipient of subsidies in the transportation sector is biofuels. Global subsidies to biofuels are estimated at about $20 billion and growing rapidly.

Environmental Externalities

In addition to subsidy reform, economic theory also supports internalizing externalities. The price of each energy source should reflect its full social costs. Various studies of energy externalities suggest that if the price of all energy sources included externality costs, a transition toward renewables would already be much further along.

---

[f] In addition, there are implicit subsidies to the nuclear industry related to limiting accident liability. The Price-Anderson Act in the United States limits nuclear operator liability to less than half a billion dollars, although the potential costs of a major accident could be much greater.

Figure 12.12   **Externality Cost of Various Electricity Generating Methods, European Union**

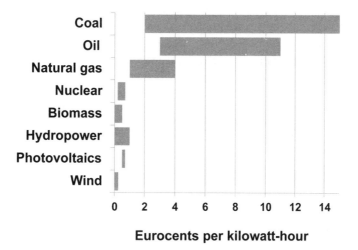

Eurocents per kilowatt-hour

Source: Owen, 2006.

Figure 12.12 provides a summary of the range of external costs associated with different electricity sources, based on European analyses. The externality cost of coal is particularly high, ranging between 2 and 15 eurocents per kilowatt-hour. This is consistent with other research that estimates the external cost of coal electricity in the United States at about 6 cents per kilowatt-hour.[21] The externalities associated with natural gas are lower, but still range between 1 and 4 eurocents per kilowatt-hour, a result that is also consistent with U.S. estimates.

The externality costs associated with renewable energy are much lower, less than one eurocent per kilowatt-hour. So while fossil fuels may currently have a cost advantage over renewables based solely on market prices, if externalities were included, several renewables would likely become the most affordable energy sources—in particular, onshore wind, geothermal, and biomass energy. Similarly, the cost advantage of oil in transportation would likely disappear if externalities were fully included in the price.[22]

The operating externalities of nuclear energy are relatively low, as the life cycle of nuclear power generates low levels of air pollution and greenhouse gas emissions. But the potentially most significant externalities from nuclear power are the risks of a major accident and the long-term storage of nuclear wastes. These impacts are difficult to estimate in monetary terms (remember the analysis in Chapter 6 of the assessment of risk and uncertainty). Whether nuclear power will play an increased or decreased role in future energy supplies remains a controversial topic (for more on the debate over nuclear energy, see Box 12.4).

Our discussion suggests that the biggest factor currently preventing a transition to renewable energy is the failure to account for externalities. Getting the prices "right" would send a clear signal to businesses and consumers that continued reliance on fossil fuels is bad economics. But even without full internalization of externalities, the declining cost of renewable means that a transition from fossil fuels will occur in the future.

Figure 12.13 shows a projected comparison of the cost of electricity generation in 2020 using traditional fossil-fuel methods and various renewable alternatives.

BOX 12.4   NUCLEAR POWER: COMING OR GOING?

In the 1950s nuclear power was promoted as a safe, clean, and cheap source of energy. Proponents of nuclear power stated that it would be "too cheap to meter" and predicted that nuclear power would provide about one-quarter of the world's commercial energy and most of the world's electricity by 2000 (Miller, 1998).

Currently, nuclear power provides only about 6 percent of the world's energy and 14 percent of the world's electricity. Most of the world's capacity to produce nuclear power predates 1990. The decommissioning of older plants, which had an expected lifespan of thirty to forty years, has already begun. However, some people were predicting a "nuclear renaissance" several years ago, mainly because carbon emissions from the nuclear power lifecycle are much lower than with fossil fuels.

The 2011 Fukushima accident has caused many countries to reevaluate their nuclear power plans.

> In Japan, the world's most catastrophic nuclear crisis since the 1986 Chernobyl disaster has other nuclear energy-dependent nations on edge. Citizens and politicians, fearful of the same tragedies in their own backyards, are calling on governments around the world to rethink their nuclear power programs. Riding the wave of growing fear, investors have been pulling out of nuclear and uranium stocks as some in the markets are calling for the end of the nuclear renaissance and the death of the uranium bull. (*The Citizen*, 2011)

As Japan reevaluates its use of nuclear power, Germany has decided to phase out the use of nuclear power entirely by 2022. In Italy, the debate over nuclear power was put to voters, with 94 percent rejecting plans for an expansion of nuclear power. But other countries are moving ahead with plans to expand their use of nuclear power, particularly China. Currently about 20 nuclear plants are under construction as China plans to increase its use of nuclear power about twentyfold by 2030. Other countries moving ahead with expanded use of nuclear power are India, Russia, and South Korea.

Thus the role of nuclear power in the future global energy mix remains uncertain. The Fukushima accident has slightly lowered baseline projections of future energy supplies from nuclear power. While some see the accident as evidence that we need to focus more on renewables like wind and solar, others worry that a decline in nuclear power will result in "higher energy costs, more carbon emissions and greater supply uncertainty" (Macalister, 2011).

Based solely on production costs, the renewable sources of onshore wind, wave energy, concentrated solar, and potentially offshore wind are all expected to be cost competitive with fossil fuels. When the impacts of externalities are included, all renewable sources become less expensive than fossil fuels. These results imply that there are good economic reasons for promoting a transition to renewables. In the final section of this chapter, we turn to policy proposals to encourage a more rapid transition.

12.6 POLICIES FOR THE GREAT ENERGY TRANSITION

What kinds of government policies are most important to foster a timely and efficient transition to a shift to renewable energy sources? As discussed, one policy goal agreed on by many of the world's largest countries is to phase out inefficient fossil-fuel subsidies. One concern is that in the short term this could lead to higher energy prices and a decrease in economic growth. But the money that governments save could be invested in ways that would reduce the cost of renewable alternatives and encourage a more rapid transition from fossil fuels.

Figure 12.13   Cost of Electricity Generating Approaches, 2020

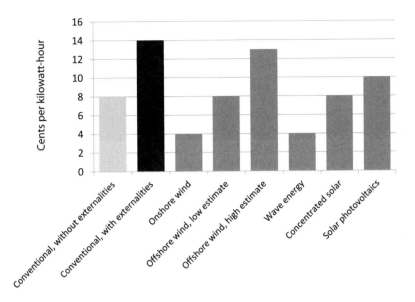

Source: Jacobson and Delucchi, 2011b.

In the long run,

> fossil fuel subsidy reform would result in aggregate increases in gross domestic product (GDP) in both OECD and non-OECD countries. The expected [increase is as high as] 0.7 per cent per year to 2050. . . . Results from a wide variety of global and single-country economic modeling studies of subsidy reform suggest that on an aggregate level, changes to GDP are likely to be positive, due to the incentives resulting from price changes leading to more efficient resource allocation.[23]

One major issue is the need to internalize the negative externalities of different energy sources. A common form of Pigovian tax is a tax on gasoline. Even though governments use this tax primarily to raise revenue, it also serves the function of internalizing externalities. While the price of crude oil is determined in a global market, the retail price of gasoline varies widely across countries due to differences in gasoline taxes. In late 2010 the price of gasoline ranged from less than $1/gallon in countries such as Venezuela, Saudi Arabia, and Kuwait, where gas is subsidized rather than taxed, to as much as $8/gallon in France, Norway, the United Kingdom, and other countries where gas is heavily taxed.

Economic theory suggests that the "correct" tax on gas should fully account for the negative externalities. In the United States, the current federal gas tax is 18.4 cents per gallon, in addition to state taxes that range from 8 to 50 cents per gallon. Virtually all economists agree that these taxes are too low, although there is disagreement about how much higher the tax should be. While some economists suggest it should be only about 60 cents higher, others suggest that gas taxes should be over $10 per gallon.[24]

Pigovian taxes can also be applied to the electricity sector. As we see in Figure 12.14, electricity prices vary across countries, primarily due to variations in tax rates. In general, higher electricity prices are associated with lower per capita consumption rates. For example, the United States has relatively low electricity

Figure 12.14 **Electricity Prices and Consumption Rates**

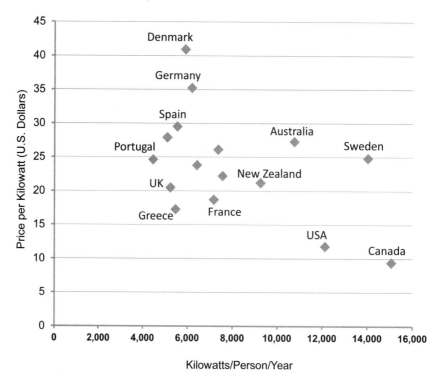

Sources: U.S. Energy Information Administration, International Energy Statistics database; International Energy Agency, Energy Prices and Statistics online database.

prices and relatively high consumption rates. Electricity prices in Germany, Spain, and Denmark are much higher, and per capita consumption rates are about half the rate of the United States. But we need to be careful about drawing conclusions based on a simple comparison like this because it fails to account for many other variables that could influence electricity demand other than prices, such as income levels, climate, and the availability of different heating options. For example, Sweden has both higher electricity prices and higher consumption rates than the United States. Explaining this difference would require additional information not presented in Figure 12.14.

Beyond reducing fossil-fuel subsidies and implementing externality taxes, other policy options to encourage a transition to renewable energy include:

1. Energy research and development
2. Feed-in tariffs
3. Subsidies for renewable sources, including favorable tax provisions and loan terms
4. Renewable energy targets
5. Efficiency improvements and standards

Increasing research and development (R&D) expenditures will speed the maturation of renewable energy technologies. Global energy R&D expenditures have been increasing in recent years, from $18 billion in 2004 to $122 billion in

2009. Countries that invest heavily in energy R&D will likely gain a competitive advantage in this area in the future.

> Those nations—such as China, Brazil, the United Kingdom, Germany and Spain—with strong, national policies aimed at reducing global warming pollution and incentivizing the use of renewable energy are establishing stronger competitive positions in the clean energy economy. Nations seeking to compete effectively for clean energy jobs and manufacturing would do well to evaluate the array of policy mechanisms that can be employed to stimulate clean energy investment. China, for example, has set ambitious targets for wind, biomass and solar energy and, for the first time, took the top spot within the G-20 and globally for overall clean energy finance and investment in 2009. The United States slipped to second place. Relative to the size of its economy, the United States' clean energy finance and investments lag behind many of its G-20 partners. For example, in relative terms, Spain invested five times more than the United States last year, and China, Brazil and the United Kingdom invested three times more.[25]

Feed-in tariffs guarantee renewable energy producers access to electricity grids and long-term price contracts. Those that take advantage of feed-in tariffs need not be companies. For example, homeowners who install solar PV panels could sell excess energy back to their utility at a set price. Feed-in tariff policies have been instituted by dozens of countries and several U.S. states. The most ambitious is in Germany, which has become the world's leader in installed solar PV capacity.

Feed-in tariffs are intended to be reduced over time as renewables become more cost competitive with traditional energy sources. A reduction in feed-in tariff rates has already begun in Germany. A 2008 analysis by the European Union of different approaches for expanding the share of renewables in electricity supplies found that "well-adapted feed in tariff regimes are generally the most efficient and effective support schemes for promoting renewable electricity."[26]

Subsidies can take the form of direct payments or other favorable provisions, such as tax credits or low-interest loans. As mentioned earlier, the bulk of current subsidies go to fossil fuels. Yet subsidies make more sense for developing, rather than mature, technologies. Subsidies for renewable energy can promote economies of scale that lower production costs. Like feed-in tariffs, output subsidies can be gradually reduced as renewables become more competitive.

renewable energy targets
regulations that set targets for the percentage of energy obtained from renewable energy sources.

Renewable energy targets set goals for the percentage of total energy or electricity obtained from renewables. More than sixty countries have set renewable energy targets. The European Union has set a goal of 20 percent of total energy from renewables by 2020, with different goals for each member country. The 2020 targets include goals of 18 percent for Germany, 23 percent for France, 31 percent for Portugal, and 49 percent for Sweden. While the United States does not have a national renewable goal, most states have set goals. Some of the most ambitious goals include Maine (40 percent by 2017), Minnesota (25 percent by 2025), Illinois (25 percent by 2025), New Hampshire (24 percent by 2025), and Connecticut (23 percent by 2020).[27]

energy demand-side management
an energy policy approach that seeks to reduce energy consumption, through policies such as information campaigns or higher energy prices.

Most of the discussion in this chapter has focused on energy supply-side management—adjusting the energy supply mix to include a greater share of renewable sources. However, **energy demand-side management** is generally considered the most cost effective and environmentally beneficial approach to energy policy. In other words, while shifting a kilowatt of energy supply from coal to solar or wind is desirable, eliminating that kilowatt of demand entirely is even better. As the U.S. Environmental Protection Agency has noted:

> Improving energy efficiency in our homes, businesses, schools, governments, and industries—which consume more than 70 percent of the natural gas and electricity used in the country—is one of the most constructive, cost-effective ways to address the challenges of high energy prices, energy security and independence, air pollution, and global climate change.[28]

In some cases energy efficiency improvements can be obtained by technological changes, such as reducing fossil fuel use by driving a hybrid car. In other cases, energy efficiency means changing behavior, such as drying clothes on a clothesline instead of a clothes dryer, or switching off lights and appliances when not in use. The potential for demand-side management to reduce the projected growth of energy consumption is significant.

Under a BAU scenario, global energy demand is projected to nearly double between 2003 and 2050. However, based on the untapped potential for energy efficiency, it has been estimated that global demand could be held steady during this period, as shown in Figure 12.15. In developed countries, energy demand could actually decrease relative to current levels. In developing countries, energy consumption would still increase, but only by about 40 percent, instead of by 160 percent under a BAU scenario.

Figure 12.15 **Global Potential for Energy Efficiency**

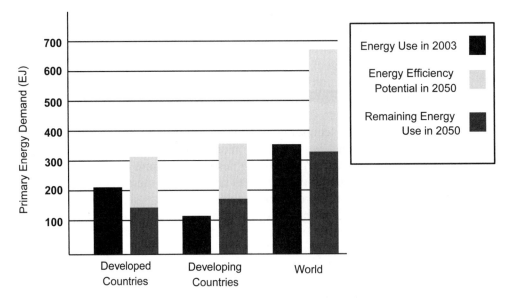

Source: Blok et al., 2008.

Realizing such gains from energy efficiency will require substantial investment, estimated at about 0.2 percent of global GDP.[29] However, investments in energy efficiency are typically much cheaper than meeting demand growth through developing new energy supplies. Well-designed energy efficiency programs cost, on average, only about half the cost of providing new energy supplies.[30] Another analysis estimates the cost of energy efficiency at 0 to 5 cents per kilowatt-hour.[31] Comparing this estimate to the cost of energy sources in Figure 12.8, we see that improving energy efficiency is the most economical option for addressing energy demand.

In addition to expanding R&D, two other policies can be effective at promoting energy efficiency. One is to set energy **efficiency standards**. Fuel-economy standards are one example. In 2011, fuel-economy standards in the United States were 30 miles per gallon (mpg) for passenger cars and 24 mpg for light trucks, a category that includes pickups, minivans, and sport utility vehicles. After about twenty years in which fuel-economy standards were little changed, in 2011 the Obama administration announced new standards that would raise the average fuel efficiency of new vehicles to 54.5 mpg in 2025. Compared to 2010 model year vehicles, total fuel savings for 2025 vehicles would total more than $8,000 over the lifetime of the vehicle. Other energy efficiency standards exist for buildings, appliances, electronics, and light bulbs.

Efficiency labeling informs consumers about the energy efficiency of various products. For example, in the United States the U.S. Environmental Protection Agency and U.S. Department of Energy manage the Energy Star program. Products that meet high-efficiency standards, above the minimum requirements, are entitled to receive the Energy Star label. About 75 percent of consumers who purchased an Energy Star product indicated that the label was an important factor in their purchase decision. In 2011 the energy savings from Energy Star products totaled about $23 billion.[32]

Even with informative labels, many consumers do not purchase high-efficiency products because the upfront costs may be higher. For example, light-emitting diode (LED) and compact fluorescent light bulbs cost more than traditional incandescent light bulbs. However, the energy savings from efficient bulbs means that the additional cost will be recovered in a relatively short period, normally less than one year. While people may resist buying efficient bulbs for other reasons, one problem is that people often have high implicit discount rates, focusing on the upfront cost while discounting the long-term savings (see Box 12.5).

BOX 12.5   IMPLICIT DISCOUNT RATES AND ENERGY EFFICIENCY

A major problem in increasing energy efficiency of appliances arises from high implicit discount rates. Suppose that a consumer can purchase a standard refrigerator for $500 and an energy-efficient model for $800. The energy efficient model will save the consumer $15 per month in energy costs. From an economic point of view, we can say that the return on the extra $300 invested in the efficient model is $15 x 12 = $180/year, or 60 percent. Thus in less than two years, the consumer will actually come out ahead by buying the more efficient refrigerator.

Anyone offered a stock market investment that would have a guaranteed 60 percent annual return would consider this a tremendous opportunity. But it is likely that the refrigerator buyer will turn down the chance to make this fantastic return. The reason is that he or she will weigh more heavily the immediate decision to spend $500 versus $800 and therefore choose the cheaper model. We could say that the consumer is implicitly using a discount rate of greater than 60 percent to make this judgment—a consumer behavior that is difficult to justify economically, yet very common.

Summary

Energy is a fundamental input for economic systems. Current economic activity depends overwhelmingly on fossil fuels, including oil, coal, and natural gas. These fuels are nonrenewable. Renewable sources such as hydroelectric, wind, and solar power currently provide less than 10 percent of global energy.

World energy use has expanded rapidly and is projected to continue growing, with an increase in energy demand of 50 percent by 2035. Supplies of oil are sufficient for at least several decades, but the era of cheap oil may be over as more oil must be obtained from expensive unconventional sources. Supplies of coal are more abundant, but its use also results in greater environmental damage. While a continued heavy reliance on fossil fuels is projected under a business-as-usual scenario, the potential exists to obtain all global energy from renewables by 2050.

Considering only market costs, fossil fuels tend to be cheaper than renewables. However, we need to consider that fossil fuels receive a disproportionate share of energy subsidies and that energy costs fail to account for negative externalities. If the price of different energy sources reflected their full social costs, then several renewables would gain a competitive advantage over fossil fuels. Also, the price of renewables is declining and relatively predictable, while the projected prices of fossil fuels are expected to rise and are highly uncertain. Thus even without internalizing externalities, renewables should be cost competitive with fossil fuels in the next decade or two.

The speed of the transition to renewable energy will be highly influenced by policy choices. Reforming fossil-fuel subsidies and instituting Pigovian taxes are two policies that can yield more economically efficient outcomes. Other potential policies include increasing energy research and development expenditures, feed-in tariffs, and renewable energy targets. Finally, the most cost-effective approach to address energy demand is to promote energy efficiency. The projected increase of global energy demand over the next few decades can be avoided through policies that focus on improving energy efficiency.

Key Terms and Concepts

biomass
capital stock
depletion allowances
economic efficiency standards
efficiency labeling
energy demand-side management
energy infrastructure
energy subsidies
energy transition

feed-in tariffs
Hubbert curve
hydropower
levelized costs
nonrenewable stock
present value
renewable energy targets
renewable flow
solar energy

Discussion Questions

1. Since energy production represents only about 5 percent of economic output, why should any special importance be placed on this sector? Is there any significant difference between an economic system that relies on nonrenewable energy supplies and one that uses

primarily renewable sources? Should policy decisions about energy use be implemented by governments, or should the patterns of energy use be determined solely by market allocation and pricing?

2. In the 1970s, energy shortages had a significant impact on economies throughout the world. Was this a one-time phenomenon or could it recur? Was it related primarily to demand-side or supply-side factors? How have demand and supply for energy changed since the 1970s, and how have these changes affected prices and consumption patterns for energy? Are further significant changes likely?

3. Many people argue that a transition to renewable energy sources would be good policy from both an economic and an environmental point of view. Yet such a transition has not occurred and does not seem imminent. Do you think that it would be beneficial to shift away from dependence on fossil fuels? What economic factors and policy decisions are likely to have a significant impact on whether and how rapidly such a shift occurs?

NOTES

1. IEA, 2011a.
2. For the classic assertion of energy's critical role in the economy, see Georgescu-Roegen, 1971. An overview of differing analytical perspectives on energy is in Krishnan et al., 1995.
3. See, e.g., Hall and Klitgaard, 2012.
4. Morton, 2006.
5. IEA, 2011a.
6. For detailed discussion of global climate analysis and policy, see Chapters 18 and 19.
7. IEA, 2010, Executive Summary, 6–7.
8. IEA, 2011a, Executive Summary, 3.
9. Natural Gas Supply Association, naturalgas.org.
10. See Howarth et al., 2011, and Wigley, 2011.
11. U.S. Energy Information Administration, 2011b.
12. Clean Air Task Force, 2010.
13. Jacobson and Delucchi, 2011a, p. 1154.
14. Ibid.
15. Jacobson and Delucchi, 2011b.
16. IEA et al., 2011.
17. IEA, 2011c.
18. Kitson et al., 2011.
19. Badcock and Lenzen, 2010.
20. Charles and Wooders, 2011.
21. Jacobson and Delucchi, 2011b.
22. See, e.g., Odgen et al., 2004.
23. Ellis, 2010, 7, 26.
24. CTA, 1998; Parry and Small, 2005.
25. Pew Charitable Trusts, 2010, 4–5.
26. Commission of the European Communities, 2008, 3.
27. Wiser and Barbose, 2008.
28. National Action Plan for Energy Efficiency, 2008, p. ES-1.
29. Blok et al., 2008.
30. National Action Plan for Energy Efficiency, 2006.
31. Lazard, 2009.
32. U.S. Environmental Protection Agency, 2011.

REFERENCES

Badcock, Jeremy, and Manfred Lenzen. 2010. "Subsidies for Electricity-Generating Technologies: A Review." *Energy Policy* 38: 5038–5047.

Blok, Kornelis, Pieter van Breevoort, Lex Roes, Rogier Coenraads, and Nicolas Müller. 2008. *Global Status Report on Energy Efficiency 2008*. Renewable Energy and Energy Efficiency Partnership, www.reeep.org.

British Petroleum. 2012. *Statistical Review of World Energy 2012*, June.

Charles, Chris, and Peter Wooders. 2011. "Subsidies to Liquid Transport Fuels: A Comparative Review of Estimates." International Institute for Sustainable Development, September.

The Citizen (Dar es Salaam). 2011. "Countries Assess Safety of Nuclear Power Plants." March 22.

Commission of the European Communities. 2008. "The Support of Electricity from Renewable Energy Sources." SEC(2008) 57, Brussels, January 23.

Clean Air Task Force. 2010. *The Toll from Coal*. www.catf.us/resources/publications/.

Cleveland, Cutler. 1991. "Natural Resource Scarcity and Economic Growth Revisited: Economic and Biophysical Perspectives." In *Ecological Economics,* ed. Robert Costanza. New York: Columbia University Press.

Department of Energy and Climate Change. 2011. "Review of the Generation Costs and Deployment Potential of Renewable Electricity Technologies in the UK," Study Report REP001, October.

Ellis, Jennifer. 2010. "The Effects of Fossil-Fuel Subsidy Reform: A Review of Modelling and Empirical Studies." International Institute for Sustainable Development, March.

Georgescu-Roegen, Nicholas. 1971. *The Entropy Law and the Economic Process*. Cambridge, MA: Harvard University Press.

Hall, Charles A.S., and Kent A. Klitgaard. 2012. *Energy and the Wealth of Nations: Understanding the Biophysical Economy*. New York: Springer.

Howarth, Robert W., Renee Santoro, and Anthony Ingraffea. 2011. "Methane and the Greenhouse Gas Footprint of Natural Gas from Shale Formations," *Climatic Change* 106 (4): 679–690.

International Center for Technology Assessment (CTA). 1998. "The Real Price of Gasoline." Report No. 3: An Analysis of the Hidden External Costs Consumers Pay to Fuel Their Automobiles.

International Energy Agency (IEA). 2010. *World Energy Outlook 2010*. Paris.

———. 2011a. *World Energy Outlook 2011*. Paris.

———. 2011b. *Key World Energy Statistics*. Paris.

———. 2011c. *World Energy Outlook 2011 Factsheet*. Paris.

International Energy Agency, Nuclear Energy Agency, and Organization for Economic Cooperation and Development. 2010. Projected Costs of Generating Electricity.

International Energy Agency, Organization for Economic Cooperation and Development, Organization of the Petroleum Exporting Countries, and World Bank. 2011. "Joint Report by IEA, OPEC, OECD and World Bank on Fossil-Fuel and Other Energy Subsidies: An Update of the G20 Pittsburgh and Toronto Commitments." Report prepared for the G20 Meeting of Finance Ministers and Central Bank Governors (Paris, 14–15 October 2011) and the G20 Summit (Cannes, November 3–4).

Jacobson, Mark Z., and Mark A. Delucchi. 2011a. "Providing All Global Energy with Wind, Water, and Solar Power, Part I: Technologies, Energy Resources, Quantities and Areas of Infrastructure, and Materials." *Energy Policy* 39: 1154–1169.

———. 2011b. "Providing All Global Energy with Wind, Water, and Solar Power, Part II: Reliability, System and Transmission Costs, and Policies." *Energy Policy* 39: 1170–1190.

Johnson, Kirk. 2011. "E.P.A. Links Tainted Water in Wyoming to Hydraulic Fracturing for Natural Gas." *New York Times*, December 9.

Kitson, Lucy, Peter Wooders, and Tom Moerenhout. 2011. "Subsidies and External Costs in Electric Power Generation: A Comparative Review of Estimates." International Institute for Sustainable Development, September.

Krishnan, Rajaram, Jonathan M. Harris, and Neva Goodwin, eds. 1995. *A Survey of Ecological Economics*. Washington, DC: Island Press.

Lazard. 2009. "Levelized Cost of Energy Analysis—Version 3.0," February. http://blog.cleanenergy.org/files/2009/04/lazard2009_levelizedcostofenergy.pdf.

Macalister, Terry. 2011. "IEA Says Shift from Nuclear Will Be Costly and Raise Emissions." *The Guardian*, June 17.

Miller, G. Tyler, Jr. 1998. *Living in the Environment*, 10th ed. Belmont, CA: Wadsworth.

Morales, Alex. 2010. "Fossil Fuel Subsidies Are Twelve Times Renewables Support." Bloomberg, July 29.

Morton, Oliver. 2006. "Solar Energy: A New Day Dawning? Silicon Valley Sunrise." *Nature* 443: 19–22.

Murphy, David J., and Charles A.S. Hall. 2010. "Year in Review—EROI or Energy Return on (Energy) Invested." *Annals of the New York Academy of Science* 1185: 102–118.

National Action Plan for Energy Efficiency. 2006. "National Action Plan for Energy Efficiency." July.

———. 2008. "Understanding Cost-Effectiveness of Energy Efficiency Programs: Best Practices, Technical Methods, and Emerging Issues for Policy-Makers." Energy and Environmental Economics and Regulatory Assistance Project.

Nemet, Gregory F., and Daniel M. Kammen. 2007. "U.S. Energy Research and Development: Declining Investment, Increasing Need, and the Feasibility of Expansion." *Energy Policy* 35: 746–755.

Odgen, Joan M., Robert H. Williams, and Eric D. Larson. 2004. "Societal Lifecycle Costs of Cars with Alternative Fuels/Engines." *Energy Policy* 32: 7–27.

Owen, Anthony D. 2006. "Renewable Energy: Externality Costs as Market Barriers." *Energy Policy* 34: 632–642.

Parry, Ian W.H., and Kenneth A. Small. 2005. "Does Britain or the United States Have the Right Gasoline Tax?" *American Economic Review*, 95(4): 1276–1289.

Parsons Brinckerhoff. 2010. "Powering the Nation." www.pbworld.com/pdfs/regional/uk_europe/pb_ptn_update2010.pdf.

Pew Charitable Trusts. 2010. "Who's Winning the Clean Energy Race? Growth, Competition, and Opportunity in the World's Largest Economies." Washington, DC.

Rosenthal, Elisabeth. 2010. "Portugal Gives Itself a Clean-Energy Makeover." *New York Times*, August 9.

U.S. Energy Information Administration. 2011a. Annual Energy Review. U.S. Department of Energy.

———. 2011b. International Energy Outlook. U.S. Department of Energy.

———. 2011c. "Levelized Cost of New Generation Resources in the Annual Energy Outlook 2011." U.S. Department of Energy.

———. 2012. *Annual Energy Outlook*. U.S. Department of Energy.

U.S. Environmental Protection Agency. 2011. "Energy Star Overview of 2011 Achievements."

Wigley, Tom M. 2001. "Coal to Gas: The Influence of Methane Leakage," *Climatic Change* 108 (3): 601–608.

Wiser, Ryan, and Galen Barbose. 2008. *Renewables Portfolio Standards in the United States: A Status Report with Data Through 2007*. Lawrence Berkeley National Laboratory.

WEB SITES

1. **www.eia.gov**. Web site of the Energy Information Administration, a division of the U.S. Department of Energy that provides a wealth of information about energy demand, supply, trends, and prices.

2. **www.cnie.org/nle/crsreports/energy/**. Access to energy reports and issue briefs published by the Congressional Research Service.

3. **www.nrel.gov**. The Web site of the National Renewable Energy Laboratory in Colorado. The NREL conducts research on renewable energy technologies including solar, wind, biomass, and fuel cell energy.

4. **www.rmi.org**. Home page of the Rocky Mountain Institute, a nonprofit organization that "fosters the efficient and restorative use of resources to create a more secure, prosperous, and life-sustaining world." The RMI's main focus has been promoting increased energy efficiency in industry and households.

5. **www.eren.doe.gov**. Web site of the Energy Efficiency and Renewable Energy Network in the U.S. Department of Energy. The site includes a large amount of information on energy efficiency and renewable energy sources as well as hundreds of publications.

6. **www.iea.org**. Web site of the International Energy Agency, an "autonomous organisation which works to ensure reliable, affordable and clean energy for its 28 member countries and beyond." While some data are available only to subscribers, other data are available for free, as well as access to informative publications such as the "Key World Energy Statistics" annual report.

7. **www.energystar.gov**. Web site of the Energy Star program, including information about which products meet guidelines for energy efficiency.

CHAPTER 13

Renewable Resource Use: Fisheries

13.1 PRINCIPLES OF RENEWABLE RESOURCE MANAGEMENT

The expansion of human economic activity, as we noted in Chapter 2, has had major impact on the planet's renewable natural resources. In the early twenty-first century, many of the world's major fisheries are depleted or in decline, tropical forest area continues to shrink by about 20 million acres per year, and groundwater withdrawals continue to deplete aquifers in all major water-scarce regions of the world.[1] Clearly, management of renewable resources remains a major continuing issue. What economic and ecological principles underlie sustainable—or unsustainable—management of renewable resources?

We can view resources simply as inputs into the economic production process or, in a broader view, analyze **renewable resources** in terms of their own internal logic of equilibrium and regeneration. In some resource management approaches, these two perspectives are compatible, but in others they clash. For example, should the governing principle in managing natural systems be ecological diversity or maximum yield? The problem of integrating economic and ecological goals is essential to the management of natural resource systems such as fisheries.

In Chapter 1, we identified the relationships between the human economy and natural systems in terms of **source functions** and **sink functions**. The source function is the provision of materials for human use, and the sink function is the absorption of waste products from human activity. We have already considered aspects of these functions in dealing with agriculture and nonrenewable resources. **Sustainable management** of renewable resources involves maintaining the resource's source and sink functions in such a way that its quality and availability remain stable overtime. Although this certainly seems like a desirable goal, some forms of management tend to encourage unsustainable use.

renewable resources
a resource that is supplied on a continuing basis by ecosystems; renewable resources such as forests and fisheries can be depleted through exploitation.

source function
the ability of the environment to make services and raw materials available for human use.

sink function
the ability of natural environments to absorb wastes and pollution.

sustainable (natural resource) management
management of natural resources such that natural capital remains constant over time, including maintenance of both stocks and flows.

We have already seen an example of how managing a fishery as an **open-access resource** can lead to overfishing and depletion of stocks (Chapter 4). However, management by a private owner or by a government authority can also lead to unsustainable practices. The reason lies in the difference between economic principles and ecological principles.

Economic principles of resource management include profit maximization, efficient production, and efficient intertemporal resource allocation. We saw in Chapters 4 and 5 how these principles apply in general to resource use. When we examine fisheries, forests, and water systems in more detail, we see that these economic principles are sometimes, but not always, consistent with sustainable management.

The ecological principles underlying renewable resource systems are a little more difficult to express in simple terms. One basic rule derived from ecological principles is that of **maximum sustainable yield (MSY)**—no more of the resource should be harvested or withdrawn annually than can be regenerated or replenished by the natural processes of resource cycling and the capture of solar energy.

We must also consider that most natural systems are characterized by **ecological complexity**. Fisheries typically include many species of fish as well as other forms of animal and vegetable marine life. Natural forests usually have a variety of tree species and provide habitat for many animal species, as well as symbiotic or parasitic insects, fungi, and microbial life. Water systems generally include different kinds of aquatic habitat, some of which, like wetlands, play a crucial role in balancing the water cycle and maintaining water quality.

Human management of natural ecosystems must of necessity be a compromise between economic and ecological goals. In almost every case, human use of natural ecosystems will alter their state to some degree. Even so, we can usually manage ecosystems without destroying their **resilience**—defined as the capacity to recover from adverse impacts—or exceeding their maximum sustainable yield. To do so, however, requires a degree of restraint that may or may not be consistent with economic principles of profit maximization and economic institutions of resource ownership. In this and the next two chapters, we investigate this tension between economic and ecological principles as it applies to the management of fisheries, forests, and water systems.

13.2 Ecological and Economic Analysis of Fisheries

In our initial analysis of fisheries in Chapter 4, we viewed the fishery as a productive system whose output—fish—was an economic good. But fisheries are fundamentally biological systems, so a more complete view should start with a biological analysis and examine its economic implications.

The field of **population biology** identifies a general theory of population change for an organism, such as a species of fish, in the natural environment. Figure 13.1 shows a basic pattern of population change over time characteristic of many species in a natural state. This graph shows two paths for population change over time. Above a minimum critical population necessary for survival (X_{min}), population will grow from point A to a natural equilibrium, in balance with food supply, following a **logistic curve** of growth over time.[a]

---

[a]A logistic curve is an S-shaped growth curve that tends toward an upper limit. For an exposition of the mathematical analysis of logistic growth, see Hartwick and Olewiler, 1998, chap. 4.

Figure 13.1 **Species Population Growth over Time**

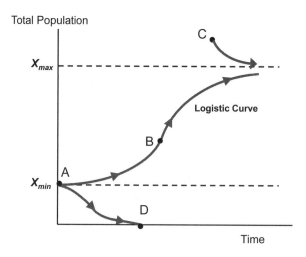

inflection point

the point on a curve where the second derivative equals zero, indicating a change from positive to negative curvature or vice versa.

carrying capacity

the level of population and consumption that can be sustained by the available natural resource base.

unstable equilibrium

a temporary equilibrium, for example, of the stock level of a renewable resource, that can be altered by minor changes in conditions, resulting in a large change in stock levels.

Starting from a low base and with an abundant food supply, the population initially grows at a steady rate, in a near-exponential pattern. Limits on food supply and living space slow the rate of population growth. Beyond point B, known as an **inflection point**, annual growth declines and population eventually approaches an upper limit X_{max}.[b] Should the population ever exceed this limit—for example, reaching point C due to a temporary increase in available food—it will rapidly decline from point C to X_{max} after normal food supply conditions return.

If the population falls below the critical X_{min} level, it will decline to extinction (point D). This can happen if disease, predation, or excessive harvesting by humans reduces the population to an unsustainably low level. The passenger pigeon in North America provides a classic case in which excessive harvesting led to extinction of a wild species. Abundant food supply in the forests of North America once made the passenger pigeon perhaps the most numerous species on the continent. Unrestrained hunting reduced it to a few scattered remnants, which died out by the early twentieth century.

In general, species populations in a natural state are determined by the environment's **carrying capacity**—the supply of food and other life support naturally available. Human exploitation of renewable resources must be consistent with this carrying capacity to avoid ecological disruption and possible population collapse.

The population growth pattern shown in Figure 13.1 can be viewed in a different way by relating the stock (population size) to its growth per year (Figure 13.2). Stock size now appears on the x-axis and annual growth on the y-axis. The arrows indicate the direction of population change. When growth rates are positive (above X_{min}), the population is expanding toward X_{max}, while below X_{min} it is declining toward zero.

We can now see that X_{min} is an **unstable equilibrium**. At this population, a slight increase will set the species on the road to recovery; a slight decrease will head it to extinction. Many endangered species are in this position. For example, barely

[b]At an inflection point, the curvature of the line changes from positive (upward) to negative (downward). In the terminology of calculus, the second derivative goes from positive to negative and equals zero at the inflection point.

Figure 13.2 **Species Population and Annual Growth**

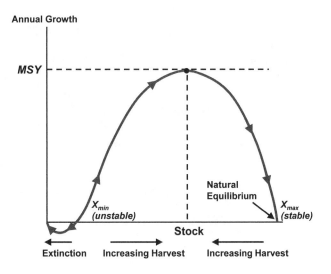

Note: MSY = maximum sustainable yield.

enough North American whooping cranes survive to maintain a nesting population, and scientists hope to nudge the number upward to recovery. But a single major incidence of natural disaster or disease could eliminate the species.

By contrast, X_{max} is a **stable equilibrium**. In a natural state, the population will approach this equilibrium. A smaller population will grow, while a larger population will shrink. Thus while some oscillation might occur around the equilibrium, the population will not tend to explode or to crash.[2]

In this form, the population growth graph clearly shows the maximum sustainable yield (MSY) at the top of the curve. The potential sustainable harvest of fish equals the total annual growth. If this amount is taken for human use, the population will remain constant. It will therefore be possible to exploit the fish stock at any population level between X_{max} and X_{min}, with the maximum possible harvest at point B.

Deriving an Economic Analysis from Biological Principles

Note that so far we have followed a strictly biological analysis, without considering economic implications. But we have derived a graph close to the economic graph of **total product** used for the fishery in Chapter 4. If we view Figure 13.2 from right to left, starting at the natural population equilibrium X_{max}, we can see how the economic graph of total product is derived.

Suppose that Figure 13.2 describes a fish population in its natural state—say, the cod population off New England when the first European colonists arrived.[c] As fishing effort increases, the stock will decline. However, this leads to a *higher* annual increment of fish. This is because a somewhat smaller stock of fish, with an unchanged food supply, can reproduce more rapidly. This pattern continues until point B, the maximum sustainable yield.

stable equilibrium
an equilibrium, for example of the stock level of a renewable resource, to which the system will tend to return after short-term changes in conditions affecting stock level of the resource.

total product
the total quantity of a good or service produced with a given quantity of inputs.

---

[c]The levels of fishing engaged in by Native American tribes before European colonization would have had little impact on the natural equilibrium.

If fishing continues beyond MSY, however, the pattern changes. Both the fish stock and the annual increment decline. Larger harvests progressively reduce both stock and yield until eventually the fish population may face danger of extinction as it approaches X_{min}.

The economic view of this biologically derived pattern is shown in Figures 13.3 and 13.4. Figure 13.3 relates fishing effort (measured in number of boat-days) to total returns. The total product, measured in tons of fish, can be converted to money terms by multiplying by the price of fish.[d] The resulting total revenue (TR) curve has the same general shape as the yield curve in Figure 13.2 and in fact corresponds closely to that curve. Increased fishing effort goes from right to left in Figure 13.2, but left to right in Figure 13.3. We measure the horizontal axes on the two graphs in different units, because one measures fish population and the other fishing effort, but in general as fishing effort increases fish population decreases.

Figure 13.3 **Total Revenues and Total Costs in a Fishery**

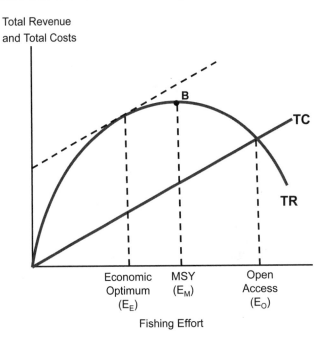

Fishing, of course, also involves costs. The total cost (TC) curve shown in Figure 13.3 is linear, implying a constant cost per unit of fishing effort. Other patterns for total cost curves are possible, but in general total costs will increase as fishing effort increases. The combination of costs and revenues shown here allows us to identify two possible equilibrium positions:

economic optimum

a result that maximizes an economic criterion, such as efficiency or profits.

open-access equilibrium

the level of use of an open-access resource that results from a market with free entry; this level of use may lead to depletion of the resource.

1. The **economic optimum** E_E, where the slopes of the total revenue and total cost curves are equal, or Marginal Revenue = Marginal Cost;
2. The **open-access equilibrium** E_O, where TR = TC, or Average Revenue = Marginal Cost.

---

[d]For this example, we assume a stable market price for fish.

Figure 13.4 **Marginal Revenues and Marginal Costs in a Fishery**

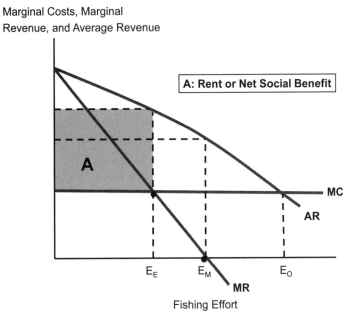

These equilibria can be identified more easily using the marginal and average cost and revenue curves shown in Figure 13.4. The maximum sustainable yield appears on the economic graphs as E_M where TR is maximized and MR = 0.

The open-access equilibrium E_O, as discussed in Chapter 4, occurs only when average revenue equals marginal cost, which means that profits throughout the fishing industry have fallen to zero. So long as the industry is profitable, new entrants will continue to increase the pressure on the fish population, driving total revenues down until TR = TC. This position is both economically and ecologically undesirable, but is the likely outcome unless policies to limit entry are in place.

From the economist's point of view, the open-access equilibrium leads to **rent dissipation**—the loss of much of the potential social benefit from the fishery. A single owner of the fishery could capture the potential **economic rent** by limiting operations to E_E. This potential rent is the shaded area A in Figure 13.4. The difference between average revenue and marginal cost shows the rent per unit of effort, and area A shows the total rent. With open access, this economic benefit is lost.

Note the relationship of the economic optimum (E_E), maximum sustainable yield (E_M), and open-access equilibrium (E_O) in Figure 13.4. The economic optimum lies to the left of maximum sustainable yield, and the open-access equilibrium lies to the right. As we saw in Chapter 4, the economic optimum might be achieved through use of a **license fee** or **quota system**.

In cases in which the fishery is localized, such as on a small lake, the economic optimum could be achieved through **private ownership**. A profit-seeking owner, or group of owners acting together, would have an incentive to limit fishing effort to E_E. This would maximize profits, and would also have the effect of avoiding overexploitation of the fishery.

Referring to the biological graph (Figure 13.2), we see that the economic optimum will lie to the right of MSY (point B), in a sustainable range. Although total

rent dissipation
the loss of potential social and economic benefits in a market because of market failure.

economic rent
income that accrues to the owner of a scarce resource.

license fee
the fee paid for access to a resource, such as a fishing license.

quota/quota system
a system of limiting access to a resource through restrictions on the permissible harvest of the resource.

private ownership
the provision of certain exclusive rights to a particular resource, such as the right of a landowner to restrict trespassing.

fish stocks will decrease as a result of the fishing effort, a high annual growth rate will allow the system to maintain resilience, or bounce-back capacity. The open-access equilibrium, in contrast, lies to the left of MSY.

As we move farther to the left of MSY, both harvest and annual growth decline, and eventually the fish stock may be in danger of exhaustion. As fish harvests decline, fish prices are likely to rise, increasing the marginal and average revenue curves in Figure 13.4, thus pushing the open-access equilibrium farther to the right and hastening the spiral toward collapse of the fishery.[e]

Unfortunately, the open-access equilibrium is common in fisheries throughout the world. Figure 13.5 shows data from Philippine fisheries, in which open access has led to effort levels exceeding first the maximum economic yield MEY (corresponding to E_E in the above analysis), then the maximum sustainable yield MSY (corresponding to E_M). It is interesting to note how this actual historical data corresponds closely to our theoretical patterns for the economics of a fishery. We can clearly see how, by the 1980s, fishing had exceeded the maximum sustainable yield and catches of both demersal (sea-bottom) and pelagic (ocean) fisheries had begun to decline.

13.3 THE ECONOMICS OF FISHERIES IN PRACTICE

tragedy of the commons
the tendency for common property resources to be overexploited because no one has an incentive to conserve the resource while individual financial incentives promote expanded exploitation.

institutional failure
the failure of governments or other institutions to prevent overexploitation of a resource.

overfishing
a level of fishing effort that depletes the stock of a fishery over time.

Fishing in open seas is a typical illustration of a situation in which the **tragedy of the commons**, as discussed in Chapter 4, is likely to occur. Individual fishers tend to have little incentive to practice conservation, for they know that if they do not catch the available fish, someone else probably will. Without limits in place, fishers try to catch as many fish as they possibly can. Technological improvements that make it easier to find and catch fish only make matters worse.

Many traditional societies have evolved rules limiting the seasons or days when particular seafood species may be harvested (e.g., prohibiting fishing at spawning season) or the amount to be taken. In recent years, these rules have in many cases been swept aside, in part due to population pressures. Other reasons the balance might break down include **institutional failure**, such as when an outside interest acquires the power to override the community's traditional patterns of property rights.[3]

Overfishing is currently occurring in many fisheries throughout the world as human demands exceed regenerative capacities.

> Approximately 25 percent of the world's marine fish stocks are considered overexploited, and an additional 50 percent are fully exploited. The depleted state of wild fish stocks is due to overfishing and increasing degradation of coastal, marine and freshwater ecosystems and habitats, as growing coastal populations exert increasing pressures on natural resources.
>
> Seven of the 10 top marine fish species—which together account for about 30 percent of all capture fisheries production—are fully exploited or overexploited (see below for definitions). The ability of the overexploited stocks to recover from human pressure or from natural disturbances (e.g., adverse climate conditions, pollution, and disease outbreaks) is severely compromised.[4]

---

[e]The process of fishery collapse cannot be fully shown in a static-equilibrium model such as Figure 13.4. More complex dynamic models are required to show the effects of disequilibrium leading to collapse (see, e.g., Clark, 1990).

Figure 13.5   **Open Access in Philippine Fisheries**

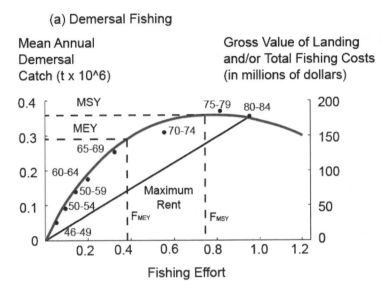

(a) Demersal Fishing

Mean Annual
Demersal
Catch (t x 10^6)

Gross Value of Landing
and/or Total Fishing Costs
(in millions of dollars)

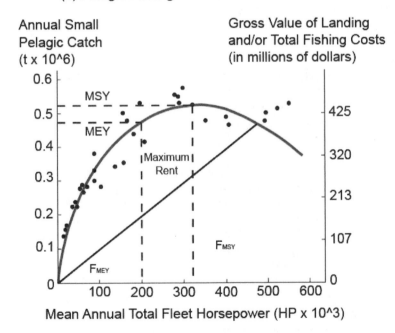

(b) Pelagic Fishing

Annual Small
Pelagic Catch
(t x 10^6)

Gross Value of Landing
and/or Total Fishing Costs
(in millions of dollars)

Mean Annual Total Fleet Horsepower (HP x 10^3)

Source: Adapted from Pauly and Thia-Eng, 1988.

The scale of fishing operations has increased dramatically with the introduction of modern vessels such as commercial trawlers. Between 1970 and 2005, global fleet capacity increased by a factor of six, whereas the average catch per ton of fleet capacity (catch rate) has steadily declined (see Figure 13.6).

Figure 13.6 **Global Fleet Capacity and Catch Rate, 1970–2005**

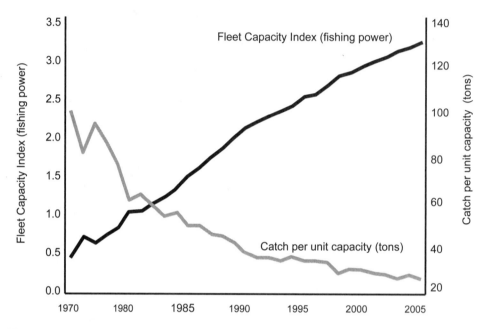

Source: World Bank and FAO, 2009.

bycatch

the harvesting of aquatic organisms other than the intended commercial species.

Clearly, an open-access situation is economically irrational. It also poses further ecological problems because modern fishing methods often cause a high death rate among nontarget species. One-fourth of all catches are discarded because they are either undersize or nonmarketable. This wasted portion of the global harvest is called "**bycatch**." A 2009 paper found that:

> 38.5 million tonnes of annual bycatch can be identified, representing 40.4 percent of the estimated annual global marine catch of 95.2 million tones. . . . [E]normous quantities of biomass are being removed from the ocean without any form of effective management. The approach outlined in this paper therefore exposes bycatch as an insidious problem of invisible fishing resulting from widespread unmanaged fisheries. . . . Few industries would tolerate levels of wastage and/or lack of sustainable management of around 40 percent.[5]

Although identifying the maximum sustainable yield for a fishery can help maintain an individual species, the issues of ecological sustainability are more complex. Depleting one species can lead to an irreversible change in ocean ecology as other species fill the ecological niche formerly occupied by the harvested species.[6] For example, dogfish and skate have replaced overfished cod and haddock in major areas of the North Atlantic fishery and are now themselves threatened with overfishing. Fishing techniques such as trawling, in which nets are dragged along the bottom of the ocean, are highly destructive to all kinds of demersal benthic (bottom-dwelling) life. In large areas of the Atlantic, formerly productive ocean-floor ecological communities have been severely damaged by repeated trawling.

Fisheries are classified into three categories, roughly based on a comparison between catch rates and the MSY:[f]

1. **Non–fully exploited**: Harvest levels are below MSY (i.e., fish catch increases with increasing effort).
2. **Fully exploited**: Harvest levels are at or near MSY.
3. **Overexploited**: Catch levels are above MSY (i.e., harvest levels have significantly declined from a peak without a decline in harvest effort).

Thus harvest levels can be sustainably increased only for fish stocks classified as non–fully exploited. Further increases in effort for fully exploited or overexploited fisheries would only lead to lower harvests. Figure 13.7 shows the status of fish stocks on a global level. In 2009 only 13 percent of fish stocks were classified as non–fully exploited, 57 percent were fully exploited, and 30 percent were overexploited. We see that the percentage of stocks classified as non–fully exploited has declined from 40 percent to only a little above 10 percent since the 1970s, while the percentage of stocks classified as overexploited has increased steadily over the same period.

non-fully exploited
term used to describe a fish stock that is being harvested below the maximum sustainable yield.

fully exploited
term used to describe a fish stock that is being harvested at the maximum sustainable yield.

overexploited
term used to describe a fish stock that is being harvested beyond the maximum sustainable yield.

Figure 13.7　**Global Trends in the Status of Fish Stocks, 1974–2009**

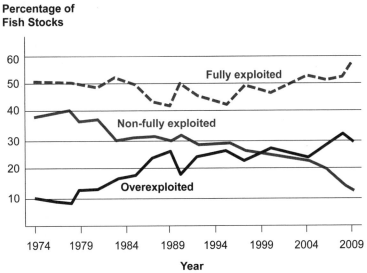

Source: FAO, 2012b.

As a 2008 report indicates:

Humans are now capable of finding and capturing marine resources in the most productive habitats around the world, and have done so better than ever before. As a result, we can no longer expect to find any hidden reserves of fish. In fact, many scientists have

---

[f]The classification scheme, devised by the UN Food and Agriculture Organization, also considers spawning potential, size and age composition, and stock abundance. See FAO, 2012b.

warned of impending collapses in fish populations within decades. While the exact timing may be debatable, the trend is not—and new stresses, including most notably, climate change, threaten to make the situation worse. . . . As the United Nations Food and Agriculture Organization (FAO) points out, "the maximum long-term potential of the world marine capture fisheries has been reached."[7]

13.4 POLICIES FOR SUSTAINABLE FISHERIES MANAGEMENT

The World Bank and FAO stress the critical need for reform of institutional fisheries:

> Failure to act implies increased risks of fish stock collapses, increasing political pressure for subsidies, and a sector that, rather than being a net contributor to global wealth, is an increasing drain on society. . . . The most critical reform is the effective removal of the open access condition from marine capture fisheries and the institution of secure marine tenure and property rights systems. Reforms in many instances would also involve the reduction or removal of subsidies that create excess fishing effort and fishing capacity. Rather than subsidies, the World Bank has emphasized investment in quality public goods such as science, infrastructure, and human capital, in good governance of natural resources, and in an improved investment climate.[8]

market failure
the failure of certain markets to provide a socially efficient allocation of resources.

From an economic point of view, **market failure** occurs in open-access fisheries because important productive resources—lakes and oceans—are treated as free resources and are therefore overused. A simple solution is to place a price on the resource.

Certainly no private owner of a small lake, for example, would allow unlimited numbers of people to fish for free, depleting the stock of fish until the resource was worthless. The owner would charge a fee to fish, yielding income for the owner (part of which might be used to restock the lake) and limiting the number of people who would fish. Although the owner's motivation would be to collect economic rent, the people fishing would also benefit—despite having to pay a fee—because they would have access to continued good fishing instead of suffering depletion of the fish stock.

Law of the Sea
a 1982 international treaty regulating marine fisheries.

Exclusive Economic Zone (EEZ)
the area normally within 200 nautical miles of the coast of a country, in which that country has exclusive jurisdiction over marine resources.

An ocean fishery does not allow the private ownership solution. The oceans have been called a common heritage resource—they belong to everyone and no one. But under the 1982 **Law of the Sea** treaty, agreed to under the auspices of the United Nations, countries can claim territorial rights to many important offshore fisheries. They can then limit access to these fisheries by requiring a fishing license within their **Exclusive Economic Zones (EEZs)**, which normally extend 200 miles from their coastline.

Fishing licenses can be sold for a set fee, or a limited number can be sold at auction. In effect, this establishes a price for access to the resource. Note that we can also view this as internalizing a negative externality. Each fisher now must pay a price for the external costs imposed on one fishery by adding one extra boat. The economic signal that such a price sends will result in having fewer people enter the fishery.

This approach, however, will not necessarily solve the problem of overinvestment. A boat owner who buys a license will have added incentive to obtain the maximum catch by investing in new equipment, such as sonar devices to track fish, bigger nets, and more powerful engines to travel farther. He or she will be more likely to spend as much time as possible at sea, to earn the maximum return on the investment in the license and equipment. If all fishers do this, the depletion problem may remain serious. Governments can respond by imposing quotas on total catch, but areawide quotas are often difficult to enforce and meet fierce resistance from fishers.[9]

One possible policy response that combines regulation with the use of market mechanisms is a system of **individual transferable quotas (ITQs)**. Like transferable emissions permits, ITQs impose a maximum limit on the quantity of fish that can be taken. Anyone purchasing such a permit can catch and sell a certain number of fish—or can sell the permit and fishing rights to someone else. Assuming that the quota limits can be enforced, the total catch from the fishery will not exceed a predetermined level.

To determine the maximum sustainable yield level, policy makers must consult marine biologists, who can estimate the sustainable level of fish population. After ecological sustainability has been assured, the permit market will promote **economic efficiency**. Those who can fish most effectively will be able to outbid others to acquire the ITQs. Although ITQ systems have been successful in certain areas, they have also led to complaints that they promote concentration in the fishing industry and squeeze out small fishers.[10]

A more difficult problem concerns species that are highly migratory. Tuna and swordfish, for example, continually travel between national fishing areas and the open ocean. Even with good policies for resource management in national waters, these species can be harvested as an open-access global resource, which almost inevitably leads to stock declines. Only an international agreement can address an issue concerning global commons.

In 1995, the first such agreement was signed: the Convention on Highly Migratory and Straddling Stocks. This convention embodies a principle of ecological economics introduced in Chapter 7: the **precautionary principle**. This principle suggests that, rather than waiting until depletion is obvious, fishery access should be controlled before problems appear, with measures to limit the total catch rate, establish data collection and reporting systems, and minimize bycatch through the use of more selective gear.[11]

Demand-Side Issues: Changing Consumption Patterns

People in developed countries currently consume 26 percent of the global fish catch; the other 74 percent is consumed in the developing world, where fish is an important protein source.[12] Increasing population and income in developing countries will likely produce steady growth in global demand for fish and fish products, but supply expansion, at least from wild fisheries, may be close to its limits.

World fish harvest has steadily increased in the past several decades (Figure 13.8). On a per capita basis, fish harvest increased steadily in the 1950s and 1960s and has increased slightly since then. As noted earlier, it is seems unlikely that the total global fish harvest can increase much further given that most fish stocks are either fully exploited or overexploited. Atlantic fisheries have been especially pressured as many fishing countries compete for access, and fishery management within the 200-mile EEZs has been inadequate.[13]

---

individual transferable quotas (ITQs)
tradeable rights to harvest a resource, such as a permit to harvest a particular quantity of fish.

economic efficiency
an allocation of resources that maximizes net social benefits; perfectly competitive markets in the absence of externalities are efficient.

precautionary principle
the view that policies should account for uncertainty by taking steps to avoid low-probability but catastrophic events.

Figure 13.8 **World Seafood Harvest, Total and Per Capita, 1950–2005**

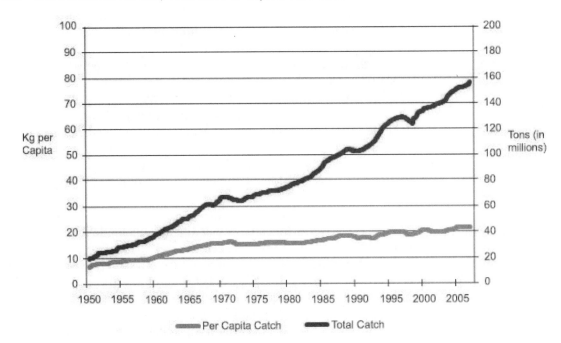

Source: Worldwatch Institute, 2009; population data from U.S. Census Bureau, 2013.

About 20 percent of world fish production—over 20 million tons—is used for nonfood uses such as fishmeal and oils.[14] Alternative use of soymeal and other sources of protein in animal and fish feed would relieve pressure on fisheries and potentially make more fish available for direct human consumption. This would depend, of course, on increased output of land-grown protein products such as soybeans, which as we saw in Chapter 10 may pose other environmental issues.

Changes in human consumption patterns are also important. Public education campaigns that identify fish and seafood produced with environmentally damaging techniques may lead consumers to avoid these species. For example, a boycott of swordfish aimed at stopping the decline of this species gained the support of numerous restaurant chefs and consumers.

Ecolabeling, which identifies products produced in a sustainable manner, has the potential to encourage sustainable fishing techniques. Products of certifiably sustainable fishing practices can often command a slightly higher market price. By accepting this price premium, consumers implicitly agree to pay for something more than the fish they eat. They pay a little extra for the health of the ocean ecosystem and the hope of a supply of fish to feed people in the future as well as in the present. These consumer choices give the fishing industry a financial incentive to use sustainable methods.

In economic terminology, we can say that consumers are *internalizing the positive externalities* associated with sustainable fishing techniques through their willingness to buy ecolabeled products. Governments or well-respected private agencies

ecolabeling
a label on a good that provides information concerning the environmental impacts that resulted from the production of the good.

certification

the process of certifying products that meet certain standards, such as certifying produce grown using organic farming techniques.

subsidy/subsidies

government assistance to an industry or economic activity; subsidies can be direct, through financial assistance, or indirect, through protective policies.

can oversee **certification** of sustainable fish products. A prominent example is "dolphin-safe" ecolabeling, which has been instrumental in reducing the number of dolphin killed as bycatch during tuna fishing.

Another area in which government policies can assist in internalizing positive externalities is the judicious use of **subsidies**—for example, to assist in developing or acquiring equipment designed especially to release bycatch or to avoid major disturbances of the seabed. This may moderate political opposition from fishing communities to government intervention aimed at eliminating destructive fishing practices. Unfortunately, most current fishery subsidies are counterproductive, increasing economic incentives for overfishing (see Box 13.1).

BOX 13.1 FISHERY POLICIES IN PRACTICE: SUCCESSES AND FAILURES

Environmental economics shows that fisheries often require some form of community or government management to avoid overuse of a common property resource. But many government fishery management policies have been counterproductive, worsening overfishing and hastening depletion of stocks. This is especially true of fishery subsidies, which include grants, loans, tax incentives, discounted insurance, and fuel tax credits, as well as support for research and development on more effective fishing methods. Globally, fishery subsidies total about $20 billion per year, and almost all these subsidies contribute to excess capacity and overfishing.

Policies that impose catch limits have been more successful in preventing depletion of stocks and, in some cases, helping stocks to recover. But these policies are often bitterly contested, since limits on fishing days or permitted catch reduce fishing incomes. In New England fisheries, for example, a 2002 decision by a federal judge found that catch restrictions have not succeeded in rebuilding cod and other groundfish stocks; the court imposed even more stringent rules, which the fishers contend will destroy their livelihood. In 2013, restrictions on cod fishing in New England were tightened further, by 77 percent for Gulf of Maine cod and 61 percent for Georges Bank cod. Canada recently closed its historic Atlantic cod fishery, citing a catastrophic decline in fish stocks.

Is there a better way? Countries such as New Zealand and Australia have pioneered the use of transferable fishing quotas. In effect, this establishes property rights in ocean fisheries. New entrants into the industry must purchase licenses from current owners. Because overall catch is strictly limited, fish stocks have flourished, and the value of the fishing permits has steadily risen. This gives fishers an incentive to conserve. "Why hurt the fishery?" says an Australian lobsterman. "It's my retirement fund. No one's going to pay me $35,000 a pot if there are no lobsters left. If I rape and pillage the fishery now, in ten years my licenses won't be worth anything."

Unlike New England lobstermen, who must tend up to 800 lobster traps to squeeze out a living from scarcer, smaller, and short-lived lobsters, their Australian counterparts can make an excellent living from 60 traps, in which they catch larger lobsters. "Fishing may be the only economic activity in which you can make more money by doing less work," says a biologist who monitors the Australian lobster fishery. "By fishing less, the fishermen leave more lobsters out there to produce more eggs, which will make it easier for them to catch lobsters in the future. The lobsters are thriving and the fishermen are spending more time at home with their families."

(continued)

BOX 13.1 *(continued)*

Transferable quota systems face opposition from critics who fear that corporations will take over public waters by buying up licenses. But it would be possible to protect small operators by limiting the number of permits any individual or corporation can own. According to Richard Allen, a Rhode Island lobsterman who is lobbying for an Australian-type system, "Many people complain that it's unfair to lock anyone out of the fishery . . . but with the current system we have fisheries that we're all locked out of. I can't go out and fish for halibut and swordfish—there aren't any left. I would rather have a healthy fish stock and the option to buy access to it."

Sources: Fishermen and biologist quotes from John Tierney, "A Tale of Two Fisheries," *New York Times*, August 27, 2000; Beth Daley, "Drastic Cuts Ordered in New England Fishing: Judge's Decision Seen as Heavy Blow to Industry," *Boston Globe*, April 27, 2002; Colin Nickerson, "Canada Declares and End to Cod Fishing," *Boston Globe*, April 25, 2003; Jay Lindsay, "New England Regulators Approve Steep Fish Cut," *Boston Globe*, January 30, 2013; subsidy estimate from Myers and Kent, 2001.

Aquaculture: New Solutions, New Problems

aquaculture
the controlled cultivation of aquatic organisms, including fish and shellfish, for human use or consumption.

The most rapidly growing area of fish production is **aquaculture**—fish farming, often in large offshore pens. Aquaculture is largely responsible for recent increases in world fish production (see Figure 13.9). However, from an environmental point of view aquaculture may pose as many problems as it solves.

Figure 13.9   **Global Fish Harvest, Wild Catch and Aquaculture, 1950-2007**

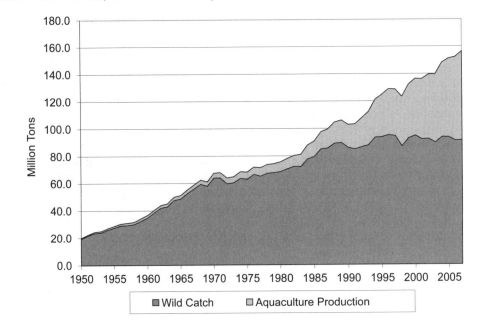

Sources: FAO, 2012c; World Watch Institute, 2009.

monoculture
an agricultural system involving the growing of the same crop exclusively on a piece of land year after year.

While traditional aquaculture systems often raised several species of fish in ecologically healthy combination with crops and animals, modern systems rely on **monoculture** of economically profitable species such as salmon and shrimp. Such systems have significant negative externalities (see Box 13.2). Excess food and fish waste contaminate the aquatic environment, and captive fish can spread disease to wild stocks or, if they escape, degrade the wild gene pool. Shrimp farms, which often replace mangrove forests, are especially ecologically destructive:

BOX 13.2   SCIENTISTS CRITICIZE SALMON AND SHRIMP AQUACULTURE

Despite their image as potential saviors of the world's beleaguered fisheries, some of the most successful forms of fish farming may do more harm than good by depleting marine resources and polluting the water, according to a paper in the journal *Science*.

Researchers from Stanford University and the Environmental Defense Fund argue that salmon and shrimp aquaculture are especially damaging to the environment because the animals are carnivorous, consuming smaller fish that could have been eaten by other marine life or by humans.

The world's salmon farmers fed their fish 1.8 million tons of wild fish to harvest just 644,000 tons of salmon. At the same time, water pollution from shrimp and salmon farms has grown. Salmon farms in Norway alone discharge nutrients in their feces equivalent to a city of at least 1.7 million people. In addition, farmed fish can spread diseases and parasites to wild stocks, and escaped fish can degrade the wild genetic pool.

Shrimp farming, which has grown 700 percent since the 1980s, also leaves a trail of ecologically crippled ponds in China, Thailand, and Indonesia, where low-income people formerly harvested shellfish.

"Rapid growth in shrimp and salmon farming has clearly caused environmental degradation, while contributing little to world food security," the paper concludes.

Sources: Scott Allen, "Fish Farming Pollutes, Harms Marine Life," *Boston Globe*, October 30, 1998, p. A13; R.L. Naylor, J. Eagle, and W.L. Smitl, "Salmon Aquaculture in the Pacific Northwest: A Global Industry," *Environment* 45, 8 (October 2003).

In the short term, intensive shrimp farming is highly profitable: in a year, an individual shrimp farmer can make up to $10,000 per hectare for intensive production rates of 4 or 5 tons per hectare. This compares to the roughly $1,000 per hectare that a species such as milkfish or carp generates. But these economic returns do not account for ecological— and economic—losses such as habitat degradation. By converting diverse ecosystems to simple ones, fish farmers and the public lose a host of ecological goods such as fish, shellfish, timber, charcoal, and other products. They also lose services that coastal ecosystems provide, such as filtering and purifying water, cycling nutrients, removing contaminants and buffering the land from coastal storms and severe weather. A study of the Matang mangrove in Malaysia revealed that its value for coastal protection alone exceeded the value of farmed shrimp by 170 percent.[15]

On a modest local scale, inland aquaculture can be environmentally beneficial, encouraging multiple use of water systems for crops such as rice as well as fish ponds. Asia has a long tradition of ecologically sound aquaculture, and developing countries in Africa and other regions show considerable potential for its further development.[16] Whether ocean aquaculture can be practiced on a large scale without irreversible damage to ecosystems remains to be seen.

Given the rapid growth in aquaculture, regulatory policy should encourage less resource-intensive forms of production. Reviving and encouraging traditional pond systems, which integrate well with local environment and available resources, would help minimize aquaculture's impact on the environment.

Aquaculture will undoubtedly be a component of a strategy for sustainable fisheries management, but it cannot compensate for the damage done by unrestricted access to wild fisheries. A comprehensive approach including supply management, demand modification, and sustainable forms of aquaculture will be required to meet the needs of a still-growing world population.

SUMMARY

A renewable natural resource system such as a fishery involves both economic and ecological principles. In a natural state, fish populations reach an equilibrium level based on the carrying capacity of the environment. Human exploitation of the resource can be sustainable provided that it is consistent with this natural carrying capacity.

Economic analysis of fisheries suggests that economically efficient resource use should be compatible with ecological sustainability. However, open-access conditions in many fisheries create a strong tendency toward overexploitation.

On a global scale, fishing fleet capacity and harvest has continued to increase, with the result that 87 percent of the world's fisheries are classified as either fully exploited or overexploited. The potential to increase the global fish harvest further seems limited. Destructive fishing techniques have damaged marine habitat and altered ocean ecology, diminishing productivity.

Policies for maintaining sustainable yield and rebuilding depleted fisheries can involve a combination of regulation and market mechanisms. International conventions have set guidelines for territorial rights and management practices. Countries can require fishing licenses or impose quotas to limit access to the fishery. Regionwide quotas can be difficult to enforce, but systems of individual transferable quotas have been successfully implemented.

Fish is an important protein source, especially in the developing world, where demand can be expected to grow as population and income rise. More efficient consumption patterns and increased aquaculture will be important as wild fish catches reach or exceed sustainable limits.

Consumption patterns can be modified to promote more sustainable fisheries management through consumer awareness and certification or ecolabeling programs. Aquaculture has great potential but can also involve significant environmental costs. Small-scale and traditional inland aquacultural systems often tend to be more environmentally beneficial than large-scale commercial operations.

Key Concepts

aquaculture
bycatch
carrying capacity
certification
complexity
ecolabeling
economic efficiency
economic optimum
economic rent
Exclusive Economic Zone (EEZ)
fully exploited
individual transferable quotas (ITQs)
inflection point
institutional failure
Law of the Sea
license fee
logistic curve
market failure
maximum sustainable yield (MSY)
monoculture

non–fully exploited
open-access equilibrium
open-access resource
overexploited
overfishing
population biology
precautionary principle
private ownership
quota system
renewable resources
rent dissipation
resilience
sink function
source function
stable equilibrium
subsidies
sustainable management
total product
tragedy of the commons
unstable equilibrium

Discussion Questions

1. What is the basic reason for depletion of fisheries? Which factors have made this problem especially severe in the modern period? How can this issue be related to the difference between economic and ecological analyses of a fishery?

2. What are the advantages and disadvantage of the following policies for fisheries management: private ownership, government regulation through licensing, the use of individual transferable quotas? In what circumstances might each one be appropriate?

3. Explain the interrelationship between the following concepts as they relate to fisheries: economic rent, maximum sustainable yield, economic efficiency, ecological sustainability. How should these concepts be used to guide fisheries management policies?

EXERCISES

1. Suppose that a fishery is characterized by the following relationship between total fish stock and annual growth:

STOCK (thousand tons biomass)	10	20	30	40	50	60	70	80	90	100	120
GROWTH (tons)	0	800	1,600	2,400	2,800	3,000	2,800	2,200	1,200	0	–1,200

Construct one graph showing the relationship between stock and growth and another graph showing the growth *rate* at each stock level (e.g., at stock = 60,000 tons, yield = 3,000 tons, growth rate = 5 percent). What stock level corresponds to the maximum growth rate? What stock level gives the maximum sustainable yield? What will be the stable and unstable equilibrium stock levels for this fish population in a natural state?

2. Now assume that we can translate this population/yield relationship into an economic relationship between fishing boats operating and total product:

BOATS	0	100	200	300	400	500	600	700	800	900
TOTAL PRODUCT (tons)	0	1,200	2,200	2,800	3,000	2,800	2,400	1,600	800	0

Fish prices average $1,000/ton, and it costs $4,000 to operate a fishing boat for a year.

Construct a graph showing total revenues and total costs in the fishery as a function of the number of boats in operation. Now derive graphs showing marginal and average revenue and marginal cost. Now use your graphs to analyze equilibrium in the fishery under the following conditions:

(a) A natural state with no fishing industry.
(b) A fishing industry obtaining the maximum sustainable yield from the fishery.
(c) A fishing industry operating under an efficient management plan, with economically optimal returns.
(d) A fishing industry characterized by open access.

What does this economic analysis suggest concerning government policy on fisheries management? Should such policies be based on the maximum sustainable yield concept? Are there other significant considerations not reflected in this analysis?

NOTES

1. UNEP, 2002; World Resources Institute et al., 2000.
2. For an advanced treatment of the dynamics of fisheries, see Clark, 1990.
3. See Ostrom, 1990; McGinnis and Ostrom, 1996.
4. World Bank, 2006, p. 2.
5. Davies et al., 2009.
6. See Hagler, 1995; Ogden, 2001.
7. Freitas et al., 2008, introduction.
8. World Bank and FAO, 2009, p. xxi.
9. For a survey of the effects of entry restrictions in fisheries, see Townsend, 1990.
10. See Arnason, 1993; Duncan, 1995; Young, 1999.
11. McGinn, 1998.
12. FAO, 2012a.
13. On Atlantic fisheries, see Harris, 1998.
14. FAO, 2012a.
15. McGinn, 1998, pp. 48–49.
16. See Brummett and Williams, 2000.

REFERENCES

Arnason, R. 1993. "The Icelandic Individual Transferable Quota System: A Descriptive Account." *Marine Resource Economics* 8: 201–18.

Brummett, Randall E., and Meryl J. Williams. 2000. "The Evolution of Aquaculture in African Rural and Economic Development." *Ecological Economics* 33 (2) (May): 193–203.

Clark, Colin. 1990. *The Optimal Management of Renewable Resources*, 2d ed. New York: John Wiley.

Davies, R.W.D., S.J. Cripps, A. Nickson, and G. Porter. 2009. "Defining and Estimating Global Marine Fisheries By-catch." *Marine Policy*, 33 (4) (July): 661–672.

Duncan, Leith. 1995. "Closed Competition: Fish Quotas in New Zealand." *Ecologist* 25 (2/3) (March/April, May/June): 97–104.

Food and Agriculture Organization (FAO). 2012a. *The State of World Fisheries and Aquaculture 2012*. Rome.

———. 2012b. "Review of the State of World Marine Fishery Resources." FAO Fisheries and Aquaculture Technical Paper 569. Rome.

———. 2012c. FAOSTAT Agriculture Database. www.fao.org.

Freitas, B., L. Delagran, E. Griffin, K.L. Miller, and M. Hirshfield. 2008. "Too Few Fish: A Regional Assessment of the World's Fisheries." *Oceana* (May).

Hagler, Mike. 1995. "Deforestation of the Deep: Fishing and the State of the Oceans." *The Ecologist* 25:74–79.

Harris, Michael. 1998. *Lament for an Ocean: The Collapse of the Atlantic Cod Fishery*. Toronto: M&S.

Hartwick, John M., and Nancy D. Olewiler. 1998. *The Economics of Natural Resource Use*. Reading, MA: Addison Wesley Longman.

McGinn, Anne Platt. 1998. *Rocking the Boat: Conserving Fisheries and Protecting Jobs*. Worldwatch Paper No. 142. Washington, DC: Worldwatch Institute.

McGinnis, Michael, and Elinor Ostrom. 1996. "Design Principles for Local and Global Commons." In *The International Political Economy and International Institutions*, vol. 2. Cheltenham, UK: Edward Elgar.

Myers, Norman, and Jennifer Kent. 2001. *Perverse Subsidies: How Tax Dollars Can Undercut the Environment and the Economy*. Washington, DC: Island Press.

Ogden, John C. 2001. "Maintaining Diversity in the Oceans." *Environment* 43 (3) (April): 28–37.

Ostrom, Elinor, 1990. *Governing the Commons: The Evolution of Institutions for Collective Action*. Cambridge, UK: Cambridge University Press.

Pauly, Daniel, and Chua Thia-Eng. 1988. "The Overfishing of Marine Resources: Socioeconomic Background in Southeast Asia." *Ambio* 17(3): 200–206.

Townsend, Ralph E. 1990. "Entry Restrictions in the Fishery: A Survey of the Evidence." *Land Economics* 66: 361–378.

United Nations Environment Programme (UNEP). 2002. *Global Environmental Outlook 3: Past, Present, and Future Perspectives*. London: Earthscan.

United States Census Bureau. 2013. World Population website, http://www.census.gov/population/international/data/worldpop/table_population.php.

World Bank. 2006. *PROFISH Fisheries Factsheet Number 2* (November).

World Bank and FAO. 2009. "The Sunken Billions: The Economic Justification for Fisheries Reform." Washington, DC.

World Resources Institute, United Nations Development Programme, United Nations Environment Programme, and the World Bank. 2000. *World Resources 2000–2001: People and Ecosystems*. Washington, DC: World Resources Institute.

Worldwatch Institute. 2009. *Vital Signs 2009: The Trends That Are Shaping Our Future*. Washington, DC.

Young, Michael D. 1999. "The Design of Fishing Rights Systems: The New South Wales Experience." *Ecological Economics* 31 (2) (November): 305–316.

WEB SITES

1. **www.fao.org/fishery/en/**. The Food and Agriculture Organization's main fisheries and aquaculture Web page. It includes links to their biennial "State of World Fisheries and Aquaculture" report, which contains detailed data on fish production and consumption.

2. **http://worldbank.org/fish/**. The World Bank's main fisheries and aquaculture Web page. It includes links to various publications and projects.

3. **http://oceana.org/en/**. Web site of Oceana, the "largest international organization focused solely on ocean conservation." The site describes various ocean conservation projects that Oceana is working on, as well as links to publications.

CHAPTER 14

Ecosystem Management—Forests

CHAPTER 14 FOCUS QUESTIONS

- What are the economic and ecological principles of forest management?
- What are the causes of forest loss, and what regions of the world are losing or gaining forest cover?
- How can policies for sustainable forestry be implemented?

---

logistic curve/logistic growth
an S-shaped growth curve tending toward an upper limit.

assets
something with market value, including financial assets, physical assets, and natural assets.

stock
the quantity of a variable at a given point in time, such as the amount of timber in a forest at a given time.

flow
the quantity of a variable measured over a period of time, including physical flows such as the flow of a river past a given point measured in cubic feet per second or financial flows such as income over a period of time.

use values
the value that people place on the use of a good or service.

14.1 THE ECONOMICS OF FOREST MANAGEMENT

Forests, like fisheries, are primarily biological systems. When we exploit them for human use, both ecological and economic analyses can help us understand principles of effective management. As with fisheries, the natural growth rate is fundamental in forest ecology and provides a link between ecological and economic analyses. An important factor in forest management policy is the cumulative nature of forest growth: biomass accumulated years, decades, or even centuries ago will remain available for use if left undisturbed. Thus, choices about the time of harvesting are important in forest management.

If we measure the volume of standing timber in a forest over time, we obtain a **logistic curve** similar to that for the growth of a fishery (Figure 14.1). However, the logic of harvesting is somewhat different. From an economic point of view, we can see a standing forest as an **asset**, or **stock**, that can also yield a **flow** of **use value** to humans. If a forest is privately owned, the owner will balance the asset value against the stream of income available from use. A simplified example will demonstrate the economic principle involved. Initially, we assume that the only financial value of the forest to the owner is as a source of timber.

Consider a forest with 100,000 tons of standing timber and a growth rate of 5,000 tons additional biomass per year. At a price of $100/ton, the value of the forest if it is **clear-cut** (logged all at one time) is $10 million. A policy of **sustainable management**, in which the annual harvest is no more than the annual growth, would yield $500,000 per year.

Which is economically preferable? It depends on the **discount rate**. At 4 percent, the Present Value (PV) of the sustainable yield alternative is:

Figure 14.1 **Forest Growth over Time**

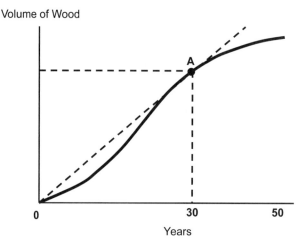

Volume of Wood

A

0   30   50

Years

clear-cut
the process of harvesting all trees within a given area.

sustainable (natural resource) management
management of natural resources such that natural capital remains constant over time, including maintenance of both stocks and flows.

discount rate
the annual rate at which future benefits or costs are discounted relative to current benefits or costs.

mean annual increment (MAI)
the average growth rate of a forest; obtained by dividing the total weight of timber by the age of the forest.

biomass
an energy supply from wood, plant, and animal waste.

$$PV = \$500,000/0.04 = \$12.5 \text{ million}.$$

At 6 percent it is:

$$PV = \$500,000/0.06 = \$8.33 \text{ million}.$$

Comparing these figures with the $10 million present value of an immediate clear-cut, we find that at the lower discount rate, sustainable management is economically preferable, but at the higher rate the owner will do better with a clear-cut.

Another way of seeing this is to note that from the owner's point of view, the clear-cut revenue of $10 million can be invested at 6 percent to earn $600,000 per year, a more lucrative option than the $500,000 from sustainable management. Thus a financial variable, the commercial rate of interest, will dominate private forest management policy. Forests with a growth rate below the going rate of interest are destined to be harvested as fast as possible. U.S. corporate forest management frequently applies this logic, especially when forest owners have high-interest debt to pay off.

This simple example fails to consider forest replanting and regrowth. We can apply a more sophisticated version to determine economically optimum harvesting periods (years from planting to cutting in plantation forestry).

Consider a forest's biological growth pattern. Figure 14.1 shows that a relatively young forest grows more rapidly than a mature forest. The **mean annual increment (MAI)**, or average growth rate, is obtained by dividing the total **biomass**, or weight of timber, by the age of the forest. Graphically, the MAI at any point on the growth curve is defined by the slope of a straight line from the origin to that point. The maximum MAI occurs where a line from the origin is exactly tangent to the curve (point A in Figure 14.1).

One possible rule for harvesting would be to clear-cut the forest at a period that maximized the MAI (thirty years in Figure 14.1). This would result in the highest total volume of timber and highest average annual revenues over time, assuming a constant price for timber.

To find an economic optimum, however, we must consider two other factors. The first is the cost of harvesting—the labor, machinery, and energy required to cut the timber and transport it to market. The second, as our earlier example showed, is the discount rate. Both revenues and costs must be discounted to calculate the present value of various harvesting policies.

The economic optimum can be determined by comparing total revenue to total cost for different possible harvesting periods (Figure 14.2), then discounting this figure to obtain the present value of expected future profits (Figure 14.3). Total revenue (TR) is equal to the volume of timber harvested multiplied by its price. The shape of the TR curve therefore resembles that of the logistic curve in Figure 14.1.

Figure 14.2 **Timber Revenues and Costs over Time**

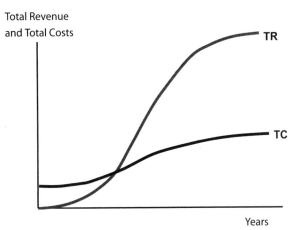

Figure 14.3 **Optimum Harvest Period with Discounting**

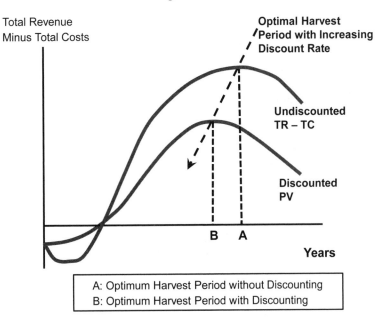

A: Optimum Harvest Period without Discounting
B: Optimum Harvest Period with Discounting

Total costs (TC) include planting and harvesting costs, with harvesting costs rising proportionately to the volume of timber. Total revenue minus total cost (TR − TC) indicates the profit from harvesting at some future point. Profits expected at a future time must be discounted to calculate their present value. The point at which the discounted value of (TR − TC) is maximized gives the **optimal rotation period** for harvesting, from the point of view of economic profitability.

At higher discount rates, the present value of expected future income shrinks. Thus the higher the discount rate, the shorter will be the optimal harvesting period. Figure 14.3 shows undiscounted TR − TC and the present value of discounted TR − TC. The discounted PV (TR − TC) curve is lower, and its maximum occurs earlier. As discount rates rise, the optimal rotation period shortens, as indicated by the arrow.[1]

This principle helps to explain why plantation forestry is generally based on faster-growing softwood trees. Slower-growing hardwoods or mixed forest might be profitable over the long term, but at a commercial rate of discount the present value of slower-growing trees will be too low to be attractive to timber companies. The determination of commercial interest rates depends on financial factors unrelated to ecological systems, but interest rates can have significant impact on forest management.

This economic logic also helps explain pressure on old-growth forests. Standing forests that may have taken hundreds of years to grow represent an economic asset that can be harvested for immediate profit. Replanting tends to be in faster-growing species. Although replanting an entire forest with a single faster-growing species or an agricultural crop represents a significant ecological loss, commercially speaking it may be the most profitable option.

The principles of commercial forest management can thus often conflict with ecological goals. Although it may be possible to internalize some of the social costs and benefits related to forest management, for vast areas of privately owned or open-access forest, market profitability is the only management principle. This is one of the factors that have led to serious problems of forest and biodiversity loss throughout the world (see Box 14.1).

BOX 14.1 FORESTS UNDER SIEGE

The Chaco forest in Paraguay covers an expanse of territory about the size of Poland. While much of the Chaco has remained impenetrable for centuries, huge tracts are now being razed in a scramble to convert the land for ranching. "Paraguay already has the sad distinction of being a deforestation champion," says José Luis Casaccia, a former environment minister. Much of the Atlantic forest in eastern Paraguay has already been cleared for soybean farms; little more than 10 percent of the original forest remains.

So much land is being bulldozed and so many trees are being burned that the sky sometimes turns "twilight gray" in the daytime. "If we continue with this insanity," says Casaccia, "nearly all of the Chaco's forests could be destroyed within 30 years." Much of the forest loss is attributed to Brazilian ranchers who have acquired vast tracts of land in the Chaco.

In Brazil, the site of massive deforestation during the 1980s and 1990s, the rate of deforestation has been reduced by 80 percent since 2006, as the government carved out about 150 million acres for conservation—an area roughly the size of France. But recently there have been signs of a shift in the government's attitude toward the Amazon. A provisional measure now allows the president to decrease the land allocated for conservation.

(continued)

"What is happening in Brazil is the biggest back-sliding that we could ever imagine with regard to environmental policies," says Marian Silva, former environmental minister. Agricultural interests with strong influence on the Brazilian Congress are pressing for legislation that would further weaken the Forest Code, a central piece of environmental legislation. Environmentalists argue that the proposed changes would open the door to a surge in deforestation.

Polls show that 85 percent of Brazilians believe that the reformed code should give priority to forest conservation, even at the expense of agricultural production. But commercial pressures favor economically profitable activities. "We have to reconcile the generation of income with sustainability," according to Izabella Teixeira, the current environment minister.

The government claims the code will reforest about 60 million acres, much of it in the Amazon, which the environment ministry calls "the largest reforestation program in the world." The government's goal is to achieve a situation in which the amount of forest being replanted is larger than the amount being deforested. But who will pay for all these new trees? And will the government enforce replanting requirements? "The small producers don't have the money to replant," says Marcos Jank of the Brazilian Sugarcane Industry Association. "You need to develop programs to help them."

Sources: S. Romero, "A Forest Under Siege in Paraguay," *New York Times,* January 20, 2012; A. Barrionuevo "In Brazil, Fears of a Slide Back for Amazon Protection," *New York Times,* January 25, 2012.

Clear-cut logging and conversion to agriculture often prove more profitable than sustainable forest management. Income from sustainable forest management might offer long-term benefits, but the present value of clear-cutting or of annual agricultural output is greater. As we will see, this economic calculation might be altered by considering positive externalities associated with forest conservation, but these values are generally not reflected in the market.

14.2 FOREST LOSS AND BIODIVERSITY

Human activity has reduced forest area in some cases and increased it in others, as well as changing forest biodiversity. Worldwide, about two-thirds of tropical deforestation results from conversion of land for agriculture rather than directly from timbering. However, opening up forest areas with logging roads often allows access and encourages destructive agricultural techniques.

As human populations have increased, natural forests have typically been cut down and at a later stage replaced with planted forests. This gives rise to a U-shaped curve showing the change in total forested area as population densities increase (Figure 14.4). Most tropical areas of the world are still on the downward-sloping portion of this curve, suffering net forest loss. Many temperate zones have a stable or increasing forest area, having eliminated most of their natural forest and replaced it with planted or second-growth forest.[2]

Losses of tropical forest have been severe over the past several decades. Tropical forest loss between 2000 and 2010 was 850,000 km^2, a rate of about 85,000 km^2 (8.5 million hectares) per year. From 1990 to 2010, Africa and Latin America lost about 10 percent of their forests, while Asia (excluding China) and Oceania lost 5–6 percent.[3]

Figure 14.4 Deforestation and Tree Cover

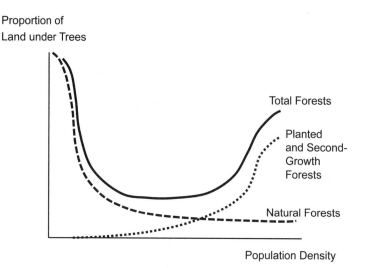

In terms of total forest area, South America suffered the largest net loss of forests between 2000 and 2010—about 4.0 million hectares/year—followed by Africa, which lost 3.4 million ha/yr.[4] Asia, which had a net loss of some 0.6 million ha/yr in the 1990s, reported an average net gain of more than 2.2 million ha/yr between 2000 and 2010, due to large-scale reforestation in China (see Box 14.2) and a reduction in the rate of deforestation in some countries, including Indonesia.

Figure 14.5 Regional Breakdown of Drivers of Deforestation

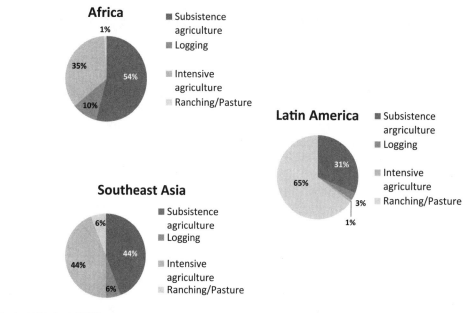

Source: Project Catalyst, 2009.

Conversion of forests to agriculture, ranching, or pasture is the primary cause of forest loss throughout the developing world (Figure 14.5). In Latin America, the main driver is conversion of forest land for ranching or pasture, while in Southeast Asia and Africa it is agriculture, with intensive agriculture more significant in Southeast Asia and subsistence agriculture the main driver in Africa.

Figure 14.6 **Threatened and Endangered Species**

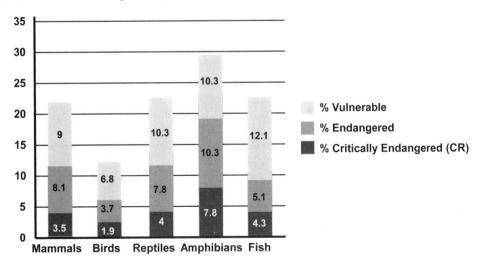

Source: IUCN, 2011.

monoculture

an agricultural system involving the growing of the same crop exclusively on a piece of land year after year.

Even in areas where forest area is stable or increasing, the threat to biodiversity from economic uses of forests may still be great. Cultivated forests tend to be **monoculture**—huge stands planted with a single species selected for maximum economic return. Such artificial forests displace natural forests, which provide habitat for many more species. Over a long period of time, it is possible to regenerate diverse forests, but economic incentives to manage forests for diversity are often lacking.

The maximum sustainable yield principle may not be enough to achieve ecosystem sustainability. Forest managers can maintain sustainable yield merely by replanting all logged areas with a single species of fast-growing tree. This offers sustainable flows of timber and income for the forest owner but destroys the original complexity of the forest ecosystem, to the detriment of many animals and plants that thrive in a multispecies forest.

resilience

the capacity of ecosystem to recover from adverse impacts.

The principle of **resilience** is central to ecosystem sustainability.[5] Resilience is a "bounce-back" capacity: the ability of an ecosystem to recover from disruption (e.g., a forest fire or pest infestation). In general, complex ecosystems display more resilience than simple systems. If a plantation forest contains only one species of tree, an attack by a single pest may destroy the entire forest. A forest with many species is much more likely to withstand pest attacks. The proportion of species within the forest may change, but its ecological integrity and health will survive.

biodiversity (biological diversity)

the maintenance of many different interrelated species in an ecological community.

Species extinction has accelerated in the past decades, and loss of **biodiversity** is likely to be one of the most critical environmental problems of the twenty-first century (see Box 14.3).[6] Biological diversity can be viewed economically as a significant set of positive externalities associated with preservation of existing forests and ecosystems—or as a negative externality associated with their loss. These externalities are not reflected in the commercial exploitation of forests for timber. We must account for them, however, in any policy for sustainable forest management.

BOX 14.3 LOSS OF BIODIVERSITY

Why does biodiversity loss matter? The loss of, say, a single species of beetle may never be noticed and have no apparent economic impact. But any species could turn out to have significant pharmaceutical or medical value, and cumulatively the existence of many species provides crucial ecosystem resilience. In 1990, a compound derived from twigs and leaves from a tree in the Malaysian rainforest was found to stop the spread of one of the two strains of HIV that causes AIDS. But when researchers returned for more samples, they found that the stand of trees had been felled, and no other trees in the vicinity yielded the crucial ingredient.

In addition to possible medical and commercial losses, the loss of even a single species can alter the balance of an ecosystem, causing ripple effects on other species and on ecosystem function and resilience. Our knowledge of the world's biodiversity, and of the scale of biodiversity losses, is limited.

A 2011 study estimated the number of species on the planet at 8.7 million, with tropical rainforests containing more biodiversity than any other ecosystem. But less than two million species have been identified. Ecologists warn that many species will become extinct before they can be identified and studied.

An extensive review of worldwide animal species conservation conducted by the International Union for the Conservation of Nature (IUCN) in 2011 concluded that about 12 percent of birds and 20 percent of mammals face a threat of extinction, and 22 percent of reptiles, 30 percent of amphibians, and 21 percent of fishes surveyed were considered threatened (see Figure 14.6, p. 341).

Sources: Allen, 1992; Black, 2011.

Figure 14.7   **Regional Change in Forest Area**

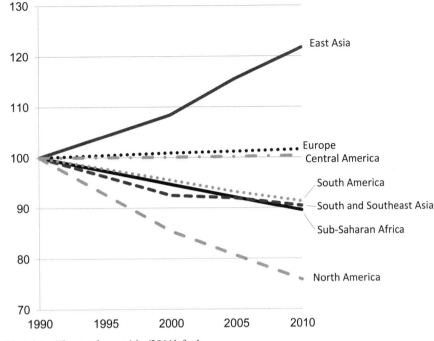

Source: FAOSTAT, 2011, http://faostat.fao.org/site/291/default.aspx.

Economic and Demographic Pressures on Forests

institutional failure

the failure of governments or other institutions to prevent overexploitation of a resource.

open access

unrestricted availability of a resource, without payment.

underpricing of forest resources

prices of goods or services, such as timbering rights, that are lower than the price that would result from taking full social costs into account.

demographic pressure

the impact of growing population on resources such as forests and water supplies.

Economic forces that promote forest destruction include a steadily increasing global market for wood products, leading to declining forest area or conversion to ecologically less desirable plantation forestry (see Figure 14.7). Rising demand alone, however, does not fully explain forest destruction. Overexploitation is often the result of **institutional failure**. Many governments either allow **open access** to forests or encourage **underpricing of forest resources** by selling logging rights well below their market value.[7]

In some cases, local communities have traditionally managed forests in a sustainable manner—until their control over the resource is lost to governments and logging companies. Governments often grant logging concessions and sometimes monopolies to timber companies. They have also encouraged large agricultural firms to encroach on the forest for extensive cattle ranching (Brazil and Central America) or cash-crop cultivation of coffee, tobacco, and other tropical crops (Indonesia, other Asian countries, and Latin America).

Demographic pressure also contributes to forest loss. Governments have encouraged settlements in formerly undisturbed forest areas to reduce pressure in heavily populated places. These new settlers often lack knowledge of forest management and their practices of exploitation and agricultural encroachment may have deep and lasting ecological impacts.[8] Although poor policies are usually more to blame for forest loss than simple population pressure, rising global population has been accompanied by a general trend of decline in forested area.

14.3 POLICIES FOR SUSTAINABLE FOREST MANAGEMENT

Both economic and ecological theory can offer guidance in devising better approaches to forest management. Better policy approaches can be implemented both on the supply side, by promoting sustainable forestry, and on the demand side, by changing consumption patterns, reducing waste and expanding recycling.

Supply Side: Property Rights and Pricing Policies

secure property rights
clearly defined and legally binding rights of property ownership.

One major issue in forest management throughout the developing world is the need for **secure property rights**. Individuals and communities whose land tenure is insecure, including many migrants, have little incentive to conserve forests. Economic necessity forces them to exploit the forest for maximum short-term gain and then move on. If granted secure tenure, they will have an interest in a continuing flow of income from the forest, including forest products other than timber, such as fruits, latex (from rubber-tapping), or shade-grown coffee.[a]

positive externalities
the positive impacts of a market transaction that affect those not involved in the transaction.

Stable communities also have incentives to maintain forests in order to enjoy their accompanying **positive externalities**. A village or community situated in the mountains, for example, may undertake a program of reforestation both to sustain the supply of wood and because trees retain soil on the slopes, preventing erosion. Forested ecosystems also help to provide a stable supply of fresh water and prevent flooding.

Some positive externalities associated with forest maintenance or reforestation are global in nature. Forests remove and store atmospheric carbon, reducing the concentration of carbon dioxide in the atmosphere and lowering the risks of global climate change. This may bring no immediate benefit to the local community, but future global climate change agreements may well provide compensation to countries that preserve or expand their forest cover.[b] In the future, a country might be able to earn income from its forests by keeping them in place rather than by cutting them down for timber export. The carbon storage function of tropical forests has been estimated at $3.7 trillion, assuming a carbon storage value of $20 per ton (see Box 14. 4).[9]

full pricing
the inclusion of both internal and external costs in the price of a product.

Another critical issue is **full pricing** of forest concessions. Government policies of low-cost sales of timber constitute a **subsidy** to major logging corporations as well as an inducement to corrupt practices, such as payoffs to government officials for valuable concessions. Since overexploitation of forests, as we have seen, has many **negative externalities**, this is a particularly inappropriate use of a subsidy, which economic theory tells us should be used only where clear positive externalities exist.[10]

subsidy/subsidies
government assistance to an industry or economic activity; subsidies can be direct, through financial assistance, or indirect, through protective policies.

negative externality/ externalities
negative impacts of a market transaction affecting those not involved in the transaction.

Economic theory supports secure property rights and full pricing of resources. But the ecological perspective adds another important dimension to forest management issues. Forests have to be seen as complex ecosystems to be managed as such, both to preserve healthy ecosystems and to supply of a wide array of

---

[a]Shade-grown coffee leaves forest trees standing, with coffee bushes beneath, while sun-grown coffee requires complete removal of forest cover.

[b]Under the Kyoto Protocol negotiated in December 1997, countries committed to reducing their greenhouse gas emissions must include in their calculations the changes to their carbon stock resulting from "afforestation, deforestation, and reforestation." See discussion in Chapter 18.

BOX 14.4 FOREST CARBON STORAGE VALUATION

One of the many benefits of forests is that trees and other plants store carbon dioxide (CO_2) in their tissue, called carbon sequestration. Net increases in plant biomass generally increase carbon storage, essentially removing CO_2 from the earth's atmosphere. As discussed in Chapter 18, CO_2 is an important greenhouse gas that influences the global climate. Thus, efforts to increase forest cover or prevent forest loss provide a positive externality by tempering climate change. According to the Intergovernmental Panel on Climate Change (IPCC) Fourth Assessment Report, forestry mitigation options have the potential to store between 1.2 billion and 4.2 billion metric tons (t) of CO_2 per year by 2030. This represents around 5–20 percent of total global CO_2 emissions, and about 50 percent of this amount is achievable at a cost of less than US$20/$tCO_2$.

One of the reasons for overexploitation of forests is that positive externality values are not reflected in market transactions. Estimates of these values can used to support efforts to preserve forests. An article in the journal *Ecological Economics* (Kundhlande et al., 2000) provides estimates of the carbon sequestration benefits for the savanna region of Zimbabwe.

The authors use a value of $25 per ton for the benefits of carbon sequestration. Future benefits are discounted at a rate of 5 percent annually. The present value of carbon sequestration is estimated at around $300 per hectare. This value is significant but less than the potential agricultural value of land, which is around $600 per hectare. Thus based on carbon storage benefits alone, policies to prevent the conversion of forests to agricultural land are not economically justified. In combination with other forest values, however, carbon storage values might alter the economic logic of forest conversion.

A study of forest management in Australia (Creedy and Wurzbacher, 2001) indicates that inclusion of carbon storage values increases the optimal rotation period for harvesting, and including other ecological values of the forest may increase it to infinity (i.e., that it would be economically optimal to conserve the forest indefinitely).

Forests also have other value, including watershed protection, wildlife habitat, recreational values, and marketable products. A complete accounting of forest benefits may indicate that forest preservation is justified but, as we saw in Chapter 6, obtaining valid estimates of all values may be difficult. Forest policies based solely on market behavior "fail to fully account for the numerous functions and values that are not captured through market transactions. Forest use decisions that ignore those benefits that are not normally exchanged in markets introduce distortions in resource allocation, often with detrimental environmental consequences" (Kundhlande et al., p. 410).

Sources: Creedy and Wurzbacher, 2001; IPCC, 2007; Kundhlande et al., 2000; Wertz-Kanounnikoff, 2008.

---

goods and services for current and future generations. These ecological goals will often differ from the priorities of private landowners, who will seek to manage the forest for profitability, often selecting faster-growing species and cutting timber on a short cycle rather the longer, natural cycle, which allows a mature forest to develop.

total economic value
the value of a resource considering both use and nonuse values.

certification
the process of certifying products that meet certain standards, such as certifying produce grown using organic farming techniques.

Ecological values of forests include provision of water services and maintenance of water quality, carbon sequestration value, biodiversity value, recreation, tourism, and cultural values.[11] Thus the **total economic value** of forests can considerably exceed the value of timber and other commercial products.

Government policy can encourage sound forest management by such measures as tax breaks for sustainable forestry or limitations on clear-cutting. From an economic theory perspective, the positive externalities associated with good forest management justify such policies. Programs have also begun for **certification** of sustainably produced wood so that consumers and public agencies can encourage sound practices by their purchasing choices. Experience shows that many consumers are willing to pay a premium above market price for sustainably produced wood. In 2012, the Forest Stewardship Council (FSC) identified 162 million acres of certified forest in 80 countries, of which 24 million acres were in developing countries.[12]

In cases in which complex and old-growth forest ecosystems can be effectively protected only through preservation as parkland, government or private conservation agencies can acquire them as **public goods**. In many developing countries, buffer zones around parkland allow local communities to pursue sustainable exploitation of forest products. This can overcome local hostility to parks among villagers who resent the loss of access to forest resources. Otherwise, encroachment into protected areas can be a major problem—some conservation areas in developing countries are referred to as "paper parks" since the protection exists only on paper.

The **availability of credit** on reasonable terms to villagers for investment in replanting and **agroforestry** (mixing tree crops with food crops) is often a key factor. As we have seen, a high interest rate encourages a short planning horizon, and low-cost credit can make it profitable to invest in long-term resource conservation.

Interest has risen in programs that provide compensation for forest conservation by linking financial incentives for conservation with the carbon stored in forests. Forest owners or managers receive credits for "avoided deforestation" or reforestation. A United Nations program aimed at reducing greenhouse gas emissions from forests and boosting livelihoods in tropical countries has approved $67 million for projects in 44 partner countries across Africa, Asia-Pacific, Latin America, and the Caribbean.[13] A 2008 report calls for "an international climate change deal . . . to halve deforestation emissions by 2020 and make the forest sector carbon neutral by 2030—with emissions from forest loss balanced by new forest growth."[14]

Demand Side: Changing Consumption Patterns

As we have noted, overall demand for wood products has risen steadily. The increase in demand for paper has been especially rapid (Figure 14.8). Like other forms of consumption, paper consumption is unequally distributed: U.S. use of paper is 335 kilograms (kg) per person per year, while in Germany per capita consumption is 200 kg, in Brazil 35 kg, and in India only 4 kg.

> If everyone in the world consumed as much as the average American, the world would be using nearly seven times as much paper. And by 2050 it would be 11 times as much. If, on the other hand, paper use stabilized at today's global average—50 kilograms a year per person—paper consumption in 2050 could be held to 1.7 times today's level.[15]

Expanded recycling of paper and other wood products has significant potential to reduce pressure on forests. Worldwide, 43 percent of wastepaper is now recycled. Developing countries such as India typically recover and reuse paper products and often import and recycle scrap paper from industrialized countries.

Low prices for paper and other wood products serve as both an incentive for greater consumption and a disincentive to expanded recycling. In some cases, direct and indirect subsidies for forest exploitation encourage the use of virgin rather than recycled paper. Internalizing environmental externalities into prices would

Figure 14.8 **World Paper and Wood Production, 1961–2009**

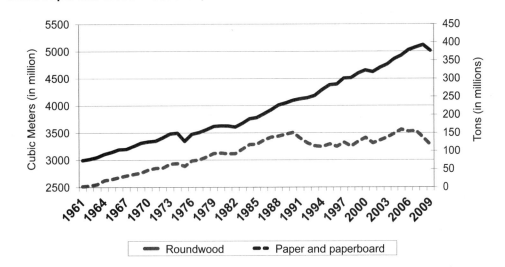

Source: FAO online database, 2011, http://faostat.fao.org/.

encourage greater efficiency at all stages of the production cycle. Properly pricing wood products would increase prices for nonrecycled paper and all one-time-use wood products relative to recycled-materials prices, thereby encouraging a higher recycling rate.[16]

In addition to reducing demand through recycling, certification programs can enable consumers to identify sustainably produced wood products. Rural communities that produce sustainable wood products can gain an increased flow of income if consumers are willing to pay a premium for these certified products.[17]

14.4 Conclusion: Reconciling Economic and Ecological Principles

A general conclusion from the basic economic theory of renewable resource management is that economically efficient use of natural resources, while generally more sustainable than open-access exploitation, is not necessarily sustainable from an ecological perspective. One important goal of forest management, therefore, must be to reconcile the differing principles of economics and ecology.

As we have noted, ecological sustainability has dimensions not reflected in the economic analyses of resource use. Whereas economic sustainability is concerned primarily with sustaining a flow of income over time, ecological sustainability depends on resilience—the "bounce-back" capacity of ecosystems affected by economic exploitation or by natural phenomena such as disease or weather extremes. Resilience depends on ecological complexity, an essential element of sustainable natural systems.

Economic harvesting with maximum profit in mind often destroys complexity. Old-growth forests are doomed to clear-cutting in a forestry regime that places a premium on rapid growth and shorter harvesting periods and that can bring to bear powerful equipment for timber removal. Total forested area may not decline, but natural forest will be replaced with ecologically less diverse second-growth forest or with faster-growing plantation monocultures. In rapidly growing developing economies, many natural resource systems, traditionally harvested in a relatively sustainable manner, come under much heavier pressure as a market logic prevails and modern technology penetrates remote areas.

At the same time, technologies such as sustainable forestry, paper recycling and efficient materials use have great potential for conservation of scarce resources. Given the proper incentives, ecologically friendly technology and management can promote conservation, less wasteful resource use, recycling, and more efficient consumption. Recognizing the total economic value of forests, with proper internalization of positive and negative externalities, can help to create such incentives.

social sustainability
the maintenance of social structure and traditions consistent with a well-functioning society.

A related issue is **social sustainability**. Indigenous communities dependent on forest products are threatened by more intensive, "modernized" methods of forest exploitation. Social sustainability and resource sustainability are mutually dependent.

Policies for forest management must also consider continuing growth in overall demand. Although policies aimed at increasing economic efficiency can improve resource management at the microeconomic level, they can also increase overall stress on natural systems at the macroeconomic level. More efficient resource use requires less resource input per unit of consumption, but may also encourage expanded consumption by lowering prices.

ecosystems management
a system of resource management that stresses the long-term sustainability of ecosystems.

An **ecosystems management** model stressing the ecological integrity of forests may provide more appropriate policy guidance. In such a model, economic efficiency principles can be extremely important, as reflected in the need for secure land tenure institutions, suitable price incentives, and credit extension to rural communities. But the principles of economic efficiency alone can also conflict with long-term natural resource sustainability. Effective forest management must therefore consider both economic and ecological principles.

SUMMARY

Forest management policies can be derived from the ecological principles of forest growth. Forest growth patterns imply an optimal rotation period for commercial timber. However, this commercial optimum neglects other ecological functions of forests.

Deforestation and conversion of natural forest to plantation cause significant biodiversity loss. Values associated with biodiversity represent significant externalities rarely reflected in market prices.

Growing demand for wood and wood products increases pressure on forests. Open access to many forests creates incentives for short-term exploitation without investment in replanting or sustainable forestry. In addition, many governments subsidize excessive forest clearance by making public lands available to timber companies at low prices.

Policies that encourage secure tenure and support for small-scale forestry enterprises and agroforestry can create incentives to maintain environmentally stable forests. In addition to timber, forests can provide income from other products, such as fruit and latex. Certification programs for sustainably produced forest products can benefit from some consumers' willingness to pay a premium for certified wood. Public good and carbon storage functions also represent positive economic values of standing forest, and internalizing these values can help promote forest conservation.

KEY TERMS AND CONCEPTS

agroforestry
assets
availability of credit
biodiversity (biological diversity)
biomass
certification
clear-cut
demographic pressure
discount rate
ecosystems management
flow
full pricing
institutional failure
logistic curve
mean annual increment (MAI)

monoculture
negative externalities
open access
optimal rotation period
positive externalities
public goods
resilience
secure property rights
social sustainability
stock
subsidy
sustainable management
total economic value
underpricing of forest resources
use values

DISCUSSION QUESTIONS

1. Unlike ocean fisheries, forests can be privately owned, and in fact many millions of acres of forests are owned and managed by private corporations. In economic theory, private ownership should create incentives for efficient management. To what extent is this true of privately owned forests? Is efficient management also beneficial to the environment?

2. How can the timber values of forests be balanced with their value in supporting biodiversity? What changes in property regimes and forest management policies could be used to help achieve the dual goals of economic profitability and environmental preservation?

3. How can consumer action affect forest conservation and forest loss? What are the most effective ways of changing consumption patterns of wood and wood products in ways that promote forest sustainability?

EXERCISE

XYZ Forest Products owns a 2,000-acre tract of forest land, of which 1,000 acres are currently planted in hardwood trees (oak, beech, etc.) and 1,000 in softwoods (pine). An acre of either kind of forest contains a biomass (standing timber) of 200 tons/acre. But hardwoods are slower-growing: An acre of hardwoods will add 10 tons/acre/year of new growth, whereas an acre of softwoods will add 20 tons/acre/year.

The going price is $500/ton for hardwood and $300/ton for softwood. These prices are expected to remain stable for the indefinite future (in real terms). Two management practices are possible: clear-cutting, in which all trees are removed; and sustainable timbering, in which the amount of biomass removed annually is just equal to annual growth. The cost of clear-cutting is $40/ton (for either kind of tree), while that for sustainable timbering is $70/ton.

Analyze the profit-maximizing forest management policy that XYZ corporation will pursue if:

(a) Real interest rates are 3 percent per annum;

(b) Real interest rates are 5 percent per annum.

Now assume that XYZ is taken over by the Gargantua conglomerate, which has $100 million in debt at a 10 percent real interest rate. Analyze its probable forest management practice.

Comment on the role of the interest rate here, and suggest a government policy on forest management. Are there other considerations not apparent in the data given here that would affect policy decisions? What would you recommend if the forest were publicly rather than privately owned? How might your recommendations differ for forest management in developed versus developing countries?

NOTES

1. For a more detailed treatment of the economics of timber harvesting and optimal rotation periods, see Hartwick and Olewiler, 1998.

2. For an overview of the state of world forests, see FAO, 2010, 2011.

3. Computed from FAO, 2011, data annex. China had a significant increase in forested land due to an extensive reforestation program (see Box 14.3). One km^2 equals 100 hectares.

4. FAO, 2010.

5. See Common and Perrings, 1992; Holling, 1986.

6. See Ehrlich and Daily, 1993; Wilson, 1988, 1992.

7. For discussion of policy failures in forest management, see Contreras-Hermosilla, 2000; Panayotou, 1993, chap. 3.

8. For specific examples of destructive government forest policies, see Abramovitz, 1998.

9. See Myers, 1996; Wertz-Kanounnikoff, 2008.

10. On policies for full pricing of forest concessions, see Panayotou, 1998, pp. 78–79.

11. For assessment of non-market values of forests, see Krieger, 2001; Pearce, 2001.

12. Forest Stewardship Council, *Facts and Figures 2012,* www.fsc.org.

13. See "Partner Countries" at www.un-redd.org.

14. Eliasch, 2008.

15. Abramovitz, 1998.

16. Data on paper consumption and recycling from Abramovitz, 1998; Abramovitz and Mattoon, 1999.

17. See Forest Stewardship Council at www.fsc.org; World Bank, 2004.

REFERENCES

Abramovitz, Janet N. 1998. *Taking a Stand: Cultivating a New Relationship with the World's Forests.* Worldwatch Paper no. 140. Washington, DC: Worldwatch Institute.

Abramovitz, Janet N., and Ashley T. Mattoon. 1999. *Paper Cuts: Recovering the Paper Landscape.* Worldwatch Paper no. 149. Washington, DC. Worldwatch Institute.

Allen, Scott. 1992. "Loss of a Tree Means Loss of an HIV Blocker." *Boston Globe,* November 10, 1992.

Black, Richard. 2011. "Species Count Put at 8.7 Million." *BBC News,* August 23, 2011.

Common, Mick, and Charles Perrings. 1992. "Towards an Ecological Economics of Sustainability." *Ecological Economics* 6 (July): 7–34.

Contreras-Hermosilla, Arnoldo. 2000. *The Underlying Causes of Forest Decline.* Center for International Forestry Research, Occasional Paper no. 30. Jakarta.

Creedy, J., and A.D. Wurzbacher. 2001. "The Economic Value of a Forested Catchment with Timber, Water, and Carbon Sequestration Benefits." *Ecological Economics* 38: 71–83.

Ehrlich, Paul R., and Gretchen C. Daily. 1993. "Population Extinction and Saving Biodiversity." *Ambio* 22(2–3): 64–68.

Eliasch, John. 2008. *Climate Change: Financing Global Forests: The Eliasch Review*. www.official-documents.gov.uk/document/other/9780108507632/ 9780108507632.pdf.

Food and Agriculture Organization (FAO). 2010. *Global Forest Resources Assessment*. Rome.

———. 2011. *State of the World's Forests 2011*. Rome.

Hartwick, John M., and Nancy D. Olewiler. 1998. *The Economics of Natural Resource Use*, 2nd ed. New York: Addison Wesley.

Holling, C.S. 1986. "The Resilience of Terrestrial Ecosystems: Local Surprise and Global Change." In *Sustainable Development of the Biosphere,* ed. W.C. Clark and R.E. Munn. Cambridge: Cambridge University Press.

Intergovernmental Panel on Climate Change (IPCC). 2007. *Climate Change 2007: Mitigation of Climate Change*. Cambridge: Cambridge University Press.

International Union for Conservation of Nature. 2011. *The Red List of Threatened Species*. www.iucnredlist.org/documents/summarystatistics/2011_1_RL_Stats_Table_2.pdf.

Krieger, Douglas J. 2001. *Economic Value of Forest Ecosystem Services: A Review*. Washington, DC: Wilderness Society.

Kundhlande, G., W.L. Adamowicz, and I. Mapaure. 2000. "Valuing Ecological Services in a Savanna Ecosystem: A Case Study from Zimbabwe." *Ecological Economics* 33: 401–41.

Li, Jie, Marcus W. Feldman, Shuzhuo Li, and Gretchen C. Daily. 2011. "Rural household income and inequality under the Sloping Land Conversion Program in Western China." *Proceedings of the National Academy of Sciences*, April 25, www.pnas.org/content/early/2011/04/20/1101018108.short/.

Myers, Norman. 1996. "The World's Forests: Problems and Potentials." *Environmental Conservation* 23(2): 156–168.

Panayotou, Theodore. 1993. *Green Markets: The Economics of Sustainable Development*. San Francisco: Institute for Contemporary Studies Press.

———. 1998. *Instruments of Change: Motivating and Financing Sustainable Development*. London: Earthscan.

Pearce, David W. 2001. "The Economic Value of Forest Ecosystems." *Ecosystem Health* 7(4), December.

Project Catalyst. 2009. Towards the Inclusion of Forest-Based Mitigation in a Global Climate Agreement, www.project-catalyst.info/focus-areas/forestry.html.

Wertz-Kanounnikoff, Sheila. 2008. *Estimating the Costs of Reducing Forest Emissions*. Center for International Forestry Research, Working Paper no. 42. Jakarta.

Wilson, E.O. 1992. *The Diversity of Life*. New York: W.W. Norton.

Wilson, E.O., ed. 1988. *Biodiversity*. Washington, DC: National Academy Press.

World Bank. 2004. *Sustaining Forests: A Development Strategy*. Washington, DC.

WEB SITES

1. **www.cifor.org**. Web site of the Center for International Forestry Research, a nonprofit, global facility that conducts research to enable more informed and equitable decision making about the use and management of forests in less developed countries, including analysis of the underlying drivers of deforestation and degradation.
2. **www.fs.fed.us/sustained/siteindex.html**. The U.S. Forest Service's Web site, with links to information on sustainable forest management.
3. **http://ran.org/forests/**. Information about rainforests from the Rainforest Action Network, an environmental group that campaigns to protect rainforests around the world.

Water Economics and Policy

CHAPTER 15 FOCUS QUESTIONS

- What is the extent of global water scarcity?
- Can water shortages be addressed by expanding supplies?
- Can water pricing promote more efficient water use?
- What is the potential for water markets to improve the allocation of water?

15.1 GLOBAL SUPPLY AND DEMAND FOR WATER

hydrologic cycle
the natural purification of water through evaporation and precipitation.

Water is a unique natural resource that forms the basis for life on earth. Water can be characterized as a renewable resource, since it can generally be reused indefinitely as long as it is not severely polluted. Also, water is continually purified in a process known as the **hydrologic cycle** (Figure 15.1). Water evaporates from lakes, rivers, oceans, and land and then returns to these sources as precipitation.

In addition to surface water, stocks of groundwater are found in underground aquifers. While aquifers are replenished as a result of infiltration, most aquifers have very long replenishment times, making them essentially nonrenewable resources on a human time scale.[a] Thus the analysis of water systems combines elements of renewable and nonrenewable resource theory.

Many of the principles of renewable resource management apply to water systems, but although surface water can be considered a renewable resource, it is still available in limited supply.

> [E]vaporation fueled by the sun's energy lifts 500,000 cubic kilometers of moisture into the atmosphere each year—86 percent from the oceans and 14 percent from the land. An equal amount falls back to earth as rain, sleet, or snow, but it is distributed in different proportions: whereas the continents lose about 70,000 cubic kilometers through evaporation, they gain 110,000 through precipitation. As a result, roughly 40,000 cubic kilometers are transferred from the sea to the land each year.[1]

---

[a]Aquifers under the Sahara, for example, are thousands of years old and are sometimes referred to as "fossil water."

Figure 15.1 **The Hydrologic Cycle**

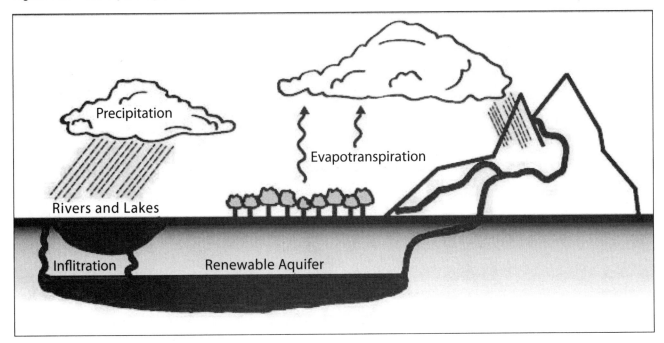

The total available supply of 40,000 cubic kilometers converts to about 5,700 cubic meters per person per year. Hydrologists have established that, considering the water needs of modern societies, a threshold of 2,000 cubic meters per person per year represents the level above which a population can be sustained comfortably.[b] But while the total global water supply is sufficient to meet human needs, not all water can be captured for human use. As much as two-thirds of the total water supply runs off as floods. Some water must also be allocated to meet ecological demands, such as supplying wetlands and wildlife habitat.

Most important, water is not evenly distributed geographically and seasonally. Some regions of the world have abundant water resources, while others suffer from a scarcity of water. A country that has an available water supply between 1,000 and 1,700 cubic meters per person per year is classified as **water stressed**.[2] If water supplies are below 1,000 cubic meters per person, the country is classified as **water scarce**, causing a severe constraint on food production, economic development, and protection of natural systems.

Figure 15.2 shows the countries that are already experiencing water stress or water scarcity. The countries with the most limited water supplies are in North Africa and the Middle East. Water stressed countries include India, South Africa, and Poland. As the human population increases, the available freshwater per person will decrease. Particularly in Africa, where the population is projected to triple by 2100, the number of countries experiencing water stress and water scarcity is expected to increase.

> [According to projections], more than 2.8 billion people in 48 countries will face water stress or scarcity conditions by 2025. Of these countries, 40 are in West Asia, North

water stressed

term used for countries where freshwater supplies are between 1,700 and 1,000 cubic meters per person per year.

water scarce

term used for countries where freshwater supplies are less than 1,000 cubic meters per person per year.

---

[b]Hydrology is the scientific study of the distribution and movement of water on the earth's surface, underground, and in the atmosphere.

Figure 15.2 **Global Freshwater Availability, 2007**

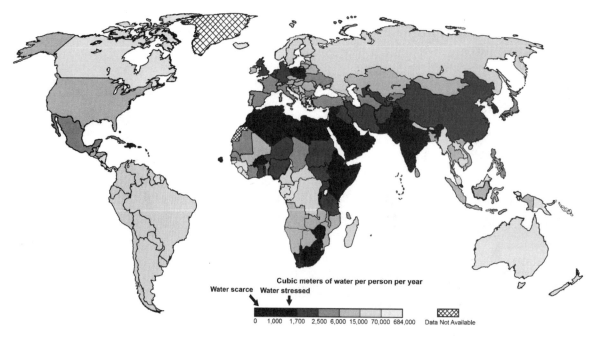

Source: UNEP, 2008.

Africa or sub-Saharan Africa. Over the next two decades, population increases and growing demands are projected to push all the West Asian countries into water scarcity conditions. By 2050, the number of countries facing water stress or scarcity could rise to 54, with a combined population of four billion people—about 40 percent of the projected global population of 9.4 billion.[3]

Water shortages will be exacerbated in some regions because of climate change. Warmer temperatures speed up the hydrological cycle. In general, already wet areas will become wetter, increasing the likelihood of flooding. But already arid areas are likely to become drier, increasing the probability of droughts.[4] (For more on the impact of climate change on precipitation patterns in the western United States, see Box 15.1).

In addition to providing for basic human needs such as drinking, cooking, and sanitation, water is a critical input for economic production. Most important, water is used to irrigate crops and raise livestock. Although 83 percent of the world's cropland is rain fed, the 17 percent that requires irrigation produces more than 40 percent of the world's food supply.[5] A total of 70 percent of global water consumption is for agricultural purposes.[6] Another 19 percent of global water use is for industrial demands, including electricity generation. Only 11 percent of water is used to meet municipal demands.

Like energy consumption, water consumption per capita varies significantly across different countries, as shown in Figure 15.3. Unlike energy use, water use is not mainly a function of economic development. Some countries with relatively high water use, such as Turkmenistan and Iraq, are not high-income countries yet heavily rely on water for agriculture. While China has a higher gross domestic product (GDP) per capita than India, India uses more water

Figure 15.3   **Water Consumption per Capita, Select Countries**

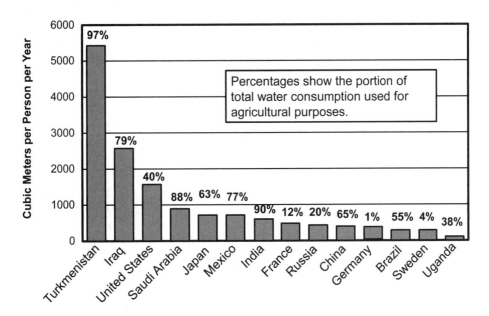

Source: Food and Agriculture Organization, Aquastat database. http://www.fao.org/nr/water/aquastat/main/index.stm.

per person, 90 percent of it for agricultural purposes. German water use per capita is similar to that in China, but hardly any water in Germany is used for agriculture.

Global water demand is projected to increase by 55 percent between 2000 and 2050, as shown in Figure 15.4. All the demand growth is expected to occur in

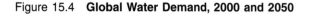

Figure 15.4 **Global Water Demand, 2000 and 2050**

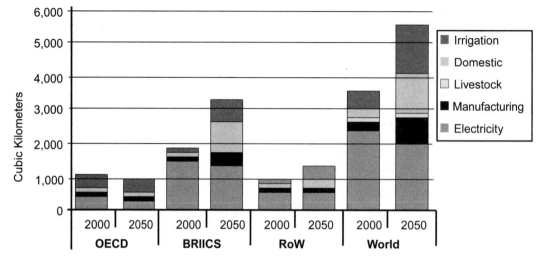

Source: OECD, 2012.

Note: BRIICS = Brazil, Russia, India, Indonesia, China, South Africa; OECD = Organization for Economic Cooperation and Development; RoW = rest of world.

countries that are not members of the Organization for Economic Cooperation and Development (OECD), mainly China and India. While the global demand for irrigation water is actually projected to decline in the coming decades due to increased irrigation efficiency, significant growth is expected for manufacturing, domestic, and electricity needs. According to the OECD, "In the absence of major policy changes and much better water management the situation will deteriorate and water availability will become increasingly uncertain."[7]

One piece of good news is that access to safe drinking water supplies is expanding in developing countries. One of the Millennium Development Goals set by the United Nations was to halve the proportion of the world's population without access to safe drinking water between 1990 and 2015. This goal was met ahead of schedule, in 2010, when an estimated 89 percent of the world's population had access to safe drinking water.[8] However, progress in expanding access to safe water has been uneven. About half the progress occurred in China and India, while in some African countries safe water access has declined since 1990.

The United Nations further emphasized the importance of access to safe water supplies in 2010 by declaring "the right to safe and clean drinking water and sanitation as a human right that is essential for the full enjoyment of life and all human rights."[9] The resolution also voiced deep concern that "approximately 884 million people lack access to safe drinking water and that more than 2.6 billion do not have access to basic sanitation" and called on member states to provide the financial and technical resources "to scale up efforts to provide safe, clean, accessible and affordable drinking water and sanitation for all." This resolution was approved in a vote of 121 to 0. However, forty-one countries, including the United States, abstained from voting on the resolution, because of concerns about national sovereignty.

15.2 ADDRESSING WATER SHORTAGES

Water shortages can be addressed using two basic approaches: from the supply side or the demand side. Given the extent of projected water shortages in some regions, a "magic bullet" solution is unlikely. A range of options will be needed.

> We have a menu of options, but the status quo is not one of them. In the United States, the usual response to water shortages is to divert more water from rivers, build more dams, and drill more groundwater wells. These traditional alternatives are not viable solutions. Other ideas—surreal ones—include towing icebergs from the Arctic, importing water from British Columbia, and seeding clouds. These ideas reflect a misguided hope that there is a new oasis out there, somewhere, that will obviate the need to examine carefully how and for what we use water. More sensible approaches include conservation, desalination, and reuse of treated municipal effluent. Yet even communities that have embraced these measures still face ominous water futures.[10]

Increasing Water Supply: Aquifers, Dams, and Desalination

Past water management policies have generally focused on ways to increase the supply of water. In regions where freshwater supplies are insufficient to meet demand, additional water has often been obtained by extracting groundwater from aquifers. While underground aquifers are normally recharged by water seepage, in most cases withdrawal rates greatly exceed the rates of recharge.

Countries such as Saudi Arabia and Libya rely on "fossil" groundwater from ancient aquifers in desert areas, which now have practically no recharge and are likely to be depleted in the next forty to sixty years. In the western United States, the Ogallala Aquifer is also severely depleted, and as a result irrigated area has started to shrink. Similar problems affect aquifers in North China and in India. (For more on the exploitation of aquifers around the world, see Box 15.2).

BOX 15.2   DEMAND FOR WATER OUTSTRIPS SUPPLY

According to an analysis of global groundwater supplies published in 2012, nearly one-quarter of the world's population lives in areas where groundwater is being withdrawn faster than it can be replenished. This includes many of the world's major agricultural regions, including the Central Valley in California, the Nile delta in Egypt, and the Upper Ganges in India. In addition to providing water for irrigation, water stored in underground aquifers for thousands of years supplies basic human needs, manufacturing demands, and water for wildlife habitat.

"This overuse can lead to decreased groundwater availability for both drinking water and growing food," says Tom Gleeson, a hydrogeologist at McGill University in Montreal, Quebec, and lead author of the study. Eventually, he adds, it "can lead to dried up streams and ecological impacts."

The study found that some aquifers are being depleted at an alarming rate. For example, the geographical area dependent upon the Upper Ganges aquifer is more than 50 times the size of the aquifer itself. Gleeson notes that "the rate of extraction is quite unsustainable there."

However, Gleeson points out that remaining groundwater supplies, overall, are quite large. As much as 99 percent of the fresh, unfrozen water on the planet is groundwater. "It's this huge reservoir that we have the potential to manage sustainably," he says. "If we choose to."

Source: Mascarelli, 2012.

Another way to increase water supplies is to construct dams. Dams can capture seasonal floodwater that would otherwise be unavailable for human use and provide hydroelectric power. Worldwide about 48,000 large dams are in operation, about half of them in China.[11] These dams provide 19 percent of the world's electricity. More dams are still being built, mainly in China, Iran, Japan, and Turkey, but the best sites are already in use. Existing dams are often affected by problems of siltation, and new large dam proposals have been criticized for the environmental and social damage that results from the flooding of large areas.[12] For example the Three Gorges Dam in China, the largest hydroelectric dam in the world, displaced 1.3 million people and disrupted the habitat of dozens of endangered species.

desalination
the removal of salt from ocean water to make it usable for irrigation, industrial, or municipal water supplies.

Because of the vast amounts of seawater on the planet, **desalination** has appeal as a potential source of virtually unlimited supply. However, cost is a significant barrier to desalination. Removing salt from seawater requires large amounts of energy. While desalination costs have declined as technology has improved, it currently costs about $0.50 to $1.00 per cubic meter to desalinate seawater,[13] which is usually more expensive than obtaining water supplies from surface water or groundwater. For example, in an analysis of water supply options in San Diego, California, desalination costs were estimated to be $1,800–$2,800 per acre-foot (AF) while the supply costs were $400–$800/AF for surface water and $375–$1,100/AF for groundwater.[14, c] While desalination may make economic sense in some very dry regions, it is unlikely to supply a significant amount of the planet's water in the future:

> Despite major advancements in desalination technologies, seawater desalination is still more energy intensive compared to conventional technologies for the treatment of fresh water. There are also concerns about the potential environmental impacts of large-scale seawater desalination plants.[15]

Water Demand Management

One of the ways that we can alter the projected trend of increasing water demand in Figure 15.4 is to increase water use efficiency. The greatest efficiency gains can be made in agriculture. Whereas traditional irrigation by flooding or channeling water by gravity is inefficient (60 percent of the water is lost by evaporation or infiltration), new techniques of **micro-irrigation** by drip systems allow an efficiency of 95 percent.[16] Also, technologies that permit better monitoring of soil and weather conditions can more accurately determine appropriate irrigation needs.

micro-irrigation
irrigation systems that increase the efficiency of water use by applying water in small quantities close to the plants.

For nonagricultural uses, recycling and reuse of wastewater can reduce water demand. For example, through a graywater system, water used for such purposes as laundry and bathing can also be used to irrigate landscaping. Water use standards for devices such as dishwashers, toilets, and showerheads can reduce domestic water needs. Leak detection and repair, especially in municipal water supply lines, can also help reduce water consumption.

Economic research shows that conservation is generally the cheapest way to address water shortages. In the San Diego study mentioned above, the cost of

---

[c]An acre-foot is an amount of water covering one acre one foot deep. It is equivalent to 1,233 cubic meters.

conservation was estimated at between \$150 and \$1,000 per AF, based on a range of conservation options. The study concludes:

> Conservation appears as the most attractive of the seven water solutions analyzed for San Diego County by a wide margin. These findings suggest that solving San Diego County's water challenge may rest significantly on the demand side.[17]

Water conservation can be realized using several approaches, including price-based and nonprice approaches. Nonprice approaches can be classified into three basic categories:[18]

1. *Required or voluntary adoption of water-conserving technologies*: This includes setting standards for appliance efficiency or offering water customers rebates or even free items such as low-flow showerheads.
2. *Mandatory water use restrictions:* These are often implemented in response to drought conditions and may include restrictions on watering lawns, washing cars, or filling swimming pools.
3. *Education and information:* These include mailing information to customers about ways to reduce water use, offering talks on water conservation, or airing public service messages on TV or the Internet.

water pricing
setting the price of water to influence the quantity consumed.

While these nonprice methods are effective to some extent, economists tend to focus on **water pricing** as the most effective way to induce water conservation. Prices should serve as indicators of economic scarcity, reflecting physical limits and environmental externalities. For various social and political reasons, however, governments have maintained low water prices, particularly for agriculture. We now turn to a discussion of water pricing, in theory and in practice.

15.3 WATER PRICING

Our study of water pricing requires us to recall several of the concepts discussed earlier in the text. First we need to differentiate between value and price.[19] The value of water to consumers is reflected in willingness to pay for it, as discussed in Chapter 3. The difference between willingness to pay for water and its price is its net benefit, or consumer surplus. In theory, consumers will continue to purchase water as long as their willingness to pay for it exceeds the price. But this market analysis does not tell the whole story. While water has obvious use values, including for domestic uses and irrigation, it also has nonmarket and nonuse values, such as for recreation and wildlife habitat.[20]

We must also differentiate between the average cost of supplying water and its marginal cost. The marginal cost is the cost of supplying one additional unit of water. The average cost is simply the total supply cost divided by the number of units supplied. The distinction is important because water utilities are normally **regulated monopolies**. A company seeking to maximize profits will produce as long as marginal revenue exceeds marginal supply costs (i.e., as long as it is making a profit on each unit). While an unregulated monopolist can set its price to maximize profits, a regulated monopolist such as a water utility is normally restricted in its ability to set prices.

regulated monopolies
monopolies that are regulated by an external entity, for example through controls on price or profits.

average-cost pricing
a water pricing strategy in which price is set equal to the average cost of production (or equal to average cost plus a profit mark-up if the water utility is a for-profit entity).

Water utilities in the United States are either privately or publicly owned. Private water utilities are permitted to make a reasonable profit, while municipal utilities' prices are set to cover their total supply costs, considering both fixed and variable costs. In either case, regulatory bodies normally set water prices using **average-cost pricing**, without any consideration of marginal costs. For a municipal utility, setting price equal to average cost means that they will just break even.[21] A private utility would be allowed to charge a price somewhat above average cost in order to make a profit.

But does average cost pricing result in an efficient level of water supply? We know that the socially efficient level of provision for a good occurs where marginal benefits equal marginal costs. Thus average-cost pricing is unlikely to result in an efficient level of water supply. Normally the marginal cost of water supply is quite low relative to its average cost because supplying water requires significant up-front capital costs, such as for pipes and treatment facilities. This might seem to imply that the efficient price for water should be lower than its average cost. But we also need to consider the externality costs of supplying water, which may include such impacts as the loss of wetlands and wildlife habitat. For a socially efficient price, any externality costs should be considered when calculating the average cost of supply, as discussed in Chapter 3. In this respect, failing to account for water's externality costs implies that average-cost pricing may result in a price that is too low. So it is unclear whether average-cost pricing results in a price that is too high or too low from the perspective of economic efficiency.

For the management and pricing of groundwater, a nonrenewable resource, we also need to consider our analysis from Chapter 5. Recall that the efficient allocation of a nonrenewable resource over time requires us to take into account the externality costs imposed on future generations if future supplies will be insufficient to meet their demands. We concluded that these costs can be internalized by charging a user cost to the current generation. This is rarely done in practice for groundwater, again suggesting an inefficient allocation of water.

Further complicating our analysis is the fact that water is often subsidized by the government, in particular for irrigation uses.

> Many authors have called for the elimination of irrigation subsidies, at times suggesting that water is a commodity and should be priced accordingly. They describe the potential gains in irrigation efficiency and the public value of communicating scarcity conditions through market-based prices. Other authors suggest that subsidies can be justified because irrigation projects provide both public and private goods, or that higher water prices will reduce agricultural net revenues without motivating notable reductions in irrigation diversions.[22]

In regions where irrigation has significant environmental impacts, it may be more appropriate to tax water rather than subsidize it. Consider some of the environmental damage caused by irrigation:

> An excessive withdrawal of water for irrigation is clearly impacting the environment in some areas. For example, the Colorado River often contains essentially no water by the time it crosses the border into Mexico, owing to both urban and agricultural withdrawals. In fact, in most years, the Colorado River doesn't make it to the ocean. This has consequences for the river and its riparian ecosystems, as well as for the delta and estuary system at its mouth, which no longer receives the recharge of fresh water

and nutrients that it normally did. The same is true for the Yellow River in China. The San Joaquin River in California is so permanently dewatered that trees are growing in its bed and developers have suggested building housing there. In the last 33 years, the Aral Sea has lost 50 percent of its surface area and 75 percent of its volume, with a concomitant tripling in its salinity, owing largely to diversion of water from its feeding rivers for irrigating cotton.[23]

A supply and demand graph helps to illustrate the inefficiency of subsidizing irrigation water even though its withdrawal and use have negative externalities. In Figure 15.5, the market equilibrium for irrigation water occurs where the marginal cost curve (MC) intersects the demand curve, resulting in a price of P_E and a quantity of Q_E. But suppose that irrigation is subsidized such that its price is P_S, below the equilibrium price. The quantity sold will increase from Q_E to Q_S.

In order to analyze the welfare effects, we also need to account for the negative externalities. The true marginal social cost of irrigation water is represented by the curve MSC, which includes the externality costs. For every unit above Q^*, the marginal social cost exceeds the marginal benefit (recall that the demand curve indicates the marginal benefits).

Figure 15.5 **Effects of Subsidizing Irrigation Water**

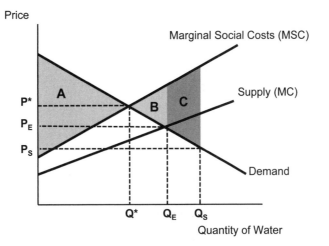

Area A represents the amount of net benefits of irrigation water at a quantity of Q^*. In other words, it is economically efficient to supply irrigation water up to Q^*. At the market equilibrium, Q_E, the net social welfare would be (A − B). At the subsidized quantity, Q_S, the net social welfare would be (A − B − C), a lower level of social welfare than at the market equilibrium. B and C represent areas of net loss resulting from a failure to internalize negative externalities and from subsidizing the price of water.

In this example, the maximum social welfare would be obtained at a quantity of Q^*. We could obtain this level of welfare by taxing water, as discussed in Chapter 3, instead of subsidizing it.

So far we have discussed water as if it has a single price. But the price of water varies in several respects. First, the price of water normally depends on its use.

Specifically, water prices charged by utilities are different for domestic, agricultural, and industrial users. The cost of agricultural water in the United States is approximately $5–$100 per thousand cubic meters.[24] Meanwhile, a typical household monthly water bill is about $20–$120 per month, which equals a cost of about $400–$2,500 per thousand cubic meters.[25]

While it may initially seem inefficient, and perhaps unfair, to charge different users different rates, there is some justification for charging agricultural and industrial users less than households. Household water requires a high degree of treatment because it must meet drinking water standards. Irrigation water is not required to meet the same quality standards and thus is cheaper to supply. After use, domestic water must also be removed for treatment. In many municipalities, households are charged a separate "sewer rate" for water disposal in addition to a charge for their water supply.

The price ranges presented above indicate that the price of water can vary regionally. Figure 15.6 shows the average monthly water bill in different American cities,[d] presented in relation to average precipitation. We might expect that water prices would be highest where water is the most scarce (i.e., precipitation is the lowest). While some arid cities, such as Santa Fe and San Diego, do charge high water rates, other dry regions, such as Las Vegas and Fresno, charge very low rates. This reflects the kind of government subsidy for water discussed in the example above.

Figure 15.6 **Average Monthly Water Bill vs. Precipitation in U.S. Cities**

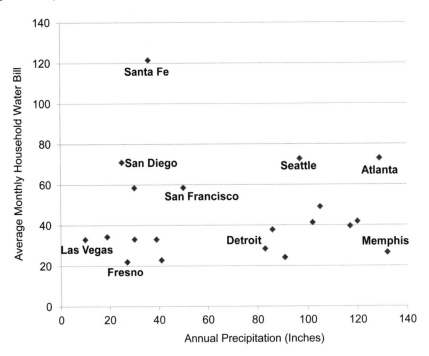

Source: Walton, 2010.

___

[d]Water bill based on a family of four using 100 gallons per person per day. About 264,000 gallons is equivalent to a thousand cubic meters.

Water rates in relatively wet cities can also vary considerably. In fact, there seems to be no discernible relationship between water rates and precipitation. Of course, other factors can determine water availability besides precipitation. Water is relatively cheap near the Great Lakes because they provide a low-cost supply of water. Some cities may have access to sufficient groundwater while others may not. Some cities can store water in reservoirs to keep supplies relatively constant throughout the year.

Water prices are generally rising, particularly in regions where supplies are scarce and population is increasing. Additional supplies can often be obtained only by relying upon relatively expensive sources such as desalination. As water levels in underground aquifers fall, pumping becomes more expensive. As mentioned earlier, the alternative to obtaining additional supplies is to manage demand. By raising prices, utilities send consumers a signal about the increasing scarcity of water.

Higher water prices will induce a behavioral response in households and other water users. Irrigators are more likely to invest in efficient irrigation methods. Households are more likely to purchase low-flow showerheads and wash cars less frequently. But how much will water users reduce their water consumption in response to higher rates? This depends on the **price elasticity of demand**.[e] The elasticity of demand for water tends to be inelastic, meaning that the percent change in the quantity demanded tends to be smaller in absolute value than the percent change in price.

price elasticity of demand

the responsiveness of the quantity demanded to price, equal to the percentage change in quantity demanded divided by the percentage change in price.

A significant amount of research has been conducted to estimate the elasticity of demand for water, particularly for residential users. A 2003 meta-analysis identified more than 300 elasticity estimates from 64 studies.[26] The mean elasticity was –0.41, with a median of –0.35. A meta-analysis of studies on irrigation water found a mean elasticity of –0.51 and a median of –0.22, based on 53 estimates.[27] A review of several studies on industrial water use finds that the elasticity varies considerably across different industries, ranging from about –0.10 to –0.97.[28] As expected, water demand also tends to be more elastic in the long run than in the short run.

Based on these estimates, water managers can determine how to adjust the price to meet conservation objectives. For example, suppose that a water utility is experiencing a potential water shortage and needs to lower water usage by 10 percent: If the elasticity of demand is –0.41, then the water utility would need to raise price by 41 percent to achieve a 10 percent reduction in quantity demanded.

But the relationship between water demand and price is not as simple as this example. One reason is that elasticity is not constant across regions or seasons. In the meta-analysis of residential water mentioned above, water demand tends to be more elastic in arid Western states than in the eastern United States. Also, water demand tends to be less elastic in winter months than in summer months. In the summer, more water use is for relatively nonessential purposes such as irrigating lawns and washing cars. In the winter, a higher percentage of total water use is for more essential tasks, such as bathing and washing dishes. So in the summer, households can more easily reduce water use in response to a price increase.

[e]See Appendix 3.1 for a discussion of the elasticity of demand.

Another complication in pricing water is that water commonly is not sold at a constant price per unit. In some cases, water users simply pay a flat monthly fee and then are able to essentially consume all the water they wish with no marginal increase in cost. While rare in the United States, in some countries, including Canada, Mexico, Norway, and the United Kingdom, water is not normally metered.[29] Where water usage is metered, there are three basic pricing structures, as illustrated in Figure 15.7:

- **Uniform Rate Structure**: The price per unit of water is constant regardless of the amount of water used.
- **Increasing Block Structure**: The price per unit of water increases as the amount of water used increases. The price is constant within each block, but the price per unit is higher for successive blocks.
- **Decreasing Block Structure**: The price per unit of water decreases as the amount of water used increases.

Figure 15.7 **Water Pricing Structures**

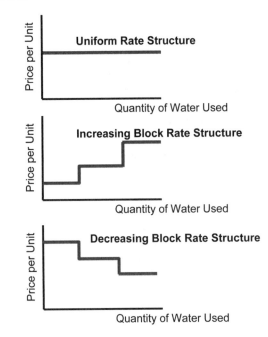

An increasing block structure encourages more water conservation, as water users will wish to avoid moving into the higher-priced blocks. The rationale behind a decreasing block structure is that it provides a price break for large water users, typically for commercial or industrial users. Water may also be priced differently by season, with rates normally higher during the summer season to discourage nonessential water consumption.

In the past, decreasing block rate structures used to be the most common pricing method for public water supplies in the United States.[30] As concerns about water conservation have grown, increasing rate block structures have now become the most common approach. In 2008, 32 percent of U.S. public water systems used uniform rates, 28 percent used decreasing block rates, and 40 percent used increasing block rates.

Internationally, rate structures vary widely. An international survey of water utilities found that in OECD countries, 49 percent used increasing block pricing, 47 percent used uniform rates, and only 4 percent used decreasing block rates. In non-OECD countries, 63 percent of water utilities used uniform pricing, and nearly all others used increasing block pricing.[31]

While an increasing block structure tends to promote higher rates of water conservation, other factors are also relevant when determining which rate structure and prices to adopt. Other considerations include:

- Utility rates are regulated; thus they cannot simply raise rates to induce a specific amount of conservation.
- Raising water rates disproportionately affects low-income households. Thus utilities may also try to take equity into consideration when setting water rates. In South Africa, the right to "sufficient water" is written into the constitution. This is operationalized by making the first block of water free (successive blocks are normally charged using an increasing block structure) so that even poor households can afford a baseline amount of water.
- Increasing block structures are somewhat more difficult to understand. Users should clearly understand when their usage moves into higher-priced blocks.
- Finally, raising water prices or changing the water rate structure may be politically difficult. While involving customers in rate discussions can increase support for conservation programs, utilities need to balance political feasibility with conservation objectives.

15.4 WATER MARKETS AND PRIVATIZATION

An economically efficient distribution of water implies that water should be allocated toward uses that generate the highest marginal values (i.e., the highest willingness to pay). In theory, transferring water from low-valued uses to higher-valued uses increases overall social welfare. At the efficient allocation, the marginal value of water would be constant across different uses, such that further transfers would not clearly result in a net increase in overall welfare.[f]

Table 15.1 provides estimates of the marginal value of water for several different uses, based on a review of existing studies from the mid-1990s in the United States. We see that the value of water can vary significantly among uses—highest for industrial and domestic uses, lowest for generating power and recreation/wildlife.[g] The uses are not all mutually exclusive. For example, water could be used for recreation and then further downstream for irrigation.

The table suggests that there may be some potential for reallocating water from relatively low-valued uses to higher-valued uses. However, the allocation of water in the United States and elsewhere is rarely determined by concerns about economic efficiency. Instead, water rights are allocated based on various historical and legal considerations.

---

[f]As mentioned earlier, we need to account for differences in water quality. The marginal WTP for residential water would not be equal to the marginal willingness to pay for irrigation water at the efficient allocation because the water quality needs of these users differ.

[g]Note that a large difference between the average and median values indicates that a relatively small number of particularly large estimates shifts the average upward.

Table 15.1

Marginal Value per Acre-Foot (AF) of Water in Various Uses

Water use	Average value per AF	Median value per AF
Navigation	$146	$10
Recreation/wildlife habitat	$48	$5
Hydropower	$25	$21
Thermoelectric power	$34	$29
Irrigation	$75	$40
Industrial	$282	$132
Domestic	$194	$97

Source: Frederick et al., 1996.

riparian water rights
a system of water rights allocation based on adjacent land ownership.

prior appropriation water rights
a system of water rights allocation in which rights are not based on land ownership but on established beneficial uses.

beneficial use
term used to refer to the use of water for productive purposes, such as irrigation or municipal supplies.

In the eastern United States, water rights are commonly allocated based on **riparian water rights**. Under this doctrine, the right to reasonable use of water is granted to those who own the land adjacent to a water source. Where demands exceed the available water supply, rights may be allocated based on the amount of water frontage of each owner. Riparian water rights generally do not allow for irrigation withdrawals or the transfer of water to lands nonadjacent to bodies of water.

While riparian water rights were initially applied in the western United States, by the late 1800s the water demands of agriculture and mining necessitated a different water rights system. **Prior appropriation water rights** separate the right to water from land ownership. Under this system, a right to water is recognized when someone establishes a **beneficial use** for it, such as for irrigation or municipal use. This system is also called "first in time, first in right" because rights are assigned on the basis of when a beneficial use first occurs.

Say, for example, that a farmer begins to withdraw 1,000 AF of water per year from a river. Then suppose that several years later a factory wishes to withdraw 5,000 AF per year from the same river. The farmer would be recognized as the "senior appropriator," and the factory (the "junior appropriator") would only have access to water after the farmer takes 1,000 AF. Anyone else who starts to withdraw water after the factory has established its right could still establish a prior appropriation right, but only after both the farmer and factory have taken their full allotment. In the case of a drought, if only 3,000 AF were available from the river, the farmer could get his or her full allocation of 1,000 AF, the factory would get the remaining 2,000 AF, and any other more-junior water users would get nothing.

Obviously, the doctrine of prior appropriation does not allocate water in an economically efficient manner. In fact, it tends to discourage conservation because if senior water right holders start using less than their full allocation, over time the amount of water associated with their rights could be legally reduced. Also, prior appropriation rights tend to make no allowance for ecological needs. Thus in the case of water shortages, ecosystems may suffer significant damage.

water markets
mechanism to sell water or water rights to potential buyers.

The creation of **water markets** has been proposed as a way to increase the economic efficiency of water allocation in the presence of prior appropriation rights. In a water market, water rights holders can sell some of their water to willing buyers. One example is a farmer who sells some of his or her water to a municipality. The municipality might buy the water in a one-time purchase (referred to as a lease) or could buy the actual water rights, which would establish it as the senior appropriator for a given amount of water per year.

As in any other market transaction, a water market in theory increases social welfare because both the buyers and sellers perceive that they will benefit from the transaction. But efficiency gains may need to be weighed against the impact of water markets on existing inequities. If poor people hold secure water rights, then water markets could provide an additional source of income. More likely, though, is that water could be directed away from the needs of the poor toward profitable uses by large-scale farmers, corporations, or other interests. For example, water markets were established in Chile in the early 1980s but led to higher water prices as a result of speculation and the monopolization of water rights. In 2005 the Chilean water market laws were revised to limit the potential for speculation and monopolization.

A water market does not necessarily require the direct transportation of water. An upstream water right holder could easily sell her rights to a downstream user. The upstream right holder would simply withdraw less water, allowing the downstream user to withdraw more. The sale of a water rights from a downstream user to an upstream user could also be conducted similarly. But in some cases a water sale may require water to be transported through canals or pipes. A fairly complex system for water transfers has already been established in the western United States. The California State Water Project and the Central Arizona Water Project are examples of engineering projects that transport water hundreds of miles to its final users.

The conditions necessary for a successful water market to form have been identified as:

- Water rights must be clearly defined.
- Water demand must exceed water supply. There must be some water users or potential users who are unable to obtain all water they seek at prevailing prices.
- Water supplies must be transferable to where water is desired for purchase and available when it is needed. Also, transaction costs must be relatively low.
- Water buyers must be confident that purchase contracts will be honored, with appropriate regulation and oversight.
- A system must be in place to resolve conflicts. This could involve both legal proceedings and less-formal resolution options.
- The cultural and social context must be considered. Some regions may resist water markets if most people believe that water is not a salable commodity.[32]

Water markets are in place in several countries, including Australia, Chile, South Africa, the United Kingdom, and the United States. An analysis of water markets in the United States identified about 1,400 water sales between 1990 and 2003.[33] Most of the water volume transferred involved short-term leases rather than outright purchases of water rights. Municipalities were the most common purchaser of water (normally from irrigators), but transfers between irrigators were also common.

About 17 percent of the water purchased was for environmental purposes, including purchases by municipalities and environmental organizations. The potential for water market transfers to meet environmental objectives, such as maintaining sufficient in-stream flows for wildlife habitat, is receiving increased attention. Some analysts see great potential for water markets to improve the environment:

> Overcoming [barriers to water market trades] is an increasingly important challenge as populations and western economies continue to grow. With this growth comes increasing demands for environmental and recreational amenities. . . . Removing barriers to trade will reduce transaction costs, promote more efficient water allocation among offstream and instream uses, create incentives for improved water use, and improve environmental quality.[34]

Even where environmental values exceed the values of other water uses, the proper institutions must exist to obtain the necessary funding. The problem is similar to our public goods discussion in Chapter 4. Voluntary contributions to environmental organizations can raise some funds to purchase water rights, but the presence of free riders means that environmental water purchases will be undersupplied to society. Also, water markets can harm as well as help the environment. Water transfers can degrade water quality and excessively deplete aquifers.[35] And as in any market, negative externalities may require government intervention to internalize the externalities.

Water Privatization

water privatization

the management of water resources by a private for-profit entity as opposed to a public utility.

A related issue is whether water should be supplied as a public good by government agencies or as a commodity by private companies. **Water privatization** has been promoted by international organizations such as the World Bank and International Monetary Fund on the grounds that private companies can provide more efficient and reliable service than public entities, particularly in developing countries. In theory, if a private company can provide water at a lower cost, then these cost savings can be passed on to customers, and perhaps more people can obtain access to water. But without appropriate regulation a private company may be able to charge excessive rates or fail to address the water needs of low-income households.

Water privatization has occurred, to some extent, in many countries, including Brazil, China, Colombia, France, Mexico, and the United States. The experience with water privatization has been mixed. According to the World Bank, water privatization in Manila, Philippines, has been successful in expanding water supplies to poor households:

> By expanding the provision of reliable and affordable services to customers, the program has benefited some 107,000 poor households since its inception in 1997. Near-to-regular access to potable/piped water supplies and increased community sanitation facilities has been achieved in low-income residential centers. Furthermore, the program established customer facilities to encourage communities to discuss and participate in the process of expanding services, and to resolve their concerns.[36]

However, in other cases water privatization has failed to deliver on its promise. Perhaps the most dramatic example was the experience in Bolivia.

> In April 2000, after seven days of civil disobedience and angry protest in the streets, the president of Bolivia was forced to terminate the water privatization contract granted to Aguas del Tunari, subsidiary of the giant Bechtel corporation. The Bolivian government had granted a 40-year contract to Aguas del Tunari in 1999.

. . . Water rates increased immediately—by 100 to 200 percent in some cases. Small farmers and the self-employed were especially hard hit. In a country where the minimum wage is less than $100 per month, many families were paying water bills of $20 or higher.[37]

Water markets and privatization are clearly not a universal panacea for water problems. The challenge is to ensure that markets and privatization operate in a manner to meet broader social and environmental goals, rather than simply maximize profits. For more on this debate, see Box 15.3.

BOX 15.3   THE NEW OIL: SHOULD PRIVATE COMPANIES CONTROL OUR MOST PRECIOUS NATURAL RESOURCE?

Nearly everyone agrees that global water supplies are being used unsustainably. Can privatization lead to more sustainable practices, with market prices motivating water conservation?

Privatization of water supplies has traditionally been implemented in developing countries. In the late 1990s the World Bank pushed scores of poor countries to privatize their water supplies as a condition for receiving desperately needed economic assistance. In several cases, most infamously Bolivia, private companies raised the price of water so much that poor families couldn't afford enough to meet basic needs.

But more recently emphasis has shifted to privatizing water in richer countries. "These are the countries that can afford to pay," says water rights attorney James Olson. "They've got huge infrastructure needs, shrinking water reserves, and money."

The need for better water management is especially acute in China. As groundwater demands increase in Beijing, wells dug around the city must reach ever-greater depths (nearly two-thirds of a mile or more, according to a recent World Bank report) to hit fresh water. With contracts to supply water becoming more lucrative, the number of private water utilities has skyrocketed. But in order to recover investment costs, companies have dramatically raised the price of water. "It's more than most families can afford to pay," says Ge Yun, an economist with the Xinjiang Conservation Fund. "So as more water goes private, fewer people have access to it."

The World Bank continues to promote privatization, noting that higher water prices are necessary to induce conservation. Public utilities rarely charge enough to reflect the true economic and social costs of water, which privatization advocates argue is the root cause of unsustainable water use. From the perspective of social welfare, even market prices are too low if they fail to account for externalities. But economic efficiency may conflict with the goal of equity. Privatization may work best when combined with policies ensuring that poorest can afford enough water to meet their basic needs, as in the South African system that provides a basic supply of water for free, with increasing prices for larger quantities.

Source: Interlandi, 2010.

SUMMARY

Water systems are under pressure from steadily growing agricultural, industrial, and urban demand. Many countries currently experience permanent water stress, defined as less than 1,700 cubic meters per capita available supply. Shortages will become more serious as population grows and climate change affects precipitation patterns and glacial runoff.

Increasing supply by pumping from aquifers has led to groundwater overdraft in major water-scarce areas throughout the world. Construction of dams also increases available supply, but most major dam sites are already being exploited, and new dam construction often involves major environmental and social costs. Desalination offers the potential to tap into a virtually unlimited supply of ocean water, but it is energy intensive and expensive.

Proper water pricing can promote conservation and encourage technologies for efficient water use. Government policies, however, often subsidize water, thereby encouraging overuse. Higher prices will reduce demand, but since water demand is inelastic, relatively large price increases are necessary to induce significant conservation. Well-designed price structures, such as increasing block pricing, can also promote conservation.

In theory, water markets can increase the economic efficiency of water allocation by allowing transfers from low-valued uses to higher-valued uses. Water markets can also be used to meet environmental objectives, although the results have been mixed. Privatization of water supplies has also produce mixed results, expanding affordable access in some situations while leading to dramatic price increases and reduced access in other cases. The evidence indicates that while both the private and public sectors have a role to play in meeting water challenges, regulation and institutions are needed to ensure that water is optimally managed.

KEY TERMS AND CONCEPTS

average-cost pricing	regulated monopolies
beneficial use	riparian water rights
desalination	water markets
hydrologic cycle	water pricing
micro-irrigation	water privatization
price elasticity of demand	water scarce
prior appropriation water rights	water stressed

DISCUSSION QUESTIONS

1. Suppose you were managing a public water utility facing a shortage due to drought conditions. What steps would you take in response to the drought?
2. Human demands for water can lead to an insufficient supply for maintaining natural resources such as wetlands and fish habitat. How would you balance the allocation of water between human and environmental demands?
3. Do you believe that access to safe drinking water is a fundamental human right? How should water be priced in developing countries, considering the potentially conflicting issues of affordability and conservation?

NOTES

1. See Figure 15.1; Postel, 1992.
2. Center for Strategic and International Studies, 2005.

3. UNEP, 2008.

4. Dore, 2005.

5. Postel, 1999, 42 ; www.fao.org/nr/water/aquastat/water_use/index.stm.

6. Aquastat, Food and Agriculture Organization, www.fao.org/nr/water/aquastat/water_use/index.stm.

7. OECD, 2012, 1.

8. Ford, 2012.

9. See www.un.org/ga/search/view_doc.asp?symbol=A/RES/64/292/.

10. Gleick, 2011, xi–xii.

11. http://wwf.panda.org/what_we_do/footprint/water/dams_initiative/quick_facts/. Large dams are defined as those over 15 meters in height.

12. See World Commission on Dams, 2000.

13. WaterReuse Association, 2012.

14. Equinox Center, 2010.

15. Elimelech and Phillip, 2011, 712.

16. Postel, 1992, chap. 8.

17. Equinox Center, 2010, 18.

18. Olmstead and Stavins, 2007.

19. See Hanemann, 2005, for a discussion of the value and price of water.

20. Recall the discussion of use and nonvalues in Chapter 6.

21. See Carter and Milton, 1999.

22. Whichelns, 2010, 7.

23. Stockle, 2001, 4–5.

24. Wichelns, 2010.

25. Walton, 2010.

26. Dalhuisen et al., 2003.

27. Scheierling et al., 2004.

28. Olmstead and Stavins, 2007.

29. OECD, 2009.

30. Tietenberg and Lewis, 2012.

31. OECD, 2009.

32. Conditions adapted from Simpson and Ringskog, 1997.

33. Brown, 2006.

34. Scarborough, 2010, 33.

35. Chong and Sunding, 2006.

36. World Bank, 2010, 2.

37. Public Citizen, 2003.

REFERENCES

Brown, Thomas C. 2006. "Trends in Water Market Activity and Price in the Western United States." *Water Resources Research*, 42, W09402, doi:10.1029/2005WR004180.

Carter, David W., and J. Walter Milton. 1999. "The True Cost of Water: Beyond the Perceptions." Paper presented at the CONSERV99 meeting of the AWWA, Monterey, February 1.

Center for Strategic and International Studies. 2005. "Addressing Our Global Water Future." Sandia National Laboratory.

Chong, Howard, and David Sunding. 2006. "Water Markets and Trading." *Annual Review of Environment and Resources* 31: 239–264.

Dalhuisen, Jasper M., Raymond J.G.M. Florax, Henri L.F. de Groot, and Peter Nijkamp. 2003. "Price and Income Elasticities of Residential Water Demand: A Meta-Analysis." *Land Economics* 79(2): 292–308.

Dore, Mohammed H.I. 2005. "Climate Change and Changes in Global Precipitation Patterns: What Do We Know?" *Environment International* 31(8): 1167–1181.

Elimelech, Menachem, and William A. Phillip. 2011. "The Future of Seawater Desalination: Energy, Technology, and the Environment." *Science* 333: 712–717.

Equinox Center. 2010. "San Diego's Water Sources: Assessing the Options." http://www.equinoxcenter.org/assets/files/pdf/AssessingtheOptionsfinal.pdf.

Ford, Liz. 2012. "Millennium Development Goal on Safe Drinking Water Reaches Target Early." *The Guardian*, March 6.

Frederick, Kenneth D., Tim VandenBerg, and Jean Hanson. 1996. "Economic Values of Freshwater in the United States." Resources for the Future Discussion Paper 97-03. http://www.rff.org/rff/documents/rff-dp-97-03.pdf.

Gleick, Peter H. 2011. *The World's Water Volume 7: The Biennial Report on Freshwater Resources.* Washington, DC: Island Press.

Hanemann, W. Michael. 2005. "The Value of Water." University of California, Berkeley, www.ctec.ufal.br/professor/vap/Valueofwater.pdf.

Interlandi, Jeneen. 2010. "The New Oil: Should Private Companies Control our Most Precious Natural Resource?" *Newsweek*, October 18.

Mascarelli, Amanda. 2012. "Demand for Water Outstrips Supply." *Nature* (News), August 8.

Olmstead, Sheila M., and Robert N. Stavins. 2007. "Managing Water Demand: Price vs. Non-Price Conservation Programs." Pioneer Institute White Paper, no. 39. http://www.hks.harvard.edu/fs/rstavins/Monographs_&_Reports/Pioneer_Olmstead_Stavins_Water.pdf.

Organization for Economic Cooperation and Development (OECD). 2009. *Managing Water for All: An OECD Perspective on Pricing and Financing.* Paris: OECD. http://www.oecd-ilibrary.org/environment/managing-water-for-all_9789264059498-en.

———. 2012. *Environmental Outlook to 2050: The Consequences of Inaction, Key Findings on Water.* Paris, France: OECD. http://www.oecd.org/env/indicators-modelling-outlooks/49844953.pdf.

Postel, Sandra. 1992. *Last Oasis: Facing Water Scarcity.* New York: W.W. Norton.

———. 1999. *Pillar of Sand: Can the Irrigation Miracle Last?* New York: W.W. Norton.

Public Citizen. 2003. "Water Privatization Fiascos: Broken Promises and Social Turmoil." March. http://www.citizen.org/documents/privatizationfiascos.pdf.

Scarborough, Brandon. 2010. "Environmental Water Markets: Restoring Streams Through Trade," PERC Policy Series, no. 46. http://perc.org/sites/default/files/ps46.pdf.

Scheierling, Susanne M., John B. Loomis, and Robert A. Young. 2004. "Irrigation Water Demand: A Meta Analysis of Price Elasticities,." Paper presented at the American Agricultural Economics Association Annual Meeting, Denver, August 1–4.

Schwalm, Christopher R., Christopher A. Williams, and Kevin Schaeffer. 2012. "Hundred-Year Forecast: Drought." *New York Times*, August 11.

Simpson, Larry, and Klas Ringskog. 1997. "Water Markets in the Americas." Directions in Development, World Bank, Washington, DC.

Strockel, Claudio O. 2001. "Environmental Impact of Irrigation: A Review." State of Washington Water Research Center. Pullman, Washington: Washington State University. http://www.swwrc.wsu.edu/newsletter/fall2001/IrrImpact2.pdf.

Tietenberg, Tom, and Lynne Lewis. 2012. *Environmental and Natural Resource Economics*, 9th ed. Boston: Pearson.

United Nations Environment Programme (UNEP). 2008. *Vital Water Graphics, An Overview of the State of the World's Fresh and Marine Waters*, 2d ed. Nairobi, Kenya: UNEP. http://www.unep.org/dewa/vitalwater/index.html.

Walton, Brett. 2010. "The Price of Water: A Comparison of Water Rates, Usage in 30 U.S. Cities." Circle of Blue, April 26. www.circleofblue.org/waternews/2010/world/ the-price-of-water-a-comparison-of-water-rates-usage-in-30-u-s-cities/.

WaterReuse Association. 2012. Seawater Desalination Costs. White Paper, January. http://www.watereuse.org/sites/default/files/u8/WateReuse_Desal_Cost_White_Paper.pdf.

Wichelns, Dennis. 2010. "Agricultural Water Pricing: United States." Paris, France: Organization for Economic Cooperation and Development.

World Bank. 2010. "Private Concessions: The Manila Water Experience." IBRD Results. Washington, DC.

World Commission on Dams. 2000. *Dams and Development: A New Framework for Decision-Making.* London: Earthscan Publications. www.dams.org.

WEB SITES

1. **www.epa.gov/gateway/learn/water.html**. The U.S. Environmental Protection Agency's water portal, with links to information about watershed protection, oceans, drinking water, and freshwater.
2. **www.unesco.org/new/en/natural-sciences/environment/water/wwap/wwdr/**. Web site for the United Nations' World Water Development Report, published every three years. Current and past reports can be freely downloaded.
3. **www.fao.org/nr/water/**. The Food and Agriculture Organization's water portal, with reports and links to a database of water information.

PART SIX

POLLUTION

IMPACTS AND POLICY RESPONSES

Pollution: Analysis and Policy

CHAPTER 16 FOCUS QUESTIONS

- What are the best policies for controlling pollution?
- How can we balance the costs and benefits of pollution regulation?
- Should industries be allowed to purchase permits to pollute?
- How can we deal with long-lived and cumulative pollutants?

16.1 THE ECONOMICS OF POLLUTION CONTROL

sink function
the ability of natural environments to absorb wastes and pollution.

One of the ecological services provided by natural systems is a **sink function**—the capacity to absorb waste and pollution. Although essential to human life and economic systems, this function has often been abused by excessive pollution. This raises two questions for environmental policy. First, how much pollution is acceptable—given that any society must emit some waste products? Second, how can we best control or reduce pollution to this acceptable level?

How Much Pollution Is Too Much?

optimal level of pollution
the pollution level that maximizes net social benefits.

You may think the answer to this question is that any pollution is too much. As noted in Chapter 3, economists think in terms of the concept of an **optimal level of pollution**. While some might believe that the optimal level of pollution is zero, economists would argue that the only way to achieve zero pollution is to have zero production. If we want to produce virtually any manufactured good, some pollution will result. We as a society must decide what level of pollution we are willing to accept. Of course, we can strive to reduce this level over time, especially through better pollution control technologies, but as long as we wish to produce goods we will have to determine the "optimal" level of pollution.

We've already discussed pollution as a negative externality in Chapter 3. According to the logic of external costs and benefits, an unregulated market outcome for a good that generates pollution results in "too much" production. The "optimal" level of production occurs when the externality is fully internalized, resulting in a lower level of production and a lower level of pollution. We can now broaden this analysis by considering the overall emissions of a particular pollutant, recognizing that the pollutant is emitted through the production of a wide range of goods and services. If the pollutant is unregulated, then firms essentially have no incentive to take steps to reduce their emissions. We refer to this unregulated level of pollution as Q_{max}, as shown in Figure 16.1. Firms can reduce pollution below Q_{max}, but it will involve costs such as installing pollution control equipment or substituting low-polluting materials. If firms must reduce pollution below Q_{max}, then a rational, profit-maximizing approach implies that firms will institute the lowest-cost pollution-reduction options first, then proceed to more expensive actions.[a] As pollution levels are reduced closer to zero, the cost of additional pollution reduction will rise. Thus we see in Figure 16.1 that the marginal cost of pollution reduction (curve MCR) rises as we move from Q_{max} to lower levels of pollution (i.e., moving from right to left).

Figure 16.1 **The Optimal Level of Pollution**

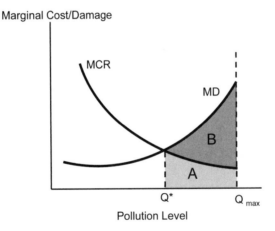

Next, consider the marginal damage associated with pollution. We will take air pollution as an example. Considering the concept of total economic value discussed in Chapter 6, this damage includes effects on human health, reduced air visibility, and harm to ecosystems. The first few units of pollution cause relatively little damage because ecosystems can process and break down a certain amount of pollution, and the levels are generally too low to have significant health impacts. Eventually, levels become high enough to start causing damage such as asthma, noticeable reductions in visibility, and ecological degradation. A small amount of automobile exhaust on a clear day may be a minor annoyance, but the same amount added to a smoggy area at rush hour could trigger significant breathing and health problems. Thus the marginal damage of pollution starts off small and grows as the level of pollution rises. This is represented by curve MD in Figure 16.1. Note that this curve can also be viewed as the marginal benefits of pollution reduction, or the avoided damage. Starting at Q_{max} and moving from right to left on the graph, there are very great benefits from the first units of pollution reduced

---

[a]Note that firms could also reduce pollution by simply producing less. We can assume firms will take the most cost-effective steps to reduce pollution, either by maintaining production levels but with lower pollution levels, or by reducing production and forgoing potential profits.

(since the damages caused by these units were very high), and the marginal benefit declines as cleanup proceeds.

At Q_{max} the marginal damage of pollution is high, while the costs to reduce pollution are relatively low. Social welfare would increase if pollution were reduced below Q_{max}. This is true for every unit of pollution above Q^*, which is the optimal level of pollution. At this point the marginal benefits of pollution reduction just equal the marginal costs. This balancing of marginal costs and marginal benefits is known as the **equimarginal principle**.[b]

equimarginal principle
the balancing of marginal costs and marginal benefits to obtain an efficient outcome.

The total cost to firms of reducing pollution from Q_{max} to Q^* is area A—the area under their marginal cost curve. The total social benefits of reducing pollution to Q^* are represented by areas (A + B). Thus the net increase in social welfare from reducing pollution is area B.

It is easy enough to find Q^* on our graph, but how can we identify it in real life? This is not so easy, because we are unlikely to know the shape and location of these curves with any precision. As we saw in Chapter 6, valuation of environmental damage is an imprecise science and involves many judgment calls. Control costs may be easier to estimate based on industry estimates, but they also are often uncertain.

Industries often estimate control costs that turn out to be too high once control policies actually go into effect. For example, the automobile industry has often argued that proposals to reduce tailpipe emissions would boost vehicle costs by a large margin. In practice, the implementation of significantly tighter vehicle emission standards has had little impact on costs.

Similarly, the electrical power industry predicted high costs for sulfur oxide (SO_x) reduction, but the real costs (as shown by the price of SO_x emissions permits, discussed below) were considerably lower. On the other hand, control costs can sometimes run higher than estimated, as has often proved the case for cleaning up toxic waste facilities.

Despite these uncertainties, the equimarginal principle is central to the economic analysis of pollution control policies. Even if we cannot define the precise goal, we know that it will be better to use efficient policies—those that give the greatest result for the lowest cost—rather than inefficient policies that bring relatively higher costs and reduced benefits. Economic analysis can help us to formulate efficient policies and analyze the advantages and disadvantages of different approaches. In the following sections, we consider possible options for pollution control policies from this point of view.

Picking a Pollution Control Policy

There are four basic approaches to pollution control:

Pigovian (pollution) tax
a per-unit tax set equal to the external damage caused by an activity, such as a tax per ton of pollution emitted equal to the external damage of a ton of pollution.

tradable pollution permits
permits that allow a firm to emit a specific amount of pollution.

1. **Pigovian (or pollution) taxes**: as discussed in Chapter 3, Pigovian taxes amount to a charge levied per unit of pollution emitted.
2. **Tradable pollution permits**: these allow firms to emit only the level of pollution for which they have permits. Tradability implies that firms can buy

[b]The equimarginal principle can also apply to marginal reduction costs for different firms or different techniques, as we will see in our discussion of pollution control approaches. Tietenberg and Lewis (2011) distinguish between the "first equimarginal principle" of equating marginal costs and marginal benefits at the overall social level and the "second equimarginal principle" of equalizing marginal reduction costs among firms.

pollution standards

a regulation that mandates firms or industries to meet a specific pollution level or pollution reduction.

technology-based regulation

pollution regulation by requiring firms to implement specific equipment or actions.

and sell these permits, with low-emitting firms able to sell extra permits and high-emitting firms able to purchase additional permits.

3. **Pollution (or emissions) standards**: standards require all firms to pollute below maximum allowable levels or reduce pollution to a certain percentage below a baseline level. These standards can also specify a given level of efficiency for products such as appliances and motor vehicles.

4. **Technology-based regulations**: these include requirements that all firms use a certain type of technology or install specific equipment.

There is no universal answer regarding which pollution control approach is the best. Different approaches may be preferable in different circumstances. In the real world, normally a combination of approaches is used.

In this chapter, we approach questions about the level and method of pollution control primarily in terms of economic analysis. At the same time, we bear in mind the limitations of a purely economic perspective. In dealing with the impacts of pollution, we may not be able to measure all the relevant costs and benefits in economic terms. This is especially true when multiple pollutants affect the environment, when cumulative ecosystem damage and degradation are at issue, or when subtle effects of persistent pollutants are poorly understood.

In such cases, economic analysis may not capture the full scope of ecosystem effects. Economic analysis, however, is essential for understanding how pollution control policies affect firms and individuals and the role that economic incentives play in altering behavior with regard to the production and consumption of pollution-generating products. We now consider each of the four pollution control approaches in more detail.

16.2 POLICIES FOR POLLUTION CONTROL

Emissions Standards

emissions standards

regulations that set the maximum amount of pollutants that may be legally emitted by an industrial facility or product.

Setting **emissions standards** is a common approach to reducing pollution. Government departments such as the Environmental Protection Agency can set standards for particular industries or products, subject to legislative guidelines. Many people experience the use of standards at an annual automobile inspection. Cars must meet certain standards for tailpipe emissions; a car that fails must have the problem corrected before it can receive an inspection sticker.

What are the advantages and disadvantages of standards from an economic perspective? The clear advantage is that standards can specify a definite desired result. This is particularly important in the case of substances that pose a clear hazard to public health. By imposing a uniform rule on all producers, we can be sure that no factory or product will produce hazardous levels of pollutants. In extreme cases, a **regulation** can simply ban a particular pollutant, as has been the case with DDT (a toxic pesticide) in most countries.

regulation

a law that seeks to control environmental impacts by setting standards or controlling the uses of a product or process.

Systems that require all economic actors to meet the same standard, however, may have the problem of inflexibility.[c] Fixed standards work well when pollution-

---

[c]Some economists refer to government-set standards as **command-and-control** systems, comparing them unfavorably to market-based mechanisms. We avoid this terminology here, since it may convey unnecessary bias. Rather, we seek to evaluate different policies on their merits, without preconceptions as to which is better. Goodstein (2010, chap. 14) shares this reservation about the use of the term.

generating firms or products are relatively similar. For example, different models of automobiles are sufficiently alike to impose the same emissions rules on all. Light-duty trucks in the United States, including sport utility vehicles, must therefore meet the same emissions standards as passenger cars. But consider an industry with many plants of different sizes and ages. Will it make sense to have the same rule for every plant? A particular standard might be too difficult for the older plants to meet, forcing owners to shut them down. But the same standard might be too lax for more modern plants, allowing them to emit pollution that could have been eliminated at low cost.

Requiring all firms or products to meet the same standards is normally not cost-effective. It is cheaper for firms that can reduce pollution at a low marginal cost to reduce pollution more than firms that have a high marginal reduction cost. Thus requiring all firms to reduce pollution by the same amount, or meet the same standards, is not the cheapest way to achieve a given level of pollution reduction.

Another problem with standards is that after firms meet them they have little incentive to reduce pollution further. An illustration of this problem is the motor vehicle fuel economy program in the United States, known as CAFE (Corporate Average Fuel Economy). After automakers met the fuel economy standards, and consumers did not demand further fuel efficiency gains, automakers stopped trying to make further efficiency gains, as shown in Figure 16.2.

Figure 16.2 **CAFE Standards and Actual Average Fuel Economy for New Passenger Cars, 1978–2011**

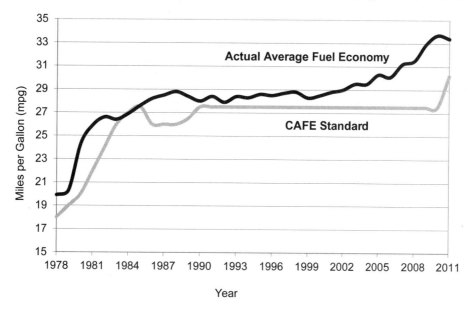

Source: U.S. Department of Transportation, 2011.
Note: CAFE = Corporate Average Fuel Economy.

In the late 1970s and early 1980s the average fuel efficiency of new passenger cars increased from about 20 to 28 miles per gallon (mpg) in order to meet a CAFE standard of 27.5 mpg. But the standard stayed the same for about 20 years, and during most of that period, the average fuel economy of new cars also stayed about the same. Only when gas prices rose in the later 2000s did average fuel efficiency increase in response to consumer demand and the awareness that CAFE standards were set to start increasing in 2011. For more on the recent increase in CAFE standards, see Box 16.1.

BOX 16.1   U.S. SETS HIGHER FUEL EFFICIENCY STANDARDS

In August 2012 the Obama administration announced new rules that will require automakers to nearly double the fuel efficiency of new vehicles by 2025. The combined corporate average fuel economy (CAFE) standard for cars and light trucks is scheduled to rise from 29.7 miles per gallon (mpg) in 2012 to 54.5 mpg in 2025.

"These fuel standards represent the single most important step we've ever taken to reduce our dependence on foreign oil," said President Obama. "This historic agreement builds on the progress we've already made to save families money at the pump and cut our oil consumption. By the middle of the next decade our cars will get nearly 55 miles per gallon, almost double what they get today. It'll strengthen our nation's energy security, it's good for middle class families and it will help create an economy built to last."

"Simply put, this groundbreaking program will result in vehicles that use less gas, travel farther, and provide more efficiency for consumers than ever before—all while protecting the air we breathe and giving automakers the regulatory certainty to build the cars of the future here in America," said Transportation Secretary Ray LaHood. "Today, automakers are seeing their more fuel-efficient vehicles climb in sales, while families already saving money under the Administration's first fuel economy efforts will save even more in the future, making this announcement a victory for everyone."

The new rules were endorsed by thirteen major automakers and generally considered a victory for environmentalists. While the new rules could increase the price of new vehicles by $2,000 to $3,000, these costs will be more than offset by projected fuel savings of about $8,000 per vehicle by 2025. In addition to the new standards, new incentives will encourage the spread of fuel-efficient technologies, including incentives for electric, plug-in hybrid, and natural gas vehicles.

The administration also said the new rules would cut vehicle greenhouse gas emissions in half by 2025, eliminating 6 billion tons of emissions over the course of the program. The program could generate hundreds of thousands of jobs by increasing the demand for new technologies.

"Our nation will be more secure, our environment will be cleaner, and consumers will have more money in their pockets as a result of the new rule," said Phyllis Cuttino, director of the Pew Clean Energy Program, an environmental organization based in Washington, DC.

Sources: NHTSA, 2012; Vlasic, 2012.

Technology-Based Approaches

best available control technology
a pollution regulation approach in which the government mandates that all firms use a control technology deemed most effective.

A second approach to environmental regulation is to set requirements that firms or products incorporate a certain pollution-control technology. For example, in 1975 the United States required that all new automobiles include a catalytic converter to reduce tailpipe emissions. While auto manufacturers are free to design their own catalytic converters, each must meet certain emissions specifications.

A similar concept is that firms adopt the **best available control technology (BACT)**.[d] An example of this is the Clean Water Act in the United States, which

---

[d]Various other terms are used to describe the "best" technology, including "best available technology" (BAT), "reasonable available control technology" (RACT), and "maximum available control technology" (MACT).

requires that effluents be controlled using "the best practicable control technology currently available."[1] Similar technology-based regulations have been enacted to control air pollution in the United States and the European Union. Technology-based approaches generally do take costs into consideration. For example, in the UK water pollution regulations require the adoption of the best technology "not entailing excessive costs."

The mandated BACT can change over time as technologies improve. However, BACT regulations may create little incentive for innovation. If a firm invents a new technology for pollution control that increases costs, it may withhold the technology from regulators in order to avoid a requirement that it be adopted.

technology-based regulation

pollution regulation by requiring firms to implement specific equipment or actions.

Perhaps the main advantage of **technology-based regulation** is that enforcement and monitoring costs are relatively low. Unlike a pollution standard, which requires that firms' pollution levels be frequently monitored to ensure compliance, a BACT regulation might require only occasional checks to ensure that the equipment is installed and functioning properly.

Technology-based approaches are unlikely to be cost-effective because they do not provide firms with the flexibility to pursue a wide range of options. Like compliance in meeting pollution standards, BACT implementation costs will vary among firms. Thus it is unlikely that a given level of pollution reduction will be achieved at the lowest cost. Technology-based approaches may, however, offer a cost advantage due to standardization. If all firms must adopt a specific technology, then widespread production of that technology may drive down its production cost over time.

Pollution Taxes

market-based pollution control

pollution regulations based on market forces without specific control of firm-level decisions, such as taxes, subsidies, and permit systems.

internalizing external costs/externalities

using approaches such as taxation to incorporate external costs into market decisions.

Pollution taxes, along with tradable pollution permits, are considered **market-based approaches** to pollution regulation because they send information to polluters about the costs of pollution without mandating that firms take specific actions. Individual firms are not required to reduce pollution under a market-based approach, but the regulation creates a strong incentive for action.

As we saw in Chapter 3, a pollution tax on emissions reflects the principle of **internalizing external costs**. If producers must bear the costs associated with pollution by paying a per-unit charge, they will find it in their interests to reduce pollution so long as the marginal control costs are less than the tax.

Figure 16.3 illustrates how an individual firm will respond in the presence of a pollution tax. Once again, Q_{max} is the level of pollution emitted without any regulation. If a uniform charge, or pollution tax, equal to T_1 is imposed, pollution will fall to Q_1. Producers will find it preferable to reduce pollution to this level, at a total cost of E, equal to the area under the marginal cost of reduction (MCR) curve between Q_1 and Q_{max}. Otherwise, if the firm maintained pollution at Q_{max} it would have to pay a fee of (E + F) on these units of pollution. Thus the firm saves area F by reducing pollution.

After reducing pollution to Q_1, the firm will still need to pay the tax on its remaining units of pollution, equal to areas (B + D). The total cost to the firm from the pollution tax is the sum of its reduction costs and tax payments, or areas (B + D + E). This is less than areas (B + D + E + F), which is what they would have to pay in taxes if they undertook no pollution reduction. The firm's response to

Figure 16.3 **A Pollution Tax**

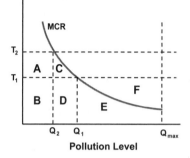

Marginal Costs/Tax Level

Pollution Level

the tax is cost-effective, as any other level of pollution different from Q_1 would impose higher costs.

If the per-unit charge is set higher, at T_2, producers will reduce pollution further, to Q_2. This will involve control costs of (C + D + E), and pollution charges of (A + B). The extra units of pollution reduction involve higher marginal costs, but so long as these costs are less than T_2, producers will find it worthwhile to undertake the extra expense and thus avoid paying the fee on the units of pollution between Q_1 and Q_2.

This cost-minimizing logic ensures that cleanup expenses are directed to wherever they can achieve the most. Here we have a different application of the equimarginal principle—marginal control costs are being equalized among all producers.[2] If the tax level reflects the true damage costs, it will also be true that marginal control costs for all producers are equal to marginal benefits from damage reduction.

We can note that the same goal of efficient pollution reduction may be achieved by the use of a subsidy for pollution reduction rather than a tax on pollution emitted. If producers are paid per unit of pollution reduced, they will make a similar judgment about the level of pollution reduction that is most profitable. For example, if a subsidy equal to T_1 is offered for each unit of pollution reduction, producers will find it worthwhile to cut pollution to Q_1, paying area E in control costs but collecting (E + F) in subsidy for a net profit of F. This has the same policy effect as a tax of T_1, but a different distributional implication. Rather than collecting revenues (B + D), the government pays (E + F), leaving the producers better off by (B + D + E + F). Politically, this approach may be more acceptable to industry, but it may also make pollution control unacceptably costly in terms of government budgets.

We can use a simple mathematical example to further demonstrate how a firm will respond in the presence of a pollution tax. Suppose a firm has a marginal cost of pollution reduction of:

$$MCR = 30 + 2Q$$

where Q is the quantity of pollution reduced, in tons, relative to Q_{max} (the amount of pollution emitted in the absence of regulation). Thus without any regulation, Q would be zero. Let's assume that Q_{max} is 100 tons. We can draw the firm's MCR

Figure 16.4 **Pollution Tax Example**

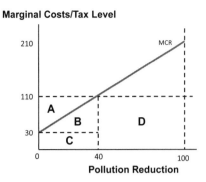

curve in Figure 16.4. Note that in this case we have reversed the *x*-axis—we are measuring *pollution reduction* rather than the level of pollution. So the maximum potential pollution reduction is 100 tons, going left to right.

Suppose that a pollution tax of $110 per ton is enacted. If the firm did not reduce its pollution at all, it would have to pay $110 for all 100 tons of pollution, or $11,000. This is shown as areas (A + B + C + D) in Figure 16.4. But instead the firm should act in a cost-effective manner, reducing pollution as long as its reduction costs are less than the tax. We can solve for the optimum quantity of pollution reduction by setting the MCR equal to the tax amount:

$$110 = 30 + 2Q$$
$$80 = 2Q$$
$$Q = 40$$

Thus the firm will reduce pollution by 40 tons, leaving 60 tons of remaining pollution. The firm will still have to pay the $110 tax on 60 tons of pollution, or $6,600. This is represented by area D in Figure 16.4. The firm's total pollution reduction cost is the area under its MCR curve for each ton reduced, or areas (B + C). Note that area B is a triangle with a base of 40 and a height of 80 (110 – 30), and area A is a rectangle with a base of 40 and a height of 30. So we can calculate the firm's pollution reduction costs as:

$$Reduction\ costs = (40 * 80 * 0.5) + (30 * 40)$$
$$= \$1,600 + \$1,200$$
$$= \$2,800$$

Considering both its reduction costs and the tax, the total cost to the firm is $9,400, which is cheaper than paying $11,000 in taxes on every ton of pollution. Any other level of pollution reduction other than 40 tons will entail higher overall costs to the firm.

Note that firms with different MRC curves will reduce pollution by different amounts. Those with higher MCR curves will reduce pollution less, while those with lower costs will reduce pollution more. The effect of each firm operating in a cost-minimizing manner is that a given level of total pollution reduction will be achieved at the lowest overall cost. Unlike standards and technology-based approaches, pollution taxes are thus economically efficient.

Tradable Pollution Permits

Economic efficiency in pollution control is clearly an advantage. One disadvantage of pollution taxes, however, is that it is very difficult to predict the total amount of pollution reduction that a given tax will produce. It depends on the shape of each firms' MCR curve, which as we have noted is usually not known to policy makers.

Suppose that the policy goal is a more precise and definite reduction in pollution levels either throughout a country or within a certain region. For example, in 1990 the U.S. Environmental Protection Agency set a goal of 50 percent reduction in sulfur and nitrogen oxide (SO_x and NO_x) emissions that cause acid rain. What is the best way to achieve such a specific target, while also achieving economic efficiency?

One approach, used in the U.S. Clean Air Act Amendments of 1990, is to set up a system of tradable pollution permits. The total number of permits issued equals the desired target level of pollution. These permits can then be allocated freely to existing firms or sold at auction. Once allocated, they are fully tradable, or transferable, among firms or other interested parties. Firms can choose for themselves whether to reduce pollution or to purchase permits for the pollution they emit— but the total volume of pollution emitted by all firms cannot exceed the maximum amount set by the total number of permits.[3]

In this system it is also possible for private groups interested in reducing pollution to purchase permits and permanently retire them, thus reducing total emissions below the original target level. The permits may expire after a given time period, after which fewer new permits could be issued, resulting in lower overall pollution levels. Figure 16.5 illustrates a simplified version of a tradable permit system.

Figure 16.5 **A Tradable Pollution Permit System**

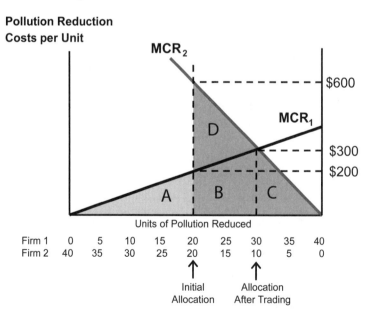

In this simplified example, we have assumed that there are only two firms, each emitting 50 units of pollution before any regulation, for total emissions of 100 units. The policy goal is a total reduction of 40 units of pollution. The sum of the reductions by the two firms must therefore equal 40. Figure 16.5 shows the different ways in which a total reduction of 40 units can be distributed between the two firms, as measured along the x-axis. Note that every point on the x-axis represents a total reduction of 40 units, but split in different ways among the two firms.

The marginal reduction costs for the two firms differ. The MCR curves for the two firms are plotted in different directions on the same axis, with pollution reduction by Firm 1 going from left to right and by Firm 2 from right to left. This is merely a graphical trick to make it easy to identify the point at which the equimarginal principle is satisfied (i.e., the point at which the marginal control costs for the two firms are equal).

Before the permit trading system is put in place, the two firms together are emitting 100 units of pollution. To achieve the reduction goal of 40 units, a total of 60 pollution permits must be issued. Suppose that the initial allocation of permits is 30 to each firm. If permits cannot be traded, each firm must cut back its emission from 50 to 30—a reduction of 20. This is shown in the middle of the graph (the "Initial Allocation"). At this point, the marginal control cost is $200 for Firm 1 and $600 for Firm 2. This is the same result that would occur if a uniform regulation limited each firm to a maximum of 30 emissions units.

This result achieves the policy goal in terms of emissions reductions, but it is economically inefficient. Each firm's total control cost can be seen on the graph as the area under their MCR curve.[e] Since the MCR curves are linear, each firm's total reduction costs equal the area of a triangle. Firm 1's total cost for pollution reduction is shown as area A, which equals:

$$Firm\ 1\ reduction\ costs = 20 * 200 * 0.5$$
$$= \$2,000$$

Total reduction costs for Firm 2 are represented by areas (B + C + D), or:

$$Firm\ 2\ reduction\ costs = 20 * 600 * 0.5$$
$$= \$6,000$$

The combined cost to achieve 40 units of pollution reduction is (A + B + C + D), or $8,000.

Now let's suppose that the firms are allowed to trade permits. Firm 2 is incurring relatively high marginal costs to reduce pollution by 20 units. At the margin, it must spend $600 to achieve the last unit of reduction. Thus it would be willing to spend up to $600 to purchase an additional permit so that it does not have to reduce pollution so much. Would Firm 1 be willing to sell a permit to Firm 2? If Firm 1 sells one pollution permit, it would then have to reduce its pollution by an additional unit to avoid exceeding its allowance. We see that at the margin it would cost Firm 1 about $200 to reduce its pollution by one more unit (from 20 units of reduction to 21 units). So Firm 1 would require at least $200 in compensation to sell a permit.

Because Firm 1 needs a minimum of $200 to sell a permit, and Firm 2 is willing to pay up to $600, we have considerable space in which to negotiate an agreement. Note that this is essentially the same situation that we had in Chapter 3 with the Coase Theorem.

---

[e]In mathematical terms, Total Cost = TC = $\int$ [0 to q] $MC\ dq$, where q is units of pollution reduced.

Firm 1 will continue to offer permits for sale to Firm 2 as long as it can receive a price greater than its reduction costs. Firm 2 will continue to purchase permits as long as it can buy them for less than their reduction costs. Trading will continue until the MCR curves are equal, with Firm 1 selling 10 permits to Firm 2 (the "Allocation After Trading"). Note that beyond this point (i.e., moving further to the right), Firm 1 would ask a price higher than $300 while Firm 2 would be willing to pay less than $300, thus no further trades can be negotiated. The price for the last permit sold will be $300, which represents the marginal reduction costs for both firms at the point where Firm 1 is reducing pollution by 30 units and Firm 2 by 10 units. For simplicity, assume that all permits sell for the equilibrium price of $300 each.

We can now compare the total costs to each firm before and after trading, as shown in Table 16.1. At the new equilibrium, total reduction costs for Firm 1 are represented by the triangle (A + B), which is equal to:

$$Firm\ 1\ reduction\ costs = 30 * 300 * 0.5$$
$$= \$4,500$$

However, Firm 1 also receives $300 per permit for 10 permits, for an income of $3,000. Thus Firm 1's net costs are only $1,500, as shown in Table 16.1. Compared to their pre-trading costs of $2,000, Firm 1 is now better by $500.

Firm 2's reduction costs at the new equilibrium are represented by triangle C, which is equal to:

$$Firm\ 2\ reduction\ costs = 10 * 300 * 0.5$$
$$= \$1,500$$

But Firm 2 must also purchase 10 permits, for an additional cost of $3,000. Thus Firm 2's total costs are $4,500. Firm 2 is also better off than before trading, when its costs were $6,000.

As the permit trades are simply a transfer of income across the two firms, not an additional total cost, the total reduction costs after trading are now $6,000. The same pollution reduction goal has now been achieved at a lower cost as a result

---

Table 16.1

Cost Efficiency of a Tradable Permit System

	Before trading	
	Units reduced	Reduction costs
Firm 1	20	$2,000
Firm 2	20	$6,000
Total	40	$8,000

	After trading			
	Units reduced	Reduction costs	Permit income or cost	Net costs
Firm 1	30	$4,500	+ $3,000	$1,500
Firm 2	10	$1,500	− $3,000	$4,500
Total	40	$6,000	0	$6,000

of trading. Area D (equal to $2,000) represents the net savings from this more efficient solution.

In a sense, a tradable permit system combines the advantages of direct regulation and an emissions tax. It allows policy makers to set a definite limit on total pollution levels, while using the market process to seek an efficient (i.e., cost minimizing) method of achieving the goal. It is economically advantageous for the firms involved, as our example shows, achieving a given amount of pollution reduction for the minimum economic cost. In addition, other interested parties can strengthen pollution control by purchasing and retiring permits, and pollution controls can be tightened over time by reducing the overall number of permits issued.

The trading equilibrium shown in Figure 16.5 is consistent with the equimarginal principle, because at the trading equilibrium the marginal reduction costs for all firms are equal. For simplicity, our example used only two firms, but the principle can easily apply to an industry with many firms. Firms will benefit by purchasing permits whenever the permit price is below their marginal reduction costs or selling permits whenever the permit price exceeds these costs.

It does not necessarily follow, however, that a tradable permit system is always the ideal pollution control policy. Tradable permits have been used successfully for sulfur dioxide reduction under the Clean Air Act Amendments of 1990 and have been widely discussed as a tool for reduction of global carbon dioxide emissions (for more on the sulfur dioxide trading program, see Box 16.2). But numerous factors must be considered in deciding whether pollution taxes, permits, technology-based approaches, or direct regulation are the best policy tools for a particular goal. We now consider some of the factors to keep in mind when deciding which pollution policy approach may be most effective in a particular circumstance.

BOX 16.2 SULFUR DIOXIDE EMISSIONS TRADING

The 1990 Clean Air Act Amendments created a national program to allow trading and banking of sulfur dioxide (SO_2) emissions, the primary cause of acid rain. The program applies to more than 2,000 large electricity plants, which must hold permits in order to emit SO_2. Most permits are freely allocated to plants based on their capacity to generate electricity. About 3 percent of the permits are auctioned off every year. Permits may then be traded, normally with brokers facilitating trades. While most trades occur between two electricity-generating plants, some permits are purchased by environmental groups or individuals (and even environmental economics classes!) and then "retired" to reduce the overall quantity of SO_2 emissions.

Economic theory suggests that a system of tradable permits can reduce pollution at a lower overall cost than a uniform standard. Dallas Burtraw, an economist with Resources for the Future, notes that the "SO_2 allowance market presents the first real test of economists' advice, and therefore merits careful evaluation" (2000, p. 2). After about twenty years in operation, how has the program performed?

To evaluate the policy, the effects of emissions trading must be isolated from other factors. Declining prices for low-sulfur coal in the 1990s and technological advances would have reduced the cost of lowering emissions even without a trading system. Economic simulation models comparing the SO_2 program to an emissions standard suggest that the cost savings from trading were about 50 percent. The savings are even greater than in a technology-based approach.

(continued)

The emissions targets of the SO_2 program have been met at lower cost than originally anticipated. Acidification problems in the northeastern states, widespread in the past, have declined. However, aquatic systems in the southeastern states are expected to continue to decline without further emissions reductions. And while the program has been effective, analysis of the marginal benefits and marginal costs of emissions suggests that further emissions reductions would produce even larger net benefits.

Burtraw concludes that the SO_2 market has "been liquid and active, and according to most observers [has] worked well in achieving the emissions caps at less cost than would have been achieved with traditional approaches to regulation. There is evidence that both process and patentable types of innovation are attributable to the [SO_2 program]. At the same time, there is evidence that some cost savings have not been realized. Moreover, despite substantial emissions reductions, ultimate environmental goals have not been achieved" (Burtraw and Szambelan, 2009, p. 2).

Sources: Burtraw, 2000; Burtraw and Szambelan, 2009.

16.3 THE SCALE OF POLLUTION IMPACTS

nonlinear or threshold effects

pollution damages that are not linearly correlated with pollution levels.

One of the major questions in formulating effective pollution control policies is the nature of the pollution involved. Are its effects primarily local, regional, or global? Do the effects increase linearly with the amount of pollutant, are there **nonlinear** or **threshold** effects? (See Figure 16.6.)

Figure 16.6   **Linear and Nonlinear/Threshold Pollution Damage Effects**

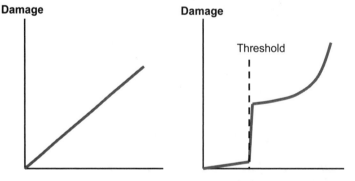

(a) Pollutant with Linear Damage Effect

(b) Pollutant with Nonlinear and Threshold Damage Effects

Consider, for example, a heavy metal pollutant such as lead. If a production facility is emitting lead as a pollutant, those living in the vicinity of the plant face a grave health threat. A small amount of lead in the blood can lead to serious neurological and mental damage, especially in children. We can say that the threshold for acceptable levels of lead in the environment is low, and above this threshold damage can be severe (Figure 16.6b).

Another important factor in this case is the distribution of the pollutant's impact. Lead can be a **local pollutant**, meaning that its health and ecosystem impacts occur relatively close to where it is emitted into the environment.[f]

Market mechanisms such as pollution taxes or permits are generally ineffective in preventing damage from lead pollution. Under a permit system, a high-polluting but profitable plant could simply purchase permits and continue polluting, with serious consequences for local residents if concentrations are above the threshold level. Similarly, the managers of such a plant might choose to pay a pollution tax rather than cut back emissions. These market-based systems might achieve regional or national control of overall lead emissions, but they would fail to protect local residents. In a case like this, regulations must specify strong emissions standards for *every* plant in order to protect the public. A technology-based approach could also work for a local pollutant, as long as it keeps pollution concentrations to an acceptable level. For some widely used substances, such as leaded gasoline or lead paint, complete prohibition is the only effective policy.

Market-based policies work better in the case of regional and global pollutants. Sulfur oxides (SO_x) are **regional pollutants**. These gases, which contribute to acid rain, are emitted by many facilities, especially coal- and oil-fired power plants. They are carried by the wind over wide areas, creating regional pollution. In devising policies to limit these regional damages, it makes little difference which sources reduce pollution output, provided that the desired reduction targets are met over a region. This is therefore a good case for the application of a tax or permit scheme.

As we have noted, the Clean Air Act Amendments of 1990 used tradable permits with successful results. Considerable overall reduction in SO_x emissions has been achieved, and the price of an emissions permit has fallen as emissions reduction technology has improved (see Box 16.2).[4] But tradable permits may not be the best choice in all cases. Even if they can succeed in reducing overall emissions, they may still allow high levels of pollution in certain localities. Here it is important to distinguish between **uniformly mixed** and **nonuniformly mixed** pollutants. A uniformly mixed pollutant is emitted by many different sources and has relatively uniform concentration levels across the region. Nonuniformly mixed pollutants may be emitted in varying concentrations and remain at different levels in different locations.

uniformly mixed pollutants
any pollutant emitted by many sources in a region resulting in relatively constant concentration levels across the region.

nonuniformly mixed pollutants
pollutants that cause different impacts in different areas, depending on where they are emitted.

hotspots
locally high levels of pollution, for example, surrounding a high-emitting plant; hotspots can occur under a pollution trading scheme.

Nonuniformly mixed pollutants may create **hotspots**, which are local areas with unacceptably high levels of pollution. While a tradable permit system specifies the total level of pollution, one or more firms in a local area may purchase an excessive amount of permits, leading to very high localized pollution. Similarly, firms with high MCR curves may choose to maintain pollution levels at Q_{max} and pay the tax on all emissions. Standards set at a local level or technology-based approaches are generally better at eliminating hotspots.

An example of a nonuniformly mixed pollutant is mercury. During the administration of George W. Bush, a tradable permit system was proposed for mercury emissions from power plants. The proposal was strongly opposed on the grounds that it would allow high levels of mercury pollution in the vicinity of some plants. The proposal was struck down in court, leading to an appeal by the Bush administration. But in 2009 the Obama administration dropped the appeal, in favor of more stringent standards for mercury emissions (see Box 16.3).

---

[f]In the case of leaded gasoline, the pollution is spread widely through automobile exhaust, and in this case lead becomes a regional pollutant.

BOX 16.3 OBAMA ADMINISTRATION REVERSES BUSH APPROACH ON MERCURY

In one of its early environmental policy decisions, the Obama administration signaled an intention to seek more stringent controls on mercury pollution from the country's power plants, abandoning an earlier approach by the administration of George W. Bush that the industry had supported. The Justice Department submitted papers to the Supreme Court to dismiss the Bush administration's appeal of the rule, which a lower court struck down in 2008.

Power plants are the biggest source of mercury, which finds its way into the food supply. It is commonly found in high concentrations in fish. Mercury can damage developing brains of fetuses and very young children.

The rule put into place by the Bush administration, but suspended by the courts, would have used a tradable permits scheme to allow some power plants to release more mercury pollution than others. States and environmental groups argued that this would create localized "hot spots" with high mercury concentrations. The law requires all facilities to install the best technology available to curb emissions.

In December 2011, the Environmental Protection Agency (EPA) announced a regulation that for the first time requires coal- and oil-fired power plants to control emissions of mercury and other poisons. About 40 percent of the country's roughly 1,400 coal- and oil-fired utilities lack modern pollution controls on toxic emissions; the new requirement is expected to prompt the closure of some of the oldest and dirtiest plants.

The EPA estimates the new regulation's safeguards—which are slated to take effect in 2014—will prevent as many as 11,000 premature deaths and 4,700 heart attacks a year by 2016 and will cost the industry $9.6 billion in compliance that year. By comparison, the agency projects that reducing these emissions will save between $37 billion and $90 billion in 2016 in annual health-care costs and lost workdays.

Source: J. Eilperin, "Environmental Protection Agency Issues New Regulation on Mercury," *Washington Post*, December 21, 2011; "Obama Reverses Bush in Case over Mercury," Associated Press, February 6, 2009.

Cumulative and Global Pollutants

cumulative pollutants
pollutants that do not dissipate or degrade significantly over time.

Pollution problems are often long lived. Organochloride pesticides such as DDT, polychlorinated biphenyls (PCBs), and chlorofluorocarbons (CFCs) remain in the environment for many decades. As emissions of such **cumulative pollutants** continue, the total amounts in land, air, water, and living things steadily increase. Even if pollution levels are reduced to zero, concentrations can remain at harmful levels for decades.

flow pollutants
a pollutant that has a short-term impact and then dissipates or is absorbed harmlessly into the environment.

The analysis that we have discussed regarding marginal costs of pollution damage is appropriate for **flow pollutants**—those that have a short-term impact and then dissipate or are absorbed harmlessly into the environment. For cumulative or **stock pollutants**, however, we need a different kind of analysis and different control policies.

stock pollutant
pollutants that accumulate in the environment, such as carbon dioxide and chlorofluorocarbons.

The issues of cumulative pollution are especially important for **global pollutants**. Carbon, methane, and chlorofluorocarbons emitted into the atmosphere last for decades and have worldwide effects. It does not matter whether a ton of carbon is emitted in the United States or China, as its impact will be essentially the same. Pollutants like DDT and other persistent pesticides also spread worldwide and are found in high concentrations in the bodies of people and animals in the Arctic, where these substances have never been used.

global pollutant
pollutants that can cause global impacts such as carbon dioxide and chlorofluorocarbons.

Polychlorinated biphenyls (PCBs), formerly used as insulators in electrical systems, have caused severe river pollution that remains a major problem decades after their use was banned. Methyl mercury absorbed by fish in rivers and oceans can remain for many years, becoming more concentrated as it moves up the food chain. As the importance of such issues increases, we must consider appropriate responses. Often these may be quite different from the policies used to respond to shorter-term air and water pollution.

Consider the case of ozone-depleting substances, which include chlorofluorocarbons (CFCs) as well as other chemicals, such as the pesticide methyl bromide. The damaging effects of CFCs were first identified in the 1970s, but many years passed before the scale of the problem was sufficiently well understood to motivate significant action on a global scale. These gases, used for cooling equipment, such as air conditioners as well as other industrial applications, eventually migrate to the upper atmosphere, where they attack the earth's protective ozone layer.

As the ozone layer thins, damaging solar radiation penetrates, causing problems such as increased incidence of skin cancer as well as complex ecological damage. Complete destruction of the ozone layer would end most life on earth, as few organisms could withstand the intense radiation that would result. Thus the problem is extremely grave, and alarm has increased as holes in the ozone layer have widened over the polar regions.[5] (See Box 16.4.)

BOX 16.4 OZONE LAYER FACES RECORD LOSS OVER ARCTIC

In spring 2011 the ozone layer reached an unprecedented low over the Arctic. From the start of winter until late March the ozone layer, which shields the earth from ultraviolet rays, thinned by about 40 percent, according to the World Meteorological Organization (WMO). The WMO blames the ozone reduction on the accumulation of ozone-depleting chemicals in the stratosphere and unusually cold temperatures.

The 1987 Montreal Protocol initiated a phase-out of ozone-depleting chemicals, including chlorofluorocarbons and halons, which were mainly used as coolants and fire retardants. The United Nations treaty, ratified by 197 nations, has generally been successful at dramatically reducing the emissions of these chemicals. However, they have long atmospheric lifetimes and recovery of the ozone layer will take some time. Thus even as emissions decline, the ozone layer has continued to thin. According to United Nations projections, the ozone layer will not achieve full recovery to pre-1980 levels until 2030–2040.

Source: "Ozone layer faces record loss over Artic," Associated Press, April 5, 2011.

To analyze the issue of ozone depletion, we must consider both emissions and the accumulated concentration of CFCs. Figure 16.7 shows the relationship between the two in simplified form. Unlike our previous graphs, this one includes time, shown on the horizontal axis. The top graph shows a simplified emission pattern over four periods of twenty years each. In the first period, emissions increase steadily. In the second, a freeze is imposed on emissions levels, with no further increase permitted—but emissions continue at the level that they had already reached. In

Figure 16.7 **Emissions and Accumulated Concentration of a Stock Pollutant**

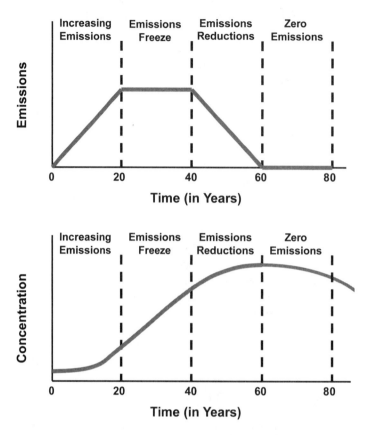

the third period, there is a steady reduction of emissions to an eventual zero level.[g] In the fourth period, emissions remain at zero.

Note the relationship between emissions and the concentration. As emissions rise at a steady rate, shown by the straight line in the first part of the upper graph, concentration rises at an increasing rate.[h] The concentration continues to rise steadily even when a freeze is imposed on emissions during the second period. Only when emissions are reduced to zero in the third period does the rate of increase in the concentration start to slow, finally reaching a maximum accumulation that occurs forty years after the maximum emission level was reached. And only in the final period, after emissions have been held steady at zero, do concentrations finally begin to decline.

This simplified diagram conveys the essence of the problem. Since damages are related to accumulated concentrations, not annual emissions, environmental impacts become steadily more severe, continuing for many years after control measures are taken. Dealing with cumulative pollutants requires urgent action and stringent policy measures. Even with such measures, irreversible damage may occur. The environmental accumulations on our graph may take many decades after year 80 before they decline to a safe level.

---

[g]For CFCs and other ozone-depleting substances, this is overly optimistic, since the goal of zero emissions has proved elusive due to loopholes in international agreements as well as illegal production and trade.

[h]In mathematical terms, this relationship can be expressed as $A = \int e\, dt$, meaning that accumulation can be measured as the integral of emissions over time.

16.4 ASSESSING POLLUTION CONTROL POLICIES

Policy Making Under Uncertainty

We saw in Figure 16.1 that the "optimal" level of pollution balances the marginal damages and the marginal costs of reduction. Pollution taxes and tradable permits can achieve the "optimal" level of pollution, but normally we do not have enough information to fully plot out the damage and cost curves. In the case of a tax, we may set the tax at the "wrong" level, leading to a socially inefficient level of pollution, possibly too much but also potentially too little. In the case of a permit system, we may allocate too many or too few permits, also leading to inefficiency.

In the likely case of uncertainty the choice between a tax or permit system is partially dependent upon the shapes of the marginal cost of reduction (MCR) and marginal damage (MD) curves shown in Figure 16.1. Even if we do not know the exact curves, we may know whether each curve is likely to be relatively steep or relatively flat. We can use this information to help us decide which policy would be preferable.

Suppose that for a particular pollutant the marginal damage curve is relatively steep, meaning that damage rises quickly as the level of pollution increases. At the same time, assume the per-unit costs of pollution reduction for this pollutant tend to be fairly stable, with marginal costs rising only slowly as pollution reduction increases. This is shown in Figure 16.8. Note that as in Figure 16.1 we again show the pollution level on the x-axis, rather than the level of pollution reduction.

Figure 16.8 **Pollution Regulation under Uncertainty with Steep Marginal Damages**

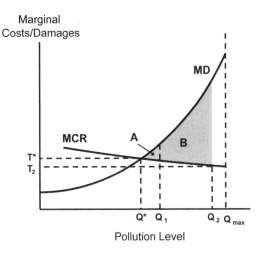

We know the optimal level of pollution is Q^*. We could achieve this by allocating a number of permits equal to Q^* or by setting a pollution tax equal to T^*. But suppose that we lack the information to determine either of these values accurately. First let's consider the impact of allocating the wrong number of permits. Suppose that we allow too much pollution by setting the number of permits equal to Q_1 instead of Q^*. For every unit of pollution between Q_1 and Q^* the marginal damages exceed the marginal reduction costs, so Q_1 is inefficient relative to the optimal level of pollution. The amount of the inefficiency is equal to area A in the graph. This represents a loss of potential benefits.

Now suppose instead that we institute a pollution tax but set the tax slightly too low, at T_2 instead of T^*. With a relatively flat MCR curve, a small error in the tax level results in a pollution level of Q_2—significantly more pollution than optimal. Now the unrealized benefits, relative to pollution at Q^*, are areas (A + B). Getting the tax wrong has resulted in a much larger inefficiency than allocating too many permits.

This pattern of damage costs might be associated with a pollutant like methyl mercury, which can cause serious nerve damage above a low tolerance threshold. In this case, a quantity-based control system would be a more effective policy. If we allocate slightly too few or too many permits, the inefficiency will be relatively small. However, a small error in a pollution tax could result in large inefficiency and a very high pollution level.

A contrasting case occurs when the marginal damage curve is relatively flat, but the marginal reduction cost curve is steep, as shown in Figure 16.9. Here, pollution reduction costs rise rapidly, while per unit damage is fairly stable.

Figure 16.9 **Pollution Regulation under Uncertainty with Steep Marginal Reduction Costs**

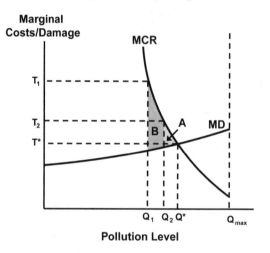

In this case, quantity controls pose the more serious risk of error. The ideal quantity control would be at Q^*, but an excessively strict control at Q_1 would cause a rapid rise in marginal control costs, to T_1, with net social loss shown by areas (A + B). But a tax policy could deviate from the appropriate level of T^* without having much negative effect either in excessive cost or excessive damage. For example, the impact of a tax policy with a tax level set too high at T_2 causes only a small deviation from the Q^* level, with net social losses equal to the small triangle of area A.

Industry spokespeople often argue that excessively rigid government regulations force high control costs for limited benefits. As we have seen, these arguments sometimes amount to crying wolf. But in cases where industry-wide control costs may genuinely be high, the use of a tax or pollution charge will allow firms to make their own decisions about pollution control. They will not be forced to undertake per-unit pollution reduction expenditures that are higher than the tax level, since they always have the option of paying the tax instead of reducing pollution. At the same time, the tax will require them to take account for the internalized social costs of pollution. For example, a tax on fertilizer or pesticides could encourage farmers to seek more environmentally friendly production techniques while allowing the use of chemical inputs where they are cost-effective.

The Impact of Technological Change

When considering the effectiveness of different policies, we should evaluate their relationship to technological progress in pollution control. The marginal reduction cost curves that we have used in our analysis are not fixed over time. With technological progress, control costs can be reduced. This raises two issues. First, how will changing control costs affect the policies that we have discussed? Second, what incentives do these policies create for the development of improved pollution control technologies?

Figure 16.10 shows how the level of pollution control will vary with different policies and technological change. Suppose that we start with control costs of MCR_1 and an initial pollution level of Q_{max}. A pollution tax at the level T_1 will lead to reduction of pollution to the level Q_1. A permit allocation of Q_1 permits will have the same effect, with a market-determined permit price of P_1. Now suppose that technological progress lowers control costs to MCR_2. How will firms react?

Figure 16.10 **The Impact of Technological Change**

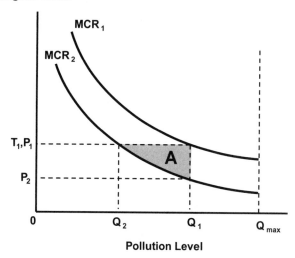

In the pollution tax case, firms will have an incentive to increase pollution control, reducing pollution levels to Q_2. By doing so they save area A (the difference between the new control costs and the pollution taxes that they were formerly paying on units Q_1 to Q_2). With a permit system, however, the result will be different. Given the lower control costs, the permit price will fall to P_2. (Recall from Figure 16.5 that the equilibrium permit price is based on firms' marginal reduction costs.) The total units of pollution reduced will remain the same at Q_1—equal to the total number of permits issued.

In fact, the permit system may have a seemingly perverse effect. If control costs fall drastically for some firms (those using newer technology), the permit price will fall, allowing plants with older technology to purchase more permits and actually increase emissions. This surprising effect of better pollution control technology leading to *more* pollution by some firms could, however, be avoided by reducing the total number of permits issued.

Both a pollution tax and a permit system create an incentive for technological improvement. But with a permit system regulators need to adjust the number of permits to account for changing technology. Since the level of a pollution tax is based on the marginal damage cost of pollution, it does not need to be adjusted as technology changes.

With a pollution standard, firms have an incentive to invest in technologies that may allow them to meet the standard at a lower cost, but they do not have a strong incentive to pursue technologies that may result in pollution levels below the standard. Finally, as mentioned previously, with a technology-based standard firms have little incentive to research new technologies, especially if these require higher costs.

Structuring Pollution Control Policies

A few other issues in designing pollution control policies are worth mentioning. First, under a tradable permit system there are two main ways in which to allocate permits. The first approach is to issue permits at no cost to existing firms, usually based on historical emissions. Obviously, polluting firms tend to prefer this approach because they receive something of value (the permits) at no charge. Yet by giving away the permits for free, the government misses an opportunity to raise revenues. Basing allocations on past emissions may also unfairly reward an inefficient plant. New firms, potentially with more efficient technologies, would be at a disadvantage because they would need to purchase permits on the open market from existing firms.

The second approach is a **permit auction**, in which permits are sold to the highest bidders. This has the advantage of bringing in government revenues that could be used to repair existing environmental damage or to lower taxes elsewhere in the economy. Tradable permits sold at auction would theoretically raise the same amount of revenue as an equivalent pollution tax. Under an auction, existing firms would not have an advantage over new firms.

A related issue is **grandfathering** of existing plants. This refers to a system in which strict pollution control regulations are applied to new plants, but existing plants are allowed to comply with less-demanding standards (or no standards at all). This is intended to avoid excessively high marginal control costs, but is clearly biased toward existing plants and is open to abuse.

When market-based policy instruments are used (i.e., taxes and tradable permits), an **upstream policy** is generally preferable. This means that the tax or permit applies as far upstream in the production process as possible, in order to minimize the administrative complexity of the policy. For example, consider levying a tax on petroleum. A downstream tax would require collecting the tax from over 120,000 gas stations in the United States.[6] But an upstream tax, at the refinery level, would require obtaining the tax from only about 150 refineries in the United States.[7]

Finally, issues of monitoring and enforcement must be considered when designing pollution control policies. Monitoring of emissions must be conducted to ensure

permit auction
a system that allocates pollution permits to the highest bidders.

grandfathering
the process of exempting existing industrial facilities from complying with new environmental standards or regulations.

upstream policy
a policy to regulate emissions or production as near as possible to the point of natural resource extraction.

compliance under policies of taxes, standards, and tradable permits. Monitoring is less critical with technology-based approaches, although inspections may be necessary to ensure that equipment is properly installed and operating. Major air and water pollution sources are increasingly being monitored using electronic equipment that provides continuous data on emissions. Facilities are also monitored using site visits from regulators, which can include interviews, review of records, collecting samples, and observing operations.

Regardless of which policy approach is taken, the punishments must be sufficient to deter violations. For example, the fine for emitting a unit of pollution without a permit should be substantially larger than the cost of a permit. In 2011 the U.S. EPA initiated over 3,000 cases against potential violators, collecting over $150 million in penalties. The EPA also brought criminal charges against 249 defendants (197 individuals and 52 companies) in 2011, resulting in jail time for some individuals.[8]

Summarizing the Advantages and Disadvantages of Pollution Control Policies

The most appropriate pollution control policy depends upon the circumstances. While pollution taxes and tradable permits are generally preferred by economists because they are efficient (i.e., achieving a given level of pollution reduction for the least cost), there are situations when these policies might not be the best choices. Table 16.2 summarizes some of the main characteristics of each of the four policy options.

Table 16.2

Summary of Characteristics of Pollution Policy Approaches

	Pollution standards	Technology-based approaches	Pollution taxes	Tradable permit system
Is policy economically efficient?	No	No	Yes	Yes
Does policy create an incentive for innovation?	Only for meeting the standard	Generally no	Yes, resulting in lower pollution	Yes, resulting in lower permit price
Does policy require monitoring?	Yes	Minimal	Yes	Yes
Does policy generate public revenues?	No	No	Yes	Yes, if permits are auctioned
Does policy provide direct control over pollution levels?	Yes	No	No	Yes
Can policy eliminate hotspots?	Yes, if localized standards	Yes	No	No
Other advantages of policy?	Allows for flexibility in meeting standards	Can lead to lower costs for the best available control technology	Revenues can be used to lower other taxes	Individuals or organizations can buy and retire permits
Other disadvantages of policy?	Possibly no incentive to go beyond the standard	Doesn't allow for flexibility	Taxes generally politically unpopular	Permit system can be difficult to understand

We have already discussed some of these characteristics, such as economic efficiency, the incentive for innovation, and monitoring. With standards and tradable permits, the government can set a cap on total emissions. With technology-based approaches and taxes, the resulting pollution level will be unknown in advance. Thus if the policy objective is to keep pollution levels below a known level with certainty, standards and permits may be the best options. But if encouraging innovation and minimizing control costs are major objectives, a pollution tax may be preferable.

Enacting pollution taxes can be politically difficult, especially in the United States, where new taxes are normally unpopular. In theory, a pollution tax can be **revenue-neutral** if the revenues from the tax are offset by lowering other taxes—but this may or may not occur in practice. Tradable permit systems tend to be more politically popular, especially if firms believe they can lobby policy makers to receive free permits. But a system of permit allocations can result in a large transfer from consumers (who will pay higher prices) to companies that receive the valuable permits. If the permits are fully auctioned, however, the government can use the auction revenues to compensate ratepayers, or to lower other taxes.

16.5 POLLUTION CONTROL POLICIES IN PRACTICE

In this section, we look at policies that have been enacted to regulate pollution, with a focus on the United States. Early pollution regulations in the 1960s and 1970s primarily used standards and technology-based approaches. Market-based approaches have become more common in recent years, particularly in policy responses to acid rain and **global climate change**.

Countries obviously vary in the stringency of their environmental policies. While it is conceptually difficult to compare pollution policies across countries, one measure that has been used to compare policies is the degree of environmental taxation across countries. Figure 16.11 shows environmental tax revenue in several countries that are members of the Organization for Economic Cooperation and Development (OECD), measured as a percentage of the gross domestic product (GDP).

Countries with relatively large environmental tax revenues include Denmark, Italy, the Netherlands, and Sweden. Among developed countries, environmental taxes are lowest in the United States. However, we should not necessarily conclude that the United States has the laxest environmental policies, as we need to consider other policy instruments, such as standards and technology-based policies. In fact, air pollution levels in the United States are slightly lower than the OECD average.[9] We now consider in more detail the pollution control policies of the United States.

Air Pollution Regulation

The major federal law governing air quality in the United States is the **Clean Air Act** (CAA), first passed in 1970 and significantly revised in 1990.[i] The goal of the CAA is to set regional air pollution standards to protect human health with an "adequate margin of safety."[10] The Act specifies that standards are to be set based

revenue-neutral (tax policy)
term used to describe a tax policy that holds the overall level of tax revenues constant.

global climate change
the changes in global climate, including temperature, precipitation, and storm frequency and intensity, that result in changes to the concentrations of greenhouse gases in the atmosphere.

---

[i]A Clean Air Act was passed by Congress in 1963, but this law only established funding to address air pollution, without any standards or other direct efforts to reduce pollution.

Figure 16.11 Environmental Tax Revenues as a Percentage of GDP, Selected OECD Countries, 2004

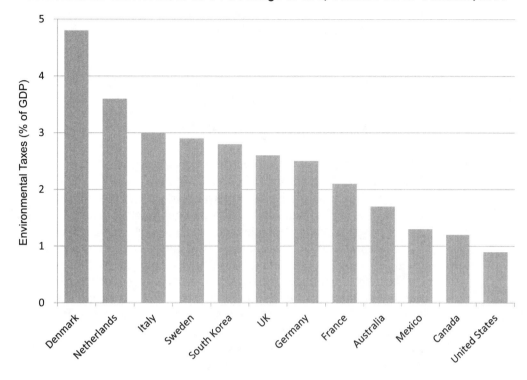

Source: OECD, 2007.
Note: GDP = gross domestic product.

criteria air pollutants

the six major air pollutants specified in the U.S. Clean Air Act.

on the best scientific evidence, explicitly ruling out cost-benefit analysis. The standards may be adjusted over time as more information becomes available.

The CAA divides air pollutants into two categories. The first category includes six major or **criteria air pollutants**: particulate matter, ground-level ozone, carbon monoxide, sulfur oxides, nitrogen oxides, and lead. Atmospheric concentrations of the criteria pollutants have declined substantially since the passage of the CAA, with an aggregate decrease of 68 percent between 1970 and 2011.[11] The decline in lead has been particularly dramatic; lead concentrations have declined 97 percent, primarily as a result of banning leaded gasoline. Despite this progress, more than 100 million Americans live in counties where the criteria pollutant standards were exceeded in 2010, mainly due to high ground-level ozone concentrations (also known as smog).

The 1990 CAA Amendments established a tradable permit system to address acid rain. The original objective of the permit system was to reduce emissions of sulfur dioxide (SO_2) by 50 percent by 2010, compared to 1980 levels.[12] The program is widely considered a success, with a decline in SO_2 emissions of 83 percent over 1980–2010 and costs significantly lower than expected (for more on the SO_2 trading program, see Box 16.2).

toxic air pollutants

harmful air pollutants other than the six criteria pollutants, as specified in the U.S. Clean Air Act.

The second category of pollutants regulated by the CAA is **toxic air pollutants**. These pollutants are emitted in smaller quantities but cause dangerous health effects such as cancer, birth defects, and respiratory damage. Examples of toxic air pollutants include mercury, arsenic, and vinyl chloride. Initial progress on addressing toxic air pollutants was slow, but the 1990 CAA Amendments directed the EPA to establish technology-based regulations for large sources emitting one or more of nearly 200 toxic air pollutants. The EPA has issued rules regulating more than eighty major industrial sources, such as chemical plants, oil refineries, and steel mills. These regulations have reduced toxic air pollution from large sources by about 70 percent, although further regulations are still needed for smaller sources and to address the complete list of toxic air pollutants.

Water Pollution Regulation

Clean Water Act (CWA)
the primary federal water pollution law in the United States, passed in 1972.

The main federal law regulating surface waters in the United States is the **Clean Water Act (CWA)**, passed in 1972 and amended in 1977. The CWA set very ambitious goals: to make all the country's lakes and rivers safe for fishing and swimming by 1983 and to eliminate all discharges of pollutants into navigable waters by 1985. While progress has been made, none of these goals have been attained, even now. For example, a 2007 assessment of the country's lakes found that 56 percent were rated as "good," 21 percent as "fair," and 22 percent as "poor."[13]

point-source pollution
pollution that is emitted from an identifiable source such as a smokestack or waste pipe.

The CWA primarily focused on **point-source pollution**—pollution from a definite source such as a drainpipe. The CWA relies upon both standards and technology-based approaches to regulate point sources. For example, it directs the EPA to specify the "best available technology" for various types of facilities. The most significant progress has been made in reducing industrial discharge. Major point sources of pollution must receive a permit to ensure they are in compliance with the CWA and report discharge to the EPA.

nonpoint-source pollution
pollution that is difficult to identify as originating from a particular source, such as groundwater contamination from agricultural chemicals used over a wide area.

The original CWA did not address **nonpoint-source pollution**—pollution from sources such as stormwater and agricultural runoff. Because of the diffuse nature of nonpoint source pollution, it is more difficult to control. Subsequent legislation has primarily placed the responsibility for regulating nonpoint-source pollution with the individual states, although the EPA has established numerous guidelines, such as suggested measures to limit runoff pollution from agriculture, forestry, and urban areas.

Other Pollution Regulation

Resource Conservation and Recovery Act (RCRA)
the primary federal U.S. law regulating the disposal of hazardous waste.

Other pollution regulation focuses on hazardous wastes and chemicals. The **Resource Conservation and Recovery Act (RCRA)** was enacted in 1976 to regulate the disposal of hazardous wastes. Under the RCRA, the EPA has designated hundreds of chemicals as hazardous, not just because of toxicity but also for other reasons such as corrosiveness and flammability. The RCRA requires "cradle-to-grave" tracking of hazardous materials, including any transportation of materials. It also sets safety standards for facilities that treat, store, or dispose of hazardous materials. The RCRA has been effective in reducing hazardous waste generation, which declined from about 300 million tons annually in the 1970s to 35 million tons in 2009.[14]

Toxic Substances Control Act (TSCA)
the primary federal U.S. law regulating the use and sale of toxic chemicals.

Regulation of other chemicals in the United States is covered under the **Toxic Substances Control Act (TSCA)**, passed in 1976. The Act gives the EPA the authority to review the safety of new chemicals and restrict the use of existing chemicals. Unlike most other major pollution laws, the TSCA does direct the EPA to consider economic costs and benefits explicitly when evaluating chemicals. For existing chemicals (those already in use before 1980) the burden of proof is on the EPA to prove that a chemical poses an "unreasonable risk." This essentially grandfathered the use of 62,000 chemicals, in most cases without information about potential health and environmental impacts. Since the passage of the Act, the EPA has required testing of about two hundred existing chemicals and regulated only five.[15]

The TSCA is more stringent in regulating new chemicals. The EPA must be notified when a new chemical is to be produced, providing time for the EPA to review the potential risks of the chemical. However, even then it is up to the EPA to request testing from the manufacturer, which is normally not done. Of the approximately 50,000 new chemicals submitted to the EPA under the TSCA, less than 10 percent have been subject to regulatory action such as additional testing or restrictions.[16]

In contrast to the United States, the European Union has enacted a significantly more powerful chemical policy that embodies the **precautionary principle** (see Chapter 7). Called REACH (Registration, Evaluation, Authorization, and Restriction of Chemicals), the policy places the burden of proof on chemical manufacturers to prove the safety of their chemicals (for more details on REACH, see Box 16.5).

precautionary principle
the view that policies should account for uncertainty by taking steps to avoid low-probability but catastrophic events.

BOX 16.5   EUROPEAN CHEMICALS POLICY

The European Union's ambitious chemicals policy, REACH, went into effect in 2007, and is being phased in over an 11-year period. According to the EU's website for REACH, one of the "main reasons for developing and adopting the REACH Regulation was that a large number of substances have been manufactured and placed on the market in Europe for many years, sometimes in very high amounts, and yet there is insufficient information on the hazards that they pose to human health and the environment. There is a need to fill these information gaps to ensure that industry is able to assess hazards and risks of the substances, and to identify and implement the risk management measures to protect humans and the environment."

Unlike TSCA, REACH applies the same safety standards to new and existing chemicals. Another difference is that the burden of proof regarding a chemical's safety is on the chemical manufacturers, not the regulating agency. If a manufacturer cannot demonstrate the safety of the chemical, its use may be restricted or banned.

Multiple manufacturers of the same chemical may join together to reduce the costs of testing. In addition to requiring testing for all new chemicals, REACH requires manufacturers to provide test results for existing chemicals. The initial focus has been on testing those chemicals produced in high volumes (greater than 1000 metric tons per year) or of the greatest concern. By 2018 all chemicals produced in excess of one metric ton annually will need to meet REACH's requirement that the chemical be registered, evaluated for safety, and been approved for manufacture. REACH's requirements apply to all chemicals produced in or imported into the EU.

The EU has estimated the costs of complying with REACH to be €2.8 to €5.2 billion ($3.6 to $6.7 billion) over 11 years. If the program reduces chemical-related diseases by 10 percent, the estimated benefits would be about €50 billion ($65 billion) over 30 years, a benefit/cost ratio of 10:1. An independent economic analysis of REACH concludes:

> Ultimately, REACH will provide the long-term benefit of helping to create sustainable industry and a healthy environment in Europe. As other parts of the world move to adopt similar standards in the future, European industry will gain the competitive advantage that comes from being the first to move toward cleaner and safer production and use of chemicals. (Ackerman and Massey, 2004, p. 12)

Sources: European Commission, 2006; Ackerman and Massey, 2004.

SUMMARY

The principle of economic efficiency in environmental policy implies a balance between the marginal costs of pollution reduction and the marginal damage of pollution. This has implications for both the level of control and the policies used to achieve it. Although the principle of balancing marginal costs and benefits is simple in theory, its application to real-world issues is often complex and involves judgment about both goals and policies.

Pollution levels can be regulated in four basic ways. The most commonly used approaches have been to set pollution standards and mandate certain technologies. While these two policies have certain advantages, economists tend to prefer market-based approaches, such as pollution taxes and tradable permit systems. With a pollution tax, the tax level should reflect the damage caused by the pollution. A pollution tax allows individual firms to decide how much pollution reduction to undertake. Least-cost pollution control options will be selected first. However, choosing the tax level requires an accurate estimate of damage costs, which may be difficult to determine in monetary terms.

Tradable pollution permits allow the setting of a target for total pollution reduction. The permit price is then set through the market mechanism, as firms trade permits. This, in theory, combines the advantages of a definite amount of pollution reduction with an economically efficient process. But it is only best suited for specific pollution control efforts under particular conditions, and may not be appropriate in all cases.

Market-based policies often fail to control pollutants that exhibit nonlinear and threshold damage effects, as well as pollutants with local rather than regional impact. Specific emissions standards may be needed for these pollutants, especially those that produce potentially severe health or ecological damage. Important considerations in the choice of pollution policy include the patterns of costs and damage as well as options for improved pollution-control technology. Policies should be selected with a view toward minimizing unnecessary costs or damage and promoting technological progress in pollution control.

Pollution policies in practice have led to major pollution reduction in some cases, but not in others. In the United States, emissions of criteria air pollutants have been significantly reduced since the 1970s, and progress has been made in reducing toxic pollutants. Water pollution policies have reduced point source pollution, with less progress on addressing nonpoint source pollution. For potentially toxic chemicals, the burden of proof in the United States is on regulators to determine whether a chemical is safe. Meanwhile, recent chemicals policy in the European Union places the burden of proof on manufacturers to demonstrate a chemical's safety.

KEY TERMS AND CONCEPTS

best available control technology
Clean Air Act (CAA)
Clean Water Act (CWA)
command-and-control policies
criteria air pollutants
cumulative pollutants
emissions standards

equimarginal principle
flow pollutants
global climate change
grandfathering
hotspots
internalizing external costs
local, regional, and global pollutants

market-based approaches
nonlinear or threshold effects
non–point-source pollution
nonuniformly mixed pollutants
optimal level of pollution
permit auction
Pigovian (pollution) taxes
point-source pollution
pollution standards
pollution taxes
precautionary principle
regulation

Resource Conservation and Recovery Act
  (RCRA)
revenue-neutral
sink function
stock pollutants
technology-based approaches
technology-based regulation
toxic air pollutants
Toxic Substances Control Act (TSCA)
tradable pollution permits
uniformly mixed pollutants
upstream policy

DISCUSSION QUESTIONS

1. How practical is the idea of an optimal pollution control level? How is it possible to establish such a level in practice? Can this be done solely based on economic analysis, or do other factors have to be taken into account?

2. Suppose that your state has a problem with pollution of rivers and lakes, from both residential and industrial sources. You are asked to advise on appropriate pollution control policies. Which kinds of policies would be appropriate? How would you decide whether to recommend standards, technology-based approaches, pollution taxes, or permits, or another policy? What factors (e.g., different kinds of pollution) would affect your decision?

3. Why is a freeze on emissions not an adequate policy response to a cumulative pollutant such as chlorofluorocarbons? What kinds of policies are more appropriate, and why is it often especially difficult to implement these policies?

4. What stories have you seen in the news recently regarding pollution policies? Considering the information that you have learned in this chapter, what are your policy recommendations in these cases?

EXERCISES

Two power plants are currently emitting 8,000 tons of pollution each (for a total of 16,000 tons). Pollution reduction costs for Plant 1 are given by $MCR_1 = 0.02Q$ and for Plant 2 by $MCR_2 = 0.03Q$, where Q represents the number of tons of pollution reduction. Analyze the effects of the following policies in terms of pollution reduction costs for each firm, government revenues, and total pollution reduction:

A regulation requiring each plant to reduce its pollution by 5,000 tons.

A pollution tax of $120 per ton of pollution emitted.

A tradable permit system in which permits for emissions of 6,000 tons of pollution are issued, 3,000 to each plant. Use a diagram similar to Figure 16.5, showing 10,000 tons of total pollution reduction. Indicate which firm will sell permits (and how many), and which firm will buy permits.

Are there different circumstances in which one of these policies might be preferable over the others? What factors should policy makers take into account when deciding on a pollution control policy?

NOTES

1. CWA section 301(b), 33 U.S.C. § 1311(b).
2. Tietenberg (2011) refers to this as the "second equimarginal principle."
3. For an in-depth account of the background and implementation of the 1990 Clean Air Act, see Goodstein, 2005, chaps. 14 and 17.
4. Sanchez (1998) discusses how the Clean Air Act promoted technological progress in emissions reduction; Joskow et al. (1998) and Stavins (1998) examine the operation of the market for emissions rights. Burtraw et al. (1998) finds that Clean Air Act Amendments benefits considerably outweigh costs, and Jorgenson and Wilcoxen (1998) evaluate the act's overall economic impact.
5. For details and data on ozone depletion and ozone holes, see www.theozonehole.com/polarozone. htm.
6. Number of gas stations from the U.S. Census Bureau.
7. Number of refineries from the Energy Information Agency (EIA).
8. U.S. Environmental Protection Agency, 2011.
9. Based on particulate matter (PM10) concentrations; data from the World Bank, World Development Indicators database. http://data.worldbank.org.
10. Information for this section is based on Goodstein (2005) and U.S. Environmental Protection Agency (2007).
11. http://epa.gov/airtrends/images/comparison70.jpg.
12. U.S. Environmental Protection Agency, 2002a.
13. U.S. Environmental Protection Agency, 2010a.
14. U.S. Environmental Protection Agency, 2002b, 2010b.
15. NRDC, 2010.
16. U.S. Environmental Protection Agency data as of September 2010, www.epa.gov/oppt/newchems/pubs/accomplishments.htm.

REFERENCES

Ackerman, Frank, and Rachel Massey. 2004. "The True Costs of REACH." Study performed for the Nordic Council of Ministers, TemaNord. http://www.ase.tufts.edu/gdae/Pubs/rp/TrueCostsREACH.pdf.
Burtraw, Dallas. 2000. "Innovation Under the Tradable Sulfur Dioxide Emission Permits Program in the U.S. Electricity Sector." Washington, DC: Resources for the Future Discussion Paper 00–38.
Burtraw, Dallas, and Sarah Jo Szambelan. 2009. "U.S. Emissions Trading Markets for SO_2 and NO_x." Washington, DC. Resources for the Future Discussion Paper 09–40 (October).
Burtraw, Dallas, Alan Krupnick, Erin Mansur, David Austin, and Deidre Farrell. 1998. "Costs and Benefits of Reducing Air Pollutants Related to Acid Rain." *Contemporary Economic Policy* 16 (October): 379–400.
European Commission. 2006. "Environmental Fact Sheet: REACH—A New Chemicals Policy for the EU." (February). http://ec.europa.eu/environment/pubs/pdf/factsheets/reach.pdf.
Goodstein, Eban. 2010. *Economics and the Environment*, 6th ed. New York: John Wiley and Sons.
Jorgenson, Dale W., and Peter J. Wilcoxen. 1998. "The Economic Impact of the Clean Air Act Amendments of 1990." In *Energy, the Environment, and Economic Growth*, ed. Dale Jorgenson. Cambridge, MA: MIT Press.
Joskow, Paul L., Richard Schmalensee, and Elizabeth M. Bailey. 1998. "The Market for Sulfur Dioxide Emissions." *American Economic Review* 88 (4) (September): 669–85.

National Highway Traffic Safety Administration (NHTSA). 2012. "Obama Administration Finalizes Historic 54.5 mpg Fuel Efficiency Standards." Press Release, (August). www.nhtsa.gov/About+NHTSA/Press+Releases/2012/Obama+Administration+Finalizes+Historic+54.5+mpg+Fuel+Efficiency+Standards.

Natural Resources Defense Council (NRDC). 2010. "Now Is the Time to Reform the Toxic Substances Control Act." NRDC Legislative Facts (April).

Organization for Economic Cooperation and Development (OECD). 2007. *OECD Environmental Data Compendium 2006/2007.* Paris: Environmental Performance and Information Division, OECD.

Sanchez, Carol M. 1998. "The Impact of Environmental Regulations on the Adoption of Innovation: How Electric Utilities Responded to the Clean Air Act Amendments of 1990." In *Research in Corporate Social Performance and Policy*, vol. 15, ed. James E. Post. Stamford, CT: JAI Press.

Stavins, Robert. 1998. "What Can We Learn from the Grand Policy Experiment? Lessons from SO_2 Allowance Trading." *Journal of Economic Perspectives* 12 (3) (Summer): 69–88.

Tietenberg, Tom, and Lynne Lewis. 2011. *Environmental and Natural Resource Economics*, 9th ed. Upper Saddle River, NJ: Prentice Hall.

U.S. Department of Transportation. 2011. "Summary of Fuel Economy Performance." NHTSA, NVS-220 (April). Washington, DC.

U.S. Environmental Protection Agency. 2002a. "Clearing the Air: The Facts about Capping and Trading Emissions." Publication No. EPA-430F-02–009 (May). Washington, DC.

———. 2002b. "25 Years of RCRA: Building on Our Past To Protect Our Future." Publication No. EPA-K-02–027 (April). Washington, DC.

———. 2007. "The Plain English Guide to the Clean Air Act." Publication No. EPA-456/K-07–001 (April). Washington, DC.

———. 2010a. "National Lakes Assessment Fact Sheet." Publication No. EPA 841-F-09–007 (April). Washington, DC.

———. 2010b. "National Analysis: The National Biennial RCRA Hazardous Waste Report (Based on 2009 Data)." Publication No. EPA530-R-10–014A (November). Washington, DC.

———. 2011. "Fiscal Year 2011 EPA Enforcement & Compliance Annual Results" (December). Washington, DC.

Vlasic, Bill. 2012. "U.S. Sets Higher Fuel Efficiency Standards." *New York Times*, August 28.

WEB SITES

1. **www.epa.gov/airmarkets/**. The EPA's Web site for tradable permit markets for air pollutants, including links to extensive information about the SO_2 emissions trading program.
2. **http://rff.org/Pages/default.aspx**. Web site of Resources for the Future, featuring many publications on the benefits of pollution reduction and different approaches for regulating pollution.
3. **http://ec.europa.eu/environment/chemicals/reach/reach_intro.htm.** The European Union's Web site for REACH, including Fact Sheets, background documents, and updates on the process of implementing REACH.
4. **www.edf.org/approach/markets/**. Environmental Defense Fund Web page on using economic incentives to improve environmental quality, with links to articles and videos.

CHAPTER 17

Greening the Economy

CHAPTER 17 FOCUS QUESTIONS

- Is a "green economy" possible?
- What economic theories provide insight into the relationship between the economy and the environment?
- Is protecting the environment bad for the economy?
- What policies can promote a transition to a green economy?

17.1 THE GREEN ECONOMY: INTRODUCTION

Economic and environmental objectives are often presented as conflicting goals. A common theme in political debates in recent years is that certain environmental regulations result in unacceptable job losses. Thus the choice is presented as being between improved environmental quality on one hand, and a robust economy on the other (see Box 17.1 for a recent example of this debate).

But is the choice this simple? Can't we have *both* sufficient environmental quality and plentiful, good jobs? In this chapter we explore the relationship between protecting the environment and economic growth. We'll consider the research on the topic to determine if there is necessarily a tradeoff between the environment and the economy. While protecting the environment clearly involves some costs, including job losses in some sectors, economists focus on whether the benefits justify these costs. Environmental regulations may also create jobs in some sectors—for example, environmental restrictions on coal plants may lead to expansion of wind power production. Thus it may be possible that at least some environmental regulations actually lead to net job gains.

Some recent policy proposals suggest that a well-designed response to current environmental and energy challenges can actually be the engine for future economic growth. Companies and countries that make the investments necessary to create a low-environmental-impact society may gain a competitive advantage over those that continue to pursue business as usual. In addition, excessive rates of natural capital degradation can reduce economic productivity, measured in traditional terms as a reduction in GDP, or in broader terms using the measures we discussed in Chapter 8. Thus maintaining natural capital may be a critical factor to ensure future economic growth.

BOX 17.1   KEYSTONE XL PIPELINE PITS JOBS AGAINST THE ENVIRONMENT

Clashes over the proposed extension of the Keystone XL pipeline took place throughout the Great Plains states as public hearings allowed supporters and opponents to make their case for or against what is proposed as the longest oil pipeline in North America.

A State Department environmental impact statement released in late August said the pipeline, operated by TransCanada, would cause minimal impact on the environment. Union organizations and business interests say the pipeline will reduce the nation's dependence on overseas oil and create jobs while environmentalists, local farmers and some state government leaders question the company's safety record.

Opponents of Keystone XL also say the government has been lax in regulating oil companies. Two examples from last year that were frequently referenced at the hearings: the Gulf of Mexico oil spill and another, smaller, spill in Michigan that polluted a 35-mile stretch of the Kalamazoo River.

At particular risk, they say, is the Ogallala Aquifer, an underground water supply that is the greatest irrigation source to the nation's farmland, supplying eight states. Because 65 percent of the aquifer is in Nebraska, the national fight is focused there.

Nebraska Governor Dave Heineman (R), who is against the pipeline, is asking the State Department to require TransCanada to reroute the pipeline away from the aquifer if it eventually wins approval.

In Atkinson, Neb. Thursday, Ron Kaminski, a business manager of Laborers' Local 1140 in Omaha, told the Associated Press his organization "believes deeply in the jobs [the pipeline] will create." Union representatives and workers who traveled long distances to attend the meetings expressed the same sentiment: that the U.S. should not dismiss an opportunity to create jobs, especially in a troubled economy. TransCanada says the pipeline will create 20,000 jobs and add $20 billion to the U.S. economy.

Detractors raised anxieties about the coarse mixture the pipelines will carry. Oil sands are more corrosive than crude oil, they say, which not only will make it more susceptible to damaging a pipeline but make it more difficult to mitigate the damage following a spill. TransCanada officials dismiss those claims, saying the Keystone XL will be thicker in construction, making it more durable, and will be monitored by sensors to ensure safety.

Source: Guarino, 2011.

---

green economy
an economy that improves human well-being and social equity, while reducing environmental impacts.

A more ambitious goal is to create a new "**green economy**" that embodies the concept of sustainable development. The United Nations Environment Program (UNEP) has defined a green economy as:

> . . . one that results in improved human well-being and social equity, while significantly reducing environmental risks and ecological scarcities. In its simplest expression, a green economy can be thought of as one which is low carbon, resource efficient and socially inclusive.
>
> [In] a green economy, growth in income and employment is driven by public and private investments that reduce carbon emissions and pollution, enhance energy and resource efficiency, and prevent the loss of biodiversity and ecosystem services. These investments need to be catalyzed and supported by targeted public expenditure, policy reforms and regulation changes. This development path should maintain, enhance and, where necessary, rebuild natural capital as a critical economic asset and source of public benefits, especially for poor people whose livelihoods and security depend strongly on nature.[1]

Note that the concept of a green economy does not necessarily reject economic growth, but instead seeks to foster growth that is compatible with sustainability. It explicitly rejects the standard jobs vs. the environment choice:

Perhaps the most widespread myth is that there is an inescapable trade-off between environmental sustainability and economic progress. There is now substantial evidence that the "greening" of economies neither inhibits wealth creation nor employment opportunities, and that there are many green sectors which show significant opportunities for investment and related growth in wealth and jobs.[2]

In addition to environmental sustainability, the green economy should promote social equity. Thus advocates of a green economy reject the notion that sustainability must limit the economic aspirations of the world's poorest.

Later in the chapter we'll discuss specific policy proposals to transition to a green economy, some of which build on policies mentioned in earlier chapters, such as removing fossil fuel subsidies and internalizing externalities. We'll also look at some empirical analysis that compares the economic and environmental performance of the green economy to a business-as-usual scenario. But first we turn to a discussion of economic theories of the relationship between the economy and the environment.

17.2 THE RELATIONSHIP BETWEEN ECONOMY AND ENVIRONMENT

We can study the relationship between the economy and the environment in both directions. We can look at how environmental protection impacts economic performance, or we can look at how economic growth impacts environmental quality. In this chapter we will consider both perspectives.

Environmental Kuznets Curves

First, let's consider how economic growth impacts environmental quality. Specifically, as a nation gets richer over time, how will this affect its environmental quality? The answer isn't obvious. On one hand, a richer nation is likely to use more resources, demand more energy, and produce more waste and pollution. On the other hand, a richer nation can afford to invest in renewable energy, install state-of-the-art pollution control equipment, and implement effective environmental policies.

normal good
a good for which total expenditures tend to increase as income increases.

luxury good
a good that people tend to spend a higher percentage of their income on as their incomes increase.

In economic terms, it is widely accepted that environmental quality is a **normal good**—meaning that people will seek to "purchase" more of it as their income increases. What is more debatable is whether environmental quality is also a **luxury good**—meaning that spending on it increases disproportionately as income grows. It may be that environmental quality is a luxury good over some income levels, and merely a normal good at other income levels.[3]

An appealing hypothesis is that economic growth will eventually provide a nation with the resources to reduce its environmental impacts. As a 1992 paper argued:

> . . . there is clear evidence that, although economic growth usually leads to environmental deterioration in the early stages of the process, in the end the best—and probably the only—way to attain a decent environment in most countries is to become rich.[4]

This notion that environmental impacts tend to increase initially as a country becomes richer, but then eventually decrease with further income gains, has

Environmental Kuznets Curve (EKC)

the theory that a country's environmental impacts increase in the early stages of economic development but eventually decrease above a certain level of income.

become known as the **Environmental Kuznets curve (EKC)** hypothesis.[a] This hypothesis proposes that the relationship between income and environmental impacts is an inverted-U shape. The concept is illustrated in Figure 17.1, based on actual data on sulfur dioxide emissions. We see that per-capita SO_2 emissions increase with income up to a per-capita income of around $4,000. But above that income level, SO_2 emissions per capita decline steadily. This is an encouraging result because the "turning point" occurs at a relatively modest income level. Thus a moderate amount of economic growth can lead to substantial SO_2 emission reductions.

Figure 17.1   Environmental Kuznets Curve for Sulfur Dioxide Emissions

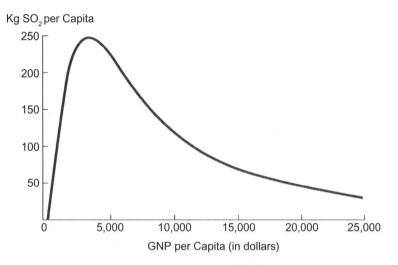

Source: Adapted from Panayotou, 1993.
Note: GNP = gross national product; kg = kilogram; SO_2 = sulfur dioxide.

While the EKC hypothesis seems to apply to SO_2, further analysis indicates that it does not apply to all environmental impacts. Perhaps most importantly, the EKC hypothesis does not match the data on carbon dioxide emissions (the primary greenhouse gas), as shown in Figure 17.2. The figure shows an attempt to fit an inverted-U trendline through the data.[b] The trendline shows that there is no turning point—per-capita CO_2 emissions continue to rise as per-capita income increases. A more sophisticated statistical analysis tested the EKC hypothesis for carbon emissions and concluded that "despite these new [statistical] approaches, there is still no clear-cut evidence supporting the existence of the EKC for carbon emissions."[5] Thus promoting economic growth does not appear to be a means to address the issue of global climate change.

The EKC hypothesis has been tested for numerous other environmental impacts. While it may be valid for some air pollutants such as SO_2, particulate matter, and nitrogen oxides, it does not seem to apply more broadly to other environmental impacts. A 2003 review of the evidence concluded that:

---

[a] The EKC hypothesis is named after Simon Kuznets, an economist who proposed a similar relationship between income inequality and economic growth in the 1950s.

[b] The trendline is a second-degree polynomial, which could show a U-shaped or inverted-U pattern.

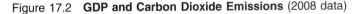

Figure 17.2 **GDP and Carbon Dioxide Emissions** (2008 data)

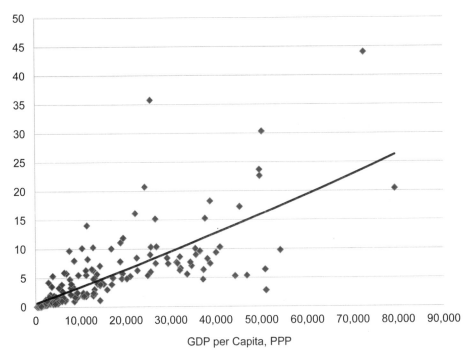

GDP per Capita, PPP

Source: World Bank, World Development Indicators database, http://data.worldbank.org/data-catalog/world-development-indicators
Note: CO_2 = carbon dioxide; GDP = gross domestic product; PPP = purchasing power parity.

The evidence presented in this paper shows that the statistical analysis on which the environmental Kuznets curve is based is not robust. There is little evidence for a common inverted U-shaped pathway which countries follow as their income rises. There may be an inverted U-shaped relation between urban ambient concentrations of some pollutants and income though this should be tested with more rigorous time series or panel data methods. It seems unlikely that the EKC is a complete model of emissions or concentrations.[6]

Even in situations where the EKC hypothesis seems valid, we should be wary of concluding that economic growth alone will result in environmental improvements.

Improvement of the environment with income growth is not automatic but depends on policies and institutions. GDP growth creates the conditions for environmental improvement by raising the demand for improved environmental quality and makes the resources available for supplying it. Whether environmental quality improvements materialize or not, and when and how, depend critically on government policies, social institutions and the completeness and functioning of markets.[7]

The Porter Hypothesis and the Costs of Environmental Regulation

Another hypothesis looks at the interaction between the economy and environment in the opposite direction. Traditional economic theory indicates that firms minimize their costs in order to remain competitive. Thus any environmental regulation imposes an additional cost to firms, and thus reduces their profits. This doesn't mean that the benefits of environmental regulations can't outweigh these costs, but that firms will end up worse off as a result of environmental regulations.

This notion was challenged in a 1995 paper that suggested that the key to competitiveness, whether it be for a firm or a nation, rests in the ability to continually innovate.[8] Well-designed environmental regulations provide an impetus for innovation, and thus can actually lower costs and provide a competitive advantage.

> In short, firms can actually benefit from properly crafted environmental regulations that are more stringent (or are imposed earlier) than those faced by their competitors in other countries. By stimulating innovation, strict environmental regulations can actually enhance competitiveness.[9]

Porter hypothesis
the theory that environmental regulations motivate firms to identify cost-saving innovations that otherwise would not have been implemented.

The idea that environmental regulation can lead to lower costs for firms has become known as the **Porter hypothesis**. Like the EKC hypothesis, the Porter hypothesis is controversial. The main reason is that it contradicts the common economic assumption that firms minimize costs. If such cost-saving innovations were available, then standard economic theory would suggest that firms would pursue such options without the spur of regulation. But the Porter hypothesis notes that firms may not be focused on ways to reduce environmental impacts, thus missing potential cost-saving innovations. Regulations may make firms more aware of new technologies and direct investments into new areas of research.

The Porter hypothesis was never intended to apply to all environmental regulations. Obviously some regulations do impose net costs on firms, even after technological innovations are implemented. The Porter hypothesis has been empirically tested by comparisons of both firms and nations.[10] For example, a firm-level study in India found evidence of the Porter hypothesis among water-polluting firms. Those firms with the lowest levels of water pollution also performed the best economically.

Other analyses have tested whether nations with more stringent environmental regulations gain an advantage in terms of international trade. The results generally don't support the Porter hypothesis at a national level. A 2011 study based on data from over 4,000 facilities in seven developed nations found that environmental regulation does induce innovations but that the net effect of regulations is still negative (i.e., they impose net costs on firms).[11]

Even if the Porter hypothesis is only true in a limited number of situations, the potential for innovation to at least reduce compliance costs may still be generally underestimated. Proposed environmental regulations often prompt opposition by industries on the basis of their anticipated **compliance costs** and negative impacts on the economy. A 1997 study sought instances where compliance costs estimated before an environmental regulation was enacted could be compared with actual compliance costs after the law went into effect.[12] A dozen such cases were found, including regulations on sulfur dioxide, CFCs, asbestos, and mining. In all cases the original estimates were higher than actual compliance costs, with the original estimates at least 29 percent higher. In most cases, the actual compliance costs were less than half the original estimates. The report concluded:

compliance costs
the cost to firms and industries of meeting pollution regulations.

> The case studies reviewed in this report clearly show that environmental regulations that mandate emission reduction at the source generally cost much less than expected. It is not clear to what extent businesses overstate their expected costs for strategic reasons, or to what

extent they fail to anticipate process and product technology changes when making early estimates. It is clear, however, that input substitution, innovation, and the flexibility of capital have allowed actual costs to be consistently much lower than early predictions.[13]

This doesn't mean that compliance costs are insignificant. A 2012 report sponsored by an organization representing U.S. manufacturers found that the cumulative effect of federal regulations was to reduce GDP by $240 to $630 billion annually, and reduce labor compensation by 1.4 percent to 5.0 percent.[14] The report also noted that the greatest share of the federal regulatory burden was a result of environmental regulations. However, the report mentioned that it did not consider the benefits of these regulations—an issue which we will return to later in the chapter. Also, one may question the objectivity of the analysis. For example, cost estimates for many regulations were obtained from a survey of manufacturing companies, who may have a strategic interest in over-stating costs.

Decoupling

We have emphasized the ways in which environmental protection and the economy are linked, but it is also worthwhile to think about ways the two can be separated. In many ways, economic growth has been associated with an increase in environmental impacts. Consider Figure 17.3a, which shows that between 1961 and 1978 global economic growth (measured using GDP) was associated with a similar upward trend in global carbon dioxide emissions. During this period, economic activity increased by a factor of 2.2 while CO_2 emissions increased by a factor of 2.0.

Since 1978, we see in Figure 17.3b that while global economic activity and CO_2 emissions both increased, they were not linked as closely as in Figure 17.3a. We can say that the two variables have become somewhat "decoupled" since the late 1970s. Economic activity increased by a factor of 2.3 while CO_2 emissions increased by only a factor of 1.6.

The term **decoupling** has been defined by the OECD as breaking the link between "environmental bads" and "economic goods."[15] We can differentiate between relative decoupling and absolute decoupling:

> **Relative decoupling**: The growth rate of the environmental bad is positive but less than the economic growth rate. We would say that since the 1970s carbon emissions and economic growth have become relatively decoupled.
>
> **Absolute decoupling**: The level of the environmental bad is either stable or decreasing at the same time that the economy is growing. Thus absolute decoupling breaks the linkage between economic growth and environmental degradation.

An example of absolute decoupling is shown in Figure 17.4. In the United Kingdom, real GDP increased by a factor of 2.6 between 1970 and 2008. But during this same period total CO_2 emissions in the country actually decreased by about 20 percent. Even during the period of rapid economic growth in the 1990s, CO_2 emissions stayed constant or decreased. This was in large part a result of a major shift in energy sources away from coal and towards natural gas, resulting from discoveries of large deposits of relatively inexpensive natural gas in the British North Sea. Also, CO_2 data don't account for "**exported emissions**"—emissions that are emitted in other countries to produce goods that are exported. Thus some of the decoupling efforts in developed countries have occurred merely because manufacturing has shifted to developing countries.

---

decoupling
breaking the correlation between increased economic activity and similar increases in envrionmental impacts.

relative and absolute decoupling
breaking the correlation between increased economic activity and increases in environmental impacts; in absolute decoupling, an increase of economic activity is associated with a decrease in environmental impacts.

exported emissions/ pollution
shifting the impacts of pollution to other countries by importing goods whose production involves large environmental impacts.

Figure 17.3a   Global Real GDP and Carbon Dioxide Emissions, 1961–1978

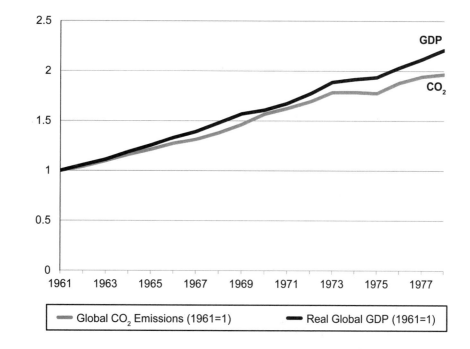

Source: World Bank, World Development Indicators database, http://data.worldbank.org/data-catalog/world-development-indicators.
Note: CO_2 = carbon dioxide; GDP = gross domestic product.

Figure 17.3b   Global Real GDP and Carbon Dioxide Emissions, 1979-2008

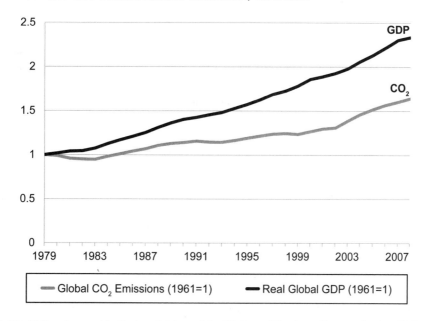

Source: World Bank, World Development Indicators database, http://data.worldbank.org/data-catalog/world-development-indicators.

Figure 17.4 **Absolute Decoupling: Real GDP and Carbon Dioxide Emissions in the United Kingdom, 1970–2008**

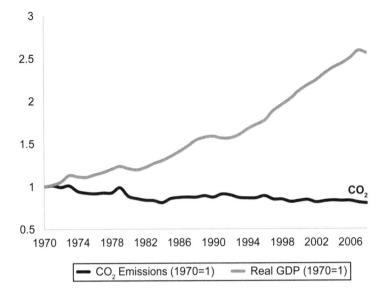

Source: World Bank, World Development Indicators database, http://data.worldbank.org/data-catalog/world-development-indicators; example taken from Smith et al., 2010.

Note: CO_2 = carbon dioxide; GDP = gross domestic product.

A 2011 report by the United Nations looks at the extent of global decoupling across a range of resources including fossil fuels, minerals, and wood.[16] The results suggest that a certain amount of relative decoupling has occurred in recent decades "spontaneously," rather than a direct result of policy intervention. This relative decoupling reflects an increase in the efficiency of production arising from technological improvements. However, some resource extraction rates exceed recent global GDP growth rates. For example, extraction of iron ore, copper, and zinc grew faster than global GDP over the period 1990–2007.[17]

The UN report found that achieving absolute decoupling will require ambitious policies. According to a business-as-usual scenario, global resource use is projected to triple by 2050. Absolute decoupling would keep global resource use constant at or below current levels, which has profound implications for developed and developing countries. In developed countries, resource use would need to decline by a factor of 3 to 5 to allow enough resource availability for developing countries to improve their living standards. Even then, the more advanced developing nations would still need to reduce their resource use by 10–20 percent in order to permit the poorest countries to somewhat increase their resource use. Thus absolute decoupling at the global level:

> . . . is only conceivable if it is accepted that sustainability-oriented innovations can result in radical technological and system change. Taken as a whole, this would be a scenario of tough restraint that would require unprecedented levels of innovation. . . . Most politicians are likely to regard this scenario as too restrictive in terms of developmental goals such as reducing poverty and providing for the material comfort of a rapidly expanding middle class.[18]

contraction and convergence
the concept that overall environmental impacts or economic activity should be reduced at the same time that economic inequalities are reduced.

More feasible is a scenario of moderate **contraction and convergence**, in which the resource use of developed countries declines (i.e., absolute decoupling), allowing the developing countries to increase their resource use enough to decrease global inequality. According to the UN report, in this scenario global resource use still increases 40 percent by 2050—declining by a factor of two in developed countries but increasing by a factor of about three in developing countries. Even this scenario "would require substantial economic structural change and massive investments in innovations for resource decoupling."[19]

Decoupling suggests that economic growth can be possible without an accompanying growth in physical throughput. However, current rates of decoupling need to increase in order to avoid a dramatic increase in resource use and pollution over the coming decades. Some nations are already taking the lead with innovative policies to encourage decoupling (see Box 17.2 on Japan's decoupling effort). But major decoupling on a global scale will require a degree of international cooperation not currently evident. In particular, developed countries must be willing to lower their resource use sufficiently to meet sustainability objectives and provide enough resource availability for developing countries to eradicate poverty.

17.3 INDUSTRIAL ECOLOGY

Economic growth has tended to rely on the increased extraction of raw materials and an increase in waste generation. Manufacturing processes have typically been designed to minimize production costs, without consideration of the associated ecological costs. Transitioning to a green economy will require a reassessment of the manufacturing process so that ecological concerns are incorporated into production decisions.

Traditional manufacturing is a "straight-line" process by which raw materials are transformed into final products, generating wastes (including waste heat) that are disposed of into the air, the land, or water, as shown in Figure 17.5. These final products are eventually disposed of as they wear out, also becoming waste products.

BOX 17.2 DECOUPLING IN JAPAN

Japan's unique culture norms and geopolitical limits have encouraged creative and effective solutions for decoupling. Japan's high population density and reliance on imports for natural resources have pushed Japan to decouple economic growth from ecological damage. In addition, Japanese culture has a long-standing concept of *mottainai*, meaning essentially that it is a shame when a resource is not utilized to its full potential.

In the 1980s, public concern over pollution from incineration, landfills nearing capacity, and the *mottainai* spirit lead to numerous solid waste reforms, such as replacing old incinerators with state-of-the-art facilities that decoupled dioxin emissions from the voluminous waste incineration. Japan has continued to innovate in solid waste disposal, both on the technical and policy level and has successfully decoupled it from economic growth.

Perhaps Japan's most successful modern decoupling initiative has been the Top Runner Programme (TRP). TRP searches the market for the most efficient product in a category, and makes that the new minimum efficiency standard, with which all companies must comply within four to eight years. As discussed in Chapter 16, standards typically create little incentive for innovation. But the TRP program motivates firms to become the industry efficiency leader, leaving other firms to catch up.

The TRP program has proven remarkably effective. In 10 out of 11 product categories, the efficiency gain was greater than initially expected. For example, diesel freight vehicles were expected to achieve a 6.5 percent efficiency improvement, but instead improved 21.7 percent. Like the Porter hypothesis, the TRP program demonstrates the significant potential for innovation when incentives are well-designed.

Source: UNEP, 2011c.

Figure 17.5   Straight-Line Process of Traditional Manufacturing

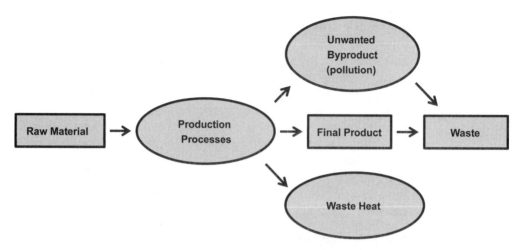

Natural systems, in contrast to economic systems, typically follow a cyclical pattern, with wastes being recycled and reused. Healthy natural systems show no buildup of pollution and wastes. Inorganic elements such as water and nitrogen cycle through the environment. Dead and decayed organic materials form the basis of fertile soils from which new plant life can grow, in turn supporting new animal life. Rather than creating a problem requiring a solution or disposal, wastes become inputs at a new stage in the cycle.

industrial ecology

the application of ecological principles to the management of industrial activity.

The emerging field of **industrial ecology** seeks to model human manufacturing systems on the closed-loop cycles found in nature. The concept of industrial ecology is illustrated in Figure 17.6. Taking this perspective, wastes can potentially become inputs into secondary production. Recycling rates are maximized to reduce the extraction of raw materials. Even waste heat that is typically unutilized can be directed toward productive uses such as heating water or living/working spaces.[20]

Figure 17.6   **Cyclical Production Processes of Industrial Ecology**

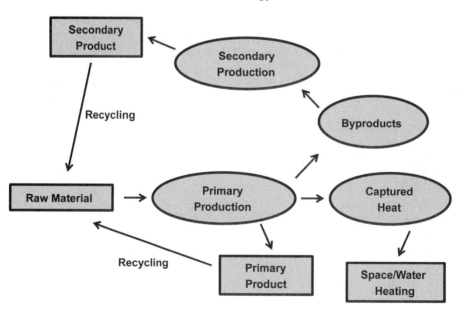

Recycling rates in the United States and elsewhere have been steadily increasing in recent years, as shown in Figure 17.7. Across the entire U.S. municipal waste spectrum, about one-third of total wastes by weight are recycled. Another 13 percent is incinerated to generate heat or electricity. The total amount of waste sent to municipal landfills has actually declined in recent years, from about 145 million tons in 1990 down to 135 million tons in 2010.[21]

The profitability of recycling depends on the demand for recycled products and the relative costs of recycled and virgin materials. One of the reasons that paper recycling rates have increased significantly over the last few decades is that it is generally cheaper to produce many paper products using recycled materials rather than virgin inputs. A 2007 study of recycling in New Zealand found that the overall recycling rate could be increased from 38 percent to 80 percent while providing society with net economic benefits.[22] The study found that recycling is particularly profitable for paper, used oil, metals, glass, and concrete. The economics of plastic recycling is mixed—while it generally makes economic sense to recycle PET (polyethylene terephthalate; recycling code #1) and HDPE (high density polyethylene; recycling code #2), it is generally not profitable to recycle PVC (polyvinyl chloride; recycling code #3) or LDPE (low density polyethylene; recycling code #4).

Figure 17.7   **Recycling Rates in the United States, 1960–2010**

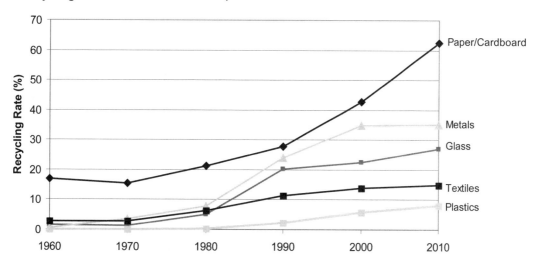

Source: U.S. EPA, 2011.

dematerialization
the process of achieving an economic goal through a decrease in the use of physical materials, such as making aluminum cans with less metal.

In addition to increasing recycling rates, industrial ecology also promotes **dematerialization**—achieving the same economic goal with less materials use. Aluminum beverage cans, for example, contain about 30 percent less metal than they did in the 1970s, and aluminum cans themselves replaced cans made of much heavier metal used in previous decades. Achieving the same function (delivering a beverage to consumers) using less material benefits the supplier, as well as the environment, cutting resource use and transportation costs, and reducing wastes even if the cans aren't recycled.

materials substitution
changing the materials used to produce a product, such as using plastic pipe instead of copper in plumbing systems.

Another principle of industrial ecology is **materials substitution**—replacing a scarce, hazardous, or highly polluting material with a more environmentally benign substitute. Many uses for copper, for example, have been replaced by plastics, optical fibers, and lighter metals such as aluminum. Government regulation has contributed to the partial replacement of metal-based pigments in paints with organic pigments, reducing the dangers of lead poisoning and the amount of lead and other heavy metals in the waste stream.

17.4 DOES PROTECTING THE ENVIRONMENT HARM THE ECONOMY?

What is the evidence regarding efforts to "green" the economy? Specifically, is there a tradeoff between protecting the environment and the economy and job creation? The conventional wisdom, particularly in the United States, seems to be that such a tradeoff exists:

> Environmental regulation in the United States stands accused of causing a broad array of undesirable economic consequences. The view that environmental regulation seriously harms the U.S. economy is so firmly established that it has become the centerpiece in the series of attempts over the last few years to roll back the very rules that have produced such dramatic improvements in environmental quality.[23]

A 1999 report to the U.S. EPA considered four approaches to assess the impact of environmental protection on the economy:[24]

1. Is environmental protection too expensive?
2. Does protecting the environment result in job losses?
3. Does environmental protection reduce economic growth?
4. Does environmental protection harm international competitiveness?

Let's now consider the empirical evidence to answer each of these questions.

Is Environmental Protection Too Expensive?

The first step to answering this question is to estimate how much is spent on environmental protection. One of the most comprehensive estimates of total environmental spending in the United States was produced in a 1990 EPA report which calculated total pollution control expenditures as 2.1 percent of GDP in 1990 (about $100 billion), rising to 2.6–2.8 percent of GDP in 2000.[25] These costs include the cost of complying with environmental regulations, as well as costs that would be incurred in the absence of such regulations, including basic water treatment and trash collection and disposal.

Using a slightly different methodology, the OECD estimated that pollution control expenditures in the U.S. in the mid-1990s were 1.6 percent of GDP.[26] More recent estimates are less comprehensive, and not comparable to these numbers. For example, 2005 data estimate U.S. pollution abatement capital and operating costs of only about $27 billion, or about 0.2 percent of GDP.[27]

Thus overall it seems the U.S. is spending 2–3 percent of its GDP protecting the environment. Is this too much? One answer would consider how environmental protection spending compares with other categories of spending. The 1990 EPA report mentioned above noted that "national environmental pollution control expenditures [are] less than half those for clothing and shoes, one-third those for national defense, one-third those for medical care, one-fifth those for housing, and one-sixth those for food."[28] Thus environmental spending is well within the range of what we spend on other essentials.

Another way to assess U.S. environmental spending is to compare it to spending in other countries. Table 17.1 shows that environmental spending in the U.S. is comparable to spending in other industrialized countries. U.S. pollution control spending is higher, as a share of GDP, than in Canada and the UK, but lower than in Austria and the Netherlands.

Table 17.1

Pollution Control and Abatement Expenditures, Select Countries (data from mid-1990s)

Country	Pollution abatement and control expenditures (as a percent of gross domestic product)
Austria	2.4
Netherlands	2.0
France	1.6
Germany	1.6
United States	1.6
Canada	1.1
United Kingdom	0.7

Source: OECD, 2003.

From the point of view of economic analysis, the most appropriate way to determine whether environmental expenditures are justified is to compare these costs to the benefits society receives. Using the techniques discussed in Chapter 6, one could theoretically estimate the market and non-market benefits of environmental expenditures. However, no comprehensive estimate has been made of the benefits of all environmental regulations in the United States or any other country. Instead, cost-benefit analyses have been conducted for many individual federal regulations. Under various executive orders in the United States, starting with Ronald Reagan and reaffirmed by Barack Obama, federal agencies proposing major regulations must quantify the costs and benefits of the proposal to the extent possible.[c] This requirement applies for nonenvironmental regulations as well as those related to the environment.

Each year the U.S. Office of Management and Budget publishes a report summarizing the results of cost-benefit analyses for all major regulations enacted that year, and also the aggregate impact of all regulations over the previous 10 years. Table 17.2 presents the cost-benefit results for various major federal agencies covering the period 2000–2010.[29]

During these 10 years, the U.S. EPA enacted more regulations (33) than any other federal agency, or about 31 percent of all major federal regulations. The annual costs of these 33 regulations are estimated to be $24–$29 billion. However, the annual benefits are estimated to be $82–$550 billion, implying a benefit-cost ratio of at least 2.8:1 and as high as 23:1.

---

[c]A major regulation is generally defined as one that has an impact on the economy of at least $100 million annually.

Table 17.2

Costs and Benefits of Major Federal Regulations, 2000–2010

Agency	Number of rules	Annual benefits (billions)	Annual costs (billions)
Department of Agriculture	6	0.9–1.3	1.0–1.34
Department of Energy	10	8.0–10.9	4.5–5.1
Department of Health and Human Services	18	18.0–40.5	3.7–5.2
Department of Homeland Security	1	< 0.1	< 0.1
Department of Housing and Urban Development	1	2.3	0.9
Department of Justice	4	1.8–4.0	0.8–1.0
Department of Labor	6	0.4–1.5	0.4–0.5
Department of Transportation	26	14.6–25.5	7.5–14.3
Environmental Protection Agency	33	81.7–550.4	23.8–29.0
Joint DOT and EPA	1	9.5–14.7	1.7–4.7
Total	106	136.2–651.2	44.2–62.2

Source: U.S. OMB, 2011.

While the EPA regulations impose about half of all federal regulatory costs, these regulations generate 60–85 percent of the benefits of all regulations. Thus EPA regulations result in higher benefit-cost ratios, on average, than other federal regulations. These results suggest that while environmental expenditures are large, and the EPA does enact more regulations than any other federal agency, environmental regulations provide significant net benefits to society.

Does Environmental Protection Result in Job Losses?

As mentioned earlier, the purported tradeoff between jobs and the environment is a common critique of environmental regulation. Several research studies have explored the relationship between employment and environmental regulation. While increased environmental spending leads to the loss of certain jobs, it creates other jobs. These effects may cancel out or actually result in a net gain of jobs. For example, a 2002 paper analyzed U.S. data in four industries: pulp and paper mills, plastic manufacturers, petroleum refiners, and iron and steel mills. The results found that:

> . . . increased environmental spending generally does *not* cause a significant change in employment. Our average across all four industries is a net gain of 1.5 jobs per $1 million in additional environmental spending.[30]

A broader 2008 national analysis also dispelled the notion that environmental protection results in job losses.[31] Using a model of the United States economy, the study was able to estimate how environmental spending and regulation affects employment in various industries. Their major finding was that:

> . . . contrary to conventional wisdom, [environmental protection (EP)], economic growth, and jobs creation are complementary and compatible: Investments in EP create jobs and displace jobs, but the net effect on employment is positive.[32]

Further, the study found that states that have the strongest environmental regulations also have the best job opportunities. The authors suggested that state-level policies integrate environmental protection as a key component of job creation proposals.

A 2007 study in the United Kingdom also studied the effect of environmental regulation on employment. The results found that regulations had a slightly negative impact on employment, although the results were not statistically significant. They concluded that their analysis found "no evidence of a trade-off between jobs and the environment."[33]

While environmental regulations clearly lead to job losses in specific industries, such as coal mining and oil refining, they also create many jobs. According to one estimate, environmental protection is responsible for about 5 million jobs in the United States.[34] This study found that just like spending in any other sector, environmental spending creates a broad range of jobs:

> [W]e found that classic environmental jobs constitute only a small portion of the jobs created by EP [environmental protection]. The vast majority of the jobs created by EP are standard jobs for accountants, engineers, computer analysts, clerks, factory workers, truck drivers, mechanics, etc. In fact, most of the persons employed in these jobs may not even realize that they owe their livelihood to protecting the environment.[35]

A 2009 study found that the "clean energy economy" has grown considerably, creating jobs at a higher rate than the economy as a whole.[36] While overall national job growth during 1997–2008 was 3.7 percent, clean energy jobs increased by 9.1 percent during the same period. The report also noted that an increasing share of venture capital is flowing into the clean energy sector.

Does Environmental Protection Reduce Economic Growth?

Another criticism of environmental protection is that it reduces economic growth, based on the results of studies showing that environmental regulations reduce GDP growth rates. For example, a comprehensive analysis of the Clean Air Act in the United States estimated that GNP in 1990 was about 1 percent lower than it would have been without the policy. The aggregate macroeconomic loss from the Act over the period 1973–1990 was estimated to be about $1 trillion. Analysis of the economic impact of major environmental regulations in Europe suggests an aggregate economic loss of about 0.2 percent of GDP.[37]

computable general equilibrium
economic models that aim to estimate the effect of policy changes throughout an entire economy.

The aggregate macroeconomic impacts of environmental regulations are estimated using **computable general equilibrium** (CGE) models. These models allow economists to determine how impacts in one sector of the economy carry through to employment and income changes in other sectors. The models include feedback loops to model longer-term impacts, particularly how capital investments respond to supply and demand changes in different sectors. However, the results of CGE models must be interpreted with caution.

> CGE models *have to* predict reduced economic growth because of environmental compliance. After all, pollution control costs in these models are treated as extra expenditures necessary to produce the same level of valued output. . . . The outcome is implicit in how the model is constructed. So this finding isn't necessarily a complete picture for what people and policymakers want to know about real world regulation, where a pollution control sector emerges as part of the economy, and helps to produce environmental protection, which is also an "output" with value.[38]

CGE models do not estimate the benefits of regulation, particularly those that don't appear in markets. For example, the CGE costs mentioned above regarding the Clean Air Act provide no insight into the benefits of the Act, which can only be obtained with additional economic analysis. When an estimate of the Clean Air Act benefits was made, it was found that the central estimate of the 1973–1990 benefits was $22 trillion, or a benefit cost ratio of 22:1.[39] CGE models also fail to account for positive feedback loops such as the increase in productivity as negative health impacts decline with better air quality.

So while there appears to be a slight negative impact of environmental regulation on economic growth as traditionally measured, we need a more complete analysis to determine its effect on social welfare. As we saw in Chapter 8, GDP was never intended to measure social welfare, and economists have developed alternative national accounting approaches to supplement or replace GDP. These alternatives may present a better framework for fully assessing the impacts of environmental regulations on social welfare. We need to analyze environmental regulations in light of both their benefits and their costs. The studies reviewed above indicate that environmental regulations provide society with significant net benefits.

Does Environmental Protection Harm International Competitiveness?

Finally, we consider whether environmental regulation makes a nation less competitive than nations with less stringent regulations. Assuming environmental regulations lead to higher production costs, firms having to meet stricter regulations would seem to be at a competitive disadvantage.

Various studies have addressed this issue, commonly looking at how regulations affect the quantity of exports in various sectors of the economy. A 1995 study collected the results of the available research at the time and concluded that "there is relatively little evidence to support the hypothesis that environmental regulations have had a large adverse effect on competitiveness."[40] Some recent analysis finds that regulations can have negative impacts on certain sectors, particularly those reliant upon fossil fuels, but positive impacts on other sectors. For example, a 2010 paper found that environmental regulations have a positive effect on exports of wood, paper, and textile products, but negative impacts on most other sectors.[41]

A 2011 study of U.S. manufacturing found that highly polluting manufacturing plants tend to be associated with lower overall productivity. The study estimated that inefficiencies associated with the failure to meet Clean Air Act standards lowers productivity by about 5 percent.[42] Finally, a 2012 study of European regulations also found evidence that certain regulations can have a positive impact on competitiveness:

> . . . the overall effect of environmental policies does not seem to be harmful for export competitiveness of the manufacturing sector, whereas specific energy tax policies and innovation efforts positively influence export flows dynamics, revealing a Porter-like mechanism. These results show that public policies and private innovation patterns both trigger higher efficiency in the production process through various complementarity mechanisms, thus turning the perception of environmental protection actions as a production cost into a net benefit.[43]

What Conclusions Can We Draw?

The evidence suggests that the common notion that environmental regulation harms the economy is a myth. While regulations may harm particular industries and reduce international competitiveness in some instances, the benefits of environmental regulations consistently outweigh the costs. Further, well-designed regulations can actually have a net positive impact on economic growth and competitiveness, and foster job creation.

17.5 CREATING A GREEN ECONOMY

The transition to a greener economy is occurring slowly, driven by economics and government policies. However, rates of decoupling, recycling, and dematerialization are generally not occurring fast enough to achieve sustainability targets such as reducing CO_2 emissions or protecting biodiversity. The United Nations concludes that "we are very far from being a green economy."[44]

Creating a green economy will require a significant shift in investments in infrastructure, research, and development. UNEP has developed a complex model to analyze the economic and environmental impacts of directing investments to promote a transition to a green economy.[45] They consider a green scenario where 2 percent of global GDP is invested in various ways to promote sustainability, including energy efficiency, renewable energy, waste management, infrastructure improvements, agricultural production methods, and water management. They compare the results of this green economy scenario to a business-as-usual scenario where investment rates follow existing trends.

The results are shown in Figure 17.8, indicating the percentage difference in various variables for the green economy scenario relative to the BAU scenario. In the short-term (2015), the green economy scenario results in about 1 percent lower real GDP and lower GDP per capita. But in the longer term the green economy shows substantially better economic performance than the BAU scenario. By 2050 real GDP in the green economy scenario is 16 percent higher than in the BAU scenario. The environmental differences between the two scenarios are initially small, but become dramatic over the following decades. By 2050 global energy demand is 40 percent lower in green economy scenario, and the ecological footprint is 48 percent lower.

Green investments are also relatively job-intensive, particularly in the agricultural, forestry, and transport sectors. In the energy sector, employment would initially decline as jobs related to fossil fuel use decline, but in the long run (after about 2030) net employment rises, primarily as a result of the creation of millions of jobs related to energy efficiency.

The UNEP model finds that investments for the green economy particularly benefit the world's poorest. The poor disproportionately depend upon natural resources for their livelihood. So investments in natural capital, including water resources, sustainable agriculture, and forests increase incomes while also improving the environment. Investments in natural capital also foster ecotourism, which offers another way to increase incomes in developing countries. In the energy sector, investment in renewable energy can also benefit the world's poor. There are about 1.6 billion people in the world who lack access to electricity. Given the lack of an existing distribution grid in many poor regions, small-scale off-grid solar energy is currently more cost-effective than electricity generated using traditional fossil fuels.

The transition to a green economy will require more than investment, it will require major policy shifts at the national and international levels. The policy recommendations from the UNEP report include:

Figure 17.8 **Environmental and Economic Projections, Green Economy Scenario versus Business as Usual**

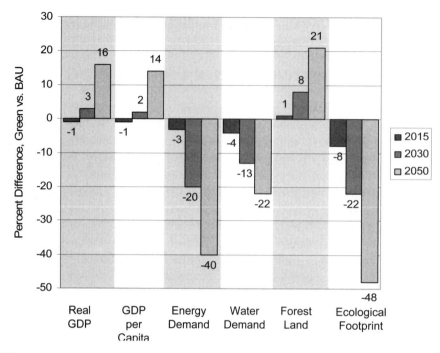

Source: UNEP, 2011a.
Note: BAU = business as usual; GDP = gross domestic product.

- *Use taxes and other market-based instruments to internalize negative externalities.* As we've seen in other instances in the book, pricing pollution promotes more efficient resource use and encourages innovation. Well-designed taxes or permit systems can also be net job creators. For example, a German tax on fossil fuels and electricity, introduced in 1999 and slowly phased in over several years, used the revenues to reduce the costs of hiring employees by lowering firms' required social security contributions. The tax was estimated to have created 250,000 full-time equivalent jobs while also reducing carbon emissions.

- *Decrease government spending that depletes natural capital.* We discussed the distortionary impact of fossil fuel subsidies in Chapter 12. And as noted in Chapter 13, at least 60 percent of global fishery subsidies have been identified as harmful, leading to over-exploitation of fisheries. Subsidy reforms should be phased in slowly to reduce negative economic impacts, and be supplemented with policies to protect the poor. In Indonesia, for example, reductions in energy subsidies in 2005 and 2008 were implemented along with cash transfers to low-income households.

- *Efficiency and technology standards can sometimes be more cost-effective and easier to administer than market-based instruments.* Developing countries often lack the institutions for complex tax and tradable permits systems. Technology standards are easier to enforce, and can ensure a rapid transition to the best available technologies. The challenge is to set appropriate standards, and adjust them as new technologies become available. Standards for government procurement have been demonstrated to be an effective way to jump-start the demand for environmentally friendly goods and services.

- *Temporary support measures are needed to ensure an employment transition for affected workers.* As shown in Figure 17.8, in the short term the transition to a green economy will cause a slight decline in GDP. Training will be needed to provide displaced workers with the skills to gain new jobs in the green economy. In many cases workers will remain employed in their current jobs, but through skill enhancement they can learn to do their jobs in new ways. Construction workers will still build houses, but construction techniques can incorporate better insulation, solar photovoltaic systems, and more efficient lighting.
- *International environmental governance needs to be strengthened.* Even with the potential economic benefits of green economy policies, individual nations remain hesitant to act alone. Strong international agreements create a level playing field and are the only effective way to deal with global environmental issues such as climate change and ozone depletion. An important step toward a green economy would be reform international trade laws, as we'll discuss further in Chapter 20. For example, international trade agreements can be set to reduce harmful subsidies while lowering certain tariffs to foster trade in environmental goods and services. Current trade laws on intellectual property rights have been criticized for failing to meet the needs of developing countries, and actually inhibiting the development of green markets. In some cases developing countries will need greater flexibility in protecting infant industries. Finally, developing countries often have an advantage in markets for ecosystem services such as carbon sequestration and watershed protection. International agreements that create markets for these services can reduce poverty while enhancing natural capital.

While some of these recommended policies will require major changes in current political institutions, others, such as reducing harmful subsidies or increasing efficiency standards, can be relatively easily and quickly implemented. The transition to a green economy will be a major issue confronting all economic policy makers in the coming decades. Significant steps are already being taken, as a greater share of public investment is directed toward greening the economy. According to the World Bank, about 16 percent of the global stimulus spending enacted as a response to the 2007 financial crisis was classified as "green" stimulus—spending on renewable energy, energy efficiency, waste management, and water sustainability.[46] The leader was China, spending $221 billion on green stimulus, about half of it directed toward rail transport. The United States allocated $112 billion as green stimulus, with about $30 billion each invested in renewable energy and energy efficient buildings. The European Union allocated about 60 percent of its stimulus spending toward green measures, including carbon capture and storage and electricity grid efficiency.

But the transition to a green, sustainable economy will require a sustained commitment. Countries that are proceeding as "first movers" are already starting to realize the benefits. South Korea has pledged 2 percent of its GDP toward investment in green sectors. Recent efforts there to increase recycling rates have saved billions of dollars and created thousands of jobs.[47] The UK is another country investing heavily in the green economy. Over a third of the UK's economic growth in 2011 and 2012 is estimated to be a result of green businesses.[48] The challenge is to maintain and extend these efforts through bold initiatives, long-term thinking, and international cooperation.

SUMMARY

The concept of a "green economy" is that improved human well-being and reduced inequality can be driven by investments to reduce environmental impacts. It is based on the finding that economic growth is compatible with protecting the environment.

We explored the relationship between the economy and the environment based on several theories. The Environmental Kuznets curve (EKC) hypothesis is that economic growth eventually leads to a reduction in environmental impacts. The empirical evidence supports the EKC hypothesis for some pollutants, but it does not apply to other environmental impacts, most importantly to carbon emissions. The Porter hypothesis states that well-designed environmental regulations can actually result in lower costs for firms. Again, the theory is valid in some cases but the evidence finds it does not apply to all regulations. Decoupling suggests that economic growth can be "delinked" from negative environmental impacts. Absolute decoupling has occurred in some instances, but much greater decoupling progress is needed to achieve sustainability targets.

The field of industrial ecology seeks to maximize resource efficiency and recycling. It promotes using the wastes from one industry as the inputs into additional production. Through dematerialization products can be constructed using a smaller volume of materials. Another focus of industrial ecology is to use materials that are nontoxic, recyclable, and low-polluting.

We explored the common perception that protecting the environment harms the economy. The evidence indicates that the benefits of environmental regulations far exceed their costs. Rather than leading to job losses, protecting the environment can actually be a source of net job creation. Environmental protection does not harm international competitiveness and has little effect on GDP growth rates.

While creating a green economy will entail short-term costs, the long-term benefits are projected to be significant. Rates of GDP growth are expected to be higher under a green economy scenario than a business as usual scenario, while environmental impacts are significantly reduced. The transition to a green economy will require strong policy action, including eliminating harmful subsidies, training workers, using economic policy instruments such as taxes and tradable permits, and meaningful international agreements.

KEY TERMS AND CONCEPTS

compliance costs	green economy
computable general equilibrium	industrial ecology
contraction and convergence	luxury good
decoupling	materials substitution
dematerialization	normal good
exported emissions	Porter hypothesis
Environmental Kuznets Curve (EKC)	relative and absolute decoupling

DISCUSSION QUESTIONS

1. What news stories have you heard recently that refer to the interaction between the environment and the economy? Was environmental protection presented as compatible with

economic growth? What were the various points of view presented in the story? What is your opinion of the story?

2. What steps, if any, do you think should be taken to promote a green economy in your country or region? What steps do you think would be most effective? Can you propose policies that businesses may support?

3. What groups would be hurt most by the transition to a green economy? What groups would most benefit from the transition? Can you think of scenarios in which those who gain could compensate those who would be hurt?

Notes

1. UNEP, 2011a, p. 16.
2. UNEP, 2011b, pp. 1–2.
3. Yandle, et al., 2004.
4. Beckerman, 1992, p. 482.
5. Aslanidis, 2009.
6. Stern, 2003, p. 11.
7. Yandle, et al., 2004, p. 29.
8. Porter and van der Linde, 1995.
9. Ibid., p. 98.
10. Wagner, 2003.
11. Lanoie, et al., 2011.
12. Hodges, 1997.
13. Ibid, p. 12.
14. NERA Economic Consulting, 2012.
15. OECD, 2002.
16. UNEP, 2011c.
17. Jackson, 2009.
18. Ibid., pp. 30, 32.
19. Ibid., p. 31.
20. See Ayres and Ayres, 1996 and Socolow ed., 1994, for an overview of industrial ecology, and Cleveland and Ruth, 1999, on materials flows in the industrial process.
21. U.S. EPA, 2011.
22. Denne, et al., 2007.
23. Arnold, 1999, Summary.
24. Arnold, 1999.
25. Carlin, 1990.
26. OECD, 2003.
27. United States Census Bureau, 2008.
28. Carlin, 1990, pp. 4–9.
29. U.S. Office of Management and Budget, 2011.
30. Morganstern, et al., 2002, p. 412.
31. Bezdek, et al., 2008.
32. Ibid., p. 63.
33. Cole and Elliott, 2007, p. 1.
34. Bezdek, et al., 2008.
35. Ibid., p. 69.
36. The Pew Charitable Trusts, 2009.
37. Commission of the European Communities, 2004.

38. Arnold, 1999, p. 10.
39. Commission of the European Communities, 2004.
40. Jaffe, et al., 1995, p. 157.
41. Babool and Reed, 2010.
42. Greenstone, et al., 2011.
43. Constantini and Mazzanti, 2012, p. 132.
44. UNEP, 2011b, p. 3.
45. UNEP, 2011a.
46. Strand and Toman, 2010.
47. http://www.unep.org/greeneconomy/AdvisoryServices/Korea/tabid/56272/Default.aspx.
48. CBI, 2012.

REFERENCES

Arnold, Frank S. 1999. "Environmental Protecting: Is It Bad for the Economy? A Non-Technical Summary of the Literature." Report prepared under EPA Cooperative Agreement CR822795-01 with the Office of Economy and Environment, U.S. Environmental Protection Agency.

Aslanidis, Nektarios. 2009. "Environmental Kuznets Curves for Carbon Emissions: A Critical Survey." FEEM Working Paper 75.09.

Ayres, Robert U., and Leslie W. Ayres. 1996. *Industrial Ecology: Towards Closing the Materials Cycle*. Cheltenham, UK: Edward Elgar.

Babool, Ashfaqul, and Michael Reed. 2010. "The Impact of Environmental Policy on International Competitiveness in Manufacturing." *Applied Economics* 42(18): 2317–2326.

Beckerman, Wilfred 1992. "Economic Growth and the Environment: Whose Growth? Whose Environment?" *World Development*. 20(4): 481–496.

Bezdek, Roger H., Robert M. Wendling, and Paula DiPerna. 2008. "Environmental Protection, the Economy, and Jobs: National and Regional Analyses." *Journal of Environmental Management* 86: 63–79.

Carlin, Alan. 1990. "Environmental Investments: The Cost of a Clean Environment, a Summary." EPA report EPA-230-12-90-084.

CBI. 2012. "The Colour of Growth: Maximising the Potential of Green Business." http://www.cbi.org.uk/media/1552876/energy_climatechangerpt_web.pdf.

Cleveland, Cutler, and Matthias Ruth. 1999. "Indicators of Dematerialization and the Materials Intensity of Use." *Journal of Industrial Ecology* 2(3): 15–50.

Cole, Matthew A., and Rob J. Elliott. 2007. "Do Environmental Regulations Cost Jobs? An Industry-Level Analysis of the UK." *Journal of Economic Analysis and Policy: Topics in Economic Analysis and Policy* 7(1): 1–25.

Commission of the European Communities. 2004. The EU Economy: 2004 Review. ECFIN (2004) REP 50455-EN. Brussels.

Constantini, Valeria, and Massimiliano Mazzanti. 2012. "On the Green and Innovative Side of Trade Competitiveness? The Impact of Environmental Policies and Innovation on EU Exports." *Research Policy*. 41(1): 132–153.

Denne, Tim, Reuben Irvine, Nikhil Atreya, and Mark Robinson. 2007. "Recycling: Cost-Benefit Analysis." Report prepared for the Ministry for the Environment (New Zealand), Covec, Ltd.

Guarino, Mark. 2011. "Keystone XL Pipeline Pits Jobs against the Environment." *Christian Science Monitor*.

Hodges, Hart. 1997. "Falling Prices: Cost of Complying with Environmental Regulations Almost Always Less Than Advertised." EPI Briefing Paper No. 69.

Jackson, Tim. 2009. *Prosperity Without Growth*. Earthscan: London.

Jaffe, Adam B., Steven R. Peterson, Paul R. Portney, and Robert N. Stavins. 1995. "Environmental Regulation and the Competitiveness of U.S. Manufacturing: What Does the Evidence Tell Us?" *Journal of Economic Literature* 33(1): 132–163.

Lanoie, Paul, Jeremy Laurent-Lucchetti, Nick Johnstone, and Stefan Ambec. 2011. "Environmental Policy, Innovation and Performance: New Insights on the Porter Hypothesis." *Journal of Economics and Management Strategy* 20(3): 803–842.

Morganstern, Richard D., William A. Pizer, and Jhih-Shyang Shih. 2002. "Jobs Versus the Environment: An Industry-Level Perspective." *Journal of Environmental Economics and Management* 43(3): 412–436.

NERA Economic Consulting. 2012. "Macroeconomic Impacts of Federal Regulation of the Manufacturing Sector." Report commissioned by Manufacturers Alliance for Productivity and Innovation.

Organization for Economic Cooperation and Development (OECD). 2003. "Pollution Abatement and Control Expenditures in OECD Countries." Report ENV/EPOC/SE (2003).

Organization for Economic Cooperation and Development (OECD). 2002. "Indicators to Measure Decoupling of Environmental Pressure from Economic Growth." Report SG/SD(2002)1/FINAL.

Panayotou, T. 1993. "Empirical Tests and Policy Analysis of Environmental Degradation at Different Levels of Development." Geneva: International Labour Office Working Paper WP238.

Porter, Michael E., and Claas van der Linde. 1995. "Toward a New Conception of the Environment-Competitiveness Relationship." *Journal of Economic Perspectives* 9(4): 97–118.

Smith, Michael H., Karlson "Charlie" Hargroves, and Cheryl Desha. 2010. Cents and Sustainability: Securing Our Common Future by Decoupling Economic Growth from Environmental Pressures. London: Earthscan.

Socolow, R., C. Andrews, F. Berkhout, and V. Thomas, eds. 1994. *Industrial Ecology and Global Change*. Cambridge, UK: Cambridge University Press.

Stern, David I. 2003. "The Environmental Kuznets Curve." Internet Encyclopaedia of Ecological Economics.

Strand, Jon, and Michael Toman. 2010. "'Green Stimulus,' Economic Recovery, and Long-Term Sustainable Development." The World Bank, Development Research Group, Environment and Energy Team, Policy Research Working Paper 5163.

The Pew Charitable Trusts. 2009. "The Clean Energy Economy: Repowering Jobs, Businesses, and Investments across America."

United Nations Environment Program (UNEP). 2011a. "Towards a Green Economy: Pathways to Sustainable Development and Poverty Eradication." www.unep.org/greeneconomy.

———. 2011b. "Towards a Green Economy: Pathways to Sustainable Development and Poverty Eradication, A Synthesis for Policymakers."

United Nations Environment Program (UNEP). 2011c. "Decoupling Natural Resource Use and Environmental Impacts from Economic Growth." A Report of the Working Group on Decoupling to the International Resource Panel. Fischer-Kowalski, M., Swilling, M., von Weizsäcker, E.U., Ren, Y., Moriguchi, Y., Crane, W., Krausmann, F., et al.

United States Census Bureau. 2008. "Pollution Abatement Costs and Expenditures: 2005." Report MA200(05), U.S. Government Printing Office, Washington, DC.

United States Environmental Protection Agency. 2011. "Municipal Solid Waste Generation, Recycling, and Disposal in the United States Tables and Figures for 2010."

United States Office of Management and Budget. 2011. "Draft 2011 Report to Congress on the Benefits and Costs of Federal Regulations and Unfunded Mandates on State, Local, and Tribal Entities."

Wagner, Marcus. 2003. "The Porter Hypothesis Revisited: A Literature Review of Theoretical Models and Empirical Tests." Center for Sustainability Management.

Yandle, Bruce, Madhusudan Bhattarai, and Maya Vijayaraghavan. 2004. "Environmental Kuznets Curves: A Review of Findings, Methods, and Policy Implications," PERC Research Study 02-1 Update.

WEB SITES

1. **http://www.unep.org/greeneconomy/**. The United Nations' page on the Green Economy, including their Green Economy report, national case studies, and several videos.
2. **http://is4ie.org/**. Homepage for the International Society for Industrial Ecology, with links to their journal, job postings, and events.

3. **http://www.epa.gov/gateway/learn/greenliving.html**. The U.S. EPA's site on green living, including numerous tips on how to reduce your environmental impacts.
4. **http://www.thegreeneconomy.com/**. Homepage for "The Green Economy" magazine, with articles and news stories targeted toward businesses leaders seeking to take advantage of green opportunities.
5. **http://www.guardian.co.uk/environment/green-economy**. Web page assembled by The Guardian, a UK newspaper, which collects stories related to the green economy.

Global Climate Change

CHAPTER 18 FOCUS QUESTIONS

- How serious a problem is global warming/global climate change?
- Can economic theory help evaluate the impact of climate change?
- How can we model the long-term impacts of climate change?

18.1 CAUSES AND CONSEQUENCES OF CLIMATE CHANGE

global climate change
the changes in global climate, including temperature, precipitation, and storm frequency and intensity, that result with changes in the concentrations of greenhouse gases in the atmosphere.

greenhouse gases
gases such as carbon dioxide and methane whose atmospheric concentrations influence global climate by trapping solar radiation.

environmental externalities
externalities that affect the environment, such as the impact of pollution on wildlife.

common property resources
a resource that is not subject to private ownership and is available to all, such as the oceans or atmosphere.

Concern has grown in recent years over the issue of **global climate change**.[a] In terms of economic analysis, **greenhouse gas** emissions, which cause planetary warming and other changes in weather patterns, represent both an **environmental externality** and the overuse of a **common property resource**.

The atmosphere is a **global commons** into which individuals and firms can release pollution. Global pollution creates a "public bad" affecting everyone—a negative externality with a wide impact. Many countries have environmental protection laws limiting the release of local and regional air pollutants. In economic terminology, such laws to some degree internalize externalities associated with local and regional pollutants. But until recently, few controls existed for carbon dioxide (CO_2), the major greenhouse gas, which has no short-term damaging effects at ground level.

A wide scientific consensus has formed that atmospheric accumulations of carbon dioxide and other greenhouse gases will have significant effects on global temperature and weather. There is uncertainty about the probable scale and timing of these effects, but impacts may have already begun to affect climate patterns (see Box 18.1). If indeed the effects of climate change are likely to be severe, it is in everyone's interest to lower emissions for the common good. If no agreement or rules on emissions exist, actions by individual firms, cities, or countries will be inadequate. Climate change can thus be viewed as a **public good** issue, requiring collaborative action. Since the

---

[a]The problem often referred to as **global warming** is more accurately called global climate change. A basic warming effect will produce complex effects on climate patterns—with warming in some areas, cooling in others, and increased climatic variability and extreme weather events.

BOX 18.1   WHAT IS THE GREENHOUSE EFFECT?

The sun's rays travel through a greenhouse's glass to warm the air inside, but the glass acts as a barrier to the escape of heat. Thus plants that require warm weather can be grown in cold climates. The global greenhouse effect, in which the earth's atmosphere acts like the glass in a greenhouse, was first described by French scientist Jean Baptiste Fourier in 1824.

Clouds, water vapor, and the natural greenhouse gases carbon dioxide (CO_2), methane, nitrous oxide, and ozone allow inbound solar radiation to pass through but serve as a barrier to outgoing infrared heat. This creates the natural **greenhouse effect,** which makes the planet suitable for life. Without it, the average surface temperature on the planet would average around–18° C (0° F), instead of approximately 15°C (60° F).

"The possibility of an *enhanced* or *man-made* greenhouse effect was introduced by the Swedish scientist Svante Arrhenius in 1896. Arrhenius hypothesized that the increased burning of coal, which had paralleled the process of industrialization, would lead to an increased concentration of carbon dioxide in the atmosphere and warm the earth" (Fankhauser 1995). Since Arrhenius's time, the emissions of greenhouse gases have grown dramatically. CO_2 concentrations in the atmosphere have increased by 40 percent over preindustrial levels. In addition to increased burning of fossil fuels such as coal, oil and natural gas, manmade chemical substances such as chlorofluorocarbons (CFCs) as well as methane and nitrous oxide emissions from agriculture and industry contribute to the greenhouse effect.

Scientists have developed complex computer models that estimate the effect of current and future greenhouse gas emissions on the global climate. While considerable uncertainty remains in these models, a broad scientific consensus has formed that the human-induced greenhouse effect poses a significant threat to the global ecosystem. The global average temperature increased by about 0.7°C (1.3°F) during the twentieth century. The Intergovernmental Panel on Climate Change (IPCC) concluded in 2007 that the global atmospheric concentrations of greenhouse gas (GHG) emissions have increased markedly as a result of human activities since 1750. The report also emphasized, "Most of the observed increase in global average temperatures since the mid-twentieth century is very likely due to the observed increase in anthropogenic GHG concentrations."

Current emissions trends will lead to a doubling of greenhouse gas concentration over preindustrial levels by around 2050. The IPCC projects a global average temperature increase of 1°C to 6°C, or 2°F to 10°F, which would have a significant impact on climate throughout the world.

Sources: Cline 1992; Fankhauser 1995; IPCC 2007a.

---

global commons

global common property resources such as the atmosphere and the oceans.

public goods

goods that are available to all (nonexclusive) and whose use by one person does not reduce their availability to others (nonrival).

problem is global, only a strong international agreement binding countries to act for the common good can prevent serious environmental consequences.

Because CO_2 and other greenhouse gases continuously accumulate in the atmosphere, stabilizing or "freezing" emissions will not solve the problem. Greenhouse gases persist in the atmosphere for decades or even centuries, continuing to affect the climate of the entire planet long after they are emitted. This is a case of a **stock pollutant**. As discussed in Chapter 16, only major reductions in emissions levels of a stock pollutant will prevent ever-increasing atmospheric accumulations. Atmospheric accumulations may eventually dissipate through natural processes but only on a time-scale of decades or centuries.

Development of national and international policies to combat global climate change is a huge challenge, involving many scientific, economic, and social issues. In this chapter we address the issues of analysis of climate change, using techniques and concepts developed in earlier chapters, and in Chapter 19 we turn to policy implications.

Trends and Projections for Global Carbon Emissions

Global emissions of CO_2 from the combustion of fossil fuels increased dramatically during the twentieth century, as illustrated in Figure 18.1. The use of liquid fuel (primarily oil) is currently responsible for about 35 percent of global carbon emissions from fossil fuels, while solid fuel (coal) is the source of another 45 percent and combustion of natural gas accounts for 20 percent. China surpassed the United States in 2006 as the largest carbon emitter in the world. In 2010, China released about 26 percent of global carbon emissions, followed by the United States with about 18 percent.[1]

Figure 18.1 **Carbon Emissions from Fossil Fuel Consumption, 1860–2008**

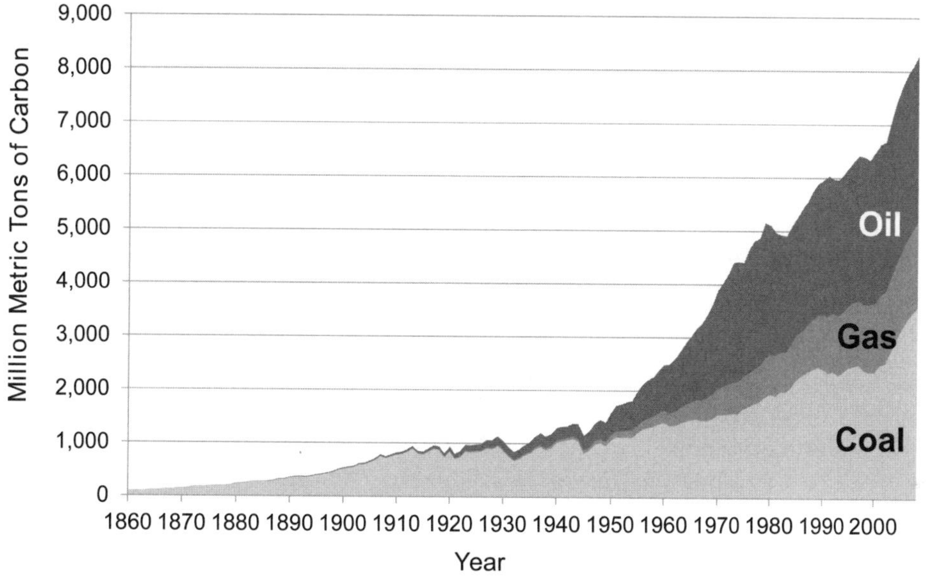

Source: Carbon Dioxide Information Analysis Center (CDIAC), http://cdiac.ornl.gov/trends/trends.htm, accessed August 2012.
Note: Emissions in million tons (MMt) of carbon. To convert to MMt of CO_2, multiply by 3.67.

Progress on combating global climate change has been slow, despite many global conferences dealing with the issue—including the 1992 United Nations Conference on Environment and Development (UNCED) at Rio de Janeiro, also known as the Earth Summit, a 1997 meeting in Kyoto, Japan, that produced the agreement known as the Kyoto Protocol, and the World Summit on Sustainable Development in 2002, the Copenhagen Conference in 2009, and the Doha Climate Change Conference in 2012.

As Figure 18.2 shows, the growth in carbon emissions is expected to continue in the coming decades. According to the U.S. Energy Information Administration, global CO_2 emissions are projected to increase by approximately 30 percent over 2012 levels by 2035.[2] These projections are for the Energy information Administration's "reference case," which assumes a **business as usual (BAU)** scenario, with no major additional efforts to reduce carbon emissions. As we will see, strong policies to shift away from carbon-based fuels could alter these projections.

stock pollutant
pollutants that accumulate in the environment, such as carbon dioxide and chlorofluorocarbons.

business as usual
a scenario in which no significant policy, technology, or behavioral changes are expected.

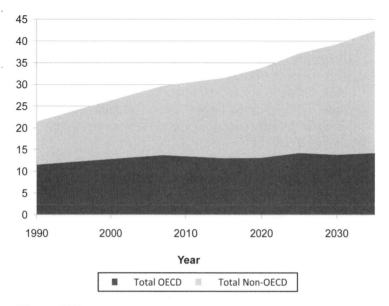

Year

■ Total OECD ■ Total Non-OECD

Source: U.S. Department of Energy, 2011.

Notes: OECD = Organization for Economic Cooperation and Development. The vertical axis in Figure 18.2 measures million metric tons of carbon dioxide (the vertical axis in Figure 18.1 shows million metric tons of carbon; the weight of a given amount of emissions measured in tons of carbon dioxide is about 3.67 times the total weight in carbon).

As of 2012, the industrialized countries were responsible for about half of global carbon emissions. As seen in Figure 18.2, most of the future growth in carbon emissions is expected to come from rapidly expanding developing countries such as China and India. For example, CO$_2$ emissions in China are projected to grow by 52 percent between 2013 and 2035.[3]

Per capita emissions are much higher in developed countries, as shown in Figure 18.3. Although carbon emissions are projected to grow fastest in developing countries, per capita emissions in 2035 will still be much higher (about six times higher) in the industrialized countries, reflecting higher per-capita income levels. The developing countries argue that they should not be required to limit their emissions while the industrial countries continue to emit so much more on a per capita basis. The global imbalance in per capita emissions is a critical issue that has yet to be adequately addressed in the policy debate on global climate change, and disagreement on this issue of relative responsibilities has accounted for much of the deadlock at global climate talks (more on this in Chapter 19).

Trends and Projections for Global Climate

The earth has warmed significantly since reliable weather records began to be kept in the mid-nineteenth century (Figure 18.4). In the past hundred years the global average temperature has risen about 0.7°C, or about 1.3°F. Twelve of the fourteen warmest years in the modern meteorological record have occurred since 2000.[4] Evidence indicates that the rate of warming, currently about 0.13°C per decade, is increasing.[5] Not all areas are warming equally. The Arctic and Antarctic regions have been warming at about double the global rate.[6]

Figure 18.3 **Per-Capita Emissions of Carbon Dioxide by Country**

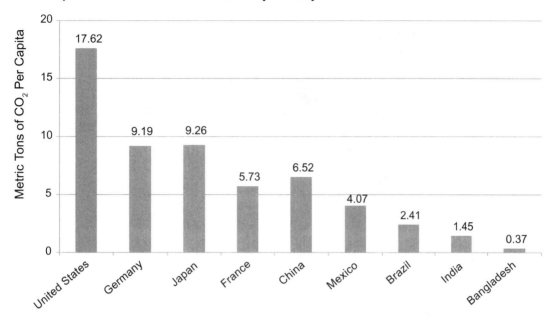

Source: U.S. Energy Information Administration, www.eia.gov.

Figure 18.4 **Global Annual Temperature Anomalies (°C), 1850–2010**

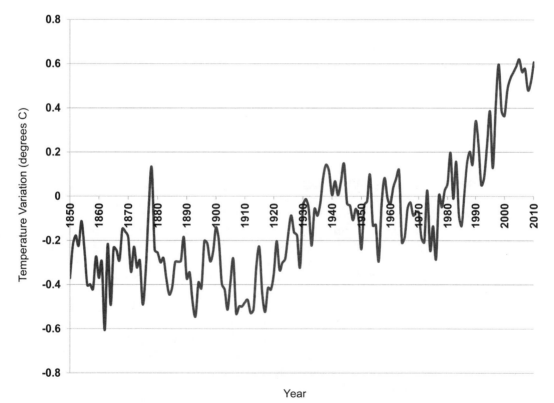

Source: CDIAC, accessed 2011, http://cdiac.ornl.gov/ftp/trends/temp/jonescru/global.txt.
Note: The zero baseline represents the average global temperature from 1961 to 1990.

Warmer temperatures have produced noticeable effects on ecosystems. In most regions of the world, glaciers are retreating. For example, Glacier National Park in Montana had 150 glaciers when the park was established in 1910. As of 2010 only 25 glaciers remained, and by 2030 it is estimated that the park will no longer have any of its namesake glaciers. Climate change is also leading to rising sea levels. Sea-level rise is attributed to the melting of glaciers and ice sheets and to the fact that water expands when it is heated. In 2012 the global average ocean temperature was about 0.5°C above the twentieth-century average. The combination of warmer oceans and melting ice has led sea levels to rise about 2 millimeters per year (see Figure 18.5 and Box 18.2).[7]

Figure 18.5   **Sea-Level Rise, 1880–2000**

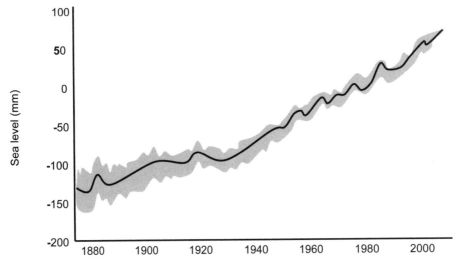

Source: IPCC, 2007a.
Note: Solid line shows average of different studies; shaded area shows 90 percent confidence intervals.

BOX 18.2   PACIFIC ISLANDS DISAPPEAR AS OCEANS RISE

Two islands in the Pacific Ocean country of Kiribati—Tebua Tarawa and Abanuea—have disappeared as a result of rising sea level. Others, both in Kiribati and in the neighboring island country of Tuvalu, are nearly gone. So far the seas have completely engulfed only uninhabited, relatively small islands, but the crisis is growing all around the shores of the world's atolls. Scientists estimate the current sea level rise in the Pacific at about 2 millimeters per year and expect that rate to accelerate due to climate change.

Populated islands are already suffering. The main islands of Kiribati, Tuvalu, and the Marshall Islands (also in the Pacific) have suffered severe floods as high tides demolish sea walls, bridges and roads, and swamp homes and plantations. Almost the entire coastline of the twenty-nine Marshall Islands atolls is eroding. World War II graves on its main Majuro atoll are washing away, roads and subsoils have been swept into the sea, and the airport has been flooded several times despite the supposed protection of a high sea wall.

(continued)

The people of Tuvalu are finding it difficult to grow their crops because the rising seas are poisoning the soil with salt. In both Kiribati and the Marshall Islands families are desperately trying to keep the waves at bay by dumping trucks, cars, and other old machinery in the sea and surrounding them with rocks. The situation is so bad that the leaders of Kiribati are considering a plan to move the entire population of 103,000 to Fiji. The inhabitants of some villages have already moved.

It is much the same story far away in the Maldives. The Indian Ocean is sweeping away the beaches of one-third of its 200 inhabited islands. "Sea-level rise is not a fashionable scientific hypothesis," says President Gayoom. "It is a fact."

The seas are rising partly because global warming is melting ice sheets and glaciers and nibbling away at the polar ice caps, but mainly because the oceans expand as their water warms. Scientists' best estimate is that these processes will raise sea levels by about 1.5 feet over the next century, enough to destroy several island countries.

The higher the seas rise, the more often storms will sweep the waves across the narrow atolls carrying away the land—and storms are expected to increase as the world warms up. Many islands will become uninhabitable long before they physically disappear, as salt from the sea contaminates the underground freshwater supplies on which they depend.

Sources: "Kiribati Global Warming Fears: Entire Nation May Move to Fiji," Associated Press, March 12, 2012; Geoffrey Lean, "They're Going Under; Two Islands Have Disappeared Beneath the Pacific Ocean—Sunk by Global Warming," *The Independent*, June 13, 1999, p. 15. Also see the documentary "The President's Dilemma," http://youtube/nZLWqa5irog.

ocean acidification
increasing acidity of ocean waters as a result of dissolved carbon from CO_2 emitted into the atmosphere.

In addition to rising ocean temperatures, increased CO_2 in the atmosphere results in **ocean acidification**. According to the U.S. National Oceanic and Atmospheric Administration, "around half of all carbon dioxide produced by humans since the Industrial Revolution has dissolved into the world's oceans. This absorption slows down global warming, but it also lowers the oceans pH, making it more acidic. More acidic water can corrode minerals that many marine creatures rely on to build their protective shells and skeletons."[8] A 2012 report in *Science* magazine finds that the oceans are turning acidic at what may be the fastest pace in 300 million years, with potential severe consequences for marine ecosystems.[9] Among the first victims of ocean warming and acidification are coral reefs, because corals can form only within a narrow range of temperatures and acidity of seawater. Oyster hatcheries, which have been referred to as "canaries in a coal mine" since they may predict effects on a wide range of ocean ecosystems as ocean acidification increases, are also affected.[10]

Although some warming may be a natural trend, the Intergovernmental Panel on Climate Change (IPCC) in 2007 concluded:

> Most of the observed increase in global average temperatures since the mid-twentieth century is very likely due to the observed increase in anthropogenic greenhouse gas concentrations. Discernible human influences now extend to other aspects of climate, including ocean warming, continental-average temperatures, temperature extremes, and wind patterns.[11]

Future projections of climate change depend on the path of future emissions. Even if all emissions of greenhouse gases ended today, the world would continue warming for many decades, and effects such as sea-level rise would continue for centuries, because the ultimate environmental effects of emissions are not realized immediately.[12] Based on a wide range of models with different assumptions about future emissions, the IPCC estimates that during the twenty-first century global average temperatures will rise between 1.1°C (2°F) and 6.4°C (11°F), with the range more likely to be between 1.8°C (3°F) and 4°C (7°F). The range of possible temperature increases is shown in Figure 18.6.

Figure 18.6   **Global Temperature Trends, 1900–2100**

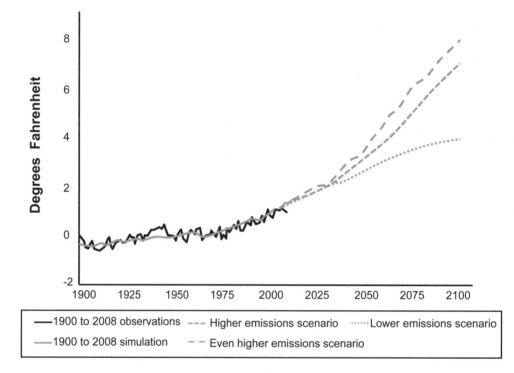

Source: U.S. Global Change Research Program, www.globalchange.gov.

CO_2 equivalent (CO_2e)
a measure of total greenhouse gas emissions or concentrations, converting all non-CO_2 gases to their CO_2 equivalent in warming impact.

The magnitude of actual warming and other effects will depend upon the level at which atmospheric concentrations of CO_2 and other greenhouse gases are ultimately stabilized. The current atmospheric CO_2 concentration is around 395 parts per million (ppm). When we consider the contribution of other greenhouse gases, the overall effect is equivalent to a concentration of 430 ppm of CO_2, referred to as **CO_2 equivalent (CO_2e)**.

Figure 18.7 relates the stabilization level of greenhouse gases, measured in CO_2e, to the resulting rise in global average temperatures, incorporating the degree of uncertainty. The solid bar at each level of CO_2e represents a range of temperature outcomes that is likely to occur with a 90 percent probability. The dashed line extending beyond this interval at either end represents the full range of predicted results from the major existing climate models. The vertical line around the middle of each bar represents the midpoint of the different predictions.

Figure 18.7 **The Relationship Between the Level of Greenhouse Gas Stabilization and Eventual Temperature Change**

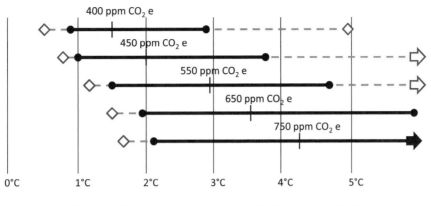

Eventual Temperature change (relative to pre-industrial)

Source: Stern, 2007.
Note: CO$_2$e = CO$_2$ equivalent; ppm = parts per million.

This projection suggests that stabilizing greenhouse gas concentrations at 450 ppm CO$_2$e would be 90 percent likely to eventually result in a temperature increase between 1.0 and 3.8°C, with a small probability that the rise could be significantly more than this. With current greenhouse gas concentrations in the atmosphere at 430 ppm CO$_2$e, stabilization at 450 ppm would be extremely challenging. As we see below, even stabilization at 550 ppm CO$_2$e would require dramatic policy action.

18.2 RESPONSES TO CLIMATE CHANGE

**preventive measures/
preventive strategies**
actions designed to reduce the extent of climate change by reducing projected emissions of greenhouse gases.

adaptive strategies
See "adaptive measures."

The onset of climate change poses a choice between **preventive strategies** and **adaptive strategies**. Consider, for example, the damage caused by rising sea levels. The only way to stop this would be to prevent climate change entirely—something that is now impossible. It might be possible in some cases to build dikes and sea walls to hold back the higher waters. Those who live close to the sea—including whole island nations that could lose most of their territory to sea-level rise—will suffer major costs under any adaptation strategy. But a prevention strategy that could slow, though not stop, sea-level rise would require convincing most of the world's countries to participate. Is it in their interest to do so? To answer this question, we have to find a way of evaluating the effects of climate change.

Scientists have modeled the results of a projected doubling of accumulated carbon dioxide in the earth's atmosphere. Some of the predicted effects are:

- Loss of land area, including beaches and wetlands, because of sea-level rise
- Loss of species and forest area
- Disruption of water supplies to cities and agriculture
- Increased air conditioning costs
- Health damage and deaths from heat waves and spread of tropical diseases
- Loss of agricultural output due to drought

Beneficial outcomes might include:

- Increased agricultural production in cold climates
- Lower heating costs
- Fewer deaths from exposure to cold

In addition, other less-predictable but possibly more damaging and permanent effects include:

- Disruption of weather patterns, with increased frequency of hurricanes, droughts, and other extreme weather events.
- Sudden major climate changes, such as a shift in the Atlantic Gulf Stream, which could change the climate of Europe to that of Alaska.
- Positive **feedback effects**, such as an increased release of CO_2 from warming arctic tundra, which would speed up global warming.[b]

feedback effect
the process of changes in a system leading to other changes that either counteract or reinforce the original change.

The IPCC projects that with increasing emissions and higher temperatures, negative effects will intensify and positive effects diminish (Table 18.1). As shown in Figure 18.6, there is considerable uncertainty about the expected global warming in the next century. We need to keep such uncertainties in mind as we evaluate economic analyses of global climate change.

Given these uncertainties, some economists have attempted to place the analysis of global climate change in the context of **cost-benefit analysis**. Others have criticized this approach as an attempt to put a monetary valuation on issues with social, political, and ecological implications that go far beyond dollar value. We first examine economists' efforts to capture the impacts of global climate change through cost-benefit analysis and then return to the debate over how to assess potential greenhouse gas reduction policies.

cost-benefit analysis (CBA)
a tool for policy analysis that attempts to monetize all the costs and benefits of a proposed action to determine the net benefit.

18.3 ECONOMIC ANALYSIS OF CLIMATE CHANGE

Without policy intervention, carbon emissions can be expected to continue to rise approximately as projected in Figure 18.2. Aggressive and immediate policy action would be required first to stabilize and then to reduce total CO_2 emissions in the coming decades. In performing a cost-benefit analysis, we must weigh the consequences of the projected increase in carbon emissions versus the costs of current policy actions to stabilize or even reduce CO_2 emissions. Strong policy action to prevent climate change will bring benefits equal to the value of damages that are avoided.[c] These benefits must be compared to the costs of taking action. Various economic studies have attempted to estimate these benefits and costs. The results of five such studies for the U.S. economy are shown in Table 18.2.

The studies are based on average temperature increases of 2.5°C to 4°C. When the monetized costs are added up, the total annual U.S. damages are estimated at between $60 billion and $140 billion (1990 dollars). This is about 1–3 percent of

---

[b]A feedback effect occurs when an original change in a system causes further changes that either reinforce the original change (positive feedback) or counteract it (negative feedback).

[c]These benefits of preventing damage can also be referred to as **avoided costs**.

Table 18.1

Possible Effects of Climate Change

| Type of Impact | Eventual Temperature Rise Relative to Pre-Industrial Temperatures | | | | |
	1°C	2°C	3°C	4°C	5°C
Freshwater Supplies	Small glaciers in the Andes disappear, threatening water supplies for 50 million people	Potential water supply decrease of 20–30% in some regions (Southern Africa and Mediterranean)	Serious droughts in southern Europe every 10 years 1–4 billion more people suffer water shortages	Potential water supply decrease of 30–50% in southern Africa and Mediterranean	Large glaciers in Himalayas possibly disappear, affecting ¼ of China's population
Food and Agriculture	Modest increase in yields in temperature regions	Declines in crop yields in tropical regions (5–10% in Africa)	150–550 million more people at risk of hunger Yields likely to peak at higher latitudes	Yields decline by 15–35% in Africa Some entire regions out of agricultural production	Increase in ocean acidity possibly reduces fish stocks
Human Health	At least 300,000 die each year from climate–related diseases Reduction in winter mortality in high latitudes	40–60 million more exposed to malaria in Africa	1–3 million more potentially people die annually from malnutrition	Up to 80 million more people exposed to malaria in Africa	Further disease increase and substantial burdens on health care services
Coastal Areas	Increased damage from coastal flooding	Up to 10 million more people exposed to coastal flooding	Up to 170 million more people exposed to coastal flooding	Up to 300 million more people exposed to coastal flooding	Sea-level rise threatens major cities such as New York, Tokyo, and London
Ecosystems	At least 10% of land species facing extinction Increased wildfire risk	15–40% of species potentially face extinction	20–50% of species potentially face extinction Possible onset of collapse of Amazon forest	Loss of half of Arctic tundra Widespread loss of coral reefs	Significant extinctions across the globe

Sources: IPCC, 2007b; Stern, 2007.

U.S. gross domestic product (GDP). Although different economic studies come up with different estimates, most of them are in the same range of 1–3 percent GDP. Cost estimates for larger temperature change over the longer term rise to around 10 percent of global GDP (Figure 18.8).

Note, however, that there are also some "Xs" in the totals—unknown quantities that cannot easily be measured. The damage from species extinction, for example, is difficult to estimate in dollar terms: The estimates shown here indicate a cost of at least $1.4–5 billion, with additional unknown costs, which rise with additional warming.

In addition to the Xs, other monetized estimates could also be challenged on the grounds that they fail to capture the full value of potential losses. For example, oceanfront land is more than just real estate. Beaches and coastal wetlands have great social, cultural, and ecological value. The market value of these lands does not reflect the full scope of the damage society will suffer if they are lost.

Table 18.2

Estimates of Annual Damages to the U.S. Economy from Global Climate Change
(billions of 1990 dollars)

	Cline (2.5°C)	Fankhauser (2.5°C)	Nordhaus (3°C)	Titus (4°C)	Tol (2.5°C)
Agriculture	17.5	3.4	1.1	1.2	10
Forest loss	3.3	0.7	X	43.6	X
Species loss	4	1.4	X	X	5
Sea-level rise	7	9	12.2	5.7	8.5
Electricity	11.2	7.9	1.1	5.6	X
Nonelectric heating	−1.3	X	X	X	X
Mobile air conditioning	X	X	X	2.5	X
Human amenity	X	X		X	12
Human mortality and morbidity	5.8	11.4		9.4	37.4
Migration	0.5	0.6		X	1
Hurricanes	0.8	0.2		X	0.3
Leisure activities	1.7	X	0.75% of GDP	X	X
Water supply availability	7	15.6		11.4	X
Water supply pollution	X	X		32.6	X
Urban infrastructure	0.1	X		X	X
Air pollution	3.5	7.3		27.2	X
Total in billions	61.1	69.5	55.5	139.2	74.2
Total as percent of GDP	1.1	1.3	1	2.5	1.5

Source: Nordhaus and Boyer, 2000, p. 70.
Note: "X" denotes items that are not assessed or quantified. GDP = gross domestic product.

Monetizing the value of human health and life is very controversial, as discussed in Chapter 6. These studies follow a common cost-benefit practice of assigning a value of about $6 million to a life, based on studies of the amounts that people are willing to pay to avoid life-threatening risk, or are willing to accept (e.g., in extra salary for dangerous jobs) to undertake such risks.

In addition, these estimates omit the possibility of the much more catastrophic consequences that *could* result if weather disruption is much worse than anticipated. A single hurricane, for example, can cause tens of billions in damage, in addition to loss of life. Hurricane Katrina in August 2005, for example, caused over $100 billion in damage, in addition to loss of over 1,800 lives. Hurricane Sandy, in 2012, caused about $50 billion in damages, disrupting power to nearly 5 million customers and leaving lasting effects on an extensive area of shoreline in New York and New Jersey. If climate change causes severe hurricanes to become much more frequent, the estimate given in Table 18.2 of less than $1 billion in annual losses could be much too low. Another of the unknown values—human morbidity, or losses from disease—could well be enormous if tropical diseases extend their range significantly due to warmer weather conditions.

In a 2008 study, the total annual cost of damage to the U.S. economy in a business as usual (BAU) case in 2025 is predicted to be $271 billion or 1.36 percent of total GDP. The cost of damage rises over time (Table 18.3). Higher ranges of temperature change lead to dramatically increased damage estimates, as shown in Figure 18.8.

These monetized estimates of damage may be subject to controversy and may not cover all aspects of damage (recall the Xs in Table 18.2), but suppose that

Table 18.3

Damage to the U.S. Economy from Climate Change

	in billions of 2006 dollars				as a percentage of GDP			
	2025	2050	2075	2100	2025	2050	2075	2100
Hurricane damages	10	43	142	422	0.05	0.12	0.24	0.41
Real estate losses	34	80	173	360	0.17	0.23	0.29	0.35
Energy sector costs	28	47	82	141	0.14	0.14	0.14	0.14
Water costs	200	336	565	950	1.00	0.98	0.95	0.93
Total costs	271	506	961	1873	1.36	1.47	1.62	1.84

Source: Ackerman and Stanton, 2008.

Figure 18.8 **Increasing Damages from Rising Global Temperatures**

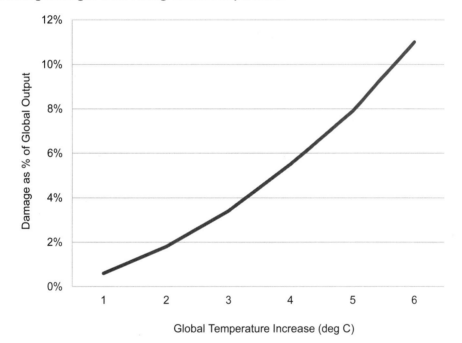

Source: Nordhaus, 2000, p. 95.
Note: National damages are weighted by population to derive global output damage.

we decide to accept them—at least as a rough estimate. We must then weigh the estimated benefits of policies to prevent climate change against the costs of such policies. To estimate these costs, economists use models that show how inputs such as labor, capital, and resources produce economic output.

To lower carbon emissions, we must cut back the use of fossil fuels, substituting other energy sources that may be more expensive. Some economic models predict that this substitution would reduce GDP growth. One major study showed GDP losses of 1–3 percent of GDP for most countries, with higher potential long-term losses for coal-dependent developing countries such as China.[13]

If costs and benefits of an aggressive carbon abatement policy are both in the range of 1–3 percent of GDP, how can we decide what to do? Much depends on

future costs and benefits

benefits and costs that are expected to occur in the future, usually compared to present costs through discounting.

discount rate

the annual rate at which future benefits or costs are discounted relative to current benefits or costs.

our evaluation of **future costs and benefits**. The costs of taking action must be borne today or in the near future. The benefits of taking action (the avoided costs of damages) are further in the future. Our task, then, is to decide today how to balance these future costs and benefits.

As we saw in Chapter 6, economists evaluate future costs and benefits by the use of a **discount rate**. The problems and implicit value judgments associated with discounting add to the uncertainties that we have already noted in valuing costs and benefits. This suggests that we should consider some alternative approaches—including techniques that can incorporate the ecological as well as the economic costs and benefits.

Economic studies dealing with cost-benefit analysis of climate change have come to very different conclusions about policy. According to studies by William Nordhaus and colleagues, the "optimal" economic policies to slow climate change involve modest rates of emissions reductions in the near term, followed by increasing reductions in the medium and long term.[14]

Until recently, most economic studies of climate change reached conclusions similar to those of the Nordhaus studies, although a few recommended more drastic action. The debate on climate change economics changed significantly in 2007, when Nicholas Stern, a former chief economist for the World Bank, released a 700-page report, sponsored by the British government, titled "The Stern Review on the Economics of Climate Change." [15] Publication of the Stern Review generated significant media attention and has intensified the debate about climate change in policy and academic circles. While most previous economic analyses of climate change suggested relatively modest policy responses, the Stern Review strongly recommends immediate and substantial policy action:

> The scientific evidence is now overwhelming: climate change is a serious global threat, and it demands an urgent global response. This Review has assessed a wide range of evidence on the impacts of climate change and on the economic costs, and has used a number of different techniques to assess costs and risks. From all these perspectives, the evidence gathered by the Review leads to a simple conclusion: the benefits of strong and early action far outweigh the economic costs of not acting.

Using the results from formal economic models, the Review estimates that if we don't act, the overall costs and risks of climate change will be equivalent to losing at least 5 percent of global GDP each year, now and forever. If a wider range of risks and impacts is taken into account, the estimates of damage could rise to 20 percent of GDP or more. In contrast, the costs of action—reducing greenhouse gas emissions to avoid the worst impacts of climate change—can be limited to around 1 percent of global GDP each year.[16]

What explains the difference between these two approaches to economic analysis of climate change? One major difference is the choice of the discount rate to use in valuing future costs and benefits.

The present value (PV) of a long-term stream of benefits or costs depends on the discount rate. A high discount rate will lead to a low present valuation for benefits that are mainly in the longer term, and a high present valuation for short-term costs. In contrast, a low discount rate will lead to a higher present valuation for longer-term benefits. The estimated net present value of an aggressive abatement policy will thus be much higher if we choose a low discount rate.

While both the Stern and Nordhaus studies used standard economic methodology, Stern's approach gives greater weight to long-term ecological and economic effects. The Stern Review uses a low discount rate of 1.4 percent to balance present and future costs. Thus even though costs of aggressive action appear higher than benefits for several decades, the high potential long-term damages sway the balance in favor of aggressive action today. These are significant both for their monetary and nonmonetary impacts. In the long term, damage to the environment from global climate change will have significant negative effects on the economy, too. But the use of a standard discount rate in the 5–10 percent range has the effect of reducing the present value of significant long-term future damages to relative insignificance. As shown in Figure 18.9, the assessment of the net benefits of action on climate change depends heavily on the weighting of future damages, since short-term costs of action tend to exceed benefits.

Figure 18.9 **Long-Term Costs and Benefits of Abating Global Climate Change, 1990–2270**

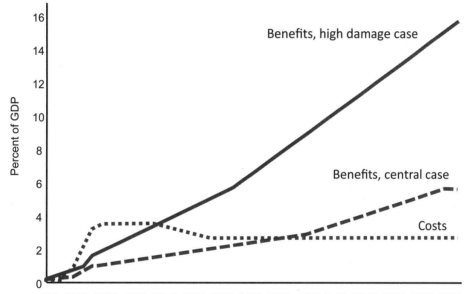

Source: Adapted from Cline, 1992.

precautionary principle
the view that policies should account for uncertainty by taking steps to avoid low-probability but catastrophic events.

Another difference between the two studies concerns their treatment of uncertainty. Stern's approach gives a heavier weighting to uncertain but potentially catastrophic impacts. This reflects the application of a **precautionary principle**: If a particular outcome could be catastrophic, even though it seems unlikely, strong measures should be taken to avoid it. This principle, which has become more widely used in environmental risk management, is especially important for global climate change because of the many unknown but potentially disastrous outcomes possibly associated with continued greenhouse gas accumulation (see Box 18.3).

A third area of difference concerns the assessment of the economic costs of action to mitigate climate change. Measures taken to prevent global climate change will have economic effects on GDP, consumption, and employment, which explain the

BOX 18.3 CLIMATE TIPPING POINTS AND SURPRISES

Much of the uncertainty in projections of climate change relates to the issue of feedback loops. A feedback loop occurs when an initial change, such as warmer temperatures, produces changes in physical processes, which then amplify or lessen the initial effect (a response that increases the original effect is called a positive feedback loop; a response that reduces it is a negative feedback loop). An example of a positive feedback loop is when warming leads to increased melting of arctic tundra, releasing carbon dioxide and methane, which add to atmospheric greenhouse gas accumulations and speed up the warming process.

As a result of various feedback loops associated with climate change, recent evidence suggests that warming is occurring faster than most scientists predicted just five or ten years ago. This is leading to increasing concern over the potential for "runaway" feedback loops, which could result in dramatic changes in a short period. Some scientists suggest that we may be near certain climate tipping points, which, once exceeded, pose the potential for catastrophic effects.

Perhaps the most disturbing possibility is the rapid collapse of the Greenland and West Antarctic Ice Sheets. While the International Panel on Climate Change forecasts a sea-level rise of 0.2 to 0.6 meters (6 inches to 2 feet) by 2100, the melting of these two ice sheets would raise sea levels by 12 meters (nearly 40 feet) or more. Such a scenario is still controversial and considered unlikely to occur in the twenty-first century, but new research suggests that changes can occur much more quickly than originally expected.

In recent studies, scientists found that methane emissions from the Arctic have risen by almost one-third in just five years. The discovery follows a string of reports from the region in recent years that previously frozen boggy soils are melting and releasing methane in greater quantities. Such arctic soils currently lock away billions of tonnes of methane, a far more potent greenhouse gas than carbon dioxide, leading some scientists to describe melting permafrost as a ticking time bomb that could overwhelm efforts to tackle climate change. They fear the warming caused by increased methane emissions will itself release yet more methane and lock the region into a destructive cycle that forces temperatures to rise more rapidly than predicted.

Sources: David Adam, "Arctic Permafrost Leaking Methane at Record Levels, Figures Show," *The Guardian*. 2010, www.guardian.co.uk/environment/2010/jan/14/arctic-permafrost-methane/; Fred Pearce, "Melting Ice Turns up the Heat," *Sydney Morning Herald*, November 18, 2006.

---

reluctance of governments to take drastic measures to reduce significantly emissions of CO_2. But these effects will not all be negative.

The Stern Review conducted a comprehensive review of economic models of the costs of carbon reduction. These cost estimates depend on the modeling assumptions that are used. The predicted costs of stabilizing atmospheric accumulations of CO_2 at 450 ppm range from a 3.4 percent decrease to a 3.9 percent *increase* in GDP. The outcomes depend on a range of assumptions including:

"backstop" energy technologies

technologies such as solar and wind that can replace current energy sources, especially fossil fuels.

least-cost options

actions that can be taken for the lowest overall cost.

- The efficiency or inefficiency of economic responses to energy price signals
- The availability of noncarbon **"backstop" energy technologies**[d]
- Whether countries can trade **least-cost options** for carbon reduction using a tradable permits scheme

---

[d]The economics of tradable permits were presented in Chapter 16.

- Whether revenues from taxes on carbon-based fuels are used to lower other taxes
- Whether external benefits of carbon reduction, including reduction in ground-level air pollution, are taken into account.[17]

Depending on which assumptions are made, policies for emissions reduction could range from a minimalist approach of slightly reducing emissions to drastic CO_2 emissions reduction of 80 percent or more.

Climate Change and Inequality

The effects of climate change will fall most heavily upon the poor of the world. Regions such as Africa could face severely compromised food production and water shortages, while coastal areas in South, East, and Southeast Asia will be at great risk of flooding. Tropical Latin America will see damage to forests and agricultural areas due to drier climate, while in South America changes in precipitation patterns and the disappearance of glaciers will significantly affect water availability.[18] While the richer countries may have the economic resources to adapt to many of the effects of climate change, poorer countries will be unable to implement preventive measures, especially those that rely on the newest technologies.

Recent studies have used geographically distributed impacts models to estimate the impacts of climate change across the global domain. As Table 18.4 indicates, the number of coastal flood victims and population at risk of hunger by 2080 will be relatively larger in Africa, South America, and Asia, where most developing countries are located.

Table 18.4

Regional-Scale Impacts of Climate Change by 2080 (millions of people)

Region	Population living in watersheds with an increase in water-resources stress	Increase in average annual number of coastal flood victims	Additional population at risk of hunger (figures in parentheses assume maximum CO_2 enrichment effect)
Europe	382–493	0.3	0
Asia	892–1197	14.7	266 (–21)
North America	110–145	0.1	0
South America	430–469	0.4	85 (–4)
Africa	691–909	12.8	200 (–2)

Source: Adapted from IPCC, 2007b.

Note: These estimates are based on a business-as-usual scenario (IPCC A2 scenario). The CO_2 enrichment effect is increased plant productivity, which at maximum estimates could actually decrease the number at risk of hunger.

The way in which economists incorporate inequality into their analyses can have a significant impact on their policy recommendations. If all costs are evaluated in money terms, a loss of, say, 10 percent of GDP in a poor country is likely to be much less, in dollars, than a loss of 3 percent of GDP in a rich country. Thus the damages from climate change in poor countries, which may be large as a percentage of GDP, would receive relatively little weight because the losses are relatively small in dollar terms. The Stern Review asserts that the disproportionate effects of climate change on the world's poorest people should increase the estimated costs of climate change. Stern estimates that, without the effects of inequity, the costs of a BAU scenario could be as much as 11–14 percent of global GDP annually. Weighing the impacts on the world's poor more heavily gives a cost estimate of 20 percent of global GDP.[19]

Assumptions about the proper way to evaluate social and environmental costs and benefits can make a big difference to policy recommendations. As we have seen, cost-benefit analyses mostly recommend action to mitigate climate change, but differ widely in the strength of their recommendations based on assumptions about risk and discounting. An ecologically oriented economist would argue that the fundamental issue is the stability of the physical and ecological systems that serve as a planetary climate-control mechanism. This means that **climate stabilization**, rather than economic optimization of costs and benefits, should be the goal. Stabilizing greenhouse gas *emissions* is insufficient; at the current rate of emissions carbon dioxide and other greenhouse gases will continue to accumulate in the atmosphere. Stabilizing *accumulations* of greenhouse gases will require a significant cut below present emission levels. Figure 18.10 shows the IPCC estimates of required reductions in emissions to achieve stabilization at levels of 450 ppm and 550 ppm of CO_2 in the atmosphere.

Clearly, reduction of this magnitude would imply major changes in the way that the global economy uses energy. As we saw in Chapter 12, energy efficiency and the use of renewable energy could have a major effect in reducing emissions. But what kinds of policies are needed to move in this direction, and how have the countries of the world responded to the issue thus far? Chapter 19 addresses these issues in detail.

climate stabilization

the policy of reducing fossil-fuel use to a level that would not increase the potential for global climate change.

Figure 18.10 **Carbon Stabilization Scenarios (450 and 550 ppm CO₂), 1980–2120**

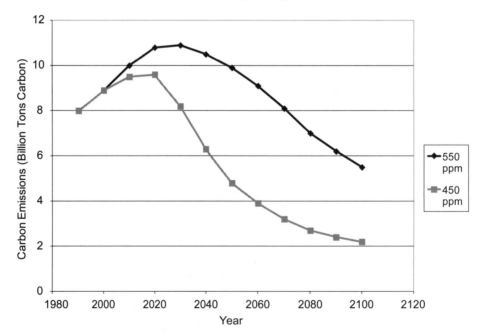

Source: Adapted from IPCC, *Climate Change 2001: The Scientific Basis,* www.ipcc.ch.
Note: ppm = parts per million.

SUMMARY

Climate change, arising from the greenhouse effect of heat-trapping gases, is a global problem. All countries are involved in both its causes and consequences. Currently, greenhouse gas emissions are approximately equally divided between developed and developing countries, but emissions by developing countries will grow considerably in the coming decades.

The most recent scientific evidence indicates that effects during the twenty-first century may range from a global temperature increase of 1°C (2°F) to as much as 6°C (10°F). In addition to simply warming the planet, other predicted effects include disruption of weather patterns and possible sudden major climate shifts.

An estimate of costs and benefits can serve as an economic analysis of climate change. The benefits in this case are the damages potentially averted through action to prevent climate change; the costs are the economic costs of shifting away from fossil-fuel dependence, as well as other economic implications of greenhouse gas reduction.

Cost-benefit studies have estimated both costs and benefits in the range of 1–3 percent of GDP. However, relative evaluation of costs and benefits depends heavily on the discount rate selected. Because damage tends to worsen over time, the use of a high discount rate leads to a lower evaluation of the benefits of avoiding climate change. In addition, effects such as species loss and effects on life and health are difficult to measure in monetary terms. Also, depending on the assumptions used in economic models, the impacts of policies to avoid climate change could range from a 3 percent decrease to a 4 percent increase in GDP.

Impacts of global climate change will fall most heavily on developing countries. Most economic analyses recommend some form of action to mitigate climate change, but vary widely in terms of the urgency and the extent of proposed remedies. Stabilizing carbon dioxide accumulations in the atmosphere at levels below 550 ppm will require drastic action to reduce emissions, implying major changes in global patterns of energy use.

KEY TERMS AND CONCEPTS

adaptive strategies

avoided costs

"backstop" energy technologies

business as usual

climate stabilization

CO_2 equivalent (CO_2e)

common property resources

cost-benefit analysis

discount rate

environmental externality

feedback effect

future costs and benefits

global climate change

global commons

global warming

greenhouse effect

greenhouse gases

internalizing externalities

least-cost options

local and regional air pollutants

ocean acidification

precautionary principle

preventive strategies

public good

stock pollutant

Discussion Questions

1. What is the main evidence of global climate change? How serious is the problem, and what are its primary causes? What issues does it raise concerning global equity and responsibility for dealing with the problem?
2. Do you think that the use of cost-benefit analysis to address the problem of climate change is useful? How can we adequately value things like the melting of Arctic ice caps and inundation of island nations? What is the appropriate role of economic analysis in dealing with questions that affect global ecosystems and future generations?
3. What goals would be appropriate in responding to climate change? Since it is impossible to stop climate change entirely, how should we balance our efforts between adaptation and prevention/mitigation?

Notes

1. Boden et al., 2011.
2. U.S. Energy Information Administration, 2011.
3. Ibid.
4. National Oceanic and Atmospheric Administration, 2012.
5. Adapted from U.S. Environmental Protection Agency, www.epa.gov/climatechange/science/recenttc.html; also from IPCC 2007a.
6. IPCC, 2007a, Working Group I: The Physical Science Basis.
7. NOAA, 2012.
8. NOAA, 2010.
9. Hönish et al., 2012; Deborah Zabarenko, "Ocean's Acidic Shift May Be Fastest in 300 Million Years," Reuters, March 1, 2012.
10. Roger Bradbury, "A World Without Coral Reefs," *New York Times,* July 14, 2012; NOAA, "Scientists Find Rising Carbon Dioxide and Acidified Waters in Puget Sound," 2010, www.noaanews.noaa.gov/stories2010/20100712_pugetsound.html and www.pmel.noaa.gov/co2/story/Going+Green%3A+Lethal+waters/.
11. IPCC, 2007a, Summary for Policymakers, 10.
12. Jevrejeva, et al., 2012; http://www.skepticalscience.com/Sea-levels-will-continue-to-rise.html.
13. Manne and Richels, 1992.
14. Nordhaus 2007, 2008; Nordhaus and Boyer, 2000.
15. Stern, 2007.
16. Stern, 2007, Short Executive Summary, vi.
17. Stern, 2007, chap. 10.
18. IPCC, 2007b; Stern, 2007, chap. 4.
19. Stern, 2007, chap. 6.

References

Ackerman, Frank, and Elizabeth A. Stanton. 2008. "The Cost of Climate Change." Natural Resource Defense Council, www.nrdc.org/globalwarming/cost/cost.pdf.
———. 2011. "Climate Economics: The State of the Art." Stockholm Environment Institute–U.S. Center. http://sei-us.org/Publications_PDF/SEI-ClimateEconomics-state-of-art-2011.pdf.

Ackerman, Frank, Elizabeth A. Stanton, and Ramón Bueno. 2013. "CRED: A New Model of Climate and Development." *Ecological Economics* 85: 166–176.

Boden, T.A., G. Marland, and R.J. Andres. 2011. "Global, Regional, and National Fossil-Fuel CO2 Emissions." Carbon Dioxide Information Analysis Center (CDIAC), Oak Ridge National Laboratory, http://cdiac.ornl.gov/trends/emis/tre_glob_2008.html.

Cline, William R. 1992. *The Economics of Global Warming*. Washington, DC: Institute for International Economics.

———. 2007. *Global Warming and Agriculture: Impact Estimates by Country*. Washington, DC: Center for Global Development and Peterson Institute for International Economics.

Fankhauser, Samuel. 1995. *Valuing Climate Change: The Economics of the Greenhouse*. London: Earthscan.

Hönisch, Bärbel, et al. 2012. "The Geological Record of Ocean Acidification." *Science* 335(6072):1058–1063 (March).

Intergovernmental Panel on Climate Change (IPCC). 2007a. *Climate Change 2007: The Physical Science Basis*. Cambridge, UK, and New York: Cambridge University Press.

———. 2007b. *Climate Change 2007: Impacts, Adaptation, and Vulnerability*. Cambridge, UK, and New York: Cambridge University Press.

———. 2007c. *Climate Change 2007: Mitigation of Climate Change*. Cambridge, UK, and New York: Cambridge University Press.

Jevrejeva, S., J.C. Moore, and A. Grinsted, 2012. "Sea Level Projections to AD2500 with a New Generation of Climate Change Scenarios. *Journal of Global and Planetary Change* 80–81: 14–20.

Manne, Alan S., and Richard G. Richels. 1992. *Buying Greenhouse Insurance: The Economic Costs of CO₂ Emissions Limits*. Cambridge, MA: MIT Press.

National Oceanic and Atmospheric Administration (NOAA). 2010. "Ocean Acidification, Today and in the Future." www.climatewatch.noaa.gov/image/2010/ocean-acidification-today-and-in-the-future/.

———. 2012. "Global Climate Change Indicators." www.ncdc.noaa.gov/indicators/index.html.

National Oceanic and Atmospheric Administration (NOAA). 2012. State of the Climate, Global Analysis Annual 2012. National Climatic Data Center. www.ncdc.noaa.gov/sotc/global/.

Nordhaus, William. 2007. "The Stern Review on the Economics of Climate Change." http://nordhaus.econ.yale.edu/stern_050307.pdf.

———. 2008. *A Question of Balance: Weighing the Options on Global Warming Policies*. New Haven: Yale University Press.

Nordhaus, William D., and Joseph Boyer. 2000. *Warming the World: Economic Models of Global Warming*. Cambridge, MA: MIT Press.

Roodman, David M. 1997. "Getting the Signals Right: Tax Reform to Protect the Environment and the Economy." Worldwatch Paper 134, Worldwatch Institute, Washington, DC.

Stanton, Elizabeth A. 2012. "Development Without Carbon: Climate and the Global Economy Through the 21st Century." Stockholm Environment Institute–U.S. Center. http://sei-us.org/Publications_PDF/SEI-Development-Without-Carbon-Ph1.pdf.

Stern, Nicholas. 2007. *The Economics of Climate Change: The Stern Review*. Cambridge: Cambridge University Press. www.hm-treasury.gov.uk/independent_reviews/stern_review_economics_climate_change/sternreview_index.cfm.

———. 2009. *The Global Deal: Climate Change and the Creation of a New Era of Progress and Prosperity*. Philadelphia: Perseus Books Group.

U.S. Energy Information Administration. 2011. *International Energy Outlook*. www.eia.gov/analysis/projection-data.cfm#intlproj/.

World Bank. 2010. *World Development Report 2010: Development and Climate Change*. Washington, DC.

WEB SITES

1. **http://epa.gov/climatechange/index.html**. The global warming Web site of the U.S. Environmental Protection Agency. The site provides links to information on the causes, impact, and trends related to global climate change.

2. **www.ipcc.ch/**. The Web site for the Intergovernmental Panel on Climate Change, a UN-sponsored agency "to assess

the scientific, technical, and socioeconomic information relevant for the understanding of the risk of human-induced climate change." Its Web site includes assessment reports detailing the relationships between human actions and global climate change.

3. **www.hm-treasury.gov.uk/sternreview_index.htm**. Web site for the Stern Review, providing an extensive analysis of the economics of climate change including impacts, stabilization, mitigation, and adaptation.

Global Climate Change: Policy Responses

CHAPTER 19 FOCUS QUESTIONS

- What are the possible policy responses to global climate change?
- What does economic theory suggest about appropriate policy response?
- What are some specific policies that have been proposed or implemented to address global climate change?

19.1 ADAPTATION AND MITIGATION

adaptive measures

actions designed to reduce the magnitude or risk of damages from global climate change.

preventive measures/ preventive strategies

actions designed to reduce the extent of climate change by reducing projected emissions of greenhouse gases.

As discussed in Chapter 18, the scientific evidence regarding the seriousness of global climate change supports policy action. Economic analyses of climate change have generally recommended policy changes, although with considerable variability. The Stern Review on the Economics of Climate Change, in particular, calls for "an urgent global response."[1]

Policy responses to climate change can be broadly classified into two categories: **adaptive measures** to deal with the consequences of climate change and mitigation, or **preventive measures** intended to lower the magnitude or timing of climate change. Adaptive measures include:

- Construction of dikes and seawalls to protect against rising seas and extreme weather events such as floods and hurricanes.
- Shifting cultivation patterns in agriculture to adapt to changing weather conditions.
- Creating institutions that can mobilize the needed human, material, and financial resources to respond to climate-related disasters.

Mitigation measures include:

- Reducing emissions of greenhouse gases by meeting energy demands from sources with lower greenhouse gas emissions (e.g., switching from coal to wind energy for electricity).
- Reducing greenhouse gas emissions by increasing energy efficiency (e.g., demand-side management, as discussed in Chapter 12).

- Enhancing **carbon sinks**.[a] Forests recycle carbon dioxide (CO_2) into oxygen; preserving forested areas and expanding reforestation have a significant effect on net CO_2 emissions.

Economic analysis can provide policy guidance for nearly any particular preventive or adaptive measure. **Cost-benefit analysis**, discussed in Chapters 6 and 18, can present a basis for evaluating whether a policy should be implemented. However, as discussed in Chapter 18, economists disagree about the appropriate assumptions and methodologies for cost-benefit analyses of climate change. A less controversial conclusion from economic theory is that we should apply **cost-effectiveness analysis** in considering which policies to adopt. The use of cost-effectiveness analysis avoids many of the complications associated with cost-benefit analysis. While cost-benefit analysis attempts to offer a basis for deciding upon policy goals, cost-effectiveness analysis accepts a goal as given by society and uses economic techniques to determine the most efficient way to reach that goal.

In general, economists favor approaches that work through market mechanisms to achieve their goals (see Box 19.1). Market-oriented approaches are considered cost effective; rather than attempting to control market actors directly, they shift incentives so that individuals and firms will change their behavior to take external costs and benefits into account. Examples of market-based policy tools include **pollution taxes** and **transferable, or tradable, permits**. Both of these are potentially useful tools for greenhouse gas reduction. Other relevant economic policies include measures to create incentives for the adoption of renewable energy sources and energy-efficient technology.

Most of this chapter focuses on mitigation policies, but it is becoming increasingly evident that mitigation policies need to be supplemented with adaption policies. Climate change is already occurring, and even if significant mitigation policies are implemented in the immediate future, warming and sea-level rise will continue well into the future, even for centuries.[2] The urgency and ability to institute adap-

---

BOX 19.1   ECONOMISTS' STATEMENT ON CLIMATE CHANGE

In 1997, more than 2,500 economists, including eight Nobel laureates, signed the following public statement calling for serious steps to deal with the risks of global climate change:

I. The review conducted by a distinguished international panel of scientists under the auspices of the Intergovernmental Panel on Climate Change has determined that "the balance of evidence suggests a discernible human influence on global climate." As economists, we believe that global climate change carries with it significant environmental, economic, social, and geopolitical risks, and that preventive steps are justified.

(continued)

---

[a]Carbon sinks are areas where carbon may be stored. Natural sinks include the oceans and forests. Human intervention can either reduce or expand these sinks through forest management and agricultural practices.

BOX 19.1 *(continued)*

II. Economic studies have found that there are many potential policies to reduce greenhouse-gas emissions for which the total benefits outweigh the total costs. For the United States in particular, sound economic analysis shows that there are policy options that would slow climate change without harming American living standards, and these measures may in fact improve U.S. productivity in the longer run.

III. The most efficient approach to slowing climate change is through market-based policies. In order for the world to achieve its climatic objectives at minimum cost, a cooperative approach among nations is required—such as an international emissions trading agreement. The United States and other nations can most efficiently implement their climate policies through market mechanisms, such as carbon taxes or the auction of emissions permits. The revenues generated from such policies can effectively be used to reduce the deficit or to lower existing taxes.

Source: www.motherjones.com/toc/1997/05/economists-statement-climate-change. A more recent statement of scientists and economists, including eight Nobel Prize winners in science or economics, is the *U.S. Scientists and Economists' Call for Swift and Deep Cuts in Greenhouse Gas Emissions* at www.ucsusa.org/global_warming/solutions/big_picture_solutions/scientists-and-economists.html.

tive measures varies across the world. It is the world's poor who face the greatest need to adapt but also most lack the necessary resources.

> [Climate change's] adverse impacts will be most striking in the developing nations because of their geographical and climatic conditions, their high dependence on natural resources, and their limited capacity to adapt to a changing climate. Within these countries, the poorest, who have the least resources and the least capacity to adapt, are the most vulnerable. Projected changes in the incidence, frequency, intensity, and duration of climate extremes (for example, heat waves, heavy precipitation, and drought), as well as more gradual changes in the average climate, will notably threaten their livelihoods—further increasing inequities between the developing and developed worlds.[3]

The Intergovernmental Panel on Climate Change (IPCC) classifies adaptation needs into seven sectors, as shown in Table 19.1. Some of the most critical areas for adaptation include water, agriculture, and human health. Climate change is expected to increase precipitation in some areas, mainly the higher latitudes including Alaska, Canada, and Russia, but decrease it in other areas, including Central America, North Africa, and southern Europe. A reduction in water runoff from snowmelt and glaciers could threaten the water supplies of more than a billion people in areas such as India and parts of South America. Providing safe drinking water in these regions may require building new dams for water storage, increasing the efficiency of water use, and other adaptation strategies.

Changing precipitation and temperature patterns have significant implications for agriculture. With moderate warming, crop yields are expected to increase in some colder regions, including parts of North America, but overall the impacts on agriculture are expected to be negative, and increasingly so with greater warming. Agricultural impacts are expected to be the most severe in Africa and Asia. More research is necessary to develop crops that can grow under anticipated weather

Table 19.1

Climate Change Adaptation Needs, by Sector

Sector	Adaptation strategy
Water	Expand water storage Expand desalination Increase water-use and irrigation efficiency
Agriculture	Adjust planting dates and crop varieties Crop relocation Improved land management to deal with floods/draughts
Infrastructure	Relocate vulnerable communities Build and strengthen seawalls and other barriers Create marshlands for flood control Dune reinforcement
Human health	Health plans for extreme heat Increase tracking of heat-related diseases Address threats to safe drinking water supplies Increase medical services for affected communities
Tourism	Relocation of ski areas More reliance on artificial snowmaking
Transport	Relocation of some transport infrastructure New design standards to cope with climate change
Energy	Strengthen distribution infrastructure Address increased demand for cooling Increase use of renewables

Source: IPCC, 2007.

conditions. Agriculture may need to be abandoned in some areas but expanded in others.[4]

The impacts of climate change on human health are already occurring. The World Health Organization (WHO) has estimated that more than 140,000 people per year are already dying as a direct result of climate change, primarily in Africa and Southeast Asia.[5] The WHO recommends strengthening public health systems, including increased education, disease surveillance, vaccination, and preparedness. The spread of tropical diseases such as malaria can be limited by insect control and the provision of mosquito nets and adequate hygiene.

Various estimates exist for the cost of appropriate adaptation measures. The United Nations has estimated that by 2030 the total cost of adapting to climate change will be between about $60 billion and $190 billion annually.[6] While adaptation costs for water, agriculture, and human health will be higher in developing countries, infrastructure adaptation will be higher in developed countries because the existing infrastructure is much more extensive. The report noted the need for "policy changes, incentives, and direct financial support" to encourage a shift in investment patterns.

A review of these UN estimates concludes that its costs were probably too low by a factor of two to three and even more when the costs for excluded sectors, such as tourism and energy, are also considered.[7] Further, adaptation costs are expected to increase after 2030 as warming and other impacts become more severe. In 2010 the World Bank estimated the costs of adaptation in developing countries at $75 billion to $100 billion annually from 2010 to 2050.[8] The report notes that funding for adaptation measures could be met by doubling current foreign aid from developed countries. It also mentions that fostering economic development will provide developing countries with greater internal resources to adapt to climate change.

19.2 CLIMATE CHANGE MITIGATION: ECONOMIC POLICY OPTIONS

The release of greenhouse gases in the atmosphere is a clear example of a negative externality that imposes significant costs on a global scale. In the language of economic theory, the current market for carbon-based fuels such as coal, oil, and natural gas takes into account only private costs and benefits, which leads to a market equilibrium that does not correspond to the social optimum. From a social perspective, the market price for fossil fuels is too low and the quantity consumed too high, as discussed in Chapter 12.

Carbon Taxes

carbon tax
a per-unit tax on goods and services based on the quantity of carbon dioxide emitted during the production or consumption process.

A standard economic remedy for internalizing external costs is a per-unit tax on the pollutant. In this case, what is called for is a **carbon tax**, levied on carbon-based fossil fuels in proportion to the amount of carbon associated with their production and use. Such a tax will raise the price of carbon-based energy sources and so give consumers incentives to conserve energy overall (which would reduce their tax burden), as well as shifting their demand to alternative sources of energy that produce lower carbon emissions (and are thus taxed at lower rates).

> Carbon taxes would appear to consumers as energy price increases. But since taxes would be levied on primary energy, which represents only one part of the cost of delivered energy (such as gasoline or electricity) and more important, since one fuel can in many cases be substituted for another, overall price increases may not be jolting. Consumers can respond to new prices by reducing energy use and buying fewer carbon-intensive products (those that require great amounts of carbon-based fuels to produce). In addition, some of these savings could be used to buy other less carbon-intensive goods and services.
>
> Clearly, a carbon tax creates an incentive for producers and consumers to avoid paying the tax by reducing their use of carbon-intensive fuels. Contrary to other taxed items and activities, this avoidance has social benefits—reduced energy use and reduced CO_2 emissions. Thus, declining tax revenues over time indicate policy success—just the opposite of what happens when tax policy seeks to maintain steady or increasing revenues. [9]

Table 19.2 shows the impact that different levels of a carbon tax would have on the prices of coal, oil, and natural gas. Based on energy content, measured in Btus, coal is the most carbon-intensive fossil fuel, while natural gas produces the lowest emissions.[b] Calculating the impact of a carbon tax relative to the standard commercial units for each fuel source, we see that a $10/ton carbon tax, for example, raises the price of a barrel of oil by about a dollar (see Box 19.2 for a discussion of the difference between a tax on carbon and a tax on CO_2). This is equivalent

---

[b]One Btu (British thermal unit) is approximately the amount of energy needed to raise the temperature of one pound of water one degree Fahrenheit (from 39 to 40 degrees).

Table 19.2

Alternative Carbon Taxes on Fossil Fuels

	Coal	Oil	Natural Gas
Tons of carbon per billion Btu	25.6	17.0	14.5
Tons of carbon per standard unit of fuel	0.574/ton	0.102/barrel	0.015/Mcf (thousand cubic feet)
Average price (2012)	$43.34/ton	$95.55/barrel	$3.20/Mcf
Carbon tax amount per unit of fuel:			
$10/ton of carbon	$5.74/ton	$1.02/barrel	
			$0.15/Mcf
$100/ton of carbon	$57.42/ton	$10.15/barrel	$1.49/Mcf
$200/ton of carbon	$114.85/ton	$20.31/barrel	$2.98/Mcf
Carbon tax as a percent of fuel price:			
$10/ton of carbon	13%	1%	5%
$100/ton of carbon	132%	11%	47%
$200/ton of carbon	265%	21%	93%

Source: Carbon emissions calculated from carbon coefficients and thermal conversion factors available from the U.S. Department of Energy. Oil price is August 2012 world average. Natural gas price is August 2012 average U.S. wellhead price. Coal price is August 2012 U.S. average over 5 different types of coal. All price data from the U.S. Energy Information Administration.

Note: Btu = British thermal unit.

to only about 2 cents per gallon.[c] A $100/ton carbon tax equates to an increase in gasoline prices of about 24 cents per gallon. Even though natural gas has a lower carbon content than oil, its relatively low price in 2012 means that a carbon tax would increase its price by a higher proportion. The impact of a carbon tax would be most significant for coal prices—a $100/ton carbon tax would more than double coal prices.

BOX 19.2 CARBON TAX CONVERSIONS

A common point of confusion is that a carbon tax can be expressed as either a tax per unit of carbon or per unit of carbon dioxide. When comparing different carbon tax proposals we need to be careful that we are expressing each tax in the same units. Say, for example, that an economist proposes a tax of $100 per ton of carbon, while another economist proposes a tax of $35 per ton of carbon dioxide. Which one is proposing the larger tax?

To convert between the two units, we first note the relative molecular weights of carbon and carbon dioxide (CO_2). Carbon has a molecular weight of 12, while CO_2 has a molecular weight of 44. So if we want to convert a tax of $100 per ton of carbon into a tax per ton of CO_2, we would multiply the tax by 12/44, or 0.2727:

$$\$100 * 0.2727 = \$27.27$$

So a tax of $100 per ton of carbon is equivalent to a tax of about $27 per ton of CO_2. If we wanted instead to convert the tax of $35 per ton of CO_2, we would multiply by the inverse ratio of 44/12, or 3.6667:

$$\$35 * 3.6667 = \$128.33$$

So a tax of $35 per ton of CO_2 is equivalent to a tax of about $128 per ton of carbon. Using either comparison, we can conclude that a tax of $35 per ton of CO_2 is larger than a tax of $100 per ton of carbon.

---

[c]A barrel of oil contains 42 gallons.

Will these tax amounts affect people's driving or home heating habits very much, or impact industry's use of fuels? This depends on the **elasticity of demand** for these fuels. As noted earlier (see Chapter 3 Appendix), elasticity of demand is defined as:

$$Elasticity\ of\ demand = \frac{Percent\ change\ in\ quantity\ demanded}{percent\ change\ in\ price}$$

Economists have measured the elasticity of demand for different fossil fuels, particularly gasoline. One study surveyed all the available research on the elasticity of demand for motor fuels and found that in the short term (about one year or less) elasticity estimates averaged –0.25.[10d] This means that a 10 percent increase in the price of gasoline would be expected to decrease gasoline demand in the short term by about 2.5 percent.

In the long term (about five years or so) people are more responsive to gasoline price increases, as they have time to purchase different vehicles and adjust their driving habits. The average long-term elasticity of demand for motor fuels, based on fifty-one estimates, is –0.64.[11] According to Table 19.2, a $200 carbon tax would increase the price of oil by 21 percent, which would add 48 cents per gallon to the price of gasoline. Assuming a retail price of $3 per gallon, this would translate to a 16 percent price increase. A long-term elasticity of –0.64 suggests that after people have time to fully adjust to this price change, the demand for gasoline should decline by about 10 percent.

Figure 19.1 shows a cross-country relationship between gasoline prices and per capita consumption. (Since the cost of producing a gallon of gasoline varies little across countries, variations in the price of a gallon in different countries is almost solely a function of differences in taxes.) Note that this relationship is similar to that of a demand curve: Higher prices are associated with lower consumption, and lower prices with higher consumption.

The relationship shown here, however, is not exactly the same as a demand curve; since we are looking at data from different countries, the assumption of "other things equal," which is needed to construct a demand curve, does not hold. Differences in demand may, for example, be in part a function of differences in income levels rather than prices. Also, people in the United States may drive more partly because travel distances (especially in the western United States) are greater than in many European countries, and public transportation options fewer. But there does seem to be a clear price/consumption relationship. The data shown here suggest that it would take a fairly big price hike—in the range of $0.50–$1.00 per gallon or more—to affect fuel use substantially.

Would a large gasoline tax increase, or a broad-based carbon tax, ever be politically feasible? Especially in the United States, high taxes on gasoline and other fuels would face much opposition, especially if people saw it as infringing on their freedoms to drive and use energy. As Figure 19.1 shows, the United States has by far the highest gasoline consumption per person and the lowest prices outside the Middle East. But let us note two things about the proposal for substantial carbon taxes:

---

[d]The short-run price elasticity of demand for gasoline may have declined significantly in recent years. Hughes et al. (2008) estimate an elasticity of demand for 2001–2006 of –0.03 to –0.08, compared with their estimate of an elasticity of demand for 1975–1980 of –0.21 to –0.34.

Figure 19.1 **Gasoline Price Versus Consumption in Industrial Countries, 2009**

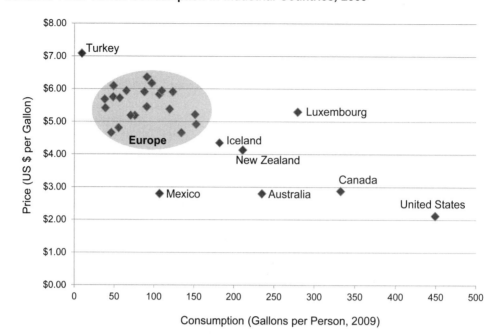

Sources: GTZ, 2009; U.S. Energy Information Administration database.
Note: Shaded area represents price/consumption range typical of West European countries.

revenue-neutral tax shift

policies that are designed to balance tax increases on certain products or activities with a reduction in other taxes, such as a reduction in income taxes that offsets a carbon-based tax.

- First, revenue recycling could redirect the revenue from carbon and other environmental taxes to lower other taxes. Much of the political opposition to high energy taxes comes from the perception that they would be an *extra* tax—on top of the income, property, and social security taxes that people already pay. If a carbon tax were matched, for example, with a substantial cut in income or social security taxes, it might be more politically acceptable.

  The idea of increasing taxes on economic "bads," such as pollution, while reducing taxes on things we want to encourage, such as labor and capital investment, is fully consistent with principles of economic efficiency. Rather than a net tax increase, this would be **revenue-neutral tax shift**—the total amount that citizens pay to the government in taxes is essentially unchanged. Some of the tax revenues could also be used to provide relief for low-income people to offset the burden of higher energy costs.

- Second, if such a revenue-neutral tax shift did take place, individuals or businesses whose operations were more energy efficient would actually save money overall. The higher cost of energy would also create a powerful incentive for energy-saving technological innovations and stimulate new markets. Economic adaptation would be easier if the higher carbon taxes (and lower income and capital taxes) were phased in over time.

Tradable Permits

An alternative to a carbon tax is a system of tradable carbon permits, also called cap and trade. A carbon trading scheme could be national in scope or include several countries. An international permit system could work as follows:

- Each country would be allocated a specific permissible level of carbon emissions. The total number of carbon permits issued would equal the desired national goal. For example, if carbon emissions for a particular country are currently 40 million tons and the policy goal is to reduce this by 10 percent, then permits would be issued to emit only 36 million tons. Note that different countries could be obliged to meet different targets, which was the case under the Kyoto Protocol agreement on climate change (see Section 19.4).
- Permits are allocated to individual carbon-emitting sources in each country. Including all carbon sources (e.g., all motor vehicles) in a trading scheme is clearly not practical. It is most effective to implement permits as far upstream in the production process as possible to simplify the administration of the program and cover the most emissions.[e] Permits could be allocated to the largest carbon emitters, such as power companies and manufacturing plants, or even further upstream to the suppliers through which carbon fuels enter the production process—oil producers and importers, coal mines, and natural gas drillers.

  These permits could initially be allocated for free on the basis of past emissions or auctioned to the highest bidders. As discussed in Chapter 16, the effectiveness of the trading system should be the same regardless of how the permits are allocated. However, there is a significant difference in the distribution of costs and benefits: Giving permits out for free essentially amounts to a windfall gain for polluters, while auctioning permits imposes real costs upon firms and generates public revenues.
- Firms are able to trade permits freely among themselves. Firms whose emissions exceed the number of permits they hold must purchase additional permits or else face penalties. Meanwhile firms that are able to reduce their emissions below their allowance at low cost will seek to sell their permits for a profit. Firms will settle upon permit prices through free market negotiations. It may also be possible for environmental groups or other organizations to purchase permits and retire them—thus reducing overall emissions.
- Countries and firms could also receive credit for financing carbon reduction efforts in other countries. For example, a German firm could get credit for installing efficient electric generating equipment in China, replacing highly polluting coal plants.

A tradable permit system encourages the least-cost carbon reduction options to be implemented, as rational firms will implement those emission-reduction actions that are cheaper than the market permit price. As discussed in Chapter 16, tradable permit systems have been successful in reducing sulfur and nitrogen oxide emissions at low cost. Depending on the allocation of permits, it might also mean that developing countries could transform permits into a new export commodity by choosing a noncarbon path for their energy development. They would then be able to sell permits to industrialized countries that were having trouble meeting their reduction requirements.

While the government sets the number of permits available, the permit price is determined by market forces. In this case, the supply curve is fixed, or vertical, at the number of permits allocated, as shown in Figure 19.2. The supply of permits is set at Q_0. Firms' demand curve for permits represents their willingness to pay for them. In turn, their maximum willingness to pay for permits is equal to the poten-

---

[e]"Upstream" here denotes an early stage in the production process, as discussed in Chapter 3 regarding a pollution tax.

tial profits they can earn by emitting carbon. This is similar to the idea presented in Chapter 4 in which fishers were willing to pay up to their potential economic profits to acquire an individual transferable quota.

Figure 19.2 **Determination of Carbon Permit Price**

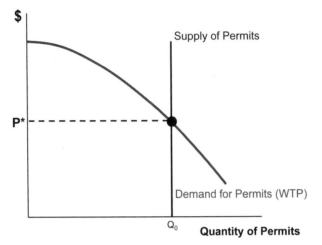

Note: WTP = Willingness to pay.

Assume that the permits will be auctioned off one by one to the highest bidders. Figure 19.2 shows that the willingness to pay for the first permit would be quite high, as a particular firm stands to make a relatively large profit by being allowed to emit one unit of carbon. For the second permit, firms that failed to obtain the first permit would be expected to simply repeat their bids. The firm that successfully bid for the first permit could also bid for the second permit, but would be expected to bid a lower amount assuming their marginal profits are declining (i.e., their supply curve slopes upward, as is normal).

Regardless of whether the same firm wins the bid for the second permit, or a new firm, the selling price for the second permit would be lower. This process would continue, with all successive permits selling for lower prices, until the last permit is auctioned off. The selling price of this permit, represented by $P*$ in the graph, is the market-clearing permit price. We can also interpret $P*$ as the marginal benefit, or profit, associated with the right to emit the Q_0^{th} unit of carbon.

While all permits could theoretically sell for different prices, tradable permit markets are normally set up so all permits sell for the market-clearing price. This is the case for the acid rain program in the United States, which has operated since 1995 and is widely considered to be a successful emissions trading program, as discussed in Box 16.1. In that program, all parties interested in purchasing permits make their bids, indicating how many permits they are willing to purchase at what price. Whoever bids the highest gets the number of permits that were requested. Then the second-highest bidders get the number of permits they applied for, and so on until all permits are allocated. The selling price of all permits is the winning bid for the very last permit available. This would be $P*$ in Figure 19.2. All bidders who bid below this price do not receive any permits.

Another important point is that each firm can choose to reduce its carbon emissions in a cost-effective manner. Firms have various options for reducing their carbon emissions. Figure 19.3 shows an example in which a firm has three carbon reduction strategies: replacing older manufacturing plants, investing in energy efficiency, and funding forest expansion to increase carbon storage in biomass. In each case, the graph shows the marginal costs of reducing carbon emissions through that strategy. These marginal costs generally rise as more units of carbon are reduced, but they may be higher and increase more rapidly for some options than others.

In this example, replacement of manufacturing plants using existing carbon-emitting technologies is possible but will tend to have high marginal costs—as shown in the first graph in Figure 19.1. Reducing emissions through greater energy efficiency has lower marginal costs, as seen in the middle graph. Finally, carbon storage through forest area expansion has the lowest marginal costs. The permit price $P*$ (as determined in Figure 19.2) will govern the relative levels of implementation of each of these strategies. Firms will find it profitable to reduce emissions using a particular strategy so long as the costs of that option are lower than the cost of purchasing a permit. In this example, we see that forest expansion would be used for the largest share of the reduction, while plant replacement would be used for the lowest share.

Firms (and countries if the program is international) that participate in such a trading scheme can decide for themselves how much of each control strategy to implement and will naturally favor the least-cost methods. This will probably involve a combination of different approaches. In an international program, suppose that one country undertakes extensive reforestation. It is then likely to have excess permits, which it can sell to a country with few low-cost reduction options. The net effect will be the worldwide implementation of the least-cost reduction techniques.

This system combines the advantages of economic efficiency with a guaranteed result: reduction in overall emissions to the desired level. The major problem, of course, is achieving agreement on the initial number of permits and whether the permits will be allocated freely or auctioned off. There may also be measurement problems and issues such as whether to count only commercial carbon emissions or to include emissions changes that result from land use changes such as those associated with agriculture and forestry.

Figure 19.3 **Carbon Reduction Options with a Permit System**

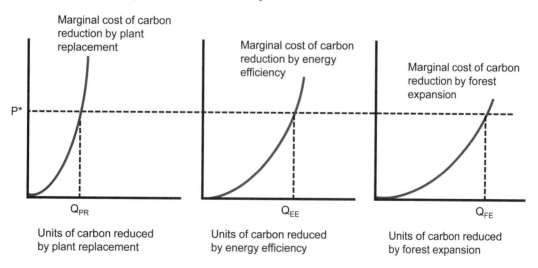

Note: Marginal costs shown here are hypothetical.

Carbon Taxes or Cap and Trade?

There is a lively debate regarding which economic approach should be used to reduce carbon emissions. Carbon taxes and a cap-and-trade approach have important similarities but also important differences.

As discussed in Chapter 16, both pollution taxes and cap and trade can, in theory, achieve a given level of pollution reduction at the least overall cost. Both approaches will also result in the same level of price increases to final consumers. Both approaches create a strong incentive for technological innovation. Both approaches can raise the same amount of government revenue, assuming all permits are auctioned off. Both approaches can be implemented upstream in production processes to cover the same proportion of total emissions.

Yet the two approaches have several important differences. Some of the advantages of a carbon tax include:[12]

- In general, a carbon tax is considered simpler to understand and more transparent than a cap-and-trade approach. Most people and businesses are familiar with paying taxes, but may be wary of a complex cap-and-trade system.
- As we saw in Chapter 16, with technological change, a carbon tax will automatically further reduce carbon emissions. In a cap-and-trade program, technological change will instead reduce the price of permits.
- A carbon tax could probably be implemented more quickly. Given the need to address climate change as soon as possible, it may be inadvisable to spend years working out the details of a cap-and-trade program.
- Perhaps the most important advantage of a carbon tax is that it provides greater price predictability. If businesses and households know what future taxes will be on fossil fuels and other greenhouse gas–emitting products, they can invest accordingly. For example, whether a business invests in an energy efficient heating and cooling system depends on its expectations of future fuel prices. In a cap-and-trade system, permit prices could vary considerably, leading to **price volatility** that makes planning difficult. A carbon tax, by contrast, provides a degree of price stability, especially if carbon tax levels are published years into the future.

price volatility
rapid and frequent changes in price, leading to market instability.

The advantages of a cap-and-trade system include:

- Even though a cap-and-trade system ultimately results in the same level of price increases to consumers and businesses, it avoids the negative connotations of a "tax." So a cap-and-trade system seems to generate less political opposition than a carbon tax.
- Some businesses favor cap-and-trade because they believe that they can successfully lobby governments for free permits, rather than having to purchase them at auction. Distributing permits for free in the early stages of a cap-and-trade program can make it more politically acceptable to businesses.
- The greatest advantage of a cap-and-trade approach is that emissions are known with certainty because the government sets the number of available permits. Since the policy goal is ultimately to reduce carbon emissions, a cap-and-trade approach does this directly while a carbon tax does it indirectly

through price increases. Using a cap-and-trade approach, we can achieve a specific emissions path simply by setting the number of permits. In a carbon tax system, achieving a specific emissions target may require numerous adjustments to the tax rates, which may be politically very difficult.

The choice of instrument—carbon tax or cap and trade—mainly depends on whether policy makers are more concerned with price uncertainty or emissions uncertainty. (Recall the discussion on price versus quantity instruments in Chapter 16). If you take the perspective that price certainty is important because it allows for better long-term planning, then a carbon tax is preferable. If you believe that the relevant policy goal is to reduce carbon emissions by a specified amount with certainty, then a cap-and-trade approach is preferable, although it may lead to some price volatility.

Other Policy Tools: Subsidies, Standards, R&D, and Technology Transfer

Political hurdles may prevent the adoption of sweeping carbon taxes or transferable permit systems in the near future. Fortunately, a variety of other policy measures have the potential to lower carbon emissions. Even with implementation of a widespread carbon tax or cap-and-trade system, supplemental policies may still be necessary to reduce carbon emissions sufficiently to keep warming within acceptable levels. These policies are generally not considered to be sufficient by themselves, but they may be important components of a comprehensive approach. To some extent these policies are already being implemented in various countries. These policies include:

efficiency standards
regulations that mandate efficiency criteria for goods, such as fuel economy standards for automobiles.

technology transfer
the process of sharing technological information or equipment, particularly among countries.

- *Shifting subsidies from carbon-based to non–carbon-based fuels.* Many countries currently provide direct or indirect subsidies to fossil fuels, as discussed in Chapter 12. The elimination of these subsidies would alter the competitive balance in favor of alternative fuel sources. If these subsidy expenditures were redirected to renewable sources, especially in the form of tax rebates for investment, it could promote a boom in investment in renewables.
- *The use of **efficiency standards** for machinery and appliances, and fuel-economy standards or requirements for low-carbon fuels.* By imposing standards that require greater energy efficiency or lower carbon use, technologies and practices can be altered in favor of a low-carbon path.
- *Research and development (R&D) expenditures promoting the commercialization of alternative technologies.* Both government R&D programs and favorable tax treatment of corporate R&D for alternative energy can speed commercialization. The existence of noncarbon "backstop" technologies significantly reduces the economic cost of measures such as carbon taxes, and if the backstop were to become fully competitive with fossil fuels, carbon taxes would be unnecessary.
- ***Technology transfer** to developing countries.* The bulk of projected growth in carbon emissions will come in the developing world. Many energy development projects are now funded by agencies such as the World Bank and regional development banks. To the extent that these funds can be

directed toward noncarbon energy systems, supplemented by other funds dedicated specifically to alternative energy development, it will be economically feasible for developing countries to turn away from fossil-fuel intensive paths, achieving significant local environmental benefits at the same time.

19.3 CLIMATE CHANGE: THE TECHNICAL CHALLENGE

Meeting the climate change challenge will require two complementary approaches. Economic policy instruments such as carbon taxes, cap and trade, and subsidies use incentives to motivate changes in behavior. For example, a carbon tax that raises the price of gasoline will lead many people to choose to drive less or buy a more fuel-efficient vehicle. But we can also look at climate change from a technical perspective rather than a behavioral perspective. Economic policies can create powerful incentives for technological changes. Because of higher gas prices as a result of a carbon tax, the increased demand for high-efficiency vehicles would motivate automobile companies to direct more of their investments to hybrid and electric vehicles.

It is worthwhile to consider what needs to be done in response to climate change from a technical perspective—not just to gain a greater understanding of the issues but to also gain some insights for appropriate policies. We now summarize two well-known analyses of the technical aspects of carbon mitigation.

Climate Stabilization Wedges

Some proposals for carbon mitigation require significant technological advancement, such as the widespread use of artificial photosynthesis or nuclear fusion. The future cost and technical feasibility of these technologies remain uncertain. Ideally, we could reduce carbon emissions sufficiently using existing technologies or those reasonably expected to be available in the near future. In 2004 physical scientists Stephen Pacala and Robert Socolow determined that carbon emissions could be stabilized over the next fifty years by scaling up existing technologies.[13]

They present the climate challenge as shown in Figure 19.4, slightly updated from their original paper.[14] Under a business as usual (BAU) scenario, carbon emissions are expected to approximately double over the next fifty years, from about 8 billion tons of carbon per year to 16 billion tons.[f] They consider which actions would effectively reduce total emissions by 1 billion tons per year by 2060. Each of these actions produces a **climate stabilization wedge** that moves emission down from the BAU scenario. Thus if eight of these wedges were implemented, carbon emissions would remain steady over the next fifty years, even as population expands and economies grow.

They then reviewed a range of technological options, focusing on technologies that were already available on an industrial level. Their proposed actions are broadly divided into three categories: increased energy efficiency, energy supply-side shifts, and carbon storage. In all, they list fifteen potential stabilization wedges:

climate stabilization wedge

a concept proposed by Pacala and Socolow (1994) in which specific mitigation actions are presented to reduce projected greenhouse gas emissions by one gigaton each (one gigaton reduction equals one wedge).

---

[f]At the time that Pacala and Socolow wrote their original paper, global carbon emissions were about 8 billion tons per year. Global carbon emissions in 2012 were approximately 9 billion tons.

Figure 19.4 **Climate Stabilization Wedges**

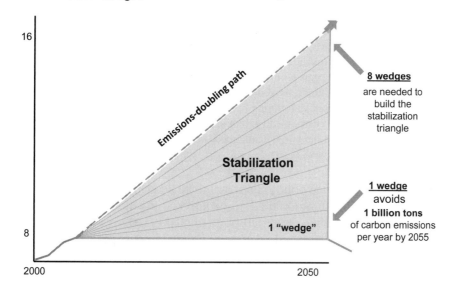

Source: Pacala and Socolow, 2004.

1. Double fuel efficiency of 2 billion cars from 30 to 60 miles per gallon (mpg).
2. Decrease the number of car miles traveled globally by half.
3. Use best-efficiency practices in all residential and commercial buildings worldwide.
4. Produce current coal-based electricity with twice today's efficiency.
5. Replace 1,400 coal electricity plants with natural gas-powered facilities.
6. Capture AND store emissions from 800 coal electricity plants.
7. Produce hydrogen from coal at six times today's rate AND store the captured CO_2.
8. Capture carbon from 180 coal-to-synfuels plants AND store the CO_2.
9. Add double the current global nuclear capacity to replace coal-based electricity.
10. Increase global wind-produced electricity capacity by ten times relative to today, for a total of 2 million large windmills.
11. Install 100 times the current global capacity of solar electricity.
12. Use 40,000 square kilometers of solar panels (or 4 million windmills) to produce hydrogen for fuel cell cars.
13. Increase ethanol production twelvefold by creating biomass plantations with area equal to one-sixth of world cropland.
14. Eliminate tropical deforestation.
15. Adopt conservation tillage in all agricultural soils worldwide.

Their proposed wedges appear daunting, especially because these actions must be implemented on a global, rather than national, scale. Such a degree of global cooperation appears lacking today. Also, as indicated by Figure 18.10 in the previous chapter, keeping emissions constant over the next fifty years will not be sufficient to keep warming to acceptable levels. Thus instead of implementing eight wedges, we may need to implement ten or more.

As in our discussion of energy in Chapter 12, we can conclude that the primary challenges are not technical but, rather, political and social.

> None of the options is a pipe dream or an unproven idea. Today, one can buy electricity from a wind turbine, PV array, gas turbine, or nuclear power plant. One can buy hydrogen produced with the chemistry of carbon capture, biofuel to power one's car, and hundreds of devices that improve energy efficiency. One can visit tropical forests where clear-cutting has ceased, farms practicing conservation tillage, and facilities that inject carbon into geologic reservoirs. Every one of these options is already implemented at an industrial scale and could be scaled up further over 50 years to provide at least one wedge.[15]

Significant policy changes will be needed to implement these wedges on a global scale. Most important, Pacala and Socolow note the need for carbon to be properly priced, with a suggested price of $100–$200 per ton of carbon ($27–$55 per ton of CO_2). This would equate to about 25 cents per gallon of gasoline.

They also address the path of carbon emissions for developing and developed countries. If members of the Organization for Economic Cooperation and Development (OECD) were to reduce their emissions by 60 percent over the next fifty years, emissions could theoretically grow by 60 percent in the non-OECD countries over the same time period, allowing them space for economic development while keeping total emissions stable. Yet even with this allocation, per capita emissions would still be twice as high in the OECD countries as in the developing countries. And, as noted, stabilizing emissions is unlikely to be sufficient to avert the worst impacts of climate change—overall global reduction will be needed.

Greenhouse Gas Abatement Cost Curves

The climate stabilization wedges analysis does not address the costs of each wedge. Obviously some wedges would be cheaper than others to implement. Depending on the social cost of carbon emissions, some wedges may not provide net benefits to society. For a more complete economic analysis, we also need to consider costs.

Another well-known analysis, by McKinsey & Company, estimates both the costs and the potential carbon reduction of more than 200 greenhouse gas mitigation, or abatement, options on a global scale.[16] Then the various options are arranged in order of cost, from lowest cost to highest. The economic logic is that it makes sense to implement actions that reduce carbon at the lowest per-unit costs first and then proceed to more costly actions. The results of their analysis are presented in Figure 19.5. The costs are estimated in euros, but the analysis covers worldwide reduction possibilities.

This figure takes a little explanation. The y-axis indicates the cost of each abatement option, measured in euros per ton of CO_2 reduction per year (or an amount equivalent to one ton of CO_2 for reductions in other gases such as methane). Note that the first option, reading from left to right, is building insulation. The thickness of the bar represents the amount of CO_2 emissions that can be avoided by each action. The cost of building insulation is *negative* 150 euros per ton of CO_2. This means that insulating buildings actually saves us money, based on a comparison of the present value of the costs to the savings from reduced power use. So even

Figure 19.5 **Global Greenhouse Gas Abatement Cost Curve to 2030**

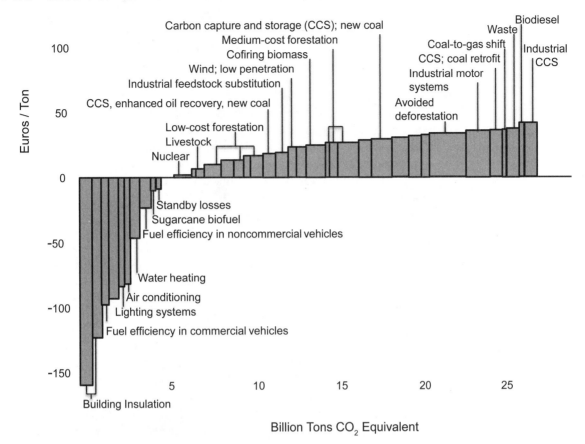

Billion Tons CO_2 Equivalent

Source: McKinsey & Company, 2007.

if we did not care about climate change and the environment, it would make sense to insulate buildings solely on long-term financial grounds. The same is true of all actions with a negative cost. For example, fuel efficiency in vehicles results in a savings of about €40—€120 per ton of CO_2 avoided.

The x-axis tells us the cumulative reduction in CO_2 equivalent emissions, relative to a BAU scenario, if we were to implement all the actions to the left. So if we were to implement all negative-cost options including improving efficiency of air-conditioning, lighting systems, and water heating, total CO_2 equivalent reduction would be about 5 billion tons (Gt) per year, all while saving money!

Moving farther to the right, actions are identified that do entail positive costs. In other words, for all these other actions it does cost us money to reduce CO_2 emissions. Figure 19.5 shows all actions that reduce CO_2 emissions for a cost of less than €40 per ton, including expanding wind energy, expanding nuclear energy, improved forest management and conservation, and implementing carbon capture and storage (CCS).[g]

---

[g]"Low penetration" wind is defined as expanding wind energy to provide as much as 10 percent of electricity supplies, while "high penetration" expands wind energy further, at slightly higher cost.

If all these actions were implemented, total CO_2 reduction would be 26 billion tons/year. Global CO_2 emissions are currently about 50 billion tons per year, projected to rise to about 70 Gt in 2030. Thus instead of emitting 70 Gt/year in 2030, we would be emitting only 44 Gt—a decrease of 6 Gt below current levels. Further reduction could be achieved at slightly higher cost, especially by more extensive expansion of wind and solar energy. (This analysis does not take into account likely costs reductions for renewable energy). This approach would be consistent with scientific estimates of what is needed to limit warming to no more than 2°C, as recommended by many scientists.

The total cost of implementing all options in Figure 19.5, considering that some options actually save money, is estimated to be less than 1 percent of global GDP in 2030. The report notes that delaying action by just ten years makes keeping warming under 2°C extremely difficult.

Four policy recommendations are made to achieve the reductions represented in Figure 19.5:

- Establish strict technical standards for efficiency of buildings and vehicles. Ideally, consumers and businesses would make rational decisions that maximize their long-term benefits. But Figure 19.5 demonstrates that people often fail to take advantage of many cost-saving actions. Efficiency standards can be enforced to ensure that efficient actions will be taken. For example, the United States passed legislation in 2007 mandating that light bulbs meet certain efficiency standards starting in 2012, and automobile efficiency standards were significantly tightened in 2011 (see Chapter 12).
- Establish stable long-term incentives for power producers and industrial companies to invest in and deploy efficient technologies.
- Provide government support for emerging efficiency and renewable energy technologies, through economic incentives and other policies.
- Ensure efficient management of forests and agriculture, particularly in developing countries.[17]

Again we see that instituting a carbon price is a part of a broader policy approach. A carbon tax or cap-and-trade program would create an incentive for the actions in Figure 19.5, but it does not guarantee that they will occur. In theory, we should already be using all the negative-cost options even in the absence of a carbon price, yet we are not. Standards and mandates can be an effective complement to a carbon price to ensure that cost-efficient actions are implemented. Potential policies could include efficiency standards for appliances, lighting, and building insulation.

How reliable is this abatement cost curve analysis? The McKinsey study has been subject to criticism both for underestimating and overestimating some costs. Also, some actions that are technically feasible, like reducing emissions from agricultural and forestry practices, may be difficult to achieve in practice due to political and institutional barriers.[h] Nonetheless, abatement costs curves such as those presented in the McKinsey study illustrate the basic principle that many low-cost or no-cost actions could be taken to reduce carbon emissions. Emissions growth is therefore not inevitable; substantial emissions reduction below current levels can be achieved at modest economic cost.

---

[h]See Kesicki and Ekins (2011) for a critique of abatement cost curves.

19.4 CLIMATE CHANGE POLICY IN PRACTICE

Climate change is an international environmental issue. Each individual country has little incentive to reduce its emissions if other countries do not agree to similar reductions, because unilaterally reducing emissions could impose significant costs (at least in the short term) while having a negligible effect on overall emissions. Thus a binding international agreement is necessary, especially if the policy goal is to reduce global emissions by 50–80 percent over the next few decades.

The most comprehensive international agreement on climate change was the Kyoto Protocol, which has now expired. Under the treaty industrial countries agreed to emission reduction targets by 2008–2012 compared to their baseline emissions, normally set to 1990 levels. For example, the United States agreed to a 7 percent reduction, France to an 8 percent reduction, and Japan to a 6 percent reduction. Developing countries such as China and India were not bound to emissions targets under the treaty, an omission that the United States and some other countries protested.

By 2012, 191 countries had signed and ratified the Kyoto Protocol. The United States was the only country that signed the treaty but never ratified it. In 2001, the George W. Bush administration rejected the Kyoto Protocol, arguing that negotiations had failed and that a new approach was necessary. Despite the U.S. withdrawal, the Kyoto Protocol entered into force in early 2005 after Russia ratified the treaty in November 2004.

To achieve the goals of the protocol in a cost-effective manner, the treaty includes three "flexibility mechanisms." The first is the trading of emissions permits among countries that are bound by specific targets. Thus one country unable to meet its target could purchase permits from another country that reduces its emissions below its requirements.

joint implementation
cooperative agreements between countries to reduce carbon emissions.

The second flexibility mechanism is **joint implementation**, in which an industrial nation receives credit for financing emission-reducing projects in other countries bound to emissions targets, mainly in transitional countries such as Russia and Lithuania. The third mechanism is the **clean development mechanism (CDM)**, in which industrial countries can obtain credit for financing emission-reducing or emission-avoiding projects in developing countries not bound to specific emissions targets, including China and India.

clean development mechanism (CDM)
a component of the Kyoto Protocol that allows industrial countries to receive credits for assisting developing countries to reduce their carbon emissions.

As of the time this chapter was written (early 2013), it appeared that the Kyoto Protocol target of a 5 percent overall reduction for participating countries would be met. However, as we see in Figure 19.6 the results for individual countries vary significantly. The figure compares the target of each country to its actual emission change between their baseline year and 2010. So, for example, Germany's target under the Protocol was an 8 percent reduction, but by 2010 it had already achieved a 22 percent reduction.

Other countries on target to meet their Kyoto commitments include France, Russia, and the United Kingdom. Russia's dramatic decline in emissions is a result of its economic collapse in the early 1990s rather than a result of policies to reduce emissions. Without the significant drop in Russian emissions, the overall Kyoto target would clearly not be met. Russia has been able to gain income through trading emissions reductions under the flexibility mechanism, but these emissions reductions would have occurred anyway.

Countries not on target to meet their Kyoto commitments include the United States, Australia, Canada, Spain, and Sweden. In December 2011 Canada formally

Figure 19.6 **Progress Toward Meeting Kyoto Protocol Targets, Select Countries, as of 2010**

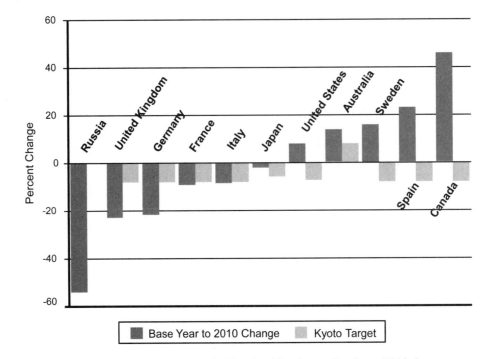

Source: UNFCCC greenhouse gas data from http://unfccc.int/ghg_data/ghg_data_unfccc/items/4146.php.
Note: Includes land use and forestry adjustments.

withdrew from the agreement because it would obviously fail to meet its obligation. The United States agreed to a 7 percent reduction in emissions relative to its 1990 baseline when it initially signed the treaty, but by 2010 its emissions had instead increased by 8 percent. In addition, Kyoto placed no restrictions on emissions from developing countries, meaning that overall global emissions have continued to grow, as shown in Figure 18.1.

Countries that fail to meet their commitments will need to make up for it during the post-Kyoto commitment period. Negotiations have been under way for several years to draft a successor to the Kyoto Protocol, as shown in Table 19.3. Previous international climate change meetings have set deadlines to reach a post-Kyoto agreement, without success. Currently it seems unlikely that a binding international agreement will be in effect before 2020.

Perhaps the most contentious point of disagreement is still whether developing countries should be bound by mandatory cuts in emissions. While some countries, particularly the United States, argue that all participants must agree to reductions in order to properly address the problem, developing countries contend that mandatory cuts would limit their economic development and reinforce existing global inequities.

While progress on an international agreement continues to languish, climate change policies are being put into effect at other levels, from multinational agreements down to individual municipalities. To help it meet its obligations under the Kyoto Protocol, the European Union set up a carbon trading system that went into effect in 2005 (see Box 19.3). Carbon taxes have been instituted in several countries, including a nationwide tax on coal in India (about $1/ton, enacted in

Table 19.3

Important Events in International Climate Change Negotiations

Year, Location	Outcome
1992, Rio de Janeiro	Negotiations start with completion of UN Framework Convention on Climate Change (UNFCCC). Countries agree to voluntarily reduce emissions with "common but differentiated responsibilities."
1995, Berlin	The first annual Conference of the Parties to the framework, known as a COP. United States agrees to exempt developing countries from binding obligations.
1997, Kyoto	COP-3 diplomats approve the Kyoto Protocol. Mandates developed countries to cut greenhouse gas emissions relative to baseline emissions by 2008-2012 period.
2000, The Hague	Outgoing Clinton administration and Europeans differ on some COP-6 terms, mainly over credit for carbon sinks such as agriculture and forests. Talks collapse.
2001, Bonn	A second session of the COP-6 talks works out terms for compliance and financing. However, by this time the Bush administration had rejected the Kyoto Protocol and the United States was only an observer to the talks.
2004, Buenos Aires	United States blocks formal negotiations on post-Kyoto treaty. COP-10 diplomats try informal talks.
2007, Bali	COP-13 diplomats approve schedule for post-Kyoto negotiations to end in 2009. This time the United States cooperates as presidential candidates appear supportive of climate change policies.
2009, Copenhagen	COP-15 fails to produce a binding post-Kyoto agreement. Instead, the Copenhagen Accord declares the importance of limiting warming to under 2°C, yet without any binding targets. Developed countries pledge to provide financing to developing countries of $30 billion annually, rising to $100 billion by 2020.
2010, Cancun	Nations meet to work out details of the "Green Climate Fund" agreed to in Copenhagen. The framework is set for a possible new binding treaty in 2011.
2011, Durban	COP-17 participating countries agreed to adopt a universal legal agreement on climate change as soon as possible, and no later than 2015, to take effect by 2020.

2010), a tax on new vehicles based on their carbon emissions in South Africa (also enacted in 2010), a carbon tax on fuels in Costa Rica (enacted in 1997), and local carbon taxes in the Canadian provinces of Quebec, British Columbia, and Alberta that apply to large emitters or motor fuels.

International negotiations as part of the Kyoto process following the original Kyoto accords on climate change in 1997 have also led to the adoption of a program known as **REDD (Reduction of Emissions from Deforestation and Degradation).** The Copenhagen Accord (2010) acknowledged the need to act on reducing emissions from deforestation and forest degradation and established a mechanism known as REDD-plus. The Accord emphasizes funding for developing countries to enable action on mitigation, including substantial finance for REDD-plus, adaptation, technology development and transfer and capacity building.[i]

The United States has no national climate change economic policies, but there have been numerous state and local-level initiatives to reduce emissions. A multistate regional agreement has been in place since 2008. The Regional Greenhouse Gas Initiative (RGGI) is a cap-and-trade program for emissions from power plants in nine Northeastern states.[18] Permits are mostly auctioned off (some are sold at a fixed price), with the proceeds used to fund investments in clean energy and energy efficiency. As of 2011 about a billion dollars had been

Reduction of Emissions from Deforestation and Degradation (REDD)

a United Nations program adopted as part of the Kyoto process of climate negotiations, intended to reduce emissions from deforestation and land degradation through providing funding for forest conservation and sustainable land use.

---

[i]For an extensive discussion of REDD, see Harris and Birjandi Feriz, 2011.

BOX 19.3 THE EUROPEAN UNION CARBON TRADING SYSTEM

In 2005 the European Union (EU) launched its Emissions Trading Scheme (EU-ETS), which covers more than 11,000 facilities that collectively emit nearly half the EU's carbon emissions. In 2012 the system was expanded to cover the aviation sector, including incoming flights from outside the EU. Under the EU-ETS, each country develops a national allocation plan to determine the overall number of permits available. Permits are both auctioned off and allocated to some firms for free based on historical emissions. Any unneeded permits can be sold on the open market.

The initial phase (2005–2007) of the EU-ETS produced disappointing results as permits were overallocated, leading to a drop in the permit price from more than €30 per tonne to less than €1 by the end of 2007. (Note: In early 2013 €1 was equivalent to about $1.35.) In the second phase (2008–2012), fewer permits were initially allocated, leading to relatively stable prices of around €15–€20/tonne for a few years. But by mid-2012 prices had fallen to €5–€10/tonne as the market again experienced a glut of permits. Despite the volatility in prices, according to the EU the EU-ETS led to a reduction in emissions from large emitters of 8 percent between 2005 and 2010. Also, the costs of the EU-ETS have been less than expected, around 0.5 percent of European gross domestic product (GDP).

The EU is currently moving into the third phase of the ETS, which will cover 2013–2020. This phase will require more of the permits to be auctioned, include more greenhouse gases, and set an overall EU cap rather than allowing individual countries to determine their own cap. By the end of the third phase, the program's goal is to reduce overall EU emissions 20 percent relative to 1990 levels.

Sources: EU-ETS, http://ec.europa.eu/clima/policies/ets/index_en.htm; Grubb et al., 2009.

raised. In early 2013, the participating states announced a nearly 50 percent cut in the target for allowable emissions, which will raise additional revenues for energy efficiency programs.[19] Permit auction prices have ranged from about $2 to $4 per ton of CO_2.

Other regional initiatives, including one among Western states and one among Midwestern states, have faltered as most states have decided to withdraw from the process. But in early 2013, California initiated a legally binding cap-and-trade scheme, "establishing a state-wide limit on total emissions of 162.8 million metric tons of carbon dioxide and imposing emission allowances on around 350 companies generating more than 25,000 metric tons of carbon dioxide a year. The bulk of the allowances will be handed to companies for free, but some allowances will be auctioned and any firm exceeding its emissions cap will have to purchase additional allowances to cover the excess."[20]

At the local level, more than 1,000 U.S. mayors have signed the U.S. Conference of Mayors' Climate Protection Agreement.[21] Under this voluntary program, cities agree to:

- strive to meet or beat the U.S. Kyoto target in their own community
- urge their state, and the federal government, to enact policies to meet or beat the U.S. Kyoto target
- urge Congress to enact greenhouse gas reduction legislation, including a national cap-and-trade program

19.5 Economic Policy Proposals

In the final section of this chapter, we take a look at three specific economic proposals for climate change policies: a U.S. carbon tax, a global cap-and-trade system, and an international analysis of climate change financing. While none of these proposals have been seriously considered by any governments, they represent applications of the economic theories we discussed earlier in the text to the issue of climate change and give some perspective on the kinds of policies that are needed to achieve major emissions reductions, as urged by the Intergovernmental Panel on Climate Change (IPCC) (see Figure 18.10).

A Distributionally Neutral Carbon Tax in the United States

regressive tax
a tax in which the rate of taxation, as a percentage of income, decreases with increasing income levels.

Placing a price on carbon emissions in developed countries would result in unequal impacts on households of different income levels. Specifically, a carbon tax would be a **regressive tax**, meaning that as a percentage of income the tax would affect lower-income households more than higher-income households. The reason is that lower-income households spend a higher percentage of their income on carbon-intensive goods such as gasoline, electricity, and heating fuels. Thus a carbon tax, implemented alone, would increase the overall level of income inequality.

A carbon tax does not necessarily mean that overall taxes must increase. Instead, implementing a carbon tax could be coupled with a decrease in one or more existing taxes such that the overall amount of taxes paid by the average household stays the same. Thus a carbon tax could be revenue neutral, meaning that the overall amount of tax revenue collected by the government is unchanged.

progressive taxes
taxes that comprise a higher share of income with higher income levels.

But the distributional impacts depend on which tax is reduced. Some taxes are regressive, affecting lower-income households more heavily, while other taxes are **progressive taxes**, affecting higher-income households more heavily. Given that a carbon tax is regressive and increases inequality, we probably would not want to counter this by decreasing a progressive tax, because that would benefit mainly higher-income households and further increase inequality. So most proposals for a revenue-neutral carbon tax suggest achieving revenue neutrality by decreasing a regressive tax. In the United States, regressive taxes include sales taxes, the payroll tax, and excise taxes.[j] Could one of these taxes be reduced such that the overall distributional impact of a carbon tax would be relatively constant across income levels?

distributionally neutral tax shift
a change in the pattern of taxes that leaves the distribution of income unchanged.

An economic analysis by Gilbert Metcalf reveals that offsetting a carbon tax in the United States with a decrease in the payroll tax could produce a result that is approximately **distributionally neutral**, meaning that the impact on households at different income levels would be nearly the same as a percentage of income.[22] Metcalf's analysis starts by assuming that an upstream carbon tax of $15 per ton of CO_2 is implemented on coal, natural gas, and petroleum products. As an upstream tax, it would be imposed at coal mines, natural gas wellheads, and petroleum refineries. Credits could be obtained for any downstream carbon capture and storage.

The upstream tax would translate to price increases for various products, which Metcalf estimates based on an economic model of manufacturing flows.

[j]Excise taxes are taxes on specific products such as cigarettes and alcohol.

Then, using consumer expenditure data, he calculates how much the carbon tax would cost households of different income levels. Table 19.4 presents his results. We see the average annual household cost of the carbon tax increases as income increases, ranging from $276 for the lowest income decile to $1,224 for the highest decile.[k] Yet as a percentage of income, the cost is 3.4 percent for the lowest income group and only 0.8 percent for the highest. Thus the carbon tax alone is regressive.

Table 19.4

A Distributionally Neutral Carbon Tax in the United States

	Change in annual household income			
Income decile	Average cost of the carbon tax	Average payroll tax credit	Net impact (dollars)	Net impact (as a percentage of income)
1 (lowest)	–$276	$208	–$68	–0.7%
2	–$404	$284	–$120	–1.0%
3	–$485	$428	–$57	–0.2%
4	–$551	$557	+$6	+0.1%
5	–$642	$668	+$26	+0.1%
6	–$691	$805	+$115	+0.3%
7	–$781	$915	+$135	+0.2%
8	–$883	$982	+$99	+0.2%
9	–$965	$1,035	+$70	+0.0%
10 (highest)	–$1,224	$1,093	–$130	–0.0%

Source: Metcalf, 2007.

Metcalf proposes offsetting the carbon tax by providing a tax credit for a worker's payroll tax up to a maximum credit of $560 per year per individual—an amount that allows the overall effect on taxes to be revenue-neutral.[l] For low-income households, this tax credit is relatively large as a percentage of income (over 2 percent), but for higher-income households this credit is only about 1 percent or less of income. Table 19.4 indicates that the credit averages from about $200 to over $1,000, depending on household income level.

The tax credit is remarkably similar to the impact of the carbon tax for each income group. The net effect, considering both the carbon tax and the tax credit, is never more than an average of $135 for any income group. Households in the middle and upper-middle income groups tend to end up slightly ahead, while households in the lowest income groups end up losing slightly. But the overall impact is nearly distributionally neutral. Some further minor adjustments could be instituted to eliminate the slightly negative impact on lower income households. Thus Metcalf's analysis demonstrates that a carbon tax in the United States could achieve carbon reductions without increasing overall taxes or having a disproportionate impact on any income group.

---

[k] A decile is a group comprising 10 percent of the population.
[l] The payroll tax in the United States is the tax that funds Social Security, Medicare, and Medicaid. It is a tax of 15.3 percent, applicable to a worker's first $110,100 of income in 2012. The tax is paid equally by employees and employers, 7.65 percent each. The employee tax was temporarily reduced by 2 percent during 2011 and 2012 in response to the economic downturn.

An Earth Atmospheric Trust

Just as a national carbon tax can have a regressive impact, an international climate change agreement could hurt the economic opportunities of the world's poorest. A global carbon price, even a small one, would translate to higher costs for everyone. As mentioned earlier, developing countries currently have little incentive to agree to a binding international treaty if it will limit their chances for much-needed economic growth.

The atmosphere is essentially a global public good, as discussed in Chapter 4. Therefore, no individual, organization, or countries has a greater fundamental right to emit pollutants into it than another. Further, as discussed in Chapter 3, carbon emissions amount to a negative externality that should be priced to fully compensate external parties that are damaged. In the case of carbon emissions, the external party is essentially everyone who lives on the planet.

An ambitious proposal for an **Earth Atmospheric Trust** is based on these principles.[23] The policy has six key features:

1. Create a global cap-and-trade system for all greenhouse gas emissions. The permits would be instituted upstream, as close to the beginning of the manufacturing process as possible.
2. Auction off all permits to the highest bidders. Permit holders may then freely trade permits to willing buyers.
3. Reduce the number of permits over time to achieve stabilization of the atmospheric concentration of greenhouse gases at an acceptable level, ideally 450 parts per million (ppm) CO_2 equivalent (CO_2e) or lower.
4. Deposit all revenues from the auctions into an Earth Atmospheric Trust, administered by a nongovernmental organization with a mandate to protect the earth's climate, composed of trustees who serve long terms.
5. Return a portion of the Trust to all people on earth as an annual per capita payment. This payment serves as compensation for each year's carbon emissions. Given that each person has an equal right to the atmosphere, the payment should be the same for all people.
6. Use the remainder of the Trust to restore the atmosphere, encourage technical innovation, and administer the Trust.

Obviously, the proposal faces significant logistical and political hurdles, although it is based on established economic principles. The logistics of implementing a global cap-and-trade system for all greenhouse gases are daunting, and distributing an annual payment to all people on the planet would be even more challenging. The authors suggest that people without access to banks or electronic delivery mechanisms could receive their dividends through microcredit institutions. The annual payment would be relatively minor for the world's rich, but for the world's poor it could provide a significant economic benefit—enough to lift many people out of absolute poverty.

Some additional analysis illustrates how the proposal would affect the average person in different countries.[m] Global CO_2 emissions in 2010 were about 32 Gt, not including other greenhouse gases. The authors suggest that the appropriate price

---

[m]This analysis is based on the approach described by Barnes et al., but uses slightly updated data from the U.S. Energy Information Administration.

on carbon would be \$20–\$80 per ton of CO_2. Thus the Trust could generate annual revenues of about \$600 billion to \$2.6 trillion and even more if other greenhouse gases were included. As a share of the world's economy, this represents about 1–4 percent of total economic activity.

The authors suggest returning half the auction revenues to everyone on the planet as an equal annual payment. At 7 billion people, this annual payment would be between about \$43 and \$183 per person, depending on the carbon price. For a person in a developed country, this payment would be relatively small. But for a person in a developing country, the payment could dramatically increase annual income. Consider that GDP per capita in the world's poorest countries currently ranges between \$300 and \$900. Thus the Trust proposal could significantly reduce the number of people living in abject poverty.

We also need to consider the costs of the global cap-and-trade system. A carbon price of \$20–\$80 per ton of CO_2 would lead to price increases on final products. The impact of the system on the average person can be estimated by simply multiplying the average carbon emissions per person in a country by the carbon price. For example, in the United States per capita emissions are 18.1 tons of CO_2. At a price of \$20–\$80 per ton of CO_2, this translates to increased costs of \$362 to \$1,448 per year.[n] Like everyone else in the world, Americans would get an annual payment of \$43 to \$183 per person. Thus the average American would end up losing money, as the annual payment is not enough to offset the costs of the carbon price.

Table 19.5 estimates the impact of the Trust on the average citizen of different countries, based on an assumed carbon price of \$80 per ton of CO_2. This higher price leads to higher cost impacts on consumers (relative to a \$20 tax) but also higher auction revenues and higher annual payments, which means greater poverty reduction in poor countries. As mentioned above, this carbon price generates as much as \$2.6 trillion in annual revenues, equivalent to 4 percent of global GDP. According to the Stern Review, the necessary funding for an adequate response to climate change is 1 percent of global GDP. Thus in this scenario it is possible to return three-quarters of the revenues as an annual per capita dividend payment, which would be \$274.

The results in Table 19.5 illustrate how some countries receive net gains while others have net losses. Consider India, where average emissions are 1.4 tons per person per year. A carbon price of \$80 per ton equals an average annual cost of \$112 per person. However, each person receives a dividend payment of \$274, so they come out ahead by \$162/year. Given that GDP per capita in India is only \$1,489, this amounts to an 11 percent net income gain. China, by contrast, has net losses because its emissions per capita are relatively high—similar to those in France despite a much lower GDP per capita. Brazil, which has a higher GDP per capita than China, receives net payments because its emissions are relatively low.

The poorest countries are the biggest gainers. In Uganda, the price of carbon is minimal since the average person's use of fossil fuels is very small. The average net gain in Uganda of \$266 is an income increase of more than 50 percent—enough to make a big difference in people's economic well-being. The average person in the United States, which has very high emissions, loses over \$1,000 annually even after receiving the dividend payment. So the program would create a strong incentive for lower carbon emissions in the richer countries while reducing pov-

---

[n]Note that this simple analysis assumes emissions stay constant, at least at the start of the program. Over time, emissions would decline but the market price for permits would likely increase.

Table 19.5

Average Impacts of an Earth Atmospheric Trust, Select Countries

Country	GDP per capita (2011)	CO_2 emissions per capita (tons)	Cost of carbon price per capita ($80/ton)	Net effect after annual payment of $274
Brazil	$12,594	2.3	$184	+$90
China	$5,430	6.3	$504	−$230
France	$42,377	6.2	$496	−$222
Germany	$43,689	9.6	$768	−$494
India	$1,489	1.4	$112	+$162
Mexico	$10,064	4.0	$320	−$46
Russia	$13,089	11.7	$938	−$662
Turkey	$10,498	3.4	$272	+$2
Uganda	$487	0.1	$8	+$266
United States	$48,442	18.1	$1,448	−$1,174

Sources: U.S. Energy Information Administration database; World Bank, World Development Indicators database.

Note: GDP = gross domestic product.

erty in the poorer countries. But, of course, it would be politically very difficult to persuade the richer countries to accept a plan that would lead to net per capita losses for their residents.

These estimates are average impacts—individual impacts will vary depending on one's income level and use of fossil fuels. Of course, individuals could take actions to reduce their carbon emissions, which would reduce their costs. To determine the overall effect of the program, one would also need to account for the benefits of lower emissions over the long term.

Greenhouse Development Rights

greenhouse development rights (GDR)

an approach for assigning the responsibility for past greenhouse gas emissions and the capability to respond to climate change.

The final economic proposal we consider here approaches the climate change challenge from a different perspective. Rather than focusing on the implementation of a carbon tax or cap-and-trade system, it focuses on the obligations of different countries to pay for the necessary mitigation and adaptation costs. The **greenhouse development rights (GDR)** framework contends that only those people living above a certain economic threshold of development should be obliged to address the climate change problem.[24] Those who live below the threshold should instead be allowed to focus on economic growth, without any climate obligations.

The GDR analysis essentially develops a methodology for assigning each country's obligation to provide financing for an international climate change mitigation and adaptation fund. It considers two factors to determine a country's obligation:

- *Capacity:* The capacity of a country to provide financing is based on its GDP, yet all income below a defined development threshold is excluded. The GDR analysis sets the development threshold at $7,500 per capita, a level that generally allows one to avoid the problems of severe poverty, such as malnutrition, high infant mortality, and low educational attainment. Figure 19.7 illustrates the concept using China as an example. The graph shows the income distribution curve for China, starting with the person with the lowest income and moving to the right as incomes increase. All income below

Figure 19.7 **Climate Change Capacity for China, Greenhouse Development Rights Framework**

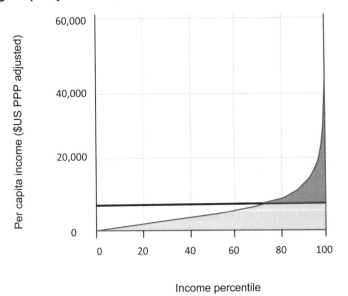

Income percentile

Source: Baer et al., 2008.
Note: PPP = purchasing power parity.

the horizontal line at the $7,500 development threshold is excluded from China's capacity. The area above the development threshold line represents China's total capacity to provide financing for climate change.

- *Responsibility:* The GDR approach defines responsibility for greenhouse gas emissions as a country's cumulative emissions since 1990, the same baseline year used for the Kyoto Protocol. As with capacity, emissions associated with consumption below the development threshold are excluded from the responsibility calculation. Thus a country whose emissions result mainly from biomass burning to provide subsistence-level heating and cooking would not be held responsible for these emissions. Each country's share of the global responsibility would be calculated by dividing its cumulative emissions by the global total.

The results indicate each country's share of the global capacity and responsibility. Then, a responsibility-capacity index (RCI) is calculated as the unweighted average of the two values. The RCI represents each country's obligation for financing a response to climate change.

The results for select countries and country groups are presented in Table 19.6. The United States, which has by far the greatest cumulative responsibility for emissions, would be allocated one-third of the global bill for addressing climate change. The European Union would receive more than one-quarter of the bill. Japan would be asked to finance about 8 percent of the response, China about 6 percent, and Russia about 4 percent. The least developed countries are collectively asked to pay a negligible share of the global bill. These shares would change over time, as developing countries' share of global emissions increases and their capacity to respond (assuming successful development) increases also.

Table 19.6

Responsibility Capacity Indices, Greenhouse Development Rights Framework, Select Countries/Regions (percent of global total)

Country or group	Population	Capacity	Responsibility	RCI
United States	4.5	29.7	36.4	33.1
EU-27	7.3	28.8	22.6	25.7
Japan	1.9	8.3	7.3	7.8
China	19.7	5.8	5.2	5.5
Russia	2.0	2.7	4.9	3.8
Brazil	2.9	2.3	1.1	1.7
Mexico	1.6	1.8	1.4	1.6
South Africa	0.7	0.6	1.3	1.0
India	17.2	0.7	0.3	0.5
Least-developed countries	11.7	0.1	0.04	0.1

Source: Baer et al., 2007.

The GDR proposal, like the Earth Atmospheric Trust, does not seem politically feasible in today's environment. However, the authors make a strong case that the time has come for dramatic action.

> [O]ne can reasonably ask if an approach like this, which compounds the climate challenge with the development challenge, and by so doing makes it even more overwhelming, is at all politically realistic. Our response is to ask another question—are we yet serious about facing down the climate crisis? For as others have noted before us, the outer bounds of today's realism are still far shy of the inner bounds of scientific necessity.
>
> The bottom line is that, without an unprecedented level of global cooperation, the 2°C emergency pathway, or anything like it, will quickly recede out of range. Climate change is a threat—perhaps humankind's first such threat—that demands cooperation, even across the rich-poor divide.[25]

19.6 CONCLUSION

Climate change is an issue that embodies many of the analyses discussed in this text, including externalities, common property resources, public goods, renewable and nonrenewable resources, and resource allocation over time. It has economic, scientific, political, and technological dimensions. Economic analysis alone cannot adequately respond to a problem of this scope, but economic theory and policy have much to offer in the search for solutions.

An effective response to the climate change problem requires much more sweeping action on a global scale than anything so far achieved. But whether we are discussing local initiatives or broad global schemes, we cannot avoid the issue of economic analysis. Economic policy instruments that have the power to alter patterns of energy use, industrial development, and income distribution are essential to any plan for mitigating or adapting to climate change. As noted in Chapter 18, evidence of climate change is already clear, and the issue is likely to become more pressing as emissions accumulation continues. The tools of economic analysis will provide critical insights as the world grapples with this continuing crisis.

SUMMARY

Policies to respond to global climate change can be preventive or adaptive. One of the most widely discussed policies is a carbon tax, which would fall most heavily on fuels that cause the highest carbon emissions. The revenues from such a tax could be recycled to lower taxes elsewhere in the economy, or they could be used to assist people in lower income brackets, who will suffer most from higher costs of energy and goods. Another policy option is tradable carbon emissions permits, which could be bought and sold by firms or countries, depending on their level of carbon emissions. Both these policies have the advantage of economic efficiency, but it has been difficult to obtain the political support necessary to implement them. Other possible policy measures include shifting subsidies from fossil fuels to renewable energy, strengthening energy efficiency standards, and increasing research and development on alternative energy technologies.

Global carbon emissions could be stabilized by scaling up existing technologies, according to the idea of climate stabilization wedges. The greenhouse gas abatement cost curve indicates that numerous opportunities exist for actions that could reduce carbon emissions and also save households and businesses money. One implication of the cost curve is that efficiency standards can be an important complement to a carbon pricing policy.

The Kyoto Protocol mandating reductions of greenhouse gases by industrialized countries went into force in 2005, but the United States refused to participate. It appears the overall Kyoto target will be met, but only because of the economic collapse of Russia in the early 1990s. Negotiations to draft a successor to the Kyoto Protocol have failed to produce an agreement, mainly because developing and developed countries disagree over how to allocate emissions reductions. Yet it is becoming increasingly clear that adequate climate change policy in the future will require the involvement of the United States as well as China, India, and other developing countries.

Many well-designed economic analyses provide potential blueprints for effective national and international climate change policies. For example, a carbon tax in the United States can be designed to be both revenue- and distributionally neutral. A more ambitious proposal, the Earth Atmospheric Trust, addresses both climate change and global poverty by recognizing the atmosphere as a global public good. Finally, the greenhouse development rights framework allocates the financing for a sufficient response to climate change based on each country's responsibility for past emissions and economic capacity, while still allowing poor countries to achieve economic development.

KEY TERMS AND CONCEPTS

adaptive measures
carbon sinks
carbon tax
clean development mechanism (CDM)
climate stabilization wedge
cost-benefit analysis
cost-effectiveness analysis
distributionally neutral taxes
Earth Atmospheric Trust
efficiency standards
elasticity of demand
greenhouse development rights (GDR)

joint implementation
pollution taxes
preventive measures
price volatility
progressive taxes
reduction of emissions from deforestation and
    degradation (REDD)
regressive tax
revenue-neutral tax shift
technology transfer
transferable (tradable) permits

DISCUSSION QUESTIONS

1. Which economic climate change policy do you prefer: a carbon tax or a cap-and-trade system? Why? What are the main barriers to effective policy implementation?
2. Climate change policies can focus on changing behaviors or changing technology. Which approach do you think could be more effective? What policies can be used to encourage changes in each?
3. The process for formulating and implementing international agreements on climate change policy has been plagued with disagreements and deadlocks. What are the main reasons for the difficulty in agreeing on specific policy actions? From an economic point of view, what kinds of incentives might be useful to induce countries to enter and carry out agreements? What kinds of "win-win" policies could be devised to overcome negotiating barriers?

EXERCISES

1. Suppose that under the terms of an international agreement, U.S. CO_2 emissions are to be reduced by 200 million tons and those of Brazil by 50 million tons.

    Here are the policy options that the United States and Brazil have to reduce their emissions:

United States:

Policy options	Total emissions reduction (million tons carbon)	Cost ($ billion)
A: Efficient machinery	60	12
B: Reforestation	40	20
C: Replace coal-fueled power plants	120	30

Brazil:

Policy options	Total emissions reduction (million tons carbon)	Cost ($ billion)
A: Efficient machinery	50	20
B: Protection of Amazon forest	30	3
C: Replace coal-fueled power plants	40	8

a. Which policies are most efficient for each country in meeting their reduction targets? How much will be reduced using each option, at what cost, if the two countries must operate independently? Assume that any of the policy options can be partially implemented at a constant marginal cost. For example, the United States could choose to reduce carbon emissions with efficient machinery by 10 million tons at a cost of $2 billion. (Hint: start by calculating the average cost of carbon reduction in dollars per ton for each of the six policies).

b. Suppose a market of transferable permits allows the United States and Brazil to trade permits to emit CO_2. Who has an interest in buying permits? Who has an interest in selling permits? What agreement can be reached between the United States and Brazil so that they can meet the overall emissions reduction target of 250 million tons at the least cost? Can you estimate a range for the price of a permit to emit one ton of carbon? (Hint: use your average cost calculations from the first part of the question.)

2. Suppose that the annual consumption of an average American household is 2,000 gallons of oil in heating and transportation and 50 Mcf (thousand cubic feet) of natural gas. Using the figures given in Table 19.2 on the effects of a carbon tax, calculate how much an average American household would pay per year with an added tax of $10 per ton of carbon. (One barrel of oil contains 42 gallons.) Assume that this relatively small tax initially causes no reduction in the demand for oil and gas. If there are 100 million households in the United States, what would be the revenue to the U.S. Treasury of such a carbon tax?

What would be the national revenue from a tax of $200 per ton of carbon? Consider the issue of the impact of increased prices on consumption—a reasonable assumption about consumption elasticity might be that a $200 per ton tax would cause the quantity of oil and gas consumed to decline by 20 percent. How might the government use such revenues? What would the impact be on the average family? Discuss the difference between the short-term and long-term impacts.

NOTES

1. Stern, 2007.
2. IPCC, 2007, 46.
3. African Development Bank et al., 2003, 1.
4. Cline, 2007; U. S. Global Change Research Program, 2009, Agriculture Chapter.
5. World Health Organization, 2009.
6. UNFCCC, 2007.
7. Parry et al., 2009.
8. World Bank, 2010.
9. Dower and Zimmerman, 1992.
10. Goodwin et al., 2004.
11. Ibid.
12. Carbon tax advantages summarized from www.carbontax.org/faq/.
13. Pacala and Socolow, 2004.
14. See http://cmi.princeton.edu/wedges/intro.php.
15. Socolow and Pacala, 2006.
16. McKinsey & Company, 2007 and 2009.
17. Ibid.
18. www.rggi.org.
19. Beth Daley, "Mass. And 8 other States Lower Greenhouse Gas Emissions Cap," *Boston Globe*, February 8, 2013.

20. Will Nichols, "California Carbon Trading Scheme Gets Underway," businessGreen January 3, 2013. http://www.businessgreen.com/.
21. www.usmayors.org/climateprotection/agreement.htm.
22. Metcalf, 2007.
23. Barnes et al., 2008; see also www.uvm.edu/~msayre/EAT.pdf.
24. Baer et al., 2008.
25. Ibid. 9.

REFERENCES

African Development Bank, Asian Development Bank, Department for International Development (UK), Directorate-General for Development (European Commission), Federal Ministry for Economic Cooperation and Development (Germany, Ministry of Foreign Affairs), Development Cooperation (The Netherlands), Organization for Economic Cooperation and Development, United Nations Development Programme, United Nations Environment Programme, and World Bank, 2003. *Poverty and Climate Change Reducing the Vulnerability of the Poor Through Adaptation.* www.unpei.org/PDF/Poverty-and-Climate-Change.pdf.

Baer, Paul, Tom Athanasiou, Sivan Kartha, and Eric Kemp-Benedict. 2008. "The Greenhouse Development Rights Framework: The Right to Development in a Climate Constrained World." 2d ed. Heinrich Böll Foundation, Christian Aid, EcoEquity and the Stockholm Environment Institute.

Barnes, Peter, Robert Costanza, Paul Hawken, David Orr, Elinor Ostrom, Alvaro Umana, and Oran Young. 2008. "Creating an Earth Atmospheric Trust." *Science* 319:724.

Cline, William R. 2007. *Global Warming and Agriculture: Impact Estimates by Country.* Washington, D.C.: Center for Global Development and Petersen Institute for International Economics. http://www.cgdev.org/content/publications/detail/14090.

Dower, Roger C., and Mary Zimmerman. 1992. *The Right Climate for Carbon Taxes, Creating Economic Incentives to Protect the Atmosphere.* Washington, DC: World Resources Institute.

Goodwin, Phil, Joyce Dargay, and Mark Hanly. 2004. "Elasticities of Road Traffic and Fuel Consumption with Respect to Price and Income: A Review." *Transport Reviews* 24(3): 275–292.

Grubb, Michael, Thomas L. Brewer, Misato Sato, Robert Heilmayr, and Dora Fazekas. 2009. "Climate Policy and Industrial Competitiveness: Ten Insights from Europe on the EU Emissions Trading System." German Marshall Fund of the United States, Climate & Energy Paper Series 09.

GTZ. 2009. "International Fuel Prices 2009," 6th ed., on behalf of Federal Ministry for Economic Cooperation and Development (Germany).

Harris, Jonathan M., and Maliheh Birjandi Feriz, 2011. *Forests, Agriculture, and Climate: Economics and Policy Issues.* Tufts University Global Development and Environment Institute, http://www.ase.tufts.edu/gdae/education_materials/modules.html#REDD.

Hughes, Jonathan E., Christopher R. Knittel, and Daniel Sperling. 2008. "Evidence of a Shift in the Short-Run Price Elasticity of Gasoline Demand." *Energy Journal* 29 (1), 113–134.

Intergovernmental Panel on Climate Change (IPCC). 2007. *Climate Change 2007: Synthesis Report.*

Kesicki, Fabian, and Paul Ekins. 2011. "Marginal Abatement Cost Curves: A Call for Caution." *Climate Policy* 12(2): 219–236.

McKinsey & Company. 2007. "A Cost Curve for Greenhouse Gas Reduction." *The McKinsey Quarterly* 1: 35–45, available at http://www.epa.gov/air/caaac/coaltech/2007_05_mckinsey.pdf.

———. 2009. *Pathways to a Low-Carbon Economy.* https://solutions.mckinsey.com/ClimateDesk/default.aspx.

Metcalf, Gilbert E. 2007. "A Proposal for a U.S. Carbon Tax Swap." Washington, DC: Brookings Institution. Discussion Paper 2007–12.

Pacala, Stephen, and Robert H. Socolow. 2004. "Stabilization Wedges: Solving the Climate Problem for the Next 50 Years with Current Technologies." *Science* 305(5686): 968–972.

Roodman, David M. 1997. "Getting the Signals Right: Tax Reform to Protect the Environment and the Economy." Worldwatch Paper no. 134. Worldwatch Institute, Washington, DC.

Parry, Martin, Nigel Arnell, Pam Berry, David Dodman, Samuel Fankhauser, Chris Hope, Sari Kovats, Robert Nicholls, David Satterthwaite, Richard Tiffin, and Tim Wheeler. 2009. "Assessing the Costs of Adaptation to Climate Change: A Review of the UNFCCC and Other Recent Estimates." Report by the Grantham Institute for Climate Change and the International Institute for Environment and Development. London.

Socolow, Robert H., and Stephen W. Pacala. 2006. "A Plan to Keep Carbon in Check." *Scientific American* (September): 50–57.

Stern, Nicholas. 2007. *The Economics of Climate Change: The Stern Review*. Cambridge: Cambridge University Press.

United Nations Framework Convention on Climate Change (UNFCCC). 2007. "Investment and Financial Flows to Address Climate Change." Climate Change Secretariat, Bonn.

United States Global Change Research Program. 2009. *Second National Climate Assessment*. http://globalchange.gov/publications/reports/scientific-assessments/us-impacts.

World Bank. 2010. "The Costs to Developing Countries of Adapting to Climate Change: New Methods and Estimates." Consultation Draft.

World Health Organization. 2009. "Protecting Health from Climate Change: Connecting Science, Policy, and People."

WEB SITES

1. **http://climate.wri.org**. World Resource Institute's Web site on climate and atmosphere. The site includes several articles and case studies, including research on the Clean Development Mechanism.
2. **www.unfccc.de**. Home page for the United Nations Framework Convention on Climate Change. The site provides data on the climate change issue and information about the ongoing process of negotiating international agreements related to climate change.
3. **http://rff.org/focus_areas/Pages/Energy_and_Climate.aspx**. Publications by Resources for the Future on issues of energy and climate change. The site includes several research papers on the trading of greenhouse gas emissions permits.

PART SEVEN

ENVIRONMENT, TRADE, AND DEVELOPMENT

World Trade and the Environment

CHAPTER 20 FOCUS QUESTIONS

- What effects does expanded trade have on the environment?
- Should regional and global trade agreements include environmental protection?
- What policies can promote sustainable trade?

20.1 ENVIRONMENTAL IMPACTS OF TRADE

World trade expansion has raised the issue of the relationship between trade and the environment. Is trade good or bad for the environment? The answer is not obvious. The production of goods for import and export, like other production, often has environmental effects. Will these effects increase or decrease with expanded trade? How will they affect the exporting country, the importing country, or the world as a whole? Who is responsible for responding to environmental problems associated with trade? Questions like these have received increasing attention in recent years.

International attention first focused on these issues in 1991, when the Mexican government challenged a U.S. law banning tuna imports from Mexico. The U.S. Marine Mammal Protection Act prohibited tuna-fishing methods that killed large numbers of dolphins and banned tuna imports from countries that used such fishing methods. The Mexican government argued that this U.S. law violated the rules of the **General Agreement on Tariffs and Trade (GATT)**.

According to the free-trade principles that provided the basis for the GATT and for its successor in 1994, the **World Trade Organization (WTO)** countries cannot restrict imports except in limited cases such as protecting the health and safety of their own citizens. A GATT dispute panel ruled that the United States could not use domestic legislation to protect dolphins outside its own territorial limits.

Although Mexico did not press for enforcement of this decision, the tuna/dolphin decision opened a major controversy over issues of trade and environment. In a similar case in 1999, the WTO ruled that the United States could not prohibit shrimp imports from countries using fishing methods that killed endangered sea turtles.

General Agreement on Tariffs and Trade (GATT)
a multilateral trade agreement providing a framework for the gradual elimination of tariffs and other barriers to trade; the predecessor to the World Trade Organization.

World Trade Organization (WTO)
an international organization dedicated to the expansion of trade through lowering or eliminating tariffs and nontariff barriers to trade.

The controversy over these issues introduced a period of debate over many aspects of international environmental issues, including forest protection, ozone depletion, hazardous wastes, and global climate change. All these issues are linked to international trade. If individual countries are prohibited from using trade measures to protect the global environment, how will it be possible to devise effective policies to respond to these issues?

To address these questions, we need to reexamine the theory and practice of international trade. A basic principle of standard economic theory is that expanded trade is generally beneficial, promoting increased efficiency and greater wealth among trading countries. But what if expanded trade causes environmental damage?

At the national level, the standard economic policy response to environmental impact is to implement policies that internalize externalities, as discussed in earlier chapters. At the international level, however, the picture is more confusing. The burden of environmental externalities associated with trade may be borne by importers, exporters, or by others not directly involved in producing or consuming traded goods. The authority to formulate and enforce environmental policies usually exists only at the national level. This can create significant problems when environmental impacts are transnational, because most international trade agreements make no provision for environmental protection.

comparative advantage
the theory that trade benefits both parties by allowing each to specialize in the goods that it can produce with relative efficiency.

environmental externalities
externalities that affect the environment, such as the impact of pollution on wildlife.

Comparative Advantage and Environmental Externalities

We can use economic theory to analyze gains and losses associated with environmental effects of trade. The theory of **comparative advantage** tells us that both trading partners gain from trade by specializing in the goods that they can produce most efficiently. This basic theory does not consider **environmental externalities** associated with the production or consumption of goods. Consider Figure 20.1, which uses automobiles as an example of an imported good's welfare effects.

Figure 20.1 **Gains and Losses from Importing Automobiles**

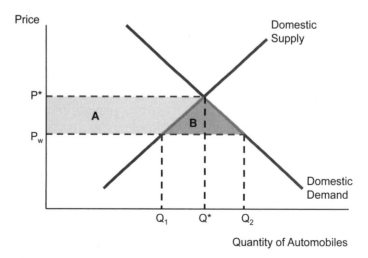

In the absence of trade, domestic supply and demand would be in equilibrium at Q^*, with a domestic price of P^*. With trade, both production and consumption of automobiles will change in the importing country. If there are no barriers to trade, automobiles can be imported at the world price P_w, which is typically lower than the domestic price for an imported good.[a] Domestic production falls to Q_1, as domestic producers lose market share to cheaper imports, while domestic consumption rises to Q_2, as domestic consumers expand purchases of automobiles in response to lower prices. The quantity of imports is shown as $(Q_2 - Q_1)'$.

How does trade affect domestic economic welfare? Using the kind of welfare analysis presented in Chapter 3, we can say that domestic producers of automobiles lose area A because they now sell fewer cars at a lower price. Domestic consumers gain areas A + B because they can now buy more cars at the same lower price. The net gain from trade is therefore (A + B) – A = B.

But this leaves out any environmental externalities associated with trade. Consider Figure 20.2, which adds curves that show two types of environmental externalities: **production externalities** caused by automobile production and **consumption externalities** resulting from automobile use.[b] The production externalities are shown as added costs on the supply side and the consumption externalities as lowered benefits on the demand side. The resulting welfare impacts from trade are represented by the shaded areas C and F. The reduction in domestic production means that the country gains area C in reduced environmental costs—costs that are shifted to countries that produce cars for export. Increased automobile consumption and use, however, cause increased environmental damage equal to area F.

production externalities

externalities associated with the production of a good or service, such as emissions of pollutants from a factory.

consumption externalities

externalities associated with consumption of a good, such as pollutant emissions from vehicles.

Figure 20.2 **Environmental Impacts of Importing Automobiles**

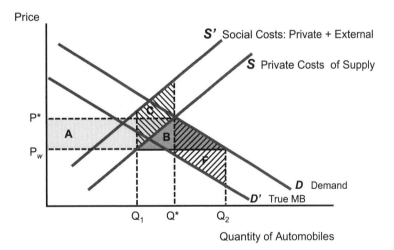

gains from trade

the net social benefits that result from trade.

This has important implications for trade theory. In the basic trade case without externalities, we can unambiguously claim overall **gains from trade**. Even though one group (automobile producers) loses, consumer gains outweigh these losses. After we introduce externalities, however, we can no longer be so sure of net gains

[a]This example shows trade in a relatively small country whose demand has no significant effect on world price, so world price is shown as constant (technically, an infinitely elastic supply curve at P_w). For a country large enough to affect world price, the world supply curve would be shown as upward sloping.

[b]In Chapter 3, we combined both types of externality for simplicity. Here, because production and consumption can take place in different countries, we must treat them separately.

from trade. It depends on the nature and size of the environmental damages C and F. Policy actions by the importing and exporting countries could internalize these external costs, but unless we know that such policies will be implemented, we cannot be sure of a net gain from trade.

Environmental Effects of Expanding Resource Exports

Environmental effects must also be figured into the analysis of the effects of trade on an exporting country. This is shown in Figure 20.3. Here we use timber exports as our example. In the ordinary analysis of trade without externalities, timber producers gain areas A′ + B′ because with trade they can produce and sell more timber, at the higher world price P_w. Domestic consumers of timber lose A′, being able to afford less timber at the higher price. The net gain to the country is B′.

Figure 20.3 **Gains and Losses from Exporting Timber**

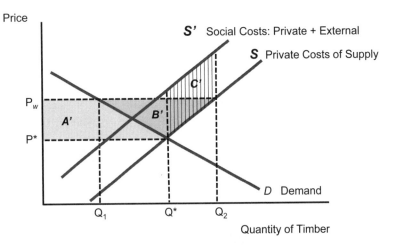

When we add the external costs associated with additional timber production—which could include land and watershed degradation as well as user costs, option values, and ecological costs—there is an additional cost to the exporting country of C′. (There could also be changes in consumption externalities associated with consuming timber, but since these are probably much less significant than in the case of automobiles, we omit them from Figure 20.3.) We cannot tell for sure how B′ and C′ compare in size. Thus we cannot say unambiguously that there are net benefits from trade to this exporting country.

Our examples, of course, represent a very simple model of trade, but the conclusion that environmental costs may seriously affect net gains from trade is far-reaching. In the real world, countries trade trillions of dollars' worth of products. Where there are significant environmental externalities, trade will reallocate these externalities among countries.

It may be possible to **export pollution** by importing goods whose production creates heavy environmental impact. In addition, expanded trade tends to increase the **scale of production** for the individual countries and world as a whole, meaning that the total volume of pollution and environmental damage is likely to increase. Trade also necessarily involves energy use for transportation, with resulting air

exported emissions/ pollution

shifting the impacts of pollution to other countries by importing goods whose production involves large environmental impacts.

scale of production

size or output level of an industry.

indirect environmental effects of trade

environmental impacts arising from trade, for example, when export agriculture displaces peasant farmers onto marginal lands, leading to deforestation and soil erosion.

pollution and other environmental consequences such as introduction of alien invasive species.[1] **Indirect environmental effects of trade** might also occur, for example when larger-scale export agriculture displaces peasant farmers onto marginal lands such as hillsides and forest margins, leading to deforestation and soil erosion. Specific kinds of trade, such as trade in toxic wastes or endangered species, can have obvious negative environmental impacts.

Trade may also have environmentally beneficial effects. Freer trade may help spread environmentally friendly technology, and the tendency of trade to promote more efficient production may reduce materials and energy use per unit of output. In addition, trading countries may come under pressure to improve environmental standards when product quality or transboundary impacts are at issue.[c] How can we balance the economic gains from trade against the reality that trade shifts environmental impact, sometimes increasing and sometimes decreasing total external costs?

20.2 TRADE AND ENVIRONMENT: POLICY AND PRACTICE

Let us consider some practical examples of the environmental impacts of trade. Many developing countries grow agricultural crops for domestic sale as well as for export. With increased trade—often a major feature of "structural adjustment" policies required by international agencies such as the International Monetary Fund (IMF) and the World Bank,[2] the area devoted to export crops increases. What are the environmental effects of shifting to export crops? In some cases, they can be significant and harmful. A study of Mali, for example, finds that development of cotton as a cash export crop "has substantially increased the cultivated area and markedly reduced the fallow period. . . . The environmental effects are evident in land degradation and soil erosion owing to over cultivation, insufficient fallow, and the use of marginal land against a backdrop of increasing aridity."[3]

But export crops can sometimes be more environmentally friendly than the domestic crops that they replace. In Latin America and Africa, tree crops such as coffee and cocoa can help prevent erosion. In Kenya, the rapidly expanding horticulture export sector has had mixed environmental effects. Some flower growers apply pesticides intensively, which has both health and environmental impacts. Excessive water use for irrigation is also an issue in water-poor Kenya. Prime agricultural land used for horticulture may displace food production; however, employment on flower farms can provide an alternative to exploitation of marginal lands for subsistence farming. The flowers are flown to Europe by jet, raising the issue of transportation energy use, but the energy consumed in jet fuel approximately equals the energy needed to grow similar flowers in heated greenhouses in Europe. Some Kenyan growers produce "fair-trade" flowers under a code that reduces water and pesticide use and guarantees workers higher wages, giving them a steady and reliable income.[4]

dualistic land ownership

an ownership pattern, common in developing countries, in which large landowners wield considerable power and small landowners tend to be displaced or forced onto inferior land.

Much depends not on trade alone but on domestic political conditions. **Dualistic land ownership**, with large landowners wielding considerable political power and small farmers being displaced by export-oriented agriculture, can be doubly damaging to the environment. In Central America, for example, improved transportation and trade infrastructure led to "a technical shift to higher-profit, input-dependent

---

[c]Examples could include pesticide residues in food or water pollution in rivers that cross national boundaries.

farming. Maize and beans gave way to cotton, tomatoes, strawberries, and bananas. The value of farmland naturally increased, which benefited privileged landowning elites but led many poor farmers to be promptly evicted. These farmers had no choice but to move on to drier lands, forests, hillsides, or lands with shallow and less fertile soils." At the same time, the affluent farmers "use their influence to demand environmentally damaging input subsidies, which in turn lead them to over-mechanize, over-irrigate, and overspray."[5]

Health and safety issues that arise from trade are not always easily resolved at either the domestic or international level. For example, domestic regulations that prohibit the sale of toxic pesticides may not apply internationally. "Goods that are restricted in domestic markets, on the grounds that they present a danger to human, animal or plant life or health, or to the environment, may often be legally exported. This may cause a problem for the importing country, where information is lacking on whether and why the product is banned: exporters may make false declarations, customs authorities (particularly in developing countries) may lack adequate product testing facilities."[6]

According to the **WTO's Article XX**, countries may restrict trade in order to "conserve exhaustible natural resources" or to protect "human, animal or plant life or health." However, interpretation of this special exception to free trade rules has led to fiercely contested disputes among countries.

For example, starting in the 1990s, European countries refused to allow imports of U.S. and Canadian beef produced with hormone supplements. The United States and Canada argued that since there is no proven harm to human health from beef hormones, this ban constituted an illegal barrier to trade. The Europeans, however, cited the **precautionary principle**: Because their consumers are concerned about the possible effects of hormones, shouldn't they have the prerogative to decide what they will allow for domestic consumption? The long-standing trade dispute was eventually settled in 2012, with an agreement that allowed the European Union to maintain its ban on imports of hormone-treated beef, in return for increasing its quota for imports of high-quality beef from the United States and Canada.[7]

Product and Process Issues

A similar issue has arisen over the use of genetically engineered crops. Although unlabeled genetically engineered foods are allowed in the United States, they are widely opposed in Europe. Should European countries be able to ban the importation of genetically engineered foods? The issue has enormous implications both for agribusinesses that see great profit potential in genetic engineering and for many consumers who strongly oppose it.

The issue is further complicated because the opposition to genetic engineering is based in part not on human health effects (which, if proved, would be a valid reason for trade restrictions under Article XX) but on the likely environmental impacts of genetically engineered crops. Pollen from such crops can easily spread into the environment, disrupting fragile ecosystems and possibly creating "superweeds" resistant to herbicides. But under GATT and WTO rules, the process by which a product is produced is not an acceptable cause for trade restrictions. Only if the product itself is harmful can a country impose controls.

For example, if pesticide residues at dangerous levels are detected on fruit or vegetables, imports of those products can be banned. But if the overuse of pesticides

WTO's Article XX
a World Trade Organization rule allowing countries to restrict trade in order to conserve exhaustible natural resources or to protect human, animal, or plant life or health.

precautionary principle
the view that policies should account for uncertainty by taking steps to avoid low-probability but catastrophic events.

is causing environmental damage in the producing areas, the importing country has no right to act. Similarly, if rainforests are being destroyed by unrestricted logging, it is not permissible for countries to impose a ban on the importation of unsustainably produced timber.

The **process and production methods (PPM)** rule removes an important potential weapon for international environmental protection. If a country fails to act to protect its own environment, other countries have no trade leverage to promote better environmental practices. Only if a specific **multilateral environmental agreement (MEA)** such as the Convention on International Trade in Endangered Species (CITES) is in place are import restrictions permissible.

This principle was at issue in the tuna/dolphin and shrimp/turtle decisions, in which trade authorities ruled that countries had no jurisdiction over extraterritorial environmental issues. But such issues are more and more common in an increasingly globalized world. Simply waiting for the producing country to "clean up its act" is likely to be insufficient.

Globalization of trade can also create "boomerang" effects through the transboundary exchange of externalities. For example, pesticides banned in the United States are often exported to developing countries. Farm laborers who apply pesticides without safety precautions suffer harmful effects, as do adults and children who drink water from streams polluted by runoff. In addition, harmful effects return to the United States through trade in fruits containing residues of dangerous chemicals.

Trade can affect domestic as well as international policy, weakening the autonomy of countries to define their own environmental and social policies. Concerns have arisen of a "**race to the bottom**," in which countries reduce environmental and social standards in order to gain competitive advantage.

> Producers located in member states enforcing strict process standards will suffer a competitive disadvantage compared with producers located in member states enforcing less strict standards. . . . [F]aced with the prospect of their industries suffering a competitive disadvantage when compared with companies located in low-standard jurisdictions, member states may choose not to elevate environmental standards or may even relax current standards.[8]

According to several economic studies, there is "relatively little evidence to support the hypothesis that environmental regulations have had a large adverse effect on competitiveness," and few cases exist of **pollution havens**—countries that attract manufacturing firms due to weak environmental regulations.[9] But competitive pressures may nonetheless exert a "chilling" effect on countries considering strict environmental laws.

The North American Free Trade Agreement (NAFTA) has produced cases in which corporations have challenged environmental regulations as barriers to trade. The Canadian asbestos industry sought to remove U.S. restrictions on the sale of cancer-causing asbestos products, and the U.S. pesticide industry challenged strong Canadian pesticide regulations. In one case, Ethyl Corporation (based in the United States) successfully overturned a Canadian ban on the importation and sale of the gasoline additive MMT, a chemical suspected of causing nerve damage. Canada was required not only to eliminate the ban but also to pay $13 million to compensate Ethyl Corporation for legal costs and lost sales.[10]

process and production methods (PPMs)

international trade rules stating that an importing country cannot use trade barriers or penalties against another country for failure to meet environmental or social standards related to the process of production.

multilateral environmental agreements (MEAs)

international treaties between countries on environmental issues, such as the Convention on Trade in Endangered Species.

"race to the bottom"

the tendency for countries to weaken national environmental standards to attract foreign businesses or to keep existing businesses from moving to other countries.

pollution haven

a country or region that attracts high-polluting indistries due to low levels of environmental regulation.

Environmentally Beneficial Effects of Trade

distortionary subsidies
subsidies that alter the market equilibrium in ways that are harmful to economic efficiency.

Trade expansion may also have direct or indirect beneficial effects on the environment. According to comparative advantage theory, trade causes countries to become more efficient in their use of resources, thereby conserving resources and avoiding waste. Trade liberalization also removes **distortionary subsidies** and pricing policies, improving the efficiency of resource allocation. For example, widespread subsidies on chemical fertilizers and pesticides promote environmentally harmful farming methods, but trade agreements often prohibit such subsidies to domestic producers. Eliminating these subsidies would promote both economic efficiency and environmental sustainability.

Trade may also encourage the spread of environmentally friendly technology. In energy production, for example, many developing and formerly communist countries depend heavily on old, inefficient, highly polluting power plants. Trade can facilitate the replacement of these plants with modern, highly efficient facilities or (as in India) encourage a growing wind-power sector. Multinational companies, sometimes seen as offenders in the exploitation of developing country resources, can also introduce efficient technologies in industrial sectors. Multinationals may respond to domestic political pressures to develop cleaner industrial processes and then disseminate those processes throughout their worldwide operations.[11]

> Foreign investment affects the environment in many ways. In resource-based industries, especially oil extraction and mineral mining, it can lead to significant local environmental degradation as demonstrated in, for example, Nigeria, Indonesia, and Papua New Guinea. Foreign investment in the manufacturing sector, on the other hand, can lead to the employment of later vintage and possibly less resource- and pollution-intensive technology.[12]

scale, composition, and technique effects
the impacts of trade on economic growth, industrial patterns, and technological progress; the combination of effects may be environmentally negative, positive, or neutral.

One way of capturing trade's differential effects on the environment is to distinguish among **scale, composition, and technique effects**. Trade promotes growth (increased scale), changes in industrial patterns (composition), and improvements in technological efficiency (technique). "If the nature of [an economic] activity is unchanged but the scale is growing, then pollution and resource depletion will increase along with output."[13] Composition effects may shift a country's production in the direction of either more or less polluting industries. Technique effects can lead to a decline in pollution due to more efficient production and the use of cleaner technologies. The combination of the three effects may increase or decrease pollution levels or balance out to leave pollution levels unchanged. One study of sulfur dioxide pollution found that, on balance, trade reduces pollution levels[14]— but this may not be true for other pollutants.

Trade and Global Climate Change

Trade has important effects on the emission of carbon dioxide and other gases that contribute to global climate change. As noted above, increased transportation resulting from expanded trade can result in higher transport-related emissions. Trade also shifts the patterns of carbon emissions, with a significant amount of "exported pollution"—carbon emissions associated with consumption of imported goods. Figure 20.4 shows major carbon flows in international trade, based on an analysis of the carbon content of internationally traded goods. Clearly, a significant portion of carbon emissions, especially from China, is associated with goods produced for export in the developing countries of the "global South" and consumed in the United States and Europe (the "global North"). This has important implications for international negotiations on global climate change. It would seem that those who consume the goods, not those who produce them, have the responsibility to reduce emissions.[15]

Figure 20.4 **Carbon Flows in International Trade**

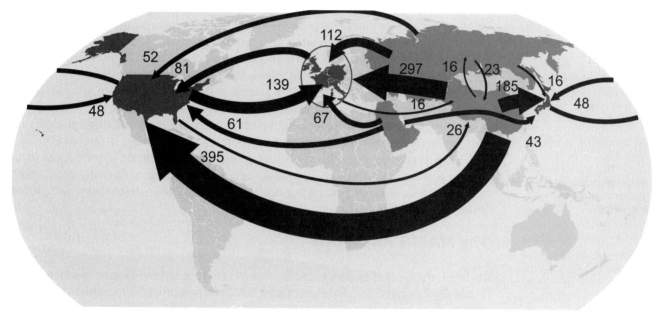

Source: Davis and Caldeira, 2010.

Note: Figures are in million metric tons of CO_2/year). Carbon flows to and from Western Europe are aggregated to include the United Kingdom, France, Germany, Switzerland, Italy, Spain, Luxembourg, the Netherlands, and Sweden.

20.3 TRADE AGREEMENTS AND THE ENVIRONMENT

A variety of institutional and policy approaches have been suggested to balance the goals of trade benefits and environmental protection, some similar to the standard free-trade model and others significantly different. We examine several of them.

The World Trade Organization Approach

This approach retains the overarching policy goal of free or "liberalized" trade, pursued for five decades through "rounds" of trade agreements under the GATT, and its successor the WTO. The WTO, whose membership now comprises 157 countries, have worked to lower tariffs (taxes imposed on traded goods) and non-tariff barriers to trade as well as eliminate subsidies for export industries.

Although the WTO recognizes a special exception to trade rules under Article XX for resource conservation and environmental protection, its panel rulings have interpreted this fairly narrowly. WTO authorities tend to be suspicious of "green protectionism"—the use of trade barriers to protect domestic industry from competition under the guise of environmental regulation. They are also unsympathetic to countries' efforts to affect environmental policy outside their borders through trade measures.

The WTO has established a Committee on Trade and the Environment, which has addressed some environmental concerns but in rather general terms. According to the WTO Web site, the committee "has contributed to identifying and understanding the relationship between trade and the environment in order to promote sustainable development" and "helps set the framework for members to design and implement measures to address environmental concerns."[16]

From the WTO perspective, environmental policy responsibility should remain primarily at the national level. As far as possible, decisions on international trade policy should not be complicated with environmental issues. This is consistent with an economic principle known as the **specificity rule**: Policy solutions should directly target the source of the problem. Using trade measures to accomplish environmental policy goals is therefore a **second-best solution** likely to cause other, undesired effects such as economic losses from trade restriction.

This argument, which places the responsibility for environmental policies on national governments, has been criticized on several grounds. It fails to consider the competitive pressures that may encourage trading countries to reduce environmental protections, as well as the weak regulatory institutions in many developing countries. It is also inadequate for dealing with truly **transboundary** and **global pollution problems**.

The NAFTA Approach

In 1993, the United States, Canada, and Mexico signed the North American Free Trade Agreement (NAFTA), lowering trade barriers across North America. During negotiations, environmental groups argued strongly that freer trade could have negative environmental consequences, pointing to the severe environmental problems already affecting the *maquiladoras*, which are industrial zones along the Mexican border in which materials and equipment can be imported duty-free for assembly and re-export. As a result, a **side agreement**, the North American Agreement on Environmental Cooperation (NAAEC), set up the tripartite Commission for Environmental Cooperation (CEC), and another side agreement, the North American Agreement on Labor Cooperation (NAALC), dealt with labor issues.

This specific attention to social and environmental aspects of trade was remarkable and almost unprecedented in trade agreements. Although this unusual aspect of NAFTA persuaded some environmental groups in the United States to support the agreement, the CEC has few enforcement powers. It may respond to a country's failure to enforce existing environmental regulations, but its role is generally limited to producing a fact-finding report and offering recommendations to the government involved.

The opening of agricultural sector trade under NAFTA has both social and environmental effects, as small corn farmers in Mexico are unable to compete with cheaper grain imported from the United States. The migration of displaced farmers from rural to urban areas has intensified urban environmental pressures as well as creating greater pressure for illegal migration across the U.S.-Mexican border. In addition, the genetic diversity characteristic of small-scale farming maybe threatened, which could result in the loss of a "living seed bank" of great importance to world agriculture.[17]

specificity rule
the view that policy solutions should be targeted directly at the source of a problem.

second-best solution
a policy solution to a problem that fails to maximize potential net social benefits, but that may be desirable if the optimal solution cannot be achieved.

transboundary and global pollution problems
pollution that is carried beyond the borders of a specific region or country and impacts those outside the region.

side agreement
a provision related to a trade treaty dealing with social or environmental issues.

In the area of industrial pollution, NAFTA has had both positive and negative impacts. Mexican environmental enforcement has improved, but increased industrial concentrations have led to worsened local environmental quality in some areas. A review of NAFTA's environmental provisions concluded that it has "fallen well short of the aspirations of the environmental community" and "should be strengthened in the next phase of NAFTA."[18] But efforts to expand NAFTA to Central and South America, in the Free Trade Area of the Americas (FTAA) and Central America Free Trade Agreement (CAFTA), have drawn opposition from critics who argue that these proposed agreements have even weaker social and environmental provisions.

One of the most controversial aspects of NAFTA is its Chapter 11, which protects foreign investors. Under this provision, investors who claim damage to their business from environmental regulations can sue governments to recover damages, and several suits have been successful. In 1999, when California ordered a phase-out of the gasoline additive and groundwater contaminant MTBE, the Canadian manufacturer Methanex sued for $1 billion in compensation. After a long legal battle, the claim was finally rejected by a NAFTA tribunal in 2005.[19] The issue of investor rights agreements has since become a major issue in other international trade agreements. In trade agreements with the Dominican Republic, Central American countries, and Peru, the United States has agreed on language that protects "bona fide environmental regulations" from being the subject of expropriation suits by corporations.[20]

The European Union Approach

harmonization of environmental standards
the standardization of environmental standards across countries, as in the European Union.

The European Union (EU) is unusual in being a free-trade area with its own legislative and administrative institutions. Unlike the North American CEC, the EU has the power to make environmental regulations binding on its member countries. This is known as **harmonization of environmental standards**. Note, however, that this policy solution involves more than free trade; it entails the creation of a supranational authority with the power to set environmental standards.

Regional trade area policies also raise the issue of "harmonizing up" versus "harmonizing down." Some countries may be forced to tighten their environmental policies to meet EU standards. But others may find their environmental standards weakened. The EU overturned a law requiring returnable bottles in Denmark as a barrier to trade, and Norway chose not to join the EU in part out of fear that it would be compelled to modify strict domestic environmental regulations.

It is relatively rare for trade agreements to include the kind of enforceable supranational environmental regulations that exist in the EU. Although the Standards Code adopted after the Uruguay Round of GATT trade negotiations in 1992 calls for international harmonization of environmental standards, no basis exists for this process to be other than voluntary.

Multilateral Environmental Agreements (MEAs)

It has long been recognized that some environmental problems require international solutions. The first international treaty dealing with trade and the environment was the Phylloxera agreement of 1878, restricting trade in grapevines to prevent the spread of pests that damage vineyards. In 1906 an international convention was adopted banning the use of phosphorus in matches. Phosphorous was responsible for serious occupational disease among match workers, but it was the cheapest ingredient for matches. An international convention was required to prevent any exporting country from gaining a competitive advantage by using phosphorus in match production.[21]

Since then, numerous international treaties have responded to specific environmental issues, such as conventions protecting fur seals, migratory birds, polar bears, whales, and endangered species. Transboundary and global environmental issues have been addressed in the Montreal Protocol on Substances that Deplete the Ozone Layer (1987), the Basel Convention on Hazardous Wastes (1989), the Antarctica Treaty (1991), the Convention on Straddling and Highly Migratory Fish Stocks (1995), the Kyoto Protocol on Climate Change (1997), the Convention on Biological Diversity (2002), and the Cartagena Protocol on Biosafety (2003). These international treaties have addressed the environmental consequences of production methods in ways that individual countries cannot.

> The local imposition of PPM (Process and Production Measures) standards on domestic manufacturing industry is obviously a national prerogative, but it should not be used to restrict imported products, whatever the process used for their production. This kind of action would be in conflict with [world trade rules]. If PPMs are included as appropriate measures within a Multilateral Environmental Agreement (MEA), however, this would be much more acceptable, as their imposition would be multilateral rather than unilateral.[22]

Serious questions remain, however, about the compatibility of MEAs with WTO rules. Which set of international agreements should take precedence in case of a conflict? For example, the Kyoto Protocol encourages the subsidized transfer of energy efficient technology to developing countries—but this provision could violate the WTO's prohibition of export subsidies. Whereas national laws such as the U.S. Marine Mammal Protection Act have been found incompatible with WTO rules, so far no major test case has addressed conflict between an MEA and a trade agreement. But some analysts have argued that the possibility of a conflict with WTO rules has a "chilling" effect on the ability of MEAs to achieve their objectives.[23]

20.4 STRATEGIES FOR SUSTAINABLE TRADE

The emerging twenty-first-century global economy will be characterized both by resource and environmental limits and by a much more important role for developing countries. Global trade continues to increase rapidly:

> There have indeed been large increases in the volumes of international trade and investment in the world economy. According to the World Bank, trade (imports plus exports) as a percent of world gross domestic product (GDP) was 24 percent in 1960, 38 percent in 1985, and 52 percent in 2005.[d]

Expanded global trade will bring benefits in terms of increased efficiency, technology transfer, and the importation and exportation of sustainably produced

---

[d]Note that the World Bank figure adds both exports and imports. Exports alone represent 28 percent of GDP. This means that about 28 percent of global economic production in 2010 was traded across country borders (Gallagher, 2009; World Bank, 2008).

products. But we must also evaluate the effects of trade in terms of social and ecological impacts.

A World Bank review of trade and environment issues found that "many participants in the debate now agree that (a) more open trade improves growth and economic welfare, and (b) increased trade and growth without appropriate environmental policies in place may have unwanted effects on the environment."[25] This implies that future trade agreements must take environmental sustainability more explicitly into account. Introducing sustainability into trade policy will require institutional changes at global, regional, and local levels.

"Greening" Global Environmental Organizations

World Environmental Organization (WEO) a proposed international organization that would have oversight of global environmental issues.

At the global level, advocates of institutional reform have proposed setting up a **World Environmental Organization (WEO)** that would counterbalance the WTO much as national environmental protection agencies balance departments of finance and commerce.[26] This would create a global environmental advocacy organization but might also lead to conflict and deadlock with other transnational institutions.

Another approach would be to "green" existing institutions, broadening the environmental and social provisions of the WTO's Article XX, and altering the missions of the World Bank and IMF to emphasize sustainable trade development objectives (discussed further in Chapter 21).

The idea of a world environmental organization may seem visionary, but it has gained significant support. According to Sir Leon Brittan, vice president of the European Commission: "Setting environmental standards within a territory may be fine, but what about damage that spills over national borders? In a rapidly globalizing world, more and more of these problems cannot be effectively solved at the national or bilateral level, or even at the level of regional trading blocs like the European Union. Global problems require global solutions."[27]

A WEO could also play a role in negotiating trade agreements on agricultural subsidies, seeking to redirect farm subsidies to soil conservation and development of low-input agricultural techniques. As global CO_2 emissions continue to rise, energy sector trade may need to accommodate a carbon tax or tradable permit scheme, as discussed in Chapter 19. Global agreements on forest and biodiversity preservation are also likely to involve specific trade restrictions, tariff preferences, or labeling systems. In all these areas, a powerful institutional advocate for environmental interests would have a major impact on the shaping of trade treaties and regulations.

Local, Regional, and Private Sector Policies

The trend toward globalization, which increasingly makes communities subject to the logic of the global marketplace, may come into conflict with the goal of strengthening local and regional policies promoting sustainable development. Reserving powers of resource conservation and management to local and national institutions is important to the sustainable management of resources. Most environmental protection policies are implemented at the national level, and it is important to maintain national authority to enforce environmental standards.

In regional groupings such as NAFTA that involve no supranational rule-making body, trade agreements could give special status to national policies aimed at sustainable agriculture and resource management. NAFTA rules currently give precedence to international environmental treaties (such as the Basel Convention on hazardous wastes, the Montreal Protocol on ozone-depleting substances, and CITES on endangered species). This principle could be expanded to all national environmental protection policies, and effective sanctions for environmental violations could be established.

Regional trade and customs unions such as the EU, with elected supranational policy-making bodies, can be responsible for environmental and social regulation to the extent that their legitimate democratic mandate allows. Transboundary issues are a logical area for supranational bodies to carry on environmental rule making. Where they are empowered to intervene in national policy-making, the process can be oriented toward "harmonizing up" rather than "harmonizing down" environmental standards. This means that countries within a free-trade area must retain the power to impose higher social and environmental standards where they see fit.

The development of **certification and labeling** requirements for sustainably produced products can arise from public or private initiative. Germany's "green dot" system for recyclable and recycled goods is one example. Private, nongovernmental organizations have also set up certification systems for goods such as coffee and timber. "Fair trade" networks certify socially and environmentally responsible production of traded goods. Although it represents only a tiny proportion of trade, the fair-trade industry has experienced a rapid rate of sales growth.[28]

It is evident that there are many different approaches to reconciling the goals of trade and environment policy. In an article reviewing the debate on trade and environment, Daniel Esty concludes that "there is no real choice about whether to address the trade and environment linkage; this linkage is a matter of fact. . . . Building environmental sensitivity into the trade regime in a thoughtful and systematic fashion should therefore be of interest to the trade community as well as environmental advocates."[29] Achieving this goal will be a major challenge for trade negotiators at both the regional and global level for the foreseeable future.

SUMMARY

Trade expansion can often have environmental implications. Trade may increase environmental externalities at the national, regional, or global level. Although it is usually economically advantageous for countries to pursue their comparative advantage through trade, trade may have environmental repercussions, such as increased pollution or natural resource degradation.

The environmental impacts of trade affect both importers and exporters. Agricultural cropping patterns altered by the introduction of export crops may involve environmental benefit or harm. Secondary effects of trade may arise from the disruption of existing communities, increased migration, and impact on marginal lands. Industrial pollution may increase, decrease, or shift regional impact.

International trade agreements make provisions for resource conservation and environmental protection, but these are usually limited exceptions to a general principle of free trade. In the

World Trade Organization (WTO), countries may consider the environmental impact of a product but not of its production processes. This has led to numerous trade disputes over whether specific measures are justified on the grounds of protection of life and health or are simply disguised protectionism.

Policy responses to trade and environment issues can occur at the national, regional, or global level. The European Union is an example of a free-trade area that includes institutions for transnational environmental standards enforcement. The North American Free Trade Agreement was accompanied by a side agreement setting up an environmental monitoring authority, the Commission for Environmental Cooperation, but this body has little enforcement power.

Multilateral environmental agreements (MEAs) address specific transboundary or global environmental issues. Conflicts between MEAs and WTO rules are possible, but have so far been avoided. Proposals have also been made for a World Environmental Organization to oversee global environmental policy and to advocate for environmental interests in the world trade system.

Where effective environmental protection policies are lacking at the regional or global level, national policies must address trade-related environmental issues. Certification and labeling requirements, instituted by governments or by private nongovernmental organizations, can help to promote consumer awareness and "greener" corporate practices in international trade.

KEY TERMS AND CONCEPTS

certification and labeling
comparative advantage
consumption externalities
distortionary subsidies
dualistic land ownership
environmental externalities
exporting pollution
gains from trade
General Agreement on Tariffs and Trade (GATT)
harmonization of environmental standards
indirect environmental effects of trade
multilateral environmental agreements (MEAs)
pollution havens

precautionary principle
process and production methods (PPMs)
production externalities
"race to the bottom"
scale of production
scale, composition, and technique effects
second-best solution
side agreement
specificity rule
transboundary and global pollution problems
World Environmental Organization (WEO)
World Trade Organization (WTO)
WTO's Article XX

DISCUSSION QUESTIONS

1. What are the welfare implications of trade in toxic wastes? Should such trade be banned or can it serve a useful function? Who should have the power to regulate trade in toxic wastes, individual countries, local communities, or a global authority?
2. Can harmonization of environmental standards solve the problem of environmental externalities in trade? How would the issues of harmonization differ in NAFTA, the EU, and the WTO? Would harmonization promote economic efficiency as well as environmental improvement, or might it lead to lower environmental standards?

3. What should be done if the provisions of a Multilateral Environmental Agreement conflict with the principles of the WTO? Which should take precedence, and who should have the authority to decide? Which economic, social, and ecological principles should be used to decide such issues?

NOTES

1. See Gallagher, 2009; McAusland and Costello, 2004.
2. For more on the IMF, the World Bank, and structural adjustment, see Chapter 21.
3. Reed, 1996, 86, 96.
4. See "Kenya's Flower Industry Shows Budding Improvement," *Guardian,* April 1, 2011, www.guardian.co.uk/environment/2011/apr/01/kenya-flower-industry-worker-conditions-water-tax/.
5. Paarlberg, 2000, 177.
6. Brack, 1998, 7.
7. See www.europarl.europa.eu/news/en/pressroom/content/20120314IPR40752/html/Win-win-ending-to-the-hormone-beef-trade-war/.
8. Brack, 1998, 113.
9. See Jaffe et al., 1995 (quoted); Gallagher, 2004.
10. See www.cela.ca/article/international-trade-agreements-commentary/how-canada-became-shill-ethyl-corp/.
11. See Zarsky, 2004.
12. Neumayer, 2001, x.
13. Gallagher, 2009.
14. Antweiler et al., 2001.
15. See Davis and Caldeira, 2010; Giljum and Eisenmenger, 2004.
16. See www.wto.org/english/tratop_e/envir_e/envir_e.htm; Charnovitz, 2007.
17. See Wise, 2007, 2011.
18. Hufbauer et al., 2000, 62. See also Deere and Esty, 2002; Gallagher, 2004.
19. See Mann, 2005.
20. Gallagher, 2009, 296.
21. Charnovitz 1996, 176–177.
22. Brack, 1998, 65.
23. Gallagher, 2009; Neumayer, 2001.
24. Note that the World Bank figure adds both exports and imports. Exports alone represent 28 percent of GDP. This means that about 28 percent of global economic production in 2010 was traded across country borders (Gallagher, 2009; World Bank, 2008).
25. Fredriksson, 1999, 1.
26. See Biermann and Bauer, eds., 2005; Esty, 1994, chap. 4; Runge, 1994, chap. 6.
27. Brack, 1998, 19, 20.
28. See www.fairtraderesource.org and www.fairtradefederation.org for a review of fair trade initiatives.
29. Esty, 2001, 114, 126–127. See also Harris, 2000.

REFERENCES

Antweiler, Werner, Brian R. Copeland, and M. Scott Taylor. 2001. "Is Free Trade Good for the Environment." *American Economic Review* 91(4) (September): 877–908.

Biermann, Frank, and Steffen Bauer. 2005. *A World Environment Organization: Solution or Threat For Effective International Environmental Governance?* Aldershot, UK: Ashgate Publishing.

Brack, Duncan, ed. 1998. *Trade and Environment: Conflict or Compatibility?* London: Royal Institute of International Affairs.

Charnovitz, Steve. 1996. "Trade Measures and the Design of International Regimes." *Journal of Environment and Development* 5(2): 168–169.

———. 2007. "The WTO's Environmental Progress." *Journal of International Economic Law* 10(3): 685–706.

Davis, Steven J., and Ken Caldeira. 2010. "Consumption-based Accounting of CO_2 Emissions." *Publications of the National Academy of Sciences,* March 8. www.pnas.org/content/early/2010/02/23/0906974107.full.pdf+html.

Deere, Carolyn L., and Daniel C. Esty. 2002. *Greening the Americas: NAFTA's Lessons for Hemispheric Trade.* Cambridge, MA: MIT Press.

Esty, Daniel C. 1994. *Greening the GATT: Trade, Environment, and the Future.* Washington, DC: Institute for International Economics.

Fredriksson, Per G., ed. 1999. "Trade, Global Policy, and the Environment." World Bank Discussion Paper no. 402, Washington, DC.

Gallagher, Kevin P. 2004. *Free Trade and the Environment: Mexico, NAFTA, and Beyond.* Palo Alto: Stanford University Press.

———. 2009. "Economic Globalization and the Environment." *Annual Review of Environment and Resources* 34: 279–304.

Giljum, Stefan, and Nina Eisenmenger. 2004. "North-South Trade and the Distribution of Environmental Goods and Burdens: A Biophysical Perspective." *Journal of Environment and Development* 13(1): 73–100.

Harris, Jonathan M. 2000. "Free Trade or Sustainable Trade? An Ecological Economics Perspective." In *Rethinking Sustainability: Power, Knowledge, and Institutions,* ed. Jonathan M. Harris, Ann Arbor: University of Michigan Press.

Hufbauer, Gary C., Daniel C. Esty, Diana Orejas, Luis Rubio, and Jeffrey J. Scott. 2000. *NAFTA and the Environment: Seven Years Later.* Washington, DC: Institute for International Economics.

Jaffe, Adam B., et al. 1995. "Environmental Regulation and the Competitiveness of U.S. Manufacturing." *Journal of Economic Literature* 33(March 5): 132–163.

Mann, Howard. 2005. *The Final Decision in Methanex v. U.S.: Some New Wine in Some New Bottles.* Winnipeg: International Institute for Sustainable Development. www.iisd.org/pdf/2005/commentary_methanex.pdf.

McAusland, Carol, and Christopher Costello. 2004. "Avoiding Invasives: Trade-Related Policies for Controlling Unintentional Exotic Species Introductions." *Journal of Environmental Economics and Management* 48: 954–977.

Neumayer, Eric. 2001. *Greening Trade and Investment: Environmental Protection without Protectionism.* London: Earthscan.

Paarlberg, Robert. 2000. "Political Power and Environmental Sustainability in Agriculture." In *Rethinking Sustainability: Power, Knowledge, and Institutions,* ed. Jonathan M. Harris, Ann Arbor: University of Michigan Press.

Reed, David, ed. 1996. *Structural Adjustment, the Environment, and Sustainable Development.* London: World Wide Fund for Nature.

Runge, C. Ford. 1994. *Freer Trade, Protected Environment: Balancing Trade Liberalization and Environmental Interests.* New York: Council on Foreign Relations Press.

Wise, Timothy A. 2007. "Policy Space for Mexican Maize: Protecting Agro-biodiversity by Promoting Rural Livelihoods." Tufts University Global Development and Environment Institute Working Paper no. 07–01, February, Medford, MA. www.ase.tufts.edu/gdae/policy_research/MexicanMaize.html.

———. 2011. "Mexico: The Cost of U.S. Dumping." North American Congress on Latin America, *Report on the Americas,* January/February. www.ase.tufts.edu/gdae/Pubs/rp/WiseNACLADumpingFeb2011.pdf.

World Bank. 2008. *World Development Indicators.* Washington, DC.

Zarsky, Lyuba. 2004. *International Investment Rules for Sustainable Development: Balancing Rights with Rewards.* London: Earthscan.

WEB SITES

1. **www.wto.org/english/tratop_e/envir_e/envir_e.htm**. The World Trade Organization's Web site devoted to the relationship between international trade issues and environmental quality. The site includes links to many research reports and other information.
2. **www.cec.org**. Home page for the Commission on Environmental Cooperation, created under the North American Free Trade Agreement "to address regional environmental concerns, help prevent potential trade and environmental conflicts, and to promote the effective enforcement of environmental law." The site includes numerous publications on issues of trade and the environment in North America.
3. **www.oecd-ilibrary.org/environment/**. The Web site for the environment division of the Organization for Economic Cooperation and Development, including many publications dealing with trade and environmental policy.
4. **www.iisd.org/trade/handbook/**. This handbook, a joint effort of the International Institute for Sustainable Development and the United Nations Environment Programme, provides a guide to trade, environment, and development issues.
5. **www.fairtradefederation.org**. Home page for the Fair Trade Federation, an organization dedicated to promoting socially and ecologically sustainable trade.

CHAPTER 21

Institutions and Policies for Sustainable Development

- Can the goals of economic development and environmental sustainability be reconciled?
- How can current development institutions be "greened"?
- How can sustainability be pursued at global, regional, and local levels?
- What are the central environment and development issues for the twenty-first century?

21.1 THE CONCEPT OF SUSTAINABLE DEVELOPMENT

In the past four decades, the role of the environment in economic development has moved from a neglected to a central issue in both developed and developing countries. This shift in perceptions, however, has not always translated into effective policies at the national and global level. One of the greatest impediments to designing and implementing policies to promote environmental sustainability has been the belief that such policies would hinder job creation and economic growth (an issue addressed in Chapter 17). This supposed contradiction found some resolution in the emergence of the concept of sustainable development in the late 1980s—a concept that has gained wide support in the past twenty-five years but also has been criticized as being too vague to lead to any significant change.

This chapter discusses the origins of the concept, the economic issues involved in sustainable development, and its strengths and limitations as a blueprint for new sets of policies. We explore how global institutions have responded to the concept of sustainable development and to what extent they have reoriented concepts of economic development toward the objectives of environmental sustainability.

We also focus on the limitations of these global institutions. Especially in the area of climate change, recent international conferences, such as the Copenhagen Conference in 2009 and the Rio + 20 Summit and Doha Climate Change Conference in 2012, have had disappointing results (as discussed in Chapter 19).[a] In the face of obstacles at the global level, we explore how local initiatives,

---

[a]Rio + 20, the United Nations Conference on Sustainable Development, also known as Earth Summit 2012, was held twenty years after the original United Nations Conference on Environment and Development held in Rio de Janeiro in 1992.

in urban and rural areas in both the global North and South, have been able to integrate the objectives of economic development and ecological sustainability and what lessons can be learned from such examples to address the challenges of the twenty-first century.[b]

21.2 THE ECONOMICS OF SUSTAINABLE DEVELOPMENT

All countries seek economic development. Economic development policies, however, have taken limited heed of the environment until relatively recently. Only within the past forty years have currently developed countries recognized the need for specific policies to protect the environment. In many countries, the concept of environmental protection is even more recent.

The United States, for example, set up its Environmental Protection Agency in 1970. Prior to this, a conservation movement, active for nearly a century, had focused primarily on protection of public lands. The idea that the industrial system should be subject to some sort of environmental controls was not an integral part of economic development theory or practice for most of the twentieth century.

By the end of the twentieth century, however, it had become clear that the issues of environment and development could not be separated. This gave rise to the concept of **sustainable development**. In 1987, the World Commission on Environment and Development (WCED) addressed the issue of conflicts between environment and development by proposing a definition:

> Sustainable development is development that meets the needs of the present without compromising the ability of future generations to meet their own needs.[1]

According to the WCED (whose findings are also known as the Brundtland Report), the definition of sustainable development must reconcile two key concepts:

- the concept of "needs"—in particular the basic needs of the world's poor—which implies the issue of setting priorities dealing with ethical questions regarding the value of equity
- the idea of limits imposed by the environment's ability to meet both present and future needs, raising questions about balancing current and future needs

The concept of sustainable development originated by the WCED can also be conceptualized as having three dimensions: ecological, social, and economic, often represented in a diagram similar to Figure 21.1.

Full sustainability occurs at the intersection of these three dimensions—meeting the requirements of environmental resilience (the ability of natural ecosystems to renew and regenerate themselves), social equity (the necessity to meet human basic needs so that each individual can live a dignified life), and economic sufficiency (the requirement to provide sufficient economic production and employment). Each of these dimensions matters.

sustainable development
development that meets the needs of the present without compromising the ability of future generations to meet their own needs.

---

[b]The "Global North" and "Global South" are terms used to refer generally to the more economically developed countries primarily in the Northern Hemisphere and developing countries primarily in the Southern Hemisphere.

Figure 21.1 **A Conceptualization of Sustainable Development**

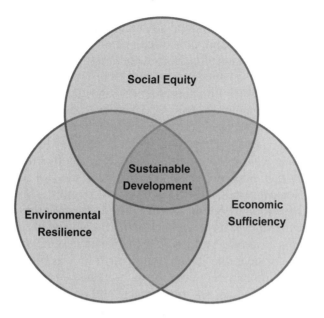

At the intersection of economic necessities and environmental concerns and limits is the dimension of ecological sustainability. The focus of this textbook has been primarily to address the issues dealing with that intersection. But related social issues are no less critical to address:

- How societies deal with ecological limits and constraints raises the question of how social and cultural (including religious) norms can help or hinder the transition toward ecological sustainability. These norms can be transformed through education in order to make the transition to ecological sustainability socially, culturally and politically acceptable.
- Social equity is also an essential part of the concept of sustainable development. An equitable society does not necessarily imply complete equality but, rather, economic justice and the provision of basic needs for all.

The concept of sustainable development has been widely accepted by various constituencies, including the business world, the political world, the scientific world, and the world of environmental activists and advocates. But precisely because of its all-encompassing nature, the term has been used and abused in many different ways, meaning different things to different people. In this chapter, we attempt to identify the meaning of sustainability more specifically, both in theoretical and practical terms.

Sustainable Development: Implications for Developed and Developing Countries

capital stock
the existing quantity of capital in a given region, including manufactured, human, and natural capital.

The implications of making development socially and ecologically sustainable differ for developed and developing countries. Currently developed countries typically have large **capital stocks** and extensive infrastructure including power plants, highways, factories, extensive urban and suburban business and residential construction, dams, and irrigation systems, and many other elements essential to modern economic production. This is both an advantage and disadvantage in trying to achieve environmental sustainability.

On the one hand, greater economic capacity and advanced technology makes it more possible and affordable to put environmental protection systems in place. On the other hand, the large existing stock of resource-using, waste- and pollution-generating capital, together with consumer demands for a continual flow of products, mean that developed countries may be locked into unsustainable methods of production. This lock-in may be technological—for example, a dependence on fossil fuels and the technologies associated with them. It may also be social, for example, the reluctance of Americans to consider alternatives to automobile-based transport. In terms of the three-part graph presented in Figure 21.1, this is a situation in which impediments to ecological sustainability may be both economic and sociocultural.

Developing countries have a different set of problems in achieving sustainability. Because they start from much lower income levels, their major social and economic goal is to increase production. As we have seen, developing countries also tend to have considerable population growth momentum. The combination of increased population and economic growth creates strong pressure for rising resource use and increased generation of waste and pollution.

As shown in Table 21.1, developing countries, which for the most part still have a low environmental impact per capita, also have the demographic and economic potential to "catch up" to the high levels of environmental impact of most developed countries, if they follow similar patterns of development. Total energy consumption in China, for example, already exceeds that of the United States, although per capita energy consumption in China is less than a quarter of that in the United States. India's per capita energy consumption is less than one-tenth of U.S. levels. If China and India both consumed energy at U.S. per capita levels, total world energy consumption would more than double. And if the whole world's population emitted CO_2 at the per capita levels of U.S. residents, global CO_2 emissions would quadruple.

Table 21.1

Environmental Data for Selected Countries

Country	2011 population (millions)	Energy consumption[1]		CO_2 emissions[2]		Motor vehicles[3]	
		Per capita	Total	Per capita	Total	Per 1,000 people	Total
Bangladesh	150	201	30	0.3	46	3	0.5
China	1,344	1,695	2,257	5.3	7,049	47	62.6
France	65	3,959	256	5.9	366	598	37.7
India	1,241	560	676	1.5	1,722	18	21.1
Japan	127	3,700	472	9.5	1,207	589	74.8
Mexico	112	1,559	175	4.3	473	276	30.4
Thailand	70	1,504	103	4.2	273	134	9.0
United States	311	7,051	2,163	18.0	5,472	802	246.2
World	6,974	1,790	12,483	4.8	32,102	137	933.0

Source: World Bank, World Development Indicators database, http://data.worldbank.org/topic/.

[1]Commercial energy from all sources, measured in kilograms of oil equivalent per capita, 2009 data. Totals in million metric tons of oil equivalent.

[2]Emissions from industrial processes, measured in metric tons of CO_2 per capita, 2008 data. Totals in million metric tons.

[3]Includes automobiles, buses, and freight vehicles, date of data varies (generally 2009, Thailand 2006). Totals in millions of vehicles.

Developing countries, however, may have greater choice as to which development path to pursue. They are not necessarily committed to following a resource-intensive, high waste-generating pattern of economic growth. As later participants in development, they may have access to improved technologies, especially with the assistance of developed countries, and can avoid costly environmental errors made by the developed countries (a phenomenon sometimes called "late-comers" advantage). But they will also find themselves competing with developed countries for limited resources and a limited environmental absorption capacity for global pollutants such as CO_2 (see Box 21.1).

BOX 21.1   CHINA AND THE FUTURE OF THE GLOBAL ENVIRONMENT

A major factor affecting the future of the global environment is China's ability to develop economically without causing serious and irreversible ecological damage. With a population of more than 1.3 billion, China already uses about 18 percent of the world's commercial energy and is responsible for emitting about 22 percent of global carbon dioxide (CO_2) emissions. China has experienced the most rapid economic growth in the world, with an average of over 8 percent per year of real gross domestic product (GDP) growth from 2000 to 2012.[1]

What will happen to the environment if China's growth continues? Even with relatively low per capita impacts, the large total population in China (about 19 percent of global population) means that China already causes significant global environmental impacts. China has already passed the United States as the world's largest energy consumer and emitter of CO_2.

As a result of rapid growth in industrial and agricultural production, China is facing an ecological and health crisis. In 2004, a report stated that "heavy air pollution contributes to respiratory illnesses that kill up to 300,000 people a year" (Yardley, 2004). In 2007, the World Health Organization estimated that "17 percent of all deaths in the Western Pacific region—in which China contributes the bulk of the population—are linked to one or more environmental health risk. . . . The Chinese Ministry of Water Resources reported that 70 percent of China's rivers and lakes are polluted."

In the past decade, China has started to take climate change seriously, by investing massively in wind and solar energy, becoming the world's largest manufacturer of wind turbines and solar panels and a leader in the development of carbon sequestration technology. In 2011, China presented its twelfth five-year plan, claiming that it would reduce its carbon intensity (amount of carbon emitted per unit of GDP) by 17 percent during the period 2012–2017 and would aim to obtain 50 percent of its energy needs from renewable sources by 2050.

China's ambitious long-term goal is considered unattainable by many observers, since renewable energy represents less than 1 percent of the country's energy use today. Chinese consumption of coal has been increasing at about 17 percent each year, and the International Energy Agency estimates that by 2030, about 80 percent of China's energy needs will still be met by coal and oil—making the Chinese announcement of its ecological sustainability goals look unrealistic.

Sources: Brown, 2005; International Monetary Fund, 2012; Lee, 2011; U.S. Energy Information Administration, 2012; World Health Organization, 2007.

Note: [1]China real GDP growth rate: www.indexmundi.com/china/gdp_real_growth_rate.html.

21.3 REFORMING GLOBAL INSTITUTIONS

International institutions often have conflicting agendas, mirroring the tensions between the demand for economic growth and the need for human development and environmental protection. Major global institutions such as the World Bank, the International Monetary Fund (IMF), and the World Trade Organization (WTO) have as their overarching goal the promotion of economic development, which often comes at an environmental cost. As we saw in Chapter 20, environmental issues remain controversial at the WTO. The IMF does not include environmental factors in its mandate, but its monetary policies have significant implications both for the environment and for relations between developed and developing countries. As for the World Bank, whose function is to provide financing for development, only relatively recently have environmental considerations taken a prominent role in its policy making.[c]

structural adjustment
policies to promote market-oriented economic reform in developing countries by making loans conditional on reforms such as controlling inflation, reducing trade barriers, and privatization of businesses.

environmental sink functions
see "sink function."

natural capital
the available endowment of land and resources including air, water, soil, forests, fisheries, minerals, and ecological life-support systems.

In the 1980s and 1990s the World Bank was frequently a target of protest for funding environmentally destructive projects such as large dams and forest clearance. A study conducted in the 1990s by the World Wildlife Fund (WWF) concluded that **structural adjustment**[d] policies supported by the World Bank had led to increased consumption of renewable and nonrenewable resources, greater pressure on **environmental sink functions** of pollution absorption, a drawdown of **natural capital**, and a weakening of environmental institutional capacity.[2] The WWF study recommended integrating environmental issues into the planning of macroeconomic reforms. This WWF analysis, as well as other reports, pointed out that neglecting the environment would lead to long-term problems that would undermine economic goals as well.

Partly as a result of the many criticisms of its policies, the World Bank began to give more prominence to environmental considerations in its lending, with some projects specifically focused on the environment and natural resource management. The World Bank's environment and natural resource management (ENRM) portfolio represented 17.2 percent of total lending in 1994 but in the past decade has fallen to around 10 percent (Figure 21.2).[3]

As presented in an assessment of the World Bank by the Independent Evaluation Group (IEG), total World Bank commitments between fiscal 1990 and 2007 were $401.5 billion in 6,792 projects—of which 2,401 projects were specifically identified as involving ENRM. Cumulatively between 1994 and 2007, the official estimate of relevant ENRM projects totaled about $59 billion (almost 15 percent of total Bank lending).[4]

These projects include both a "brown agenda" (pollution management) and a "green agenda" (natural resource conservation) including forest management,

---

[c]Both the World Bank and the IMF were founded in 1944 to stabilize the world financial system. The IMF "is charged with overseeing the international monetary system to ensure exchange rate stability and encouraging members to eliminate exchange restrictions that hinder trade," while the World Bank is "not a bank in the ordinary sense but a unique partnership to reduce poverty and support development," by providing loans, sometimes at reduced interest rates, to developing nations to "support a wide array of investments in such areas as education, health, public administration, infrastructure, financial and private sector development, agriculture, and environmental and natural resource management." See www.imf.org and www.worldbank.org.

[d]Structural adjustment policies refer to a package of conditions linked to loans to developing countries, intended to promote market-oriented economic reform. Generally these conditions include fiscal and monetary measures aimed at balancing government budgets and restraining money supplies to avoid inflation. In addition, countries often must reduce barriers to trade, correct overvalued exchange rates, and privatize state-controlled enterprises.

Figure 21.2   **The Active World Bank Environmental Portfolio, Fiscal Year 1993 to Fiscal Year 2010**

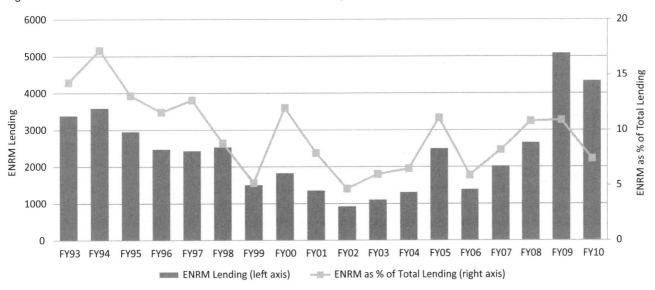

Source: World Bank, 2004, 2010.
Note: ENRM = Environmental and natural resource management.

integrated pest management, watershed rehabilitation, energy efficiency and renewables, and water management and sewer systems, sometimes in collaboration with other international environmental and development organizations.

In addition, all World Bank projects are screened for potential environmental impact. Rural development projects increasingly emphasize land resource management, soil and water conservation, and training in sustainable farming techniques. Urban development projects include water and sanitation upgrading and solid waste management. Energy lending includes promotion of energy efficiency and renewable energy sources, as well as development of cleaner fossil fuels such as natural gas. Examples of the World Bank's investment in projects with a dual goal—eradication of poverty and environmental sustainability—include large-scale efforts in rural solar electrification in Bangladesh (see Box 21.2).

As part of its "greening" efforts, the World Bank has also established a Carbon Finance Unit (CFU), which does not lend or grant resources to projects but, rather, contracts to purchase emission reductions, using money contributed by government and companies in Organization for Economic Cooperation and Development (OECD) member countries, under carbon trading schemes such as those discussed in Chapter 19. The World Bank's CFU is helping developing countries establish programs of reforestation that, at a larger scale, could mitigate some of the effects of climate change. Several of the poorest African countries, including Ethiopia and the Democratic Republic of Congo (DCR), are benefiting from such projects (see Box 21.3).

Despite significant improvement in the environmental content of World Bank policies, critics have argued that "the World Bank and the IMF pay insufficient heed to the profound effects of [their] policies on the ecological health and the social fabric of the recipient countries."[5] A report from the World Resources Institute showed that between 2005 and 2007, less than 30 percent of the World Bank's lending to the energy sector had integrated climate considerations into project decision

BOX 21.2   RURAL ELECTRIFICATION AND RENEWABLE ENERGY DEVELOPMENT IN BANGLADESH

About half of Bangladesh's 150 million people lack access to reliable electricity. A large-scale rural electrification and renewable energy development project was launched in 2009, for which the World Bank approved a $130 million zero-interest International Development Association (IDA) loan and another $172 million loan in 2011. In two years, more than 1.4 million low-income rural households have gained access to electricity, delivered by solar photovoltaic (PV) panels, most of which are imported from China.

In addition to delivering power to unserved communities, it is helping to reduce carbon emissions from avoided use of kerosene and diesel for lighting. The solar electrification industry and its supply chain in Bangladesh have also helped create, directly and indirectly, a total of about 50,000 jobs.

According to Vijay Iyer, the director of the Sustainable Energy Department at the World Bank: "The drop in price of solar PV panels, combined with high prices for fossil fuels, slow pace of grid connections, along with the scale of cell-phone penetration among the poor, which is driving demand, has created vast new potential for off-grid solar—not just in Bangladesh, but in many other low-income countries."

Source: World Bank, "Energy from Solar Panels Transforms Lives in Rural Bangladesh," http://go.worldbank. org/SJPS5X0RG0/.

BOX 21.3   REFORESTATION IN ETHIOPIA AND THE DEMOCRATIC REPUBLIC OF CONGO

Ethiopia has lost 97 percent of its original forest, with dramatic consequences for both the livelihoods of local communities and on biodiversity. The Humbo Ethiopia Assisted Natural Regeneration project (supported by the World Bank's Carbon Finance Unit) is restoring 2,700 hectares of a biodiverse native forest, while supporting local income and employment generation.

On the Batéké plateau in the Democratic Republic of Congo, the ecosystem is composed of dry forest, and the lands are subject to uncontrolled degradation and deforestation due to charcoal production and subsistence agriculture. The Ibi Batéké Degraded Savannah Afforestation Project is converting 4,200 hectares of natural grassy savannah into an abundant and sustainable fuelwood supply for charcoal production. The project is encouraging the local population and farmers to stop the destruction of the natural forests and to concentrate on planting managed forests.

Source: World Bank Carbon Finance Unit, http://wbcarbonfinance.org.

making—whereas more than 50 percent of the World Bank's $1.8 billion energy-sector portfolio did not include climate change considerations (Figure 21.3).[6]

Because the World Bank provides loans, not grants, the funds must eventually be repaid. To promote debt repayment, the lenders emphasize export promotion, which can lead countries to liquidate natural assets, undermining their long-term economic prospects. In addition, large bureaucratic institutions dealing in billions of dollars often are poorly prepared to connect to sustainable initiatives at the local level.

The establishment of the Global Environmental Facility (GEF) was an attempt to develop a joint effort among several international institutions to promote sustainable development. Established in 1991 as a joint operation between ten international

Figure 21.3   World Bank Energy Finance and Climate Change, 2000–2007

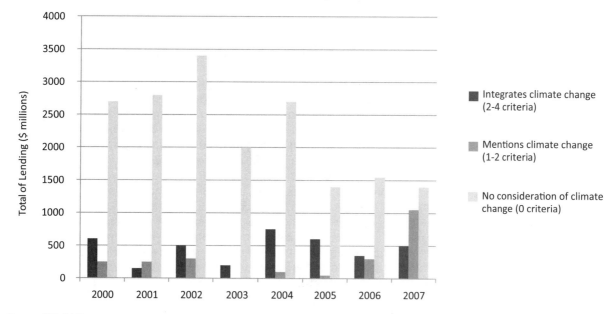

Source: World Resources Institute, 2008.

incremental costs

costs of environmental protection in developing countries in excess of what the country is prepared to pay without foreign assistance.

organizations, the GEF provides grants to developing countries and countries with economies in transition for projects related to biodiversity, climate change, international waters, land degradation, the ozone layer, and chemicals. These projects benefit the global environment, linking local, national, and global environmental challenges and promoting sustainable livelihoods.

In the past twenty years, the GEF has allocated $10 billion, supplemented by more than $47 billion in cofinancing, for more than 2,800 projects in more than 168 developing countries and countries with economies in transition. (See Box 21.4.)

BOX 21.4   THE GLOBAL ENVIRONMENTAL FACILITY

The Global Environmental Facility (GEF) unites 182 member governments. It is jointly administered by ten international agencies, including the United Nations Development Programme (UNDP), the United Nations Environment Programme (UNEP), the World Bank, the United Nations Food and Agriculture Organization (FAO), the United Nations Industrial Development Organization (UNIDO), and regional development banks. Unlike the World Bank and the International Monetary Fund, the GEF provides grants and concessional funds rather than loans. Often a GEF grant may be paired with a World Bank environmental loan to increase its impact at lower cost to the receiving country.

The economic rationale for the GEF's operations is that the **incremental costs** of environmental protection, over and above what developing countries are prepared to pay, should be borne by the global community as a whole. For example, installation of energy-efficient and renewable power sources will be of local benefit, but will also benefit the global effort to limit greenhouse gas emissions. It seems

(continued)

BOX 21.4 *(continued)*

reasonable, therefore, that some of the cost should be paid by the recipient country, in the form of loan repayments, but some should be underwritten by wealthier countries through the GEF.

In practice, the implementation of this incremental-cost concept has been tricky. Critics have argued that it is difficult to separate global and national benefits. Also, the pairing of regular World Bank grants with GEF loans may actually promote greater environmental damage in some cases. For example in Ecuador, a logging company received $4 million in World Bank funds as well as a $2.5 million GEF grant. The company was required to set up a forest reserve, but was able to expand logging on a much greater area. In Egypt, a $242 million World Bank loan to develop a coastal resort was paired with a $4.75 million GEF loan for conservation activity. In such cases, the GEF component may serve as a rationale for accelerated resource exploitation.

The GEF is currently managing 619 projects in 117 countries, of which China has the largest number of projects. A 2005 survey of the impact of GEF projects in China concluded that these programs played an important role in raising awareness on climate change and biodiversity issues in the country, but that there was difficulty in coordinating the roles of the various agencies involved with government institutions there.

Most of the GEF's grants are channeled through national institutions (following the same model as World Bank's loans). Only 5 percent of the GEF's grants are tailored directly to address the needs of rural and urban communities and are channeled through local **nongovernmental organizations (NGOs)**. But the GEF's Small Grants Program have been acknowledged as one of the most effective tools in achieving global environmental benefits while addressing the livelihood needs of local populations, with special attention to reaching the poor.

Small grants program examples include training pastoral communities in Yemen to build cisterns to collect rain, improving water resources management in one of the driest areas on earth; providing local artisans in Senegal with solar cookers, each of which saves the equivalent of twelve trees per year (3 metric ton of carbon equivalent).

As modest as these projects may seem (each reaching communities of about 1,000 people, with a budget often under $50,000), evaluations have shown that small grants programs have a higher rate of success in achieving global environmental benefits, and a significantly higher rate in sustaining them, than GEF medium- and full-size projects. About 90 percent of small grants programs were rated as successful, and 80 percent of these projects showed benefits likely to be sustained into the future.

Sources: Barnes et al., 1995; GEF's Annual monitoring report interactive map at www.thegef.org/gef/RBM/; GEF Evaluation Office, 2010; Heggelund et al., 2005; Shiva, 2001; UNDP, 2012; World Bank, 1995, 2004.

nongovernmental organizations (NGOs)
privately funded, and commonly nonprofit, organizations involved in research, lobbying, provision of services, or development projects.

The Shortcomings of Global Environment Governance

Between the first United Nations Conference on the Human Environment, held in Stockholm in 1972, and the Rio+20 Summit in 2012, an ambitious agenda emerged to push the international community of nation-states in the direction of greater commitments to environmental sustainability.[e] It has often been difficult, however, to reach any international consensus on meaningful targets.

A critical issue is whether developed and developing countries can cooperate to promote environmentally sustainable development paths. As we saw in the discussion of global climate policy in Chapter 19, agreement can be difficult to reach.

[e]For a detailed historical account of the major benchmarks in the building on international institutions for sustainable development, see International Institute for Sustainable Development 2012, Sustainable Development Timeline, www.iisd.org/pdf/2012/sd_timeline_2012.pdf.

Developing countries argue that the richer countries should "clean up their act" first. Developed countries worry that the vast growth of production expected in the developing world will swallow up gains from efficiency and pollution control, unless developing countries modify their economic goals. This difference in perspectives need not lead to deadlock. Many possibilities exist for mutual progress toward environmental improvement, but the scale of the problems is daunting.

The United Nations Climate Change Conference in Copenhagen in 2009 was described as a bitter failure by many observers. On that occasion, China and India walked out of the negotiations, and no significant binding agreement was arrived at. Another disappointment was the 2012 Rio + 20 Summit, intended as a follow up to the 1992 Earth Summit, which had put in place the ambitious conventions on climate change and biodiversity, as well as commitments on poverty eradication and social justice. Major world leaders were absent from the Rio Summit in 2012, and the final document, called "The Future We Want" was decried as an empty declaration of intentions rather than a real plan for action.

To address the shortcomings in international environmental governance, several attempts have been made in the past forty years to propose the establishment of a United Nations Environment Organization. Three structural models are being discussed at the international level for such an organization, from a modest scenario of an upgrading of UNEP into a specialized UN agency with full-fledged organizational status, similar to the World Health Organization, to a more ambitious and far-reaching model of a "hierarchical intergovernmental organization on environment issues that would be equipped with majority decision making as well as enforcement powers vis-à-vis states that fail to comply with international agreements on the protection of global commons."[7] Forty-six countries have already affirmed their support for the creation of a United Nations Environment Organization.[f]

Despite such efforts, a former head of the Global Environmental Facility offered a sobering assessment of limited international progress:

> In less than fifteen years, the response of the international community to the challenges of environment and sustainable development included four international summits, four ministerial conferences, three international conventions, two protocols and a new financial entity—the Global Environment Facility (GEF). On the face of it, these are remarkable achievements. But in spite of the high-powered gatherings, agreements and commitments, little progress has been achieved in improving the environment and in pursuing sustainable development. Global environmental trends continue to be negative and the promise of significant financial resources to address the challenges of environment and development has not materialized.[8]

Action at the Local level: Sustainability from the Ground Up

As we have seen, the international record on moving toward sustainable development is very uneven. But, as noted earlier regarding the GEF's Small Grants Program (Box 21.4), great diversity and creativity have emerged at the local level, in cities, and in rural areas, in the North as well as in the South.

---

[f]Under the leadership of France, the Netherlands, and Norway, which since the 1980s have promoted the creation of such an agency, members of the European Union (EU) joined the "Paris Call for Action" in 2007, as did several developing countries (including Algeria, Morocco, Ecuador, and Cambodia). However the main emitters of greenhouse gases, the United States and the BRIC countries (Brazil, Russia, India, China) declined to sign on to the document. See www.reuters.com/article/2007/02/03/us-globalwarming-appeal-idUSL0335755320070203/.

In the past twenty years, thousands of local initiatives have sprouted that respond to the necessities of ecological sustainability while improving people's livelihoods, through innovative initiatives in agriculture, forestry, resource management, biodiversity conservation, energy production, industrial recycling, and other areas.[9] Such programs include:

extractive reserves
a forested area that is managed for sustainable harvests of nontimber products such as nuts, sap, and extracts.

- Organic farming cooperatives in the Philippines.
- **Extractive reserves** in the Brazilian rainforest promoting multiple-product forest management and conservation.
- Sustainable forestry and reforestation in the Peruvian Amazon and Costa Rica.
- Rural solar power installation in the Dominican Republic.
- Soil restoration and conservation technologies in Honduras.
- Women's cooperatives for farming, food processing, and light industry in Nigeria.

agroforestry
growing both tree and food crops on the same piece of land.

- **Agroforestry** programs in Guatemala, Haiti, and Indonesia.
- Solar cooker project in Senegal.
- Conservation of native potatoes, tubers, grains, and beans in Bolivia.
- Community seed banks to protect local indigenous varieties of grains (wheat, barley, corn, etc.) in Asia, Africa, and Latin America.
- Forest regeneration projects in Congo and in Ethiopia (see Box 21.3).
- Reforestation in the Atlas Mountains, in Morocco.[10]
- Coastal afforestation in Bangladesh.[11]

These examples of local sustainable development in practice demonstrate that the goals of economic development, poverty reduction, and environmental improvement can be successfully combined. Unfortunately, the principles embodied in these small-scale projects are rarely reflected in national and global economic priorities. This indicates the continuing need for a major reorientation of economic development policies.

Sustainability issues are increasingly important for urban areas. More than half the world's population lives in urban areas today, and by 2050 this proportion will be closer to 80 percent. Cities account for 50 percent of all waste, generate 60–80 percent of all greenhouse gas emissions, and consume 75 percent of natural resources, while occupying only 3 percent of the earth's land area.[12]

Transportation systems are a key issue for urban areas. Urban planners are seeking ways to design cities for people, not cars: "after a point, as their numbers multiply, automobiles provide not mobility but immobility."[13] At the Rio + 20 Summit in 2012, a Global Town Hall was set up in which mayors from hundreds of cities exchanged ideas on best practices, showing that cities are among the most committed institutional actors in global sustainability, while also facing some of the most challenging problems (see Box 21.5).[14]

21.4 NEW GOALS AND NEW PRODUCTION METHODS

Promoting ecological sustainability implies a major shift from existing techniques and organization of production. Examining the implications in terms of specific sectors of economic activity and drawing on the discussion in earlier chapters, we can summarize some of the needed changes.

BOX 21.5 SUSTAINABLE URBAN MANAGEMENT IN CURITIBA, BRAZIL

The city of Curitiba, Brazil, has been a pioneer in investing in sustainability, public transportation systems, and reduced carbon emissions. Heralded as an example for other cities in the developing and the developed world, Curitiba is nonetheless facing several challenges in keeping its promise of sustainability in the face of rapid demographic growth.

A key component of Curitiba's success is the attention given to transportation issues. Zoning laws foster high-density development along transportation corridors served by buses. The bus system transports more than a million passengers per day. Gasoline use per capita and air pollution levels in Curitiba are among the lowest in Brazil. Although 60 percent of people own cars in Curitiba, busing, biking, and walking dominate, accounting for 80 percent of all trips in the city. The city emits 25 percent less carbon per capita than most Brazilian cities.

The city has protected drainage areas to control flooding by converting these areas into public parks. Curitiba could not afford a large-scale recycling plant, but public education programs have been successful in reducing wastes and increasing recycling rates. In areas where streets are too narrow for garbage trucks to enter, incentives for community garbage collection have been created by exchanging filled garbage bags for bus tokens, parcels of surplus food, and school notebooks. In another program, older public buses are converted to mobile schools and travel to low-income neighborhoods.

The example of Curitiba shows that progress toward environmental sustainability is possible even in an urban area with increasing population and high poverty rates. "The lesson to be learned from Curitiba is that creativity can substitute for financial resources. Any city, rich or poor, can draw on the skills of its residents to tackle urban environmental problems" (World Resources Institute, 1996).

These successes have not been without significant problems, however. The city has grown in population from 300,000 in 1950 to around 3 million today (including its greater metropolitan area). The city has had difficulty keeping up with demographic growth, and its landfill regularly overflows. It is no longer the Brazilian city with the most green space, and its development has led to dramatic deforestation: 99 percent in the state of Parana, of which Curitiba is the largest city. So, despite the success of aggressive urban planning measures undertaken forty years ago, Curitiba must continue to update its initiatives and adapt to the times.

Sources: Green Planet Monitor, 2009; World Resources Institute, 1996.

Agriculture

Feeding an expanding population at higher per capita levels of consumption will impose a significant strain on global soil and water systems. The response to this must be twofold. On the production side, current high-input techniques associated with soil degradation and water pollution and overdraft must give way to organic soil rebuilding, integrated pest management, and efficient irrigation. This, in turn, implies much greater reliance on local knowledge and participatory input into the development of farming systems.[15]

On the consumption side, probable resource limitations on production will necessitate both population growth limits and greater food distribution equity and efficiency. As discussed in Chapter 9, effective policies can simultaneously promote social equity and moderate population growth, including women's education and health-care and family planning services. Distribution and dietary patterns will need to emphasize affordable basic food stuff and vegetable-based proteins and nutrients.

Industry

As the scale of global industrial production grows well beyond current levels, which represent a quadrupling of 1950 levels, the inadequacy of "end-of-pipe" pollution control will be increasingly apparent. As we saw in Chapter 17, the concept of **industrial ecology** implies the restructuring of entire industrial sectors based on a goal of reducing emissions and reusing materials at all stages of the production cycle. A broad cooperative effort between corporations and government is essential to achieve this goal.

Energy

Both supply limits and environmental impacts, in particular the accumulation of greenhouse gases, mean that it will be necessary to accomplish a transition away from fossil fuels well before 2050, as discussed in Chapters 13 and 19. A restructured energy system would be significantly less centralized, adapted to local conditions, and take advantage of opportunities for wind, biomass, and off-grid solar power systems. This is unlikely to occur without a major mobilization of capital resources for the development of renewable energy sources in countries now rapidly expanding their energy systems.

Renewable Resource Systems

As discussed in Chapters 13, 14, and 15, world fisheries, forests, and water systems are severely overstressed. With even greater demands on all systems expected in the next century, all levels of institutional management must be urgently reformed. Multilateral agreements and global funding are needed to conserve transboundary resources; national resource management systems must be shifted from goals of exploitation to conservation and sustainable harvesting; and local communities must be strongly involved in resource conservation.

Toward a Redefinition of Development

The goals of sustainable development policies can be viewed in terms of strong and weak sustainability, as discussed in Chapters 7 and 8. In general, advocates of **strong sustainability** argue that natural systems should be maintained intact wherever possible. They identify **critical natural capital**—such as water supplies—as resources to preserve under all circumstances. In this view, for example, maintaining soil's natural fertility is essential, even if it is possible to compensate for degraded soils with extra fertilizer. Under the more moderate approach of **weak sustainability**, some degradation or loss of natural capital is acceptable if it is compensated for by accumulation of **manufactured capital**.

Either concept of sustainability—but especially the strong version—implies changes in the standard conception of economic growth. Economic activity that relies heavily on natural resources, raw materials, and fossil fuels cannot grow indefinitely. Because the planetary ecosystem has certain limits, limits must also apply on a **macroeconomic scale**—the overall level of resource use and goods output, as discussed in Chapter 7. Herman Daly has argued for the long-term need to reach a plateau, a **steady state** economy in terms of the consumption of material and energy resources.[16]

---

industrial ecology
the application of ecological principles to the management of industrial activity.

strong sustainability
the view that natural and human-made capital are generally not substitutable and, therefore, natural capital levels should be maintained.

critical natural capital
elements of natural capital for which there are no good human-made substitutes, such as basic water supplies and breathable air.

weak sustainability
the view that natural capital depletion is justified as long as it is compensated for with increases in human-made capital; assumes that human-made capital can substitute for most types of natural capital.

manufactured capital
productive resources produced by humans, such as factories, roads, and computers, also referred to as produced capital or human-made capital.

macroeconomic scale
the total scale of an economy; ecological economics suggests that the ecosystem imposes scale limits on the macroeconomy.

steady state
an economy that maintains a constant level of natural capital by limiting the throughput of material and energy resources.

exponential growth

a value that increases by the same percentage in each time period, such as a population increasing by the same percentage every year.

This concept differs radically from the standard view of economic growth, in which GDP increases indefinitely on an **exponential growth** path—for example, GDP growth of 4 percent per year. In the limits-to-growth perspective, national and global economic systems must follow what is called a **logistic growth** pattern in which economic activity approaches a maximum, at least in terms of resource consumption (Figure 21.4).

Figure 21.4   **Growth Reaching a Steady State**

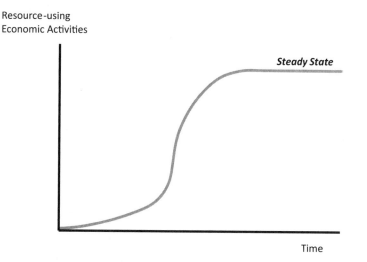

logistic curve/logistic growth

an S-shaped growth curve tending toward an upper limit.

post-growth economy

an economy that has completed the process of economic growth and operates with no further increase, and possibly a decrease, in resource and energy use.

This analysis implies constraints on material consumption, but activities that involve no resource consumption or are environmentally neutral or environmentally friendly, could grow indefinitely. Such activities could include services, arts, communication, and education. After basic needs are met and moderate levels of consumption are achieved, economic development could be increasingly oriented toward these kinds of inherently "sustainable" activities.[17]

Currently much of development theory and policy promote continuous economic growth. What kind of policies would promote sustainability? Are the goals of economic growth and sustainability compatible?

Some ecological economists view "sustainable growth" as a contradiction in terms. They point out that no system can grow without limit. However, certain kinds of economic growth are essential. The large number of people in the world who cannot satisfy basic needs require more and better food, housing, and other goods.

In high-consumption societies, improved well-being might be achieved through expanded educational and cultural services that, as we have noted, have little negative environmental impact. People might also choose more leisure time rather than expanded goods consumption. But unregulated economic growth is unlikely to be either equitable or environmentally benign. A global transition to more sustainable growth would involve major investments in health, water, sanitation, and education, as well as alternative energy sources and environmental protection. Currently, no national governments or international institutions are prepared to undertake such investments on anything near the necessary scale. But some theorists have proposed a **post-growth economy** that would be "slower by design, not by disaster."[18]

One model of a transition to a steady-state economy has been presented by Peter Victor.[19] An economic model called LOWGROW applied to the Canadian economy models "socio-eco-environmental" paths that offer attractive social and environmental outcomes without requiring economic growth.

In the scenario presented in Figure 21.5 the Canadian government is assumed to introduce a tax on greenhouse gas (GHG) emissions, creating incentives to switch from high GHG sources of energy to lower ones, making energy in general more expensive and encouraging conservation and efficiency. The revenues from the GHG tax are used to reduce other taxes, so that the net effect on revenues is zero. In this scenario, GDP per capita stabilizes after 2025, and GHG emissions decrease by 22 percent by 2035. Poverty levels as well as unemployment decrease significantly, and fiscal balance is reached, with a steady decrease in the debt-to-GDP ratio. A shorter work week allows for full employment, with less growth in material consumption but more spending on health care and education.

Figure 21.5 **A No-Growth Scenario for the Canadian Economy**

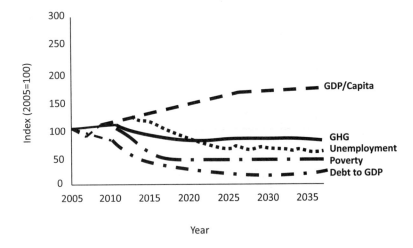

Source: Adapted from Victor, 2008, p. 182.
Note: GDP = gross domestic product; GHG = greenhouse gases.

Such models show that slower growth, leading eventually to a steady-state economy, can be consistent with full employment, virtual elimination of poverty, more leisure, considerable reduction in GHG emissions, and fiscal balance.

Specific Policy Proposals

Which specific policies would be consistent with environmentally sound development? Some of the possibilities that we have already touched on in previous chapters include:

green taxes
taxes based on the environmental impact of a good or service.

revenue-neutral (tax policy)
term used to describe a tax policy that holds the overall level of tax revenues constant.

- **Green taxes** that would shift the tax burden away from income and capital taxation and onto fossil-fuel use, resource extraction, and pollution generation. This would discourage energy- and material-intensive economic activities while favoring the provision of services and labor-intensive activities. A **revenue-neutral (tax policy)** shift could match every dollar collected in new energy and resource taxes with a dollar of income, payroll, corporate, or capital gains tax reductions.[20]

- Elimination of agricultural and energy subsidies that encourage overuse of energy, fertilizer, pesticides, and irrigation water. This could be matched with promotion of sustainable agricultural systems including nutrient recycling, crop diversification, and natural pest controls, minimizing the use of artificial chemicals and fertilizer.
- Greater recycling of materials and use of renewable energy. The principles of industrial ecology suggest redesigning industrial systems to imitate the closed-cycle patterns of natural systems and reuse as many materials as possible with minimal waste output.
- Efficient transportation systems that replace energy-intensive automotive transport with high-speed trains, public transit, increased bicycle use, and redesign of cities and suburbs to minimize transportation needs. The use of highly fuel-efficient cars would be important in countries such as the United States that have extensively developed automobile-centered systems. Some developing countries might avoid large-scale automobile dependence by relying instead on bicycles and efficient public transit.
- Accelerated development of **renewable energy** systems such as solar, hydroelectric, wind, and geothermal power, as well as new technologies such as fuel cells and high-efficiency industrial systems. As we saw in Chapter 12, redirection of current fossil-fuel subsidies to create market incentives for alternative energy sources is essential to this process.

renewable energy sources
energy sources that are supplied on a continual basis such as wind, water, biomass, and direct solar energy.

Conclusion

Analysis of development policy must take long-term sustainability into account. Policies oriented toward economic growth alone risk damage to the broader "circular flow" of the **biosphere** discussed in Chapter 1, unless they include consideration of environmental impact and sustainable scale. This adds a new dimension to the debate over development policy, a dimension that will be increasingly important for both developed and developing countries.

biosphere
all areas on earth that contain life forms, including air, soil, land, and water.

Future sustainable paths will differ drastically between the industrialized countries of the developed world and the emerging and developing countries that are still in their growing phase, both demographically and economically.

In the Global South, the necessity to provide basic needs for hundreds of millions of poor people in rural areas and urban slums will push economic growth forward. But economic growth need not be pursued using the same growth model that has created current ecological crises. As local sustainability initiatives show, the improvement of sustainable livelihoods can be achieved without a significant impact on natural resources. A more sustainable path is conceivable for developing countries, through scaling up initiatives that combine social goals with environmental goals, including increased use of renewable energy, as well as integrated approaches to restoring soil fertility, securing access to water, and reforesting to protect biodiversity.

As the world population continues to grow, and economic activity continues to expand, sustainability will become both more important and more difficult to achieve. This is the major challenge of the twenty-first century, and both economic and ecological understanding will be needed to formulate global, national, and local responses.

SUMMARY

Sustainable development has been defined as development that meets present needs without damaging the basis for meeting future needs. This implies increasing and improving manufactured capital without destroying natural capital. The needs of a growing population must be met without increasing resource demands and pollution generation beyond the supportive capacity of ecosystems.

For developed countries, this implies both moderation in consumption growth and adoption of more environmentally friendly technologies. Developing countries, for which growth in consumption is essential, can avoid production methods that have high resource demands and environmental repercussions. Mutual cooperation between developed and developing countries toward these goals is essential but often difficult to achieve.

Major reforms must occur in agricultural, industrial, and energy systems, as well as in renewable resource management. Low-input and organic agriculture, energy-efficient and ecologically sound industrial development, as well as better fishery and forest management, are all important components of a balanced economic/environmental system. In addition, population stabilization is central to sustainability in all these areas.

An inherent tension exists between the ideas of sustainability and economic growth. Although the two are not necessarily incompatible, we cannot have unlimited economic growth with finite resources. Future economic growth must therefore turn more toward areas such as services, communication, arts, and education that contribute to human welfare but have relatively low resource requirements.

Major global finance institutions such as the World Bank have begun to recognize the necessity of specific policy initiatives to promote more sustainable development and reorient their development lending accordingly. However, resource-intensive and pollution-generating development strategies remain common. Small-scale projects financed privately or by individual countries have often been more successful in achieving the dual goals of poverty reduction and environmental conservation.

Sustainable development strategies attempt to balance the imperatives of economic growth with the limits of planetary resources and pollution absorption capacity. Modification of global goals of economic growth will be essential for sustainability in the twenty-first century.

KEY TERMS AND CONCEPTS

agroforestry
biosphere
capital stock
critical natural capital
environmental sink functions
exponential growth
extractive reserves
green taxes
industrial ecology
logistic growth
macroeconomic scale

manufactured capital
natural capital
post-growth economy
renewable energy
revenue-neutral tax policy
steady state
strong and weak sustainability
structural adjustment
sustainable development
technological and social lock-in

Discussion Questions

1. Comment on the original definition of sustainable development: "development that meets the needs of the present without compromising the ability of future generations to meet their own needs." Do you think this definition is useful, or is it so ambiguous or vague that it lacks applicability? Can you think of ways to make it more precise or alternative definitions?
2. How would you balance the goals of economic growth and environmental sustainability? To what extent are these goals necessarily in conflict?
3. Which specific policies do you think are of greatest importance in promoting environmentally sustainable development? In which areas is the world making progress toward sustainability, and where are the most serious problems?

Notes

1. World Commission on Environment and Development, 1987.
2. Reed, 1997, 351.
3. World Bank, 1995, 2004, and 2010.
4. Report available at http://go.worldbank.org/BD8MP7T5B0/.
5. French, 2000, 196.
6. World Resources Institute, 2008.
7. Biermann, 2011.
8. Mohamed El-Ashry, former CEO of the Global Environmental Facility in the 1990s, quoted in Swart and Perry, 2007.
9. Examples drawn from Barnes et al., 1995; Global Environmental Facility, 2012, www.thegef.org/gef/.
10. High Atlas Foundation, www.highatlasfoundation.org.
11. See www.thegef.org/gef/news/bangladesh-wins-earth-care-award-2012-ldcf-project/.
12. Brown, 2009.
13. UN News Center, "UN and Partners Unveil New Initiative to Achieve Sustainable Cities," June 18, 2012, www.un.org/apps/news/story.asp?NewsID=42264#. UFObSbJlT6l/; quotation from Molly O'Meara, *Reinventing Cities for People and the Planet*, Worldwatch Paper 147 (Washington, DC: Worldwatch Institute, June 1999), pp. 14–15.
14. See www.iclei.org for specific examples of sustainable city efforts.
15. Pinstrup-Andersen and Pandya-Lorch, 1988.
16. See Daly, 1996; Daly and Townsend, 1993.
17. See Durning, 1992, and Harris, 2013.
18. See Jackson, 2009; Victor, 2008.
19. Victor, 2008, chap. 10.
20. See Frank, 2012; Hamond et al., 1997.

References

Barnes, James N., Brent Blackwelder, Barbara J. Bramble, Ellen Grossman, and Walter V. Reid. 1995. *Bankrolling Successes: A Portfolio of Sustainable Development Projects*. Washington, DC: Friends of the Earth and the National Wildlife Federation.

Biermann, Frank. 2011. *Reforming Global Environmental Governance: the Case for a United Nations Environment Organization*. www.stakeholderforum.org/fileadmin/files/WEO%20Biermann%20FINAL.pdf.

Brown, Lester R. 2005. *China Replacing the U.S. as World's Leading Consumer*. www.earth-policy.org/plan_b_updates/2005/update45/.

———. 2009. *Plan B 4.0: Mobilizing to Save Civilization*. New York: W.W. Norton.

Daly, Herman E. 1996. *Beyond Growth: The Economics of Sustainable Development*. Boston: Beacon Press.

Daly, Herman E., and Kenneth N. Townsend, ed. 1993. *Valuing the Earth: Economics, Ecology, Ethics*. Cambridge, MA: MIT Press.

Durning, Alan. 1992. *How Much Is Enough: The Consumer Society and the Future of the Earth*. New York: W.W. Norton.

Frank, Robert. 2012. "Nation's Choices Needn't Be Painful." *New York Times,* September 22.

French, Hilary. 2000. "Coping with Ecological Globalization." In *State of the World 2000*, ed. Brown et al., New York: W.W. Norton.

GEF Evaluation Office. 2010. *Fourth Overall Performance Study of the GEF*. www.thegef.org/gef/.

Green Planet Monitor. 2009. *Smart Solutions for a Developing World—Curitiba*. www.greenplanetmonitor.net/news/2009/03/curitiba-sustainable-city/.

Hamond, M. Jeff, et al. 1997. *Tax Waste, Not Work*. Washington, DC: Redefining Progress.

Harris, Jonathan M., 2013. "The Macroeconomics of Development Without Throughput Growth." Chapter 2 in *Innovations in Sustainable Consumption: New Economics, Socio-technical Transitions, and Social Practices*, eds. Maurie J. Cohen, et al. Cheltenham and Northampton, MA: Edward Elgar. Also available at: http://www.ase.tufts.edu/gdae/Pubs/wp/10-05MacroeconomicsofDevelopmentwithoutThroughputGrowth.pdf.

Harris, Jonathan M., Timothy A Wise, Kevin P. Gallagher, and Neva R. Goodwin, ed. 2001. *A Survey of Sustainable Development: Social and Economic Dimensions*. Washington, DC: Island Press.

Heggelund, Gorild, Andresen Steinar, and Ying Sun. 2005. "Performance of the Global Environmental Facility (GEF) in China: Achievements and Challenges as Seen by the Chinese." *International Environmental Agreements* 5: 323–348. www.springerlink.com/content/f000235438327217/.

International Monetary Fund. 2012. *World Economic Outlook: Growth Resuming, Dangers Remain*. www.imf.org/external/pubs/ft/weo/2012/01/index.htm.

Jackson, Tim. 2009. *Prosperity Without Growth: Economics for a Finite Planet*. London: Earthscan.

Lee, John. 2011. "The Greening of China, a Mirage." *The Australian*, September 9.

Pinstrup-Andersen, Per, and Rajul Pandya-Lorch. 1998. "Food Security and Sustainable Use of Natural Resources: A 2020 Vision." *Ecological Economics* 26(1): 1–10.

Pretty, Jules, and Robert Chambers. 2000. "Towards a Learning Paradigm: New Professionalism and Institutions for Agriculture." In Jonathan M. Harris, ed., *Rethinking Sustainability: Power, Knowledge, and Institutions*. Ann Arbor: University of Michigan Press.

Reed, David, ed. 1997. *Structural Adjustment, the Environment, and Sustainable Development*. London: Earthscan.

Shiva, Vandana. 2001. "Conflicts of Global Ecology: Environmental Activism in a Period of Global Reach." Original publication in *Alternatives* 19 (1994), pp. 195–207; summarized version in Harris et al. eds., *A Survey of Sustainable Development*.

Swart, Lydia, and Estelle Perry, ed. 2007. *Global Environmental Governance: Perspectives on the Current Debate*. Center for UN Reform Education, www.centerforunreform.org/node/251/.

United Nations Development Programme (UNDP). 2012. "The GEF Small Grants Program, 20 years—Community Action for the Global Environment," www.thegef.org/gef/pubs/20-years-community-action-global-community/.

U.S. Energy Information Administration. 2012. *China: Country Analysis*. www.eia.gov/countries/cab.cfm?fips=CH/.

Victor, Peter. 2008. *Managing Without Growth, Slower by Design, not Disaster*. Northampton, MA: Edward Elgar.

World Bank. 1995. *Monitoring Environmental Progress: A Report on Work in Progress*. Washington, DC.

———. 2004. *Environment Matters: Annual Review*. Washington, DC.

———. 2010. *Annual Report 2010: Development and Climate Change*. Washington DC.

World Commission on Environment and Development. 1987. *Our Common Future*. Oxford: Oxford University Press.

World Health Organization. 2007. *Environment and Health in China Today*. http://www2.wpro.who.int/china/sites/ehe/.

World Resources Institute. 1996; *World Resources 1996–97: The Urban Environment*. New York: Oxford University Press.

———. 2008. *Can the World Bank Lead on Climate Change?* www.wri.org/press/2008/06/can-world-bank-lead-climate-change/.

Yardley, Jim. 2004. "Rivers Run Black, and Chinese Die of Cancer." *New York Times,* September 12.

Web Sites

1. **www.thegef.org/gef/**. Home page of the Global Environmental Facility, a funding agency established "to address global environmental issues while supporting national sustainable development initiatives. The GEF provides grants for projects related to biodiversity, climate change, international waters, land degradation, the ozone layer, and persistent organic pollutants."
2. **www.unep.org**. Web site of United Nations Environmental Program, including the *GEO Yearbook 2012* (www.unep.org/yearbook/2012/) focusing on major policy developments and instruments that have a bearing on sustainable development.
3. **www.iisd.org**. The International Institute for Sustainable Development offers policy recommendations on international trade and investment, economic policy, climate change, measurement and indicators, and natural resources management. The site includes free software for modeling complex relationships between economic, social, and environmental issues.
4. **www.maweb.org**. Reports by the Millennium Ecosystem Assessment, a United Nations project "strengthening capacity to manage ecosystems sustainability for human well-being" including Synthesis Reports on biodiversity, desertification, business and industry, wetlands and water, and health.
5. **www.wri.org**. Web site of the World Resources Institute, a global environmental think tank that produces research reports and conducts projects on aspects of global climate change, sustainable markets, ecosystem protection, and environmentally responsible governance.
6. **www.earth-policy.org**. Web site of the Earth Policy Institute (EPI), an advocacy think tank founded in 2011 by Lester Brown, the founder and former president of the Worldwatch Institute, to provide a plan for a sustainable future.
7. **www.greenplanetmonitor.net/news/**. Web site of the Green Planet Monitor presenting case studies of local sustainable solutions all over the world
8. **www.iclei.org**. Web site of Local Governments for Sustainability, a Global Association of 1200 local governments that provide tools and technical assistance to local governments, cities, and municipalities, all over the world, to set and achieve their climate protection and sustainability goals.

Glossary

absolutely diminishing returns: an increase in one or more inputs results in a decrease in output. (4)

absorptive capacity of the environment: the ability of the environment to absorb and render harmless waste products. (2, 7)

adaptive measures: actions designed to reduce the magnitude or risk of damages from global climate change. (19)

adaptive strategies: See "adaptive measures." (18)

adjusted net saving (ANS): a national accounting measure developed by the World Bank which aims to measure how much a country is actually saving for it future. (8)

aggregation: in reference to environmental asset accounts, the degree to which different types of natural capital are combined. (8)

agroforestry: growing both tree and food crops on the same piece of land. (10, 14, 21)

anthropocentric viewpoint: a human-centered approach to managing natural resources. (6)

aquaculture: the controlled cultivation of aquatic organisms, including fish and shellfish, for human use or consumption. (13)

assets: something with market value, including financial assets, physical assets, and natural assets. (1, 14)

availability of credit: terms on which loans are provided, especially relevant for agricultural and natural resource management and conservation investments. (14)

average cost: the average cost of producing each unit of a good or service; equal to total cost divided by the quantity produced. (4)

average-cost pricing: a water pricing strategy in which price is set equal to the average cost of production (or equal to average cost plus a profit mark-up if the water utility is a for-profit entity). (15)

average revenue: the average price a firm receives for each unit of a good or service; equal to total revenue divided by the quantity produced. (4)

avoided costs: costs that can be avoided through environmental preservation or improvement. (18)

"backstop" energy technologies: technologies such as solar and wind that can replace current energy sources, especially fossil fuels. (18)

backstop resource: a substitute resource that becomes a viable alternative after the price of the initial resource reaches a certain high price. (11)

beneficial use: term used to refer to the use of water for productive purposes, such as irrigation or municipal supplies. (15)

benefit transfer: assigning or estimating the value of a resource based on prior analysis of one or more similar resources. (6)

bequest value: the value that people place on the knowledge that a resource will be available for future generations. (6)

best available control technology: a pollution regulation approach in which the government mandates that all firms use a control technology deemed most effective. (16)

Better Life Index (BLI): an index developed by the OECD to measure national welfare using 11 well-being dimensions. (8)

biocentric viewpoint: a perspective on the management of natural resources that recognizes the inherent value of nature and seeks to maintain ecological functioning. (6)

biodiversity (biological diversity): the maintenance of many different interrelated species in an ecological community. (1, 10, 14)

biofuels: fuels derived from crops, crop wastes, animal wastes, or other biological sources (10)

biomass: an energy supply from wood, plant, and animal waste. (2, 12, 14)

biophysical cycles: the circular flow of organic and inorganic materials in ecosystems. (10)

biosphere: all areas on earth that contain life forms, including air, soil, land, and water. (21)

business as usual: a scenario in which no significant policy, technology, or behavioral changes are expected. (18)

bycatch: the harvesting of aquatic organisms other than the intended commercial species. (13)

capital depreciation: a deduction in national income accounting for the wearing-out of capital over time. (7)

capital formation: addition of new capital to a country's capital stock. (9)

capital shallowing: a decrease in the availability of capital per worker, leading to reduced productivity per worker. (9)

capital stock: the existing quantity of capital in a given region, including manufactured, human, and natural capital. (2, 12, 21)

carbon sinks: portions of the ecosystem with the ability to absorb certain quantities of carbon dioxide, including forests and oceans. (19)

carbon tax: a per-unit tax on goods and services based on the quantity of carbon dioxide emitted during the production or consumption process. (19)

carrying capacity: the level of population and consumption that can be sustained by the available natural resource base. (1, 2, 9, 10, 13)

certification: the process of certifying products that meet certain standards, such as certifying produce grown using organic farming techniques. (13, 14)

certification and labeling: see "certification" and "ecolabeling." (20)

choke price: the minimum price on a demand curve where the quantity demanded equals zero. (11)

circular flow: a diagram that indicates the ways resources, such as goods, money, waste, and energy, move through an economy or ecosystem. (1)

Clean Air Act (CAA): the primary federal air pollution law in the United States, passed in 1970, with major amendments in 1990. (16)

clean development mechanism (CDM): a component of the Kyoto Protocol that allows industrial countries to receive credits for assisting developing countries to reduce their carbon emissions. (19)

Clean Water Act (CWA): the primary federal water pollution law in the United States, passed in 1972. (16)

clear-cut: the process of harvesting all trees within a given area. (14)

climate stabilization: the policy of reducing fossil-fuel use to a level that would not increase the potential for global climate change. (18)

climate stabilization wedge: a concept proposed by Pacala and Socolow (1994) in which specific mitigation actions are presented to reduce projected greenhouse gas emissions by one gigaton each (one gigaton reduction equals one wedge). (19)

closed system: a system that does not exchange energy or resources with another system; except for solar energy and waste heat, the global ecosystem is a closed system. (7)

CO_2 equivalent (CO_2e): a measure of total greenhouse gas emissions or concentrations, converting all non-CO_2 gases to their CO_2 equivalent in warming impact. (18)

coase theorem: the proposition that if property rights are well defined and there are no transactions costs, an efficient allocation of resources will result even if externalities exist. (3)

cogeneration: the generation of both electricity and useful heat from a power source. (11)

command-and-control policies: a pollution regulation approach in which individual firms must meet exact emissions standards or implement specific control technologies with little, if any, flexibility. (16)

common property resources: a resource that is not subject to private ownership and is available to all, such as the oceans or atmosphere. (1, 4, 10, 18)

comparative advantage: the theory that trade benefits both parties by allowing each to specialize in the goods that it can produce with relative efficiency. (20)

complementarity: the property of being used together in production or consumption, for example, the use of gasoline and automobiles. (7)

compliance costs: the cost to firms and industries of meeting pollution regulations. (17)

computable general equilibrium: economic models that aim to estimate the effect of policy changes throughout an entire economy. (17)

constant dollars: an adjustment of economic time series data to account for changes in inflation. (8)

constant returns to scale: a proportional increase (or decrease) in one or more inputs results in the same proportional increase (or decrease) in output. (4, 9)

consumer surplus: the net benefit to a consumer from a purchase; equal to their maximum willingness to pay minus price. (3)

consumption externalities: externalities associated with consumption of a good, such as pollutant emissions from vehicles. (20)

contingent ranking (CR): a survey method in which respondents are asked to rank a list of alternatives. (6)

contingent valuation (CV): an economic tool that uses surveys to question people regarding their willingness to pay for a good or , such as the preservation of hiking opportunities or air quality. (6)

contraction and convergence: the concept that overall environmental impacts or economic activity should be reduced at the same time that economic inequalities are reduced. (17)

cost of illness method: an approach for valuing the negative impacts of pollution by estimating the cost of treating illnesses caused by the pollutant. (6)

cost-benefit analysis (CBA): a tool for policy analysis that attempts to monetize all the costs and benefits of a proposed action to determine the net benefit. (1, 6, 18, 19)

cost-effectiveness analysis: a policy tool that determines the least-cost approach for achieving a given goal. (6, 19)

criteria air pollutants: the six major air pollutants specified in the U.S. Clean Air Act. (16)

critical natural capital: elements of natural capital for which there are no good human-made substitutes, such as basic water supplies and breathable air. (8, 21)

crop rotation and fallowing: an agricultural system involving growing different crops on the same piece of land at different times and regularly taking part of the land out of production. (10)

crop value index: an index indicating the relative value of production of different crops on a given quantity of land. (10)

cumulative pollutants: pollutants that do not dissipate or degrade significantly over time. (2, 16)

decoupling: breaking the correlation between increased economic activity and similar increases in envrionmental impacts. (7, 17)

defensive expenditures (approach): a pollution valuation methodology based on the expenditures households take to avoid or mitigate their exposure to a pollutant. (6, 8)

demand-side management: an approach to energy management that stresses increasing energy efficiency and reducing energy consumption. (2)

dematerialization: the process of achieving an economic goal through a decrease in the use of physical materials, such as making aluminum cans with less metal. (7, 17)

demographic pressure: the impact of growing population on resources such as forests and water supplies. (14)

demographic transition: the tendency for first death rates and then birth rates to fall as a society develops economically; population growth rates first increase and eventually decrease. (9)

dependency ratios: the ratio of the number of people in a society who are dependent on others for their livelihood divided by the number who are not dependent on others. (9)

depletable resource: a renewable resource that can be exploited and depleted, such as soil or clean air. (10)

depletion allowances: a tax deduction for capital investments used to extract natural resources, typically oil and gas. (12)

deposit/return systems: systems that encourage recycling by charging consumers a deposit when they purchase certain goods such as beverages in recyclable containers or batteries; the deposit is returned when the consumer returns the recyclable material to the appropriate location. (11)

depreciation: the reduction in value of a capital stock over time due to wearing out or exploitation. (8)

desalination: the removal of salt from ocean water to make it usable for irrigation, industrial, or municipal water supplies. (15)

diminishing returns: a proportional increase (or decrease) in one or more inputs results in a smaller proportional increase (or decrease) in output. (4)

direct-use value: the value one obtains by directly using a natural resource, such as visiting a national park. (6)

discount rate: the annual rate at which future benefits or costs are discounted relative to current benefits or costs. (1, 5, 6, 10, 14, 18)

discounting: the concept that costs and benefits that occur in the future should be assigned less weight (discounted) relative to current costs and benefits. (6)

distortionary subsidies: subsidies that alter the market equilibrium in ways that are harmful to economic efficiency. (20)

distributionally neutral tax shift: a change in the pattern of taxes that leaves the distribution of income unchanged. (19)

dualistic land ownership: an ownership pattern, common in developing countries, in which large landowners wield considerable power and small landowners tend to be displaced or forced onto inferior land. (20)

dynamic equilibrium: a market equilibrium that results when present and future costs and benefits are considered. (5)

Earth Atmospheric Trust: a proposal to address global climate change involving a global cap-and-trade system with the auctioning of all permits and a global per capita rebate. (19)

ecolabeling: a label on a good that provides information concerning the environmental impacts that resulted from the production of the good. (13)

ecological complexity: the presence of many different living and nonliving elements in an ecosystem, interacting in complex patterns; ecosystem complexity implies that the impacts of human actions on ecosystems may be unpredictable. (7, 13)

ecological cycles: the flow of energy and natural resources through ecosystems. (1)

ecological economics: an economic perspective that views the economic system as a subset of the broader ecosystem and subject to biophysical laws. (1, 7)

economic efficiency: an allocation of resources that maximizes net social benefits; perfectly competitive markets in the absence of externalities are efficient. (3, 13)

economic efficiency standards: an environmental regulation approach that sets minimum standards for efficiency such as electricity or fuel consumption. (12)

economic optimum: a result that maximizes an economic criterion, such as efficiency or profits. (13)

economic profit: profit measured relative to a producer's next-best alternative. (4)

economic rent: income that accrues to the owner of a scarce resource. (11, 13)

economic reserves (economically recoverable reserves): the quantity of a resource that is identified as economically feasible to extract given current prices and technology. (11)

economic supply (of a resource): the quantity of a resource that is available based on current prices and technology. (11)

economic valuation: the valuation of a resource in monetary terms. (1)

economies of scale: an expanded level of output increases returns per unit of input. (3, 9)

ecosystem services: beneficial services provided freely by nature such as flood protection, water purification, and soil formation. (6)

ecosystems management: a system of resource management that stresses the long-term sustainability of ecosystems. (14)

efficiency labeling: labels on goods that indicate energy efficiency, such as a label on a refrigerator indicating annual energy use. (12)

efficiency standards: regulations that mandate efficiency criteria for goods, such as fuel economy standards for automobiles. (12, 19)

elasticity of demand: the sensitivity of quantity demanded to prices; an elastic demand means that a proportional increase in prices results in a larger proportional change in quantity demanded; an inelastic demand means that a proportional increase in prices results in a small change. (3, 19)

elasticity of supply: the sensitivity of quantity supplied to prices; an elastic supply means that a proportional increase in prices results in a larger proportional change in quantity supplied; an inelastic supply means that a proportional increase in prices results in a small change. (3, 10)

embodied energy: the total energy required to produce a good or service, including both direct and indirect uses of energy. (7)

emissions standards: regulations that set the maximum amount of pollutants that may be legally emitted by an industrial facility or product. (16)

empty-world and full-world economics: the view that economic approaches to environmental issues should differ depending whether the scale of the economy relative to the ecosystem is small (an empty world) or large (a full world). (7)

endowment effect: the concept that people tend to place high value on something after they already possess it, relative to its value before they possess it. (6)

energy demand-side management: an energy policy approach that seeks to reduce energy consumption, through policies such as information campaigns or higher energy prices. (12)

energy infrastructure: a system that supports the use of a particular energy source, such as the supply of gas stations and roads that support the use of automobiles. (12)

energy subsidies: direct or indirect government payments to encourage the use of specific energy sources. (12)

energy supply augmentation: an approach to energy management emphasizing increase in energy supplies, such as building more power plants or increasing oil drilling. (2)

energy transition: an overall shift of energy consumption away from fossil fuels toward renewable energy sources. (12)

entropy: a measure of the unavailable energy in a system; according to the second law of thermodynamics entropy increases in all physical processes. (7)

environmental asset accounts: national accounts that track the level of natural resources and environmental impacts in specific categories, maintained in either physical or monetary units. (8)

environmental degradation: loss of environmental resources, functions, or quality, often as a result of human economic activity. (7)

environmental externalities: externalities that affect the environment, such as the impact of pollution on wildlife. (3, 18, 20)

Environmental Kuznets Curve (EKC): the theory that a country's environmental impacts increase in the early stages of economic development but eventually decrease above a certain level of income. (17)

environmental macroeconomics: an analysis approach that places the human economic system within an ecological context to balance the scale of the economic system within ecological constraints. (1)

environmental microeconomics: the use of microeconomic techniques such as economic valuation, property rights rules, and discounting to determine an efficient allocation of natural resources and environmental services. (1)

environmental services: ecosystem services such as nutrient cycling, water purification, and soil stabilization; these services benefit humans and support economic production. (1, 8)

environmental sink functions: see "sink function." (21)

environmental sustainability: the continued existence of an ecosystem in a healthy state; ecosystems may change over time but do not significantly degrade. (2, 10)

environmentally adjusted net domestic product (EDP): a national accounting measure that deducts a monetary value from net domestic product to account for natural capital depreciation. (8)

equilibrium price: the market price where the quantity supplied equals the quantity demanded. (3)

equimarginal principle: the balancing of marginal costs and marginal benefits to obtain an efficient outcome. (16)

Exclusive Economic Zone (EEZ): the area normally within 200 nautical miles of the coast of a country, in which that country has exclusive jurisdiction over marine resources. (13)

existence value: the value people place on a resource that they do not intend to ever use, such as the benefit that one obtains from knowing an area of rain forest is preserved even though he or she will never visit it. (6)

expected value: the weighted average of potential values. (6)

exponential growth: a value that increases by the same percentage in each time period, such as a population increasing by the same percentage every year. (9, 21)

exponential reserve index: an estimate of the availability of a mineral resource based on an assumption of exponentially increasing consumption. (11)

exported emissions/pollution: shifting the impacts of pollution to other countries by importing goods whose production involves large environmental impacts. (17, 20)

external cost(s): a cost, not necessarily monetary, that is not reflected in a market transaction. (1, 3, 10, 18)

external benefit(s): a benefit, not necessarily monetary, that is not reflected in a market transaction. (1, 3, 18)

externalities: an effect of a market transaction that changes the utility, positively or negatively, of those outside the transaction. (1, 3, 9, 10, 18)

externality in time: an externality that affects future periods or generations. (5)

extraction path: the extraction rate of a resource over time. (11)

extractive reserves: a forested area that is managed for sustainable harvests of nontimber products such as nuts, sap, and extracts. (21)

feedback effect: the process of changes in a system leading to other changes that either counteract or reinforce the original change. (18)

feed-in tariffs: a policy to provide renewable energy producers long-term contracts to purchase energy at a set price, normally based on the costs of production (but higher than the cost of production). (12)

fertility rate: the average number of live births per woman in a society. (9)

first and second laws of thermodynamics: physical laws stating that matter and energy cannot be destroyed, only transformed, and that all physical processes lead to a decrease in available energy (an increase in entropy). (7, 11)

fixed factors: factors of production whose quantity cannot be changed in the short run. (9)

flow: the quantity of a variable measured over a period of time, including physical flows such as the flow of a river past a given point measured in cubic-feet per second or financial flows such as income over a period of time. (14)

flow pollutants: a pollutant that has a short-term impact and then dissipates or is absorbed harmlessly into the environment. (16)

free market environmentalism: the view that a more complete system of property rights and expanded use of market mechanisms is the best approach to solving issues of resource use and pollution control. (3)

free-rider effect: the incentive for people to avoid paying for a resource when the benefits they obtain from the resource are unaffected by whether they pay; results in the undersupply of public goods. (3)

free riders: an individual or group that obtains a benefit from a public good without having to pay for it. (4)

full pricing: the inclusion of both internal and external costs in the price of a product. (14)

fully exploited: term used to describe a fish stock that is being harvested at the maximum sustainable yield. (13)

future costs and benefits: benefits and costs that are expected to occur in the future, usually compared to present costs through discounting. (18)

gains from trade: the net social benefits that result from trade. (20)

GDP growth rate: the annual change in GDP, expressed as a percentage. (2)

GDP per capita: GDP divided by population. (8)

General Agreement on Tariffs and Trade (GATT): a multilateral trade agreement providing a framework for the gradual elimination of tariffs and other barriers to trade; the predecessor to the World Trade Organization. (20)

General Mining Act of 1872: a U.S. federal law that regulates mining for economic minerals on federal lands. (11)

genuine progress indicator (GPI): a national accounting measure that includes the monetary value of goods and services that contribute to well-being, such as volunteer work and higher education, and deducts impacts that detract from well-being, such as the loss of leisure time, pollution, and commuting. (8)

global climate change: the changes in global climate, including temperature, precipitation, and storm frequency and intensity, that result in changes to the concentrations of greenhouse gases in the atmosphere. (2, 16, 18)

global commons: global common property resources such as the atmosphere and the oceans. (2, 4, 18)

global environmental problems: environmental problems having global impacts such as global climate change and species extinction. (1)

global pollutant: pollutants that can cause global impacts such as carbon dioxide and chlorofluorocarbons. (16)

global public goods: environmental goods or services that benefit all people, such as biodiversity and climate stabilization. (20)

global warming: the increase in average global temperature as a result of emissions from human activities. (18)

government procurement: programs that guarantee a certain government demand for a good or service. (11)

grandfathering: the process of exempting existing industrial facilities from complying with new environmental standards or regulations. (16)

green accounting: general term applied to efforts to incorporate natural resources and environmental quality into national accounting techniques. (8)

green economy: an economy that improves human well-being and social equity, while reducing environmental impacts. (17)

green taxes: taxes based on the environmental impact of a good or service. (21)

greenhouse development rights (GDR): an approach for assigning the responsibility for past greenhouse gas emissions and the capability to respond to climate change. (19)

greenhouse effect: the effect of certain gases in the earth's atmosphere trapping solar radiation, resulting in an increase in global temperatures and other climatic impacts. (18)

greenhouse gases: gases such as carbon dioxide and methane whose atmospheric concentrations influence global climate by trapping solar radiation. (16, 18)

gross annual population increase: the total numerical increase in population for a given region over one year. (9)

gross domestic product (GDP): the total market value of all final goods and services produced within a national border in a year. (2, 8)

gross domestic product (GDP) per capita: GDP divided by a country's population. (8)

gross investment: total investment in produced, or manufactured, capital. (8)

Gross National Happiness (GNH): the concept, originating in Bhutan, where a society and its policies should seek to improve the welfare of its citizens, as opposed to maximizing GDP. (8)

gross national product (GNP): the total market value of all final goods and services produced by citizens of a particular country in a year, regardless of where such production takes place. (8)

habitat equivalency analysis (HEA): a method used to compensate for the damages from a natural resource injury with an equivalent amount of habitat restoration. (6)

harmonization of environmental standards: the standardization of environmental standards across countries, as in the European Union. (20)

Hartwick rule: a principle of resource use stating that resource rents—the proceeds of resource sale, net of extraction costs—should be invested rather than consumed. (5)

hedonic pricing: the use of statistical analysis to explain the price of a good or service as a function of several components, such as explaining the price of a home as a function of the number of rooms, the caliber of local schools, and the surrounding air quality. (6)

holdout effect: the ability of a single entity to hinder a multiparty agreement by making disproportionate demands. (3)

Hotelling's rule: a theory stating that in equilibrium the net price (price minus production costs) of a resource must rise at a rate equal to the rate of interest. (5, 11)

hotspots: locally high levels of pollution, for example, surrounding a high-emitting plant; hotspots can occur under a pollution trading scheme. (16)

Hubbert curve: a bell-shaped curve showing the production quantity of a nonrenewable energy resource over time. (12)

human capital: the knowledge, skills, and abilities of the labor force, reflecting investments in education and training. (6)

Human Development Index (HDI): a national accounting measure developed by the United Nations, based on three factors: GDP levels, education, and life expectancy. (8)

hydrologic cycle: the natural purification of water through evaporation and precipitation. (15)

hydropower: the generation of electricity from the energy in flowing water. (12)

hypothetical (resources): the quantity of a resource that is not identified with certainty but is hypothesized to exist. (11)

identified reserves: the quantity of a resource that has been identified; includes both economic and subeconomic reserves. (11)

identity: a mathematical statement that is true by definition. (9)

income inequality: a distribution of income in which some portions of the population receive much greater income than others. (9)

incremental costs: costs of environmental protection in developing countries in excess of what the country is prepared to pay without foreign assistance. (21)

indicated or inferred (reserves): resources that have been identified but whose exact quantity is not known with certainty. (11)

indirect environmental effects of trade: environmental impacts arising from trade, for example, when export agriculture displaces peasant farmers onto marginal lands, leading to deforestation and soil erosion. (20)

indirect-use values: ecosystem benefits that are not valued in markets, such as flood prevention and pollution absorption. (6)

individual transferable quotas (ITQs): tradeable rights to harvest a resource, such as a permit to harvest a particular quantity of fish. (4, 13)

induced innovation: innovation in a particular industry resulting from changes in the relative prices of inputs. (10)

industrial ecology: the application of ecological principles to the management of industrial activity. (2, 17, 21)

inflection point: the point on a curve where the second derivative equals zero, indicating a change from positive to negative curvature or vice versa. (13)

information asymmetry: a situation in which different agents in a market have different knowledge or access to information. (10)

information-intensive techniques: production techniques that require specialized knowledge; usually these techniques substitute knowledge for energy, produced capital, or material inputs, often reducing environmental impacts. (10)

input-intensive agriculture: agricultural production that relies heavily on machinery, artificial fertilizers, pesticides, and irrigation. (2)

institutional failure: the failure of governments or other institutions to prevent overexploitation of a resource. (13, 14)

integrated pest management: the use of methods such as natural predators, crop rotations, and pest removal to reduce pesticide application rates. (10)

intensification of production: increasing production rates with a limited supply of resources, such as increasing agricultural yield per acre. (2)

intercropping: an agricultural system involving growing two or more crops together on a piece of land at the same time. (10)

intergenerational equity: the distribution of resources, including human-made and natural capital, across human generations. (7)

internalizing external costs/externalities: using approaches such as taxation to incorporate external costs into market decisions. (1, 3, 16, 18)

intertemporal resource allocation: the way resource use is distributed over time. (1)

irreversibility: the concept that some human impacts on the environment may cause damage that cannot be reversed, such as the extinction of species. (7)

joint implementation: cooperative agreements between countries to reduce carbon emissions. (19)

labor-intensive techniques: production techniques that rely heavily on labor input. (10)

law of demand: the economic theory that the quantity of a good or service demanded will decrease as the price increases. (3)

law of diminishing returns: the principle that a continual increase in production inputs will eventually yield decreasing marginal output. (9)

law of supply: the economic theory that the quantity of a good or service supplied will increase as the price increases. (3)

Law of the Sea: a 1982 international treaty regulating marine fisheries. (13)

least-cost options: actions that can be taken for the lowest overall cost. (18)

levelized costs: the per-unit cost of energy production, accounting for all fixed and variable costs over a power source's lifetime. (12)

license fee: the fee paid for access to a resource, such as a fishing license. (4, 13)

local and regional air pollutants: pollutants that cause adverse impacts only within the area where they are emitted. (16, 18)

logistic curve/logistic growth: an S-shaped growth curve tending toward an upper limit. (13, 14, 21)

luxury good: a good that people tend to spend a higher percentage of their income on as their incomes increase. (17)

macroeconomic scale: the total scale of an economy; ecological economics suggests that the ecosystem imposes scale limits on the macroeconomy. (1, 2, 21)

Malthusian hypothesis: the theory proposed by Thomas Malthus in 1798 that population would eventually outgrow available food supplies. (2)

manufactured capital: productive resources produced by humans, such as factories, roads, and computers, also referred to as produced capital or human-made capital. (21)

marginal benefit: the benefit of producing or consuming one more unit of a good or service. (4)

marginal costs: the cost of producing or consuming one more unit of a good or service. (3, 4)

marginal extraction cost: the cost of extracting an additional unit of a nonrenewable resource. (11)

marginal net benefit: the net benefit of the consumption or production of an additional unit of a resource; equal to marginal benefit minus marginal cost. (5)

marginal physical product: the additional quantity of output produced by increasing an input level by one unit. (10)

marginal revenue: the additional revenue obtained by selling one more unit of a good or service. (4)

marginal revenue product: the additional revenue obtained by increasing an input level by one unit; equal to marginal physical product multiplied by marginal revenue. (10)

market-based pollution control: pollution regulations based on market forces without specific control of firm-level decisions, such as taxes, subsidies, and permit systems. (16)

market equilibrium: the market outcome where the quantity demanded equals the quantity supplied. (3)

market failure: the failure of certain markets to provide a socially efficient allocation of resources. (9, 13)

materials substitution: changing the materials used to produce a product, such as using plastic pipe instead of copper in plumbing systems. (17)

maximum sustainable yield (MSY): the maximum quantity of a natural resource that can be harvested annually without depleting the stock or population of the resource. (13)

mean annual increment (MAI): the average growth rate of a forest; obtained by dividing the total weight of timber by the age of the forest. (14)

measured (reserves): resources that have been identified and whose quantity is known with certainty. (11)

meta-analysis: an analysis method based on a quantitative review of existing research to identify explanatory variables for differences in results. (6)

methodological pluralism: the view that a more comprehensive understanding of problems can be obtained using a combination of perspectives. (7)

micro-irrigation: irrigation systems that increase the efficiency of water use by applying water in small quantities close to the plants. (15)

micronutrients: nutrients present in low concentrations in soil, required for plant growth or health. (10)

monoculture: an agricultural system involving the growing of the same crop exclusively on a piece of land year after year. (10, 13, 14)

multiple cropping: an agricultural system involving growing more than one crop on a piece of land in the same year. (10)

multilateral environmental agreements (MEAs): international treaties between countries on environmental issues, such as the Convention on Trade in Endangered Species. (20)

natural capital: the available endowment of land and resources including air, water, soil, forests, fisheries, minerals, and ecological life-support systems. (2, 7, 8, 9, 21)

natural capital depreciation: a deduction in national accounting for loss of natural capital, such as a reduction in the supply of timber, wildlife habitat, or mineral resources. (7, 8)

natural capital sustainability: conserving natural capital by limiting depletion rates and investing in resource renewal. (7)

natural resource limitations: constraints on production resulting from limited availability of natural resources. (9)

natural resources: resources that occur in a natural state and are valuable for economic activities, such as minerals, timber, and soils. (1)

negative externality/externalities: negative impacts of a market transaction affecting those not involved in the transaction. (3, 14)

neo-Malthusian perspective: the modern version of Thomas Malthus's argument that human population growth can lead to catastrophic ecological consequences and an increase in the human death rate. (9)

net domestic product (NDP): gross domestic product minus the value of depreciation of produced, or human-made, capital. (8)

net domestic savings (NDS): a national accounting measure equal to gross domestic savings less manufactured capital depreciation. (8)

net investment and disinvestment: the process of adding to, or subtracting from, productive capital over time, calculated by subtracting depreciation from gross, or total, investment. (7, 8)

net price (of a resource): the price of a resource minus production costs. (5, 11)

net primary product of photosynthesis (NPP): the biomass energy directly produced by photosynthesis. (7)

nitrogen cycle: the conversion of nitrogen into different forms in the ecosystem, including the fixation of nitrogen by symbiotic bacteria in certain plants such as legumes. (10)

nominal GDP: gross domestic product measured using current dollars. (2)

nonexclusive good: a good that is available to all users; one of the two characteristics of public goods. (4)

non–fully exploited: term used to describe a fish stock that is being harvested below the maximum sustainable yield. (13)

nongovernmental organizations (NGOs): privately funded, and commonly nonprofit, organizations involved in research, lobbying, provision of services, or development projects. (21)

nonlinear or threshold effects: pollution damages that are not linearly correlated with pollution levels. (16)

nonmarket benefits: benefits not obtained from goods and services sold in markets. (6)

nonpoint-source pollution: pollution that is difficult to identify as originating from a particular source, such as groundwater contamination from agricultural chemicals used over a wide area. (10, 16)

nonrenewable resources: resources that are available in a fixed supply, such as metal ores and oil. (1, 2, 5, 11)

nonrenewable stock: See "nonrenewable resources." (12)

non-response bias: bias as a result of survey respondents not being representative of survey non-respondents. (6)

nonrival good: a good whose use by one person does not limit its use by others; one of the two characteristics of public goods. (4)

nonuniformly mixed pollutants: pollutants that cause different impacts in different areas, depending on where they are emitted. (16)

nonuse values: values that people obtain without actually using a resource; nonuse values include existence and bequest values. (6)

normal good: a good for which total expenditures tend to increase as income increases. (17)

normal profit: the minimum profit a business needs to remain in operation. (4)

nutrient recycling: the ability of ecological systems to transform nutrients such as carbon, nitrogen, and phosphorus into different chemical forms. (10)

nutritional deficit: the failure to meet human demands for basic levels of nutrition. (10) **ocean acidification**: increasing acidity of ocean waters as a result of dissolved carbon from CO_2 emitted into the atmosphere. (18)

open access: unrestricted availability of a resource, without payment. (14)

ocean acidification: increasing acidity of ocean waters as a result of dissolved carbon from CO_2 emitted into the atmosphere. (18)

open-access equilibrium: the level of use of an open-access resource that results from a market with free entry; this level of use may lead to depletion of the resource. (4, 13)

open-access resource(s): a resource that offers unrestricted access such as an ocean fishery or the atmosphere. (2, 4, 13, 14)

open system: a system that exchanges energy or natural resources with another system; the economic system is considered an open system because it receives energy and natural resources from the ecosystem and deposits wastes into the ecosystem. (7)

optimal depletion rate: the depletion rate for a natural resource that maximizes the net present value of the resource. (5)

optimal level of pollution: the pollution level that maximizes net social benefits. (3, 16)

optimal macroeconomic scale: the concept that economic systems have an optimal scale level beyond which further growth leads to lower well-being or resource degradation. (7)

optimum rotation period: the rotation period for a renewable resource that maximizes the financial gain from harvest; determined by maximizing the discounted difference between total revenues and total costs. (14)

option value: the value that people place on the maintenance of future options for resource use. (6)

overexploited: term used to describe a fish stock that is being harvested beyond the maximum sustainable yield. (13)

overfishing: a level of fishing effort that depletes the stock of a fishery over time. (4, 13)

overharvesting of renewable resources: rates of harvest that decrease the stock or population of a resource over time. (2)

pay-by-the-bag systems: a waste disposal system in which customers are charged a fee for each unit of waste discarded. (11)

per capita GDP growth rate: the annual change in per capita GDP, expressed as a percentage. (2)

per capita output: the total product of a society divided by population. (9)

permit auction: a system that allocates pollution permits to the highest bidders. (16)

physical accounting: a supplement to national income accounting that estimates the stock or services of natural resources in physical, rather than economic, terms. (7)

physical reserves: the quantity of a resource that has been identified; includes both economic and subeconomic reserves. (11)

physical supply (of a resource): the quantity of a resource that is available, without taking into account the economic feasibility of extraction. (11)

Pigovian (pollution) tax: a per-unit tax set equal to the external damage caused by an activity, such as a tax per ton of pollution emitted equal to the external damage of a ton of pollution. (3, 16)

point-source pollution: pollution that is emitted from an identifiable source such as a smokestack or waste pipe. (16)

polluter pays principle: the view that those responsible for pollution should pay for the associated external costs, such as health costs and damage to wildlife habitats. (3)

pollution: contamination of soil, water or atmosphere by discharge of harmful substances. (1)

pollution haven: a country or region that attracts high-polluting indistries due to low levels of environmental regulation. (20)

pollution standards: a regulation that mandates firms or industries to meet a specific pollution level or pollution reduction. (16)

pollution tax(es): a per-unit tax based on the level of pollution. (16, 19)

population age profile: an estimate of the number of people within given age groups in a country at a point in time. (9)

population biology: the study of how the population of a species changes as a result of environmental conditions. (13)

population cohort: the group of people born within a specific period in a country. (9)

population growth rate: the annual change in the population of a given area, expressed as a percentage. (2, 9)

population momentum: the tendency for a population to continue to grow, even if the fertility rate falls to the replacement level, as long as a high proportion of the population is in young age cohorts. (2, 9)

Porter hypothesis: the theory that environmental regulations motivate firms to identify cost-saving innovations that otherwise would not have been implemented. (17)

positional analysis: a policy analysis tool that combines economic valuation with other considerations such as equity, individual rights, and social priorities; it does not aim to reduce all impacts to monetary terms. (6)

positive externalities: the positive impacts of a market transaction that affect those not involved in the transaction. (3, 14)

post-growth economy: an economy that has completed the process of economic growth and operates with no further increase, and possibly a decrease, in resource and energy use. (21)

precautionary principle: the view that policies should account for uncertainty by taking steps to avoid low-probability but catastrophic events. (6, 7, 13, 16, 18, 20)

present value: the current value of a stream of future costs or benefits; a discount rate is used to convert future costs or benefits to present values. (5, 6, 10, 12)

preventive measures/preventive strategies: actions designed to reduce the extent of climate change by reducing projected emissions of greenhouse gases. (18, 19)

price elasticity of demand: the responsiveness of the quantity demanded to price, equal to the percentage change in quantity demanded divided by the percentage change in price. (3, 15)

price elasticity of supply: the responsiveness of the quantity supplied to price, equal to the percentage change in quantity demanded divided by the percentage change in price. (3, 10)

price path: the price of a resource, typically a nonrenewable resource, over time. (11)

price taker: a seller in a competitive market who has no control over the price of the product. (11)

price volatility: rapid and frequent changes in price, leading to market instability. (19)

prior appropriation water rights: a system of water rights allocation in which rights are not based on land ownership but on established beneficial uses. (15)

private ownership: the provision of certain exclusive rights to a particular resource, such as the right of a landowner to restrict trespassing. (13)

process and production methods (PPMs): international trade rules stating that an importing country cannot use trade barriers or penalties against another country for failure to meet environmental or social standards related to the process of production. (20)

producer surplus: the net benefits of a market transaction to producers, equal to the selling price minus production costs (i.e., profits). (3)

product, spending, and income approaches to calculating GDP: different approaches for calculating GDP; in theory each approach should produce the same value. (8)

production externalities: externalities associated with the production of a good or service, such as emissions of pollutants from a factory. (20)

profits: total revenue received minus total cost to producers. (4)

progressive taxes: taxes that comprise a higher share of income with higher income levels. (19)

property rights: the set of rights that belong to the owner of a resource, such as the right of a landowner to prohibit trespassing. (1)

protest bids: responses to contingent valuation questions based on the respondent's opposition to the question or the payment vehicle, rather than the underlying valuation of the resource. (6)

proxy variable: a variable that is meant to represent a broader concept, such as the use of fertilizer application rates to represent the input-intensity of agricultural production. (10)

public goods: goods that are available to all (nonexclusive) and whose use by one person does not reduce their availability to others (nonrival). (1, 4, 14, 18)

purchasing power parity (PPP): an adjustment to GDP to account for differences in spending power across countries. (8)

pure rate of time preference: the rate of preference for obtaining benefits now as opposed to the future, independent of income level changes. (6)

quota/quota system: a system of limiting access to a resource through restrictions on the permissible harvest of the resource. (4, 13)

"race to the bottom": the tendency for countries to weaken national environmental standards to attract foreign businesses or to keep existing businesses from moving to other countries. (20)

range bias: a potential bias with payment card or multiple-bounded contingent valuation questions whereby the responses are influenced by the range of values presented to the respondent. (6)

real GDP: gross domestic product corrected for inflation using a price index. (2, 8)

real or **inflation-adjusted dollars**: monetary estimates that account for changes in price levels (i.e., inflation) over time. (6)

recycling: the process of using waste materials as inputs into a production process. (11)

Reduction of Emissions from Deforestation and Degradation (REDD): a United Nations program adopted as part of the Kyoto process of climate negotiations, intended to reduce emissions from deforestation and land degradation through providing funding for forest conservation and sustainable land use. (19)

referendum format: a contingent valuation question format where the valuation question is presented as a vote on a hypothetical referendum. (6)

regressive tax: a tax in which the rate of taxation, as a percentage of income, decreases with increasing income levels. (19)

regulated monopolies: monopolies that are regulated by an external entity, for example through controls on price or profits. (15)

regulation: a law that seeks to control environmental impacts by setting standards or controlling the uses of a product or process. (16)

relative and absolute decoupling: breaking the correlation between increased economic activity and increases in environmental impacts; in absolute decoupling, an increase of economic activity is associated with a decrease in environmental impacts. (17)

renewable energy sources: energy sources that are supplied on a continual basis such as wind, water, biomass, and direct solar energy. (2)

renewable energy targets: regulations that set targets for the percentage of energy obtained from renewable energy sources. (12)

renewable flow: the continuous quantity of a renewable energy source supplied over time, such as the quantity of solar energy available each year. (12)

renewable resources: a resource that is supplied on a continuing basis by ecosystems; renewable resources such as forests and fisheries can be depleted through exploitation. (1, 2, 5, 10, 13)

rent dissipation: the loss of potential social and economic benefits in a market because of market failure. (13)

replacement cost methods: an approach to measuring environmental damages that estimates the costs necessary to restore or replace the resource, such as applying fertilizer to restore soil fertility. (6)

replacement fertility level: the fertility level that would result in a stable population. (9)

resilience: the capacity of ecosystem to recover from adverse impacts. (13, 14)

resistant pest species: pest species which evolve resistance to pesticides, requiring either higher pesticide application rates or new pesticides to control the species. (10)

Resource Conservation and Recovery Act (RCRA): the primary federal U.S. law regulating the disposal of hazardous waste. (16)

resource depletion: a decline in the stock of a renewable resource due to human exploitation. (1, 7)

resource depletion tax: a tax imposed on the extraction or sale of a natural resource. (5)

resource lifetime: the number of years the economic reserves of a resource are projected to last under expected consumption rates. (11)

resource recovery: mining or extraction of resources for economic use. (2)

resource rents: income derived from the ownership of a scarce resource. (4, 11)

resource substitution/substitutability: the use of one resource in a production process as a substitute for another resource, such as the use of aluminum instead of copper in electrical wiring. (11)

resource use profile: the consumption rates for a resource over time, typically applied to nonrenewable resources. (11)

revealed preference methods: methods of economic valuation based on market behaviors, including travel cost models, hedonic pricing, and the defensive expenditures approach. (6)

revenue-neutral (tax policy): term used to describe a tax policy that holds the overall level of tax revenues constant. (16, 21)

revenue-neutral tax shift: policies that are designed to balance tax increases on certain products or activities with a reduction in other taxes, such as a reduction in income taxes that offsets a carbon-based tax. (19)

riparian water rights: a system of water rights allocation based on adjacent land ownership. (15)

risk: term used to describe a situation in which all potential outcomes and their probabilities are known. (6)

risk aversion: the tendency to prefer certainty instead of risky outcomes, particularly in cases when significant negative consequences may result from an action. (6)

safe minimum standard: the principle that environmental policies on issues involving uncertainty should be set to avoid possible catastrophic consequences. (6)

salinization and alkalinization of soils: the buildup of salt or alkali concentrations in soil from the evaporation of water depositing dissolved salts, with the effect of reducing the productivity of the soil. (10)

satellite accounts: accounts that estimate the supply of natural capital in physical, rather than monetary, terms; used to supplement traditional national income accounting. (7, 8)

scale, composition, and technique effects: the impacts of trade on economic growth, industrial patterns, and technological progress; the combination of effects may be environmentally negative, positive, or neutral. (20)

scale limit: a limit to the size of a system, including an economic system. (7)

scale of production: size or output level of an industry. (20)

second-best solution: a policy solution to a problem that fails to maximize potential net social benefits, but that may be desirable if the optimal solution cannot be achieved. (20)

second law of thermodynamics: the physical law stating that all physical processes lead to a decrease in available energy, that is, an increase in entropy. (11)

secure property rights: clearly defined and legally binding rights of property ownership. (14)

sensitivity analysis: an analytical tool that studies how the outputs of a model change as the assumptions of the model change. (6)

shortage: a market situation in which the quantity demanded exceeds the quantity supplied. (**3**)

side agreement: a provision related to a trade treaty dealing with social or environmental issues. (20)

sink function: the ability of natural environments to absorb wastes and pollution. (1, 13, 16)

smelting: the production of a metal from a metallic ore. (11)

social benefits: the market and nonmarket benefits associated with a good or service. (4)

social cost: the market and nonmarket costs associated with a good or service. (5)

social discount rate/social rate of time preference (SRTP): a discount rate that attempts to reflect the appropriate social valuation of the future; the SRTP tends to be less than market or individual discount rates. (6)

social marginal cost curve: the cost of providing one more unit of a good or service, considering both private production costs and externalities. (3)

social sustainability: the maintenance of social structure and traditions consistent with a well-functioning society. (14)

socially efficient: a market situation in which net social benefits are maximized. (3)

solar energy: the energy supplied continually by the sun, including direct solar energy as well as indirect forms such as wind energy and flowing water. (1, 2, 12)

solar flux: the continual flow of solar energy to the earth. (7, 9)

source function: the ability of the environment to make services and raw materials available for human use. (1, 13)

species diversity: See biodiversity. (10)

specificity rule: the view that policy solutions should be targeted directly at the source of a problem. (20)

stable equilibrium: an equilibrium, for example of the stock level of a renewable resource, to which the system will tend to return after short-term changes in conditions affecting stock level of the resource. (13)

stated preference methods: economic valuation methods based on survey responses to hypothetical scenarios, including contingent valuation and contingent ranking. (6)

static equilibrium: a market equilibrium that results when only present costs and benefits are considered. (5)

static reserve index: an index that divides the economic reserves of a resource by the current rate of use for the resource. (11)

steady state: an economy that maintains a constant level of natural capital by limiting the throughput of material and energy resources. (21)

stock: the quantity of a variable at a given point in time, such as the amount of timber in a forest at a given time. (14)

stock pollutant: pollutants that accumulate in the environment, such as carbon dioxide and chlorofluorocarbons. (16, 18)

strategic bias/strategic behavior: the tendency for people to state their preferences or values inaccurately in order to influence policy decisions. (6)

strong sustainability: the view that natural and human-made capital are generally not substitutable and, therefore, natural capital levels should be maintained. (7, 8, 21)

structural adjustment: policies to promote market-oriented economic reform in developing countries by making loans conditional on reforms such as controlling inflation, reducing trade barriers, and privatization of businesses. (21)

subeconomic resources: term used to describe mineral resources that cannot be profitably extracted with current technology and prices. (11)

subsidy/subsidies: government assistance to an industry or economic activity; subsidies can be direct, through financial assistance, or indirect, through protective policies. (3, 13, 14)

substitutability (of human-made and natural capital): the ability of one resource or input to substitute for another; in particular, the ability of human-made capital to compensate for the depletion of some types of natural capital. (7)

supply constraint: an upper limit on supply, for example, of a nonrenewable resource. (5)

surplus: a market situation in which the quantity supplied exceeds the quantity demanded. (3)

sustainable agriculture: systems of agricultural production that do not deplete the productivity of the land or environmental quality, including such techniques as integrated pest management, organic techniques, and multiple cropping. (2, 10)

sustainable development: development that meets the needs of the present without compromising the ability of future generations to meet their own needs. (1, 2, 21)

sustainable (natural resource) management: management of natural resources such that natural capital remains constant over time, including maintenance of both stocks and flows. (2, 13, 14)

sustainable yield: a yield or harvest level that can be maintained without diminishing the stock or population of the resource. (7)

System of Environmental and Economic Accounts (SEEA): a guidebook developed by the United Nations to provide standards for incorporating natural capital and environmental quality into national accounting systems. (8)

tailings: the unwanted material from mining operations, often highly toxic. (11)

tax shift: reducing taxes in one area and increasing them in another, for example reducing taxes on labor and increasing taxes on pollution. (17)

technological progress: increases in knowledge used to develop new products or improve existing products. (2, 9)

technological (and social) lock-in: the tendency of an industry or society to continue to use a given technology despite the availability of more efficient or cheaper technologies. (11, 21)

technology-based regulation: pollution regulation by requiring firms to implement specific equipment or actions. (16)

technology transfer: the process of sharing technological information or equipment, particularly among countries. (19)

theoretical paradigm: the basic conceptual approach used to study a particular issue. (2)

third-party effects: effects of market transactions that affect people other than those involved in the transaction, such as industrial pollution that affects a local community. (1, 3)

throughput: the total use of energy and materials as both inputs and outputs of a process. (1, 7)

total cost: the total cost to a firm of producing its output. (4)

total economic value: the value of a resource considering both use and nonuse values. (6, 14)

total net benefit: total benefit minus total cost. (5)

total product: the total quantity of a good or service produced with a given quantity of inputs. (4, 13)

total revenue: the total revenue obtained by selling a particular quantity of a good or service; equal to price multiplied by quantity sold. (4)

toxic air pollutants: harmful air pollutants other than the six criteria pollutants, as specified in the U.S. Clean Air Act. (16)

Toxic Substances Control Act (TSCA): the primary federal U.S. law regulating the use and sale of toxic chemicals. (16)

tradable pollution permits: permits that allow a firm to emit a specific amount of pollution. (16)

tragedy of the commons: the tendency for common property resources to be overexploited because no one has an incentive to conserve the resource while individual financial incentives promote expanded exploitation. (4, 13)

transaction costs: costs associated with a market transaction or negotiation, such as legal and administrative costs to transfer property or to bring disputing parties together. (3)

transboundary and global pollution problems: pollution that is carried beyond the borders of a specific region or country and impacts those outside the region. (20)

transferable (tradable) permits: tradable permits that allow a firm to emit a certain quantity of a pollutant. (19)

travel cost method (TCM): the use of statistical analysis to determine people's willingness to pay to visit a natural resource such as a national park or river; a demand curve for the resource is obtained by analyzing the relationship between visitation choices and travel costs. (6)

uncertainty: term used to describe a situation in which some of the outcomes of an action are unknown or cannot be assigned probabilities. (6)

underpricing of forest resources: prices of goods or services, such as timbering rights, that are lower than the price that would result from taking full social costs into account. (14)

uniformly mixed pollutants: any pollutant emitted by many sources in a region resulting in relatively constant concentration levels across the region. (16)

unstable equilibrium: a temporary equilibrium, for example, of the stock level of a renewable resource, that can be altered by minor changes in conditions, resulting in a large change in stock levels. (13)

upstream policy: a policy to regulate emissions or production as near as possible to the point of natural resource extraction. (16)

upstream tax: a tax implemented as near as possible to the point of natural resource extraction. (3)

use values: the value that people place on the use of a good or service. (6, 14)

user costs: opportunity costs associated with the loss of future potential uses of a resource, resulting from consumption of the resource in the present. (5, 10, 11)

value of a statistical life (VSL): the willingness to pay of society to avoid one death based on valuations of changes in the risk of death. (6)

value-added method: the additional value of a good or service from each step in the production process. (8)

vertical addition: adding the price of more than one demand curve at the same quantity demanded. (4)

virgin resource: a resource obtained from nature, as opposed to using recycled materials. (11)

wage-risk analysis: a method used to estimate the value of a statistical life based on the required compensation needed to entice people to high-risk jobs. (6)

water markets: mechanism to sell water or water rights to potential buyers. (15)

water pricing: setting the price of water to influence the quantity consumed. (15)

water privatization: the management of water resources by a private for-profit entity as opposed to a public utility. (15)

water scarce: term used for countries where freshwater supplies are less than 1,000 cubic meters per person per year. (15)

water stressed: term used for countries where freshwater supplies are between 1,700 and 1,000 cubic meters per person per year. (15)

weak sustainability: the view that natural capital depletion is justified as long as it is compensated for with increases in human-made capital; assumes that human-made capital can substitute for most types of natural capital. (7, 8, 21)

welfare analysis: an economic tool that analyzes the total costs and benefits of alternative policies to different groups, such as producers and consumers. (3)

willingness to accept (WTA): the minimum amount of money people would accept as compensation for an action that reduces their utility. (3, 6)

willingness to pay (WTP): the maximum amount of money people are willing to pay for a good or service that increases utility. (6)

World Environmental Organization (WEO): a proposed international organization that would have oversight of global environmental issues. (20)

World Trade Organization (WTO): an international organization dedicated to the expansion of trade through lowering or eliminating tariffs and nontariff barriers to trade. (20)

WTO's Article XX: a World Trade Organization rule allowing countries to restrict trade in order to conserve exhaustible natural resources or to protect human, animal, or plant life or health. (20)

yea-saying: responding "yes" to a contingent valuation WTP question even though one's true valuation of the scenario is less, for reasons such as perceiving "yes" to be a correct answer. (6)

Index

Italic page references indicate charts, tables, and boxed text.

About the Authors

Jonathan M. Harris is Director of the Theory and Education Program at the Tufts University Global Development and Environment Institute. He is coeditor of *Twenty-First Century Macroeconomics: Responding to the Climate Challenge* (Edward Elgar, 2009) and editor of *Rethinking Sustainability: Power, Knowledge, and Institutions* (University of Michigan Press, 2000). His current research focuses on the implications of large-scale environmental problems, especially global climate change, for macroeconomic theory and policy.He has served on the boards of the U.S. Society for Ecological Economics and the International Society for Ecological Economics, and has taught environmental economics at the Fletcher School at Tufts University, Brown University, and Boston University.

Brian Roach is Senior Research Associate at the Tufts University Global Development and Environment Institute. He has written numerous articles and reports on nonmarket valuation of natural resources, including drinking water quality, outdoor recreation, wildlife, and ecosystem benefits. His research also includes global climate change policies, the role of large corporations in a global economy, and the distributional implications of tax policies. He has taught environmental economics at Tufts University, Brandeis University, and Brown University.